Handbook of Research on Global Information Technology Management in the Digital Economy

Dr. Mahesh S. Raisinghani
TWU, School of Management, Executive MBA Program, USA

Information Science REFERENCE

INFORMATION SCIENCE REFERENCE

Hershey · New York

Acquisitions Editor:	Kristin Klinger
Development Editor:	Kristin Roth
Senior Managing Editor:	Jennifer Neidig
Managing Editor:	Sara Reed
Copy Editor:	Maria Neithercott and Maria Boyer
Typesetter:	Cindy Consonery and Jamie Snavely
Cover Design:	Lisa Tosheff
Printed at:	Yurchak Printing Inc.

Published in the United States of America by
Information Science Reference (an imprint of IGI Global)
701 E. Chocolate Avenue, Suite 200
Hershey PA 17033
Tel: 717-533-8845
Fax: 717-533-8661
E-mail: cust@igi-global.com
Web site: http://www.igi-global.com

and in the United Kingdom by
Information Science Reference (an imprint of IGI Global)
3 Henrietta Street
Covent Garden
London WC2E 8LU
Tel: 44 20 7240 0856
Fax: 44 20 7379 0609
Web site: http://www.eurospanonline.com

Library of Congress Cataloging-in-Publication Data

Handbook of research on global information technology management in the digital economy / Mahesh S. Raisinghani, editor.

    p. cm.

  Summary: "This book provides comprehensive coverage and definitions of the most important issues, concepts, trends and technologies in the field of global information technology management, covering topics such as the technical platform for global IS applications, information systems projects spanning cultures, managing information technology in multi-domestic/international/global/transnational corporations, and global information technology systems and socioeconomic development in developing countries"--Provided by publisher.

  Includes bibliographical references and index.

  ISBN 978-1-59904-875-8 (hbk.) -- ISBN 978-1-59904-876-5 (ebook)

  1. Information technology--Management. I. Raisinghani, Mahesh S., 1967-

  HD30.2.H36426 2008

  658.4'038--dc22

                              2007036324

British Cataloguing in Publication Data
A Cataloguing in Publication record for this book is available from the British Library.

Table of Contents

Detailed Table of Contents

Chapter I
Economic Development: Government's Cutting Edge in IT

This chapter explores the interface between information technology (IT) and economic development. The impacts of three IT innovations are assessed in terms of how they contributed to the development of economic development practice: database management systems (DBMS), geographic information systems (GIS), and the evolution of Web sites. With regard to the close relationship between IT and economic development, the chapter primarily focuses on current and future issues in this area. The chapter is organized into the following sections: it begins with an introductory section, a second section delves into the history of economic development and its relationship with IT, a third section introduces the three IT revolutions in economic development. The sections that follow, fourth, fifth, and sixth, each address a key development in economic development/IT relationship: DBMS, GIS, and Web site development, respectively. The chapter concludes by providing a glimpse of what might be expected in the future and some recommendations for future research on this topic.

Chapter II
The Development of National ICT Policy in Kenya: The Influence of Regional Institutions and

The role that information and communication technologies could play in socio-economic development has been recognized by governments worldwide. The most important starting point in most countries is a national ICT policy. In many developing countries, ICT policy development has increasingly become a participatory process. This is largely as a result of implementing policy reforms, with a strong emphasis on governance systems. This chapter is a case study of the development of national information and communication technology policy in Kenya, the influences of regional institutions and their products, and the role of the private sector and civil society. The chapter is based on a study that was carried out by reviewing existing relevant documents and by interviewing key persons involved in national and regional ICT policy in Kenya. The chapter also presents the challenges, conclusions, recommendations, and future research directions based on the case.

Chapter III

In this chapter, the author seeks to examine this political aperture, in particular, the context through which these changes were realized. The author examines, in particular, the evolution of economic policies in Southeast Asia and how its integration into the global economy ushered in latent and corresponding social changes. Of course, it is not possible to analyze here every country in the region. As such, this study concerns itself primarily with the dominant ASEAN countries—Malaysia, Indonesia, Singapore, and Thailand. The chapter, after providing an overview of Southeast Asian economies, proceeds to provide an analysis of ICT projects in the region, focusing on the Singaporean and Malaysian experiences. It next examines the relationships and dynamics of changes effected through the intersection of economics, politics, and ICTs. I argue, drawing on the examples of Indonesia, Malaysia, and Singapore, that as these forces interact, greater political space is engendered. Similarly, economic change via privatization has a simila,r although unintended, *liberalizing* effect. The chapter further notes that states have responded to this liberalizing thrust by seeking greater control and regulation, but these attempts are unlikely to be successful.

Chapter IV

This chapter looks at a key concept called *communities of practice* that helps to facilitate organizational learning through increased knowledge sharing within global virtual teams. By using Granovetter's (1974) *weak ties* theory, the author suggests that casual acquaintances known as *weak ties* have significant implications for social relationships and context, both of which can benefit virtual organizational team members. Furthermore, based on Hofstede's (1980) cultural dimensions, the author also argues that cultural factors can impact one's willingness to share knowledge. Thus, there are three questions that guide this chapter: (1) How do social relationships and context among global virtual teams' affect the development of communities of practice? (2) How does culture affect the knowledge sharing activities? and (3) What is the impact of ICTs on knowledge sharing and the emergence of communities of practice?

Chapter V

This chapter examines Web sites created by American multinational corporations (MNCs) in the Czech Republic. Utilizing a content analysis technique, the authors scrutinized (1) the type of brand Web site functions, and (2) the similarity ratings between the home (US) sites and Czech sites. Implications are discussed from the Web site standardization versus localization perspective.

Localization of a document requires tacit knowledge of the target language and culture. Although it is promoted by many software developers and Web designers, localization is becoming increasingly inadequate as a strategy for disseminating information via the World Wide Web. The 21st century already has seen dramatic rises in the numbers of Internet users in nearly every country, making it difficult if not impossible for any translation effort to accommodate all of the 347 languages that claim at least 1 million speakers. The best way to expand the accessibility of Web content is to make it more explicit, not more tacit. This means producing and uploading clear English content that non-native speakers can easily understand. *Global English* is written with simpler sentence structure, less jargon, and no slang—characteristics that make it a viable lingua franca for countless Web users whose native language is not considered important enough to merit a localization effort.

This chapter attempts to explore the possibility of building social capital in VC by first introducing the phenomenon, its problems and context, types of VCs and the significance of knowledge sharing. The author presents the process of social capital from a sociological standpoint where two main theories will be used—*elementary theory of social structure* and *social exchange theory* as the backbone of the arguments. By integrating both theories, the author provides a conceptual framework that includes six antecedents to develop social capital. Subsequently, the propositions are expressed in terms of implications to the sociological approach of VC and some conclusions are made by including some future research agenda.

This chapter explores the theory and practice of business & IT alignment in multinational companies. In the first part of the chapter an overview of the theory is presented. In this part, the familiar frameworks for business & IT alignment are put in perspective in an *alignment development model*. The second part of the chapter presents the practical issues that are experienced in aligning IT to business in multinational companies. These issues and considerations resulted from a focused group discussion with IT managers and CIOs of medium-sized and large organizations in The Netherlands.

Intercultural collaboration is a necessity for many ICT workers since the ICT sector has become highly globalized. In the context of international market entries, mergers, network production, as well as near- and offshoring, three modes of intercultural collaboration take place: collaboration in multicultural teams, in dispersed teams, and in the context of foreign assignment. If persons with different cultural backgrounds work together, challenges occur due to different value systems, work and communication styles. They join the general difficulties of internationalization and industrialization in the ICT sector, and thus are often overlooked, but may hold risks and provoke hidden costs. This chapter describes the challenges of intercultural collaboration and methods to control the risk of intercultural friction focusing on the particular modes of collaboration. Companies should include results of intercultural research into their selection of personnel strategies. Additionally a systematic intercultural personnel development by cross-cultural trainings and coaching helps the collaborators to handle culture differences and to establish a productive collaboration.

Chapter X

Over the past two decades computer mediated communication (CMC) has become a vital form of communication for education, business, and industry, as well as simply another form of social interaction. Past authors have suggested that building online communities with the various CMC tools provides for a more egalitarian social network. However, others have suggested that this may not be the case as there are communication style differences that could impeed equity or social interactions. This chapter provides a discussion of the issues, recommendations, and trends that the future might hold for CMC, both in terms of technical advances and social implications.

Chapter XI

The scope of interests in the area of information systems (IS) has focused mainly on technological aspects so far. If the human component were taken into account, it has been analyzed from the level of an individual, so have all new concepts of rationality. This chapter argues that collective behavior, which is a basic determinant of the Global IS dynamics, does not proceed in a planned manner, but rather is adaptive and follows certain patterns found in nature. It follows that this behavior can be expressed in a model form, which enables to structure it. A model exemplification of a global information system is a modern, electronic, stock exchange. The identification of quantitative attributes of a social subsystem can provide substantial theoretical and methodological premises for the extension of the optimizing and individualistic notion of rationality by the social and adaptive aspects.

Chapter XII

Networked communication is proliferating our world. The fact that global information communication technologies (ICTs) are becoming increasingly available is facilitating human computer interaction, which permeates the use of computer-mediated communication (CMC) in various organizations, groups, and interpersonal contexts. As a result, the issue facing today's organizations is not whether to use global information technologies (GITs) in networked communication, but rather how to use them for effective functioning and as efficient coordination tools, especially how to incorporate GITs into the decision-making process. Consequently, this chapter examines the issues in designing CMC into group interactions and decision-making processes.

Chapter XIII

This chapter provides information technology (IT) project leaders, call center management, researchers and educators with an analytical tool to examine current concerns and anticipate future trends related to globalization and information technology. The authors propose to use a *multi-lens* analysis as a framework for evaluating outsourcing opportunities. This approach offers a valuable and effective *full-circle* methodology for assessing technological, political, organizational, economic, legal, educational, and cultural considerations that encourage a fuller understanding of the issues, problems, and opportunities that globalization and technological innovation creates. An understanding of these factors related to outsourcing and other technical collaborative projects can avoid costly miscalculations, reduce misunderstandings, and promote mutually beneficial results. Outsourcing is part of a larger socio-political and cultural process, and extends beyond the narrow parameters of economic and technological considerations. The discussion of the various lenses is supported by relevant material from case studies and qualitative interview data collected by the authors in Germany and India from IT experts, call center managers, and call center agents.

Enterprises within and outside the IT industry have long used offshore development and outsourcing to reduce information systems development and maintenance costs, and as a source of specialized, low-wage workers. In the last decade, there has been a spur of activities in offshore outsourcing, which is driven by the e-business revolution and a worldwide demand for IT skills. This contributed to the growth of IT-related industries in countries such as Ireland and India. Meanwhile, vendors from the Philippines, Russia, Hungary, China, Taiwan, Mexico, and other countries entered the market, and in some cases, adapting business models established by Indian firms that have dominated the services sector in the past decade. The emergence of new offshore centers has been marked by new approaches and skill sets, adding to the services and value propositions that define the offshore sector today. In this chapter, we identify the main risk factors and best practices in global IT outsourcing. In addition, we delve into some important issues on IT outsourcing, particularly the challenges along with benefits. Finally we present case studies of two Global 200 organizations and validate some of the claims made by previous researchers on IT outsourcing. This study will help the management to identify the risk factors and take the necessary remedial steps.

Chapter XV

Quality standardization contributes to the internationalization process of the ICT industry. At the policy level institutional aspects related to the definition, acknowledgement and implementation of quality standards constitute the focus of research. From an organizational point of view the influence of quality standards on working practices and outputs are related to the implementation of quality management systems. This chapter gives an overview about the quality standardization patterns at the policy level and discusses the influence of the implementation of quality management systems in off- and nearshore practices.

Off- and nearshoring in the European ICT sector represents a relative new practice that has significantly increased since the beginning of the new millenium. Cost reduction, perceived cultural and historical nearness, and institutional and legal advantages influence the decision for host country destinations, whereas hidden and transaction costs represent some of the main related risks and can lead to a repatriation of off- and nearshore projects. This chapter overviews off- and nearshoring trends in Europe and discusses the main related challenges and development chances.

Chapter XVII

This chapter outlines and maps the field of IT consulting in global information technology. In providing an overview of recent market developments, main characteristics of the field are highlighted and linked to the research on consultancy and organization development. In order to examine the role of IT consultants in modern organizations and to cover various aspects of the field, a conceptual framework is offered, which may be used for further analytical investigation of the field.

Chapter XVIII

This chapter investigates the role of IT consultants in cases where the implementation of IT systems results in changes within the organization. Given the ever-present relevance of power relations within organizations and the fact that an actor's authority is dependent on his or her access to resources and the rules of the organization, IT systems can be said to be objects of micro-political negotiations. Power relations between IT consultants and members of the client organization, for instance, between the project manager and his employees, are analysed on a micro level to illustrate the strategies actors use. Teamwork and collaboration between consultants and employees are analysed, and proposals for further research are suggested.

Current knowledge is produced, disseminated, and stored in digital format. This data will not be preserved by benign neglect; digital information will be preserved only through active management. This chapter will provide a theoretical foundation for digital preservation, an overview of current best practice for digital preservation, and a research agenda as well as a proscriptive framework by which to design digital preservation into a system.

GIT and GIS have a significant impact on the undergraduate and postgraduate programs offered in universities in Australia. Further, how to teach IT and IS to international students has been becoming a significant issue for IT and IS programs offered in Australia, in particular in the context of a fiercely competitive market of international students, and in the context of GIT and GIS. However, these topics have not drawn the attention of academic researchers so far. This chapter will fill this gap by examining the impact of global information technology (GIT) on universities in Australia in such areas as curriculum development, textbooks, and teaching, and by looking at some issues in teaching information technology (IT) and information systems (IS) to international students from different countries with different IT and IS backgrounds based on the author's working and teaching experience in three different universities in Australia. This chapter also makes a daring prediction for the impact of GIT on international education in Australia and proposes a few viable strategies for resolving some issues facing international education for IT and IS in Australia. The proposed approach is very useful for research and development of GIT and GIS, as well as for IT/IS programs in Australian universities.

Chapter XXI

In this chapter, we have proposed the importance sampling approaches to track the prevalence and growth of Web service, where an improved importance sampling scheme is introduced. We present a thorough analysis of the sampling approaches. Based on the periodic measurement of the number of active Web servers conducted over the past five years, an exponential growth of the Web is observed and modeled. Also discussed in this chapter is the increasing security concerns on Web servers.

Chapter XXII

While HTML provides the Web with a standard format for information *presentation,* XML has been made a standard for information *structuring* on the Web. The mission of the Semantic Web now is to provide *meaning* to the Web. Apart from building on the existing Web technologies, we need other tools from other areas of science to do that. This chapter shows how natural language processing methods and technologies, together with ontologies and a neural algorithm, can be used to help in the task of adding meaning to the Web, thus making the Web a better platform for knowledge management in general.

This chapter investigates opportunities to integrate mobile technologies within an organization's enterprise architecture, with an emphasis on supply chain management (SCM) systems. These SCM systems exist within the overall enterprise architecture (EA) of the business. SCM systems are further influenced by the increasing modern-day need of information and communications technologies (ICT) within a business, to bring together all their disparate applications. The resultant enterprise application integration (EAI) also stands to benefit immensely by the incorporation of mobile technologies within it. Traditionally, supply chain management systems have involved management of the flows of material, information, and finance in a complex web of networks that include suppliers, manufacturers, distributors, retailers, and customers. Thus, these traditional supply chain management systems have a great need for integration under the umbrella of "EAI." Mobile technologies can provide *time and location* independence to these

EAIs in terms of information in the supply chain systems, creating the possibilities of multiple business processes that traverse diverse geographical regions. This chapter, based on the research conducted by the authors at the University of Western Sydney, discusses the opportunities that arise in supply chain management systems due to the time and location independence offered by mobility, and the resultant advantages and limitations of such integration to the business.

Chapter XXIV

Organizations are globalising their businesses primarily due to the communications capabilities offered by the Internet technologies. As a result, there are global business processes that span across multiple geographical locations and time zones. The influence of mobility on these global business processes does not appear to have been studied in sufficient detail. Furthermore, mobile technology goes far beyond its ubiquitous use as a mobile phone for voice communication or for the exchange of messages. This chapter discusses and recommends a model for transition and integration of mobility into global business processes. Furthermore, the authors also envisage the accommodation of mobile Web services in mobile transformations enabling business applications to collaborate regardless of their technological platforms.

This exploratory research project set out to investigate the architecture and design principles of international information systems. Analysing six case vignettes in a modified grounded theory approach, a two-dimensional topology for international information systems—postulated from previous research as a seed concept—was confirmed as a useful architecture paradigm. In its terms, international information systems are configured from two elements: 'Core' systems (common for the whole enterprise) on the one hand and 'Local' systems (specific only for each site) on the other. The interface between the two is a third component. The cases showed that achieving the 'correct' balance between Core and Local can be a difficult political process and requires careful organisational engineering to be successful. One case vignette in particular highlights the logical and organisational difficulties in defining these systems elements. Object orientation as the fundamental design principle is investigated as an approach to provide a solution for this problem. Because it enables implementation differentiation and flexibility for future functional changes, it is conjectured that object technology is an optimal – technical - development strategy for international information systems. Directions for further research are outlined.

Foreword

A growing body of knowledge is being accumulated in the area of global information technologies (IT). Global IT research is a subset of IS research. It focuses on IS issues that are international in flavor. However, Global IT research is distinct from general IS research. One way of differentiating is by the research themes examined. Six major themes distinguish global IT research—namely, global enterprise management, global information resources management, culture & socio-economic issues, comparative study of nations, research frameworks/key issues, and single country studies.

Global IT research also is very diverse. There are a wide variety of variables studied and methodology used. Variables examined included those internal to the organization (e.g., characteristics of the development; operations and management environments; the characteristics of the IS being studied; and extent of adoption and diffusion of IT), as well as the external environments (e.g., culture, infrastructure, government policy, and legal system). Both quantitative and qualitative approaches have been widely employed—primarily, field and case studies.

The narrow and diverse nature of the field presents difficulties in conducting global IT research. The difficulties intrinsic in global research revolve around resource constraints and methodological problems. For example, language barriers between researchers and research participants, research instrument translation, conceptualizing and measuring culture, biasness, financial and time-related limitations.

This book brings together research from academics in countries such as Australia, China, the Czech Republic, Finland, Germany, Malaysia, Mexico, New Zealand, Poland, Spain, and the USA. The chapters cover most of the major themes in global IT mentioned earlier. In sharing their research and findings relating to global IT management in the digital economy, I hope that you will find this book a useful resource in developing further research into the subject.

Felix B. Tan is professor of information systems, director of research management, and head of the University Research Office at AUT University, New Zealand. He serves as editor-in-chief of the Journal of Global Information Management. *He is on the executive council and is a fellow of the Information Resources Management Association. He also served on the council of the Association for Information Systems as the Asia-Pacific Representative. Dr. Tan's current research interests are in electronic commerce, global information management, business-IT alignment, and the management of IT. Dr. Tan has published in* MIS Quarterly, Information & Management, Journal of Information Technology, Information Systems Journal, IEEE Transactions on Engineering Management *as well as other journals, and he has refereed numerous conference proceedings.*

Preface

Lao-Tzu, 6th century BC Chinese poet said, "Those who have knowledge do not predict. Those who predict do not have knowledge." It is not a crystal ball prediction that today's enterprises are increasingly *going global* by becoming more distributed and leveraging resource bases in all parts of the world. Whether through offshore relationships, global support, or application development programs, or by linking disparate parts of organizations, enterprises are focused on leveraging globalization and cultivating innovation.

Global Information Technology Management in the Digital Economy provides comprehensive coverage of the most important issues, concepts, trends, and technologies in the field of the emerging sub-discipline of global information technology (IT) management (also referred to within the information systems [IS] discipline as global information technology management, as international information systems, and as global management information systems). The chapters provide definitions, explanations, and applications of various pertinent topics and issues. This publication will help in providing researchers, scholars, students, and professionals access to the latest knowledge related to global IT/S, and solving related problems and challenges. *Global Information Technology Management in the Digital Economy* with its contributions from authors in Australia, China, the Czech Republic, Finland, Germany, Malaysia, Mexico, New Zealand, Poland, Spain, and the USA encompasses multiple levels of analysis:

1. The nation(s), or international policy-making body
2. The firm(s), the MultiNational Enterprise (MNE) or the IT vendors
3. The group(s) or team(s)
4. The individual
5. The technology overlay

Clearly, these five levels of analysis look to numerous referent disciplines such as political science, economics, law, management, international business, human-computer interface, cross-cultural studies, sociology, psychology, telecommunications, and computer science.

The target audience for this book are global executives, managers, and other business decision makers who need to make informed choices about how their organizations can use global information technology/systems effectively; researchers (both academic and corporate) studying global information technology/systems, and global information technology/systems business models for industry and/or academic purposes; educators and trainers who increasingly find themselves using/teaching global information technology/systems; and administrators of global/international/multi-domestic/transnational organizations who wish to leverage global information technology/systems for competitive advantage.

The subject areas and specific topics covered in this book include the following:

- Aligning global information systems (IS) strategy to global business strategy
- Issues involving the technical platform for global IS applications
- Issues involved in international sharing of data
- Issues of IS projects spanning cultures
- Key GIT issues such as: (1) managerial/strategic, (2) technological/application, (3) host country social/cultural, (4) host country economic, (5) host country technological, and (6) host country political/legal
- Issues and trends in global information technology education
- Managing information technology in multi-domestic/international/global/transnational corporations
- Global information technology/systems and socio-economic development in under-developed/developing/developed countries

One example of concrete proof of global IT management in action in the digital economy is provided by Cemex, a 101-year-old global ready-mix concrete supplier with an annual sales volume of about 70 million cubic meters. A critical element is the product's perishability since the concrete begins to harden as soon as it is loaded into a truck for delivery to a construction site. Hence, Cemex needed a way to accommodate weather and traffic delays, in addition to last-minute orders from builders. Taking a page from the handbooks of FedEx, food delivery services, and ambulance dispatchers, chief information officer Gelacio Iniguez led development of a scheduling and routing application based on dynamic synchronization of operations (DSO), which is combined with a GPS system installed on the company's cement-mixer trucks. Dubbed CemexNet, the system has increased truck productivity by 35% and cut average response time for changed orders from three hours to 20 minutes. This has enabled Cemex to charge premium prices to time-sensitive customers, and it is building brand loyalty among contractors whose costs spiral when crews wait idly for deliveries. Cemex's ability to guarantee fast delivery is a huge competitive advantage over other companies that require a half- or full-day delivery window. It allows them to charge premium prices for what is the ultimate commodity product. Cemex grew sales more than 72% last year and has a three-year growth rate of nearly 30% for sales and more than 42% for earnings per share, according to Reuters.

In manufacturing, Toyota Motor Corp. has used world-renowned just-in-time supply-chain management and business-process management technology to eliminate waste, limit inventory buildup and continually improve production. Its technology leadership finally helped the Japanese manufacturer topple General Motors as the world's No. 1 automaker, with 2007 first-quarter sales of 2.35 million vehicles, compared with GM's 2.26 million.

In the context of global sourcing in and internationalization of the information and communications technology (ICT) sector, intercultural collaboration is for many ICT workers a daily affair. Especially in the field of software development, where the needs for communication are high, intercultural collaboration poses a particular challenge. Misunderstandings and an unproductive work atmosphere may result in hidden costs for the companies. Martina Maletzky's chapter entitled, *Intercultural Collaboration in the ICT Sector* highlights the different types of intercultural collaboration in the ICT sector, identifying the special challenges that occur and suggesting ways in which companies may minimize such challenges of intercultural collaboration.

Over that past two decades computer mediated communication (CMC) has become a vital form of communication for education, business, and industry, as well as simply another form of social interaction. Past authors have suggested that building online communities with the various CMC tools provides for a more egalitarian social network. However, others have suggested that this may not be the case as there are communication style differences that could impeed equity or social interactions. The chapter entitled, *Computer-Mediated Communication: Enhancing Online Group Interactions*, by J. Michael Blocher, provides a discussion of the issues, recommendations, and trends that the future might hold for CMC, both in terms of technical advances and social implications.

The scope of interest in the area of information systems (IS) has focused mainly on technological aspects so far. If the human component were taken into account, it has been analyzed from the level of an individual. So have all new concepts of rationality. In *The Dynamics and Rationality of Collective Behavior within a Global Information System*, Jacek Unold argues that collective behavior, which is a basic determinant of the global IS dynamics, does not proceed in a planned manner, but is adaptive and follows certain patterns found in nature. It follows that this behavior can be expressed in a model form, which enables to structure it. A model exemplification of a global information system is a modern, electronic, stock exchange. The identification of quantitative attributes of a social subsystem can provide substantial theoretical and methodological premises for the extension of the optimizing and individualistic notion of rationality by the social and adaptive aspects.

The chapter entitled, *Group Decision Making in Computer-Mediated Communication as Networked Communication: Understanding the Technology and Implications*, by Bolanle Olaniran, explores networked communication using global and communication information systems in the organizational decision-making process. Specifically, the chapter examines the issues in designing CMC into group interactions and decision-making processes. For example, challenges facing communication information technologies (CITs) regarding freedom of participation and equal participation are addressed. The chapter also offers ideas for making decision processes effective when incorporating global information and communication information systems into decision-making process using the two stage process, namely, the idea generation and evaluation stages.

Subhankar Dhar's chapter entitled, *Global IS Outsourcing: Current Trends, Risks, and Cultural Issues*, states that in the last decade, there has been a spur of activities in offshore outsourcing, which is driven by the e-business revolution and a worldwide demand for IT skills. This contributed to the growth of IT-related industries in countries such as Ireland and India. Meanwhile, vendors from the Philippines, Russia, Hungary, China, Taiwan, Mexico, and other countries entered the market, and in some cases, adapting business models established by Indian firms that have dominated the services sector in the past decade. The emergence of new offshore centers has been marked by new approaches and skill sets, adding to the services and value propositions that define the offshore sector today. In this chapter, the author identifies the main risk factors and best practices in global IT outsourcing, delves into some important issues on IT outsourcing, particularly the challenges along with benefits, presents case studies of two Global 200 organizations and validates some of the claims made by previous researchers on IT outsourcing. This study will help the management to identify the risk factors and take the necessary remedial steps.

In the chapter entitled, *Teaching Information Systems to International Students in Australia: A Global Information Technology Perspective*, Zhaohao Sun examines international education in Australia and looks at IT and IS in Australian universities from a global viewpoint. He discusses impacts of global IT on IT and IS in Australia and examines his own teaching experiences in Australia as an example of GIT. He discusses the future trends for IT and IS in Australia and proposes future research directions.

In *Natural Language Processing Agents and Document Clustering in Knowledge Management: The Semantic Web Case*, Steve Legrand and JGR Pulido argue that while HTML provides the Web with a standard format for information *presentation*, XML has been made a standard for information *structuring* on the Web. The mission of the Semantic Web now is to provide *meaning* to the Web. Apart from building on the existing Web technologies, we need other tools from other areas of science to do that. This chapter shows how natural language processing methods and technologies, together with ontologies and a neural algorithm, can be used to help in the task of adding meaning to the Web, thus making the Web a better platform for knowledge management in general.

In *Electronic Highways in South East Asia: Liberality, Control, and Social Change*, Loong Wong provides an overview of Southeast Asian economies, and then proceeds to provide an analysis of ICT projects in the region, focusing on the Singaporean and Malaysian experiences. This chapter examines the relationships and dynamics of changes effected through the intersection of economics, politics, and ICTs. Drawing on the examples of Indonesia, Malaysia, and Singapore, Wong argues that as these forces interact, greater political space is engendered. Economic change via privatization has a similar, although unintended, *liberalizing* effect. This chapter further notes that states have responded to this liberalizing thrust by seeking greater control and regulation, but suggests that these attempts are unlikely to be successful.

Bhuvan Unhelkar, Ming-Chien Wu, and Abbass Ghanbary provide an insight on how mobile technologies impact the enterprise architecture (EA) with an emphasis on supply chain management (SCM) systems. This chapter entitled, *Integrating Mobile Technologies in Enterprise Architecture with a Focus on Global Supply Chain Management Systems*, is based on the research conducted by the authors at the University of Western Sydney, defining the use of mobility in the area SCM systems and explaining the time and location independence in the area of EA and SCM. It provides the advantages and limitations of mobile integration in global organizations.

The chapter entitled, *Influence of Mobile Technologies on Global Business Processes in Global Organizations*, by Dinesh Arunatileka, Abbass Ghanbary, and Bhuvan Unhelkar is based on an action research project carried out in a global organization in order to evaluate how mobility alters the existing business processes of the global organizations. It provides an insight into organizational business processes and the impact of mobility providing competitive delivery to those business processes under investigation. The chapter provides the future benefits of the Web services in mobile technology enabling global organizations to collaborate with each other while using different platforms.

In *The Development of National ICT Policy in Kenya: The Influence of Regional Institutions and Key Stakeholders*, Timothy Mwololo Waema argues that the role that information and communication technologies could play in socio-economic development has been recognized by governments worldwide. The most important starting point in most countries is a national ICT policy. In many developing countries, ICT policy development has increasingly become a participatory process. This is largely as a result of implementing policy reforms, with a strong emphasis on governance systems. This chapter is a case study of the development of national information and communication technology policy in Kenya, the influences of regional institutions and their products, and the role of the private sector and civil society. The chapter is based on a study that was carried out by reviewing existing relevant documents and by interviewing key persons involved in national and regional ICT policy in Kenya. This chapter also presents the challenges, conclusions, and recommendations based on the case.

Stacy Kowalczyk's chapter, *Digital Preservation by Design*, argues that current knowledge is produced, disseminated, and stored in digital format. This data will not be preserved by benign neglect; digital information will be preserved only through active management. This chapter will provide a theoretical foundation for digital preservation, an overview of current best practice for digital preservation, and a research agenda, as well as a proscriptive framework by which to design digital preservation into a system.

In *Economic Development: Government's Cutting Edge in IT*, Gerald A. Merwin Jr., J. Scott McDonald, and Levy C. Odera explore the interface between information technology (IT) and economic development. The impacts of three IT innovations are assessed in terms of how they contributed to the development of economic development practice: database management systems (DBMS), geographic information systems (GIS), and the evolution of Web sites. With regard to the close relationship between IT and economic development, the chapter primarily focuses on current and future issues in this area. The chapter concludes by providing a glimpse of what might be expected in the future and some recommendations for future research on this topic.

Michaela Wieandt's chapter, *Information Technology Consulting in Global Information Technology*, outlines and maps the field of IT consulting in global information technology. In providing an overview of recent market developments, main characteristics of the field are highlighted and linked to the research on consultancy and organization development. In order to examine the role of IT consultants in modern organizations and to cover various aspects of the field, a conceptual framework is offered that may be used for further analytical investigation of the field.

In *Understanding Global Information Technology and Outsourcing Dynamics: A Multi-Lens Model*, Robert C. Yoder, Vera Eccarius-Kelly and Suvarna Cherukuri provide information technology (IT) project leaders, call center management, researchers, and educators with an analytical tool to examine current concerns and anticipate future trends related to globalization and information technology. The authors propose to use a multi-lens analysis as a framework for evaluating outsourcing opportunities. This approach offers a valuable and effective *full-circle* methodology for assessing technological, political, organizational, economic, legal, educational, and cultural considerations that encourage a fuller understanding of the issues, problems, and opportunities that globalization and technological innovation creates. An understanding of these factors related to outsourcing and other technical collaborative projects can avoid costly miscalculations, reduce misunderstandings, and promote mutually beneficial results. Outsourcing is part of a larger socio-political and cultural process, and extends beyond the narrow parameters of economic and technological considerations. The discussion of the various lenses is supported by relevant material from case studies and qualitative interview data collected by the authors in Germany and India from IT experts, call center managers, and call center agents.

The Possibility of Water-Cooler Chat?: Developing Communities of Practice for Knowledge Sharing within Global Virtual Teams, by Norhayati Zakaria looks at a key concept called *communities of practice* that helps to facilitate organizational learning through increased knowledge sharing within global virtual teams. By using Granovetter's (1974) *weak ties* theory, the author suggests that casual acquaintances known as *weak ties* have significant implications for social relationships and context, both of which can benefit virtual organizational team members. Furthermore, based on Hofstede's (1980) cultural dimensions, the author argues that cultural factors also can impact one's willingness to share knowledge. Thus, there are three questions that guide this chapter: (1) How do social relationships and context among global virtual teams affect the development of communities of practice? (2) How does culture affect the knowledge sharing activities? and (3) What is the impact of ICTs on knowledge sharing and the emergence of communities of practice?

The chapter, *Understanding Brand Web Site Positioning in the New EU Member States: The Case of the Czech Republic*, by Shintaro Okazaki and Radoslav Škapa examines Web sites created by American multinational corporations (MNCs) in the Czech Republic. Utilizing a content analysis technique, we scrutinized (1) the type of brand Web site functions, and (2) the similarity ratings between the home (U.S.) sites and Czech sites. Implications are discussed from the Web site standardization versus localization perspective.

In *Information Technology Consulting and the Implementation of Information Technology*, by Michaela Wieandt, the author investigates the role of IT consultants in cases where the implementation of IT systems results in changes within the organization. Given the ever-present relevance of power relations within organizations and the fact that an actor's authority is dependent on his or her access to resources and the rules of the organization, IT systems can be said to be objects of micro-political negotiations. Power relations between IT consultants and members of the client organization, for instance between the project manager and his employees, are analysed on a micro level to illustrate the strategies actors use. Team work and collaboration between consultants and employees are analysed, and proposals for further research are suggested.

In *Offshoring in the ICT Sector in Europe: Trends and Scenario Analysis*, Esther Ruiz Ben, Michaela Wieandt, and Martina Maletzky argue that off- and nearshoring in the European ICT sector represents a relative new practice that significantly has increased since the beginning of the new millenium. Cost reduction, perceived cultural and historical nearness, and institutional and legal advantages influence the decision for host country destinations, whereas hidden and transaction costs represent some of the main related risks and can lead to a repatriation of off- and nearshore projects. This chapter overviews off- and nearshoring trends in Europe, and discusses the main related challenges and development chances.

Beyond Localization: A New Look at Disseminating Information via the Web, by Martin A. Schell, states that localization of a document requires tacit knowledge of the target language and culture. Although it is promoted by many software developers and Web designers, localization is becoming increasingly inadequate as a strategy for disseminating information via the World Wide Web. The 21st century already has seen dramatic rises in the numbers of Internet users in nearly every country, making it difficult, if not impossible, for any translation effort to accommodate all of the 347 languages that claim at least 1 million speakers. The best way to expand the accessibility of Web content is to make it more explicit, not more tacit. This means producing and uploading clear English content that non-native speakers can easily understand. Global English is written with simpler sentence structure, less jargon, and no slang—characteristics that make it a viable lingua franca for countless Web users whose native language is not considered important enough to merit a localization effort.

The chapter entitled, *Understanding Social Capital Formation for Knowledge Sharing in Virtual Communities*, by Shafiz A. Mohd Yusof, attempts to explore the possibility of building social capital in virtual communities (VC) by first introducing the phenomenon, its problems and context, types of VC, and the significance of knowledge sharing. It presents the process of social capital from a sociological standpoint employing two main theories—elementary theory of social structure and social exchange theory as the backbone of the arguments. By integrating both these theories, the chapter provides a conceptual framework that includes six antecedents to develop social capital. Subsequently, the propositions are expressed in terms of implications to the sociological approach of VC and some conclusions are made by including some future research agenda.

In the chapter, *Business & IT Alignment in a Multinational Company: Issues and Approaches*, A. J. Gilbert Silvius, explores the theory and practice of business & IT alignment in multinational companies. In the first part of the chapter, an overview of the theory is presented. In this part, the familiar frameworks for business & IT alignment are put in perspective in an *alignment development model*. The second part of the chapter presents the practical issues that are experienced in aligning IT to business in multinational companies. These issues and considerations resulted from a focused group discussion with IT managers and CIOs of medium-sized and large organizations in the Netherlands.

The chapter entitled, *Sampling Approaches on Collecting Internet Statistics in the Digital Economy*, by Song Xing, Bernd Peter Paris, and Xiannong Meng, argues that the Internet's complexity restricts analysis or simulation to assess its parameters. Instead, actual measurements provide a reality check. Many statistical measurements of the Internet estimate rare event probabilities. Collection of such statistics renders sampling methods as a primary substitute. Within the context of this inquiry, the authors have presented the conventional Monte Carlo approach to estimate the Internet event probability. As a variance reduction technique, Importance Sampling is introduced, which is a modified Monte Carlo approach resulting in a significant reduction of effort to obtain an accurate estimate. This method works particularly well when estimating the probability of rare events. It has great appeal to use as an efficient sampling scheme for estimating the information server density on the Internet.

In this chapter, the authors have proposed the importance sampling approaches to track the prevalence and growth of Web service, where an improved importance sampling scheme is introduced. They present a thorough analysis of the sampling approaches. Based on the periodic measurement of the number of active Web servers conducted over the past five years, an exponential growth of the Web is observed and modeled. Also discussed in this chapter is the increasing security concerns on Web servers.

Acknowledgment

Editing this book has been a delightful and rewarding experience. For conceptual and content contributions, I owe a debt of gratitude to all the authors that have contributed to this book. I would like to thank them all sincerely for their excellent and much committed work (as a virtual team between the editor and the author/s) and transnational tele-cooperation in the various revisions of their manuscripts. The responsibility for content and potential errors remains of course with the author/s exclusively. IGI Global management and staff are thankfully acknowledged for their efforts in making this book a success. I also would like to thank my family for their love and support during the countless hours spent in making this book a reality. Ultimately, I would consider my goal met if this book extends the existing body of knowledge in theory and practice, and serves as a valuable resource for focused research in the field of global information technology/systems management.

Mahesh S. Raisinghani, MBA, MSc, Ph.D, CEC, CISM, PMP

Live as if you were to die tomorrow. Learn as if you were to live forever.
- Mahatma Gandhi

Chapter I
Economic Development:
Government's Cutting Edge in IT

Gerald A. Merwin Jr.
Valdosta State University, USA

J. Scott McDonald
University of Texas El Paso, USA

Levy C. Odera
University of Florida, USA

ABSTRACT

This chapter explores the interface between information technology (IT) and economic development. The impacts of three IT innovations are assessed in terms of how they contributed to the development of economic development practice: database management systems (DBMS), geographic information systems (GIS), and the evolution of Web sites. With regard to the close relationship between IT and economic development, the chapter primarily focuses on current and future issues in this area. The chapter is organized into the following sections: it begins with an introductory section, a second section delves into the history of economic development and its relationship with IT; a third section introduces the three IT revolutions in economic development; the fourth, fifth and sixth sections each address a key development in economic development/IT relationship: DBMS, GIS, and Web site development, respectively. Section seven provides examples of IT in practice with descriptions of three excellent economic development Web sites. The chapter concludes by providing a glimpse of what might be expected in the future and some recommendations for future research on this topic.

SCOPE AND OVERVIEW

This chapter explores the interface between information technology (IT) and economic development. The intent is not to construct a comprehensive overview; rather, this chapter presents the key issues, especially those likely to expand in importance, resulting in a yet closer marriage of IT and economic development. The discussion encompasses a wide spectrum of local U.S. governments. The focus on the U.S. is reflective of that country's leadership in the merged domains of economic development and IT. For the most part, U.S. economic development is largely a local function with the national government playing support roles, while in most other countries, the responsibility for economic development rests firmly on the shoulders of a national government. The advantage of focusing on U.S. local governments is that with tens of thousands of these governments, considerable diversity of economic development and IT exists. While the primary focus of this chapter is on current and future issues, the chapter begins with a review of some key historic elements in the development of economic development practice. This is necessary to provide both definition to the broad area of public policy encompassed by economic development, and to establish context for discussion of current and future issues and trends. Wherever possible, emphasis is placed on an application, that is, real world perspectives rather than theoretical orientations.

This chapter will make every effort to avoid redundancy with other chapters in this volume or with the extensive literatures on economic development and IT. The principle focus of this chapter is the highly important yet under-explored issue of the identification and elaboration of the critical interfaces between economic development and IT. Specifically, this chapter looks at three key IT innovations as they impact economic development: database management systems (DBMS), geographic information systems (GIS), and the evolution of Web sites.

The chapter is organized into nine sections. Following this introductory section, the second section, delves into the history of economic development and its relationship with IT. This section focuses on key definitions and the difficulty of delineating between economic development and other areas of public policy and private activity. The second section broadly elaborates the relationships between government economic development policy and IT policy/actions. The third section introduces the three IT revolutions in economic developments. And the following fourth, fifth, sixth sections each address one key development in the economic development/IT relationship: DBMS, GIS, and Web site development, respectively. Each of these developments is treated as revolutionary because they shifted the paradigm of how practitioners approached the implementation of programming, and,

when taken together, have changed the practice of economic development in ways unimaginable just a short time earlier. The seventh section provides examples of IT in practice with descriptions of three excellent economic development Web sites. Section eight and nine focus on the future with predictions for ways economic development can further utilize IT and suggestions for future research.

ECONOMIC DEVELOPMENT: INFORMATION TECHNOLOGY INTERFACE

Economic Development Defined

Economic development has been variously defined. Practitioners and scholars have produced countless case studies and meta-studies, of the role of economic development in a community, and an almost endless collection of recipes for success. One issue is clear from this plethora of study; there is no single, widely accepted definition. Definitions tend to fall into two categories—narrow and broad. Narrow definitions focus exclusively on economic impacts of policy, almost always jobs. Broad definitions meld economic measures and social measures, such as community ambiance and quality of life. Unfortunately, the same term—economic development—is used to convey both narrow and broad concepts. Practitioners and scholars must take care to monitor the context within which the term is being used in order to understand the scope of the discussion at hand. The broader definition (economic plus social) is more accurately referred to as *community development*. It is not uncommon for two highly knowledgeable professionals, either academics or practitioners to suffer confusion regarding definition.

At a minimum, *economic development* focuses on growth, in other words, is the economy growing (narrow definition)? *Community development* is focused on growth and change, economic growth in the economy, and positive change in non-economic, socially important factors (e.g., quality of life, diversity, improved physical environment).

For a majority of communities, including states, regional organizations, cities, and counties, economic development is defined in terms of changes in employment, such as numbers of jobs created or retained in a community. Secondary measures are quality of jobs, primarily measured in terms of wages and diversity of job opportunity, that is, the economy not being dominated by a single industry or type of employment. Practitioners commonly quip that economic development success is measured in terms of three factors: (1) jobs, (2) jobs, and (3) jobs. A broader definition of economic development starts with economic growth, and incorporates one or more additional measures associated with a community's social and environmental conditions. Social conditions may be narrow or far-reaching, including such items as recreation options, youth programs, educational infrastructures and programs, public safety, and healthcare options. Environmental conditions likewise may be narrowly or broadly defined to include such matters as open space, air, surface and ground water qualities, and brownfields (abandoned industrial sites), to name a few.

A broad definition of economic development, unless otherwise noted, is employed herein. The rationale behind this decision is straightforward; the profession and much of the scholarly focus have moved or are moving toward a broader definition. This is a critical matter as communities increasingly find themselves being asked to compete on more than purely economic costs (for example, costs per unit produced), and being asked to address issues of educational attainment and availability of local amenities among other matters.

Information Technology Implications of a Broad Definition of Economic Development

The information technology implications of employing a broad definition of economic development are far-reaching. Under the broad definition almost any IT investment by a public, not-for-profit or private organization may be considered as economic development. For example, investments in classroom computers, connectivity for social welfare organizations, or a new data management tool for a local manufacturer would each fall into the scope of IT and economic development broadly defined.

Of course this would result in considerable overlap with other topics covered in this handbook, and a scope that could not be meaningfully addressed in a single chapter.

The following statistics are intended to provide a snapshot of the penetration of IT into economic development practice in the U.S. employing the most recent national-level data available. What is clear from these numbers is that, while not yet complete, the penetration, and as we shall see, the impact of IT into economic development has been enormous. The International City/County Management Association (ICMA) in a 2004 report on the economic development practices of 726 local governments in the U.S. found 96.5% had a Web site, 86% used a Web site to attract business, and 55.5% offer some online services (e.g., permit applications submitted online) (ICMA, 2004a). As early as 1999, more than half (54.1%) of these were using community resource databases (ICMA, 1999). In its *Electronic Government 2004 Survey*, ICMA reported that more than a quarter (27.2%) of local governments that responded provide GIS mapping/data on their Web site (ICMA, 2004b). Geographic information systems (GIS) mapping is the integration of data and geographic locations to display information on a map. This opened new avenues for quality services and according to the *Guide to Geographic Information Systems*, "with a geographic information system (GIS), you can link information (attributes) to location data, such as people to addresses, buildings to parcels, or streets within a network." Information Technology is defined as "computer technology (hardware and software) for processing and storing information, as well as communications technology for transmitting information" (Martin, Brown, DeHayes, Hoffer, & Perkins, 2005).

Public Impacts on IT

Following a review of approximately 2,000 super projects (e.g., the NASA moon landing, U.S./Russia nuclear weapons and waste disposal, France's TGV, among others) the Internet was identified as the number two project and the most important communications development of recent years. The Internet was selected ahead of other communications super projects such as the global library of the World Wide Web, global television, and GPS (Conway & Lyne, 2006, p. 33). It is important to note for each of these projects, while availability of each innovation was fostered by private and/or not-for-profit investment, governments (especially the U.S. government) provided initial investments and established regulatory environments enabling these innovations. This discussion highlights two of the most basic government/IT interactions: government as a capital investor in technology/networks and government as regulator.

Government Shaping IT

Government may directly impact IT in a number of ways. Most notable for the purposes of this discussion are governmental roles as regulator and infrastructure and/or service provider.

Government as Regulator

Government as regulator is an essential underlying foundation to any type of development. It is difficult to overstate the impact regulation has on economic development. Suffice to say, government regulation provides the basis upon which protections are afforded to individuals and groups within a society. For our purposes, at a minimum, regulation protects private property, both physical (e.g., theft and trespass) and intellectual (e.g., patent and copyright), fair use and access (e.g., open range, water law, and antitrust), and ensures some foundational protections regarding health and safety. Regulation creates the environment in which investors and consumers interact with some confidence that they know the rules. This is particularly important with much of IT due to its large investments, substantial risks, and the importance of intellectual property.

Government as Provider

Governments may opt to provide one or more IT services. Of course, since the fall of communism, government provision of services has been universally viewed as a less-preferred option than before.

Still, today, government provision of service is viewed as a reasonable alternative under certain market conditions, such as a solution to a natural monopoly, in situations where services offered have the properties of a public good or when capital requirements are extremely large or fraught with risk (Van Wart, Rahm, & Sanders, 2000, p. 133).

Today, local governments in the U.S. are providing Internet infrastructure in situations where the market has failed to do so, most notably in rural areas such as Iowa (Van Wart, Rahm, & Sanders, 2000, p. 131). Many national governments have played a more active role in expanding access to information, especially via infrastructure development and/or communications and Internet service provision, often with a good degree of success, for example, developing countries such as Macedonia with USAID support (Nairn, G., 2006), India (Jain, 2004), and China (Lemon, 2005); former Soviet states, for example, Estonia (Fingar, 2006), and more developed states such as Dubai (DED and Tejari, 2006), some of the Arab emirates (Ajman, 2006), Belgium (Belgium economy, 2005), and Canada (New Brunswick) (Galagan & Homer, 2005).

Government as Consumer

Thus far we have discussed two important relationships between government and IT: (1) as a provider of service, and (2) as a regulator, creating an environment conducive to IT development. Government has an additional relationship with IT, (3) as a consumer (purchaser) of service(s). Governments, especially the U.S. government, are the largest consumers of IT goods and services, and their buying habits are felt industry-wide as they influence standards (UNIX Systems Cooperative Promotion Group, n.d., Accella Communications, 2002). Like the U.S. government, state and local governments spend large amounts on IT goods and services (Info Tech Research Group, 2006).

Each of the three relationships described above impacts economic development; however, they account for just one side of the government/IT equation: governments' impacts on IT. The other side of this equation, how governments are shaping their IT practices to enhance development of local economies, is the focus of the remainder of this chapter. These mainstream applications involve government as consumer. Economic development, at the cusp of the public and private sectors, generally is a leading edge of public sector innovation. This is evident in governments' early adoption of IT and its application to a broad array of activities within the scope of the economic development function.

Economic Development Structures and Functions

Before continuing this discussion, it is useful to mention briefly economic development in terms of structures and functions. Economic development clearly is a function that almost all governments have defined as part of their core mission. All 50 states and most cities and counties have an economic development function located somewhere in their bureaucracies. National governments, including those struggling with meeting basic needs or for survival of the state, define economic development in one form or another, as a core activity, for example, Nepal, Sri Lanka, Afghanistan, Cambodia, Malawi, and Uganda, to name a few. Many national governments define the basic essence of the state in terms of economic development, although some are exceedingly poor in terms of execution.

While there is almost universal agreement that economic development is an extremely important function, this function may be assigned to any combination of a wide variety of structures. In the U.S. the economic development function is found mostly in the private sector, the free economy.

The role of government is variously defined and divided among the three basic levels of government: federal, state, and local. While all governments serve as major consumers, the federal role is mostly establishing the ground rules and providing basic high cost infrastructures and services national in scope, such as highways, air traffic control, regulation, and research institutes. The state role overlaps the federal role, with states providing an additional layer of regulation and investment. However, these roles are more diverse (50 states vs. 1 federal gov-

ernment) and more localized. Also, state policy tends to concentrate on different issue areas than the federal government, most notably education. Add to this a third major layer, local governments, that generally focus most on quality of life issues, education, and maintaining low taxes.

The diversity of economic development activity at the local level is extreme, ranging from Chicago, New York City, and Los Angeles to a long list of extremely rural counties such as Clinch County, GA; Modoc County, CA; Kemper County, PA; and Petroleum County, MN. The number of local economic development organizations is stunning, for example, in Wisconsin alone, there are an estimated 800 to 900 local economic development organizations (Anderson & Nacker, 2003, p. 1).

The specific structures assigned to managing the public interest in economic development functions at state and local levels vary enormously from specific governmental units to not-for-profits, to private sector firms. Overlapping authority, functionally and/or geographically, for a particular function is common as various state and local-level organizations share responsibility, with varying levels of cooperation and competition.

IT/Economic Development Revolutions

This review looks predominately at the external face of economic development, the external marketing of a community. This is the most clearly visible aspect of economic development and normally the cutting edge, because most community economic development efforts are geared toward marketing. Three primary applications are clearly evident as pertaining to information management: Web sites, GIS, DBMS. DBMS in turn serves two primary functions, management of clients/customers and management of inventory, that is, available sites (land, building, and associated infrastructures), and other pertinent information. Additionally, integrated systems link DBMS, GIS, and/or Web sites. Each of these applications revolutionized the way economic development was conducted. They represented more than a quantitative shift in the amount of data available; each of these applications changed the way organizations and communities approached economic development, the way they perceived the issues relevant to the economic development function, and how they interacted with clients and customers.

Also, within these three applications, from the perspective of information technology are found one new development and two paradigm shifts. The development and paradigm shifts in IT influence the way economic development professionals utilize IT: The new development, already mentioned earlier, is GIS. The first paradigm shift is within DBMS, the transition from flat file to relational databases during the 1960s and 1970s; and the second paradigm shift relates to the development of the World Wide Web in the 1990s, which followed as an expansion of the capabilities of the Internet, generally attributed to having emerged in the 1960s. These three major developments are important for different reasons that will become apparent as the story of IT and economic development emerges.

Database Management

This review begins with database management systems because DBMS is the earliest and most frequent use of IT in economic development. Prior to the introduction of the personal computer, some major organizations, for example state governments, utilities, and transportation companies, employed databases to manage inventories of sites available for development and lists of potential customers. For a time line of the developments in information technology that relate to economic development, see Figure 1.

History of Database

A brief history of the database is warranted here, although more thorough histories might be available elsewhere in this volume. The roots of what we think of today as modern database systems were first developed between 1890 and 1900. At that time the U.S. Bureau of the Census needed an automated system for processing census data (National Research Council [NRC], 1999). This earliest data management system used machines with punched cards to process the data. The company that originally developed that system later merged with another company and became International Business Machines, what we know today as IBM.

A good summary of some key early events relating government-funded projects to database and computer development is available in *Funding a Revolution: Government Support for Computing Research* (NRC, 1999):

During World War I, the government used new punched-card technology to process the various data sets required to control industrial production, collect the new income tax, and classify draftees. The Social Security Act of 1935 made it necessary to keep continuous records on the employment of 26 million individuals. For this, "the world's biggest bookkeeping job," IBM developed special collating equipment. The Census Bureau purchased the first model of the first digital computer on the commercial market, the UNIVAC I (itself based on the government-funded Electronic Discrete Variable Automatic Computer (EDVAC) project at the University of Pennsylvania). In 1959, the Pentagon alone had more than 200 computers just for its business needs (e.g., tracking expenses, personnel, spare parts), with annual costs exceeding $70 million. U.S. dominance of the punched-card data processing industry, initially established with government support, was a major factor in U.S. companies' later dominance in electronic computing. (NRC, 1999, p. 160)

Transition from Flat File to Relational Databases

Database applications in use during the 1950s and 1960s were very basic compared to the popular ones in common use today. The databases of that time generally were called *flat file* databases and were hampered by the technology of the time in many ways. All data were stored in text format in a table. What we now know as *comma-delineated files* became important because of this.

All databases store data in columns and rows, referred to as fields and records, which are defined when the table is designed. In these flat file

Figure 1. Timeline of information technology developments significant to economic development

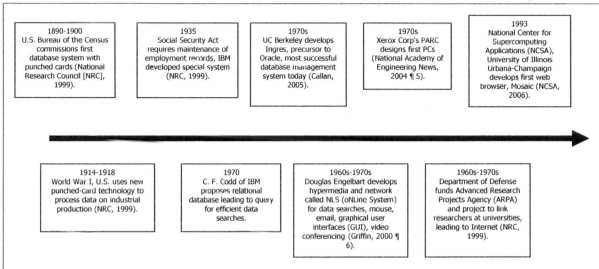

databases, one column or field was used to track the record number—a unique numeric value that incremented when each new record was added. This created an index of the data, but the index was based on only one field of each record. For example, if the table has a list of buildings available for lease, the field that stored the square footage of the buildings might be the index field. If the economic development professionals who used this database decided that they needed to have additional data, for instance, a list of major roads near the available buildings, this meant that a new field would be needed to store the information. This was not, however, a simple task.

If you needed to add new field to the flat file database, you had to create a new database file that included a field for the additional data. After the new file was created, the person in charge would have to transfer the data from the old file to the new file (not always a simple matter), and then re-index the data by hand. In these flat file databases a pointer value—or record number—was stored in a separate file with an index used to find the records. When the new database file was created with the new field and data moved, the separate file with the index had to be replaced.

In 1970, a major step in the world of databases was taken when C.F. Codd wrote the paper titled,

"A relational model of data for large shared data banks" (Codd, 1970). Codd observed that the existing database applications required users to understand and follow the structure of the tables and accept the limitations. He argued that a better database design would mean users would not need to understand the database design and they would have much more flexibility in the ways they could access the data. They should be able to find data from the user's perspective. With relational databases this would be possible.

Part of Codd's (1970) viewpoint on database design was that the relational database concept was developed with mathematical and reading concepts, not computer concepts. Codd held that a DBMS should be based on how people think and use information. The paradigm shift was the major step forward from the old flat file database designed from the standpoint of how computers work, toward the relational database designed on the basis of how people think.

Flat file databases required a user to scroll through the data in order to find the information they were seeking. There was a not a search function, such as the query we are familiar with in modern databases. In other words, the design of the databases was based on computer rules, not on the needs of the user who would view this from a point of reality. The user wants to find the data needed and not necessarily to view all data in the entire database. Consider the user visiting the library to find information about a topic. The patron might be willing to use a book, a journal, a video, or other media. With a card catalog using the subject index, the library visitor can find information on the desired topic and on whichever media it might reside.

The description of the relational model was the first indication that there would be a database model that would solve most if not all of the problems with the flat file databases. A key concept of Codd's model is that relationships could be defined for data in one table or many tables to allow manipulation of the data independent of the design of the database, the application, or the limitations of the operating system. A field can be added without having to structure a new database file and re-index the entire dataset. This was a remarkable step in the field of data management.

Codd was a researcher with IBM when he wrote his papers on the relational database and the ways it could help users find and manage data (NRC, 1999). Perhaps, in part, because he was viewed as an academic and not strictly a programmer, the methods Codd developed for creating and searching databases was not chosen by IBM as the method they would use in their new database, System R.

At about the same time that System R was being developed at IBM, a group of researchers at the University of California Berkeley also were working on a relational database to use geographic information for economic research. The UC-Berkeley project was called Ingres. Ingres stood for interactive graphics and retrieval system (NRC, p. 164). Experts on database systems generally regard Ingres as the more efficient product, and many attribute that to the research environment in which it was developed. Berkeley was not dependent on the market view or concern about the costs or profitability of the product, and so the researchers there were free to work toward what they conceived as the best relational database approach. Both conceptual and staff connections can be traced from Ingres to what became Oracle, viewed by many as the most successful DBMS today (Callan, 2005). This connection demonstrates the connections between

research and IT in economic development.

Ingres was later developed into Postgres (also from UC Berkeley), which is one of the most widely used databases on the Web. It is used to connect databases to the Web so potential economic development clients can view properties and related assets from the Web. Postgres is a free download from UC Berkeley, meaning that Web developers avoid the expense of software like Oracle, or one of the other commercial DBMSs.

The advent of low-cost PCs and support software revolutionized DBMS in economic development. The early 1990s saw the introduction of a plethora of software developed by private sector vendors, not-for-profit organizations, corporate benefactors, and governments to support local economic development organizations in managing site and client databases, and to match these via query systems. In a very real sense this revolutionized local economic development as organizations were now capable of building and editing databases that could be quickly queried and matched to clients' needs on a long list of characteristics (e.g., size, zoning, transportation availability, and utilities). Additionally, client databases greatly facilitated ongoing marketing efforts and maintaining a stream of contacts with potential customers.

Many computer users probably do not know that components we recognize today as part of the personal computer actually were developed in the 1960s and 1970s. Again, the new technology development can be traced to research facilities. The mouse, monitor, hypertext, and other innovations were developed by Douglas Engelbart, a UC Berkeley PhD, as documented by Scott Griffin as part of his graduate work in the School of Journalism and Mass Communication at the University of North Carolina at Chapel Hill:

In 1963, Engelbart set up his own research lab. He called it the Augmentation Research Center. Throughout the 1960s and 1970s his mlab developed an elaborate hypermedia—groupware system called NLS (oNLine System). NLS facilitated the creation of digital libraries and storage and retrieval of electronic documents using hypertext. This was the first successful implementation of hypertext. NLS used a new device to facilitate computer interaction—the mouse. (The mouse was not adopted for general use until the 1980s when Apple computers began using them). NLS also created new graphical user interfaces implementing a windowing environment and allowed the user to e-mail other users as well as offering a variety of word processing options. Perhaps most remarkably, NLS also provided for on-screen video teleconferencing. All of these technologies, which are now ubiquitous, were truly astonishing to most back on the 1960s (Griffin, 2000, ¶ 6).

In the early 1970s, a group of researchers at Xerox Corporation's Palo Alto Research Center (PARC) began work on development of the first personal computer. In 2004, Robert Taylor, Alan Kay, Charles Thacker and Butler Lampson, the primary researchers at PARC, were given The Charles Stark Draper Prize by the National Academy of Engineering. According to William A. Wulf, President of the National Academy of Engineering, "The creation of the first practical networked personal computer is a story that's [*sic*] dramatically affected all of us, but which few really know about. These four prize recipients were the indispensable core of an amazing group of engineering minds that redefined the nature and purpose of computing" (National Academy of Engineering News, 2004, ¶ 5).

The system designed at PARC had icons on a screen, a pointer, did word processing including cut and paste, and was connected to a network with other computers and a laser printer, another XEROX invention (Abate, 2004, ¶ 4). Some may recognize these components and think, but wait a minute, didn't Apple Computer invent those when they designed their computer? The story behind this misapprehension is that Steve Jobs, Apple's founder, visited the PARC facilities in 1979 and saw a computer with graphical user interface (GUI), object-oriented programming, networking, and other features, and then built the Lisa (Jobs, 1996, ¶ 37).

GIS

The introduction of GIS into economic development created yet another revolutionary wave.

GIS enabled communities to map available sites, infrastructures, and amenities to better market themselves by employing greater amounts of information that was timelier, more accurate, and better integrated into a user-friendly format. Economic development was possibly the first local government function to benefit from GIS. Major utilities, for example, Georgia Power and Wisconsin Public Service, among others, that employed GIS for internal functions assisted communities by applying GIS capabilities to mapping local (re)development sites. These maps were then indexed with a photographic inventory of sites. Early versions of this technology were mainframe-based utilizing for the era, enormous amounts of centralized computer resources (although by today's standards the applications were primitive and relatively small).

Web Sites

The third IT revolution to impact economic development was the World Wide Web, specifically the evolution of Web sites. Prior to this innovation, contact with potential clients (investors) was via direct mailings, trade shows, working the phones, and headquarters visits by economic development personnel. While these activities have not been wholly replaced by Web sites, today, most initial contact between potential clients and community economic development organizations is done by way of Web sites.

While there certainly are adequate and thorough histories of the Internet and Web elsewhere, it seems worthwhile to briefly review it here to set the context of the connections between academic research and the impact of the Web on economic development. The roots of the Internet and Web started with a project that involved the U.S. military and several research institutions. This research and actual development of new technologies (including TCP/IP—transmission control protocol and Internet protocol, and other networking and data transfer methods) that led to the Internet were funded by the Department of Defense, through Advanced Research Projects Agency (ARPA), and the National Science Foundation (NSF). The connection between research institutions and the federal government in terms of technology has been documented in a book, *Funding the Revolution: Government Support for Computing Research* (1999), from the National Resource Council. The following quote is from Chapter VII, "Development of the Internet and the World Wide Web":

Approximately 15 years after the first computers became operational, researchers began to realize that an interconnected network of computers could provide services that transcended the capabilities of a single system. At this time, computers were becoming increasingly powerful, and a number of scientists were beginning to consider applications that went far beyond simple numerical calculation. Perhaps the most compelling early description of these opportunities was presented by J.C.R. Licklider (1960), who argued that, within a few years, computers would become sufficiently powerful to cooperate with humans in solving scientific and technical problems. Licklider, a psychologist at the Massachusetts Institute of Technology (MIT), would begin realizing his vision when he became director of the Information Processing Techniques Office (IPTO) at the Advanced Research Projects Agency (ARPA) in 1962. Licklider remained at ARPA until 1964 (and returned for a second tour in 1974-1975), and he convinced his successors, Ivan Sutherland and Robert Taylor, of the importance of attacking difficult, long-term problems. (NLS, 1999, p. 170)

As you can tell, this sets the stage for further developments in that a true "early adopter" of technology is placed in a position of authority of a government agency that is geared to work to implement new technology. The Department of Defense, through ARPA (later changed to DARPA, for Defense Advanced Research Projects Agency), provided funding for NLS, mentioned earlier in relation to the origins of the PC, and to other projects that would help improve research by connecting university scientists around the country with government and, specifically, military project managers. Much of the motivation for this funding was related to an effort to keep up with the Soviets and the space race, and with building the missile defense system of the United States.

More on this project from the book, *Funding the Revolution: Government Support for Computing Research* (NRC, 1999);

Taylor, who became IPTO director in 1966, worried about the duplication of expensive computing resources at the various sites with ARPA contracts. He proposed a networking experiment in which users at one site accessed computers at another site, and he co-authored, with Licklider, a paper describing both how this might be done and some of the potential consequences (Licklider & Taylor, 1968). Taylor was a psychologist, not a computer scientist, and so he recruited Larry Roberts of MIT's Lincoln Laboratory to move to ARPA and oversee the development of the new network. As a result of these efforts, ARPA became the primary supporter of projects in networking during this period. (NRC, 1999, p. 171)

Thus the stage was set with a basic system that used telephone lines that already were in place to carry the data between the contractors (researchers at the universities) and the ARPA facilities. From this came e-mail, file transfer protocol (FTP), and eventually, the Web in the 1990s. It was the combined effort of researchers with funding from the government that provided the infrastructure and the technology necessary to build the "network of networks" we think of today as the Web.

The graphical user interface (GUI) pioneered at both Engelbart's Augmentation Research Center (with ARPA funding) and at Xerox Corporation's PARC, would become significant when combined with Mosaic, the first browser for the GUI and the Web. Mosaic was developed in 1993 at the National Center for Supercomputing Applications (NCSA), at the University of Illinois at Urbana-Champaign and funded by the National Science Foundation's Supercomputer Centers Program (NCSA, 2006).

The paradigm shift of the Web is posited because the medium of promoting economic development (along with most all other forms of marketing, commerce, governmental communication with the public, etc.) moved from traditional methods to the Web or new media, based on the convergence of telecommunications and computer technologies, networking, video, audio, and other media to communicate the messages. In the past, economic development professionals used mass-mailings, conference attendance, and promotional trips to get the word out about their communities. In the Web age, those methods are antiquated.

Economic development Web sites have evolved considerably from their early days. To better understand this evolution, it is necessary to briefly review a typology of Web sites. A Congressional Research Service report specifies four stages of Web site evolution: presence, interaction, transaction, and transformation (Seifert, 2003). While a site may skip one or more stages, examples of economic development Web sites are to be found at each stage (level).

- **Presence**, the first stage is the establishment of a placeholder for delivering information in the future. It is the simplest and least expensive entrance into e-government, but offers the least options for its audience. This is nothing more than an informational Web site, sometimes described as the electronic equivalent of a paper brochure.
- **Interaction** has enhanced capability (*vis-à-vis* presence). This site is still limited in its streamlining and automation of government functions. Interactions revolve around information provision and remain relatively simple. They substitute a Web site for a trip to the office or a phone call by providing 24-hour access to the most commonly requested information, forms, and instructions. Forms are downloadable for mailing of faxing back to the office. Sometimes e-mail contact is permitted.
- **Transaction(al)**, stage 3, permits more complex interactions than simple information. Customers and clients are enabled to complete entire tasks electronically, anytime. These are self-service operations typified by mostly one-way (either customer to government or government to customer) interactions, for example, submitting bids for contracts, seeking or renewing licenses, paying taxes and fees.
- **Transformational**, the highest order Web site employs the capabilities of technology to transform the way government functions are conceived, organized, and executed. These sites offer a robust customer relationship to address the full range of questions, problems, and needs. These sites often seek to remove barriers between governments (organizations) to promote customer-centric solutions. In short, a customer's complex issue (problem, situation) involving multiple organizations (governments, for profit, and/or not-for-profit) could be solved *via* a single Web site (Seifert, 2003, pp. 9-11).

Economic development as a government function arrived early on the Internet. It may have been the close relationship between government and private sector that fostered the evolution of the first sites in the early 1990s. Early on, all local economic development Web sites (and for that matter all state and national ones) were nothing more than brochures in electrons (vs. ink). They provided snapshots of their communities in pictures, words, or statistics. The best interaction a customer usually could hope for was the provision of contact information for one or more units of local government. These sites, while much less predominate today, still are frequently found.

Through a sort of natural evolution, it was not long (mid-1990s) until interactional sites arrived on the scene, especially for larger, more professional economic development organizations with full-time staff. Transactional sites first appeared in the mid- to late-1990s when customers were empowered to provide detailed specifications for their proposed project (say, a plant siting). As the process evolved, much of the key paperwork, for example, business permits, building permits, tax exemptions, and grant applications, could be submitted via a Web site. Today, these transactional sites are common. However, transformational, the highest order of sites, are rare, although we suspect that they are more frequent in economic development than other realms of government activity. In some cases, a customer can seamlessly access services and programs across governments (e.g., city and county) or across public, private, or not-for-profit sectors.

The higher frequency of transformational sites in the economic development sector may be explained by the potential for community gain from attracting new businesses to an area. The economic benefits of new business, reduces any reluctance local government officials may feel regarding expansion of services available through a transformational site. It is not unusual for an economic development site to link local governments (city, county, regional, or state), financing opportunities (public, private, or not for profit), as well as land and buildings available for purchase or lease.

The remainder of this chapter is focused on economic development Web sites because it is in enhanced Web presence that thousands of local economic development organizations in communities are investing large shares of their resources. Additionally, it is at a Web site where much of a community's efforts in BDM and GIS is most readily observed by an outsider. Finally, while GIS and DBM applications tend to be uniformly available to local organizations depending on level of investment, Web sites are highly diverse, often reflecting community values and commitment to economic development.

IT Applications in Practice: Web Sites

The advent of the Web brought a new realm of marketing to the economic development practitioners as they increased access to information for prospective target organizations (usually businesses) looking to expand or relocate. Local or regional economic development entities could provide information including photos and maps to tell the story of their area to the potential recruits they are seeking. In addition to key economic indicators, such as labor availability, wage rates, and transportation costs, economic development Web sites often present information on area "quality of life" factors, including amenities, resources, photos of scenery, maps, and links to other relevant sites (e.g., local governments and resources for entrepreneurs).

To illustrate the utility of Web applications, innovative Web sites from three communities are featured in this section. These sites were selected as examples because the communities are recognized as outstanding in some way by knowledgeable third parties. Each site has some unique qualities or features that serve as best practices from which practitioners can draw upon. Three cases

representing a small, a medium, and a large community are presented. Each site uses information from DBMS, GIS, and often other IT applications to attract new businesses to its area or to help local grow the existing.

The first of the cases is Tinley Park, IL, representing a small community with a population of 57,000 that won the 2006 EDA Economic Development Awards in the category for Urban and Suburban locations. The other finalists in the EDA Awards in the category of Urban and Suburban locations included Los Angeles, CA, and San Antonio, TX. Tampa, FL, with a population of 325,000, is the second case serving as an example of a medium-size community. Tampa has won several awards for its community Web site. While not specifically named for economic development, the site has numerous characteristics that will be helpful to those promoting the area to new businesses. The third case is Boston, a city of approximately 600,000 people in a metropolitan statistical area exceeding 4 million in population. Richard Florida (2002) listed Boston as one of the most creative communities in the U.S. Additionally, the Boston area has a reputation as a strong economic development actor. As demonstrated below, this community with a high rating among creative, technology oriented individuals and a strong economic development organization, has a superior Web site employing cutting edge technology.

Tinley Park, IL

Tinley Park won the first place award in the category of Urban or Suburban Economic Development in Excellence in Economic Development Awards 2006 from the Economic Development Administration (EDA), part of the U.S. Department of Commerce. According to the EDA Web site, "the nominations are evaluated to determine how effectively they utilize innovative, market-based strategies to improve urban or suburban economic development (EDA Awards, 2006, ¶ 3)."

The Tinley Park Economic Development site is closely connected to the site for the Village of Tinley Park local government and has a similar "look and feel" to carry over continuity and engage visitors to both sites (see Figures 2 and 3). The Tinley Park Economic Development site (see screen shot in Figure 2) has links to many important types of information for potential businesses considering the Chicago area. This seamless transition between economic development and other aspects of local government is a strength presenting the prospective client with easy access to a wealth of information.

The Tinley Park Economic Development Office makes it easy to find locations for either expanding an existing business or starting up a new business in the area. The pages on "Available Sites" have links to both local (see Figures 4, 5, and 6) and regional properties, plus some state sites through an "Advanced Search" option (Figure 7).

Following links to specific properties on the Tinley Park "Available Sites" page (Figure 4) produces a page with site-specific information, such as address, size of the property, photographs, and contact information (Figure 5). A link on that site-specific page connects visitors to "Maps and Radii Reports" and the resulting page (Figure 6) shows industrial complexes, highways, railroads, airports, shopping centers, colleges and universities, parks, bodies of water and other significant land use areas near the available site.

Most organizations considering new locations will want to know about the availability of infrastructure for information technology. The Economic Development Web site for Tinley Park has information on these resources including high-speed Internet and other data transfer options in the Chicago area (see Figure 8).

As mentioned earlier, there are close connections between the Web sites for local government in Tinley Park and the Economic Development Office. On the site for the Village of Tinley Park, visitors and residents alike can find Business News, such as the announcement of the U.S. Department of Commerce EDA Award (see Figure 9). There is a section on Downtown Redevelopment (Figure 10) with attractive photos, access to data such as traffic and market studies (Figure 11), and a Tinley Park Site Map with links to numerous pertinent pages, for example, Information for Business, such as Demographics, Transportation, Technology,

Business Licenses, and Education and Training (Figure 12). A Tinley Park Visitor Information page provides links to information about history, events, and resources in the area (Figure 13).

When asked how the community of 57,000 came to develop a Web site that won the 2006 EDA Economic Development Awards in the category for Urban and Suburban locations, Ivan Baker, Tinley Park's Director of Economic Development said consultant and widely accepted guru Mark James influenced most of the effective economic development Web sites in the U.S.:

I actually have utilized his (Mark James') guidelines in the production of three E.D. Websites. [The goal is to be] simple, basic, informative, accurate, up-to-date, colorful, and market based and not letting the graphic designer take over the project with heavy graphics and flash. [A key is to] focus only on what the target audience needs and has to have: good information, user friendliness, attractive and organized presentation, and the basics of who, what, when, where, why and how ...Basically, his ideas just make sense. A lot of great E.D. Websites in the country use his ideas, because they simply work ... no frills attached. (Ivan Baker, personal communication, October 11, 2006, by E-mail)

Apparently Tinley Park has received other accolades. According to Baker, "Tinley Park was named 1 of 12 U.S. Cities for Economic Development Leadership and Innovation from CoreNet Global, the world's largest association of corporate real estate executives. The village Mayor Ed Zabrocki was named one of the Top 10 U.S. Mayors by the World Mayor Project in London, England" (Ivan Baker, personal communication, October 11, 2006).

Tinley Park is an excellent example of how a smaller community with limited resources can produce a superior economic development Web site, one easy to navigate, seamlessly linking city departments and economic development functions, and addressing matters of key concern to business planners as they look to locate into or expand within the community.

Tampa, FL

The City of Tampa has received numerous awards for their Web site, TampaGov.net. In 2002, TampaGov won first place in both the Best of the Web and the Digital Cities Survey for excellence and leadership in local government. TampaGov won first place in the Digital Cities Survey again in 2003. The Digital Cities Survey Award for second place went to TampaGov in 2005. In 2006, Tampa's Customer Service Center was a finalist in the Public Administration Category of the Stockholm Challenge, global award for Information and Communication Technology (Stockholm Challenge, 2006). The only other finalist from the United States was FirstGov.gov, the federal government Web site.

According to the TampaGov Website, the secret of success for the city has been a *citizen centric focus* (TampaGov.net, 2006). This focus allows Web designers and administrators to provide access to the content on the Web site from many entry points within the site. Someone who comes to the site to gather information might start from the perspective of a tourist, a citizen, an individual with age-specific interests, or a person seeking information on doing business in or living in Tampa. This availability of data and easy access is likely to appeal to a new company considering a location in Tampa, because: (1) they will observe the positive orientation of the city toward its citizens as seen in the high volumes of user-friendly information provided for current citizens and business, and (2) they will be able to use this same information in their location decision.

In addition to providing excellent service to citizens and visitors through its Web site and, thereby, providing a considerable volume of high quality information to anyone interested in the doing business in the city, the city offers several other avenues for organizations to obtain information about doing business in the city. For instance, some of the pages on TampaGov.net site are clearly related to economic development: the "Economic Incentives" page provides information on local programs for loans and other assistance (Figure 14), a page on "How does Tampa rank?" showing national rankings on various economic measures such as the economy, education, quality of life, and technology (Figure 15), specific "Technology Rankings" on how Tampa compared to other cities in the U.S. (Figure 16), a page with Census Tract Data on a map of the City (Figure 17), and

Figure 2. A screen shot of the Tinley Park Economic Development Web site at http://www.tinleyparkbiz. biz/

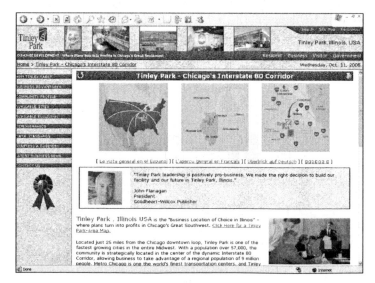

Figure 3. Web site for the Village of Tinley Park, IL http://www.tinleypark.org//index.asp

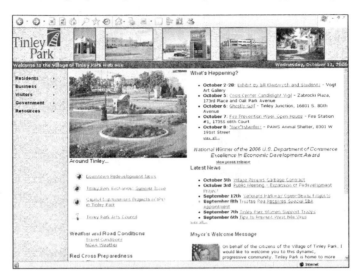

Figure 4. A screen shot of the Available Sites page on the Tinley Park Economic Development Web site

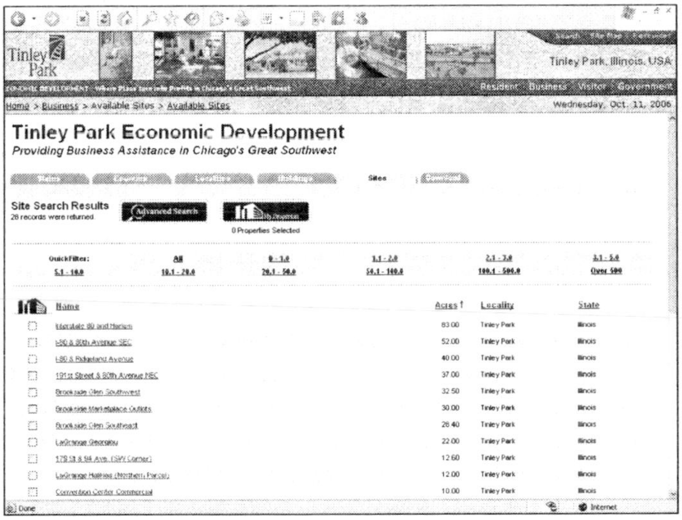

the Ybor City Development Corporation (YCDC) in a historic section of Tampa (Figure 18). A page about "Doing Business in Tampa" (Figure 19) has a long list of service contacts, for example, express permits (building and others), utility bills, parking tickets, and general customer service, all on quick links with street address. The "Doing Business" page includes links to a variety of other information including city contacts, zoning and ordinances, and access to bids and RFPs for the City Purchasing Department.

The TampaGov site has a section titled "Neighborhood Information" (Figure 20) that can be an invaluable service to small neighborhood businesses and to large firms considering Tampa as a site. A drop-down listing of the neighborhood shows

Figure 5. Tinley Park listing for a specific site which is available for development (linked from page shown in Figure 4)

Figure 6. Map produced from the link "Maps and Radii Reports" on a page with a specific site listing shown in Figure 5

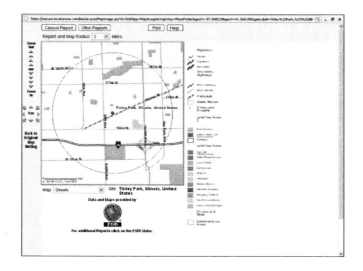

links to each of the areas. For a small business, these pages provide information on the customers in a section of town including income levels and other demographics. Representatives of a larger business can view the neighborhoods to gather information for use in considering the appropriateness of the areas for the location of the business or the desirability of the housing and other resources for employees who might be moving to Tampa.

The neighborhood pages provide both visitors and residents with an overview of the neighborhoods and links to neighborhood organizations. Corporate relocation departments might provide these neighborhood links to employees or potential recruits who will be looking for housing. These pages on specific neighborhoods contain information on strengths and weaknesses of each section of town, comparative levels of public services, indicators of health and vitality, opportunities for investment and development and more.

The site provides extensive and versatile mapping applications as evidenced in Figure 21, with a map showing Schools, Parks, Roads, and Railroads. A map of a different part of Tampa provides more neighborhood information, with a list of links to points of interest, fire stations, public schools, public parks (Figure 22).

An option on the maps pages provides links to "Property Tax Records" so viewers can go directly to the page showing Hillsborough County's Property Tax Records for that neighborhood (Figure 23). Even though the City of Tampa and Hillsborough County are separate local government entities, the link to the Property Records Page comes from a map on TampaGov.net provides search options for specific property or neighborhoods (Figure 24). In Figure 25, one will see the property search results from previous page (reached from the link on TampaGov.net).

TampaGov.net also provides an option for Hybrid Map/Satellite Images with Streets & Roads, Traffic Direction on One-Way Streets, etc. (Figure 26). All the map pages on the TampaGov Web site are linked to Google and have Application Program Interface (API) to allow the city Web staff to program addresses to GIS coordinates and to show specific buildings, city offices, etc., on the maps.

The Tampa site demonstrates what can be accomplished by a community with substantial resources and commitment to excellence in Web presence. While the primary focus of Tampa's efforts is to support citizen information and empowerment, the extensive amount of easily accessible and meaningful information addresses many of the key economic development questions. The data focused on citizen support are supplemented by extensive pages focused directly on the needs of business location decision makers. Like the Tinley Park site, Tampa has clearly focused its efforts on user friendliness, access, and a no-nonsense approach to the development of its Web site.

Boston, MA

Another way of determining Web sites for review was to use the Creativity Index described by Richard Florida (2002). Florida ranked Boston, with a 2004 population estimated at 569,000 and the center of the Boston-Cambridge-Quincy MSA with a population of 4.425 million, in the top ten (actually No. 3) in the MSAs over 1 million population on the Creativity Index. Florida's Creativity Index is a measure of a community's ability to attract and retain members of a new class of worker, the creative class that comprises about 30 percent of the workforce and includes the idea professions such as scientists, engineers, architects, educators, writers, artists, and entertainers.

Viewing the Web site for the Boston Redevelopment Authority, it is clear that the city is on the cutting edge in terms of the use of technology for

Figure 7. A screen shot of the advanced search that includes region and state search options

Figure 8. Information on telecommunications technology in Chicago area

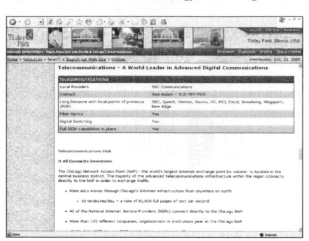

Figure 9. Tinley Park Web page announcing the award for Excellence in Economic Development from the U.S. Department of Commerce

economic development. The economic development page, likely the point of entry for a prospective client, is not overly sophisticated and does not exude high levels of technology (see Figure 27). However, linked in this set of pages is the site for the Boston Connects, a not-for-profit organization that hosts the Empowerment Zone (EZ), a resource for training and job creation (Figure 28). The offerings of the EZ program are clearly displayed and include job training, specialized technology training, education leading to graduate equivalency diplomas, plus health and wellness, and family support networks (Figure 29).

The Boston Connects site is multifunctional. One side of the site clarifies the importance of bridging the digital divide so that families can learn about training and education leading to jobs, plus the health care options available through the Web (Figure 29). The Boston Connects Technology Programs target families and intergenerational training that brings together parents and children to learn computer skills, and also to provide them with computers and Internet access. Those who are interested can take classes in computer setup, maintenance, and repair.

Figure 10. Downtown redevelopment

Figure 11. Tinley Park News on redevelopment plans and market studies

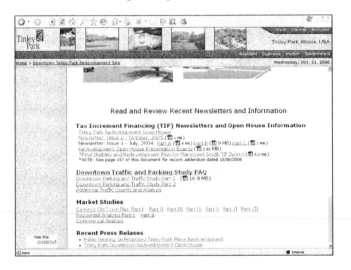

The Boston Connects program also provides meetings to coordinate efforts of community based organizations to utilize computers more effectively. Some courses, institutes, and clinics for the community based organizations on a variety of technology-related topics, such as strategic planning and budgeting, infrastructure needs assessment, board development, and even legal issues.

The other side of the site places considerable emphasis on technology applications, for example, Boston Atlas page—with links to maps, aerial photography, VRML, and 3D CAD Models (Figure 31). Any business searching for a location in a large and complex city/metro area such as Boston will need to be oriented to the community. This is where the Boston site excels with its technical sophistication. If we are looking for the real cutting edge of government technology applications, this is evidence of how these tools can be put to work to promote economic development.

The opening page of Boston Atlas site presents a hybridized map-aerial photograph (Figure 32).

Figure 12. Tinley Park Site Map with links to information for business, such as demographics, transportation, technology, business licenses, education and training, etc.

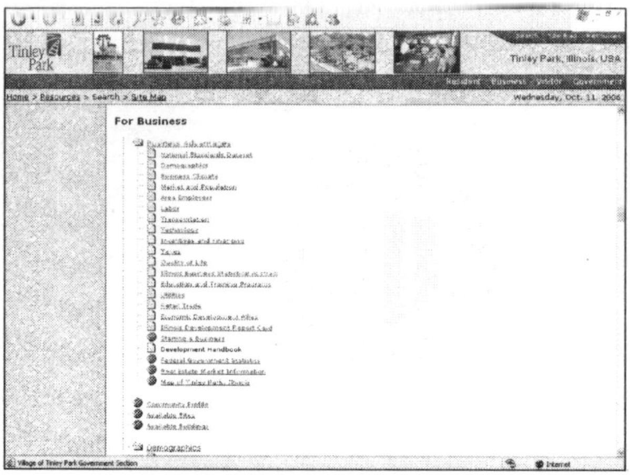

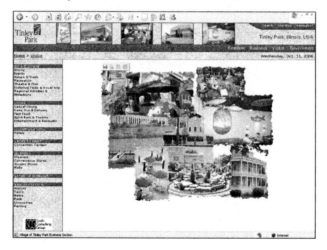

Figure 13. Tinley Park visitor information

As an example, the search option, available on each page of the Boston Atlas, was used to enter a search for "rail." This yielded a hybrid map and aerial photo/image page with information on available properties adjacent to rail access (Figure 33). A similar search for "port" produced a page with information on ports and links to images of passenger ports showing the Seaport Hotel and including information on street names, building footprints, and other relevant information (Figure 34). Another page with a different site at the International Cargo Port was linked from the same search page for ports (Figure 35).

For anyone interested in 3D images of the Boston area and specific sections, there is a page with Boston Digital 3D Models on the site (Figure 36). The page has download links for 3D images of 1 MB to 11 MB in size, which require special software to view. Three-dimensional CAD images showing buildings, terrain, bridges, and other salient features are available for sections of Boston, including Back Bay, Charlestown, Fenway, and others.

While the Boston site may not be as comprehensive or citizen-friendly as the Tampa site, the

Figure 14. Economic Incentives http://www.tampagov.net/dept_economic_and_urban_development/Incentives/Index.asp

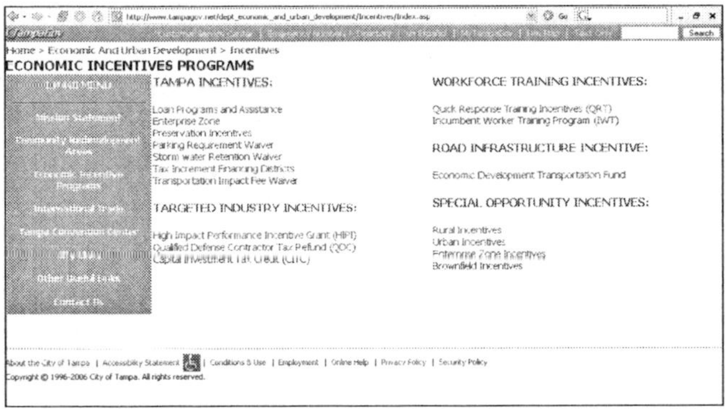

Figure 15. TampaGov Economic Development statistics "How does Tampa rank?" presented to market the City http://www.tampagov.net/dept_strategic_planning_and_technology/planning_management/statistics/index.asp

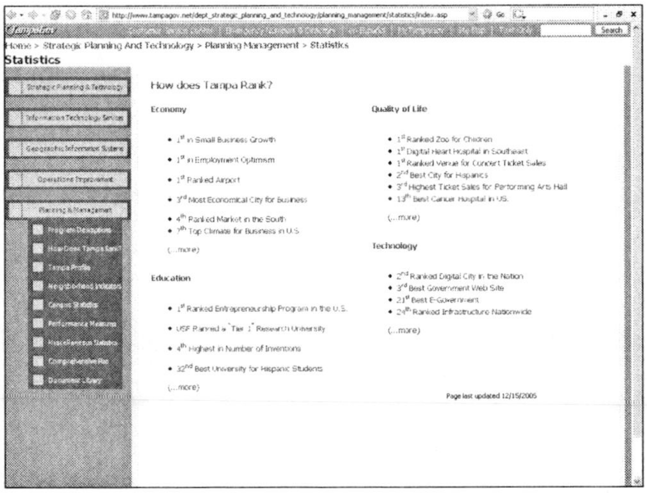

Boston site, particularly its atlas, takes technology up a notch. Its mapping functions are nothing short of spectacular, and with downloaded software, are accessible to a wide array of users from within the community and outside.

The Future

Just a few short decades ago, economic development professionals processed client information on note cards or some similar medium. They marketed their communities via printed brochures and phone contacts. Today, economic development and IT are firmly wedded, and in all likelihood the dependence of economic development on IT will continue to grow.

The revolutionary and paradigm-shifting impacts of DBMS, GIS, and Web sites continue to be felt, especially in light of new techniques to meld these innovations. While there certainly will be developments with each innovation, it is clear that economic development will see the most progress

Figure 16. TampaGov Technology Rankings http://www.tampagov.net/dept_strategic_planning_and_technology/planning_management/statistics/index.asp

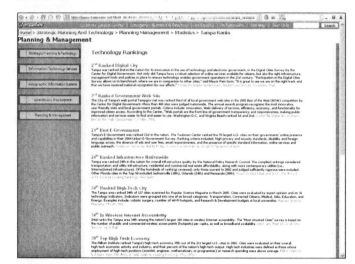

Figure 17. Census Tract Data on Tampa map (Data files are accessible by clicking on the maps, and the drop-down menu allows viewing of detailed maps for sections of the City.) http://www.tampagov. net/dept_strategic_planning_and_technology/planning_management/images/2000_census_tracts_map/ census_2000_map.asp

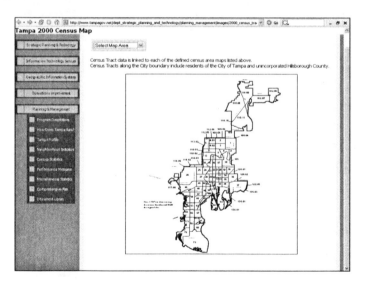

in the combination of GIS and Web sites. The availability of user-friendly systems that enable a user to manipulate and spatially present data represents a significant step forward.

The concept of future trends will depend largely on the existing level of a community's economic development and E-government operations. For those localities with Web sites at the early stages as defined by Seifert (2003), they can look to either Tinley Park or Tampa (depending on size and vision) for inspiration. Both of these local governments are doing an excellent job providing information about

Figure 18. Ybor City Development Corporation (YCDC) http://www.tampagov.net/dept_YCDC/

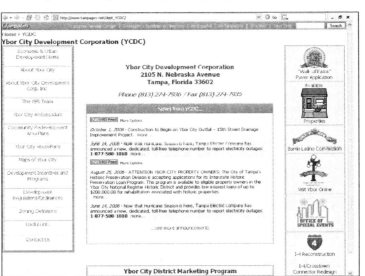

Figure 19. Doing Business in Tampa – Note building permits, utility bills, etc. on quick links, also address information with location characteristics, etc.; plus links to city contacts, information, etc. http://www.tampagov.net/guide_for_business.asp

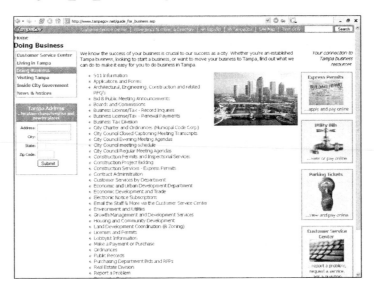

the community along with access to databases with information about site selection, etc.

One common thread that can be traced through the history of computers and economic development involves the use of data, such as the census, and collaborations with government entities and university researchers. It is likely that a model such as this will help nearly all communities move beyond their current status in using technology to promote economic development. These partnerships might be short-term or more permanent, depending on the needs and willingness of those involved.

A small community can work toward providing an online database with mapping and photos

Figure 20. TampaGov.net Neighborhood Information Page with drop-down menu of neighborhoods

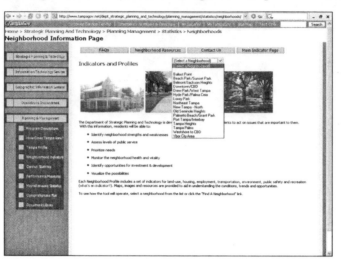

Figure 21. Map example with schools, parks, roads, railroads

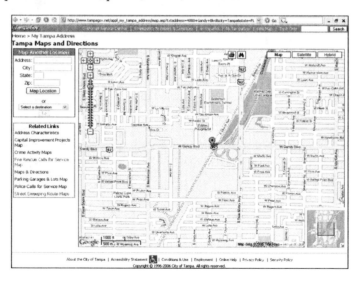

of available sites and buildings as Tinley Park has done. Add to this the use of positive characterizations of the community through photos and stories and it makes an appealing pull to those considering the area for development. This should be within the reach of most communities with some assistance from nearby experts in a university or at least some Internet consulting firms.

For the community that is truly citizen-oriented, the Tampa model provides a great way to give citizens more access to information while providing data to potential corporate citizens. The City of Tampa is working with the University of South Florida's economic development research center to increase the types and combinations of information accessible through the Web. Most

Figure 22. More neighborhood information: List of links to points of interest, fire stations, public schools, public parks

Figure 23. Map page info has "property tax records" link to Hillsborough County's property tax records (see Figure 24)

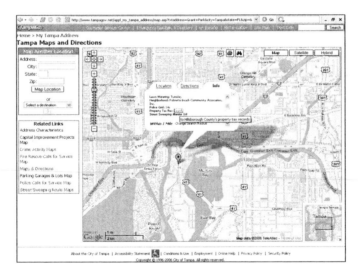

information can be linked through GIS, so that citizens can use address-based searches to find the most relevant data.

The ultimate goal for most economic development sites is to emulate Boston's search with aerial photography and mapping in one package. As with most technology developments, it is likely that the prices will fall on this advanced application before

too long. From the standpoint of the "ahhh" factors and effectiveness of delivery of site information, the Boston scenario is an ideal state or benchmark until newer and more effective applications are developed.

Going beyond the immediate capabilities of applications and more into the conceptual realm for future trends, one might consider neighbor-

Figure 24. Hillsborough County property records page linked from map on TampaGov.net providing search options

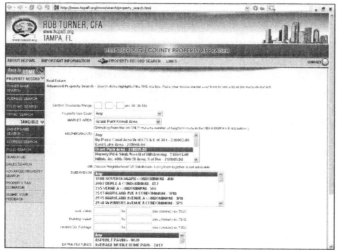

Figure 25. Property search results from property records page shown in Figure 23 (reached from link on TampaGov.net)

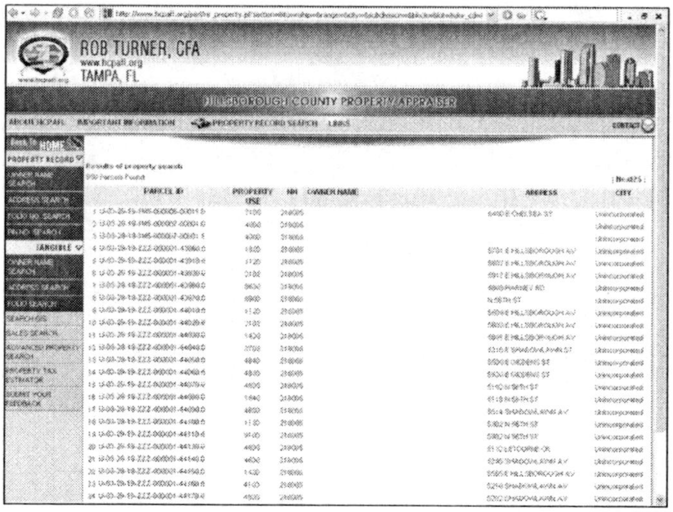

hood information systems (NIS) as described by Hwang (2006). Hwang suggests the NIS as a way to promote economic development through collaborations among universities, local governments, and community-based organizations. NIS is a combination of GIS available through the Web with data from varied sources that typically do not share their information. By hosting NIS and leading the collaboration, the universities facilitate a situation in which all gain from the sharing of data. Hwang suggests that access to varied forms of data will create synergy by giving more information and opening up new ways to use it. Another advantage of NIS is building the opportunity for participation by members of the community in planning and decision making related to economic and community development.

Figure 26. Hybrid map/satellite image with streets and roads, traffic direction on one-way streets, etc.

Figure 27. Boston Redevelopment Authority's economic development ppage: http://www.cityofboston. gov/bra/econdev/EconDev.asp

All figures related to Boston are used with permission from the Boston Redevelopment Authority and Boston Connects.

There are many types of Web applications evolving at this time that might fit the general description of "new media" and could unfold as aids to economic development. There are some early signs of the use of blogs and podcasts in e-government. It is very likely that someone engaged in economic development will find a way to promote local sites through videoblogs and use podcasting for dissemination of information about a community for organizations that might locate there in the future.

One emerging phenomenon is called Web 2.0 and has been described as a method for online social networking (World Economic Forum, 2007). A panel discussion titled The Impact of Web 2.0 and Emerging Social Network Models included Bill Gates of Microsoft, Chad Hurley, co-founder and chief executive officer, YouTube, and Caterina

Figure 28. Boston Connects – Empowerment Zone http://www.cityofboston.gov/bra/bostonez/index. htm

And one on programs (see next page)

Figure 29. Programs offered by Boston Connects: http.//www.cityofboston.gov/bra/bostonez/connect/ current1.asp

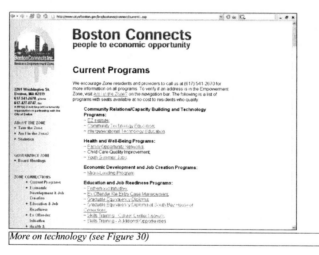

More on technology (see Figure 30)

Fake, founder, Flickr, among others. Much of the discussion among members of the panel dealt with the macroeconomic impact of Web 2.0 through virtual communities controlled by the members and contributors to the online groups with some common interests. Several nonprofit and social change organizations are utilizing the virtual communities to promote their causes. While the Web 2.0 movement includes video blogs, podcasts, and other new media applications, it remains to be seen how the tools will be used to meet micro-economic goals.

These future trends involve research and applications of the outcomes to the promotion of economic development. It is logical that communities and educators can work together to find faster ways to implement the new technologies and those that might be new to the area in this effort. Because this volume focuses on IT research, it is likely that universities will be able to help in most situations.

Figure 30. Boston Connects Technology Programs http://www.cityofboston.gov/bra/bostonez/connect/technology.asp

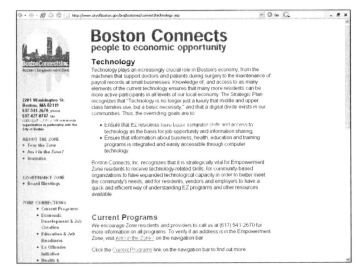

Figure 31. Boston Atlas – Maps, Aerial Photography, VRML, and 3D CAD Models http://www.cityof-boston.gov/bra/maps/maps.asp

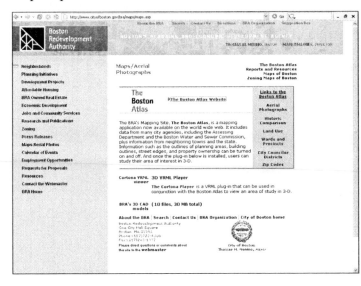

(Contact your local university to find out what resources are available for promoting economic development in your community.)

With the rapid developments in GIS and in making GIS available to users via the Web, it is reasonable to expect the cutting edge mapping features available on the Boston site to filter down to smaller, less financially endowed community Web sites. The powerful NIS evident on the Tampa site has garnered the attention of other communities. It also is reasonable to expect to see more communities enhancing NIS as part of their efforts at community revitalization, historical tourism, and grassroots economic development.

Hwang (2006) reports on a collaborative project in Pittsburgh that resulted in a NIS:

Figure 32. Boston Atlas with mapping and aerial photographs http://www.mapjunction.com/places/Boston_BRA/main.pl?ht=768

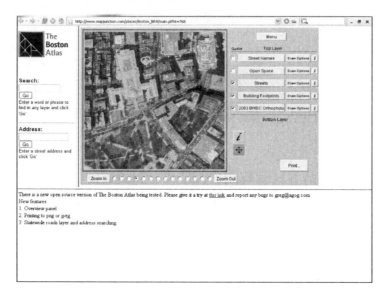

Figure 33. A search for "rail" on the Boston Atlas produced this map overlay and aerial photo/image page with information: http://www.mapjunction.com/places/Boston_BRA/main.pl?ht=768

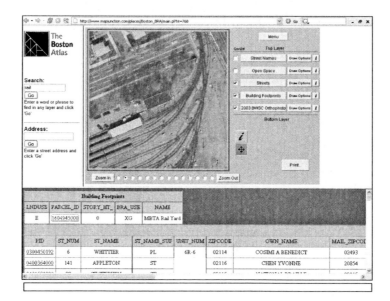

NISs are hybrid applications of geographical information system (GIS) and web technologies that provide demographic, social, and economic information to community stakeholders. Government agencies, non profit organizations, and community organizations engage in decision making process for community development and NISs are designed to help information sharing, and effective and participatory decision makings for community development stakeholders.

The NIS project described by Hwang (2006) is a collaborative effort that includes the University of Pittsburgh, Carnegie Mellon University, the City of Pittsburgh, Allegheny County, the Pittsburgh Partnership for Neighborhood Development, the

Figure 34. A search for "port" produced this page with image of the Seaport Hotel and info on shows street names, building footprints, etc.: http.//www.mapjunction.com/places/Boston_BRA/main.pl?ht=768

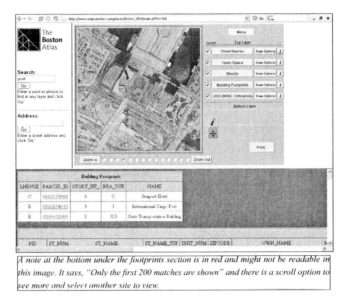

Figure 35. Another page with a different site at the International Cargo Port: http.//www.mapjunction. com/places/Boston_BRA/main.pl?ht=768

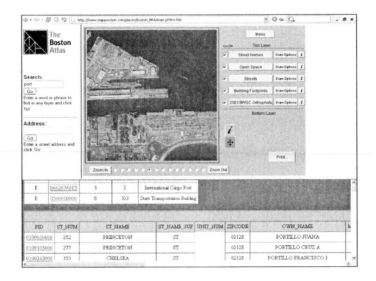

Community Technical Assistance Center, 3 Rivers Connect, and Maya Design. These entities are sharing data, with focus on governments and nonprofits working more closely toward improvements in community development.

A similar project exists in Boston with the Urban Information Systems Group at the Massachusetts Institute of Technology (MIT), Metropolitan Area Planning Council, City of Boston Department of Neighborhood Development, and The Boston Foundation as the major players. They have developed what they call Intelligent Middleware for Understanding Neighborhood Markets and suggest this is a new way to manage and share data. According to the MIT site: "These tools and methods provide a mechanism for accumulating local knowledge

Figure 36. Boston Digital 3D Models are demonstrated on this page: http://www.cityofboston.gov/bra/ BRA_3D_Models/Index.html

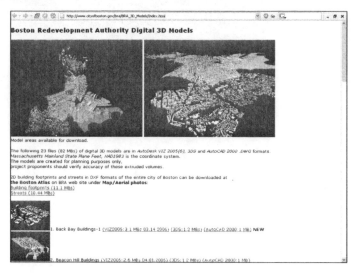

about neighborhood-scale land use, ownership, and market potential and for using that knowledge to re-interpret administrative datasets and develop customized analyses of neighborhood conditions and market potential" (MIT Urban Information Systems Group Introduction page, 2007, ¶ 3).

How the interface between economic development and IT will be impacted by new media such as blogs, podcasts, and other emerging technologies is anybody's guess. Communities will need to be increasingly proactive in posting information on their sites. It may be necessary to update portions of a community's economic development site more often, perhaps daily. Otherwise, the message that will cut through the morass of information may be the blog or podcast of a third party. Will communities get directly involved in blogging and podcasting? Certainly, stranger things have happened! If these are channels for broadcasting positive information about an area to the economic development community, a group with a history of responsiveness to technology, those areas would be foolish to not seriously consider such technologies. One thing is for certain—the future of economic development and IT will evolve at an increasingly fast pace, and when we think we will be able to predict the future, some revolutionary change will come on the scene, something like DBMS, GIS, or Web sites.

FUTURE RESEARCH DIRECTIONS

Since economic development is an early adopter of IT innovations, it is a good place to look for IT implementation in anticipation of implementation elsewhere in the public and not-for-profit sectors. This chapter painted the relationship between IT and economic development with a relatively broad brush. More detailed analyses of each key IT-economic development interfaces are warranted. Still more research is warranted into specific subject matter, for example, the convergence of NIS, Web 2.0, and IT for economic development needs. The two aspects that need particular attention are whether there is evidence that NIS actually will facilitate economic development and whether Web 2.0 might possibly help with microeconomic development. Although this chapter established that IT has considerable positive impact on economic development practice, there remains a chance that IT may fail to deliver in some areas. This chapter established that IT has substantially increased effectiveness in economic development practice, but there remains considerable room for investigations seeking to apply metrics, measurements of the magnitude of impacts. In this vein, outcome analysis is warranted to enable measurement of both the efficacy and efficiency of IT investments in the economic development realm.

The preceding analysis was focused predominately on U.S. experiences; investigation into international experiences regarding IT—economic development interfaces is definitely warranted. The revolutionary and paradigm-shifting impacts of DBMS, GIS, and Web sites on economic development continue to evolve, especially in light of new techniques to meld these innovations. Hence, further developments in these innovations are to be expected. These anticipated developments present another direction for further research. Especially notable will be the continued evolutions of interactions between economic development on one hand and GIS and Web sites on the other. As a way of maximizing the potential of IT, NIS may be widely adopted in the future. The success of NIS in economic development will depend on establishing extensive partnerships between local governments, universities, non-profit organizations, and/or community-based organizations. Analysis of these early partnerships in pursuit of establishing NIS will be beneficial as communities will then be able to knowledgeably build upon prior experiences.

ACKNOWLEDGMENT

This project was partially funded by Valdosta State University (VSU) Faculty Development Grants and the VSU Center for Applied Research. The authors appreciate the support of Valdosta State University President Ronald M. Zaccari, Dr. Louis H. Levy, Vice President for Academic Affairs, Dr. Linda T. Calendrillo, Dean of the College of Arts and Sciences, and Dr. James T. LaPlant, Assistant Dean of the College of Arts and Sciences.

The authors wish to thank the following for their assistance in gathering information for this project and for their approval in the use of images from Web sites: from Boston, Robert Tumposky, deputy director for management information services, Boston Redevelopment Authority; from Tampa, FL, Judy Lake, deputy chief IT officer, Tom Campbell, information technology services project leader, Steve Cantler, information technology services project leader, Eric Hayden, information technology services project leader, Alan Baker, planning research supervisor, Don Taylor, lead systems analyst; from Tinley Park, IL, Ivan Baker, CEcD, director of economic development.

Special thanks are due to Professor Rick D. Boulware, University of South Carolina Beaufort, for his expert assistance in editing the final document for submission. Robert D. Drury of St. Simons Island, GA, also provided advice and sources for the information on Web 2.0.

REFERENCES

Abate, Tom (2004). Digital pioneers: Xerox PARC scientists honored for groundbreaking work on early computers, *San Francisco Chronicle*. Retrieved October 19, 2006 from http://www.sfgate.com/cgi-bin/article.cgi?f=/c/a/2004/02/25/BUGDD57F741.DTL

Accella Communications (2002). Government's new IT needs spell opportunity, *IT World.com* (January 1). Retrieved August 25, 2006 from http://www.itworld.com/Tech/2987/IDG020110govit/pfindex.html

Ajman: A sound liberal economy (2006). *Global Agenda*, *4*, 60-62, January.

Anderson, A., & Nacker, N. (2003). *Survey of local economic development organizations*. Madison: University of Wisconsin Extension and Wisconsin Economic Development Association.

Belgium economy: Wallonia set out e-government plans, (2005). *EIU Newswire*, July 1.

Callan, S. (2005). Where did oracle come from? *Database Journal*. Retrieved October 4, 2006, from www.databasejournal.com/features/oracle/article.php/3519241

City Data (2006). *Population of Boston and MSA*. Retrieved October 17, 2006, from http://www.city-data.com/us-cities/The-Northeast/Boston-Population-Profile.html

Codd, E. F. (1970). A relational model of data for large shared data banks. *Communications of the ACM, 13(6), 377-387*.

Conway M. & Lyne, L. The world's top super projects: The best of the big. *The Futurist, 40*, 32-39.

Das, S., & Chandrashekhar, R. (n.d.). Capacity building for e-governance in India. *United Nations Development Program, Asia-Pacific Development Information Programme, e-Government Case Studies*. Retrieved August 23, 2006 from http://www.apdip.net/projects/e-government/cap-blg/casestudies

DED and Tejari connect Dubai's business community through 'mylinkDubai.com' (2006). *Al Bawaba,* June 6, 1.

Dutta, S., Lopez-Carlos, A., & Mia, I. (2006). The global information technology report 2005-2006. *World Economic Forum*. Geneva: Switzerland.

Economic Development Administration (EDA), part of the U. S. Department of Commerce. Retrieved October 11, 2006, from http://www.eda.gov/NewsEvents/ExcellenceAwards.xml

Fingar, C. (2006). Interview: Andrus Ansip – E is for efficiency. *Foreign Direct Investment*, March 1, 1.

Florida, R. (2002). The rise of the creative class, *Washington Monthly,* May 2002. Retrieved October 12, 2006, from http://www.washingtonmonthly.com/features/2001/0205.florida.html

Galagan, P., & Homer, J. (2005). Thinking big. *T + D 59*, December, 30-37.

Griffin, S. (2000). *Internet pioneers*. ibiblio.org (a collaboration of the Center for the Public Domain and the University of North Carolina at Chapel Hill). Retrieved October 18, 2006 from http://www.ibiblio.org/pioneers/englebart.html

Guide to Geographic Information Systems. How does GIS use geography? (2006). Retrieved September 24, 2006, from http://www.gis.com/whatisgis/index.html

Hwang, Sungsoo (2006). *Leveraging public nonprofit private partnership network for IT innovation: How to build effective neighborhood information systems*. Paper presented at the Southeastern Conference on Public Administration, Athens, GA.

Info Tech Research Group (2006). *Government: 2006 IT budget and staffing report*. London, Ontario.

International City/County Management Association (ICMA) (1999). *Economic development 1999: Survey results*. Washington, DC. Retrieved August 7, 2006, http://www.icma.org/main/ld.asp?from=search&ldid=18042&hsid=1

International City/County Management Association (ICMA) (2004a). *Economic development 1999: Survey results*. Washington, DC. Retrieved August 14 from http://www.icma.org/main/ld.asp?from=search&ldid=19347&hsid=1

International City/County Management Association (ICMA) (2004b). *Electronic government 2004: Survey results*. Washington, DC. Retrieved August 7, 2006, from http://www.icma.org/main/ld.asp?from=search&ldid=19348&hsid=1

Jain, N. (2004). Enabling e-commerce in rural India. *Express India*. Retrieved August 24, 2006, from http://www.expressindia.com/fullstory.php?newsid=38159#compstory

Jobs, Steve (1996). *Triumph of the nerds [Transcripts of the Television series]*. Public Television. Retrieved October 19, 2006, from http://www.pbs.org/nerds/part3.html

Lemon, S. (2005). Chinese official calls for expanding IT use. *Computerworld 39,* November 21, 10.

Massachusetts Institute of Technology (2007). Urban Information Systems Group Web page. Retrieved March 24, 2007, from http://uis.mit.edu/

Nairn, G. (2006). Broadband network is envy of the West: Geoff Nairn on Macedonia's transformation from poverty to the forefront of technology. *Financial Times*, March 29, 7.

National Academy of Engineering (2004). *NAE News*. Retrieved October 19, 2006, from http://www8.nationalacademies.org/onpinews/newsitem.aspx?RecordID=02242004

National Research Council (1999). *Funding a revolution: Government support for computing research.* Washington: National Academy Press. Retrieved October 15, 2006 from: http://newton.nap.edu/books/0309062780/html

Stockholm Challenge, *World's best information and communication technology (ICT) projects* (2006). Retrieved October 15, 2006, from http://event.stockholmchallenge.se/finalists.php

TampaGov.net (2006) *Awards information.* Retrieved October 15, 2006, from http://www.tampagov.net/about_Tampa/tampagov/

Tinley Park, IL, http://www.tinleyparkbiz.biz/

Seifert, J. (2003). *A primer on e-government: Sectors, stages, opportunities, and challenges of online governance.* Washington, DC: Library of Congress, Congressional Research Service.

UNIX Systems Cooperative Promotion Group (n.d.). The UNIX operating system: Mature, standardized and state-of-the-art. Retrieved August 25, 2006, from http://www.unix.org/whitepapers/wp-0897.html

Van Wart, M., Rahm, D., & Sanders, S. (2000). Economic development and public enterprise: The case of rural Iowa's telecommunications utilities. *Economic Development Quarterly, 14*, 131-145.

Wainright, M. E., Brown, C. V., DeHayes, D. W., Hoffer, J. A., & Perkins, W. C. (2005). *Managing information technology* (5th ed). Upper Saddle River, NJ: Prentice Hall.

World Economic Forum (2007). Retrieved March 25, 2007, from http://www.weforum.org/en/events/AnnualMeeting2007/index.htm and the panel video from: http://gaia.world-television.com/wef/worldeconomicforum_annualmeeting2007/default.aspx?sn=19781

ADDITIONAL READING

Apgar, W. (2003). *Accessing capital for community development.* Retrieved February 2, 2004, from http://www.harvardred.com/gsd5483m4.pdf

Bartik, T. (1991). *Who benefits from state and local economic development policies?* Kalamazoo: W. E. Upjohn Institute for Employment Research.

Blair, J. (1995). *Local economic development: Theory and practice.* Thousand Oaks: Sage.

Brice, K. (2002). *Economic development planning and finance.* Retrieved February 2, 2004, from http://www.gsu.edu/~wwwpsp/academics/courses/syllabi/paus4451_fall2002_brice.htm

Carroll, R., & Wasykenko, M. (1994). Do state business climates still matter? Evidence of a structural change. *National Tax Journal, 47*, 19-37.

Committee for Economic Development (1998). *America's basic research: Prosperity through discovery, a policy statement by the research and policy committee.* New York: Committee for Economic Development.

Curtin, Gregory G., Sommer, Michael H., & Sommer, Veronica V. (Eds.). (2003). *The world of e-government.* Haworth Press.

Dabson, B., & Rist, C. (1996). *Business climate and the role of development incentives.* Region (Federal Reserve Bank of Minneapolis). June. Retrieved January 8, 2004 from http://minneapolisfed.org/pubs/retion/96-06/dabson.cfm

Eisinger, P. (1988). *The rise of the entrepreneurial state: State and local economic development policy in the United States.* Madison: University of Wisconsin Press.

Folsenstein, D., & Persky, J. (1999). When is a cost really a benefit? Local welfare effects and employment creation in the evaluation of economic development programs. *Economic Development Quarterly 13*, 46-54.

Fitzgerald, J., & Leigh, N. (2002). *Economic revitalization: Cases and strategies for city and suburb.* Thousand Oaks: Sage.

Friar, J. (1999). Economic development incentives: A review and recommendations. *Economic Development Review, 16*, 3-7.

Garson, G. David (2006). *Public information technology and e-governance: Managing the virtual state.* Boston: Jones & Bartlett.

Gershberg, A. (2003). *Capital markets and development finance.* Retrieved February 2, 2004, from http://www.newschool.edu/milano/course/sp04/4319/oldsyllabus.pdf

Good Jobs First (2004). *Good jobs first: Promoting accountable development.* Retrieved January 30, 2004, from http://www.goodjobsfirst.org

Herbert, S., Vidal, A., Mills, G., James, F., & Gruenstein, D. (2001). *Interim assessment of the empowermentzZones and enterprisecCommunities (EZ/EC) program.* Washington, DC: U.S. HUD.

Hodge, S., Moody, J., & Warcholik, W. (2003). *State business tax climate index* (Background Paper). Washington, DC: Tax Foundation.

International Economic Development Council (n.d.). *The IEDC professional development series.* Retrieved January 5, 2004, from http://wwwiedconline.org/prodev_course_desc.html

Kottler, P., Haider, D., & Rein, I. (1992). *Marketing places: Attracting investment, industry, and tourism to cities, states, and nations.* New York: Free Press.

Labyrinth of Incentives (2002). Foreign direct investment. Retrieved January 3, 2004, from

http://www.fdimagazine.com/news/printpage.php/aid/187/Labyrinth_of_incentivesUnited

Levy, J. (1990). *Economic development programs for cities, counties and towns* (2nd ed.). New York: Praeger.

Lyons, T., & Hamlin, R. (2001). *Creating an economic development action plan: A guide for development professionals* (revised and updated edition). Westport: Praeger.

National Association of Development Organizations (n.d.). *EDFA.* Retrieved March 1, 2004 from http://www.nado.org/edfs/index.html

National Association of State Development Agencies (n.d.) *Statewide public-private partnership economic development organizations.* Retrieved February 25, 2004 from http://www.nasda.com/statewide_public_private_partner.htm

National Conference of State Legislatures (2003). *State economic development.* Retrieved January 15, 2003, from www.ncsl.org/programs/econ/topics.htm

Porter, M. (2000). Location, competition, and economic development: Local clusters in a global economy. *Economic Development Quarterly, 14*, 15-34.

Reese, L. (1992). Local economic development in Michigan: A reliance on the supply-side. *Economic Development Quarterly, 6*, 383-393.

Reese, L., & Fasenfest, D. (1997). What works best?: Values and the evaluation of local economic development policy. *Economic Development Quarterly, 11*, 195-207.

Reese, L., & Fasenfest, D. (1999). Critical perspectives on local economic development policy evaluation. *Economic Development Quarterly, 13*, 3-7.

Reich, R. (2000). *The future of success: Working and living in the new economy.* New York: Vintage Books.

U.S. Department of Housing and Urban Development (2003). *Tax Incentive Guide for Businesses in the Renewal Communities, Empowerment Zones, and Enterprise Communities.* Washington, DC.

U.S. General Accounting Office (1999). *Community development: Extent of federal influence on "Urban sprawl is unclear."* Washington, DC.

U.S. General Accounting Office (2000). *U.S. infrastructure: Funding trends and opportunities to improve investment decisions.* Washington, DC.

Wisconsin Public Service Corporation (n.d.). *Tax incentives and benefits.* Retrieved January 28, 2004, from http://www.wisconsinpublicservice. com/business/bcd_tax_incentive.asp

Wisconsin, State of (n.d.). Wisconsin business incentives. Retrieved February 4, 2004, from http://www.wisconsin.gov/state/core/wisconsin_business_incentives.html

Wolman H., & Spitzley, D. (1996). The politics of local economic development. *Economic Development Quarterly, 10,* 115-150.

Chapter II
The Development of National ICT Policy in Kenya:
The Influence of Regional Institutions and Key Stakeholders

Timothy Mwololo Waema
University of Nairobi, Kenya

ABSTRACT

The role that information and communication technologies (ICT) could play in socio-economic development has been recognized by governments worldwide. The most important starting point in most countries is a national ICT policy. In many developing countries, ICT policy development has increasingly become a participatory process. This is largely as a result of implementing policy reforms, with a strong emphasis on governance systems. This chapter is a case study of the development of national information and communication technology policy in Kenya, the influences of regional institutions and their products, and the role of the private sector and civil society. The chapter is based on a study that was carried out by reviewing existing relevant documents and by interviewing key persons involved in national and regional ICT policy in Kenya. The chapter also presents the challenges, conclusions, recommendations, and future research directions based on the case.

INTRODUCTION

The role that information and communication technologies (ICTs) could play in socio-economic development has been recognized by governments worldwide. These technologies have been seen as harbingers of prosperity as they can help guarantee access to global markets, enhance wealth creation and generation of high quality employment, enable direct foreign investment and e-commerce, and allow process innovation (new ways of doing old things), which increases productivity and creates new value added and may generate innovative socio-economic activities (new ways of doing new things). In addition, ICT represents a new factor of production, along with land, labour, and capital, which can lead to socio-economic restructuring. Finally, with smaller, faster, and cheaper ICT, the cost-to-performance ratio of its application has declined considerably, thereby raising productivity. In summary, ICTs have come to be regarded as the engines of the new or digital economy and have been key in creating a new world order of digital *haves* and *have nots,* commonly referred to as the *digital divide.*

As a result of the realization of the potential impact of ICT on socio-economic growth, the development of national ICT policies has been high on the agenda of many developing nations for the last one to two decades. In most developing countries, ICT policy development has been a new phenomenon, with many countries often grappling in the dark on the process and its outcomes. In practice, most countries have relied on the experiences and outcomes of other countries. They also have relied on recommended frameworks and models by regional bodies. Some of the United Nations agencies (such as UNECA and UNESCO), and other bilateral agencies, have committed considerable funding on work on national information and ICT policies.

This chapter is a case study of the development of national information and communication technology policy in Kenya, the influences of regional institutions and their products, and the role of the private sector and civil society. The chapter is based on a study that was carried out by reviewing existing relevant documents, and by interviewing key persons involved in national and regional ICT policy in Kenya. The chapter also presents the challenges, conclusions, recommendations, and future research directions based on the case.

BACKGROUND

This background section briefly describes key models that have been used or may be used to explain the policy process. Throughout the chapter, the author takes an interactive political perspective of the policy process. The section ends with an outline of the major stakeholders who should participate in a national ICT policy process and their roles in the process.

There are many models to explain the policy process. The most dominant in the last three decades has been the linear model, based on the traditional breakdown of process into stages. It assumes that policy process consists of various stages: agenda setting, policy formulation, implementation, evalu-

ation, and so forth (DeLeon, 1999). This model has been criticized for a number of weaknesses. Key among these is that the separation of policy formulation and policy implementation enables policy makers to escape responsibility and that a policy decision (the outcome of policy formulation) is inadequate to bring about policy change. In other words, the key weakness, like all other stage models, is the separation of process into distinct and separable stages.

Alternative models have been proposed to address some of the key weaknesses of the linear model. Key among these is the interactive model, which views all the stages of the policy process as interactive rather than linear. For example, Thomas and Grindle (1990) view policy change will always lead to a reaction. There will always be resistance by those who are against it or those who will not benefit from its implementation. This resistance leads to a pressure for change, which can be exercised at any stage of the policy process. This can, in turn, result in the alteration or even reversal of the policy. The interactive model can be extended further by viewing the interaction from different perspectives. The most popular is the political perspective. It assumes that actors in the policy process, whether individuals or groups, have ideas and interests, and that policy outcomes are shaped by a process of interactions in which actors mobilize their sources of power to pursue their ideas and interests. For example, a government will not support a policy outcome that may remove it from power or make it loose votes.

Other more sophisticated perspectives can be used to understand the policy process, its outcomes in terms of policy decisions and the context in which this takes place. One such perspective is Giddens' (1984) social theory, which has been extensively used in the information systems literature. Giddens' social theory has the following key ideas (summarized and paraphrased for clarity):

- **Human beings are knowledgeable agents:** The traditional *objectivism* fails to appreciate the complexity of social action produced by actors operating with knowledge and understanding as part of their consciousness. The extent of people's knowledge of the world is bordered on the one side by the unconscious and on the other side by the unacknowledged conditions and intended consequences of action.

- **The duality of social structure or context:** This means that social structure or context is both a medium and an outcome of human behaviour or social interactions. It is a medium in that social context is drawn on in human behaviour, for example, the current poor state of the national ICT infrastructure in making a decision on the ICT policy outcome. Social context is at the same time an outcome in that day-to-day human interactions produce and reproduce social structures or contexts.
- **The role of power in human behaviour:** Power is not a secondary issue in human behaviour—power is a means to an end and, hence, is directly involved in the actions of every person.

Although a review of these perspectives is beyond the scope of this chapter, we take an interactive political perspective of the policy process.

In many developing countries, policy development has increasingly become a participatory process. This is largely as a result of implementing policy reforms, with a strong emphasis on governance systems. The following are the major stakeholders who get involved in the ICT policy process:

- Government ministries as the key facilitators in policy development.
- Private sector, both national and international, as a key supplier of investment, finance, and technical services.
- Independent regulatory bodies as implementers of policy directives and responsible for managing regulatory systems.
- The telecommunications, IT, and broadcasting sub-sectors with vital interests in sectoral policy reform, investment, and services.
- Non-governmental organizations (NGOs) with increasing roles as providers of services in society.
- Scientists, ICT personnel, and other professional bodies as providers of input on the technological, scientific, and human resource implications and requirements.

- International and regional institutions involved in supporting ICT policy-making process.

Each stakeholder or group of stakeholders comes into this process with specific interests to pursue, in line with the political perspective. It is the management of these interests that is key to the success of the process.

THE CASE OF ICT POLICY DEVELOPMENT IN KENYA

This section describes the case of the development of ICT policy in Kenya. It starts by describing the ICT policy and regulatory environment from the time Kenya started liberalizing the telecommunications sector. It then traces the development of a national ICT policy for almost 10 years, citing, where possible, the performance of the various markets as well as the participation of key stakeholders. The section also outlines the ICT policy models and frameworks of the regional bodies and the two-way influences with the national ICT policy development in Kenya. Further, it describes how the private sector and civil society have participated in the ICT policy process. Finally, the section ends by outlining the key challenges that Kenya has faced in the development of its ICT policy and that regional institutions have faced in influencing ICT policy development in Kenya and the region.

ICT Policy and Regulatory Environment

The Kenya Posts and Telecommunications Corporation (KP&TC), the precursor to the current public licensees in the telecommunications and postal sectors, was an offshoot of the East African Posts and Telecommunications Corporation (EAP&TC). EAP&TC had been formed during the late 1960s as a common infrastructure carrier in line with what was then the East African Community (EAC). KP&TC was a state monopoly over telecommunications and postal services.

The first policy statement specific to telecommunications and postal sector liberalisation was issued in 1997. This culminated in the Kenya

Communications Act (KCA) 1998 and the Postal Corporation Act, 1998. The KCA 1998, which replaced the Kenya Posts and Telecommunications Corporation Act (Cap 411), came into effect on July 1, 1999. As a result of these acts, the KP&TC was split into three separate entities: Telkom Kenya Ltd. (TKL), the Postal Corporation of Kenya (PCK), and the Communications Commission of Kenya (CCK). At the same time, a National Communications Secretariat (NCS) was established within the Ministry of Information, Transport and Communications, to serve as the policy advisory arm of the government on matters relating to the communications sector, while an Appeals Tribunal serves as the independent arbitrator.

In general, the government has recognized the role of ICT in national development and the need to develop a national ICT policy that will act as a catalyst for responsive and growth-enhancing ICT sector for the benefit of all Kenyans. The government's economic blue print (Economic Recovery Strategy for Wealth and Employment Creation, 2003-2007), for example, recognizes that the ICT sector "is important to the realization of the required improvement in productivity and empowerment of the citizenry."

The NCS, established under the KCA 1998, has as its main objective to advise the government on the adoption of a communication policy, which among other things encourages competition and efficiency in the provision of communication services, and fosters full and efficient use of telecommunication resources, including effective use of the radio spectrum. The CCK, also established under the KCA 1998, is an independent regulator whose main objective is to license and regulate telecommunications, radio communication, and postal services. The CCK's vision is to "enable access to reliable communications services by all Kenyans," while its mission is to "ensure that the communications sector contributes to the country's overall development through efficient and enabling regulation and public participation."[1] It is not clear which arm of the government deals with matters relating to information technology (IT). At the same time, there is no regulator for the IT and broadcasting sub-sectors. With convergence of technologies, it is reasonable to expect that one independent regulator regulates telecommunications, postal, broadcasting, and IT services.

Given technological convergence, it is similarly reasonable to expect that all policy matters in telecommunications, postal, broadcasting, and IT are brought under one roof. Other than the coming together of Information and Communications in one ministry, hardly anything else has changed.

The key institutions that can influence ICT policy formulation and implementation are outlined below:

- **The Ministry of Information and Communications:** In a cabinet reshuffle in 2004, a new ministry was created, namely, the Ministry of Information and Communications. According to some observers, the previous Minister of Transport and Communications had an uneasy relationship with the private sector. As was the case with his predecessors, the Permanent Secretary's attention under the old ministry of Transport and Communications tended to focus more on the transportation sector rather than the communications sector. It is this new Ministry of Information and Communications that is in charge of national ICT policy formulation and is the one that eventually delivered the new national ICT policy, which was approved by the Cabinet in January 2006 and came into effect in March 2006.
- **National Communications Secretariat:** The National Communications Secretariat (NCS) advises the Government of Kenya, through the Ministry of Information and Communications, on ICT policy. Although NCS took several years to get started, it is the only key organization with an explicit and legislatively mandated policy function. It is expected to pay particular attention to policies that promote the development of technological capabilities, deliver social services and foster economic growth, encourage competition, and efficiency in the industry, among other goals.
- **Communications Commission of Kenya:** The Communications Commission of Kenya (CCK) is a parastatal, whose purpose is to license and regulate telecommunications, radio communications, and postal services

in Kenya. In addition, according to official documents, "CCK is responsible for developing and co-coordinating the policies and strategies with respect to telecommunications services in Kenya." CCK is recognized as a legal entity and is the regulator of the majority of the ICT services in Kenya. The Commission is managed by a board of directors. The act allows as many as 11 commissioners, and 11 currently are in office. The frontline management of the commission is vested in the Director General.

In making telecommunications regulations, the minister has a duty to consult CCK. This allows CCK to contribute in regulation formulation indirectly.

- **The Appeals Tribunal:** The Appeals Tribunal was established for arbitrating in cases where disputes arise between the parties under the act. Any dispute in the application of the act by CCK, for example, is referred to the Appeals Tribunal. The decision of the Appeals Tribunal can be appealed in the highest court—the Court of Appeal. The Tribunal jurisdiction is limited to the interpretation of the spirit of the Kenya Communications Act. By 2003, the Tribunal had delivered a judgment on interconnection rates dispute between Kencell Communications Ltd., a cellular operator, and Telkom Kenya Ltd.

- **E-government Directorate:** The E-government Directorate was founded in March 2004 and a director was appointed in September of the same year. According to interviewees, the cabinet saw the need for ICT and thus mandated the creation of this entity. The e-government Directorate is called for as part of the structural composition of the e-government strategy. The official purpose of the e-government Directorate, according to the strategy, is to oversee the implementation of e-government strategy, and to assist the government of Kenya to more effectively deliver services to citizens. The e-government strategy proposes that each ministry have its own ICT department.

- **Government Information Technology Services (GITS):** The prodecessor of the Government IT Services was the Micro-

Information Systems Department (MISD). In 2000, MISD was abolished and GITS created. GITS provides computer services to government ministries and departments, and some parastatal organizations. GITS develops relevant computer applications, updates existing systems, evaluates system design, and conducts feasibility studies. The agency aims to ensure ICT standards within government organizations. GITS remains a technical entity. The head of GITS is at a director level.•

- **Parliamentary Committee on Energy, Communications, and Public Works:** This committee provides parliamentary oversight in one aspect of ICT, communications.

- **Monopolies and Prices Commission:** The Monopolies and Prices Commission Act allows the commissioner to determine matters that may affect competition in the economy including companies in telecommunications business. Monopolies established by an act of Parliament are however excluded from the Monopolies and Prices Commission (MPC) control. Consequently, the MPC has had little effect on the telecommunications sector exclusivity until June 2004. In the liberalized segment in the Internet provision, MPC has had a role to ensure competition and control mergers. In 1999, MPC cleared the take-over of an ISP (Net, 2000) by another ISP (Africa Online) concurring that the resulting merger did not affect market concentration of Internet business. No other telecommunications related case has been handled by the MPC.

From the above outline, the state of affairs where ICT responsibilities were distributed in different arms of the government, with little, if any, coordination still prevails. This situation has to change if Kenya is to harness the potential of the whole spectrum of ICT for national socio-economic development and to exploit the inherent synergies in the sub-sectors.

As part of the liberalization process, the government intended to sell 49% of TKL in order to enable TKL to achieve increased growth. However, this move has failed for a number of reasons. According to the Economic Recovery Strategy for Wealth and

Employment Creation, the government still aims at restructuring TKL in readiness for privatization.

As part of the post-exclusivity regulatory strategy, the director general of the CCK issued a statement in September 2004 containing a new licensing framework. The general goal of this framework is "to ensure that the regulatory environment in the sector is friendly to investment and conducive to the provision of modern communication services." The specific objectives of the new licensing framework are to ensure that Kenya has a more dynamic and competitive ICT environment, improved access to ICT infrastructure and services, and choice in the provision of communication services to meet socio-economic needs of the society.

The new converged licensing framework would:

- Allow cellular mobile operators to construct and operate their own international gateways if they choose to do so; this was largely necessitated by the need for diversity in international links, high traffic volumes, need to expand and better manager roaming services, and so on
- Provide for the licensing of additional Internet backbone and gateway operators, broadcasting signal distributors and commercial VSAT operators on a first-come-first-served basis
- Allow public data network operators (PDNOs) to establish international gateways for data communications services
- Allow Internet backbone and gateway operators, broadcast signal distributors, commercial VSAT operators, and public data network operators (PDNOs) to carry any form of multimedia traffic, for example, VoIP

One notable aspect of the new licensing framework is that the CCK was abandoning licensing based on a bidding process in favour of open market-based licensing. The CCK argues that licensing through a bidding process, especially in a liberalized market, is "not only unnecessary but undesirable and inconsistent with market dynamics." The problems of using the bidding process were evident in the licensing of rural telecommunications operators (RTOs), commercial trunked radio operators (CTROs), and the third GSM operator.

The post-exclusivity statement by CCK's Director General in September 2004 states that in the medium- to long-term CCK "shall adopt a unified and absolute technology neutral licensing framework that permits any form of communications infrastructure to be used to provide any type of communications service that is technically capable of providing." It goes further to suggest that in the next two to five years, the market structure, largely driven by technological convergence, will be technology neutral.

The new licensing framework, at the time, was seen to be likely to lead to reduced costs of communication, broader choice of service providers, more rapid rollout, and more widespread coverage by operators, and better and more reliable services. However, two years after licenses were issued, there has been no significant reductions in costs, while at the same time several licensees, especially Internet backbone gateway operators and local loop operators, took a long time to roll out their networks.

THE NATIONAL ICT POLICY DEVELOPMENT PROCESS IN KENYA

1997-2004

Kenya has had very many attempts in developing national ICT policy for more than two decades (Waema, 2005). Most of these attempts, however, have not involved the stakeholders. For example, the telecommunications and postal policy statement,[2] first prepared in 1997, and subsequently revised in 1999 and 2001, was prepared by the government, and specifically, the Ministry of Information, Transport and Communications, without public involvement or even subjecting the policy to discussion and inputs from other stakeholders, as was the practice in many countries.

As an illustration of the contents of the telecommunications and postal sector policy guidelines, the objectives and targets of the 2001 policy statement were:

1. The overall government's objective for the sector is to optimize its contribution to the

development of the Kenyan economy as a whole by ensuring the availability of efficient, reliable and affordable communication services throughout the country. In the area of telecommunications services for instance, it is intended:

a. To improve penetration in the rural areas from the present 0.16 lines to 5 lines per 100 people by the year 2015.

b. To improve service penetration in urban areas from the present 4 lines to 20 lines per 100 people by the year 2015.

2. These targets translate to installation of 1.5 million fixed lines in rural areas and 2.4 million fixed lines in urban areas respectively. At an estimated average cost of about US$1,500 per line, the total investment over the 15 years period will amount to about US$5.85 billion. This means that, on average, the annual requirements will be about US$390 million. This is an enormous investment requirement which calls for new initiatives to attract capital into the sector. It is in this context that the restructuring of Telkom Kenya Limited and a step by step liberalization of the sector is being undertaken particularly with a view to attract capital from the private sector.

3. In the area of postal services, it is observed that the network is already fairly extensive. The main objective, therefore, will be to ensure high quality service, cost effective expansion and financial self-sustenance.

With respect to universal access to postal and telecommunication services, the policy statement provided in Part 3.4.1, the following:

The government will continue to emphasize the provision of basic postal and telecommunication services to all unserved or under-served areas at affordable rates. All players will be expected to contribute towards this goal. Appropriate regulations and licensing procedures will be put into place to ensure compliance. However, where the provision of such services is deemed to be uneconomical, the government will undertake to avail appropriate subventions.

The above objectives and targets set out in the official policy above were out of line with the prevailing circumstances. Targets, for example, were only set for fixed telephone lines; the policy did not address the mobile cellular market, which, by that time, was relatively a young but rapidly growing market. The seriousness of this omission is illustrated by the performance of the fixed line and mobile cellular markets as summarized in tables 1 and 2, respectively.

As can be observed from the above tables, the mobile network surpassed the fixed network in 2000/2001 and has since then experienced phenomenal growth. By 2006/2007, the mobile network was more than 20 times the size of the fixed network. The inadequacy of these early policy statements, as illustrated above, may be associated with the involvement of people who had a traditional thinking of the telecommunications sector (almost all had had their career in the monopolistic fixed network era) and the lack of stakeholder participation in thinking of the future of the sector.

The first attempt to involve stakeholders was made by the National Communications Secretariat in the Ministry of Information, Transport and Communications. NCS started preparing a national ICT policy in 2002. This effort culminated in a five-day conference in March 2003, whose objective was "to collect and collate views of stakeholders drawn from the public and private sectors as a basis for preparing Kenya's National ICT Policy and Plans." Participation was by invitation only and some of the participants were requested to prepare presentations in a pre-defined format. Participants were invited from the following:

- Office of the Attorney General
- Ministry of Education, Science and Technology
- Public universities
- Kenya Institute of Education and the National Council for Science and Technology
- Ministry of Transport and Communications, including Kenya Railways Corporation, Postal Corporation of Kenya, and Telkom Kenya Ltd.
- Ministry of Labour and Human Resource Development

- Ministry of Agriculture
- Ministry of Energy
- Ministry of Environment and Natural Resources
- Ministry of Foreign Affairs
- Ministry of Home Affairs, Heritage and Sports
- Ministry of Lands and Settlement
- Ministry of Local Government
- Ministry of Roads and Public Works
- Ministry of Tourism and Information
- Provincial Commissioners' offices
- Kenya Community Broadcasting Network
- The African Centre for Women, Information and Communication Technologies

The participation was almost exclusively drawn from the public sector, with hardly any participation of the private sector and civil society organizations. Nevertheless, a small committee was selected at the end of the workshop to put together all the presentations and discussions into a draft national ICT policy. After about a year, by June 2004, a draft document was ready. This document remained confidential, circulating only within government offices. Other stakeholders were not allowed access to the document. Unfortunately, the document never moved to the next stage to become a cabinet memorandum. It is alleged that the Ministry of Tourism and Information delayed its input, which was critical given the role of information in ICT.

E-Government Strategy (2004)

In March 2004, the government released the e-government strategy that had been developed in the Cabinet Office in the Office of the President. The objectives of the strategy were to:

a. Increase efficiency and effectiveness, enhance transparency, and accountability in the delivery of government services through the use of information technologies.
b. Improve the internal workings of government to be externally oriented and more customer-focused.
c. Facilitate collaboration and the sharing of information within and between government agencies.

Table 1. Summary of fixed telephone network performance, 2000-2006 (Source: Telkom Kenya Ltd., 2006)

Year	Exchange Capacity	Subscriber Connections	% Unused Switch Capacity	Average % Growth in Connections	Waiters	Pay-Phones
1999/2000	444,422	313,470	29		127,169	8,684
2000/2001	445,822	326,282	27	4.09	133,862	9,135
2001/2002	507,652	331,718	35	1.67	108,761	9,618
2002/2003	508,230	328,358	35	-1.01	107,938	9,964
2003/2004	531,442	299,255	44	-8.86	107,260	9,798
2004/2005	531,804	281,764	47	-5.84	85,177	8,967
2005/2006 (Feb. 2006)	513,824	293,364	43	4.12	85,177	8,915

Table 2. Performance of the mobile cellular market (Source: Communications Commission of Kenya)

	1999/2000	2001/2002	2002/2003	2003/2004	2004/2005	2005/2006	2006/2007
SafariCom	54,000	325,235	728,163	1,000,000	1,627,378	2,512,826	4.3million
Celtel	60,000	259,896	458,959	590,785	918,779	2,099,144	2.14million
Combined subscribers	114,000	585,131	1,187,122	1,590,785	2,546,157	4,611,970	6.48million
Average % growth in subscribers		413.27	102.88	34.00	60.06	81.13	

d.   Significantly reduce transaction costs leading to savings.

e.   Encourage participation and empowerment of citizens, including the disadvantaged groups, and communities in the rural and remote areas through closer interaction with the government.

f.   Attract foreign investments by providing faster access to information and government services.

The e-government priorities were instituting structural and operational reforms, review of the regulatory and legal framework, and development of a reliable and secure infrastructure. As originally conceptualized, the priority activities and implementation framework over the immediate, medium, and long terms along the dimensions of government to government (G2G), government to business (G2B) and government to citizen (G2C) communications are as shown in Table 3.

The strategy was a detailed and ambitious plan. Its release signalled a readiness to implement ICTs in the government. Whilst this was a welcome initiative, it nevertheless, once again, demonstrated the government's ad hoc approach to ICT policy and strategy development and implementation because the strategy was released before the national policy was in place. At the same time, it was not clear how the e-government Directorate in the Office of the President would work with the new Ministry of Information and Communications and Government IT Services (GITS) in the Ministry of Finance in implementing the strategy. It would be interesting to evaluate the performance of e-government strategy in 2007 when its life comes to an end.

2004-2006

When the new Ministry of Information and Communications was created in June 2004, following the reorganisation of some ministries, the new minister, who had been the Minister of Tourism and Information before the reorganisation, rejected the draft national ICT policy, referring to it as "a cut and paste job." The new Minister also rejected the draft national broadcasting policy and a draft broadcasting bill. These last two documents had been prepared by the media and broadcasting stakeholders initially under the auspices of the Ministry of Information, Transport and Communications and later under the auspices of the Ministry of Tourism and Information.

By October 2004, the draft national ICT policy was ready in the new Ministry of Information and Communications. This document appeared to be a lot similar to the June 2004 version, which had been rejected. It was unclear who provided the extra input and in what areas. The document was unveiled to the public by the Ministry of Information and Communications in November 2004, during a national ICT visioning workshop. The Permanent Secretary in the Ministry promised that the draft ICT policy document would be subjected to public discussion before its finalisation. By February 2005, the draft policy was in the Ministry's Web site, and public comments were sought through advertisements in the daily newspapers. The comments were to be sent to the permanent secretary, Ministry of Information and Communications at a given e-mail address. This seemed to herald the beginning of a truly new regime of public participation in policy making.

One of the problems facing the development of the national ICT policy then was the multiplicity of initiatives working in parallel. Several development partners interested in Kenya's ICT policy process had engaged a variety of stakeholder groups, leading to confusion and, in turn, frustrating efforts to finalize the draft policy. However, the formation of the Kenya ICT Action Network (KICTANET), a loose network of networks of all stakeholders who had been working to support the government's efforts in developing and finalising Kenya's ICT policy, marked the beginning of harmonizing all the initiatives. KICTANET and Kenya ICT Federation (KIF) had organized a two-day convention on March 8-9, 2005 to discuss the way forward on the ICT policy.

Participants were drawn from the civil society, media, academia, and the private sector, as well as development partners. This meeting, which was the Second National ICT Convention, marked the beginning of a detailed process of analysis, critique, and public input into the ICT draft policy with a view to finalizing the policy and pursuing future legislative action for implementation. At the end of the convention, the following recommendations[3] were made:

- That the Ministry for Information and Communication legitimises the policy process begun at the Second National ICT Convention and KICTANET to be part of the consultation and implementation process aimed at finalising Kenya's national ICT policy.
- That the ministry provides a forum for consensus building on the comments collected from the public and from the mailing list discussions after the 10th April, 2005 deadline.

At the end of the convention, sector-specific working groups were launched. These groups would comment on specific segments of the draft ICT policy, and the comments would be collated and forwarded to the Ministry for incorporation into Kenya's final national ICT policy.

The draft ICT policy together with the comments from stakeholders were the resource materials in the first truly stakeholder-driven national ICT workshop held over a three-day period (June 13-15, 2005). At the end of this workshop, a small group of the participants was appointed to use the inputs from the stakeholders to create the final draft ICT policy. By August 2005, the Ministry of Information and Communications had prepared a cabinet memorandum on the draft ICT policy. This policy was discussed and approved by the cabinet in January 2006[4] and an ICT policy document published in March 2006. For the first time in more than two decades of failed attempts, Kenya had an official ICT policy.

In 2006, the Ministry of Information and Communications also introduced a draft Information and Communication Bill[5]. The government also published a guide to the bill[6]. The new legislation is intended to address convergence in telecommunications, internet, etc. From the guide:

The draft Information and Communications Bill outlines the proposed new regulatory regime to be managed by the converged sector regulator. It transforms regulation in the ICT sector by providing a new regulatory framework that will adapt to the changing market. The following changes are being introduced:

a. The transformation of Communications Commission of Kenya into fully-fledged ICT sector regulator for the rapidly evolving and converging industry thereby allowing all regulatory decisions affecting the sector to be made within a single strategic framework.
b. The removal of the requirement for licensing of telecommunications, broadcasting and multimedia services separately, hence, creating a new framework where electronic communications networks, electronic communications services and associated infrastructure and services can be licensed.
c. Setting up a universal service fund.
d. Creating a one-stop shop for making decisions affecting the use of radio frequency spectrum and access networks.

This Bill has been circulated and stakeholders are still making comments on it, although there is no appropriate framework to facilitate these comments.

Influence of Regional Institutions

Kenya is an active participant in regional cooperation arrangements particularly in the Common Market for Eastern and Southern Africa (COMESA) and the East African Community (EAC) that have substantial interest in the development of ICTs in the sub-region.

COMESA's ICT vision is:

... a sub-region where the effective use and application of ICTs enhances and accelerates economic growth, social development and regional integration and contributes to the achievement of the objectives of the African Union and NEPAD.

Its overall ICT goal is:

To promote the development and application of ICTs, through the implementation of facilitative and harmonised policies, with a view to achieving the widest use of and access to information throughout the sub-region within a reasonable period.

Table 3. Priority activities and implementation framework for the e-government strategy

Short-Term Activities (by June 2004)	Medium-Term Activities (by June 2007)	Long-Term Activities
A. G2G Communications		
Institute information and communication technology (ICT) policy and e-government strategy	Increase automation and integration of government records and information	
Expand the information infrastructure	Completion of the information infrastructure within the government up to the district level	
Initiate the integration of internal government processes	Develop and implement Web-enabled databases	
Increase the efficiency and effectiveness of internal operations	Operationalize other information systems under development (e.g., civil registration, road transport, revenue collection, etc.)	
Develop Web sites for ministries		
Build capacity		
B. G2B Communications		
Operationalize a single government portal	Electronic administration of business	Electronic government payments
Establish government auctions	Electronic filing of government returns and claims	e-Trading of government securities
	Portal services-data warehousing	Government service management
	E-procurement	
	Electronic forums for discussion and feedback	
C. G2C Communications		
Interaction with citizens	Increased involvement of citizens in decision making and public activities.	Enhanced e-policing
Improving public services	Electronic property search.	E-voting
Introduction of e-policing	Legal	Integrated electronic payments
Advertising government jobs		
Education		
Provision of family entertainment, dissemination of information on social/health issues and related public events.		
Verification of the voter's register		

COMESA[7] has developed policy model for the harmonious development and application of ICTs within member states with a view to turning COMESA into an information society. The ICT policy objectives of this model are:

a. Achieving affordable, ubiquitous and high quality services.
b. Building a competitive regional ICT sector.
c. Creating an environment for sustainable ICT diffusion and development.

In a meeting of the Council of Ministers held on March 13-15, 2003 and the Heads of State Summit held on March 17, 2003 in Khartoum, Sudan,

COMESA adopted the common ICT Policy and Model Bill for use by member states in reforming their policies and legislation. COMESA used the facilitation by consultants and involved its members in workshops to develop this model policy and legislation. In this development, COMESA borrowed heavily from those member states that were ahead. It also was informed by practices in other countries in Europe and the United States of America. Kenya was involved in developing the regional ICT model for COMESA.

In January 2003, in Addis Ababa, the Association of Regulators of Information and Communications in Eastern and Southern Africa (ARICEA) was established to assist in the standardization of best regulatory practices. Since its formation, ARICEA[8] has been developing and *selling* model regulatory policies to member countries with the objective of creating one attractive market in the region. In developing the model policies, ARICEA has borrowed from countries that were ahead in regulatory matters, as well as borrowing from practices in other relevant countries. In Kenya, the communications regulator (CCK) and the National Communications secretariat have been active participants in the COMESA ICT initiatives and the director-general of CCK currently is the chairperson of ARICEA.

Several member states within the Eastern and Southern Africa (ESA) region in the last few years have embarked on the development and implementation of the ICT policies and programmes. Countries are at various stages of ICT policy development with ICT policies in place in some countries while others either do not or are still developing them. Kenya is one of the last countries in this region to develop its national ICT policy. It borrowed heavily from the COMESA model, especially the policy areas of communications, universal access, competition, and interconnection. According to sources in the National Communications Secretariat, COMESA might have to borrow from Kenya and those other countries that have incorporated IT in their ICT policy. This is because the COMESA common ICT policy excluded a serious treatment of the information technology sub-sector.

Kenya also is an active participant in the East Africa Regulatory, Postal and Telecommunications Organization (EARPTO). EARPTO is an organization whose members are drawn from regulators and operators in postal and telecommunications from the East Africa region. Its objectives are to:

- Harmonize and promote the development of postal and telecommunications services and regulatory matters, and devise ways and means to achieve fast, reliable, secure, economic, and efficient services within the community.
- Ensure the provision of tariff structure and settlement of accounts.
- Promote the development and application of ICTs.
- Serve as a consultative organization for settlement of postal and telecommunications mat-

ters, which are regional in nature, promote the development of technical facilities and their most efficient utilization with a view to improving the efficiency for telecommunications and postal services, increasing their usefulness and making them generally available to the public.
- Harmonize policies and legislation in the communications sector (i.e., managing competition and licensing requirements in the region).

Although EARPTO works very well, it is not linked to any of the *official* regional bodies (e.g., the African Union and the East African Community). Government representatives from relevant parent ministries can attend EARPTO meetings as observers. Therefore, EARPTO lacks a formal mechanism to influence ICT development in the region. The lack of a secretariat and a rotating chairmanship of EARPTO also has created difficulty in following up with its recommendations.

In March 2004, the government of Kenya launched an ambitious three-year (2003-2007) e-government strategy in line with the national development strategy for Wealth and Employment Creation. It was not clear whether this strategy was guided by any regional framework. The strategy identified the e-government priorities as:

- Instituting structural and operational reforms.
- Review of the regulatory and legal framework.
- Development of a reliable and secure infrastructure.

According to this study, Kenya is involved in developing an e-government regional framework under the East African Community. The participants are studying the Indian models, sponsored by the EAC Secretariat. Kenya has also been a participant and has moderately influenced the development of other regional frameworks, including voice over IP (VoIP), e-health and e-education.

Finally, Kenya has developed a draft IT Bill, borrowing from models developed by other bodies. For example, according to sources in the National Communications Secretariat, aspects of E-commerce and Electronic Signatures have borrowed heavily from the Model Law on Electronic Commerce of the United Nations Commission on International Trade Law (UNCITRAL) of 1996 and the UNCITRAL Model Law on Electronic Signatures of 2001 respectively[9]. This draft bill was however developed without the involvement of stakeholders. It is at the stage of public discussions.

The study found out that Kenya takes regional issues seriously, and actively participates in and influences regional ICT discussions, especially in COMESA and EAC. However, the influence of Kenya waned largely due to very slow progress in developing a national ICT policy and in implementing ICT programmes or projects. Nevertheless, Kenya has benefited to a great extent from regional ICT models. The analysis also has shown that the influence of regional institutions is only restricted to ICT policy development. From the study, regional institutions do not have any significant role in ICT policy implementation and evaluation. Although member countries are entrusted with and expected to carry out implementation and evaluation of ICT policy, most regional institutions do not have mechanisms to track implementation and to gauge the degree of compliance[10]. For Kenya, the institutional framework to ensure implementation of policy and monitor it has not been clear. In the liberalization of the communications sector, CCK has been implementing the policy guidelines. As we move into the implementation of the ICT policy, the institutional framework is once again in focus and discussions on an appropriate framework are yet to be finalized.

The Role of the Private Sector and Civil Society

The participation in regional ICT governance issues has been largely restricted to the public sector. One of the main exceptions is ARICEA where both public and private operators participate in deliberations. In Kenya, for example, the cellular operators, fixed line operator (Telkom Kenya), Postal Corporation of Kenya, private broadcasters, Telecommunications Service Providers Association of Kenya (TESPOK), and the Courier Association of Kenya are regular attendees of the ARICEA meetings. Kenya acts as a hub for major international meetings that had the effect of partly facilitating awareness and participation of civil society organizations (CSOs) and the private sector in ICT issues.

In general, private sector firms, especially the large operators, are very clear on national and regional ICT policies and programmes. In the past, they have been excluded from policy processes largely because of the view that policy development was the role of governments, a view that has significantly changed in the last few years in most countries in the region. Despite their exclusion, private sector organizations have been active and have tried to influence ICT policy in their countries as well as in the region. For example, in the past, the private sector has initiated meetings with key government departments and institutions with a view to influencing public policy. An example of one such meeting is the National Investment Conference that was held in Nairobi on November 20-21, 2003. The infrastructure (including ICT infrastructure) break out group, recommended, among other things, that the government creates an enabling climate for private investment, that the government moves to implementation rather than continue writing about what ICT can do for national development, that there be private-public partnerships, and that the government reforms public procurement procedures to enable development, and nurturing of local capacity to develop infrastructure and support services. In general, what has been lacking for private-public partnerships to take place is the government's willingness or commitment to make this a reality. In Kenya, this is beginning to happen. For example, in August 2005, the ICT Secretary convened a meeting of all ICT units in government and representatives of private sector data network operators to explore private-public partnerships in building a fiber-backbone for provision of e-government services.

The participation of civil society organizations (CSOs) in national and regional ICT processes has been very weak. One of the key reasons is that CSOs do not have formal organizations to be able to constructively engage governments. At the same time, the government is not aware of the activities of most CSOs in the ICT sector. A further reason is that most CSOs, which are mainly set up as non-governmental organizations, tend to focus on achieving objectives of the development aid organization funding them. In some cases, according to some of the respondents, the representatives of CSO organizations pursue more of their personal interests than those of the civil society and the public at large. The key strategies to increase CSO participation include, creating an umbrella organization, which can effectively articulate the views of the public and for the governments and regional bodies to create formal mechanisms through which civil society can participate.

The private sector, which tends to pursue narrow business-oriented objectives, already has created such an umbrella organization—the Kenya Private Sector Alliance (KEPSA). KEPSA[11] seeks to bring together the private sector representative organisations in Kenya, so that they can speak with a single voice in order to influence public policy formulation. Participating organisations are either sector federations (bringing together one or more associations within a specific sector) or thematic (and, therefore, cross-sector) organisations. As an example, the KEPSA ICT Board, a board that deals with the ICT sector, has received positive recognition from government, donors, and the private sector. It also has positively engaged the government on pertinent ICT policy issues and was one of the key groups in KICTANET. For example, KEPSA ICT Board members have made presentations at numerous national conferences, including the East African Business Summit of November 2002, which addressed the ICT sector in its deliberations and the national ICT stakeholders' policy workshops in March 2003 and June 2005.

There was minimal participation by other stakeholders, especially women and marginalized groups. The initial drive in Kenya was to change the framework where government dominated the ICT policy processes to a situation where there was increased participation by other stakeholders. During this period, the categories of stakeholders (e.g., women and minorities) was not as important as the general opening up of the policy processes. As the stakeholder-driven processes take route in Kenya, as illustrated toward the end of the ICT policy development process, we should expect distinct categories of stakeholders to emerge and claim their right to push their ideas and interests.

Challenges

Although regional bodies have had model ICT policies for some time, Kenya has taken a long time to develop its own ICT policy, despite having been one of the pioneers in attempting to have developed a policy more than 20 years ago. The key challenges that Kenya has faced in the development of its ICT policy have been:

- **Lack of appropriate institutional framework:** Kenya has not had appropriate institutional arrangements to coordinate ICT policy development and implementation. At times, institutions with some mandate for ICT have tried to compete in developing a policy.
- **Autonomy of policy drivers:** The main policy driver, the National Communication Secretariat, has not had the necessary autonomy to carry out its work. In the past, the tight control by the Permanent Secretary of the parent ministry was tantamount to lack of government support. At the same time, the implementers of communications policy, CCK, has not had the required autonomy from government.
- **Funding:** In the past, development aid organizations have funded most ICT policy processes and programmes in government. At the same time, most arms of government that have an ICT mandate did not have a corresponding budget that was adequate and sustainable.
- **Champions:** The majority of ministers, permanent secretaries, and legislators have not appreciated the role and potential impact of ICT in national development. They, therefore, have not been able to champion ICT in national development. At the same time, no national champion has emerged. The creation of the Ministry of Information and Communication in mid-2004 and the appointment of the ICT Secretary in the Cabinet Office (at the level of a Permanent Secretary and reporting to the Head of Civil Service and Secretary to the Cabinet) in 2005 are the early signs of the possible emergence of a national ICT champion.

The key challenges that regional institutions have faced in influencing ICT policy processes in Kenya and the region are:

a. **Myriad of initiatives and lack of ownership:** The region has a number of ICT policy and programme initiatives, some of which are in competition with each other. Some of these initiatives have their origins in the "development partners" funding the initiatives with very little ownership from African governments. In some situations, development aid organizations duplicate the funding of similar or related initiatives, resulting in waste of valuable resources.

b. **Institutional mechanisms:** Regional institutions lack institutional mechanisms to ensure compliance with model policies and frameworks, and to monitor and evaluate implementation of ICT policies in member countries. Although COMESA advocates for regional institutional arrangements for coordinating the implementation of the common policy at national and regional level, these arrangements do not exist.

c. **Differences in development:** The various countries in the region are at different stages of economic, political, and social development. This makes it difficult for member countries to have common priorities and, therefore, to adopt common models or frameworks.

d. **Sovereignty of member states:** Member states are sovereign states and have no obligation to go by policy guidelines by regional bodies. This becomes even more difficult when political considerations are involved. The COMESA ICT policy, for example, advocates for the set up of regulatory bodies, which are seen to be independent in order to supervise the implementation of the ICT policies and regulate the industry where required. Further, COMESA proposes that removal of a member of the board of a regulatory body "should be by the appointing authority and for cause, such as misconduct or incapacity, on the recommendation of a judicial committee as is usually the case with the removal of an ombudsman, an electoral commissioner or a similar official." However, COMESA and other regional institutions have no power over any member country. In Kenya, for example, the Minister of Information and Communication

was able to sack the Director General and the whole Board of the Communications Commission of Kenya, with COMESA not making any attempt to question the decision.

e. **Participants divorced from reality in ministries:** Participation in meetings and other fora of regional institutions is often dominated by the most senior persons in the concerned ministries at the expense of the more junior people who deal with the matters on a day-to-day basis. As a result, the people who get involved are often divorced from realities and may not be well briefed, thereby, creating a gap. This is worsened by lack of a mechanism to give feedback on issues discussed or agreed to by the people who will be involved in implementation.

f. **Coordination between ministries:** In most cases, there is no clear mechanism to coordinate the inputs of the various ministries involved in a regional institution's agenda. For example, the contact ministry for COMESA is the Ministry of Trade while the inter-governmental development authority (IGAD) deals with the Ministry of Foreign Affairs. With respect to ICT issues, these contact ministries may not share the information with the most relevant ministries, or may not be able to co-ordinate and get the most relevant inputs and personnel from the ministries concerned. As a result, the ICT policy models/frameworks developed can be at variance with those of the region.

g. **Stakeholder interests and participation:** Policy development involves compromises on the interests of various stakeholders. Some of the respondents felt that the agenda or interests of some of the regional institutions are not entirely that of the member countries. Others felt that regional ICT policy is conceptualized at the highest level with very little, if any, input from local stakeholders in individual country members. It is possible, therefore, that some of the policy measures fail to capture the socio-economic interests of common people in member countries. Even with the almost exclusion of the interests of local stakeholders, it is possible that the interests of the regional body, of nations represented, and of individuals representing line ministries are not quite aligned to each other. In such cases, the interests of the nations' and the region can be compromised at the expense of strong personal interests.

In addition, although the government of Kenya has made the transition from centralized ICT policy processes to a participative viewpoint, there is yet no mechanisms to institutionalize stakeholder participation. For the private sector and civil society organizations, there is the additional challenge that most interest groups do not have formal fora through which to participate in ICT policy development processes. In addition, some of the civil society groups, and generally members of the public, may not have the requisite knowledge or have adequate resources to mobilize in order to effectively participate in and influence the ICT policy process.

CONCLUSION

This chapter has described the process of developing ICT policy in Kenya and discussed the influence of regional bodies and the roles of key stakeholders. The case has illustrated how various initiatives to develop a national ICT policy took a long time before a formal outcome was realized. One of the key reasons was that ICT mandates were spread over several government bodies in a number of ministries. This arrangement resulted in poor to non-existent coordination of initiatives that, in turn, slowed down, and even frustrated, policy development. A second reason was the frequent re-organization of government arms with mandates for ICT as well as regular changes in the key officers in charge of ICT. These changes created discontinuities that frustrated the process of ICT policy development. A further reason was that the majority of ministers, permanent secretaries, and legislators involved did not appreciate the role and potential impact of ICT in national development. They, therefore, could not provide championship of ICT for socio-economic development. Finally, funding for e-government, including development of ICT policy, was heavily reliant on "development partners." At the same time, most arms of government that had an ICT

mandate did not have a corresponding budget that was adequate and sustainable.

The case also has illustrated a limited role of regional bodies in influencing the development of national ICT policy. One of the explanations is the existence of multiple ICT policy and programme initiatives, some of which are often in competition with each other, have their origins in the "development partners" funding the initiatives with very little ownership from African governments. A second explanation is that regional institutions lack institutional mechanisms to ensure compliance with model policies and frameworks as well as to monitor and evaluate implementation of ICT policy in member countries. This is made difficult by the fact that member states are sovereign states and have no obligation to go by policy guidelines of regional bodies. A further explanation is that the various countries in the region are at different stages of economic, political, and social development, making it difficult for member countries to have common priorities and, therefore, to adopt common models or frameworks. Other reasons are that participation in meetings and other fora of regional institutions is often dominated by the most senior persons in the concerned ministries at the expense of the more junior people who deal with the matters on a day-to-day basis, and that there is no clear mechanism to coordinate the inputs of the various ministries involved in a regional institution's agenda.

RECOMMENDATIONS

Given the challenges outlined in the case, we recommend that individual member countries in a region with regional cooperation need to have political commitment to regionalism and to adopting or customizing, and implementing regional model ICT policies and frameworks. Simultaneously, regional institutions need to develop obligatory measures to ensure that regional models and frameworks are of a binding nature and that there are motivational sanctions for non-compliance at both policy development and implementation stages. Further, the agencies in charge of and that drive the different stages of the ICT policy process, especially policy formulation and implementation stages, need to be given the necessary autonomy to carry out their work under institutional and legislative frameworks that are well defined. Finally, a nation requires powerful and high-level champions as well as adequate and sustainable funding for the ICT policy processes.

FUTURE RESEARCH DIRECTIONS

Many studies on ICT and developing countries in the last decade have concentrated on ICT policy development, perhaps because this was what was perceived to be required at the time. In comparison, there is limited research with respect to ICT policy implementation. We recommend that future research focuses on the implementation of ICT policy and its outcomes and impacts, especially with respect to human socio-economic development. In addition, future research should focus on the link between policy implementation and policy formulation rather than treating these as separate phenomena.

In line with the theme of the handbook, we recommend that future research also should study the influence of global forces (e.g., technological developments, funding organizations, multi-national corporations, foreign governments, etc.) on ICT policy processes in developing countries. It would be nice if these studies analyze their data from some of the more interactive policy process models.

Finally, although the chapter does not analyze the case from any of the policy process perspectives; it, nevertheless, has illustrated the importance of taking a policy perspective in order to gain a deeper understanding of the policy process. Future ICT policy researchers, therefore, should make a transition to analyzing policy processes from relevant perspective(s) in order to make their research more useful to other researchers as well as policy practitioners.

REFERENCES

DeLeon, P. (1999). In Paul A. Sabatier (Ed.), The stages approach to the policy process. What has it done? Where is it going? *Theories of the policy process* (pp. 19-32). CO: Westview Press.

Giddens, A. (1984). *The constitution of society.* Cambridge, UK: Polity Press.

Kenya (1998). The Kenya Communications Act, 1998 and The Postal Corporation Act, 1998. (Supplement No. 64 (Act No. 3) Special Issue). *The Kenya Gazette Supplement*. Nairobi: Kenya (2001). Telecommunications and postal sector policy guidelines, The Kenya Communications Act (No. 2 of 1998). *The Kenya Gazette* (Vol. CIII-No. 77, Special Issue). Nairobi.

Kenya (2003). *Economic recovery strategy for wealth and employment creation, 2003-2007.* Government of Kenya.

Kenya (2004). *E-government strategy: The strategic framework, administrative structure, training requirements and standardization framework*, Cabinet Office, Office of the President, Republic of Kenya, March.

Kenya (2005). *Economic survey 2005.* Central Bureau of Statistics.

Thomas, J. W., & Grindle, M. S. (1990). After the decision: Implementation policy reform in developing countries. *World Development, 18*(8), 1163-1181.

Waema, T. M. (2004). *Final report on universal access to communication services: development of a strategic plan and implementation guidelines.* Nairobi, Kenya: Communications Commission of Kenya, http://www.cck.go.ke/

Waema, T. M. (2005). A brief history of the development of ICT policy in Kenya. In F. E. Etta & L. Elder (Eds.), *At the crossroads: ICT policy making in East Africa* (pp. 25-43). Nairobi, Kenya: East African Educational Publishers Ltd.

ADDITIONAL READING

Adedeji, A. (1990). *African charter for popular participation in development and transformation: The politics of policy-making.* UNECA, Addis Ababa.

Alice, M. (2005). Positioning for impact: Women and ICT policy making. In F.E. Etta & L. Elder (Eds.), *At the crossroads: ICT policy making in East Africa* (pp. 183-198). Nairobi, Kenya: East African Educational Publishers Ltd.

Alison, G. et al. (2007). *Towards an African e-Index: Understanding ICT access and usage in Africa.* African Communication Ministers' Meeting, Uganda. http://www.researchictafrica.net/images/upload/UgandaMinisters_meetingE-index240207.pdf

Economic Commission for Africa (ECA), (2003). *Policies and plans on the information society: Status and impact.* ECA, Addis Ababa.

Hafkin, N. (2003). The African information initiative: 1995-2000. In I. Kakoma, & P.T. Zeleka (Eds.), *Science and technology in Africa.* Africa World Press Inc., Asmara.

ISPO (2004). *Recommendations to the European council: Europe and the global information society.* http://www.ispo.cec.be/infosoc/backg/bangeman.html

James, T. (2001). In James, T. (Ed.). An overview of information policy initiatives in Southern Africa. *An information policy handbook for Southern Africa: A knowledge base for decision-makers. IDRC,* Ottawa.

Lwakabamba, S. (2005). The development of ICTs in Rwanda: Pioneering experiences. In F.E. Etta & L. Elder (Eds.), *At the crossroads: ICT policy making in East Africa* (pp. 213-224). Nairobi, Kenya: East African Educational Publishers Ltd.

Mansell, R. et al. (Eds.). (2007). *The Oxford handbook of information and communication technologies.* Oxford University Press.

Melody, W. H. (Ed.) (1998). *Telecom reform: Principles, policies and regulatory practices.* Lyngby, Denmark: Den Private Ingeniorford, Technical University of Denmark. http://lirne.net/test/wp-content/uploads/2007/02/telecomreform.pdf

Ochuodho, S., & Matunga, M. (2005). A national orchestra? Civil society involvement in ICT policy making. In F.E. Etta, & L. Elder (Eds.), *At the crossroads: ICT policy making in East Africa* (pp. 68-83). Nairobi, Kenya: East African Educational Publishers Ltd.

KEY TERMS

ARICEA: Association of regulators of information and communications in Eastern and Southern Africa

CCK: Communications commission of Kenya

COMESA: Common market for Eastern and Southern Africa

CSO: Civil society organization

CTRO: Commercial trunked radio operator

EAC: East African community

EAP&TC: East African posts and telecommunications corporation

EARPTO: East Africa regulatory, postal and telecommunications organization

ESA: Eastern and Southern Africa

G2B: Government to business

G2C: Government to citizen

G2G: Government to government

GITS: Government IT services

GSM: Global mobile systems

ICT: Information and communications technology

IGAD: Inter-governmental development authority

IT: Information technology

KEPSA: Kenya private sector alliance

KCA: Kenya communications act

KICTANET: Kenya ICT action network

KP&TC: Kenya posts and telecommunications corporation

MISD: Micro-information systems department

MPC: Monopolies and prices commission

NEPAD: New partnership for Africa's development

NCS: National communications secretariat

NGO: Non-governmental organization

PDNO: Public data network operator

RTO: Rural telecommunications operator

TESPOK: Telecommunications service providers sssociation of Kenya

TKL: Telkom Kenya Ltd.

UNCITRAL: United Nations Commission on International Trade Law

UNECA: United Nations Economic Commission for Africa

UNESCO: United Nations Scientific and Cultural Organization

VoIP: Voice-over Internet protocol

VSAT: Very small aperture terminal

ENDNOTES

[1] http://www.cck.go.ke

[2] The policy gave exclusivity to the two public license holders for telecommunications and postal services. It gave Telkom, Kenya a five-year period of exclusivity for almost all telecommunication services. It also gave the Postal Corporation of Kenya perpetual exclusivity, on the following services: delivery of letters with weights up to a maximum of 350 grammes, printing and issuance of stamps, and the provision of letter boxes.

[3] Final communiqué of the second national ICT convention held at the Safari Park Hotel, March 8-9, 2005.

[4] http://www.information.go.ke

[5] http://www.information.go.ke/Bills/Info-com-Feb.doc

[6] http://www.information.go.ke/Bills/Guide-ICT-Bill.doc

[7] http://www.comesa.int

[8] http://www.aricea.org

[9] http://www.uncitral.org

[10] One of the respondents indicated that ARICEA had started examining returns on compliance to agreed regional models.

[11] http://www.kepsa.or.ke

Chapter III
Electronic Highways in Southeast Asia:
Liberality, Control, and Social Change

Loong Wong
University of Canberra, Australia

ABSTRACT

New information and communication technologies (ICTs), it is argued is transformative, and governments all over the world have sought to incorporate it into their development desideratum. It is clear that ICTs have transformed social, economic, and political practices and this certainly is true for Southeast Asia. In the context of Southeast Asia, it is particularly salient for it provided avenues for new political movements and expressions in the face of predominantly authoritarian regimes. Via the new ICTs, people were able to communicate freely and oppositional forces could be readily mobilized. This assertion of political rights threatened the status quo and the ruling political elites' hold on power. This was compounded by a crisis in public confidence as Southeast Asian economies found themselves caught in the maelstrom of a financial crisis precipitated by the loss of investment confidence and crony capitalism. As the crisis intensified and spread, its political fallout became clear. Governments have to accommodate and make way for social, economic, and political changes.

INTRODUCTION

Post-independent Southeast Asia has been portrayed as a lawless, corrupt, identity-less area, likely to implode, to "drift to further Balkanisa-tion ... (and so becomes) the powder keg of Asia" (Fisher, 1964, p. 10). Indeed, as a region, it only gained some recognition since the 1940s, but, since then, the region has gained some growing influence in international diplomacy, for example, over the Kampuchean conflict and fashioned for itself a form of regional identity, particularly through its regional institution, ASEAN (Association of Southeast Asian Nations). Marked by great diversity, the region has increasingly played a major role in the world economy. It has supplied key raw materials, provided markets for developed world goods, received investment, and has been the site of much multinational economic activities. Far from being an economic backwater, Southeast Asia has emerged as a dynamic economic region, and in recent decades, sought to re-engineer itself as a developed region vigorously pursuing new information and communication technologies.

The Southeast Asia region is characterized by high levels of inequality. The digital divide is real in the region and even in a country like Malaysia, which has been seen as an active promoter of information and communication technologies (ICTs), there is a lot that needs to be done. Singapore is, of course, an example readily recognized as the country with the most developed ICT networks and well-developed policies. On the other hand, the region also comprises Myanmar, Laos, and Cambodia, all of which are marked by extreme poverty and low levels of ICT penetration. This chapter attempts to provide an overview of the economic and political significance, and impact of ICTs in the region. The chapter begins with an account of the evolution of Southeast Asian economies. It then discusses the deliberative intent of ASEAN governments to transform themselves into new technologically driven economies, noting that there is no certainty that any will succeed, although Singapore appears to have significant advantages. The chapter goes on to examine the different ICT visions between Malaysia and Singapore before examining the political impact of ICTs usage and developments in the region. In particular, the chapter examines the key role ICT played in Indonesia and Malaysia during the political reform process of the late 1990s. The chapter then revisits the political economy of ICT ownership and developments suggesting that these are critical factors in affecting socio-political developments. The chapter concludes with an assessment of the problems and challenges the region faces as it seeks to promote both greater political liberation and its transformation into a knowledge-based economy.

The Growth of Southeast Asian Economies

The origins of Southeast Asia's economic structures can be found in the colonial practices that provided an initial entry into the global commercial system. How patterns emerged was a complex and varied process that depended on the colonial powers and their specific commercial objectives (Reid, 1988; Osborne, 1979). In Dutch East India, production of spices, sugar, and related goods led to the institution of plantation economies across much of what is today Indonesia (Reid, 1980; Tate, 1979). In British Malaya, which began its development later, mostly in the nineteenth century, tin mining was the key raw material. Tin from Southeast Asia fed Europe's booming food-canning industries in the 1800s (Wong, 1965). Later, as automobiles came into use in North America and Europe, the demand for rubber produced the establishment of rubber plantations across Southeast Asia, especially Malaya (Drabble & Drake, 1981; Courtenay, 1981; Voon, 1976; Jackson, 1968). Capital was imported from investors in Britain, and the various colonial authorities were active investors and planners in the development of the colonial economies (Davenport-Hines & Jones, 1989; Falkus, 1989; Lindblad, 1989; Platt, 1986; Murray, 1980). Investment, however, dealt with local primary commodities and was mainly confined to import-export and agency activities. Indeed, this control of external trade gave them a lot of power vis-à-vis local traders and producers.

One effect of the pattern of colonial development was the emergence of dual economies. Basically this refers to a two-sector economy where one depended upon western technology and capital, immigrant labor, and imported inputs and was geared to export markets; whilst the other used local labor and was organized traditionally, and produced mainly for domestic consumption (Fisher, 1971). A second effect of the process of colonial development was the dependency it engendered, particularly that of imported labor, capital, skills, and technology. A concomitant effect was that it also made the region highly susceptible to the effects of global trade and its fluctuations had tremendous impact on the local economy. Despite this, Southeast Asia continued to trek this dual economy path and on independence, continued to be wedded to such a development path. Primary commodities, particularly, food products, tin, and rubber remain important as an economic mainstay, contributing as much as 90% of its exports (Rigg, 1991, p. 187).

Independence saw a new orientation, and governments sought to industrialize their economies. Manufacturing became a strategy through which the economic linkages generated would induce greater economic growth (Hirschman, 1958). Pursuing, at first, import substitution industrialization policies (Myint, 1972), Southeast Asian governments soon found it to be self-limiting and adopted an export-oriented industrialization (EOI) policy based upon pro-market policies centered on direct foreign investment (ILO, 1980; Ariff & Hill, 1985). Moreover, it is argued that the state plays a minimal role and primarily acts to effect policies promoting growth, lowering trade and investment barriers, and liberalizing domestic markets through deregulation and privatization (Bowie and Unger, 1997). The success of EOI strategies is thus attributed to "getting the basics right" via "the application of a set of common, market-friendly economic policies" (World Bank, 1993, pp. 5, vi). As such, the lesson was that global markets and liberalization once embraced and prosecuted would enable the transformation of developing economies into *miracle economies*.

Despite this official prescription, a closer examination of policies and practices readily shows that rather than a decisive break in policies, government in the region adopted a multi-layered approach, often combining different, and sometimes, conflicting mix of policies. Barriers and other protective mechanism were judiciously used, and EOI policies pursued were more of an ad hoc adjustment to changes in the domestic and international political economies. EOI policies provided employment opportunities for growing inbound, urban migrants from rural areas, and at the same time, it simultaneously *protected* local industries by forcing foreign and ethnic Chinese minority capital to invest and develop these *new* industries. This created an economic dualism and enabled some form of economic integration, but, more importantly, it ensured the rise and consolidation of the state dominance of the domestic economy via its patronage, linkages, and protection.

An International Division of Labor and the Development of a Regional Economy

This *turn* to EOI also ushered in the rise of a new international division of labor and a growing regional political economy. As the international context of investment deepens, the growing rivalry between Japan and the USA also is played out within the region (Beeson & Berger, 2003). As the USA withdrew from the region following the Vietnam War, and pressures against Japan intensified in the USA, Japanese firms sought to defuse these criticisms by investing in the region and leveraging these national economies in their economic drive. Japanese development assistance was stepped up and investment grew, and Japan became a critical player in effecting development outcomes in the region (Doner, 1997; Unger, 1993; Nester, 1990).

The Southeast Asian region was thus drawn into the Japanese ambit as it staked out its economic role, and Japan began to give effect to its regional expression of developmentalism—the *flying geese* model (Kaname, 1998; Jomo et al., 1997; Bernard & Ravenhill, 1995; Korhonen, 1994). This model described a coordinated regional division of labor in which the structural upgrading of the Japanese economy led to a rather hierarchical but complementary structural change in its partnering economies through trade-creating foreign direct investment (Beeson, 2001; Ozawa, 1999; Katzenstein & Shiraishi, 1997; Hatch & Yamamura, 1996). Regional economic integration accelerated in the late 1980s with the lowering of tariffs and other trade barriers. Foreign direct investment flooded in and as other *foreign* capital competed with the Japanese for access to the region, the region experienced a decade of high economic growth (Beeson, 2001; Krauss, 2000; Bowie & Unger, 1997). Of particular importance was construction by U.S. and Japanese firms of offshore electronic component manufacturing plants.

As an industry, the electronics industry is distinctive because of the variety of intermediate and finished products for both the consumer and industrial markets. Because of this, the industry tends to be vertically disintegrated and can be geographically dispersed according to the particular location requirements of individual production stages. Indeed, Southeast Asia has embraced this development, and industrial parks and export processing zones mushroomed. National governments actively cultivated foreign direct investment and positive inducements also were offered.

By the 1980s, most electronic equipment employed integrated circuit (IC) components. ICs are electronic devices containing multiple transistors, diodes, resistors, and capacitors in a single package smaller than a postage stamp. Looking for locations to produce low-ICs and other components, manufacturers like Fairchild and Sony found Singapore a welcoming place, and by the early 1970s they had built huge factories (Huff, 1994; Henderson, 1986). Within a few years, other production centers were set up to the north in Malaysia, and within a few years that country had become the world's leading producer of electronic components (Sussman, 1998; Pang & Lim, 1977)—a leadership Malaysia maintained for many years afterward. An important proviso for foreign companies to gain access to Singapore and Malaysia's low-wage workers was compulsory technology transfer. This key policy allowed both countries to build human capital capable of constructing domestic industrial bases of their own. However, as Jomo has noted, "it is inconceivable that transnational corporations reliant on technological superiority to ensure profitability—will voluntarily surrender technical edge, especially to potential competitors. This does not mean that no technical transfer can ever take place. Rather, such a transfer is planned to maximize profitability, not lose it. Hence, it would

be naïve to expect that such technology transfer can eventually develop an international competitive technology capacity" (Jomo, 1987, p. 135).

Searching for High-Tech

By the end of the 1980s, Southeast Asia has become the source of much of the world's manufactured electronic components and consumer electronic equipment such as VCRs, TVs, air conditioners, CD players, boom boxes, and so on. These successes brought capital into the region and introduced Singapore, Malaysia, Thailand, and Indonesia into the club of Asian *miracle economies*. These governments saw new information and communication technologies (ICTs) as providing the opportunities to propel and transform Southeast Asia into hyper-competitive and technologically advanced economies. The new ICTs held out the promise of greater productivity and transformative potential. They are "reshaping, at [an] accelerated pace, the material basis of society," creating new cultures, new practices and actively transforming the socio-political landscape (Castells, 1996, p. 1). In enabling the transmission of large volumes of information at lower costs, a global reach, the new ICTs offer a vision of a new borderless, global market where the traditional rules of competition no longer apply (World Bank, 1999, p. 9). Small players now have the world at their feet and any company and/or nation-state can compete successfully in this new global economic market.[1]

Armed with this insight and the desire to see their countries evolve into highly developed societies and economies, governments find themselves gravitating to and embracing the new capabilities of ICTs as the next-generation tools of development. Via these tools, they would develop new strategic and competitive engines of development propelling them to the next evolutionary stage of technology. They could leapfrog development, become "third wave" societies and are no longer bound by their "traditions," space or "smallness."[2] A particularly powerful stimulus for these initiatives was the explosion in popularity of the personal computer. Each PC required a large number of ICs, and many manufacturers found it advantageous to produce the components in Malaysia or Singapore and then assemble computer sub-units at plants nearby. These locally built computers quickly found their way into domestic markets, thus providing cheap computers throughout Southeast Asia at an early date. Enthusiasm for computers generated unprecedented demand for information technology training at local universities and vocational institutions. The end result was a population that was wealthy enough to afford computers and sufficiently knowledgeable to participate in what has become known as the information revolution. Malaysia and Singapore's knowledge industry workers grew out of this particular set of conditions. To a lesser extent, this pattern also could be seen in other Southeast Asian countries (except Laos and Burma, the two countries where domestic policies and underdevelopment were barriers to participation in electronic technology initiatives).

Michael Hobday (1995) and others have noted that there are different tiers of development amongst Asian economies. According to Hobday, some Asian countries have been able to transform themselves and become fairly successful "innovative" economies, and may invest down the "technological ladder" to capitalize on economies of scale and lower labor costs. But as he also points out, the much sought-after, value-adding activities of the ICTs are not located in manufacturing's competitive advantage but rather are derived from services and creative developments arising from codes and programming, which are either nascent or non-competitive in many of these Asian economies. Upgrading is not automatic (Edgington & Hayter, 2000), and consequently, some will find their participation and development trajectories rather limited or realizable. Indeed, a number of writers have warned that ICTs have the potential to reinforce and exacerbate existing inequalities (Norris, 2001; OECD, 2001; UNDP, 1999; Graham & Marvin, 1996). New investments in ICTs are driven by market efficiencies and are often overlain on existing inequalities, for example, rural areas are and will continue to be under-serviced more than major metropolitan areas. The costs of ICTs also reinforce the digital inequalities and can further aggravate prevailing inequalities. Despite this, the seduction of infinite global opportunities arising from ICTs has captivated Southeast Asian governments, and they have sought accordingly to invest in, appropriate, and harness these technologies for their particular national projects.

Information Technology Projects

Southeast Asia, as noted above, is enamored with the pace of developments in new ICTs. Seeing themselves as having the ready platforms for the next stage of their ICT development, they have embarked on new visionary and imaginary projects. In Malaysia and Singapore, national political leaders were particularly taken by the economic potential in electronics that they devised plans to leverage their competitive advantage in this field into leadership in information technology. In Singapore, the initiative took shape as the *Intelligent Island* project, while in Malaysia the effort coalesced around what was known as the *Multimedia Super Corridor* (Wong, 2003b; Jusawalla, 1999).[3] Both governments and their plans took advantage of comparatively ready local access to personal computer technologies.

By structuring incentives to encourage development of ICT activities, the two countries believed they could emerge as regional hubs for electronic communication and commerce. Computer ownership was largely an urban phenomenon in most parts of Southeast Asia; by the end of the 1990s, slightly more than 30% of Singaporeans owned Internet accounts, and there were personal computers in roughly 40% of homes. These figures generally paralleled adoption of other electronic information gadgets. Approximately half of Singaporeans carried a pager and almost one-third carried a cellular telephone. Singapore had the best access to international telephone service in Asia, 55 telephone lines per 100 population, exceeding even Japan at 49 per 100 population (*The Economist*, July 2000) and, in early 2000, was the second highest Internet user among *developing* countries and the tenth highest in the world (*ST*, March, 2000). Table 1 profiles the penetration of ICTs in the region. It shows that within the region there is a great disparity in access and usage. By far, the most *advanced* country in this context is Singapore, followed by Malaysia. Internetworldtsts. com in their latest report confirms the great disparity in the region; penetrations of the Internet in the nine remaining countries remain low by both Asian and world standards; eight registered less than a 10% penetration rate. Of the estimated 364 million users connected to the Internet, about 44 million are in Southeast Asia, and most are registered and accessing the Internet in urban metropolitan centers. Table 2 provides greater analytical depth to the disparities of the informational revolution within the region. It clearly demonstrates that, by far, the most advanced ICT system and infrastructure is in Singapore, far outstripping its neighbors, even its nearest competitor, Malaysia.

The adoption of new ICTs was considered a prerequisite to achievement of economic goals. Asian governments accordingly promoted the active use of new information technologies—technological leadership not only would drive commercial expansion, it would legitimize national claims of modernity and technical advancement. Singapore and Malaysia pursued particularly aggressive campaigns to expand the information technology sector. Under a government-sponsored Malaysian project, it was possible in the mid-1990s to open an Internet account for the equivalent of about 10 American dollars, and online access would then be available for less than 40 cents per hour. Similar services were available in Singapore. Only a few countries showed a lack of interest in the information revolution: Burma and Laos had no Internet service at all until after 2000, and Vietnam allowed operation of only a limited number of state-owned Internet service providers.

Malaysia and Singapore: Engineering Growth

In Malaysia, the main technology thrust was the Multimedia Super Corridor (MSC). The project aims to catapult Malaysia into a *global test bed* for new ICTs. The MSC was designed to function somewhat along the lines of the Silicon Valley in the United States. The MSC was physically located in a 15km by 50km swath of the central part of the peninsula south of Malaysia's capital Kuala Lumpur—in total a territory of 270 square miles. At the southern end of the MSC is situated Putrajaya, a planned city being built as a new government administrative center. Also nearby is the Kuala Lumpur International Airport (KLIA). Putrajaya was intended to demonstrate Malaysia's technical capability and incorporated plans for paperless offices, electronic record-keeping, video conferencing, digital databases of all types, and so on. A model city also was incorporated in the MSC plan.

Table 1. Internet usage and population in Asia (Source: www.internetworldstats.com)

Country	Population (2006 Est.)	Internet Users (Year 2000)	Internet Users, Latest Data	Penetration (% Population)	(%) Users in Asia	Use Growth
Brunei	796,314	500	20,000	2.5 %	0.0 %	3,900.0 %
Cambodia	15,017,110	6,000	41,000	0.3 %	0.0 %	583.3 %
East Timor	947,401	-	1,000	0.1 %	0.0 %	0.0 %
Indonesia	221,900,701	2,000,000	18,000,000	8.1 %	4.9 %	800.0 %
Laos	5,719,497	6,000	20,900	0.4 %	0.0 %	248.3 %
Malaysia	27,392,442	3,700,000	10,040,000	36.7 %	2.8 %	171.4 %
Myanmar	54,021,571	1,000	63,700	0.1 %	0.0 %	6,270.0 %
Philippines	85,712,221	2,000,000	7,820,000	9.1 %	2.1 %	291.0 %
Singapore	3,601,745	1,200,000	2,421,000	67.2 %	0.7 %	101.8 %
Thailand	66,527,571	2,300,000	8,420,000	12.7 %	2.3 %	266.1 %
Vietnam	83,944,402	200,000	5,870,000	7.0 %	1.6 %	2,835.0 %

Known as Cyberjaya, this was to be an *intelligent city* maintaining a hub of a 2.5-10 gigabit telecommunications network for the district. The MSC's site had been open jungle and palm oil plantations, but, with the infusion of funds, the district began a transformation into a research and technology center, complete with an advanced information and electronic communication infrastructure, and a new multimedia university. The government also affirmed a number of key principles: free ownership in the corridor's IT firms; unrestricted hiring policies, including the freedom to recruit expatriate workers; a high-quality technical infrastructure; a guarantee that Malaysia would protect intellectual property rights through comprehensive cyberlaws; and, most important of all, no censorship of the Internet.

The focus of Malaysia's *cyberlaws* was legal protections against abuses of e-commerce and intellectual properties. Although the concepts embodied in the legal framework changed as time passed, the original plan was to be embodied in the Multimedia Convergence Act, which would have four objectives: (1) to create means under law for digital equivalents to personal signatures; (2) a set of laws protecting against hacking, tampering, and other attacks against computers; (3) protections

of intellectual properties; and, (4) protections for practice of medicine over public digital networks (Wong, 2003a).

Singapore's model has been and is based on long-term government planning and a direct linkage between economic, industrial, and ICTs development. Because of its size, and realizing that it could not compete and sustain its competitive advantage via low labor costs alone, the government focused on tapping and integrating into global market practices, which called for the development and transformation of the island into "a highly efficient switching centre for goods, services, capital, information and people" (NCB, 1992; see also Mansell & Jenkins, 1992). Accordingly, Singapore sought to reinvent itself into an *intelligent island*.

The Intelligent Island concept was built around a project called the *Singapore ONE* [One Network for Everyone]. This project, launched in 1997, will eventually provide for the installation of wired technology across the entire island, making a national network interconnected with the Internet available to nearly all homes, businesses, and institutions. The Singapore ONE project utilizes an optical fiber network that, when completed, is expected to total approximately 186,000 miles of fiber. Implementa-

Table 2. Selected ICT output in Asia*

Country	Personal Computer	Internet Hosts	Telephone Lines	Mobile Phones	Secure Servers	ICT per Capita
Indonesia	11	0.11	26.7	5.2	60	8.86
Malaysia	78	1.93	204.7	101.5	146	214.69
Philippines	16	0.21	31.9	19.0	68	26.75
Thailand	33	0.03	82.2	39.6	116	52.11
China	7	0.02	73.6	20.1	184	31.40
India	4	0.01	20.3	1.2	122	13.17
Japan	272	11.03	493.9	315.7	5,153	2,485.69
Hong Kong	310	20.09	583.6	430.8	538	1,820.13
S.Korea	150	4.22	467.0	304.2	345	431.95
Singapore	344	13.45	464.6	280.7	525	2,348.20
Taiwan	178	16.71	542.7	194.7	372	610.86
Mean						
Asia	127.55	6.16	271.93	155.70	636.25	731.256
OECD**	270.48	26.18	496.40	230.64	4,377.88	1396.77
Non-Asia	221.48	20.55	424.71	182.61	2,613.51	1022.39

Notes: *All data are for 1998 unless otherwise stated. Figures are based on per 1,000 people.*
**Japan and South Korea are excluded from these OECD figures

tion was to be realized in stages, with an initial goal of 400,000 subscribers by the end of 2001 (Wong, 2003b). To augment this development, the government charged the National Computer Board in 1999 to develop specific industry clusters plan, formed the Infocomm Development Authority (IDA) of Singapore and developed its Electronic Commerce (EC) Masterplan in 1998. Like Malaysia, it enacted the Electronic Transactions Act in 1998, enabling and recognizing digital signatures. The government also sought to further liberalize its economic environment and enable greater competition in the ICT area.

There is general excitement over Malaysia's and Singapore's technology projects and both their sweeping visions captured their publics' imagination. In Malaysia, this was particularly palpable. Its MSC project was closely linked to a grand concept called Wawasan [Vision] 2020. Vision 2020 referred to the then-Prime Minister's call for Malaysia to attain the status of a developed country by the year 2020, a concept heavily promoted by the entire government apparatus and the leading political parties. Enthusiasm for Vision 2020 was sustained even as the economies of Southeast Asia suffered a stunning loss of confidence beginning in 1997.

It is clear that there was a sense of competition in technological capacities between Singapore and Malaysia. This competition is, however, largely irrelevant as Malaysia and Singapore have tightly integrated economies and, if one wins, so will the other. Their governments' efforts can be better construed as one aimed at motivating the other in its global race against competitors. The policies of the two countries studied are rather similar. Both:

• Foregrounds a central role for the sta.te in policy development and implementation
• Promotes an image and desire for government control and its ability to *manage* flexibility.
• Accepts globalization as a rather unlinear process and the supremacy of market forces
• Promotes a high-tech path to development and regional dominance.

Nonetheless, there are significant differences; they differ not only in the direction but also in the rate of their technological development.

Singapore has adopted a more *global,* pro-market approach where the government plays an anchor role in shaping and managing its development ethos and trajectory (Wong, 2003). This is accompanied by a deliberate attempt to engineer for itself a regional and global stake in the ICTs industries through positive and active government policies (including incentives). A positive cultural development sympathetic and embracing a culture of high-tech developmentalism is encouraged and fostered. Over the last few years, the Singapore government and its strategists has developed and crafted new global strategies enabling the Singaporean state and its corporate assets to acquire key business assets globally.[4] This is seen as enabling the state to create a larger and more competitive market, and also to gain critical technologies and invaluable capital assets. Underlying this thrust is the recognition that Singapore needs to arm and fortify itself as it seeks to manage globalization.

Malaysia, has adopted rather similar policies to Singapore. In fact, many of its policies parallel developments in Singapore.[5] It sees for itself a global role where Malaysians can actively partake in shaping developments in the world—a *global test bed* where *collaborating companies and smart regions* will mutually enrich and benefit from its participation in the MSC (Mahathir, 1998). But where the Singaporean state has gone out to seek and acquire strategic assets to manage the globalization process and develop its educational and creative *software,* the Malaysian state has been more pre-occupied with its own internal socio-political process. Educational policies still discriminated against well-qualified Chinese Malaysians, and there is clearly a lack of skilled personnel and committed resources to education, training, research, and development.[6]

Clearly from our discussions above, in Singapore, its corporatist-like arrangements have engendered close, dense relationships, reduced transaction costs and enabled the state to harness and harvest gains from these relationships. In the case of Malaysia, the state's ethnic identity has moderated its efficacy—local Chinese affected resent the state's imprimatur and have been less than fully cooperative. Where there is trust and an acceptance of the state (and its agents), especially at the local level, there is an element of selective success. For example, in Penang, where trust-based cooperation (rooted in strong ethnic networks) allow political leaders, top management of transnational corporations, and directors of local industry to upgrade the technological capacity of both TNCs and local industry.

Economics, Politics, and ICTs

Southeast Asia's information technology ambitions were buffeted by the Asian financial crisis of 1997. Countries across East and Southeast Asia—South Korea, Japan, Thailand, Malaysia, and Indonesia were all affected by a massive outflow of foreign funds arising from a loss of confidence in Asian economies, prompting loan recalls, and a massive surge in non-performing loans regardless of their different macroeconomic and financial circumstances (Winters, 2000; Jomo et al., 1997). Particularly significant in the run-up to the crisis was the devaluation of the Thai baht in July 1997. Over succeeding months, the economic picture grew increasingly grim. Among the hardest hit was Indonesia, where the *rupiah* lost much of its value against major international currencies.

Across Southeast Asia, there is an assumption that government stability depends upon continued growth in citizens' personal incomes and wealth. This belief was sorely tested in 1997 and 1998. Indeed, it can be argued that at least two changes in government took place as a direct or indirect result of financial problems, one in Thailand and another in Indonesia. Of these, by far the more remarkable case was that of Indonesia where President Suharto had held power since the overthrow of Sukarno more than 30 years before.

Indonesia's political conditions degenerated rapidly in 1998 after B. J. Habibie became Indonesia's vice president. In the ensuing months, hundreds of student protests took place. The Internet became a crucial and credible means of communication

among dissidents and protestors, and *warungs* (internet café) became sites of alternative news and information. These alternative sites, *Suara Independen, Kabar dari Pijar, Tempo Interaktif* amongst others, enabled wide dissemination of news and also provided a focus for direct action in contrast to the mainstream media

In Indonesia, the crisis reached a turning point on May 12 when five students were killed by police in protests at Trisakti University. In the aftermath, thousands of outraged demonstrators around the country produced even more violence. This peaked on May 15 when more than 500 protesters were killed (*The Economist,* May 1998), prompting massive demonstrations and calls for Suharto's resignation. In the face of this onslaught and potential widespread bloodshed, Suharto's rule became increasingly untenable and on May 21, relentless pressure ensured his resignation (Atmakusmah, 1998; *FEER*, May 1998).

Responding to crises such as Indonesia's power transition, Southeast Asia's radio and television media found themselves overwhelmed by new technological competitors. Many of these new media had surfaced during the 1970s and 1980s, such as broadcast satellite television, video, video CDs, DVDs, and cable, but the growth of Internet presented by far the most significant and unexpected challenge to mainstream conventional over-the-air broadcast outlets. Governments had always controlled the latter and, as such, have been able to manage the flow of information within their borders. The new information and communication technologies could not, however, be controlled in the same way as before. Oppositional forces were quick to exploit the Internet. They discovered that the Internet offered them a tremendous capacity to communicate across the whole of the archipelago and over borders. Anti-Suharto activists employed Internet chat rooms, mail lists, and Web sites in their campaign to drive the government from power. The government attempted to crack down on the Internet in July 1996 but found that these new communication tools were beyond the reach of authorities who were powerless to stem the rising public sentiment against the Jakarta regime. Opposition came not only from those who wanted a new government but also from groups arrayed to seek independence or autonomy from central Indonesian governance. Most prominent among these were activists in the Aceh, East Timor, and Irian Jaya provinces.

But the Internet was not only used by opposition groups and activists, ordinary citizens mystified by the rapidly evolving political conditions found it useful as a means of staying informed on events. Perhaps, the most important and influential Internet information channel was the U.S.-based Indonesia mail list *apakabar*. This list was described as a factor that "helped accelerate Indonesian society's awareness of the need for change as it encouraged open and democratic debate on issues" (Pabico, 1999). Cyberspace became "a battleground between the pro-democracy activists (in Indonesia) and the Suharto supporters" (Wong, 2001, p. 384).

The vital role played by the Internet in the country's political transition was its critical role in unifying disaffected Indonesians no matter where they lived. The island geography of Indonesia had mitigated against any concerted country-wide action, but the Internet brought together, not only people scattered across the archipelago, but even those living abroad. One such person was Abigail Abrash, an Indonesia employed by the Robert F. Kennedy Memorial Center for Human Rights in Washington, D.C. When the confusion and violence in Jakarta made it difficult to get full accounts of events, she contributed summaries of U.S. news media reports about Indonesia to mail lists, while reading reports from other correspondents in Indonesia. Abrash was astonished to discover that "even remote towns in Indonesian Borneo [Kalimantan] were 'wired.'" On this, she concluded that "in a country that's as far-flung as Indonesia, the Net has meant that people have been able to communicate at a time like this." This *imagined community* allows for anonymity and hence greater security, enabling people to freely express their views. As one writer in a chat group said, "one or two people saying [they are opposed to Suharto] are easily dragged away and silenced. One or two million it is not so easy" (Marcus, 1998). Its reach also enables a national consciousness and dialogue

through which national ills and issues could be addressed.

Online newspapers and other news sites were additional important sources of information available on the Net. International news media such as the BBC and CNN were particularly favored by Internet users. Singapore's *Straits Times* and Hong Kong's *South China Morning Post* were popular sources and many readily access these sites for information. The *Straits Times* online edition reported a huge increase as a result of the turmoil in Indonesia. It claimed a 40% increase in hits during 1998 from the preceding year, mostly due to a 25% growth in hits from overseas readers. The newspaper guessed that coverage of the troubles in Indonesia, and the dismissal and subsequent trial of Malaysia's then-Deputy Prime Minister Anwar Ibrahim were causes of the growth. *Straits Times'* online edition journalist, Raoul Le Blond, claimed that he published messages from Chinese Indonesians containing stories of violence via the online newspaper because "access to their local media was blocked to them" (*ST Interactive*, September 1998).

In Malaysia, the Internet Revolution was initially promoted through the government's attempts and investment in the new information and communication technologies to create a developed and technologically advanced society (as encapsulated in its Vision 2020 pronouncements). This techno-developmentalist view was the dominant global view until the events of 1998. When the government cracked down on alternative print media in the fallout over the detention of sacked Deputy Prime Minister, Anwar Ibrahim, the Internet's democratic edge received a fillip. Closing traditional avenues of dissent saw a migration of readers to the Web (e.g., *laman reformasi, mahafiraun*), for information, as Malaysian citizens seek alternative news medium as opposed to the mainstream media. Opposition parties also have developed their sites and found many visitors. On top of that, there is now an online daily Web paper, *Malaysiakini.com*.

Malaysiakini.com, proclaiming itself to be an independent Internet newspaper run by professional journalists reporting *only the news that matters* has caused some alarm within some government quarters. Via its analytical and critical pieces of the government and its policies, *Malaysiakini* has engendered a new critical awareness amongst the Malaysian polity. This has prompted some members of the ruling coalition to blacklist' *Malaysiakini* journalists by excluding them from its press conferences and official functions; government officials claim *Malaysiakini* is not a licensed publication under the Printing and Publishing Act. Some officials have gone further, issuing publicly veiled threats, and repeatedly raising the issue of placing controls and restrictions on Internet publications (*New Straits Times*, September 2000). The then-Malaysian Deputy Prime Minister (Abdullah Badawi who is, incidentally the present Prime Minister) has similarly criticized postings that are "divisive" or those that "incited" or "endangered political stability." The mainstream broadcast and print media also have targeted *Malaysiakini* and sought to report its "inaccuracies," its "conspirational links" with "foreign" powers, including George Soros (who has been blamed by Malaysia's then-Prime Minister as the cause of the Asian financial crisis of 1997). Despite these criticisms, *Malaysiakini* has become an alternative mainstream source of news in Malaysia, and to its credit, the Malaysian government has committed itself to ensuring freedom of expression prevails as stipulated in its Multimedia Supercorridor pronouncement. The Malaysian government response is, however, not a shared response in Asia. Some Asian governments, in the face of these technological challenges, have adopted rather crude and blunt responses. They have detained people, seized computers or cut Web access (e.g., as done in China), but such extreme measures also carry with it invidious economic costs. As e-commerce transactions become more critical and thicker, network stability and continuity become critical concerns for both local and foreign businesses. Resentment and economic disruption can prevail, and this is one reason Singapore's censors have all but given up the fight to control the Internet.

In Singapore, alternative sites (e.g., the thinkcentre.org) exist, but they do not, as in Malaysia and Indonesia, make similar impacts. The culture

of silence and fear is still pervasive amongst the average Singaporean, and many are reluctant to voice their dissent.[7] On the other hand, there are those who argued that the *development dividend legitimacy* thesis applies in Singapore—the government has delivered development goods consistently and, as rational, material and pragmatic beings, Singaporeans are unlikely to embrace the opposition.

In recent years, either because of a more liberal attitude fostered by the government or because of its inherent nature, Singaporean academics have produced and articulated a more critical approach, albeit often within academic circles. This is often a relatively safe space as not many Singaporeans may have access to such views. Publicly articulated views are, however, systemically challenged and admonished as in the case of author and academic, Catherine Lim.

The reach of the Singaporean state also is almost legendary and occasionally manifests itself ensuring that inappropriate behavior and practices are punished. An example that comes to mind is the penalizing of two Singaporean students studying in Perth who had tried cannabis. The idea of dissent, and inappropriate behavior and practices in Singapore is still a dangerous idea and is guided, even remotely, by the Singaporean state and elite discourses. Because of its small size, the idea of possible control remains strong and overwhelms, if not moderates, the idea of the Internet as critique. For the Singaporean state, foreign, and diasporic dissent may cause some hiccups in international arenas, but they count for very little in the eventual drama of *realpolitik* of international relations. Moreover, this dissent is both foreign and safe, and since it is not rooted locally, as in having a local organizational base, it cannot influence and hurt the state and its exercise of power. As such, it can be ignored.

Thailand has a more open but diffused net culture. There is a plurality of views (e.g., www.thaidemocracy.org, www.banok.com, www.pnn.net, www.media40.org. www.sanook.com, www.pantip.com, amongst others) and clearly the Internet has engendered much public discussions. In the main, the Internet remains exclusive and serves as a rallying point for many younger, educated urban middle classes (Pongsawat, 2002) and many Thais, particularly those in rural Thailand, remain politically out of the loop. Myanmar's small Internet community is compensated by its diasporic community and global activists campaigning for greater democracy and accountability. Via the Internet and with new information and communication technologies, activists have been able to promote both international awareness and build solidarity against the ruling junta. These new technologies have become effective organizing tools enabling disparate and diffuse Burmese communities to participate in a pro-democracy movement and gradually transform it into a credible and viable alternative. Within Burma itself, the regime set up its own corporation and sought to monitor Internet activities. Laws also were passed to ensure that locals could not access external Web sites and those caught doing so were liable to punishment. Licenses were required for anyone wishing to import, possess, or use computer equipment, and the Ministry of Communications, Post and Telegraphs was given absolute power to grant or refuse licenses and to impose such conditions as it deemed necessary. Failure to obtain a license is made punishable with imprisonment between 7 to 15 years and incurring an unspecified fine (Iyer, 1999). With the help of Singaporean firms, the junta has upgraded its capacities and capabilities (Ball, 1998), including the use of e-mail viruses (Daniz & Strobel, 2000).

The Internet resistance movement in Burma has a long history. BurmaNet was established as a news group in 1994. It collected and facilitated first-hand reports of developments in Burma, fostered transnational activist links, and also served to disseminate news to Burmese in Burma and the diaspora (Keck & Sikkink, 1998). E-mail, as a cheap, speedy and easy technology became indispensable tools for Burmese dissidents. E-mail-based networking, particularly those initiated by the Free Burma movement, enabled new campaigns against the military junta in Burma (Zarni, 1997; Tyson, 1995), including the Harvard Pepsi boycott campaign and the Burma Law by the State of Massachusetts in 1996. This cyber-activism has led to

numerous other American cities banning city's governments' contracts to any companies doing business in Burma. Other companies—Heineken, Carlsberg, Ericsson, and Triumph—followed through campaigning pressures, and European parliaments took a more active and engaged interest in Burma. Today, activists are using the Web to promote greater political openness, debates, civility, and conviviality enabling a credible alternative to be articulated. In one sense, the Web has become a tool to offset the institutional and political deficit in Burma.

In the main, ASEAN governments have sought to initially control the Internet via mainstream broadcasting legislative and regulative measures. They have, however, found that effecting and implementing these measures are not as simple as previously thought. The technologies involved in Web transmission and broadcasting mean that traditional control measures are largely ineffective. Because of this, many have tempered their strategies. Of the three ASEAN states discussed, Singapore is perhaps the only state able to affect its regulative and legislative measures most effectively.[8] In part, this is because of the island's size, but the reach of the government also is critical. Its long arm has meant that the populace is easier to manage and control.

Generally, ASEAN governments have found that to counter the Internet, sheer force simply does not work: the Internet's anonymity, ubiquity and seeming speed, flexibility and invincibility protects the virtual dissenters and quarantines them from the power and reach of ASEAN governments. As such, these governments have evolved a new strategy—setting up alternative sites of information (all three countries discussed above have adopted this strategy) and waging an information war in cyberspace against their critics. This is complemented by stringent regulative measures: mandating and blocking certain IP addresses (e.g., in Singapore and China[9]), and Internet service providers (ISPs) are left to monitor and police traffic flows. Penalties are then inflicted on these breaches and, typically, results in revocation of licenses. There also is the more laborious act of physically monitoring on-screen the log of Internet traffic of every ISP, second by second and of blocking access to *unde-sirable* sites. However, this has yet to be tried by any governments in the region.

Many Asian governments have embraced the new ICTs and see them as the key to *leap-frog* development, ensuring wealth and prosperity to their nation-states. However, they could not imagine that the computer and the modem could be revolutionary tools, unleashing tsunami-like social forces, enabling new voices and pressures for change and reforms. Their visions of a technologically advanced society ensuring better, faster, and more secure economic transactions was a program they sought to implement, but the arrival of the personal computer (PC) clones, networks, and the subsequent proliferation of pirated computer programs saw new uses and the development of new configurations of power. Students, the *new* middle classes, and both emergent and oppositional groups absorb and embrace these new advances in information technology and its concomitant effects, including the pursuit of greater freedoms and voices. This raised consciousness prompts a greater interest in information and feeds on itself. In some cases, it also leads to direct action as people are mobilized and act to influence changes within the political system (Wong, 2001).

Economics, Politics, and Privatization

Like other developing regions, Southeast Asia's economies have been characterized by a significant degree of state ownership. This was particularly true in sectors such as the information and communication industries. And, as in other parts of the world, the efficiency of these state-owned enterprises was uneven at best. In Malaysia, for example, the government-owned voice and data monopoly, Malaysia Telekoms, was notoriously underproductive. In the early 1980s, the backlog of line orders numbered in the hundreds of thousands, and anyone wishing to obtain new telephone service could expect to wait about two years for a line. However, in 1981 there was a change in government signaling a shift in economic policies. On coming to power, Prime Minister Dr. Maha-

thir Mohamad immediately introduced plans to make state-owned enterprises more efficient and accountable to their stakeholders.

In Southeast Asia, as across the globe generally, an important developmental thrust was embodied in policies of neo-liberal market economics. This played a major role in reshaping Southeast Asian media through privatization, so much so that public service broadcasting came under threat in a number of countries. In Indonesia, for example, by 2002, there were six private channels on the air including RCTI, SCTV, TPI, Indosiar, ANteve, TransTV, and MetroTV. These were all arrayed against the government channel TVRI. Prior to privatization policies of the 1990s, in all of Southeast Asia only the Philippines had a dominant private system of broadcasting.

Malaysia was the region's first to privatize in 1983, partly in response to the government's general moves to shrink state ownership. To the surprise of many observers, privatization included even the information sector, including Malaysia Telekoms, which was sold off to a private corporation owned by local mostly ethnic Malay entrepreneurs (see Kennedy, 1990). Privatizing a large portion of the public sector firms reduced government costs, and, if successfully executed, public services could be enhanced as well. In addition, privatization was intended as a measure to reduce the rapid loss of Radio Television Malaysia's television audiences to VCRs—most videos in circulation were uncensored and were deemed threatening to Malaysia's unification policies. TV3 (TV-Tiga) as the first of the private stations was known, signed on the air in 1984. Further private channels soon joined the action, including MetroVision[10] starting in February 1995, and in 1998 a fifth channel was added, called NTV7, operated by business interests based in East Malaysia and intended to "foster closer relationship and better integration between the people of Sarawak, Sabah, and Peninsular Malaysia" (*NST,* November 1996).

The diversity in ownership afforded by privatization failed to produce much diversity in content. Even though Malaysia's TV3 was privately owned, its license was awarded to companies and individuals closely associated with UMNO and other parties of the national coalition, *Barisan Nasional*, and franchises that came along later were given to groups having the same types of political connections. Zaharom Nain found in his analysis of the licensing process in Malaysia that instead of producing a broader range of viewpoints, privatization merely transformed state monopolies into *private monopolies* that extended "the tentacles of the ruling coalition and its allies even wider across the Malaysian economy, adding economic and cultural domination to what is already a virtual political domination" (Zaharom Nain, 1996, p. 52).

Across Southeast Asia, similar developments in privatization were evident. Ubonrat (1997) found in Thailand, after the free-speech movement of 1992 forced government to authorize additional television stations and to deregulate cable and satellite television, that "although the deregulation policy for the Thai broadcast media has opened up the system to more actors, it is confined to a handful of large corporations" (Ubonrat, 1997, p. 74). The economic power wielded by these favored corporations prevented other firms from competing successfully against them. In recent years, this has further intensified, and the present Prime Minister of Thailand, Thaksin Shinawatra, for example, wields considerable power both through his own personal wealth and the control of the ICT sector. His telecommunication company, Shin Corporation (reportedly the largest in Thailand) and publishing interests have, in the view of the many critical Thais, compromised Thailand's democracy. In the last year, Thaksin has sought to sell his shares to Temasek Holdings (a Singapore GLC), prompting dissatisfaction and protests. This has culminated in Thaksin losing office and an investigation into his use of the media, money, and political power.

In Myanmar, the Internet arrived courtesy of a contract between a Thai-based company and the Ministry of Post and Telegraph in Myanmar, and there is a small group of companies providing Internet access. The government set up a joint venture with some business elites to establish Bagan Cybertech for screening and controlling the Internet. The government also encouraged private sector involvement in the ICT sector, but Bagan Cybertech remains in the pole position and seems to monopolize the ICT sector.

In Indonesia under Suharto, it was well-known that private stations could only win a license if they gave a significant block of ownership shares to members of the Suharto family, mainly Suharto's children. Consequently, privatization did not produce a freer and more open *market of ideas* but, instead, simply reinforced existing power structures. In each country, newly licensed stations were linked firmly to their governments and to majority political party interests. In the post-Suharto era, five new television stations were issued broadcasting licenses in Indonesia, but their startup was slow-moving due to the weak economy. Metro TV and TransTV were the only stations to start transmissions by 2002. Even without the additional broadcasters, intense competition caused by the new stations threatened to create a chaotic environment and to place extreme pressure on the troubled national public service broadcaster. This came to a head in late 2001 when the Indonesian parliament took up the problems of TVRI. The government station did not carry advertising, but was financed by the receipt of 12.5% share of the private TV stations' advertising revenues. Although there had been an increase in advertising earnings among the private stations, it was not enough to cover TVRI's rising expenses. For a number of years, many within the field of broadcasting had considered the possibility of altering the official status of the organization, either by making TVRI a public corporation, that is, publicly owned but not government-controlled, or by selling the network to private investors. As Parliament weighed options, TVRI's Director, Sumita Tobing, argued in favor of an outright sale noting, "I do not believe that TVRI will be able to improve its professionalism as long as it is run by civil servants" (*Jakarta Post*, September 2001). She rejected the notion that the organization could survive by increasing support from raising funds from viewers. According to her, "I do not think it is feasible because 70% of our viewers are poor people in rural areas."

The conversion of TVRI finally occurred in May 2002. Its new status was neither a private organization nor a public corporation. It was reorganized as a limited liability state-owned corporation, rather than as a private company. The management structure underwent review and articles of incorporation were drafted. The new company's financial position was made difficult by the fact that it had not received payments of about 300 billion *rupiah* from private stations' share of advertising. This produced debts to foreign film suppliers of approximately 260 billion *rupiah*. The biggest problem the new company faced was bloated staffing—about 7,000 persons were on TVRI's payrolls as the company started its new life (*Tempo*, May 2002).

Political Changes?

The changes introduced by technology, monetary conditions, and consequent political adjustments continue to reverberate across the region. Indonesian economic restructuring has so far been primarily aimed at balancing government finances by the sales of state assets. It has proceeded slowly, and the Director General for State enterprises, I Nyoman Tjager, had to admit in mid-2001 that no funds had been generated by the sell-off of government-owned corporations. Plans to divest in cement and pharmaceutical industries met resistance from legislators and wary foreign investors (*Jakarta Post*, August 2001). However, media privatization is still moving ahead in Indonesia and some other countries, though its pace has been distinctly slowed by the region's sluggish financial recovery and by policymakers' foot-dragging. For example, Malaysia's private station TV3, along with its print media sibling, New Straits Times Press group, were in dire financial distress by 2002. TV3's debts were forcing it into insolvency and producing such a drag on the parent holding corporation Malaysian Resources (MRCB) that its chief executive officer was forced to resign at the end of 2001 (*Financial Times*, 9 October 2001). In Thailand, privatization of Internet services brought hope that the high costs of Net access could be reduced. Internet Thailand staged its initial public offering in November 2001, but its stockholder structure ensured state involvement through 49% government-share ownership (*Bangkok Post*, 22 October 2001). In any case, as

has been shown, governmental authorities have tended to arrange privatization so that stock in new media firms are owned by corporations held by political parties or by investors aligned with political leaders, thus assuring that government officials could retain control. Still, private media have goals and interests that diverge from public media, and this means that a different menu of choices have become available since the 1980s. State stations are inclined to promote government dealings and development projects, while private broadcasters are more likely to cater to viewers' preferences, both in the sorts of programming scheduled and in the glitz and polish of their presentation. Private television stations also have tended to schedule far more program imports from the U.S. and other popular culture centers.

Nevertheless, measures have been taken to regain control over media and information channels in countries of the region, though strategies have differed. In the Philippines, the E-Commerce Act of 2001 was enacted in the aftermath of the ILOVEYOU virus that caused havoc around the world after its release by a Manila hacker. The focus of this legislation was provision of a uniform standard for e-business but, significantly, it defined broadcasting and cable as part of the telecommunications business, not as a distinct media business (*Business World*, 15 March 2001). In Malaysia, renewed interest in curbing online media content arose in 2001. Rais Yatim, then Minister in the Prime Minister's Department, spoke on this at a cyberspace seminar where he criticized "hate messages, seditious writings and e-mail advocating religious dissent." He denied any official reversal of position on Internet censorship saying "of course there will be no censorship" but continued that "… we did not exclude our right to make laws needed by the country" (*Australian Financial Review [AFR]*, 7 July 2001).

This new mood also boiled over in local media management. For example, the *Malaysia's Sun* newspaper fell afoul of officials when it ran a Christmas Day story on a purported plot to kill Malaysia's political leaders. In the ensuing furor, a total of 42 journalists were fired, apparently under government pressure (*AFR*, 16 January 2002). In

Indonesia, critics likewise claim that inflammatory reporting of communal violence has led to heightened tensions. North Maluku Governor Muhyi Effendie warned TPI and RCTI, two private television networks that had carried reports on clashes in the area. Other officials urged media to practice self-censorship in order to preserve calm (*Jakarta Post*, 28 March 2001). Subsequently, a restructuring of government oversight was announced with the creation of the State Ministry for Communication and Information, a move that was received unhappily by local journalists. The Alliance of Independent Journalists expressed dismay over the creation of an entity that resembled the discredited former Ministry of Information. AJI Secretary-General Didik Supriyanto termed the move "antidemocratic, antireform, and unproductive" (*Jakarta Post*, 10 August 2001).

However, media reform in Southeast Asia is gaining momentum and it cannot be arrested easily, even though political figures are attempting to guide and limit the process. Changes in governments across the region provide some assurance that information practices will impact on government policies and practices, ensuring a slow evolutionary path toward greater transparency and openness. This may be guided, prescribed for, as in the case of Singapore, or it may be a more belligerent, although hands-off, approach adopted, as in Malaysia.

There certainly is a new generation of political leaders in the region. Both Lee Hsien Loong (Singapore) and Abdullah Badawi (Malaysia) have sought to cultivate a modicum of liberality in their speech and public utterances, but how this new *openness* and *tolerance* is going to be played out remains to be seen. There is clearly a greater public demand and desire for greater openness and less restrictive media rules, and Southeast governments realize they cannot depend solely on their own economic recipes of low labor costs for China, to its north, out-competes them. They must, instead, harness new skills, and these new skills require and also engender greater reflexivity, openness, and tolerance. Consequentially, this is likely to create new *space* and will inadvertently subvert politicians' impulses for control. In such a

scenario, political developments in the region may evolve into enabling more open and democratic discourses that also may impact on economic developments.

CONCLUSION

It is apparent that there are clear differences between Southeast Asian countries. They are at different levels of development and their ICT capacities are similarly skewed. This digital gap is clearly important and will continue to shape the developments of national economies. In many cases, it will entrench and further exacerbate existing inequalities, and certain portions of society will be left behind. Thus, the issue of access and equity is an important consideration and has been at the forefront of many discussions. Governments have worked on a range of programs to promote access and equity, including greater liberalization and privatization, hoping to engender greater competition, more providers and lower costs in the ICT market, funding for programs, equipment and training, and, within ASEAN, greater cooperation and collaboration is necessary. As important as these initiatives are, there is the need for governments within the region to address fundamental structural issues of inequalities. Until they are addressed, the pre-occupation with ICTs will remain and reflect an elitist, urban bias, and any expenditure on ICTs will only further and enlarge the digital divide.

Therefore, as important and powerful as states are and as they can try to re-make markets, they cannot force economic actors to take innovatory initiative. This is only possible through the willing participation of economic actors. Similarly, many Asian governments could not have imagined that a piece of ordinary equipment called the computer combined with a telephone cable would unleash new tsunami-like social forces and enable new voices. In adopting and promoting the Internet and new ICTs as symbols of progress, modernity, economic prowess, and sophistry, these new technologies and practices have been warmly embraced by students, the young, the growing middle classes, and the counter-elites. Opening up a new world of linkages and possibilities, the Internet and new ICTs also provided many Asians with new lens, languages, and enlarged windows of democratic debates and discourses. Governments in East and Southeast Asia have, in particular, recognized the critical role played by these new technologies and have tried to thwart dissent on the Web by imposing restrictions on Internet access. But, like rhizomes, these Internet activists have sprout up continuously and wage their incursions against the power of their states. They also are aided by the lack of a national coordinated response by Asian governments as these governments seek to come to terms with their vulnerabilities arising from this new threat and its machinations. To expect ICTs or the Internet to deliver democracy, however, is asking a great deal more than these technologies could give. While there is a proliferation of information networks, and there is potential for greater individual freedom, ICTs enthusiasts fail to appreciate that these new technologies are embedded in social relations of power and control, and therefore, are innately political (Jordan, 1999; Golding, 2000). As such, ICTs do not and cannot guarantee democracy, nor can they ensure that democracy can be merely downloaded from the Web or shopped for online. Democracy remains a highly contested process, requiring the mobilization of social forces of power and control. Indeed, the ability to ensure that democratic space does not become truncated and continues to grow will depend on greater social, economic, and political reforms in Asia. Outcomes for greater democracy, are, however, not guaranteed (as in China and Singapore), and the task for social and political activists campaigning for greater democracy is, therefore, to craft a strategy where the local-global contradictions are successfully negotiated. This strategy would need to empower the disempowered, extend the boundaries of political debate, make political discourse more rational and informative, and bring citizens closer to interaction with centers of power. Such a task is not easy to efface, but space is emerging both online and offline as Asian activists struggle for greater autonomy and mobilize their citizens accordingly across different social sectors.

FUTURE DIRECTIONS FOR RESEARCH

From the foregoing discussion, it is apparent that there are a number of areas that need further investigation. There are different trajectories and recipes for economic and technological success. Research, therefore, needs to examine the dynamics and the relationships engendering economic and social transformations. This is little understood, and investigation will have to look at cultural and institutional factors and influences, in particularly, how these factors push the market and technological advances within each and different societies and polities. This is critical for analysts to better understand the developmental process and how innovative policies may be appropriately framed and developed. Such research may aid in developing a tool kit through which developing countries may learn and, consequently, aid in developing their societies and economies.

Future research would have to examine the impact of the Internet on the process of social and political change. This will require amongst other things, an examination of new identities and practices and how these identities and practices enhance mobilization and enable some new and alternative forms of interaction and civil disobedience. Clearly in the era of Internet-linked movements, there is a flow and exchange of information. How such exchanges of information impact on the political process in developing democracies is, however, not well understood. The research needs to examine how the Internet and new ICTs may enable new cultures and identities. This also would impact on the idea of the public sphere, and how the Internet and new ICTs may constitute a new public sphere. How such developments may affect democracy also needs to be examined and validated.

Related to these are issues of transnational linkages and networked processes, and their ability to effect political and social change. It has been argued that domestic space may be enlarged through dense and critical linkages, but how and why these linkages are effective have yet to be fully appreciated. Future research tracing particular linkages and how such flow of information affects domestic responses are critical in allowing us to better appreciate the impact of global information technology practices (van de Donk, Loader, Nisxon, & Rucht, 2004).

There is a need to better appreciate government policies, particularly its effects on the regulation of social, economic and political activities. This may result in an identification of common clustering attributes and how these attributes impinge on and are affected by the Internet. At the same time, such research would help us to better understand the possible trajectories and directions of change, and the varying responses to such changes. Such changes are contingent on and dependent on institutions, and in examining these common clustering attributes, the research would enable us to examine the varying effects of the Internet on different social and institutional arrangements.

REFERENCES

Ariff, M., & Hill, H. (1985). *Export-oriented industrialisation: The ASEAN experience*. Sydney: Allen and Unwin.

Atmaskusmah, S. (1998). Kebebasan pers untuk kebebasan masyarakat. In *Alinasi Jurnalis Indepen Reformasi Indonesia*. Jakarta: AJI.

Baker, C. (2001). Implications of rival visions of electoral campaigns. In W. Bennett & R. Entman (Eds.), *Mediated politics: Communication in the future of democracy*. New York: Cambridge University Press.

Beeson, M. (2001). Japan and Southeast Asia: The lineaments of quasi-hegemony. In G. Rodan, K. Hewison, & R. Robison (Eds.), *The political economy of South East Asia: An introduction*. Melbourne: Oxford University Press.

Beeson, M., & Berger, M. (2003). The paradoxes of parmountcy: Regional rivalries and the dynamics of American hegemony in East Asia. *Global Change, Peace and Security, 15*(1), 27-42.

Bernard, M., & Ravenhill, J. (1995). Beyond product cycles and flying geese: Regionalization, hierarchy and the industrialisation of East Asia. *World Politics, 47*(2), 171-209.

Bowie, A., & Unger, D. (1997). *The politics of open economies*. New York: Cambridge University Press.

Cairncross, F. (1997). *The end of distance: How the communications revolution will change our lives*. Cambridge: Harvard University Press.

Castells, M. (1996). *The rise of the network society, Vol. 1: The information age: Economy, society and culture*. Oxford: Basil Blackwell.

Choo, C. W. (1997). IT2000: Singapore's vision of an intelligent island. In P. Droege (Ed.), *Intelligent environments: Spatial aspects of the information revolution*. Amsterdam: Elsevier.

Courtenay, P. (1981). The plantation in Malaysian economic development. *Journal of Southeast Asian Studies, 12*(2), 329-48.

Daniz, T., & Strobel, W. (2000). *Networking dissent: Cyber activists use the internet to promote democracy in Burma*. Virtual Diplomacy Series, Washington DC: United States Institute of Peace.

Davenport-Hines, R. P. T., & Jones, G. (Eds.) (1989). *British business in Asia since 1860*. Cambridge: Cambridge University Press.

Doner, R. F. (1997). Japan in East Asia: Institutions and regional leadership. In P. Katzenstein & T. Shirashi (Eds.), *Network power: Japan and Asia*. Ithaca: Cornell University Press.

Drabble, J. H., & Drake, P.J. (1981). The British agency houses in Malaysia: Survival in a changing world. *Journal of Southeast Asian Studies, 12*(2), 297-328.

Edgington, D., & Hayter, R. (2000). Foreign direct investment and the flying geese model: Japanese electronic firms in Asia Pacific. *Environment and Planning A, 32,* 281-304.

Falkus, M. (1989). Early British business in Thailand. In R. P. T. Davenport-Hines & G. Jones (Eds.), *British business in Asia since 1860.* Cambridge: Cambridge University Press.

Felker, G. (1999). Malaysia's innovation system: Actors, interests, and governance. In K. S. Jomo & G. Felker, (Eds.), *Industrial technology development in Malaysia: Industry and firm studies.* London: Routledge.

Fisher, C. A. (1962). South East Asia: The Balkans of the Orient. *Geography, 47,* 347-67.

Fisher, C. A. (1964). *South-East Asia: A social, economic and political geography.* London: Methuen.

Fisher, C. A. (1971). South East Asia. In W. G. East, O. H. K. Spate, & C. A. Fisher (Eds.), *The changing map of Asia.* London: Methuen.

George, J. F., et al. (1995). The information society: Image versus reality in national computer plans. *Information Infrastructure and Policy, 4*(3), 181-92.

Graham, S., & Marvin, S. (1996). *Telecommunications and the city.* London: Routledge.

Hatch, W., & Yamamura, K. (1996). *Asia in Japan's embrace: Building a regional production alliance.* Cambridge: Cambridge University Press.

Henderson, J. W. (1986). The new international division of labor and American semi-conductor production in South East Asia. In C. Dixon, D. Drakakis-Smith, & H. D. Watts (Eds.), *Multinational corporations and the third world.* London: Croom Helm.

Hirschman, A. (1958). *The strategy of economic development.* New Haven, CT: Yale University Press.

Ho, J. (2000). *Cyber-tigers: How companies in Asia can prosper from e-commerce.* Singapore: Prentice-Hall.

Hobday, M. (1995). *Innovation in East Asia.* London: Edward Elgar.

Huff, W. G. (1994). *The economic growth of Singapore: Trade and development in the twentieth century.* Cambridge: Cambridge University Press.

ILO (1980). *Export-led industrialisation and employment: Proceedings of a symposium, Asian employment programme.* Bangkok: International Labor Office.

Iyer, V. (1999). *Acts of oppression: Censorship and the law in Burma.* London: Article 19.

Jackson, J. C. (1968). *Planters and speculators.* Kuala Lumpur: University of Malaya Press.

Jomo, K. S., et al. (1997). *Southeast Asia's misunderstood miracle.* Boulder: Westview Press.

Jordan, T. (1999). *Cyberpower: The culture and politics of cyberspace and the internet.* London: Routledge.

Jussawalla, M. (1999). The impact of ICT convergence on development in the Asian region. *Telecommunications Policy, 23,* 217-34.

Katzenstein, P., & Shirashi, T. (Eds.). (n.d.). *Network power: Japan and Asia.* Ithaca: Cornell University Press.

Keck, M., & Sikkink, K. (1998). *Activists beyond borders: Advocacy networks in international politics.* Ithaca, NY: Cornell University Press.

Kennedy, L. (1990). *Privatization and its policy antecedents in Malaysian telecommunications.* Unpublished doctoral dissertation, Ohio University, Athens, OH.

Korhonen, P. (1994). The theory of the flying geese pattern of development and its implications. *Journal of Peace Research, 31*(1), 93-108.

Kraus, E. (2000). Japan, the U.S. and the emergence of multilateralism in Asia. *Pacific Review 13*(3), 473-94.

LeDoeuff, M. (1991). *Hippachria's choice: An essay concerning women. Philosophy, etc.* Cambridge: Basil Blackwell.

Lindblad, J. T. (1989). Economic aspects of Dutch expansion in Indonesia, 1870-1914. *Modern Asian Studies, 23*(1), 1-23.

Mansell, R., & Jenkins, M. (1992). Networks, industrial restructuring and policy: The Singapore example. *Technovation, 12*(6), 397-406.

Murray, M. J. (1980). *The development of capitalism in colonial Indochina, 1870-1940.* Los Angeles: University of California Press.

Myint, H. (1972). *South East Asia's economy-development policies in the 1970s.* Harmondsworth: Penguin.

NCB (National Computer Board) (1992). *A vision of an intelligent island: IT 2000 Report.* NCB: Singapore.

Nester, W. (1990). *Japan's growing power over East Asia and the world economy: Ends and means.* London: Macmillan.

Norris, P. (2001). *Digital divide: Civic engagement, information poverty and the Internet worldwide.* Cambridge: Cambridge University Press.

OECD (2001). *Understanding the digital divide.* Paris: OECD.

Osborne, M. (1979). *Southeast Asia: An introductory history.* Sydney: Allen and Unwin.

Ozawa, T. (1999). Pacific economic integration and the "flying geese" paradigm. In A. M. Rugman & G. Boyd (Eds.), *Deepening integration in the pacific economies: Corporate alliances, contestable markets and free trade.* Cheltenham: Edward Elgar.

Pabico, A. (1999). *South-East Asia: The Internet, a handy political weapon.* Inter Press Service, January, 14 1999.

Pang E. F., & Lim, L. (1977). *The electronics industry in Singapore: Structure, technology, and linkages.* Singapore: Economic Research Centre, University of Singapore.

Platt, D. C. St. M. (1986). *Britain's investment overseas on the eve of the first world war.* Basingstoke: Macmillan.

Pongsawat, P. (2002). Virtual democracy in Thailand: Information technology, internet political message board and the politics of representation in Thailand after 1992. *Journal of Social Science, 33*(1), 141-66.

Prahalad, C. K. (2000). *Let's focus on the digital dividend.* Retrieved from http://www.ebfonline.com

Reid, A. (1980). An age of 'commerce' in Southeast Asian history. *Modern Asian Studies, 24*(1), 1-30.

Reid, A. (1988). *Southeast Asia in the age of commerce, 1450-1680, Volume one: The lands below the winds.* New Haven, CT: Yale University Press.

Rigg, J. (1991). *Southeast Asia: A region in transition.* London: Unwin Hyman.

Rodan, G. (1989). *The political economy of Singapore's industrialisation.* London: Macmillan Press.

Rodan, G. (1998). The Internet and political control in Singapore. *Political Science Quarterly, 113*(1), 63-89

Schein, E. H. (1996). *Strategic pragmatism: The culture of Singapore's economic development board.* Cambridge: The MIT Press.

Singapore—data communications equip market. (1999). *FT Asia Intelligence Wire.* Washington, DC: U.S. Department of Commerce.

Singh, J. P. (1999). *Leapfrogging development? The political economy of telecommunications restructuring.* Albany: State University of New York Press.

Singh, J. P. (2000). The institutional environment and effects of telecommunication privatisation and market liberalisation in Asia. *Telecommunications Policy, 24*, 885-906.

Sussman, G. (1998). Electronics, communication and labor: The Malaysia connection. In G. Sussman & J. A. Lent (Eds.), *Global productions: The making of the 'information society.'* Cresskill, NJ: Hampton Press.

Tate, D. J. M. (1979). *The making of modern South East Asia: Vol. 2. The western impact: Economic and social change.* Kuala Lumpur: Oxford University Press.

Ubonrat, S. (1997). Limited competition without re-regulating the media. *Asian Journal of Communication, 7,* 57-74.

Unger, D. (1993). Japan's capital exports: Molding East Asia. In D. Unger & P. Blackburn (Eds.), *Japan's emerging global rule.* Boulder: Lynne Reiner.

United Nations Development Programme (UNDP) (1999). *Human development report 1999: Globalisation with a human face.* New York: UNDP/ Oxford.

United Nations Education and Scientific Organisation (UNESCO) (1998). *World communication report: The media and challenges of the new technologies.* Paris: UNESCO.

Voon, P. K. (1976). *Western rubber planting in South East Asia.* Kuala Lumpur, University of Malaya Press.

Winters, J. A. (2000). The financial crisis in Southeast Asia. In R. Robison, M. Beeson, K. Jayasuriya, & H. R. Kim (Eds.), *Politics and markets in the wake of the Asian crisis.* London: Routledge.

WITSA (2000). *Digital planet 2000: The global information economy.* Vienna: World Information Technology and Services Alliance.

Wong, L. (2001). The internet and social change in Asia. *Peace Review, 13*(3), 381-7.

Wong, L. (2003a). Creating space in the global economy: Building a high-tech dream in Malaysia. *Prometheus, 21*(3), 289-301.

Wong, L. (2003b). Catalytic states and high-tech developmentalism: An analysis of institutions and the market in South East Asia. *Communications and Strategies, 52,* 49-69.

Wong, L. K. (1965). *The Malayan tin industry to 1914.* Tucson: University of Arizona Press.

Wong, P. K. (1996). Implementing the national information infrastructure vision: Singapore's experience and future challenges. *Information Infrastructure and Policy, 5*(2), 95-117.

Wong, P. K. (1998). Leveraging the global information revolution for economic development: Singapore's evolving information industry strategy. *Information Systems Research, 9*(4), 323-41.

Wong, P. K. (2003). Global and national factors affecting e-commerce diffusion in Singapore. *The Information Society, 19,* 19-32.

World Bank (1993). *The East Asian miracle: Economic growth and public policy.* New York: Oxford University Press.

World Bank (1999). *World development report: Knowledge for development.* New York: Oxford University Press.

Zaharom, Nain (1996). Rhetoric and realities: Malaysian television policy in an era of globalization. *Asian Journal of Communication, 6,* 43-64.

Zarni (1997). Foreword. Washington: Free Burma Coalition Manual.

ADDITIONAL READING

The following are indicative guides and are useful:

Becker, T. (1998). Governance and electronic innovation: A cClash of paradigms. *Information, Communication and Society, 1*(3), 339-43.

Castells, M. (1996). *The Rise of the network society, Vol. 1. The information age: Economy, society and culture.* Oxford: Basil Blackwell.

Castells, M. (1997). *The rise of the network society, Vol. 2. The power of identity.* Cambridge: Basil Blackwell.

Castells, M. (2000). Information technology and global capitalism. In W. Hutton & A. Giddens

(Eds.), *On the edge: Living with global capitalism.* London: Jonathan Cape.

Felker, G. (1999). Malaysia's innovation system: Actors, interests, and governance. In K.S. Jomo & G. Felker (Eds.), *Industrial technology development in Malaysia: Industry and firm studies.* London: Routledge.

Golding, P. (2000). Information and communication technologies and the sociology of the future. *Sociology, 34*(1), 165-84.

Henderson, J. W. (1986). The new international division of labor and American semi-conductor production in South East Asia. In C. Dixon, D. Drakakis-Smith, & H. D. Watts (Eds.), *Multinational corporations and the third world.* London: Croom Helm.

Ho, K. C., Kluver, R., & Yang, K. C. C. (2003). *Asia.com: Asia encounters the internet.* London: RoutledgeCurzon.

Hobday, M. (1995). *Innovation in East Asia.* London: Edward Elgar.

Jordan, T. (1999). *Cyberpower: The culture and politics of cyberspace and the Internet.* London: Routledge.

Jussawalla, M. (1999). The impact of ICT convergence on development in the Asian region. *Telecommunications Policy, 23,* 217-34.

Keck, M., & Sikkink, K. (1998). *Activists beyond borders: Advocacy networks in international politics.* Ithaca, NY: Cornell University Press.

Norris, P. (2001). *Digital divide: Civic engagement, information poverty and the Internet worldwide.* Cambridge: Cambridge University Press.

Pongsawat, P. (2002). Virtual democracy in Thailand: Information technology, internet political message board and the politics of representation in Thailand after 1992. *Journal of Social Science 33*(1), 141-66.

Rodan, G. (1998). The internet and political control in Singapore. *Political Science Quarterly, 113*(1), 63-89.

Rodan, G., Hewison, & Robison, R. (Eds.). *The political economy of South East Asia: An introduction.* Melbourne: Oxford University Press.

Sclove, R. E. (1995). *Democracy and technology.* NY: Guilford Press.

Singh, J. P. (1999). *Leapfrogging development? The political economy of telecommunications restructuring.* Albany: State University of New York Press.

Sussman, G., & Lent, J. A. (Eds.). *Global productions: The making of the 'information society.'* Cresskill, NJ: Hampton Press.

Van de Donk, W., Loader, B. G., Xixon, P. G., & Rucht, D. (Eds.). (2004). *Cyberprotest: New media, citizens and social movements.* London: Routledge.

Wong, L. (2003a). Creating space in the global economy: Building a high-tech dream in Malaysia. *Prometheus, 21*(3), 289-301.

Wong, L. (2003b). Catalytic states and high-tech developmentalism: An analysis of institutions and the market in South East Asia. *Communications and Strategies, 52,* 49-69.

Wong, P. K. (1998). Leveraging the global information revolution for economic development: Singapore's evolving information industry strategy. *Information Systems Research, 9*(4), 323-41.

Wong, P. K. (2003). Global and national factors affecting e-commerce diffusion in Singapore. *The Information Society, 19,* 19-32.

ENDNOTES

[1]   See for example, F. Cairncross, *The End of Distance: How the Communications Revolution Will Change Our Lives,* Harvard University Press, 1997; J. Ho, Cyber-Tigers: *How Companies in Asia Can Prosper from E-Commerce,* Singapore: Prentice-Hall, 2000.

2   This is articulated most forcefully in J. P. Singh, *Leapfrogging Development? The Political Economy of Telecommunications Restructuring*, Albany: State University of New York Press 1999; see Ho, *op.cit.*; C.K. Prahalad, "Let's Focus on the Digital Dividend," 2000 (http://www.ebfonline.com), supportive of this position.

3   For details of the Singapore's government initiative, see Wong (1996, 1998, 2003). Malaysia has been discussed in Wong (2003), and a comparative analysis of both Malaysia and Singapore's initiatives has been provided by Wong (2003).

4   This is apparent over the last year where GLCs (Government-Linked Corporations) like the Development Bank of Singapore and SingTel have expanded overseas and acquired stakes in new foreign corporations. In the present discussion, the case of SingTel is instructive. It has sought to buy over Cable & Wireless in China (Hong Kong) and Time Engineering (Malaysia) but had been rebuffed by the respective governments of these countries. More recently, it has acquired Optus (Australia) and also had bidded for a stake in India's largest telco, VSNL. SingTel's approach clearly marks a deliberate attempt to map out a greater regional and global presence by acquiring what it perceives to be strategic assets.

5   It has introduced similar financial incentives, new immigration measures, developed its cultural, social and educational amenities, developed a high-speed backbone network linked to major trading centers and, more critically, a raft of cyber-legislations that is more open and amenable to global IT economic interest.

6   This is especially clear in the educational area where a racial quota for places at universities still persist despite an affirmative policy lasting some 30 years. Many Chinese who have scored 10 distinctions (the highest possible grades) had their applications rejected at local universities over the years. This year, it became a little ridiculous when some 500 Chinese students with such outstanding results were turned down by local universities. Incidentally, Malays were never required to meet such exacting standards. Less than 1% of Malaysians have and are able to access science and technology educational courses.

7   This *development dividend legitimacy* thesis has been articulated often by many authoritarian governments and their supporters. It would be churlish to dismiss these arguments completely for these concerns clearly have some resonance with a significant portion of the population. This *authoritarian populist* tendency embodies certain elements. First, there is the horror of mixing, a binary of purity and danger. Second, there is a fear of solitude. Third, there is an apprehension of freedom (ala Fromm)——it makes life more complicated and too many decisions have to be made. Fourth, there is tense anxiety over the possibility that equality will produce uniformity. These elements lead to an emotional economy in which specific kinds of *circuits of solidarity* and *structures of feeling* are produced and reinforced. The world is to become a perpetual, small, containable, predictable, and safe place in which all know their place. Within this rather absolutist vision of the view, democracy has to be limited, or the myriad societal changes unleashed would tear this preferred ideal asunder. In a sense, these structures of feeling support structures of vassalage, which are as undemocratic as possible' (LeDoeuff, 1991, pg313).

8   The Singaporean experience is instructive as it has provided the benchmark for other countries e.g. China. ISPs are required to register with the Singapore Broadcast Authority (SBA) and site hosts are responsible for any content appearing on their sites, particularly those that threaten 'the public interest, public morality, public order, public security (and) national harmony' (as encapsulated in the Internet Code of Practice) (See www. sba. gov.sg).

9   Rather than seeing this as an Asian peculiarity, it should be pointed out that these practices are also common and mandated in 'western liberal democratic' Australia.

10   MetroVision quickly encountered financial problems and was forced to sign off the air within a few years.

Chapter IV
The Possibility of Water-Cooler Chat?
Developing Communities of Practice for Knowledge Sharing within Global Virtual Teams

Norhayati Zakaria
Universiti Utara Malaysia, Malaysia

ABSTRACT

This chapter looks at a key concept called communities of practice that helps to facilitate organizational learning through increased knowledge sharing within global virtual teams. By using Granovetter's (1974) weak ties theory, I suggest that casual acquaintances, known as weak ties have significant implications for social relationships and context, both of which can benefit virtual organizational team members. Furthermore, based on Hofstede's (1980) cultural dimensions, I also argue that cultural factors can impact one's willingness to share knowledge. Thus, there are three questions that guide this chapter: (1) How do social relationships and context among global virtual teams affect the development of communities of practice? (2) How does culture affect the knowledge of sharing activities? (3) What is the impact of ICTs on knowledge sharing and the emergence of communities of practice?

INTRODUCTION

The advent of information and communication technology (ICT) has changed the way people communicate, exchange information, and accomplish and coordinate their managerial tasks in organizations. Essentially, the use of ICTs together with the increasing pressure for globalization is driving the growth of global virtual teams. Global virtual teams is defined as a distinct entity that is organizationally dispersed and whose members come from different geographical locations, may not have a common cultural background, collaborate using asynchronous and synchronous technologies, and often assemble on an ad hoc basis (Zakaria, Amelinckx, & Wilemon, 2004). Not only that, ICT also influences the way people structure their relationships across national boundaries. The current state of ICT therefore offers opportunities for multinational corporations (MNCs) to develop communities of practice so that they can support their geographically dispersed team members who are working on a common business goal to share knowledge within them.

According to Wenger (1998) *community of practice* is defined along three main dimensions: (1) its joint enterprise as understood and continually re-negotiated by its members, (2) mutual engagement that binds members together into a social entity, and (3) the shared repertoire of communal resources (routines, sensibilities, artifacts, vocabulary, styles, etc.) that members have developed over time. With the use of ICT, the development of communities of practice is freed from constraints such as time and geographical distance. As such, it is becoming a common platform for people to collaborate and share knowledge using ICTs. Potentially, the movement toward the development of communities of practice is based on the acculturation of cultural values among team members. As Kimble, Li, and Barlow (2000) suggested, communities of practice can help alleviate the barriers of building trust and creating social bonding among virtual team members.

Research on knowledge sharing (including knowledge creation, acquisition, and transfer) or behavior change in the context of organizational learning (Duncan & Weiss, 1979; Edmondson & Moingeon, 1996; Garvin, 1993; Huber, 1991; Senge, 1990) suggests that organizational learning can be categorized into two phases: (i) knowledge sharing, and (ii) behavior change. The knowledge-sharing phase involves the creation of knowledge, the acquisition of knowledge, and the transfer of knowledge among organizational members, which enhances an organization's efficiency by emphasizing the need for understanding the existing organizational context. The behavior change phase involves modification of behaviors among global members, which enhance an organization's effectiveness through organizational restructuring. In this regard, a study by Collier and Esteban (1999) suggested that the advancement of ICT provides a plethora of opportunities for collaborative learning,

self-management, and ownership of work, which takes precedence over the traditional bureaucratic and authoritarian management structure.

It is useful to note that communities of practice are not merely geographically dispersed conventional teams separated by time and space. They also often differ in national, cultural, and linguistic attributes. What makes them prevalent and significant in today's electronic global village is the fact that organizations use ICTs to share knowledge and to collaborate. Communities of practice requires innovative communication and learning capabilities among different members across organizational and geographical boundaries, and the increasing familiarity with ICTs means an easier adaptation to communities of practice. Here, I would like to suggest that virtual intra-team social interactions and work practices should not be compared to conventional work structures, or treated as such by the managers. Instead, there is a need to understand both the social interactions and work practices in light of the process of creating and maintaining effective communities of practice. Several studies further highlight that organizational structure and culture, and communities of practice are the primary factors that impact the success of organizational learning (Inkpen, 1998; Johnson, 2001; Okunoye & Karsten, 2002; Montoya-Weiss, Massey, & Song, 2001). By looking at the concept of communities of practice, I hope to illustrate how people could develop a shared-knowledge base in a geographically dispersed environment such as the global virtual teams.

The concept of communities of practice includes the internal dynamics of the organizational members participating in the community, and the establishment of shared values within the team members. Various relevant viewpoints include practice as meaning, practice as community, practice as boundary, practice as locality, and knowing in practice (Wenger, 1998). In this regard, Inkpen (1998) argued that the acquisition of new organizational knowledge is increasingly becoming a managerial priority for ensuring the sustainability of global competitiveness. Inkpen (1998) also recognized the challenges that surface in a global knowledge-sharing setting. These challenges can be categorized as complexities of acquiring, transferring, and integrating knowledge in an organizational learning environment, particularly in a global and network environment. This priority takes a new meaning as the global competitive environment continues to intensify, consequently requiring multinational firms to make the extra effort to transfer knowledge and renew organizational skills in various diverse settings.

This chapter examines the following questions: (1) How do social relationships and context among organizational members affect the development of communities of practice? (2) How do cultural factors affect the knowledge sharing within global virtual teams? (3) What is the impact of ICTs on knowledge sharing and the emergence of communities of practice within global virtual teams? To answer these questions, the author first provides a conceptual framework, which introduces communities of practice by looking at its definition, the process of developing communities of practice, and the guiding principles to cultivate it. Second, the author examines the two main elements of communities of practice: its structure and culture. Third, the author analyzes the potential of ICTs for e-collaboration and knowledge sharing, hence facilitating communities of practice. Fourth, this chapter discusses the *weak tie theory*, which illuminates the interplay between ICT, communities of practice, and organizational learning. Lastly, several research ideas that illustrate the relationships or interplay between (1) ICT, (2) communities of practice, and (3) culture are offered as the potential future research directions.

A Conceptual Framework for Communities of Practice

The rapid adoption of ICTs, which have been the primary drivers in the development of the electronic global village, provides us with an opportunity to understand the communities of practice for global virtual teams (expressed in this chapter as new form of work arrangements that necessitates the use of new technologies). What is more important is that this new technology often requires people from different cultural backgrounds to share knowledge and create common practices among them. As a result, MNCs need innovative

strategies of enhancing organizational learning. In addition, organizations want to minimize cost, decrease time spent abroad, and reduce the cultural shock and conflicting values of diverse team members. All these demands contribute to the concept of communities of practice. In this chapter, *communities of practice* is used as the primary conceptual framework in understanding how people can develop a shared knowledge base in organizations. This chapter begins by defining the concept of social practice, which encompasses *communities of practice*. According to Wenger, social practice:

... includes what is said and what is left unsaid; what is represented, and what is assumed. It includes the language, tools, documents, images, symbol, well-defined roles, specified criteria, codified procedures, regulations, and contracts that various practices make explicit for a variety of purposes. But it also includes all the implicit relations, tacit conventions, subtle cues, untold rules of thumb. (p. 47)

Wenger (1998) also illustrates communities of practice as: (1) being engaged in an enterprise that people want to pursue over time, and (2) having the ability to learn collectively (based on social interaction and relationships between members of society or communities). In short, communities of practice are the prime context in which people can work out common sense through mutual engagement, which always involves the whole person, both acting and knowing at once. Johnson (2001) states that communities of practice consist of the following components: (i) authentic and complex problems; (ii) group activities and teamwork; (iii) constructive form of learning and negotiated learning processes; (iv) social interdependence among members; (v) shared goals; (vi) use of cognitive tools aided by process, procedures, and technology; and (vii) team members assume the role of facilitator. In support of that, Wick (2000) further refines this definition as groups of professionals with similar task responsibilities, which involve entities that help solve authentic and ill-structured problems. The existence of a group with whom to share knowledge and solve problems, in turn, promotes learning through effective communication among its members. Gherardi and Nicolini (2000) allude to this concept of *community knowledge* in which the aggregate knowledge is greater than the sum of individual participant knowledge.

Although communities of practice provide a unique and relevant concept to look at in the context of a virtual environment, developing this form of communities of practice presents many challenges. Building any communities of practice involves the following five stages (refer to Table 1) as suggested by Wenger, McDermott, and Snyder (2002). The first two stages are crucial in creating a sense of membership, encouraging and developing their shared interests. These stages involve attracting potential members, discovering, and crafting a shared interest, and participating in series of activities in order to build trust and relationships among members. The next three stages, however, involve a different set of norms and procedures. Members are actively engaged in advancing their interests, shaping their domain, exchanging and sharing knowledge, and ascertaining the sustainability and transformation of membership—a viable yet challenging process.

Cultivating Virtual CoPs

Likewise, it is equally important to understand how to cultivate communities of practice in MNCs, and how to create an environment that can be flourished by "valuing the learning process, making time and other resources available for their work, encouraging participation, and removing barriers" (Wenger, McDermott, & Snyder, 2002, p.13). One important element of cultivating communities of practice is that it is not the same as developing or designing organizational structure comprised of an established set of roles, rules, procedures of planning, and organizing activities. Instead, communities of practice involve a significant amount of negotiation among the members (the community). Subsequently, the members act based on their passion and commitment, bringing into their group identity a diverse set of knowledge and expertise. It is a dynamic process, so much so that Wenger, McDermott, and Snyder claim, "cultivating communities of practice in an organizational context is an art" (p. 14). Because it is an art, they further propose seven design principles to effectively cultivate communities of practice. These principles should not be rigidly observed as recipes, rather used as guidelines to understand how the elements of design work together. Table 2 shows the guiding principles for the development of communities of practice.

Wenger, Dermott and Snyder (2002) suggest four factors that pose challenges: distance, size, organizational affiliation, and cultural differences. On the other hand, Merali (2000, 2001) proposes that since the activities of knowledge sharing and

Table 1. Stages of developing communities of practice

STAGES		ILLUSTRATION
1. Potential	•	People begin to discover the value of practices, in which they have formed a loose or extant social network but yet are likely to form the core group of a community over time
2. Coalescing	•	Members are prepared to participate on several key activities such as hosting community events in order to build trust and relationships, and awareness of their common interests and needs
3. Maturing	•	A very active stage where tension of the members builds up, thus requiring a considerable support to continue and refine their domain, and identify knowledge gap between them
4. Stewardship	•	One of the crucial issues is how to sustain the members, that is achievable by maintaining the relevance of the domain, keeping the community in cutting edge, and ability to receive new ideas and maintaining ownership, and continuously stimulating their intellectual focus
5. Transformation	•	Subsequently, communities may transform into many ways—fade away from the domain—that is, from IT issues to organizational or personal, losing members and energy, die, split into distinct communities or merge with others, or become institutionalized

(Adopted from: Wenger, E., McDermott, R., & Snyder, W. M. (2002). Cultivating communities of practices. Boston: Harvard Business School Press)

organizational learning take place in a different social context, potential issues are:

a. People that share information are no longer collocated.
b. Knowledge sharing must transcend disparate disciplines, and backgrounds.
c. Uncertainty in the competitive context and dynamic process that demand organizational responses to support virtual knowledge networks.
d. Getting people to trust and value the contributions of others without personally (i.e., face-to-face) knowing with whom they are working or communicating in the virtual environment.

Each of these issues needs to be understood in terms of the various stages of communities of practice development. For example, how do we form an informal network across time and space at the initial (potential) stage? In many illustrated cases in organizations, people initiate communities of practice through increasing exchanges of tacit knowledge, which oftentimes arise from informal situations such as *water-cooler-talk*, or *hallway-talk* (Lave & Wenger, 1991). Can the same instances and climate exist for communities of practice in a virtual environment?

Turning to the second stage where hosting community activities paves the way for a more established relationship, how does the virtual environment affect this process? Wenger and colleagues suggest that more time needs to be in-vested in creating a higher sense of intimacy and trust level among virtual members. Ultimately, creating a *swift trust* among members can be a key challenge (Jarvenpaa & Leidner, 1999). The third and fourth stages pose the challenge of reconciling multiple agendas, such as between having the *ownership* of certain knowledge and receiving new ideas from other members. Having members from all around the globe contributes to a greater diversity of viewpoints, needs, interests, and priorities for virtual knowledge sharing and organizational learning. Yet, under certain circumstances, the opportunities for negotiations and coordination among team members may be limited—depending on the types of technology used. For instance, if the teams used e-mail—an asynchronous medium—then the feedbacks and responses will be delayed due to the different time zones. As a consequence, negotiation can take a longer time compared to teams that collaborate face-to-face. Additionally, the coordination effort can also be more challenging when scheduling a meeting with members across the globe, again due to the differences in time zone.

It is further suggested that the cultivation of communities of practice requires a careful examination of the structural and cultural challenges. Generally, communities of practice take a variety of forms depending on factors such as size, length of practice, collocated or distributed interactions, homogeneous or heterogeneous members, whether teams are within or across boundaries, spontaneous or intentional, and unrecognized or institutionalized.

Table 2. Cultivating communities of practice

GUIDING PRINCIPLES	
1.	Design for evolution
2.	Open a dialogue between inside and outside perspectives
3.	Invite different levels of participation
4.	Develop both public and private community spaces
5.	Focus on value
6.	Combine familiarity and excitement
7.	Create a rhythm for the community

(Adopted from: Wenger, E., McDermott, R., & Snyder, W. M. (2002). Cultivating communities of practices. Boston: Harvard Business School Press)

According to Wenger, McDermott, and Snyder (2002), the communities of practice structure is comprised of three elements: (1) domain of knowledge, which defines a set of issues; (2) a community of people who care about this domain; and (3) the shared practice that they are developing to be effective in their domain. It is essential to recognize that *domain* normally creates a communal or shared ground, and a sense of identity to the participating members in an organization. In this respect, the domain becomes the essential motivating factor for members to contribute, commit, learn, and participate—all of which give meaning to their actions. On the other hand, a community comes into being as a *social learning* structure, which fosters interactions and relationships guided by reciprocal trust, respect, and sense of belonging. Hence, a community is largely dependent on both the cognitive (intellectual discussions) as well as the affective process. In order for communities of practice to be successful, there is a need to identify the types of framework, ideas, tools, information, styles, language, stories, and documents that the communities share.

Bleeker (1994), Garrecht (1998), and Semich (1994) argued that a virtual organization constitutes a *network organization*, which is characterized by lateral rather than vertical relationships. In vertical relationships, the structure is based on a hierarchical organizational design that is described in organizational charts, and formalized organizational procedures (Kasper-Fuehrer & Ashkanasy, 2001). In this structure, traditional mechanisms such as hierarchical coordination, control and direct supervision, and enforcement of rules are crucial (Wiesenfeld, Raghura, & Garud, 1998). Contrariwise, these mechanistic structures are no longer relevant and applicable in virtual environments.

In this chapter, it is proposed that the concept of communities of practice is applied in the context of virtual working structure, namely global virtual teams. In order to maximize their effectiveness, two key elements must be specifically addressed: virtual structure and cultural values. As shown in Figure 1, it is proposed that the application of communities of practice on global virtual teams is based on a structure that relies on networking,

connectivity, mobility, flexibility, and speed as the main drivers to effectively form global communities of practice. This framework recognizes a new form of working context that is based on a *nontraditional* and flattened organizational structure as well as dependent on elements like distributed and heterogeneous team members who communicate, collaborate, and share knowledge across geographical boundaries. Such communities are built spontaneously and on a temporal basis.

It is useful to note that in this chapter, structure is not defined from a rigid viewpoint, such as the *logical structure* or the *reporting structure,* as often has been illustrated in an organizational chart. Rather, structure is defined from a systemic approach that takes into account the *key interrelationships that influence behaviors over time* (Senge, 1990). This approach allows us to fully comprehend the variables that influence team members who collaborate virtually. Wenger argued that "Practice must be understood as a learning process ... a community of practice is therefore an emergent structure, neither inherently stable nor randomly changeable" (p. 49, 1998).

Aside from structure, the other factor of interest is *cultural values*. This factor raises the question of the basic shared assumptions, norms, beliefs, values, behaviors, and team practices that this new form of communities of practice can or should adopt. This chapter looks at both the organizational and the national culture of the global virtual team members. Findings show that different cultural factors affect the willingness and degree of knowledge sharing. Johnson (2001) asserts that communities of practice are cultural entities that emerge from the establishment of a virtual or traditional form of organization. Both the individual and collective knowledge should support each other (i.e., common knowledge vs. diversity). This is largely a question of how organizational culture can provide sufficient mechanisms such that the experience and collaboration of the community are worked out and transformed into artifacts (e.g., symbols, procedures, rules, technology, products, etc.). The solution involves construction of common history through negotiated meetings via the electronic communicative technologies, such as e-mail, list servers, chat rooms, bulletin boards, teleconferencing, video-conferencing, and many more.

According to Schein (1992), organizational culture glues or ties people together. There are certain assumptions that people hold in common, certain procedures, norms and standards that people need to follow, in order to know how to behave and conform in an organization. This itself is a learning experience, but what is more important is to inculcate a culture that encourages knowledge sharing and exchanges so that each team member as an individual can be bonded to the group by the same grounds, purposes, and goals. Hence, the concern here is: How do organizations integrate the practices of the communities with team members from different cultures and parts of the world? How successful can that be? Furthermore, how such a situation can be translated into a virtual environment? In a virtual environment, team members communicate with strangers, people with whom they have no historical relationship. Eventually, they might be bonded by this new networking culture. Yet the organizational culture that the team members belong to will shape how they learn, exchange, and share knowledge, and sometimes it intersects or interacts with member's own cultural values. For example, some organizations provide more incentives for group effort as compared to individual effort, yet for people who ascribe to the individualistic culture, they would highly prefer individual acknowledgement and

incentives (Hofstede, 1980). Thus, it all depends on the mechanism the organizations employ and utilize to promote knowledge sharing that take into account the compatibility between task fit vs. culture fit.

The national culture further affects the level of acceptance for knowledge diffusion, and the communication and information boundaries among members. It determines to what extent people are more or less willing to share knowledge and with whom they are most comfortable sharing that knowledge. For example, individuals from different cultures vary in terms of their group behaviors and communication styles (Chen, 2001; Gudykunst & Kim, 2002; Igbaria & Tan, 1998). This chapter focuses on the four cultural dimensions introduced by Hofstede (1980), which are the following:

a. **Power distance:** According to Hofstede, power distance indicates the level of inequality that is accepted by most people in their jobs and lives. In some countries, generally one's status in organization usually bestows the same status in society. Conversely, social status may lead to status of a similar level in an organization. For example, in a high-power distance culture like Japan, subordinates approach their superior only if there is an urgent problem (Tudor & Trumble, 1996). By contrast, in low-power distance cultures such as the USA, subordinates have access to superiors due to

Figure 1. Framework for understanding the development of communities of practice in the context of global virtual teams

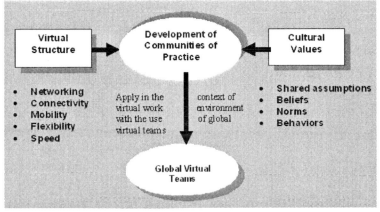

lack of significant gaps between organizational hierarchies.

b. **Individualism vs. collectivism:** A person from an individualistic society views him/herself as more important than other people, and, thus, he/she is independent from other people. This implies that when individualists intend to share knowledge, the boundaries to communication are less restrictive. Individualists can easily communicate with strangers by giving detailed descriptions of their objectives, as they are a more task-oriented society (Triandis, 2002). In contrast, collectivism views the individual as belonging to a group of people (Hofstede, 1980), and thus interdependent with others in the group (Markus & Kitayama, 1998). The communication boundaries are more rigid as they are more skeptical of whom they would share knowledge. In addition, collectivists view those within the circle of their interests, with whom they have formed a strong relationship and ties, as the *in-group* (family, close friends, and colleagues). Conversely, they have a weak relationship with *out-group* members such as strangers or acquaintances (Triandis, 1995).

c. **Uncertainty avoidance:** Hofstede considers aversion to uncertainty a very important attitude in some societies where it demonstrates the way society deals with the unknown aspects of a new or different environment. This is a significant element for effective teamwork particularly in the business negotiations setting. It further explains the extent to which people are willing to accept risks inherent in uncertain situations. In other words, Kapij and Abetti (1997) define this dimension as "the degree to which individuals prefer structured over unstructured situations" (p.168).

d. **Masculinity vs. femininity:** This dimension represents poles of continuum, which defines the importance of achievements and possessions (termed masculine values) and of the social environment and helping others (termed as feminine values). The level of masculinity also explains part of the perception that business negotiators have of each other. For a masculine cultural environment, people appreciate getting right to the business, by laying out the

rules and procedures on the tasks to be taken up. The setting of the collaboration will be defined by a contractual relationship—known as the *black and white* relationship. In contrast, in a cultural environment where relationships are highly valued, it is common for a negotiation to begin by introducing oneself—known as the *warm-up* session. The rationale of doing so is to set a conducive climate and tone for the early relationship building so that both negotiating partners can first get to know each other.

Applying the Weak Ties Theory for Understanding the Social Virtual Structure of Global Virtual Teams

Granovetter (1974) introduced the theory of *strong* and *weak* ties in the economic sociology research fields. His study used a random sample of professional, technical, and managerial personnel who had found new jobs through social contacts to determine how frequently the job seeker and the contact saw each other. The findings of his study suggest that if frequency of meetings indicates the strength of tie, then job seekers are more satisfied with using weak ties rather than strong ones due to the superiority of the social resources (social resources encompass social relations and the resources embedded in positions reached through such relations). He also asserts that interpersonal ties is classified in social network literature as either *strong* or *weak* ties (Granovetter, 1974, 1983). Granovetter (1983) then introduces four dimensions for distinguishing between a strong tie and weak tie network: (i) time, (ii) emotional intensity, (iii) mutual confidence, and (iv) reciprocal relationships. Strong ties involve frequent and emotionally intense communication where people are willing to share knowledge among the communicating members. This suggests *reciprocity* between the communicating members. In general, strong ties are reflected in relationships people have between themselves and their spouses, children, and friends. Strong ties can also be established with co-workers through the execution of work-related tasks.

Conversely, weak ties reflect less frequent communication, a lack of strong feelings and lower emotional intensity (Granovetter, 1974). Weak ties also do not share confidences, nor do they require strong reciprocity. Examples of weak ties are extended family members, co-workers who are not central to an individuals' task domain, or everyday acquaintances made in connection with work, social activities, and mutual friendships. Constant et al. (1997) points out that relative strangers (weak ties) could offer an advantage over friends and colleagues in obtaining useful information as it does not require a strong establishment of emotional closeness, nor does it require frequent contact or a history of reciprocal services. Therefore, weak ties serve as information bridges across cliques of strong ties and provide access to resources that are not found in a person's strong-tie relationships (Constant et al., 1996; Stevenson & Gilly, 1991 in Constant et al., 1996).

In this chapter, the strength of *weak ties is used* to illustrate the emergence and significance of communities of practice. By linking interpersonal ties in the virtual context, Wellman's (1997) view of *networked society* enhances our understanding of communities of practice. He operationalized the concept of a society that is socially bonded with the use of computers, proposing that "when computer networks link people as well as machines, they become social networks" (p. 213, 1996). Wellman and colleagues' (1996) research contributed to the literature by accentuating that the nature of medium—particularly in an electronic form—both constrains and facilitates social control, and thus has strong societal implications. In a networked society, boundaries are more permeable, interactions are more diverse, and the structure is flatter and more recursive (Castells, 2000; Wellman, 1997, 1999). People and organizations are also beginning to appreciate the ability of the Internet capability to transcend distance and time zones at low cost, which helps sustain relationships based on shared interests although the members are scattered, as well as providing powerful ties between people, which results in increased diffusion of information and knowledge (Rheingold, 2000).

In support of that, Wellman believes that a networked society has more freedom to communicate and develop relationships that provide sociability, support, information, and a sense of belonging. In this sense, communicative technologies are viewed more as a socio-technological means than as merely a communication and collaboration tool. However, the question here is whether this form of communication can facilitate the sharing of knowledge if limited social presence constrains the maintenance of socially close and strong ties that people have developed. This form of online communication supports or encourages the formation of weak ties because community members come to regard each other as their closest friends, although they have no opportunities to meet face-to-face (Hiltz & Turoff, 1993, Wellman, 1997). As Wellman et al. (1996) asserts, "Net members tend to base their feelings of closeness on shared interests rather than shared social characteristics such as gender and socio-economic status" (p. 222).

What is even more fascinating about this emergence of communities of practice is that people are able to reach out to the people from whom they are estranged. This is the group of people known as the *weak ties* or the *out-group* members because they are socially and physically remote, and not bound into a densely knit network or community structure. People from a collectivist culture actually can benefit from weak ties despite the fact they often need the formation of strong ties. In the virtual environment, people exchange and share information on the basis of social support, sense of belonging, shared interests, and problem-based learning (Kraut & Attewell, 1993; Rice & Love, 1987; McCormick & McCormick, 1992; Haythornwaite et al., 1995; Walther, 1996; Sproull & Faraj, 1995; Cullen, 1995), and this does not necessarily mean that they could not form a new relationship. As stipulated by Latane and Darley (1976), people are more willing to communicate with strangers online compared to in person because of factors such as anonymity, ease of withdrawal, increased visibility, and positive rewards for those who contribute (participation will be observed by a larger group), demonstrating technical expertise publicly and widely, earning respect and status, and responding to norms of helping people (Hiltz & Turoff, 1993; Walther, 1996; Rheingold, 1993; Barlow, 1995; Lewis, 1995), all of which strengthen weak ties.

However, the knowledge-sharing activities in a virtual form are less likely to be successful in sustaining strong ties because strong ties generally require a higher level of frequency and emotional intensity, mutual confidentiality, and establishment of reciprocity between members (Pickering & King, 1992). As has been discussed, for example, members of global virtual teams may consist of two different cultural values, collectivists or individualists. Collectivists or individualists differ in the ways they communicate, as well as in the level of willingness to share knowledge. With this significant observation, Lin (1999) argued that the applicability of Granovetter's work to the development of interpersonal ties in respect to different context, particularly from an Asian perspective, is debatable. She notes that there is a gap in the theory due to the differing cultural values of the team members, which needs to be considered. In the case where team members value collectivism, they may emphasize *a priori* relationship building.

Instead, in a virtual setting, many collectivists may experience feelings of isolation since team members are geographically separated and they often work without frequent group input. Although people may be eager to establish new relationships and form new friendships with strangers, building trust can be problematic because they do not have enough verbal and non-verbal cues when sharing knowledge online. The absence of physical cues actually may promote understanding once intra-team trust has developed (though not at the initial stage), since individuals will not be faced with potentially confusing, dissonant cultural signals from culturally diverse team members. As Rosa and Mazur (1979) concluded, "… when a group is composed of strangers, they very quickly make use of whatever limited status cues are immediately at hand, even such subtle signs as eye contact and speaking order." Thus the impact of ICTs can be exaggerated by the lack of these elements. On the other hand, for virtual team members from cultures that value directness and informality like the individualists, ICTs can promote dialogue since it already fits within their own cultural framework.

Since this chapter argues that the structural foundation of the communities of practice is characterized by networking, connectivity, mobility, flexibility, and speed, collaborative communicative technologies such as ICTs are more prevalent in this context. The next section discusses how and why ICTs enable the development of communities of practice.

Using ICTs for Supporting Communities of Practice in the Virtual Work Context

Without the use of collaborative communication technology, traditional teams need to be in one location to communicate and work collaboratively. Hence, matching meeting time with location is a common problem for multinational corporations. A study by McGrath and Hollingshead (1994) suggests that electronically enhanced communication systems can be used in absence of meeting face-to-face, thus defeating the time and space constraints. The use of communication technology thus supports mobility and flexibility, which are considered essential attributes of virtual teams' success.

This chapter, however, does not focus on which technology is used, or whether it is asynchronous or synchronous mode; it attempts only to understand the role of ICTs and the impact of their use on the success of communities of practice. McGrath and Hollingshead (1994) make several assumptions in regard to the effects of electronic technology on work groups: (1) improved task performance, (2) elimination of space and time constraints, and (3) increased access to information. It is not proposed that ICTs will totally eliminate the cultural differences of team members, merely that ICTs facilitate intra-team interaction by introducing a shared framework and virtual work setting. In that light, ICTs are a useful tool for facilitating cross-cultural collaboration and communication.

Strategic planning and management of technology needs to be implemented at the organizational level in order to capitalize on the technology and take full advantage of virtual teams. O'Hara, Devereaux, and Johansen (1994) suggest that information technology is not an alternative but a requirement for successful global business. Information technology can make it easier to overcome the problems of working together in a fragmented, global work environment and meet the challenges of distance and diversity. Further study is needed on issues such as the limitation of available technologies, and the unpredictability of existing global information infrastructure. Findings from group work studies have shown that cultural differences are important, be it national cultures or organizational cultures. For example, a study by Shea and Lewis (1996) has shown that in one way or another, culture plays an influential role when introducing or implementing new ICTs.

ICTs promote cross-cultural collaboration and communication by providing a common medium for work and shared meaning. For example, Strauss (1997) suggest that ICTs foster interdependence between less and more powerful team members, promote equality of participation, reduce organizational hierarchy (Kock & McQueen, 1997), and generally enhance member participation in virtual meetings compared to face-to-face meetings (Bikson, 1996; Sheffiled & Gallupe, 1994; Slater & Anderson, 1994; Williams & Wilson, 1997). Most studies on computer-mediated communication suggest that low, social presence generally is unsatisfying and leaves people in some situations, such as those involving conflict, unable to resolve differences effectively or unable to meet their goals (Ketrow, 1999). Over time, however, the lack of social and physical presence can foster positive intra-team coalitions and strengthen working relationships that would be less likely to thrive in a more traditional team framework. Table 3 summarizes some of the inherent advantages and disadvantages of ICTs as a supporting collaboration tool.

Implications of Weak Ties Theory and Cultural Dimensions on Developing Communities of Practice

The effect of weak ties on the success of building virtual communities of practice can be judged from three perspectives: (1) how social ties impact the development of virtual communities of practice, (2) how cultural factors impact knowledge-sharing activities using ICTs and, (3) how ICTs impact knowledge sharing and emergence of virtual communities of practice.

(1) The impact of social ties among team members' on the development of virtual communities of practice

Global virtual team members can benefit from the novelty and diverse ideas available to them in communities of practice. Hence, the weak ties theory suggests that people do not need to establish a prior relationship with members in an organization to get superior information and access to desired resources. The following assumptions set forth by Constant et al. (1996) with regard to the weak ties theory are, therefore, applicable to the study of communities of practice: (i) advice from more people is more useful than advice from fewer people; (2) advice from more diverse ties is more useful than advice from less diverse ties; and (3) advice from people with more resources is more useful than advice from people with fewer resources. Furthermore, weak ties have the potential to capitalize on both the diversity and range of ideas and information, and desirable resources like wealth, status, prestige, power, or access to others (Lin et al., 1981; DiMaggio & Mohr, 1985; Marsden & Hurlbert, 1988). Also Granovetter (1973) emphasized that bridging weak ties in organizations can help link culturally different groups, reduce alienation, and increase social solidarity. Effective communities of practice can be developed by defining a domain of interests and reconciling multiple agents, building the community with enhanced trust and personal relationships, creating a structure that promotes both local variations and global connection, having a strong organizational culture that demonstrates the value of sharing knowledge through the use of ICTs, and developing the private space of the community more systematically (an extension of the guiding principles of communities of practice, refer to Table 2).

(2) The impact of national culture on knowledge-sharing activities using ICTs

As clearly stated in previous sections, building trust is crucial in a collectivistic society (Walther, 1996). Conversely, an individualistic society is primarily concerned with task and is goal oriented; building relationships is secondary. The cultural boundaries described by these two differing viewpoints affect the extent to which people are willing to disclose information. Cultural values also shape the type of situation needed to facilitate knowledge sharing, and when and how sharing is made

Table 3. Summary of advantages and disadvantages of ICTs as supporting collaborative communicative technologies (Zakaria, Amelinckx, & Wilemon, 2004)

Advantages of ICTs	Disadvantages of ICTs
• Greater anonymity of team members	• Lack of communication modalities such as non-verbal or verbal cues
• Transcends space and time	
• Allows equal participation	• Lack of physical or non face-to-face interaction
• Access to wider and faster Information sources	• Deficiencies in issue of trust
• More flexible communication structures	• Implementing ICTs are costly
• Better information retrieval and repository	• Difficulty in using the technology
• Faster communication and feedbacks	• Differences in technologies used
	• Slower decision making

possible. Strangers can more easily contribute to the pool of knowledge when communicating in a virtual environment. As stipulated by Constant et al. (1996), virtual communities of practice could, perplexingly, benefit from the kindness of strangers. However, when talking about global virtual teams comprised of people of different nationalities, how would people from a collectivist society respond to knowledge received from people with whom they have no historical relationship at all? Would they trust that source of information?

In addition to having doubts about the source, people from a collectivist culture also may be more skeptical about the quality and usefulness of the information itself. Not only that, individuals from collectivist cultures may be less willing to contribute to a pool of knowledge for two reasons: saving face—they may refrain from sharing knowledge if they feel the consequences would damage their pride, face, or social standing since they need to maintain their conduct or performance in an organization (Chow, Deng, & Ho, 2000; Ting-Toomey, 2005). Studies conducted by Triandis (1989) found that a collectivist society is more hostile and distrustful when it comes to people that are considered as their out-group. In view of knowledge sharing, findings from Chow, Deng, and Ho (2000) indicated that individualistic people share more knowledge when the organizational work environment is supportive and understanding. Individualists are deterred by an organizational environment that is punitive and non-supportive. On the other hand, collectivist people are more inclined to share knowledge because of the benefits to the collective interests, work ethics, integrity, and honesty. They also noted that knowledge sharing is increased

when a relationship exists between the knowledge recipient and knowledge provider. However, if the recipient is an out-group member, knowledge sharing is less likely.

(3) The impact of ICTs on knowledge sharing and emergence of communities of practice within global virtual teams

Walther (1996) suggests that in an ICT environment collectivist people normally would take longer to evoke the social, contextual, and non-verbal cues necessary for effective collaboration and communication since ICTs evidently lacks these cues. In the same vein, for global virtual team members, the initial stage of communicating demands the most important elements or cues that the society has to offer. Hence, establishing trust and strong relationships is difficult when people are denied the necessary cues. However, Walther also argued that despite the fact that it takes a bit longer to set up the social status of the members of an electronic communication, once people become more experienced they can pick up or seek out cues relatively quickly and easily. Lea and Spears's model (1991) proposed that communication does not rely necessarily on the online communication of informational cues for the operation of social norms, or even attraction. Although open to negotiation and development, both norms and the bases of attraction are nominally encoded within the social identities of the participants at the outset. Hence the lack of social information in electronic discussions no longer serves as a barrier to effective communication (Lea & Spears, 1991; Walther, 1996). In support of that, the later work of Kiesler and Sproull (1992) and Meijer (1994) specified that although e-communication is primarily textual-oriented and lacks the social context cues, yet the notion of reduced social cues explains how members communicating via computer become more divergent than members that engage in face-to-face communications due to enhanced effects of group polarization and de-individualization. This only accentuates the positive effects of using ICTs over face-to-face.

FUTURE RESEARCH DIRECTIONS

A new social and working context for the global virtual teams to share knowledge is no longer constrained by geographical distance, space, and time. However, there are some inevitable challenges in building a sustainable knowledge-sharing base between diverse members of global virtual teams. In cultivating communities of practice in global virtual teams, these three factors really matter: (1) nature of social ties (weak ties), (2) national culture of the virtual team members (individualism vs. collectivism, power distance, uncertainty avoidance, and masculinity vs. femininity), and (3) nature of ICTs as communicative technologies—which are all translated in people's communicative behaviors and practices. Hence, Granovetter's *weak ties* together with Hofstede's *cultural dimensions* have important implications for all three above-mentioned factors.

In essence, the *weak ties* theory explains how people from outside (out-group members) are more likely to give *fresher* and *diverse* ideas since they are not circumscribed by the common reality of *group think*. Weak ties are not bounded by traditional organizational structures; in fact they are driven by the networking, connectivity, flexibility, mobility, and speed, all of which enhance the development of communities of practice. For example, the key question is: Can global virtual team members still engage in the *water-cooler-talk* in a virtual environment? The potential answer would thus be by participating in instant messaging or electronic bulletin boards in which ideas can be *tossed around* by team members from all over the world without constraints of time and space.

It is equally crucial to understand key questions such as what, why, when, how, and to whom members will share knowledge within the teams or across teams. As such, the use of cultural theoretical lens introduced by Hofstede (1980) provide the argument that people communicate and collaborate dependent on their cultural roots and consequently translates into acceptable behaviors and practices.

Inherently, the unique advantages of weak ties could provide a new solution to cultivate communities of practice for global virtual teams so that they can share knowledge and form epistemic communities at a distance. Such practices will increase organizational learning as well as individual knowledge. As a result, for both the knowledge provider and the recipient, weak ties provide a valuable way of reaching out to strangers who can, thus, contribute diverse, novel, and innovative ideas. To sum up, this chapter proposes several empirical future research directions that can be undertaken and explored based on the following questions:

- What are the challenges of building communities of practices in the virtual work environment? How do we overcome some of the barriers so that global virtual teams can be effective?
- What are the structural and cultural factors that facilitate the emergence and development of community of practices within global virtual teams?
- How does culture impact the flow of information and sharing of knowledge within global virtual teams and to what extent?
- How does IT competencies enhance task performance and, in turn, promote the emergence of communities of practice for knowledge sharing?
- What are the ways or strategies that MNCs can take in order to inculcate organizational culture that facilitates knowledge sharing within team members?

ACKNOWLEDGMENT

The initial draft of this chapter was reviewed by Dr. Liaquat Hossain, who is attached at School of Information Technology, University of Sydney.

Through time, the chapter has been worked out and revised substantially to suit the theme of the handbook project. Hence, I would like to thank him for the comments and ideas shared, which led to the success of this chapter.

REFERENCES

Barlow, J. P. (1995). Is there a cyberspace? *Utne Reader,* March-April, 50-56.

Bikson, T. K. (1996).Groupware at the World Bank. In C. U. Coborra (Ed.), *Groupware and teamwork: Invisible air or technical hindrance?* (pp. 145-183). Chichester: John Wiley.

Bleeker, S. E. (1994). The virtual organization. *The Futurist, 28*(2), 9-14.

Castells, M. (2000). The rise of the network society. Malden, MA: Blackwell.

Chen, G. M. (2001). Toward transcultural understanding: A harmony theory of Chinese communication. In V. H. Milhouse, M. K. Asante, & P. O. Nwosu (Eds.), *Transcultural realities: Interdisciplinary perspectives on cross-cultural relations* (pp. 55-70). Thousand Oaks, CA: Sage

Chow, C. W., Deng, J. F., & Ho, J. L. (2000). The openness of knowledge sharing within organizations: A comparative study in the United States and the People's Republic of China. *Journal of Management Accounting Research, 12*, 65-95.

Collier, J., & Esteban, R. (1999). Governance in the participative organization: Freedom, creativity and ethics. *Journal of Business Ethics, 21*(2/3), 173-188.

Constant, D., Sproull, L., & Kiesler, S. (1996). The kindness of strangers: The usefulness of electronic weak ties for technical advice. *Organization Science, 7*(2), 119-135.

Cullen, D. L. (1995). Psychotherapy in cyberspace. *The Clinician, 26,* 1, 6-7.

DiMaggio, P., & Mohr, J. (1985). Cultural capital, educational attainment, and marital selection. *American Journal of Sociology, 90,* 1231-1261.

Duncan, R. B., & Weiss, A. (1979). Organizational learning: Implications for organizational design. In B. M. Staw, *Research in organizational behavior,* Vol. 1 (pp. 75-123). Greenwich, CT: JAI Press.

Edmondson, A., & Moingeon, B. (1996, June 2). Organizational learning as a source of competitive advantage: When to learn how and when to learn why (pp. 691-699). *Proceedings of the first Asia Pacific DSI conference,* Hong Kong.

Garrecht, M. (1998). The origin of virtual corporations. In H. Nolte (Ed.), *Aspect of resource-oriented corporate governance* (pp. 110-133). Mering, Germany: Rainer Hampp Verlag.

Garvin, D. A. (1993). Building a learning organization. *Harvard Business Review,* 78-91.

Gherardi, S., & Nicolini, D. (2000). The organizational learning of safety in communities of practice, *Journal of Management Inquiry, 9*(1), 7-18.

Granovetter, M. S. (1974). The strength of weak ties. *American Journal of Sociology,* 78(6), 1360-1380.

Granovetter, M. S. (1983). The strength of weak ties: A network theory revisited. In R. Collins, (Ed). *Sociological theory* (pp. 210-233). Jossey-Bass Publishers.

Gudykunst, W. B., & Kim, Y. Y. (2002). *Communicating with strangers: An approach to intercultural communication.* (4th ed.). London: McGraw Hill.

Haythornthwaite, C., Wellman, B., & Mantei, M. (1995). Work relationship and media use: A social network analysis. *Group Decisions and Negotiation, 4*(3), 193-211.

Hiltz, S. R., & Turoff, M. (1993). *The network nation.* Cambridge, MA: MIT Press.

Hofstede, G. (1980). *Cultural consequences.* Beverly Hills, CA: Sage.

Huber, G. (1991). Organizational learning: The contributing processes and the literatures. *Organization Science, 2,* 88-115.

Igbaria, M., & Tan, M. (1998). *The virtual workplace.* London: Idea Group Publishing.

Inkpen, A. (1998). Learning and knowledge acquisition through international strategic alliances, *The Academy of Management Executive, 12*(4), 69-80.

Jarvenpaa, S. L., & Leidner, D. E. (1999). Communication and trust in global virtual teams. *Organization Science, 10*(6), 791-815.

Johnson, C. M. (2001). A survey of current research on online communities of practice. *The Internet and Higher Education*, 4, 45-60.

Kapij, M. I., & Abetti, P. A. (1997). An entrepreneurial venture teaming of multi-cultural groups: A case study of software factory of international ltd. *Management of Technology VI,* 1162-1171.

Kasper-Fuehrer, E. C., & Ashkanasy, N. M. (2001). Communicating trustworthiness and building trust in interorganizational virtual organizations, *Journal of Management, 27*(3), 235-254.

Ketrow, S. M. (1999). Nonverbal aspects of group communication. In L. R. Frey, D. S. Gouran, & M. S. Poole (Eds.), *The handbook of group communication theory and research.* Thousand Oaks, CA: Sage.

Kiesler, S., & Sproull, L. (1992). Group decision making and communication technology. *Organizational Behavior & Human Decision Processes,* 52, 96-123.

Kimble, C., Alexis, B., & Li, F. (2000). Effective virtual teams through communities of practice. *Strathclyde Business School Management Science Working Paper* No. 2000/9.

Kock, N., & McQueen, R. (1997). A field study of the effects of asynchronous groupware support on process improvement groups. *Journal of Information Technology,* 12, 245-259.

Kraut, R. E., & Attewell, P. (1997). Media use in a global corporation: Electronic mail and organizational knowledge. In S. K. (Ed.), *Culture of the internet* (pp. 323-342). Mahwah, NJ: Lawrence Erlbaum Associates.

Latane, B., & Darley, J. (1976). *Help in crisis: Bystander response to an emergency.* Morristown, NJ: General Learning Press.

Lave, J., & Wenger, E. (1991). *Situated leaning: Legitimate peripheral participation.* Cambridge: Cambridge University Press.

Lea, M., & Spears, R. (1992). Paralanguage and social perception in computer-mediated communication. *Journal of Organizational Computing,* 2, 231-342.

Lewis, P. H. (1995). Strangers, not their computers build a network in time of grief. *New York Times,* March 8.

Lin, N. (1999). Building a network theory of social capital. *Connections, 22,* 28-51.

Markus, H. R., & Kitayama, S. (1991). Culture and self: Implication for cognition, emotion, and motivation. *Psychological Review, 98,* 224-253.

Marsden, P. V., & Hurlbert, J. (1988). Social resources and mobility outcomes: A

replication and extension. *Social Forces, 66,* 1039-1059.

McCormick, N., & McCormick, J. (1992). Computer friends and foes: Content of undergraduates' electronic mail. *Computers in Human Behavior, 8,* 379-405.

McGrath, J. E., & Hollingshead, A. B. (1994). *Groups interacting with technology.* Thousand Oaks, CA: Sage Publications.

Meijer (1994). *Writing apart together.* Unpublished graduation thesis. [Online] Available http://infolab.kub.nl/pub/theses/w3thesis/Readthis/meijer1994.html

Merali, Y. (2000). Individual and collective congruence in the knowledge management process. *Journal of Strategic Information Management* 9(2-3), 213-234.

Merali, Y. (2001). Leveraging capabilities: A cognitive congruence framework. In R. Sanchez (Ed.),

Knowledge management and organizational competence. New York: Oxford University Press.

Montoya-Weiss, M. M., Massey, A. P., & Song, M. (2001). Getting it together: Temporal coordination and conflict management in global virtual teams. *The Academy of Management Journal, 44*(6), 1251-1262.

O'Hara-Devereaux, M., & Johansen, R. (1994). *Global work: Bridging distance, culture, and time.* San Francisco: Jossey-Bass Publishers.

Okunoye, A., & Karsten, H. (2002). Where the global needs the local: Variation in enablers in the knowledge management process. *Journal of Global Information Technology Management, 5*(3), 12-31.

Pickering, J. M., & King, J. L. (1992). Hardwiring weak ties: Individual and institutional issues in computer-mediated communication. *Proceedings of the conference on computer-supported cooperative work* (pp. 356-361). NY: ACM Press.

Rice, R. E., & Love, G. (1987). Electronic emotion: Socio-emotional content in a computer-mediated communication network. *Communication Research, 14*, 85-105.

Rheingold, H. (1993). *The Virtual community: Homesteading on the electronic frontier.* Reading, MA: Addison Wesley.

Rheingold, H. (2000). *The virtual community.* Cambridge, MA: MIT Press.

Rosa, E., & Mazur, A. (1979). Incipient status in small groups. *Social Forces, 58*, 18-37.

Schein, E. (1992). *Organizational culture and leadership* (2nd ed.). San Francisco: Jossey-Bass.

Semich, J. (1994). Information replaces inventory at the virtual corporation. *Datamation, 40*(14), 37-40.

Senge, P. M. (1990). *The fifth discipline: The art and practice of the learning organization.* NY: Doubleday/currency.

Shea, T., & Lewis, D. (1996). The influence of national culture on management: Practices and information use in developing countries. In E. Szewczak & M. Khosrow-Pour, *The human side of information technology management* (pp. 254-273). Harrisburg, PA: Idea Group Publishing.

Sheffield, J., & Gallupe, R. B. (1994). Using electronic meeting technology to support economy policy development in New Zealand: Short term results. *Journal of Management Information Systems, 10*, 97-116.

Slater, J. S., & Anderson, E. (1996). Communication convergence in the electronically supported discussions: Adaptation to Kincaid's convergence model. *Telematics and Informatics, 11*, 111-125.

Sproull, L., & Faraj, S. (1995). Atheism, sex, and databases: The net as a social technology. In B. Kahin & J. Keller (Eds.), *Public access to the internet* (pp. 62-81). MA: MIT Press.

Strauss, S. G. (1997). Technology, group process and group outcomes: Testing the connection in computer-mediated and face-to-face groups. *Human Computer Interaction, 12*, 227-266.

Ting-Toomey, S. (2005). The matrix of face: An updated face-negotiation theory. In W. B. Gudykunt, *Theorizing about intercultural communication* (pp. 71-92). Thousand Oaks: Sage.

Triandis, H. C. (1995). *Individualism and collectivism.* Boulder, CO: Westview Press.

Triandis, H. C. (2002). Generic individualism and collectivism. In M. J. Gannon & K. L. Newman (Eds.), *The Blackwell handbook of cross-cultural management* (pp. 16-46). Malden, MA: Blackwell Publisher.

Tudor, T. R., & Trumble, R. (1996), Cultural integration: An examination of success for United States and Japanese business mergers, *International Journal of Management, 13*(1), 52-59.

Walther, J. B. (1996). Computer-mediated communication: Impersonal, interpersonal, and hyperpersonal interaction. *Communication Research, 23*(1), 3-43.

Wellman, B. (1997) An electronic group is virtually a social network. In S. Kiesler (Ed.). *Culture of the Internet* (pp.179-205). Mahwah, NJ: Lawrence Erlbaum Associates.

Wellman, B. (1999). In B. Wellman (Ed.), *Networks in the global village* (pp. 1-147). Boulder, CO: Westview Press.

Wellman, B., Salaff, J., Dimitrova, D., Garton, L., Gulia, M., & Haythornthwaite, C. (1996). Computer networks as social networks: Collaborative work, telework, and virtual community. *Annual Review Sociology, 22,* 213-238.

Wenger, E. (1998). *Communities of practice: Learning, meaning and identity.* NY: Cambridge University Press.

Wenger, E., McDermott, R., & Snyder, W. M. (2002). *Cultivating communities of practices,* Boston: Harvard Business School Press.

Wick, C. (2000). Knowledge management and leadership opportunities for technical communicators. *Technical Communication, 47*(4), 515-529.

Wiesenfeld, B. M., Raghura, S., & Garud, R. (1998). Communication patterns as determinants of organizational identification in a virtual organization. *Journal of Computer Mediated Communication, 3*(4), 1-22.

William, S. R., & Wilson, R. L. (1997). Group support systems, power, and influence in an organization: A field study. *Decision Sciences, 28*(4), 911-937.

Zakaria, N., Amelinckx, A., & Wilemon, D. L. (2004). Challenges of managing global virtual teams via ICTs. In Y. A. Hosni & T. M. Khalil (Eds.), *Management of technology Internet economy: Opportunities and challenges for developed and developing regions of the world* (pp. 243-264). San Francisco: Elsevier.

ADDITIONAL READING

Brown, J. S., & Duguid, P. (1991). Organizational learning and communities of practice: Toward a unified view of working, learning and innovation. *Organization Science, 2,* 40-57.

Cramton, C. D. (2001). The mutual knowledge problem and its consequences for dispersed collaboration. *Organization Science, 12*(3), 346-371.

Cramton, C. D., & Hinds, P. J. (2004). Subgroups dynamics in internationally distributed teams: ethnocentricsm or cross-national learning? *Research in Organizational Behavior, 26.*

Daft, R. L., & Lengel, R. H. (1984). Information richness: A new approach to managerial behavior and organizational design. In L. L. Cummings & B. M. Staw (Eds.), *Research in organizational behavior, 6 (*pp. 191-233*),* Homewood, IL: JAI Press.

Earley, P. C., & Mosakowski, E. 2000. Creating hybrid team cultures: An empirical test of transnational team functioning. *Academy of Management Journal, 43,* 26-49.

Earley, P. C., & Gibson, C. B. 2002. *Multinational work teams: A new perspective.* Mahway, NJ: Erlbaum.

Gu, B., & Jarvenpaa, S. (2003). Online discussion boards for technical support: The effect of token recognition on customer contributions (pp.110-120). *Proceedings of the 24th International Conference on Information Systems.*

Gheradi, S., & Nicolini D. (2000). The organisational learning of safety in communities of practice, *Journal of Management Inquiry, 9*(1), 7-18.

Kimble, C., Alexis, B., & Li, F. (2000). *Effective virtual teams through communities of practice.* Strathclyde Business School Management Science (Working Paper No. 2000/9).

Kimble, C., Hildreth, P., & Wright, P. (2000). *Communities of practice: Going virtual.* In *Knowledge management and business model innovation* (Chapter 13, pp. 220-234). Hershey, PA: Idea Group Publishing.

Lin, N., Ensel, W. M., & Vaughn, J. C. (1988). Social resources and strength of ties: Structural factors in occupational status attainment. *American Sociological Review, 46,* 393-405.

Friedkin, N. (1982). Information flow through strong and weak ties in interorganizational social networks. *Social Networks*, 3, 273-285.

Kakabadse, N. K., Kouzmin, A., Kakabadse, A., & Savery, L. (2001). Low and high context communication patterns: Toward mapping cross-cultural encounters. *Journal of Cross-Cultural Management, 8*(2), 3-24.

Marlene, C. F., & O'Connor, E. J. (2005). Identification in face-to-face, hybrid, and pure virtual teams: Untangling the contradictions. *Organization Science, 16*(1), 19-32.

Mortensen, M., & Hinds, P. J. (2001). Fuzzy teams. Boundary disagreement in distributed and collocated teams. In P. Hinds & S. Kiesler (Eds.), *Distributed work* (pp. 283-308). Cambridge, MA: Massachusetts Institute of Technology Press.

Olaniran, B. A. (2001). The effects of computer-mediated communication on transculturalism. In V. H. Milhouse, M. K. Asante, & P. O. Nwosu (Eds.), *Transcultural realities: Interdisciplinary perspectives on cross-cultural relations* (pp. 55-70). Thousand Oaks, CA: Sage.

Palloff, R., & Pratt, K. (1999). *Building learning communities in cyberspace: Effective strategies for the online classroom.* San Francisco: Jossey Bass.

Reid, S. E. (1994). Cultural formations in text-based virtual realities (pp. 164-183). First published as Virtual worlds: Culture and imagination. In S. G. Jones (Ed.), *CyberSociety: Computer-mediated communication and community.* Thousand Oaks, CA: Sage. Publications.

Rintel, E. S., & Pittam, J. (1997). Strangers in a strange land: Interaction management on internet relay chat. *Human Communication Research, 23,* 507-534.

Robey, D., Khoo, H. M., & Powers, C. (2000). Situated learning in cross-functional virtual teams. *IEEE Transactions on Professional Communication, 43*(1), 51.

Rogers, J. (2000). Communities of practice: A framework for fostering coherence in virtual learning communities. *Educational Technology & Society, 3*(3), 384-392.

Shachaf, P. (2005). Bridging cultural diversity through email. *Journal of Global Information Technology Management, 8*(2), 46-60.

Squire, K. D., & Johnson, C. B. (2000). Supporting distributed communities of practice with interactive television, *Educational Technology Research and Development, 48*(1), 23-43. Available at http://www6.open.ac.uk/h805/resources/SupportingDistributedComms.pdf

Thorpe, M. (2002). From independent learning to collaborative learning: new communities of practice in open, distance and distributed learning (pp. 131-151). In M. Lea & K. Nicoll (Eds.), *Distributed learning: Social and cultural approaches to practice.*

Vangelisti, A. L., Knapp, M. L., & Daly, J. A. (1990). Conversational narcissism. *Communication Monographs,* 57, 251-274.

Wasko, M. M., & Faraj, S. (2000). It is what one does: Why people participate and help others in electronic communities of practices. *Journal of Strategic Information Systems, 9*(2-3), 155-173.

Wasko, M., & Faraj, S. (2005). Why should I share? Examining social capital and knowledge contribution in electronic networks of practice. *MIS Quarterly, 29*(1), 35-57.

Windsor, D. (2001). Learning to do knowledge work in systems of distributed cognition, *Journal of Business and Technical Communication, 15*(1), 5-28.

Zakaria, N., & Mohd Yusof, S. A. (2005). The dynamics of virtual teams. In M. Pagani (Ed.), *Encyclopedia of multimedia technology and networking (Volume 1)* (pp. 1-9). Hershey, PA: Idea Group References.

Chapter V
Understanding Brand Web Site Positioning in the New EU Member States:
The Case of the Czech Republic

Shintaro Okazaki
Universidad Autónoma de Madrid, Spain

Radoslav Škapa
Masaryk University, Czech Republic

ABSTRACT

This chapter examines Web sites created by American Multinational Corporations (MNCs) in the Czech Republic. Utilizing a content analysis technique, we scrutinized (1) the type of brand Web site functions, and (2) the similarity ratings between the home (U.S.) sites and Czech sites. Implications are discussed from the Web site standardization versus localization perspective.

INTRODUCTION

Both academics and practitioners have long debated whether advertising messages should be standardized. The proponents of standardization argue that the use of uniform advertising would provide significant cost benefits, thus improving company performance in the short run, while creating a consistent brand image in multiple markets. In contrast, the proponents of localization contend that ignoring the cultural, social, and economic characteristics of particular markets would cause psychological rejection by local consumers, thus decreasing profits in the long run. The debate also has produced a compromised or hybrid approach, which suggests that whether to standardize or localize advertising in a given market is a question of degree, and it is necessary to analyze many factors on a case-by-case basis (Mueller, 1991).

This debate is not limited to traditional media. As multinational corporations (MNCs) integrate their marketing communication with an emergent interactive medium, Web sites are becoming increasingly important for brand marketing and customer relationship management in multiple markets. This is because the Internet is, by definition, a *global* medium, which allows companies to create localized content with global access. In fact, many MNCs have established so-called *global gateway* sites with several language options. Consumers can first choose the language, then seek the information they desire. In this regard, the content of the local sites may need to be adapted to local consumers' tastes and preferences, in terms of design, layout, copy, message, and so forth. (Okazaki & Alonso, 2002).

Okazaki (2005) examined Web sites created by American MNCs' in four EU member states (i.e., the UK, France, Germany, and Spain), and found a high level of localization in Web site communication strategy. This research extends Okazaki's exploration into the new EU member states, by conducting a content analysis of the MNCs' Web sites created in the Czech Republic. Specifically, we address the following questions: (1) What types of brand Web site functions are used? (2) To what extent are the Czech sites standardized?

SIGNIFICANCE OF THE STUDY

This study will be an interesting addition to the literature of global information technology for two reasons. First, prior research provides little information on how the content created by the most globally diffused information technology, the Internet, has been standardized in foreign markets. Information managers in global markets should be aware of a question of transmitting culturally bound meanings into local sites. Secondly, this study addresses how design features and Web site functions can be used as a tool to create a universal imagery in global Web sites. Specifically, this study explores one of the most understudied countries in Europe: the Czech Republic. After joining the European Union, studies on information technology in this new member state is almost non-existent, thus, this research makes a unique contribution to the literature.

ENLARGEMENT OF THE EUROPEAN UNION

In 2004, the enlargement of the European Union increased its member states from 15 to 25, by adding 10 countries: Cyprus, the Czech Republic, Estonia, Hungary, Latvia, Lithuania, Malta, Poland, Slovakia, and Slovenia. In 2007, two more countries, Romania and Bulgaria became the member states, making the Union of 27 countries. This drastic expansion changed the way multinational corporations (MNCs) operate their businesses in Europe. Because of these countries' low labour costs and investment incentives (e.g., tax reduction, construction aid, etc.), many firms moved their production facilities from other regions to these new member states. For example, Sheram and Soubbotina (2000) report that "Countries seen as more advanced in market reforms—the Czech and Slovak Republics, Hungary, and Poland—attracted almost three-quarters of foreign investment" in transition economies. In fact, Poland received approximately $6.4 billion in foreign direct investment in 2003, an increase of $360 million over the previous year (MacKay, 2004).

As these new EU member states experience rapid economic expansion, global marketing influences consumers more and more. Their product experiences increasingly resemble those of their *Western* neighbours. In this light, it is reasonable to argue that the role of advertising in everyday consumption also has undergone a drastic transition, in both content and executions. For example, in the Czech Republic, advertising spending reached 563 million euros in 2004, while the average annual growth rate over the last 5 years has been 5%. Multinational corporations (MNCs) are the largest advertisers in these countries (ARBOmedia, 2005).

MEDIA USAGE IN EASTERN AND CENTRAL EUROPE

The Czech Republic

In the Czech Republic, television has traditionally been the primary vehicle for advertising, accounting for 46% of the MNCs' marketing budgets. Print media is the second medium with 34%, while outdoor advertising (i.e., billboard) is third, with 8% of total advertising expenditure (OMD Czech, 2005). However, the rapid growth of the Internet has significantly affected this media distribution. According to the Czech Publishers Association, the share of Internet advertising has been estimated at approximately 4%, or 25 million euro (760 millions CZK), with a growth rate of almost 80% in 2004 (Unie vydavatelů, 2005). The telecommunications, financial, and automobile companies are the heaviest users of the Internet as an advertising medium (Unie vydavatelů, 2005).

In 2005, nearly 30% of Czech households had a personal computer (Czech Statistical Office, 2005). Internet penetration is increasing steadily in the Czech Republic. Nowadays, 35% of the adult population in the Czech Republic uses the Internet, almost twice the number of Internet users in 2000. The Czech Republic, thus, has clearly outmatched other Central European countries: for example, Bulgaria (16%), Hungary (22%), and Poland (31%). However, it has not yet achieved the levels of Internet penetration in Estonia (51%) or Slovenia (56%). The most dynamic increase is found in older people (GfK, 2006), even though the Internet use remains the domain of younger people. A quarter of Czech citizens have an Internet connection at home.

Searching for information is one of the most frequent activities on the Internet, according to a survey by the Czech Statistical Office (2005). In the most recent quarter to be surveyed, 62% of the Internet users used the Internet to find information about goods and services, 54% used it to find and download professional texts, 38% looked for services related to travel and accommodation, 36% to read and download online newspapers and magazines, and 28% to play or download games or music. However, the number of individuals with e-shopping experience increased rapidly between 2005 and 2006 (the survey was carried out in the first quarters of 2005 and 2006): it amounted to 14% in 2006, while a year before it had been only 6% (Czech Statistical Office, 2006). The most popular items in the Internet shopping are electron-

ics, books, journals, textbooks, tickets and travel services, and accommodation. Online shopping is typically used more by men than women, and by the younger generation groups, between 25 and 45 years.

Approximately 12,500 Czech enterprises purchased goods or services via the Internet in 2003, almost 30% of the total number. The value of Internet purchases reached 2.8% of total purchases, and the value of Internet sales reached nearly 2.1% of total sales in these enterprises.

Poland and Hungary

Along with the Czech Republic, Poland, and Hungary make up the fastest-growing economic region within the new EU member states. For example, the rapid transformation of the Polish economy is reflected in the accelerated growth of its advertising market. Between 1996 and 1999, average annual growth in advertising expenditure was more than 40%, which can be attributed to the drastic structural changes, and the subsequent economic boom, in this period. With regard to media share, television was the most popular (48%), with print media second (35%). Online advertising, including Web sites, remains far behind traditional media, representing approximately 1% of total media spending (Zenith Optimedia, 2004). The telecommunications, financial, and automobile industries are the heaviest users of the Internet for advertising, promotion, and transactions (Agora, 2005).

In 2005, 30% of households in Poland had the technical possibility of the Internet access. In term of quality of connections, the survey found that only 16% of Polish households used a broadband connection. The significant disparity in the Internet infrastructure is between urban areas and the countryside, where the penetration of broadband connections is four times lower than in urban areas (Eurostat, 2005).

The Internet usage by Polish enterprises is below the EU average: in 2005, 87% of enterprises used the Internet connection. The share of broadband Internet connections was 43%. More than 67% of companies have their own Web site homepage (Eurostat, 2006). Online purchases have not yet become popular. Only 5% of Polish consumers ordered goods or services via the Internet in 2005 (Eurostat, 2006). According to the survey by GfK (2006), only 4% of the Internet users make a purchase on the Internet once a month or more. A further 6% buy online once every two to three months, while 18% go online sporadically with the intention of buying something. The most frequently purchased items include books, CDs, clothes, and shoes. Less frequently, people buy DVDs and air tickets (GfK, 2006).

In B2B the situation is similar. In 2005, only 9% of the enterprises surveyed ordered products or services via the Internet. Sales were lower, with only 4% of enterprises selling via the Internet. In 2005, turnover from e-commerce amounted to 1.6% of total turnover (Eurostat, 2005).

Similarly, the Hungarian market has shown a drastic growth in market size and advertising spending. According to the *Budapest Business Journal* (BBJ, 2004), advertising expenditure in television media reached 213 million euros by 2003. The print media also showed a drastic growth, to spending of 212 million euros. In 2003, the online advertising market expanded by approximately 30%, achieving a 2% share of the total media market. The principal reasons for this growth were an increased number of the Internet users in younger generations, and the rapid proliferation of broadband high-speed connection. The largest online advertisers include car dealers, telecommunication companies, beer makers, and cosmetics firms (BBJ, 2003).

Other EU Member States

In 2005, Slovenia had the highest rate of the Internet usage in the new member states, both for households (48%), and for enterprises (96%) (Eurostat, 2006). The lowest rates of access were in Lithuania, for households (16%), and in Latvia, for enterprises (75%). The largest disparities in Internet access between households and enterprises were recorded in the Czech Republic, Lithuania, and Slovakia. The number of individuals who have never used the Internet outweighs the number of regular users

in the new member states. That differs from the situation in the old member states.

There also is disparity in the presence of companies' Web sites on the Internet. In January 2005, 62% of enterprises in the EU were equipped with a Web site, but only 49% in the new member states. The lowest percentages of companies with Web sites were found in Latvia, Hungary, and Lithuania. Most enterprises use the content of their Web presentations mainly to market their products. Less than half use it to display catalogues of their products, services, and prices. One-quarter use Web sites to offer after-sales service to their customers. Apart from the Czech Republic, enterprises in the new member states registered lower rates than the EU average for purchases, sales, and for total sales on the Internet, as a percentage of their overall turnover (Eurostat, 2006).

The e-readiness rankings of the Economist Intelligence Unit can be seen as a complex indicator of the level of ICT of a country's infrastructure. The index is a weighted collection of nearly 100 quantitative and qualitative criteria, which assesses the *state of play* of a country's information and communications technology (ICT) infrastructure, and the ability of its consumers, businesses, and governments to use ICT to their benefit. In the 2006 e-readiness rankings, Estonia achieved the best position of all the new EU member states (27th), whereas Latvia (39th) was lowest. By comparison, 10 of the 15 old EU members were in the top 20.

The Networked Readiness Index, published annually in the Global Information Technology Report, is a similar index. This index captures such aspects as available ICT infrastructure, and actual levels of ICT usage, and its purpose is to understand more thoroughly the impact of ICT on the competitiveness of nations. In this index, Estonia again scored best amongst the new members. Latvia and Poland had the lowest ratings.

Standardization vs. Localization

The issue of standardization arises from the desirability and feasibility of using a uniform marketing mix (4Ps) across national markets (Szymanski et al.,

1993). Advertising has been examined more often than the other elements of this mix (Agrawal, 1995; Zandpour et al., 1994). A *standardized* approach is the use of uniform messages with no modification of headings, illustrations, or copy, except for translation in international markets (Onkvisit & Shaw, 1987). The standardized school of thought argues that consumers anywhere in the world are likely to share the same wants and needs (Elinder, 1961; Levitt, 1983). On the other hand, the *localized* approach asserts that consumers differ across countries, and therefore advertising should be tailored according to culture, media availability, product life cycle stages, and industry structure (Synodinos et al., 1989; Wind, 1986).

Combining these two extremes, the third school of thought states that the appropriateness of standardization depends on economic similarity, market position, the nature of the product, the environment, and organizational factors (Jain, 1989).

In the 1970s, empirical evidence showed a high degree of localization, due to both increasing nationalistic forces, and various well-publicized advertising blunders in the 1960s (Agrawal, 1995). This trend reversed, to favour standardization, in the 1980s, and went along with a drastic rise in the number of multinational advertising agencies (Yin, 1999). During this period, a series of content analysis studies attempted to identify cross-cultural differences between Japanese and U.S. advertising (Hong et al., 1987; Madden et al., 1986; Mueller, 1987).

In the 1990s, localization seemed to remain popular among MNCs operating in various regions of world markets. Harris (1994) found that 69% of 38 MNCs (19 American and 19 European) standardized their advertising campaigns to some extent throughout the EC markets, whilst the rest of the sample localized. Interestingly, only 8% of the sample used totally standardized advertising, providing "little evidence of any widespread practice of standardized pan-European advertising campaigns" (Harris, 1994). Kanso and Nelson (2002) found that 62% of 193 firms (both American and non-American subsidiaries) in Finland and Swe-

Table 1. Descriptive statistics

	Population[1]	GDP per capita[2]	Advertising spending[3]	Advertising spending as % of GDP[4]	Internet penetration[5]	Internet household penetration[6]	No of local domains[7]	Online spending[8]	Internet Advertising spending[9]
Czech Rep.	10,288.9	73.6	769,186	0.65	50	29	1,502,537	7	22,734
Cyprus	776.0	88.9	89,073	0.54	33.6	37	75846	2	n.a.
Estonia	1,339.9	59.8	107,744	0.79	51.8	46	449,036	n.a.	3,607
Hungary	10,057.9	62.5	1,029,874	0.91	30.4	32	1,176,592	7	21,302
Latvia	3,385.7	48.6	129,961	0.81	45.2	42	132,204	1	7,277
Lithuania	2,280.5	52.1	150,07	0.50	35.9	35	240,592	2	3,086
Malta	407.7	71.7	n.a.	n.a.	33	53	20,673	n.a.	n.a.
Poland	3,8101.8	49.7	1,862,672	0.55	29.9	36	5,001,786	6	32,885
Slovakia	5,391.6	57.1	n.a.	n.a.	46.5	27	486,020	0	n.a.
Slovenia	2,010.3	81.9	242,656	0.64	55.5	54	64,284	9	5,484
EU 10	74,040.3	64.6			44	39	9,149,570		

Note: (1) Data in thousands for the 1st of January 2007 (Source, Eurostat, 2007); (2) GDP (in PPS per capita) in 2005. EU25=100% (Source: Eurostat, 2007); (3) Global advertising expenditure 2006. In US$ Thousands. Initiative Innovation (2007); (4) Initiative Innovation (2007) and The World Factbook, Central Intelligence Agency (2007); (5) Internet Usage in the European Union. Penetration (% Population) in 2007. Source: Internet World Stats (2007); (6) Percentage of households who have Internet access at home in 2006 (Source: Eurostat, 2007); (7) Number of local domains based on number of top-level domain in January 2007 (Source: ISC Internet Domain Survey, 2007); (8) The Internet turnover as percentage of the total turnover of enterprises with 10 or more employees in 2006 (Source: Eurostat, 2007), (9) Global advertising expenditure 2006. In thousands of $. Initiative Innovation (2007).

Table 2. Network and e-readiness statistics

	Networked Readiness Index [1]	Networked Readiness Index (Rank) [1]	E-readiness Rankings [2]	E-readiness Rankings, General Index [2]	E-readiness Rankings, Connectivity Index [2]	e-readiness rankings, Business Environment index [2]	Enterprises selling via Internet 2005 in % [3]	Enterprises availability of the Internet 2005 in % [3]
Czech Republic	0.36	32	32	6.14	4.90	7.39	13	92
Cyprus	0.36	33	n.a.	n.a.	n.a.	n.a.	4	85
Estonia	0.96	23	27	6.71	6.60	7.81	8	90
Hungary	0.27	37	32	6.14	4.80	7.34	4	78
Latvia	-0.03	52	39	5.30	3.95	7.21	1	75
Lithuania	0.08	44	38	5.45	4.65	7.28	6	86
Malta	0.51	30	n.a.	n.a.	n.a.	n.a.	16	90
Poland	-0.09	53	32	5.76	4.30	7.28	5	87
Slovakia	0.19	41	36	5.65	4.05	7.35	7	92
Slovenia	0.34	35	28	6.34	5.90	7.45	12	96

Note: n.a. = not available.
1. *Global Information Technology Report 2005-2006*
2. *Economist Intelligence Unit (2006).*
3. *Eurostat (2005).*

den use localization, and place a strong emphasis on local cultures. Similarly, Samiee et al. (2003) found that MNCs operating in Southeast Asia tend to localize advertising. They examined 113 firms in Hong Kong, PRC, Taiwan, and Singapore, and found that both environmental and economic factors were the primary drivers of this tendency.

Web Site Positioning as Global Information Management

Although these issues have been debated for decades in traditional media, a new stream of research has emerged recently, on the standardization versus localization of global Web sites in multiple markets. With the rapid expansion of the Internet, and the resulting connections between local, regional, and international markets, an increasing number of MNCs are shifting from offline to online marketing. This frequently entails creating a diverse range of Web sites in multiple markets (Donthu & Garcia, 1999). By 2001, more than 36 million domains for commercial Web sites already had been established: these *dot coms* are projected to attract an astonishing $6.8 trillion in business by 2004 (Forrester, 2002; Internet Software Consortium, 2001).

Such numbers incline observers to see the Internet as a door to the *global village wonderland,* as advocated by Levitt (1983): that is, an entity that creates an environment for more standardized marketing communication in world markets. Product-based Web sites are replacing such shopping venues as mail-order catalogues and television-based home shopping, and also offer a new format for global advertising among culturally and linguistically diverse groups (Pastor, 2001). An increase in the quantity and quality of product/brand information on the Internet is generating extraordinary consumer interest, which extends beyond physical and political boundaries (Donthu & Garcia, 1999). Accordingly, Roberts and Ko (2001) asserted that Web sites, with their ability to uniformly blend textual and visual content, constitute the best communication medium in which to develop brand images.

One roadblock that MNCs face involves localized Web sites: primarily, the need to satisfy the linguistic requirements of a diverse population of potential customers (Warden et al., 2002). According to Quelch and Klein (1996), establishing localized relationships with international consumers is best achieved by creating regional Web content.

However, creating regional commercial Web sites may not be cost-effective if, to elicit return visits, a company is obliged to update information continuously. Such intense Web site maintenance on a regional level can jeopardize consistent brand strategies, by eliminating the "advantage of centralized management of a firm's Web sites" (Warden et al., 2002).

In a pioneering study, Okazaki and Alonso (2002) examined Japanese Web sites in Japan, Spain, and the USA, and found that cultural dimensions (power distance, uncertainty avoidance, masculinity-femininity, individualism-collectivism, and long-term orientation) and communication style (high context vs. low context) were the primary drivers of cross-cultural differences in MNCs' Web site communication strategies. Focusing on more operational aspects, Okazaki (2005) examined American brands' Web site standardization in France, Germany, Spain, and the UK. He argued that the progress of the EU enlargement and economic integration via the euro provided firms with an incentive to use a uniform Web site communication across the EU member states. However, the findings were mixed, in that the level of standardization of American brands' Web sites in the European countries was low, compared to their respective home-country (American) Web sites. On the other hand, differences within the EU were minimal: the Web sites created within the European markets were somewhat *regionalized*, especially for durable and industrial goods.

A summary of prior research on Web site content analysis is shown in Table 3.

Communication in the Global Web Site Environment

What is the primary factor influencing MNCs that operate in European markets? They now face more and more pressure to generate more comprehensive marketing strategies on the Web. Among the various forms of the online environment, Web sites have been one of the most popular platforms, allowing consumers to see, consult, and obtain product-related information at any time, anywhere. Such Web sites can be seen as a new form of global marketing communications, offering opportunities

to strengthen effective relational marketing in international markets (Robert & Ko, 2002). The creation of a localized URL in Europe, therefore, may be a necessary strategic move, because cultural and linguistic barriers are perhaps the most difficult obstacles to overcome in marketing communications across European nations (Kahle, Beatty, & Mager, 1994). Such localization, however, could cost a great deal. Hence, MNCs may intuitively favour standardization, given the benefits associated with offline marketing standardization, such as consistent brand image and corporate identity, cost savings, and organizational control. Furthermore, Web sites seem to be an effective medium for establishing a global brand image, by offering consistent textual and visual information to international consumers.

Unfortunately, there seems to be a lack of empirical research regarding the standardization vs. localization issue in the online environment, leaving important questions unanswered.

What are the determining factors in international marketing communications on the Web? In a recent criticism of the slow progress of international advertising research, Taylor and Johnson (2001) argue that the standardization debate should "focus on what executions can be standardized and when they can be standardized." Following this suggestion, this study intends to fill this gap, by identifying to what extent MNCs have adopted a standardized approach for their Web sites created in European markets. In order to ensure cross-national data equivalency, we examined only the Web sites created by America's top brands for the UK, France, Germany, and Spain. These countries differ importantly in terms of cultural and linguistic characteristics, but are relatively homogeneous in socioeconomic conditions and technological infrastructure, and have online markets of a reasonable size.

Furthermore, 3.3%, 6.5%, and 8.1% of the world's online population consist of French-, German-, and Spanish-speaking consumers, respectively, compared to 35.2% of English speakers (Global Reach, 2003). Therefore, these four countries represent an important segment of world online consumers. On the other hand, the languages spoken in the new EU member states,

Table 3. Prior research on Web site content analysis

Year	Authors	Countries examined	Unit of analysis	Analyzed content	Sample size	Statistical design
1999	Ju-Pak	U.S., UK & S. Korea	Product-based Web sites	Information content, creative strategies, design	110 (EE.UU.) 100 (UK) 100(S. Korea)	Chi-square, ANOVA
1999	Oh, Cho & Leckenby	U.S. & S. Korea	Target ads	Information content, creative strategies	50 for each country	Chi-square
1999	Yoon & Cropp	U.S. & S. Korea	Brand Web sites	Information content, emotional appeals, cultural aspects	20 for each country	Chi-square
2000	Lee & Sego	U.S. & S. Korea	*Banners*	Information content, emotional appeals, colours, etc.	252 in total	Chi-square
2000	Chung & Ahn	U.S. & S. Korea	*Banners*	Information content, "call-to-action" messages, demographics, etc.	251 (EE.UU.) 221 (S. Korea)	Chi-square
2000	Yoon	U.S.	Product-based Web sites	Information content, celebrity endorsement, etc.	200 in total	Chi-square, ANOVA
2002	Okazaki & Alonso	Japan, Spain & EE.UU.	Product-based Web sites	Information content, cultural values, creative strategies	20 for each country	Chi-square, ANOVA
2002	Dou, Nielsen & Tan	Canada, Denmark & Malaysia	Commercial Web sites	Communication systems, transactional functions, etc.	150 for each country	ANOVA
2002	Zahir, Dobing & Hunter	26 countries	National portals	Linguistic aspects, design, colours, Hofstede's cultural dimensions, etc.	26 portals	Descriptive stat
2003	Robbins & Stylianou	16 countries	Corporate Web sites	Design, presentation, links, security, information content, financial content, corporate information, etc.	90 in total	ANOVA
2005	Okazaki	U.S., UK, France, Germany & Spain	Brand Web sites	Brand Web site functions, similarity ratings	244	ANOVA, discriminant analysis, multiple regression

such as Polish or Czech, account for a very small portion of the online population. In fact, the impact of these countries, on both the world economy and the world online population, is negligible (Table 4). Thus, an important question arises: Is it worthwhile for MNCs to consider local adaptation in such new markets? Or is it better to use a standardization approach in these markets, to take advantage of cost savings and efficient Web site maintenance? To address these questions, this study will examine Web sites created by MNCs for the Czech Republic.

CONCEPTUAL FRAMEWORK

Figure 1 shows the conceptual framework for this study. These concepts are essentially based on the matrix proposed by Quelch and Klein (1996), who suggested two primary models of a Web site: the communication model and the transaction model. Originally, their matrix was not intended to be a theoretical model for formal testing, but since then it has been used as a conceptual base (e.g., see Dou, Nielsen, & Tan, 2002). In our modified matrix, the communication and transaction feature forms two ends of one axis, which should be balanced with the other axis, consisting of fact and image. The resulting four quadrants need to be effectively combined to achieve the desired level of Web site standardization. The components in each quadrant can be considered the most relevant programmes for Web site-brand communications.

The extent of Web site standardization should be determined on the basis of the two major roles of global online programmes: (1) to enhance worldwide transactions by establishing a localized relationship, and (2) to develop a standardized brand image, using the appropriate combination of content, graphics, backgrounds, and multimedia effects in all the MNC's Web sites in different languages (Roberts & Ko, 2003). In the following section, each principal feature of our proposed model is, therefore, analyzed in the light of these perspectives.

METHODOLOGY

This study adopts content analysis as a research methodology. This method has been widely used in cross-cultural research (Brislin, 1980), as well as

Table 4. World online population and language use

Language type	Internet access [1]	% of world online pop.	Total pop. [1]	GDP [2]	% of world economy	GDP per capita [3]
English	238.5	35.2	508	n.a.	n.a.	n.a.
Non-English	439.8	64.8	5,822	n.a.	n.a.	n.a.
European Languages (non-English)	238.1	35.1	1,218	12,968	30.3	n.a.
Czech	4.0	n.a.	12	121	n.a.	10.0
Dutch	13.2	2.0	20	575	n.a.	28.5
Finnish	2.8	n.a.	6	142	n.a.	23.6
French	22.7	3.3	77	1517	4.2	19.7
German	44.4	6.5	100	2,679	5.8	26.8
Greek	2.0	n.a.	12	189	n.a.	15.8
Hungarian	1.6	n.a.	10	96	n.a.	9.6
Italian	24.1	3.6	62	1,251	3.6	20.1
Polish	6.9	n.a.	44	359	n.a.	8.1
Portuguese	19.3	2.8	176	1,487	3.6	8.4
Romanian	2.4	n.a.	26	108	n.a.	4.2
Russian	18.4	2.7	167	822	1.8	4.9
Scandinavian languages (total)	13.5	2.0	20	550	1.3	27.9
Serbo-Croatian	1.0	n.a.	20	n.a.	n.a.	n.a.
Slovak	1.0	n.a.	6	47	n.a.	8.7
Slovenian	0.7	n.a.	2	22.9	n.a.	10.9
Spanish	54.8	8.1	350	2500	8.9	7.1
Turkish	4.6	n.a.	67	431	n.a.	6.4
Ukrainian	0.9	n.a.	47	115	n.a.	2.3
TOTAL EUROPEAN LANGUAGES (non-English)	238.1	35.1	1,218	12,968	33.9	n.a.
TOTAL ASIAN LANGUAGES	201.7	29.7	n.a.	n.a.	n.a.	n.a.
TOTAL WORLD	648.7		6,330	41,400	n.a.	n.a.

Note: [1] *US$ in million;* [2] *US$ in billion,* [3] *US$ in Thousand.*
Source: Global Reach (2003)

Figure 1. Conceptualization of Web site program standardization

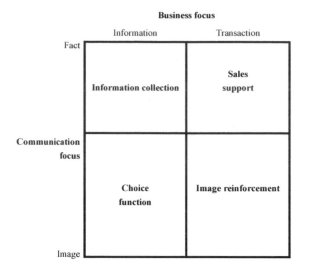

in the Internet research (McMillan, 2000; Okazaki & Alonso, 2002).

Company selection. A Web site content analysis was performed, to examine the degree of Web site standardization of American brands' Web sites created for the Czech market. Methodological recommendations from prior research were adopted, to establish a high reliability (Dou et al., 2002; Okazaki & Alonso, 2002; Philport & Arbittier, 1997). To create a dataset, a ranking of "The 100 Top Global Brands" from *BusinessWeek (2002)* was used. Only brands with America as country of origin (by the classification of *BusinessWeek*) were chosen to match home vs. host country Web site pairs. In total, 66 brands were found, of which 34 brands had Web sites in the Czech Republic. Here, it is important to note that these firms are considered as representative of American firms doing business in the Czech Republic, because their Internet presence can be considered as the initial step of market entry mode.

Coding categories. Next, a detailed coding sheet was first developed, with detailed operational definitions. The variables include (1) brand Web site functions, and (2) similarity ratings (Table 5). With regard to the former, the coding categories were adopted from Okazaki (2005), who suggested 23 Web site communication functions. Similar

categories have been suggested in the past (e.g., Ghose & Dou, 1998; Leogn, Huang, & Stanners, 1998). Each variable was measured on a categorical dichotomy as to the existence of each function on a Web site. Values of *1* and *0* were assigned for answers of *Yes* and *No*, respectively. For example, Web sites that had appropriate information associated with *job/career development* were assigned *1* for this attribute. Those that did not were assigned *0*. These values were considered dependent variables in the analysis. The similarity rating refers to the degree of similarity between home-country and host-country Web sites. This *similarity rating* measure also was adopted from Okazaki (2005), and was originally inspired by Mueller (1991). The textual and visual components of Web sites created for local markets were assessed for the extent to which they were similar or dissimilar to those created at home. The similarity rating was coded for each pair of Web sites (i.e., USA-Czech sites) on a five-point semantic scale, ranging from *very different* (coded as 1) to *very similar* (coded as 5), with an intermediate scale point *not determinable* (coded as 3). The components included copy, headlines, text, layout, colour, photographs associated with the product, with human models, and with background scenes, illustrations, charts, graphs, and interactive images.

Coding instrument. All coding instruments were originally prepared in English, and then translated into Czech, using the *back translation* technique. Each typology was supplemented with additional examples, to give a better illustration. The unit of analysis was determined as the homepage, which has been considered a central gate to Web-based communication. This is appropriate, given the primary objective of the study: to identify major differences in the main text, pictures, and graphics. We examined the first and second levels of Web sites, because it is practically impossible to scrutinize every detail of an entire site. The existence of online brand communications was primarily determined by the main menu or index provided on the homepage. For instance, if the menu included a link labelled *corporate information,* the site was coded as having this variable. The only exception occurred when analyzing direct or

Table 5. Measurement schemes

Measure	Coding categories	Scale type
Brand Web site functions	Global/Local site options, Corporate information, Corporate news release, Product/ Brand news release, General product information, Brand specific information, Investor relationships, Direct online transaction, Indirect online transaction, Office/ Store locator, Country/Language option, Search engine, Jobs/Career development, Promotion/Prizes/Sweepstakes, Education/Training, Culture/Entertainment, Client registration/Log-in, Guest book/Customer feedback, E-mail alert, FAQs, Free download, Sitemap, Links	Nominal scale (Yes=1, No=0)
Similarity ratings	Company logo, Company logo placement, Major copy, Major copy placement, Major headline, Major headline placement, Major text, Layout in top half / right half, Layout in bottom half / left half, Colour in top half / right half, Colour in bottom half / left half, Major photograph 1 (product), Major photograph 2 (human model), Major photograph 3 (background scene), Major illustrations, Major chart or graph, Interactive image 1 (flash as opening), Interactive image 2 (pop-ups), Interactive image 3 (animated banners), Interactive image 4 (layers, pop-unders, etc.)	Interval scale (1=very different, 5=very similar)

indirect online transactions, because in some cases these functions may not be listed on the main index. In this case, the coders were asked to examine the submenu of the Web sites.

Coder training and reliability. Following the recommendations by Kolbe and Burnett (1991), two bilingual Czech judges, both of whom were unaware of the purpose of the study, were hired and first trained to grasp the operational definitions of all the variables. During the training period, the coders practised independently, by examining 20 randomly chosen Web sites from non-American firms. Then, the coded results were compared, and differences were reconciled through discussion. An inter-judge reliability was calculated using the reliability index suggested by Perreault and Leigh's reliability index (I_r) (1989). Various researchers consider this estimation method to be the best among available alternatives (e.g., Kolbe & Burnett, 1991).

As Table 6 shows, the majority of the resulting indexes far exceeded a widely accepted minimum .80???, and was, thus, deemed satisfactory. It was recognized that there would be a potential loss of information in similarity evaluation between American and Czech sites, because non-native English speakers had analyzed American Web

sites. However, it was accepted that such potential bias was minimized by the coders' extensive preparation: the subjective interpretation of textual information was minimal, since the coders were responsible for examining only *major* copy, headlines, and text on the Web sites. Otherwise, they were instructed to objectively measure the similarity of non-textual information.

RESULTS

Table 7 summarizes the frequency distribution of brand Web site functions. For the sake of comparison, the information provided in Okazaki's (2005) previous exploration was used as a reference with regard to the U.S., UK, French, and German markets. This comparison should help our understanding of MNCs' Web site standardization in existing vs. new EU member states.

The Chi-square analysis detected significant differences in eight categories: global/local site options, general product information, investor relations, online purchase, e-mail contact, promotion/prizes/sweepstakes, culture/entertainment, and guest book/customer feedback. It appears that American MNCs tend to apply a different Web

Table 6. Intercoder reliability

Measure	Coding categories	Perreault & Leigh's *Ir*
Brand Web site functions	Brand-specific information	0.82
	Client registration/Log-in	0.91
	Corporate information	1.00
	Corporate news release	0.97
	Country/Language option	1.00
	Culture/Entertainment	0.97
	Direct online transaction	1.00
	Education/Training	0.94
	E-mail alert	1.00
	FAQs	1.00
	Free download	0.94
	General product information	0.97
	Global/Local site options	0.94
	Guest book/Customer feedback	1.00
	Indirect online transaction	1.00
	Investor relations	0.97
	Jobs/Career development	0.97
	Links	0.91
	Office/Store locator	1.00
	Product/Brand news release	1.00
	Promotion/Prizes/Sweepstakes	0.97
	Search engine	1.00
	Sitemap	1.00
Similarity ratings	Text	0.91
	Major photograph: product	0.75
	Major photograph: model	0.56
	Major photograph: background scene	0.92
	Major illustrations	0.82
	Major chart or graph	
	Layout in top half / right half	0.93
	Layout in bottom half / left half	0.98
	Headline placement	0.74
	Headline	0.69
	Copy placement	0.73
	Copy	0.91
	Company logo placement	0.95
	Company logo	0.96
	Colour in top half / right half	0.93
	Colour in bottom half / left half	0.91

site communication strategy in the Czech market because, in prior research, Okazaki (2005) found significant differences in only 3 of 23 variables, suggesting that the frequency of the usage of brand Web site functions in the UK, France, Germany, and Spain was relatively uniform. In observing the frequencies of brand Web site functions in the Czech sites, e-mail contact was used more frequently, but the other tools were used much less frequently than in the other markets.

Next, in order to capture the relationships between the brand Web site functions and country domain, we performed a multiple correspondence analysis via optimal scaling technique. This method is appropriate for nominal variables, from which a multidimensional map can be created. We used the existence of the brand Web site functions (yes or no) as descriptive variables, and the type of country domain (USA or Czech Republic) as classification variables. Figure 2 shows the resulting biplot

Table 7. Results of brand Web site functions

1. Brand Web site features	US (n=66)	UK (n=57)	France (n=49)	Germany (n=57)	**Czech (n=34)**	*p*
Global/Local site options	37.9	84.2	65.3	75.4	**64.4**	.000
Corporate information	89.4	86.0	87.8	84.2	**86.1**	.956
Corporate news release	53.0	54.4	55.1	59.6	**55.6**	.983
Product/Brand news release	51.5	49.1	53.1	52.6	**55.6**	.990
General product information	80.3	84.2	83.7	78.9	**47.2**	.000
Brand-specific information	75.8	68.4	73.5	68.4	**69.4**	.858
Investor relationships	45.5	26.3	16.3	22.8	**11.1**	.001
Online purchase	71.2	42.1	42.6	43.9	**25.0**	.000
E-mail contact	22.7	31.6	28.6	24.6	**77.8**	.000
Office/Store locator	33.3	33.3	32.7	26.3	**13.9**	.346
Country/Language option	62.1	57.9	71.4	61.4	**52.8**	.536
Search engine	68.2	57.9	55.1	50.9	**52.8**	.442
Jobs/Career development	62.1	47.4	46.9	54.4	**61.1**	.374
Promotion/Prizes/Sweepstakes	56.1	63.2	44.9	47.4	**11.1**	.000
Education/Training	39.4	33.3	26.5	24.6	**25.0**	.331
Culture/Entertainment	47.0	57.9	53.1	42.1	**13.9**	.001
Client registration/Log-in	51.5	36.8	38.8	36.8	**41.7**	.398
Guest book/Customer feedback	78.8	82.5	75.5	77.2	**22.2**	.000
E-mail alert	25.8	15.8	20.4	19.3	**25.0**	.483
FAQs	18.2	22.8	16.3	19.3	**8.3**	.647
Free download	19.7	26.3	26.5	28.1	**36.1**	.643
Sitemap	45.5	42.1	44.9	36.8	**38.9**	.905
Links	4.5	12.3	8.2	3.5	**19.4**	.053

Note: The data of the U.S., UK, France and Germany are based on Okazaki (2005)

component loadings. As clearly seen, the majority of brand Web site functions are more closely associated with U.S. sites (represented by *1*), while only a limited number of brand Web site functions are associated with Czech sites (represented by *2*). Specifically, global/local site options, links, and indirect online transactions are concentrated in the lower-left quadrant (which U.S. sites appear to dominate), but the rest of the brand Web site functions are concentrated in the upper-right quadrant (where Czech sites appear to dominate).

Lastly, Table 8 summarizes the results of the similarity ratings. A higher similarity rating indicates a higher degree of standardization. As the results clearly show, the similarity between the American and Czech sites was notably higher, especially in logo, copy, and colour. In comparison with the other sites, headlines and major photographs also exhibit higher similarity. On this basis, it appears clear that the American MNCs tend to create highly standardized Web sites in the Czech Republic.

DISCUSSION

This study attempts to examine the Web site communication strategy used by American MNCs in a new EU member state, the Czech Republic. We performed a content analysis of 34 Czech sites created by America's top brands in terms of brand Web site functions, and similarity between the home and host sites. The findings indicate that American MNCs appear to standardize their Czech sites. Given that the Czech Republic is a growing market that attracts more and more foreign direct investment, this case could be considered indicative of the general tendency in the other new EU member states.

First, American MNCs tend to use general product information less frequently in the Czech market than in the other EU markets, which suggests two possible scenarios. First, they have not yet commercialized their products in this market, and, therefore, dispose of little information. In this case, the primary objective of their Web sites would

Figure 2. Multiple correspondence analysis

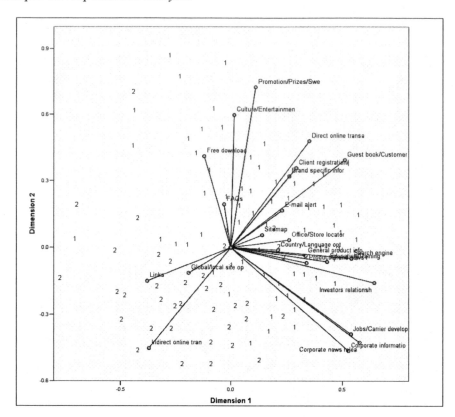

Note: Varimax principal normalization method. 1 = USA, 2 = Czech Republic

Table 8. Results of similarity ratings

Components	UK (n=57)	France (n=49)	Germany (n=57)	**Czech (n=34)**
Company logo	4.51	4.61	4.39	**4.58**
Major copy	1.43	1.36	1.14	**4.00**
Major headline	1.23	1.17	1.02	**3.47**
Major text	2.84	2.53	2.68	**2.32**
Layout	3.35	3.32	3.29	**3.88**

be to provide a preliminary information platform in a new market. Second, they might have needed to localize product information to a great extent, especially in the local language, with more adapted product usage. However, it appears that the most logical conclusion would be that the lack of online product information is because American firms are still in the very early mode of market entry in the Czech Republic.

The second scenario seems very unlikely when we address the following question: Why would large multinational firms devote resources to extensive adaptations of Czech Web sites? The country's population is only 10 million and, according to the most recent Eurostat (2006), only 19% of Czech homes had Internet access in 2005, including 5% with broadband connections. As much as 63% of the population has never used the Internet. Only one in six people who used the Internet (5.5%) bought anything online in 2005, and these purchases were limited largely to electronic goods (2.1%), books (1.6%), and clothing (1.1%). Therefore, if the total market in a given product category is currently only 100,000 or so, and if adapting the Web site is only going to improve Web site effectiveness by 5% to 10%, is there any incentive to adapt and then to continue managing that adaptation? Consistent with this argument, our findings indicate that online purchase functions are rarely used in the Czech sites. This suggests that American MNCs may have neither distribution channels nor local investors in the Czech market. Similarly, the much less frequent use of guest book/ customer feedback indicates that American brands are less willing to offer personalized contact to the local Czech consumers, probably because of the unavailability of local outlets, representatives, or staff. In contrast, in the Czech Republic, they offer general e-mail addresses more frequently than in the other countries, as an alternative contact mode for general inquiries.

Third, by the same token, culture/entertainment and promotion/prices/sweepstakes are used much less in the Czech market than in the others, because these elements need to be matched to local consumer tastes, and require more personalized content. It would make little sense to offer presents or incentives when the companies actually have no local sales activities.

Finally, a surprisingly high level of similarity ratings for both textual and visual components indicates a lack of any cultural adaptation of Web sites to the Czech market. This contrasts with Okazaki's (2005) findings regarding American MNCs' Web site strategy in the UK, France, Germany, and Spain, where clearly localized Web sites have been created in the existing EU member states. This finding is consistent with the frequency of brand Web site functions: the Czech sites use far fewer brand Web site functions with highly standardized textual and visual components.

It is clear that American MNCs consider the EU a single market, and one that is strategically dissimilar to their home market. If we observe only the Web sites created in the *older* member states,

there seems to exist a *regionalization* strategy across Europe, in that the level of similarity ratings among the European samples was relatively uniform. This may be due to the close geographical proximity of the three countries, which would, logically, provide more opportunities for personal interaction and the accumulation of greater knowledge. However, in the case of the Czech Republic, Web site adaptation has not yet advanced, probably due to many unknown factors: in particular, specific information regarding local consumers' tastes and preferences.

Limitations

While this study makes significant contributions to the global information management literature, some important limitations also must be recognized. First, content analysis is, by definition, an observational method that examines only manifest content. Our findings have little or nothing to do with marketers' *true* intentions on global Web site positioning. Second, our unit of analysis was limited to the menu and submenu of the homepages. In this regard, it will be interesting to extend this study in the future, by conducting a questionaire survey of advertisers and marketers who actually are responsible for the new EU member states. However, it is possible that a more localized strategy might have been observed in further links. Finally, we examined only one of the new EU member states, thus, any generalization of our findings should be treated with caution.

Future research should expand this study into other new EU member states, especially Poland and Hungary, these two countries, along with Czech Republic, are the most economically developed regions. Because of the extreme scarcity of research related to these countries, any such extension will contribute significantly to the literature.

FUTURE RESEARCH DIRECTIONS

First, future extensions should examine Web sites created for the other new EU member states, such as Poland, Hungary, Latvia, Lithuania, and Malta.

Information technology management for Web site positioning in these countries is virtually unknown, and analyzing brands' Web sites positioning in these countries should help us to draw more generalisable implications. In particular, researchers are planning to examine Polish and Hungarian Web sites in the next stage because, in these countries, the total online, as well as offline advertising spending, is substantial, in comparison with the other new EU member sates.

Second, in furthering our explorations, content analysis methodology should be improved. Specifically, we need to examine the level of standardization or localization at deeper levels of Web sites. While this study scrutinized the first level of Web sites or homepages, some may claim that much information was lost by ignoring the second and third levels of Web sites. For example, the lack of direct online transactions need not necessarily mean that the Web site does not have a link to the online shopping sites of different companies. This was the case for consumer electronics, in that computer or office machine products are sold on *general* e-commerce (or even auction) sites. More specific coding instructions should be established, to enable the coders to improve their analysis with a higher level of inter-coder reliability.

Third, we also should conduct a survey that targets foreign subsidiaries' managers. It will be interesting to compare the findings of this study with the managers' perceptions. In particular, several questions appear of special interest. For example, are their Web sites created or controlled locally or globally? What level of control do senior executives of foreign subsidiaries actually have of their electronic commerce planning and executions?

Finally, in an attempt to capture a clearer picture of global Web site positioning in multiple markets, more collaboration will be needed by researchers in information systems management and other disciplines, in particular, marketing management. Needless to say, a higher level of international co-operation is necessary to conduct more objective and reliable data collection in multiple markets.

REFERENCES

Agora (2005). *Advertising market*. Available http://www.agora.pl/agora_eng/1,60209,2385752.html?menu=7

Agrawal, M. (1995). Review of a 40-year debate in international advertising. *International Marketing Review, 12*(1), 26-48.

ARBOmedia (2005). *Standardní reklamní rok přinese médiím 17,8 miliard.* Available: http://www.arbomedia.cz/strany/ipwc/w2a.asp?id=133

Brislin, R. W. (1980). Translation and content analysis of oral and written material. In H. C. Triandis & J. W. Berry (Eds.), *Handbook of cross-cultural psychology* (Vol. 2, pp. 389-444). Boston: Allyn and Bacon.

Budapest Business Journal (2003). Web-based advertising making ground. September 16, 2003, from http://www.bbj.hu

Budapest Business Journal (2004). Online advertising boom August 18, 2004. Available http://www.bbj.hu

BusinessWeek (2002). *The 100 top brands.* August 5, 95-99.

Czech Publishers Association (2006). *Internetová reklama v roce 2005 přesáhla 1 miliardu Kč.* Press release, Available: http://www.unievydavatelu.cz

Czech Statistical Office (2006). *The survey on ICT usage in households and by individuals in the Czech Republic in 2006* (in Czech).

Donthu, N., & Garcia, A. (1999). The Internet shopper. *Journal of Advertising Research, 39*(5), 52-58.

Dou, W., Nielsen, U. O., & Tan, C. M. (2002). Using corporate Web sites for exporting marketing. *Journal of Advertising Research, 42*(5), 105-115.

Economist Intelligence Unit (2006), *The 2006 e-readiness rankings.*

Elinder, E. (1961). How international can advertising be? In S. W. Dunn (Ed.), *International handbook of advertising* (pp. 59-71). NY: McGraw-Hill.

Eurostat (2005). *Europe in figures: Eurostat yearbook 2005.*

Eurostat (2006). *Community survey on ICT usage in households and by individuals.*

Forrester (2002). *Forrester's global e-commerce predictions for 2004.* Available http://www.forrester.com/home/0,6092,1-0,FF.html

GfK (2006). *Increasingly more kids use the Internet. One in three Polish Internet users willing to buy music on the Internet.* Press release. Available http://www.gfk.pl/podstrona.php?page=/page.php?id=630&ltr=

Ghose, S., & Dou, W. (1998). Interactive functions and their impacts on the appeal of Internet presence sites. *Journal of Advertising Research, 38*(2), 29-43.

Harris, G. (1994). International advertising standardization: What do the multinationals actually standardize? *Journal of International Marketing, 2*(4), 13-30.

Hong, J. W., Muderrisoglu, A., & Zinkhan, G. M. (1987). Cultural differences and advertising expression: a comparative content analysis of Japanese and U.S. magazine advertising. *Journal of Advertising, 16*(1), 55-62, 68.

Internet Software Consortium (2001), *Distribution of top-level domain names by host count (July 2002).* Online: http://www.isc.org/ds/WWW-200207/dist-bynum.html

Jain, S. C. (1989). Standardization of international marketing strategy: Some research hypotheses. *Journal of Marketing, 53*(January), 70-79.

Ju-Pak, K. H. (1999). Content dimensions of Web advertising: a cross-national comparison. *International Journal of Advertising, 18*(2), 207-231.

Kanso, A., & Nelson, R. A. (2002). Advertising localization overshadows a standardization. *Journal of Advertising Research, 42*(1), 79-89.

Kolbe, R. H., & M. S. Burnett (1991). Content-analysis research: An examination of applications with directives for improving research reliability and objectivity. *Journal of Consumer Research, 18*(September), 243-250.

Koudelova, R., & Whitelock, J. (2001). A cross-cultural analysis of television advertising in the UK and the Czech Republic. *International Marketing Review, 18*(3), 286-300.

Leong, E. K. F., Huang, X., & Stanners, P. J. (1998). Comparing the effectiveness of the Web site with traditional media. *Journal of Advertising Research, 38*(5), 44-51.

Levitt, T. (1983). The globalization of market. *Harvard Business Review, 61*(May/June), 92-102.

Mackay, S. (2004). Parliament approves new government. *Executive Perspectives: Poland, Price Waterhouse Coopers.* Available http://www.pwcglobal.com/

Madden, C. S., Caballero, M. J., & Matsukubo, S. (1986). Analysis of information content in U.S. and Japanese magazine advertising. *Journal of Advertising, 15*(3), 38-45.

McMillan, S. J. (2000). The microscope and the moving target: The challenge of applying content analysis to the World Wide Web. *Journalism and Mass Communication Quarterly, 77*(1), 80-98.

Mueller, B. (1991). An analysis of information content in standardized vs. specialized multinational advertisements. *Journal of International Business Studies,* First Quarter, 23-39.

OBP (2001). *Advertising in Poland.* Available http://www.obp.pl/03-raport/2001/advertising_in_poland.htm

Oh, K. W., Cho, C. H., & Leckenby, J. D. (1999). A comparative analysis of Korean and U.S. Web advertising. *Proceedings of the 1999 Conference of the American Academy of Advertising* (pp. 73-77). Gainesville: University of Florida.

Okazaki, S. (2005). Searching the Web for global brands: How American brands standardise their

Web sites in Europe. *European Journal of Marketing, 39*(1/2), 87-109.

Okazaki, S., & Alonso, J. (2002). A content analysis of Web communication strategies: Cross-cultural research framework and pre-testing. *Internet Research: Electronic Networking, Applications and Policy, 12*(5), 380-390.

OMD Czech (2005). Odhady reklamních výdajů. Available http://www2.omd.com/OMDOffice/section/subsection.asp?CompanyID=9&SubSectionID=105

Onkvisit, S., & Shaw, J. J. (1987). Standardized international advertising: A review and critical evaluation of the theoretical and empirical evidence. *The Columbia Journal of World Business, 22*(Fall), 43-55.

Perreault, W. D., & Leigh, L. E. (1989). Reliability of nominal data based on qualitative judgments. *Journal of Marketing Research, 26*(May), 135-148.

Philport, J. C., & Arbittier, J. (1997). Advertising: Brand communications styles in established media and the Internet. *Journal of Advertising Research, 37*(2), 68-76.

Quelch, J. A., & Klein, L. R. (1996). The Internet and international marketing. *Sloan Management Review, 38*(Spring), 60-75.

Roberts, M. S., & Ko, H. (2001). Global interactive advertising: Defining what we mean and using what we have lLearned. *Journal of Interactive Advertising, 1*(2). Online http://www.jiad.org/vol1/no2/roberts/index.html

Root, F. R. (1994), *Entry strategies for international markets.* Heath, Washington DC: Lexington.

Sheram, K. & Tatyana P. Soubbotina (2000). *Beyond economic growth: Meeting the challenges of global development,* Washington DC: World Bank.

Synodinos, N., Keown, C., & Jacobs, L. (1989) Transitional advertising practices: A survey of leading brand advertisers. *Journal of Advertising Research, 29*(2), 43-50.

Taylor, C. R., Bonner, G. P., & Dolezal, M. (2002). Advertising in the Czech Republic: Czech perceptions of effective advertising and advertising clutter. In Charles R. Taylor (Ed.), *New direction in international advertising research* (Vol 12, pp. 137-149). San Diego, CA: Elsevier.

Taylor, C. R., & Johnson, C. M. (2002). Standardized vs. specialized international advertising campaigns: What we have learned from academic research in the 1990s. *New Directions in International Advertising Research, 12,* 45-66.

TNS Factum (2004). *Firemní weby a marketing.* Available http://www.factum.cz/tz93.html

TNS Factum (2005). *Češi a reklama v roce 2004.* Available http:// www.factum.cz/tz124.html

Unie vydavatelů (2005). *Internetová reklama v roce 2004 dosáhla 760 milionů Kč.* Available http://www.uvdt.cz/download.aspx?id_file=209

van REPEN, Erica, Rik Pieters, Jana Fidrmucova and Peter Roosenboom (2000). The Information Content of Magazine Advertising in Market and Transition Economies. *Journal of Consumer Policy, 23,* 257-283

West, D. C., & Paliwoda, S. J. (1996). Advertising adoption in a developing market economy: The case of Poland. *International Marketing Review, 13*(4), 82-101.

World Advertising Resource Center (WARC) (2004). *European marketing pocket book.*

Zandpour, F., Campos, V., Catalano, J., Chang, C., Cho, Y.D., Hoobyar, R., et al. (1994). Global reach and local touch: Achieving cultural fitness in TV advertising. *Journal of Advertising Research, 34*(5), 35-63.

Zenith Optimedia (2004). *Poland's advertising market in 2004.* Available http://www.eniro.com/AR/EN/2004/filter.asp?filename=eniro04_016.html

ADDITIONAL READING

Batra, R., Myers, J. G., & Aaker, D. A. (1996). *Advertising management.* Englewood Cliffs, NJ: Prentice Hall.

De Mooij, M. (1998). *Global marketing and advertising: Understanding cultural paradox.* Thousand Oaks, CA: Sage.

Duncan, T., & Ramaprasad, J. (1995). Standardized multinational advertising: The influencing factors. *Journal of Advertising, 24*(3), 55-67.

Ghose, S., & Dou, W. (1998). Interactive functions and their impacts on the appeal of Internet presence sites. *Journal of Advertising Research, 38*(3), 29-43.

Ha, L., & James, E. L. (1998). Interactivity re-examined: A baseline analysis of early business Web sites. *Journal of Broadcasting and Electronic Media, 42*(4), 457-469.

Hwang, J. S., McMillan, S. J., & Lee, G. (2003). Corporate Web sites as advertising: An analysis of function, audience, and message strategy. *Journal of Interactive Advertising, 3*(2). Available http://jiad.org/vol3/no2/mcmillan/index.htm

Jain, S. (1989). Standardization of international marketing strategy: Some research hypotheses. *Journal of Marketing, 53*(1), 70-79.

Krippendorff, K. (1980). *Content analysis: An introduction to its methodology.* Newbury Park, CA: Sage Publications.

Laroche, M., Kirpalani, V. H., Pens, F., & Zhou, L. (2001). A model of advertising standardization in multinational corporations. *Journal of International Business Studies, 32*(2), 250-65.

Lynch, P. D., Kent, R. J., & Srinivasan, S. S. (2001). The global Internet shopper: Evidence from shopping tasks in twelve countries. *Journal of Advertising Research, 41*(3), 15-22.

Okazaki, S., & Alonso, J. (2003). Beyond the net: Cultural values reflected in Japanese multinationals' Web communication strategies. *Journal of International Consumer Marketing, 16*(1), 47-70.

Okazaki, S., & Alonso, J. (2003). Right messages at the right site: On-line creative strategies by Japanese multinational corporations. *Journal of Marketing Communications, 9*(4), 221-239.

Okazaki, S. (2004). Do multinationals standardise or localise? The cross-cultural dimensionality of product-based Web sites. *Internet Research: Electronic Networking, Applications and Policy, 14*(1), 81-94.

Tharp, M., & Jeong, J. (2001). Executive insights: The global network communications agency. *Journal of International Marketing, 9*(4), 111-131.

Warden, C. A., Lai, M., & Wu, W. Y. (2003). How world-wide is marketing communication on the World Wide Web? *Journal of Advertising Research, 43*(5), 72-84.

Chapter VI
Beyond Localization:
A New Look at Disseminating Information via the Web

Martin A. Schell
New York University, USA

ABSTRACT

Localization of a document requires tacit knowledge of the target language and culture. Although it is promoted by many software developers and Web designers, localization is becoming increasingly inadequate as a strategy for disseminating information via the World Wide Web. The 21st century has already seen dramatic rises in the numbers of Internet users in nearly every country, making it difficult, if not impossible, for any translation effort to accommodate all of the 347 languages that claim at least 1 million speakers. The best way to expand the accessibility of Web content is to make it more explicit, not more tacit. This means producing and uploading clear English content that nonnative speakers can easily understand. Global English is written with simpler sentence structure, less jargon, and no slang—characteristics that make it a viable lingua franca for countless Web users whose native language is not considered important enough to merit a localization effort.

INTRODUCTION

The implementation of information technology (IT) worldwide has made huge strides in the first years of the 21st century. One milestone is that the number of people who access the Internet surpassed 1 billion by the end of 2005. As the development of IT impacts more of humanity, there is an increasing need for the development of human infrastructure, especially the ability to express oneself clearly to audiences who do not share one's cultural background.

During the past decade or two, the conventional wisdom has been that teams of translators should be summoned to render user guides, help files, Web pages, and other documents into selected languages. Ideally, content should not only be translated, but also attuned to tacit aspects of the target language that reflect the local culture of the end users. In other words, the document should be localized.

Although localization is still essential in marketing, the author challenges the assumption that all Web documents "need" to be localized in order to maximize global availability. As more and more people come online in countries that speak "minor" languages, the task of disseminating information in translated form becomes increasingly complex. One must either continually add new languages to the company repertoire, or else abandon increasingly large segments of the world's population who are not native speakers of any of the languages chosen for localization efforts.

The author does not propose that localization efforts should be relinquished; rather, the paradigm for maximizing global access to a Web site needs to be shifted. The first step is to recognize localization's declining ability to cover a Web that is populated by increasing numbers of speakers of ever more diverse languages. After we see the limits of localization as a 21st century strategy, we can take a fresh look at alternatives. The author believes that a comprehensive approach to disseminating information globally must include English-language content that is accessible to a wide range of user fluency.

This chapter explains why and how English should be written more clearly so that it can function better as a global language, not only between native and nonnative speakers but also between nonnative speakers from diverse linguistic backgrounds. The explanation extends into a discussion of how to improve Web page design by considering infrastructure logistics and cultural preferences, which impact decisions about content because they are facets of the larger question of global access. The chapter aims to show how *Global English* can facilitate the sharing of knowledge via the World Wide Web, enabling the medium to benefit more of humanity.

BACKGROUND CONCEPTS

When a child learns to tie shoelaces, or another routine task that we adults take for granted, he or she acquires a skill that is rarely, if ever, learned through words, images, or a combination of both. Such *tacit knowledge* is contrasted with *explicit knowledge* (Nonaka & Takeuchi, 1995, p. 8), *focal knowledge* (Sveiby, 1997), *codified knowledge* (Stiglitz, 1999, p. 11), or *formal knowledge* (Jarboe, 2001, p. 2). All four expressions of this fundamental dichotomy in human knowing derive from the theories of Polanyi (1962, 1966).

Tacit knowledge can be defined as knowledge that is demonstrated but not explained; it is absorbed rather than grasped. It is often acquired through learning by doing which, as Jarboe (2001) notes, is facilitated by the "web of relationships and connections" that constitutes social capital (p. 3). Such learning involves imitating other people—not only family, friends, and coworkers, but also strangers within one's community. An example would be people in a mall reinforcing a child's ability to get on an escalator without hesitating. Learning by doing also happens without guidance, which is how most video games and computer simulations are played.

In *Aspects of the Theory of Syntax*, Chomsky (1969) tells how native speakers tacitly understand their own language in ways that they often cannot explain:

Obviously, every speaker of a language has mastered and internalized a generative grammar that expresses his knowledge of his language. This is not to say that he is aware of the rules of the grammar or even that he can become aware of them, or that his statements about his intuitive knowledge of the language are necessarily accurate. Any interesting generative grammar will be dealing, for the most part, with mental processes that are far beyond the level of actual or even potential consciousness; furthermore, it is quite apparent that a speaker's reports and viewpoints about his behavior and his competence may be in error. Thus a generative grammar attempts to specify what the speaker actually knows, not what he may report about his knowledge. (p. 8)

For example, people who are fluent in English know that *I saw a big black horse* is correct but *I saw a black big horse* is incorrect. If a student of English as a foreign language (EFL) asks a native speaker why the second sentence is wrong, the latter will realize how difficult it is to turn syntax into explicit knowledge. He or she may even devise an erroneous rule such as "The color adjective always comes last," which fits *long brown hair* but not *blue suede shoes.*

Sveiby (1997) notes that we can recall the meaning of a message after reading it, but we rarely remember its exact words. He explains:

The focal and tacit dimensions are complementary. The tacit knowledge functions as a background knowledge which assists in accomplishing a task which is in focus. That which is tacit varies from one situation to another. For instance, when reading a text, words and linguistic rules function as tacit subsidiary knowledge while the attention of the reader is focused on the meaning of the text. (Tacit and Focal Knowledge section, para. 2)

With a moment's effort, someone who is literate can shift between subsidiary awareness and focal awareness while reading. This happens when an unfamiliar word catches one's attention, prompting a pause in order to look it up in a dictionary; alternatively, one can simply stare at an individual word, letter, or numeral. The process of learning to read requires familiarizing oneself with the shapes of characters and then recognizing combinations as words until one achieves the ability to scan a sentence without focusing on its component letters. Becoming literate involves converting explicit knowledge into tacit knowledge, a process that Nonaka and Takeuchi (1995) call *internalization* in their socialization, externalization, combination, and internalization (SECI) model (pp. 62-70).

Tacit knowledge has been defined in diverse ways in knowledge management (KM) literature (Sveiby, 2001). Nevertheless, there is general agreement that a major goal of KM programs is to convert tacit knowledge into explicit knowledge in order to share it throughout an organization. Nonaka and Takeuchi (1995) call this type of conversion *externalization* and consider it to be the key to knowledge creation. Examples of articulating tacit knowledge into explicit knowledge include drawing a map to guide a guest to one's home, or telling an audience how to sell successfully.

Unfortunately, there is a tendency in the field of KM to conflate *unarticulated* with *hidden*, as Jarboe (2001) does when he exhorts economic development organizations to use "knowledge creation tools" that can "capture ... knowledge hidden within the organization" (p. 2). However, the act of uncovering a seed of knowledge which can be disseminated does not prove that the knowledge was tacit. Suppose a project leader discovers that a team in another department recently developed software which can expedite the leader's project. The project leader will rejoice in finding a hidden resource (hidden from his or her viewpoint, that is), but the team who coded the software already articulated the underlying ideas into explicit knowledge. This type of "discovery" is a good example of networking, but not knowledge creation; Nonaka and Takeuchi (1995) would label it *combination*.

Tacit knowledge can be disseminated widely by *socialization* (Nonaka & Takeuchi, 1995) without ever being articulated into explicit form. For example, orchids in Southeast Asia are usually grown on a base of charcoal. Perhaps this technique was discovered accidentally by someone in Thailand, which has long been famous for its orchids. Countless amateur horticulturists adopted the technique by imitation without ever receiving an explanation about why charcoal is better than soil. An explicit reason could be codified or formalized by a botanist, but it is not essential for the propagation of the idea.

DATA AND INFORMATION

As NCR Corporation's overseas market expanded in the 1970s, their headquarters began receiving complaints from customer support representatives about confusing terminology that contributed to mistaken translations of end-user manuals. NCR management accumulated the complaints and assigned a senior technical writer, Charles "Ted" Brusaw, to look for patterns and develop guidelines.

Brusaw (1978) traced the translation errors to misunderstandings caused by word choice in the original English document. His team identified a large number of common English words that have multiple meanings which are tacitly understood by native speakers but can easily confuse nonnative speakers. They compiled the *NCR Fundamental English Dictionary*, consisting of 1175 clearly defined root words printed in boldface plus hundreds of problematic words interspersed alphabetically in regular font (each followed by a recommended substitute in parentheses).

Although NCR's database about vocabulary problems predated the concept of KM, one could say that their knowledge repository belonged to the *IT track* in the KM model formulated by Sveiby (2001). The information technology track is characterized by seeing knowledge as quantifiable objects (e.g., a list of specific words that have been mistranslated), in contrast to the *people track*, which looks at knowledge as processes (e.g., general awareness of how ambiguity results in mistranslation).

Sveiby (2001) emphasizes the differences between the two tracks in order to encourage investment in intangible assets, especially human infrastructure, but the two orientations are complementary. In the NCR case, the back-and-forth flow went like this: Accumulation of specific mistranslation incidents led to an awareness of general patterns, which led to the production of a list in a tangible book, which was distributed to employees as an informal training tool to increase their awareness.

An underlying assumption in the collection and transmission of data is that it is worth retaining and distributing. This point is often articulated by recalling the maxim *garbage in, garbage out* (GIGO): "If invalid data is entered into a system, the resulting output will also be invalid. Although originally applied to computer software, the axiom holds true for all systems, including, for example, decision-making systems" (Jupitermedia, 2001). It is essential to have confidence that one's data is reliable.

Completeness is a key aspect of data integrity, but it can be a drawback at the level of information. A Web site that has dozens or hundreds of links can be time-consuming or even bewildering to navigate. It can become a source of frustration if many of the links lead to sites that do nothing more than list links. As Jarboe (2001) notes, "There is an enormous need to be able to quickly distinguish between what information is relevant and what is irrelevant" (p. 2).

The remainder of this chapter challenges some IT-track ideas about the production of documents, especially Web content. Respective sections address how assumptions about language, infrastructure, and culture impact the dissemination of information. The author offers suggestions for expanding one's awareness to a global perspective, which will facilitate the reader's efforts to make his or her information available to everyone on our planet.

THE LIMITS OF LOCALIZATION

Web sites that aim for multinational audiences often *localize* their content by translating it into languages spoken by major groups of Internet users: Spanish, Chinese, Russian, and so forth. The Localization Industry Standards Association (LISA, 2005) defines *localization* as "taking a product and making it linguistically and culturally appropriate to the target locale (country/region and language) where it will be used and sold."

LISA's inclusion of the words *product* and *sold* focuses their definition on user guides and marketing materials rather than Web content or information in general. As the president of a Web translation agency, Hopkins (2002) agrees with the principle of multilingual sites. However, he recognizes that localization is not needed on every page because most Web content is global information that can simply be translated directly without adapting it to the audience's culture (What is a Multilingual Web site? section, para. 3).

Localizing each page of a Web site is not only *too much* in terms of translator effort and expense but also *too little* in terms of the variety of potential users. By itself, localization can never succeed in reaching a global audience because its purpose is to serve specific groups of users. Adding up a handful of regional groups—or even a few dozen local groups—does not equal a worldwide audience.

Although straight translation is simpler and cheaper than localization, it is still incomplete as a global strategy. There are 6,912 living languages, including 347 that have over 1 million speakers each (Gordon, 2005c). It is not feasible to translate content into all of them. How often do you see sites that offer the option of viewing pages in Bengali, Marathi, Telugu, or Vietnamese, each of which has over 60 million native speakers (Gordon, 2005a)?

A common explanation for excluding languages from Web site localization efforts is that they are spoken in areas that "do not have enough users to make localization worthwhile" (Nielsen, 1999, p. 315). However, the world's Internet users more than tripled during the first six years of this millennium: from 361 million at the start of 2001 to 1,244 million at the end of September 2007. Dramatic increases occurred on every continent, ranging from 117% in North America to 875% in Africa. Among the world's 10 most populous countries, the amounts of increase during this six-year period were: 620% in China, 1100% in India, 121% in the U.S., 900% in Indonesia, 683% in Brazil, 8862% in Pakistan, 3900% in Nigeria, 803% in Russia, 350% in Bangladesh, and 86% in Japan (Internet World Stats, 2007c).

The rapid increases in Internet penetration worldwide imply that localization is only a short-term strategy for global dissemination, because its coverage of the world's online population will become less complete as time goes on. The number of Internet users who speak "minor" languages is rising, increasing the complexity and cost of a comprehensive localization effort. In 2007, Internet penetration reached 33.1% in Romania (September),

25.6% in Iran (August), 20.3% in Vietnam (August), and 12.1% in Ukraine (August). Before the end of 2006, Poland had achieved 29.9% (October) and Turkey 21.1% (September), according to Internet World Stats (2007c). Each of these six "minor" countries has a national language that is spoken by over 20 million people (Gordon, 2005a).

In developing countries, many people who lack a computer at home access the Internet at cybercafes. The sharing of hardware is analogous to older forms of pass-around readership, such as joining a library or renting a video. Statistics about total Internet users in these countries are often based on multiplying the number of Internet Service Provider (ISP) accounts by a sharing factor.[1] Because each sharing factor is only an estimate, user totals should be viewed with a fair amount of skepticism.

It is also important to compare countries at the same point in time. The growth of Internet penetration by 200% (i.e., tripling) during a six-year period is equivalent to a steady rise of about 5% during each of the 24 quarters. Therefore a table that cites surveys that were done at different times of year creates unreliable information due to the inconsistent basis of comparison. As writers, we should take care to represent data faithfully, because inaccuracies are likely to be echoed by our readers.

The shortage of Web pages in many languages is obvious to people who are native speakers of those languages. If a Web site does not consider their language important enough to merit localization, users are likely to access the English version of the site. At cybercafes in Indonesia, for example, someone whose English is fluent enough to comprehend Web pages in that language will sit next to a friend who is surfing and provide impromptu translation.

In addition, there is evidence that people who speak English as a second language often choose the English version, even though the Web site offers pages in their native language. A survey conducted by Research & Research found that 8% of Hispanic American Internet users prefer Spanish-language Web sites but 41% prefer English-language sites. The remaining 51% said they are bilingual and view Web content in either English or Spanish. In other words, 92% of Hispanic American Internet users are comfortable with English-language Web sites, despite the fact that 63% of this market segment were born outside the United States (Romney, 2000).

A United States Census 2000 brief (Shin, 2003) lists the 20 most commonly spoken languages other than English in 1990 and 2000. The category "all other languages" accounted for about 10% of "total non-English" in both years, increasing to 1.7% of the total U.S. population in 2000 (p. 4, Table 1). Therefore, a localization effort that includes the top 20 languages would exclude about 4.5 million speakers of "all other languages" (1.6 million of whom speak English less than "very well").

The incompleteness of localization is even more apparent in the global arena: Translating a document into each of the 83 languages that has more than 10 million speakers would fail to serve 20.5% of the world's population (Gordon, 2005c). In terms of Internet users, 15.0% would be neglected by a localization effort involving all of the top 10 languages spoken by the online population (Internet World Stats, 2007b). Clearly, the use of a global language is an essential part of worldwide outreach.

USING ENGLISH AS A GLOBAL LANGUAGE

LISA (2005) defines *internationalization* as "generalizing a product so that it can handle multiple languages and cultural conventions without the need for redesign" and calls the process the "forerunner of localization" (question 3) because internationalization is often implemented by editing a document before translation. Another way to express the complementarity is to say that internationalization aims to make text as explicit as possible for a global audience, while localization aims to evoke a local audience's empathy by appealing to tacit aspects of their culture.

In *The Future of English?* Graddol (2000) discusses the use of English as a global language. He lists 12 "major international domains of English" including international organizations and conferences, scientific and technical publications, global advertising and mass culture, aviation and maritime communications, international tourism, universities, and the Internet (p. 8, Table 2). More than 60 countries publish at least some of their books in English (p. 9, Figure 2).

The global presence of English suggests that producing a document in that language is the best way to reach a worldwide audience. However, the English spoken by Americans, Canadians, British, Australians, New Zealanders, Indians, Singaporeans, Nigerians, Jamaicans, and others is not itself a global language. Each nation speaks and writes its own variety, colored by local idioms and slang: American English, Queen's English, and so forth.

In order to serve a worldwide audience (as suggested by the name *World Wide Web*), it is best to use *Global English*—English which is written in a way that can easily be understood by non-native speakers, as well as by native speakers in diverse parts of the planet. Global English lacks slang; it also has simpler sentence structure, less jargon, and fewer idioms than the English that is typically spoken and written in the "inner circle" (Kachru, 2005, pp. 13-14) of countries settled by the British.

The NCR dictionary produced by Brusaw (1978) was one company's attempt to encourage its writers to globalize their English in order to make "technical documents easier to read and use by NCR employees and customers around the world." One category of words that they found to be problematic for translators was "jargon that was understood only by the initiated few" (p. 1). The tendency to use obscure jargon is as widespread as ever in the IT industry today, but at least we have a word for it now: *techspeak*.

Despite LISA's stance that a document should fit the linguistic preferences of its readers, this esteemed organization sometimes indulges in techspeak. For example, LISA (2005) promotes the arcane abbreviations *G11n*, *I18n*, *L10n*, and *T9n* for the terms *globalization*, *internationalization*, *localization*, and *translation*, respectively. It is not obvious that each abbreviation's embedded numeral indicates how many letters were omitted;

everyone needs a brief initiation when encountering this alphanumeric jargon for the first time. A more serious problem is that three of the abbreviations tend to confuse the reader's eye because the numeral *1* is similar to uppercase *I* or lowercase *l* in many fonts.

Eliminating the use of slang in online content and other documents has benefits beyond enhanced readability for a global audience. A report by Stanford University's Persuasive Technology Lab (Fogg et al., 2002) listed "writing tone" among the top 10 factors that users mentioned when describing a Web site's trustworthiness. "People generally said that sensationalism or slang hurt a site's credibility, while a straightforward, friendly writing style boosted credibility" (p. 43).

It also is important to avoid the use of idioms and slang in an online discussion. This may seem counterintuitive because chatting is a way to open up and express oneself with fewer inhibitions. Instant messaging (IM) can be so fast and fluid that it seems like speech instead of writing. However, because it lacks the nonverbal clues of spoken conversation, IM is prone to misinterpretation, especially when participants are from diverse cultural backgrounds.

The moderator of an online discussion group should remind participants that clarity is important. Pointing out incomplete sentences and gently discouraging the use of the latest slang may slow the action, but such emphasis on explicit language makes a multicultural discussion more inclusive. A casual style of Internet English is great for communicating with friends who know each other's tacit linguistic habits, but it is too parochial for a chat room, Web site, or blog that aims for a worldwide audience.

HOW TO WRITE GLOBAL ENGLISH

Global English is characterized not only by its lack of slang and scarcity of idioms, but also by its avoidance of jargon and buzzwords. All four of these categories of diction ruin inclusiveness by making it harder for uninitiated people to read a document. Suppose, for example, that the following sentence ended a paragraph promoting an online clothing store:

Which is just the right feature for users who want what works.

This type of colloquial English is easy for native speakers to understand. However, the incomplete sentence may confuse nonnative speakers, many of whom would expect the sentence to end in a question mark.

Changing the initial *which* to *this* might decrease the text's trendiness in the American or British market, but it would greatly increase the number of people who could understand the sentence in the global market. In addition, the adverb *just* and the idiom *what works* should be modified. A good revision would be:

This is exactly the right feature for users who want efficient online shopping.

Using the latest buzzwords and slang is the lazy way to produce cool Web content. Many nonnative speakers became fluent in English while studying or working in the U.S., UK, or Canada 20 or more years ago. After returning to their home countries, they retained their fluency, but their tacit knowledge of English slang eventually became outdated. For example, they might not know that an expression like *It sucks* is now inoffensive enough to appear in mainstream American media.

Colloquial usage is not the only tacit aspect of language that can hinder successful global communication. Many ordinary words have multiple meanings (and even different parts of speech) that can create ambiguity in a reader's mind, particularly if he or she is less than fully fluent in English.

Ambiguity usually makes a translator's work harder, slower, and less accurate (N. Hoft, personal communication, September 6, 2005; G. Fletcher, personal communication, September 9, 2005). Writing the original document in Global English means making every paragraph, sentence, and word as explicit as possible. This process includes internationalizing the text so that it is "as culturally and technically 'neutral' as possible," which will save time and money when the document is translated from English into one or more other languages (LISA, 2005, question 3).

Here are two examples of ambiguity that native speakers of English generally read without hesitation. However, a nonnative speaker may become confused by them. And even a good translator might express one of these sentences ambiguously or incorrectly in the target language.

When used as a conjunction, the word *once* can be confusing because some readers might misinterpret it as an adverb meaning "one time." For example:

Once the prompt appears, enter the course title.

Some people may think the prompt appears only once, regardless of the number of course titles. It would be clearer to write:

After the prompt appears, enter the course title.

Similarly, confusion can occur when *since* is used as a conjunction, because it can be misinterpreted as an adverb or preposition meaning "after":

Keep a log, since the use of this device can produce momentary fluctuations in the supply of power to other electrical equipment in the room.

Someone might think the log does not need to be started until a fluctuation occurs. Using *because* as the conjunction is a simple way to remove the ambiguity:

Keep a log, because the use of this device can produce momentary fluctuations in the supply of power to other electrical equipment in the room.

After finishing a document's final draft, a writer or editor should reread its entire text, seeking points of ambiguity. Words or phrases that could hinder comprehension or translation should be replaced.

However, no writer or editor can anticipate everything that might seem unclear to the document's readers or translators.

A useful approach to reducing ambiguity is to build redundancy into one's writing. It is a good idea to provide some overlap between sentences, so they support each other and create a clear context for all of the paragraph's ideas. For example:

We recommend the purchase of this factory because it is a good medium-term investment. If our company buys the manufacturing facility this year, we will be able to upgrade it by the middle of next year. After we modernize the equipment, we will have additional production capacity to help us meet the increase in demand for our products that is expected two years from now.

Notice how this example uses synonyms to repeat ideas: *purchase ... buy, factory ... facility, upgrade ... modernize*. In addition, the time periods appear in chronological order and support the use of *medium-term*.

Although some redundancy is useful, most writing can be improved by making it more concise. In "Standards for Online Content Authors," McAlpine (2005) urges writers to limit sentences to a maximum of 21 words and paragraphs to 65 words (Style section, bullets 4 and 5). It is generally less tiring to read sentences that have fewer words, as well as paragraphs that have fewer sentences. When a writer simplifies the syntax of a document in order to achieve these targets, the content usually becomes clearer, too.

The principle that smaller "bundles" of information facilitate comprehension also operates at the level of document design. In his book *Designing Web Usability*, Nielsen (1999) recommends keeping Web pages short so that they are "optimized for online readers who frequently scan text." If a topic utilizes a lot of information, the primary page should be narrowly focused and "secondary information relegated to supporting pages" (p. 15).

Streamlining a document in all of the ways described in this section will not restrict one's writing style much, but it will greatly expand one's potential audience by making the content easier to understand. Many people who are not completely fluent in English read the language more easily than they speak it. They can also reread a written document or Web page at their own pace with a dictionary—a type of review that would be very awkward while engaging in a conversation or listening to a lecture.

LOGISTICAL CONSIDERATIONS FOR WEB DOCUMENTS

After articulating ideas in Global English, the producer of a document is ready to consider another question: How can it be shared to the widest possible extent? If one chooses to use the World Wide Web to maximize the dissemination of information, it is essential to think about the logistics of Internet access before uploading content.

Although digital subscriber line (DSL), cable, wireless, satellite, and other fast connections are now common in industrialized economies, a significant fraction[2] of users rely on older ways to access the Internet. Many Web site visitors are likely to use an integrated services digital network (ISDN), or even a 56 Kbps modem. Connection rates and speeds can be low, especially during business hours in their countries when heavy Internet traffic overloads local ISPs. Therefore, it would be a mistake to design a Web site that can only work smoothly if it is accessed via a broadband connection.

In addition, it is necessary to consider that Internet time is often charged by the minute, as is telephone time. Users of a Web site might be paying a dollar or more per hour for online access if their telecom company and ISP do not offer flat rates. Local utility costs can severely impact a site's ability to disseminate information globally.

Streamlining online content is a key factor in gaining and retaining a worldwide audience. It is wise to reduce the loading time of every page on a Web site in order to make access easier and cheaper. The Webmaster can provide feedback to the content producer about page-view failures. He or she can also advise how to make pages easy to re-access if a visitor's connection unexpectedly fails.

In the "Response Times" section of his book's second chapter, Nielsen (1999) describes three thresholds of attention span:

1. A delay equal to 0.1 second is the limit for most users to feel that the system is reacting "instantly"
2. A delay of 1 second is the limit for feeling that one's flow of thought is uninterrupted (for example, after clicking on a link to read another page of text)
3. A delay of 10 seconds is the maximum for keeping a user's attention on the display screen while a page is loading

Allowing for a half-second of latency in the system's responsiveness, Nielsen (1999) cautions that the 10-second limit for holding a person's attention on a Web page is reached with only 34 kilobytes (KB) for modem connections and 150 KB for ISDN connections (p. 48). A page over these limits will probably seem to load slowly, thereby becoming an unintentional test of the user's patience.

Connection speed does not matter much for text-rich Web pages, because they rarely exceed 10 KB. However, a Web page designer should be careful about delays in loading time due to the inclusion of photos, music, or animation. A digital photo in .jpg format usually exceeds 34 KB, and a .wav file of instrumental or vocal music is typically 5-10 KB per second of playing time.

When planning a Web page, check the size of every multimedia file that will be accessed with it. Provide links to .mov files ("Click here to see the video") instead of embedding the files in the page itself. Reduce the use of sound and carefully consider the quality of each photo in relation to its file size. A page that totals 500 KB is likely to take more than half a minute to appear on a user's screen if accessed via an ISDN connection, and longer if via a modem.

Make the text as independent of the images as possible, even when it refers directly to a photo.

Here is an example of dependent text that forces the user to wait until the image loads:

Look at the photo on the left.

By adding a few words about the photo, one can make the text independent of it and free the reader to scan past it if he or she cannot see it immediately. For example:

Look at the photo of the router (left).

It is also a good idea to insert the ALT attribute in the HyperText Markup Language (HTML) code for each page that includes an image. This attribute enables the display of descriptive text in the box that outlines an image while its file is loading.

Tables and graphs should be planned carefully to facilitate their translation into other languages. Rendering into German, for example, often expands the length of the equivalent English text by about 30% (Nielsen, 1999, p. 318). Therefore, localization can distort a table's appearance if the Web designer neglected to make the column widths flexible enough.

TRANSCENDING OUR CULTURAL PREFERENCES

Recall LISA's (2005) definition of internationalizing a document, which includes the goal of making it "culturally neutral" (question 3). Removing cultural biases before producing a globalized document streamlines the subsequent localization process and reduces the possibility that the content may alienate some readers. The following examples reveal a few ways to accommodate other worldviews.

In 1986, the author edited a speech by a Japanese businessman who asked, "Why does the term *classical* always refer to Europe? If we want to refer to the traditional arts and culture of other regions, we must insert an extra adjective: classical *Japanese* music, classical *Indian* dance, classical *Chinese* calligraphy." More than two decades later,

the unqualified term *classical music* still refers to a period in European history, and *Classics* names a field of study that focuses on ancient Greece and Rome.

One cannot anticipate every point of sensitivity, but a little research can reduce the intercultural friction that may accompany a document's publication. For example, it would be unwise to refer to Hinayana Buddhism when discussing religion in Southeast Asia, because *Hinayana* is a pejorative term coined by self-declared Mahayana Buddhists in order to contrast themselves with Theravada Buddhists (Lie, 2005).

It is common to hear people say, "History is written by the victors." For example, if a country wins a war of independence, its people date their sovereignty from the year of declaration, not the year of the subsequent peace treaty; for the United States, it is 1776 rather than 1783. However, Western history books ignore the August 17, 1945 declaration of independence by Indonesia and refer to The Hague conference late in 1949 instead.

Lists of the world's largest languages often merge the national languages of Indonesia (*Bahasa Indonesia*) and Malaysia (*Bahasa Melayu*), calling the combination *Malay* (Graddol, 2000, p. 8, Table 1; also p. 27, Table 7). The online marketing company Global Reach (2004) states, "Malay is the same language that is spoken in Indonesia" but notes that most of this market segment lives in Indonesia (footnote 26). People in Jakarta might therefore wonder why this "single" language is not called Indonesian instead of Malay. The confusion is due to the habit of conflating modern Malay with the older language of the same name, which gave birth to it and its sister Indonesian (Gordon, 2005a)—a situation analogous to combining Romanian and French into *Romance language speakers* and then saying "Romance is the same language that is spoken in France."

Other cultural assumptions are unrelated to artistic, religious, political, or linguistic favoritism; they may lead to embarrassment or confusion without arousing national pride. In his chapter about designing Web pages for a global audience, Nielsen (1999) shows a banner ad for Apple Computer that asked users to turn on a virtual light switch by clicking it. However, the switch was shown in the down position, which *is* the "on" position in many countries. Nielsen says the variation of this type of tacit knowledge from country to country is rarely mentioned in guidebooks that tell how to internationalize software or Web sites, but it can be discovered by testing the image on a sample of users overseas before uploading to the World Wide Web (p. 315).

THE RISE OF MANDARIN: DECONSTRUCTING THE HYPE

Is it likely that English will lose its role as the global language? When the British Council published the first edition of David Graddol's *The Future of English?* in 1997, the mass media began producing articles that claimed English was being surpassed by "Chinese" (Lovgren, 2004). Graddol (2000) divided the world's English speakers into three categories: those who speak it as a first language (native speakers, or L1), those who speak it fluently as a second (or third, etc.) language (L2), and those who are learning English as a foreign language (EFL) but are not yet fluent in it (p. 10).

Graddol (2000) estimated that English has 375 million L1, 375 million L2, and 750 million EFL speakers (p. 10, Figure 4). Although the rounded L1 figure is well above his estimates for Hindi (316 million) and Spanish (304 million), it is very far below the 1,113 million he claimed for "Chinese" (p. 8, Table 1). The popular press echoed these estimates without questioning why the separation of L1 and L2 speakers was being applied to English but not to "Chinese."

Linguists generally do not recognize a monolithic language called "Chinese" that is spoken as a first language throughout the People's Republic of China (PRC). "Chinese" consists of several large languages that share a common system of writing but are mutually unintelligible when spoken (C. Hurd, personal communication, December 5, 2005). It is considered a subfamily within the Sino-Tibetan family of languages (Columbia, 2001;

Gordon, 2005a). However, due to "social, cultural, or political factors," (Gordon, 2005b, The Problem of Language Identification section, para. 1), politicians often displace linguists as the authorities who determine whether two or more languages are equivalent (thereby promoting national unity) or distinct (thereby promoting ethnic identity).

Mandarin is the official language of the PRC and the standard language of instruction in China's public schools. In these respects, it is analogous to national languages that were created to unify diverse populations (e.g., Filipino in the Philippines and Indonesian in Indonesia). In its *Ethnologue* encyclopedia of world languages, SIL International states that 70% of the people in China speak Mandarin as their native language (Gordon, 2005a), which would yield an L1 of 928 million among the present population of 1,325 million (World Gazetteer, 2007).

However, in May 2005, the PRC's Xinhua news agency reported that a National Language Commission survey found that only 53% of the population can speak Mandarin, and many of them "are not frequent Mandarin users, preferring their local dialect" ("Half of all Chinese," 2005). This yields a combined L1+L2 of only 702 million. If one adds in all of the L1+L2 Mandarin speakers among the 23 million Taiwanese and 34 million (Liren, 2002) to 55 million (Seagrave, 1996, p. 14) overseas Chinese, Mandarin's total is virtually equal to Graddol's (2000) combined L1+L2 estimate of 750 million English speakers.

In *Asian Englishes: Beyond the Canon*, Kachru (2005) suggests a much higher L1+L2 figure for English. Estimating that one third of his native India uses English, as do 200 million people in the PRC, he claims those two countries have a total of 533 million L2 speakers. However, his tallies assume that people who studied English in school for only three years are "users of the language" (pp. 206-207).

In recent decades, it has been standard practice for Japanese to study English for six or more years in public school, but they are generally reluctant to speak the language. It is fair to say that Japanese have the *potential* to become L2 speakers. After conversing with many Japanese of varying levels of English fluency when I lived in Tokyo during 1984-1987, I came to the conclusion that those who were L2 usually had lived at least six months in an L1 country such as the U.S. or UK. Axtell (1995) describes a similar six-month threshold in *Do's and Taboos of Using English Around the World*, based on his encounters trotting the globe as a salesman (p. 147).

Regardless of the numbers, there are two strong reasons why Mandarin will not become popular as a global language: Tones make it hard to speak and ideograms make it hard to write. Adults who are fluent in a tonal language such as Thai, Lao, or Vietnamese sometimes learn Mandarin by overhearing conversations or watching movies, but speakers of non-tonal languages have a lot more difficulty doing so and need twice as much time in an immersion setting such as Automatic Language Growth (J. M. Brown, personal communication, 1990). Learning enough ideograms to read a newspaper requires years of diligent effort.

One benchmark of a global language is its use as a lingua franca between two nonnative speakers from separate countries, neither of whom knows the other's L1. It is common to see English used this way at international conferences. For example, a Japanese who is based in Benin would probably speak English to a Swede who is on assignment in Bolivia. The touchstone for a speaker of Global English is not the ability to communicate with native speakers of English, but rather the ability to communicate with nonnative speakers from diverse backgrounds.

Although Mandarin is used as an international lingua franca, its scope is regional; people outside Taiwan, Singapore, and other Chinese-majority areas study the language primarily to communicate with citizens of the PRC. Its recent rise in popularity as a medium for international commerce has been at the expense of Cantonese (Yue), not at the expense of English. One impulse for the shift was the return of Hong Kong in 1997. It is also noteworthy that Mandarin language schools began to operate openly in Indonesia after the dictator Suharto resigned in 1998.

FUTURE DIRECTIONS OF ENGLISH AS A GLOBAL LANGUAGE

Graddol's (2000) report suggests that English will remain globally dominant, but it will be influenced by nonnative speakers, leading to "new hybrid language varieties" (p. 36). A harbinger of the hybridization is Singapore, which has four official languages: English, Mandarin, Malay, and Tamil. English is the default language when Singaporeans of different ethnicity make each other's acquaintance, earning it an L2 (p. 11, Table 5). This L2 "Singlish" is flavored with words and structures from three non-Indo-European language families, making it a notable variety even though it has a narrow geographical range.

Graddol (2000) also foresees "migration toward L1 use of English" by middle-class professionals and university students who use it "as a primary means of social communication" in L2 countries (p. 58). Such migration has been going on for more than half a century in India, where the large anglophone sector supports the creation of literature in their own variety of English, dating back before independence.

It is widely recognized that the globalization of American entertainment and fast food make English trendy among millions, even billions, of people who are not fluent in it. This "wave" of popular culture resonates with a socioeconomic "wave" in developing countries, some of whose governments now require English to be taught as a foreign language in primary schools. It remains to be seen whether the critical mass of L1+L2 speakers attained by Singapore and India will be replicated by dozens of other countries, each of which will thereby develop its own variety of English.

Kachru (2005) describes the interaction of diverse forms of English in terms of *pluricentricity*, his concept that "world Englishes have a plurality of centres" (p. 18). These centers provide models for English language acquisition, regional codification, and literature. He puts Singapore, India, Sri Lanka, and the Philippines in the *norm-providing* group, distinct from China,

Taiwan, Japan, South Korea, and Thailand in the *norm-dependent* group (p. 19).

In a recent publication, I coined the term *colingual* (analogous to *coworker*) to refer to people who *speak a language with each other* (Schell, 2007, p. 140). People conversing in a common language are colinguals in that language. Although native speakers of a language are colinguals in their L1, they might not be colinguals in a shared L2. For example, two Japanese might both be colinguals in English with their American acquaintance but not with each other, because Japanese tend to speak English only when communicating with non-Japanese. Singaporeans, however, are likely to be colinguals in English with each other, even if they have the same L1.

The concept of colinguals is helpful for understanding Kachru's (2005) division of anglophone countries into norm-providing and norm-dependent (p. 19). A country can be categorized by determining the internal colingual level among its English speakers. Specifically, one would ask: Do compatriots speak English with each other when no foreigners are present? In the norm-dependent group, the answer is "rarely;" however, in the norm-providing group, the answer is "often enough to create a critical mass of colinguals who generate their own norms of usage."

If the number of national and regional hybrid Englishes increases, what is the future of mutual intelligibility? A Japanese acquaintance of the author recounted an experience she had while teaching her native language to Indonesians in North Sumatra. One day, Etsuko's students invited her to go hiking, pronouncing the word in Japanese fashion (*haikingu*) as part of a Japanese sentence. She was confused when they said everyone would gather in the evening, because she understood *haikingu* to be a day trip on level ground or in low hills. Instead, the students trekked up a small mountain, arriving at the summit in time for sunrise. In Indonesian, the borrowed word *hiking* refers to an activity that Japanese consider to be mountain climbing.

This anecdote illustrates how the expansion of a language can undermine itself. Recognizing common ground among the varieties of English may prove to be the best way to preserve their mutual intelligibility—it probably will be more effective than trying to repress their diversity. Global English might become essential in the future as a medium for speakers of divergent forms of English to communicate with each other. We all need to learn to express ourselves clearly to audiences who do not share our cultural background and the concomitant tacit aspects of our speech and writing.

Graddol (2000) uses a pyramid diagram (p. 12, Figure 6) to illustrate how shifts in language accompany the expansion of an Indian citizen's viewpoint from home to village to state to nation. At the base of the pyramid are local languages that are used within families and learned by infants as L1. One step higher are languages of wider geographical scope, which are used in media broadcasts and primary schools. Another step higher are official state languages (e.g., Malayalam in Kerala), which are used in government offices and secondary schools. At the top are Hindi and Indian English, both of which are used nationally and in universities. Global English is the next logical step beyond the top of this pyramid, because it can serve as a lingua franca for the World Wide Web and other channels of international communication.

CONCLUSION

Localization is very important in marketing and other communication activities that rely on tacit knowledge of a target language and culture. However, it is incomplete as a global communication strategy because it cannot accommodate everyone. The limits of localization are becoming more apparent in the 21st century, now that over 1.2 billion people have access to the Internet. Localizing a Web site into all 347 languages that each claim at least 1 million speakers is not a feasible approach to the global dissemination of information.

To make the Web truly a worldwide medium, we need to write English content in an explicit way that can be easily understood by nonnative speakers: simpler syntax, less jargon, fewer idioms, no slang. Producing a Web page or other document in Global English is the best way to ensure that people from all linguistic backgrounds have a reasonable chance of comprehending it. Global English is likely to become more important in the near future, both online and in hardcopy. It may prove to be essential for maintaining English as a lingua franca if new varieties of the language proliferate in diverse cultures throughout our world.

REFERENCES

Axtell, R. (1995). *Do's and taboos of using English around the world.* New York: John Wiley & Sons.

Brusaw, C. (1978). *NCR fundamental English dictionary.* Dayton, OH: NCR Corporation.

China Internet Network Information Center. (2006, July). *18th Statistical Survey Report on the Internet Development in China.* Retrieved November 23, 2006, from http://www.cnnic.net/download/2006/18threport-en.pdf

Chomsky, N. (1969). *Aspects of the theory of syntax.* Cambridge, MA: MIT Press.

Columbia University. (2001). *Chinese language.* In *The Columbia Electronic Encyclopedia* (6th ed.). New York: Columbia University Press. Retrieved December 6, 2005, from http://www.bartleby.com/65/ch/Chinese.html

Computer Industry Almanac. (2005, November 14). *USA leads broadband subscriber top 15 ranking.* Retrieved November 23, 2006, from http://www.c-i-a.com/pr1105.htm

Federal Communications Commission. (2005, June 10). *Frequently asked questions (FAQs) about FCC form 477 (local telephone competition and broadband reporting).* Retrieved October 2, 2005, from http://www.fcc.gov/broadband/broadband_data_faq.html

Fogg, B. J., Soohoo, C., Danielson, D., Marable, L., Stanford, J., & Tauber, E. R. (2002, November 11). *How do people evaluate a Web site's credibility?* Stanford, CA: Persuasive Technology Lab, Stanford University.

Global Reach. (2004, September 30). *Global Internet statistics: Sources & references.* Retrieved May 24, 2005, from http://www.global-reach.biz/globstats/refs.php3

Gordon, R. G., Jr. (Ed.). (2005a). Ethnologue country index: Languages of the world. In *Ethnologue* (15th ed.). Retrieved November 23, 2006, from http://www.ethnologue.com/country_index.asp

Gordon, R. G., Jr. (Ed.). (2005b). Introduction to the printed volume. In *Ethnologue* (15th ed.). Retrieved December 6, 2005, from http://www.ethnologue.com/ethno_docs/introduction.asp

Gordon, R. G., Jr. (Ed.). (2005c). Statistical summaries: Summary by language size. In *Ethnologue* (15th ed.). Retrieved May 23, 2005, from http://www.ethnologue.com/ethno_docs/distribution.asp?by=size

Graddol, D. (2000). *The future of English?* (2nd ed.). London: The British Council.

Half of all Chinese people can't speak Mandarin: Report. (2005, May 23). *Taipei Times.* Retrieved May 24, 2005, from http://www.taipeitimes.com

Hopkins, R., Jr. (2002). *Multilingual Websites: Benefits you can count on, headaches you can avoid.* Retrieved December 12, 2005, from http://www.weblations.com/eng/articles/art_2.htm

International Telecommunication Union. (2003). *Technical notes.* Retrieved May 24, 2005, from http://www.itu.int/ITU-D/ict/statistics/WTI_2003.pdf

International Telecommunication Union. (2005, April 26). *Economies by broadband penetration, 2004.* Retrieved May 24, 2005, from http://www.itu.int/ITU-D/ict/statistics/at_glance/top20_broad_2004.html

Internet World Stats. (2006a, May 11). *694 million people used the Internet in March, 2006 in all the world.* Retrieved June 1, 2006, from http://www.internetworldstats.com/usage/use002.htm

Internet World Stats. (2006b). *World Internet users and population stats.* Retrieved January 22, 2006, from http://www.Internetworldstats.com/stats.htm

Internet World Stats. (2007a). *Internet World Stats surfing and site guide.* Retrieved April 2, 2007, from http://www.internetworldstats.com/surfing.htm

Internet World Stats. (2007b, June 30). *Internet world users by language.* Retrieved November 18, 2007, from http://www.internetworldstats.com/stats7.htm

Internet World Stats. (2007c, September 30). *World Internet users and population stats.* Retrieved November 18, 2007, from http://www.internetworldstats.com/stats.htm

Ipsos. (2005, March 2). *The majority of global Internet users using a high-speed connection.* Retrieved May 26, 2005, from http://www.ipsos-na.com/news/pressrelease.cfm?id=2583

Jarboe, K. P. (2001, April). *Knowledge management as an economic development strategy.* Washington, DC: Economic Development Administration, U.S. Department of Commerce.

Jupitermedia Corporation. (2001, December 3). What is garbage in, garbage out? In *Webopedia Computer Dictionary.* Retrieved October 7, 2005, from http://www.webopedia.com/TERM/g/garbage_in_garbage_out.html

Kachru, B. (2005). *Asian Englishes: Beyond the canon.* Hong Kong, China: Hong Kong University Press.

Lie, K. A. (2005). *The myth of Hinayana.* Retrieved November 3, 2005, from http://www.lienet.no/hinayan1.htm

Liren, Z. (2002, September 12). *Distribution of the overseas Chinese population.* Retrieved January 15, 2006, from http://www.library.ohiou.edu/subjects/shao/databases_popdis.htm

Localization Industry Standards Association, The. (2005). *Frequently asked questions about LISA and the localization industry.* Retrieved September 28, 2005, from http://www.lisa.org/info/faqs.html

Lovgren, S. (2004, February 26). *English in decline as a first language, study says.* Retrieved May 23, 2005, from http://news.nationalgeographic.com/news/2004/02/0226_040226_language.html

McAlpine, R. (2005). *Standards for online content authors.* Retrieved September 5, 2005, from http://www.webpagecontent.com/arc_archive/177/5/

Nielsen, J. (1999). *Designing Web usability: The practice of simplicity.* Indianapolis, IN: New Riders.

Nonaka, I., & Takeuchi, H. (1995). *The knowledge creating company: How Japanese companies create the dynamics of innovation.* New York: Oxford University Press.

Polanyi, M. (1962). *Personal knowledge: Towards a post-critical philosophy.* Chicago: University of Chicago Press.

Polanyi, M. (1966). *Tacit dimension.* Garden City, NY: Doubleday & Co.

Romney, L. (2000, January 6). The cutting edge: Survey looks at online habits of U.S. Latinos. *Los Angeles Times.* Retrieved May 29, 2005, from http://www.latimes.com

Schell, M. (2007). Developing a global perspective for knowledge management. In H. Rahman (Ed.), *Information and Communication Technologies for Economic and Regional Developments* (pp. 122-147). Hershey, PA: Idea Group Publishing.

Seagrave, S. (1996). *Lords of the rim: The invisible empire of the overseas Chinese.* London: Transworld Publishers.

Shin, H. (2003). *Language use and English-speaking ability: 2000* (Rep. No. C2KBR-29). Washington, DC: U.S. Census Bureau.

Stiglitz, J. (1999, December). *Scan globally, reinvent locally: Knowledge infrastructure and the localization of knowledge.* Keynote Address at the First Global Development Network Conference, Bonn, Germany. Retrieved November 28, 2005, from http://www.iucn.org/themes/ceesp/Publications/CMWG/Stiegliz-local-knowledge.PDF

Sveiby, K. (1997). *Tacit knowledge*. Retrieved October 1, 2005, from http://www.sveiby.com/articles/Polanyi.html

Sveiby, K. (2001, April). *What is knowledge management?* Retrieved October 1, 2005, from http://www.sveiby.com/articles/KnowledgeManagement.html

Web Site Optimization. (2005, February 19). *January 2005 bandwidth report*. Retrieved December 11, 2005, from http://www.websiteoptimization.com/bw/0501/

World Gazetteer. (2007). *World*. Retrieved April 3, 2007, from http://www.world-gazetteer.com

ADDITIONAL READING

Suggested URLs

http://www.12manage.com/methods_nonaka_seci.html (Tom De Geytere's summary of Nonaka and Takeuchi's SECI model, including a diagram of their knowledge spiral)

http://www.algworld.com/history.htm (Automatic Language Growth and the work of J. Marvin Brown at AUA Language Center in Bangkok)

http://www.anglistik.tu-bs.de/global-english/GE_Was_ist_GE.html (A list of links to online articles that use the term Global English)

http://www.contented.com (Rachel McAlpine's tips for Web content writers)

http://www.globalenglish.info/globallyspeaking/index.htm (Tips on intercultural communication in the Internet age)

http://www.globelanguage.com (Translation company co-owned by George Fletcher)

http://www.oecd.org/document/60/0,2340,en_2649_34225_2496764_1_1_1_1,00.html (Organization for Economic Co-operation and Development's broadband statistics for 2001-2004, based on ITU data)

http://www.pulpchat.com/faq/faq215.php (List of chat room slang)

http://www.research-research.com (Research & Research)

http://www.sveiby.com/Portals/0/articles/TacitTest.htm (Karl-Erik Sveiby's hands-on exercise "Test Your Tacit Knowledge")

http://www.useit.com (Jakob Nielsen's Web site about usability)

http://www.world-ready.com/academic.htm (A list of links offered by Nancy Hoft, a consultant in "world-readiness")

ENDNOTES

[1] The International Telecommunication Union (ITU, 2003) describes a method for estimating the number of Internet users: "Countries that do not have surveys generally base their estimates on derivations from reported Internet Service Provider subscriber counts, calculated by multiplying the number of subscribers by a multiplier" (p. 4). The multiplier compensates for the undercounting that occurs when several members of a household or office share a single Internet account. According to the ITU's World Telecommunication Indicators database, some of the multipliers used in 2004 were: Myanmar 2; Argentina, Bahrain, Bangladesh 3; Nepal 4; El Salvador, Syria 5; Costa Rica 8; Latvia 9; Honduras 10; and Uganda 25 (E. Magpantay, personal communication, December 13, 2005). Other countries had more complex estimation methods, which varied the sharing factor from city to city, or even within a single city (E. de Argaez, personal communication, December 11, 2005).
Bear in mind that a multiplier exacerbates the overcounting that results from an individual having more than one account (e.g., at work or school, as well as at home). Even so, the

growing popularity of cybercafes, which have very high ratios of users to accounts, probably outweighs the distortion that is due to multiplying overcounts.

Internet World Stats (IWS, 2007a) reports various standards for tallying children. The ITU defines an Internet user as "someone aged 2 years old and above, who went online in the past 30 days" but the U.S. Chamber of Commerce restricts the definition to "those 3 years or older who 'currently use' the Internet" and the Chinese Internet Network Information Center (CNNIC) narrows it further to a citizen "aged 6 or above, who uses the Internet at least one hour per week" (Internet Usage section, para. 2).

Internet World Stats (2006a) also cites a comScore tally that found 694,260,000 unique visitors age 15 or older used the Internet during March 2006—less than 70% of the 1 billion who had online access by the beginning of that year (IWS, 2006b).

During the first five years of the 21st century, South Korea had the world's highest proportion of Internet users who subscribe to broadband. According to ITU figures for the country, 11.9 million of 31.6 million Internet users subscribed at the end of 2004, representing a broadband penetration rate of 37.7% (W. Yasandikusuma, personal communication, May 27, 2005).

However, "broadband penetration" figures are calculated in different ways, showing the greatest variance of all Internet statistics. Some authorities apply the term *broadband* to speeds that are less than the ITU minimum of 256 kilobits per second in both directions (V. Gray, personal communication, May 26, 2005). The Federal Communications Commission (FCC, 2005) of the United States defines *broadband* as a connection that "enables the end user to receive information from and/or send information to the Internet at information transfer rates exceeding 200 kilobits per second (kbps) in at least one direction" (question 5).

Also, the term *penetration* is defined in several ways. Some surveys divide the total number of broadband subscribers in a country by its total inhabitants. Although the United States had the most broadband subscribers in December 2004, the ITU (2005) ranked it only 16th globally on the basis of 11.4% penetration of its national population, compared to 24.9% for South Korea.

Other surveys divide the total number of households or users who have broadband capability installed (even if they do not subscribe to the service) by the total number of "active Internet users." For example, over 69.4 million American households had the capability in December 2004, yielding a penetration of 54.7% for home users according to Web Site Optimization (WSO, 2005). The inflated WSO figure was exaggerated even more in the "Face of the Web 2004" study by Ipsos-Insight, which announced that 68% of the entire world "accessed" the Internet via broadband in October 2004 (Ipsos, 2005).

The China Internet Network Information Center (CNNIC, 2006) claimed that 77 million of China's 123 million Internet users were "beneficiaries" of broadband access by June 30, 2006 (p. 3), yielding a broadband penetration rate of 62.6%. This seems comparable to the WSO method of counting installed capability as access; also, all Internet users counted by the CNNIC are defined as "active" (see Endnote 1 of this chapter). However, late in 2005, Computer Industry Almanac (2005) projected that there would be only 46.9 million broadband subscribers in the U.S. by the end of that year, far fewer than the 69.4 million households which had broadband capability at the end of 2004 (WSO, 2005).

If one gives more credence to tallying subscribers than to tallying installations, it is clear that the digital divide between slow and fast connections will remain for the rest of this decade. Computer Industry Almanac (2005) projects that only 500 million of the 1.8 billion Internet users in 2010 will be broadband subscribers. This will mean a worldwide broadband penetration rate of only 27.8%—significantly less than the rate achieved by Korea in 2004, according to the calculation method described at the beginning of this endnote.

Chapter VII
Understanding Social Capital Formation for Knowledge Sharing in Virtual Communities

Shafiz A. Mohd Yusof
Universiti Utara Malaysai, Malaysia

ABSTRACT

This chapter attempts to explore the possibility of building social capital in virtual community (VC) by first introducing the phenomenon, its problems and context, types of VCs and the significance of knowledge sharing. This chapter then presents the process of social capital from a sociological standpoint where two main theories will be used—the elementary theory of social structure and the social exchange theory as the backbone of the arguments. By integrating both theories, a conceptual framework that includes six antecedents to develop social capital is provided. Subsequently, the propositions are expressed in terms of implications to the sociological approach of VC and some conclusions are made by including some future research agenda.

INTRODUCTION

Over the years, the formation of virtual communities are growing and beginning to gain its popularity in the global context. Moreover, with the expansion of computer-mediated communication (CMC), these technologies provide a platform and new ways for society to meet, communicate, collaborate, socialize, and shop (Turoff, 1991; Burnett, 2000). More and more people are joining virtual communities due to the sense of belonging and the concrete experience of social networks that can bring great benefits to people (Smith, 2001).

One of the benefits gained by people involved in virtual communities is knowledge. People go back and forth to their virtual communities for knowledge. This is because knowledge sharing is a fundamentally social phenomenon (Granovetter, 1982; Boer, Baalen, & Kumar, 2001). Knowledge sharing involves a relationship between actors (same as people) that also is embedded in a structure of other social relationships. These ongoing social relationships provide the constraints and opportunities that, in combination with characteristics of individuals, organizations and knowledge, may help explain the dynamics of knowledge sharing in virtual communities (Boer, Baalen, & Kumar, 2001).

Recently, the understanding of social capital is becoming critical and significant apart from the financial, human, intellectual, and other capitals in today's communities. Social capital is the fabric or glue that holds communities and other social networks together. The basic premise here is the interaction that enables people to build communities, to commit themselves to each other, and to knit the social fabric (Smith, 2001). Those concerned with social capital have examined the density of social networks that people are involved in; the extent to which they are engaged with others in informal social activities; and their membership of groups and associations. None have observed this phenomenon in the setting of virtual communities and how it is developed.

This chapter will attempt to address the process of building social capital through knowledge sharing in virtual communities (VCs). The organization of the chapter is as follows. First, the meaning of virtual communities is defined. Then, significance of knowledge and knowledge sharing as an activity which is vital for the development of building social capital is presented. The following section will be on the concept of social capital and why it is important in today's environment where people are going virtual instead of physical. Subsequently, the Elementary Theory of Social Structure, which will be applied to this phenomenon and finally proposed some recommendations, is presented.

BACKGROUND

The Emergence of Virtual Communities

The term *community* originated from the Latin word *communis*. Fernback and Thompson (1995) suggests that *communis* can be formed by pairing (i) *cum* refers to together and *munus* refers to obligation, or (ii) *cum* meaning together and *unus* meaning one. *Community* can be referred to as a group in which individual participation is based on an obligation to one another or as

a group in which individuals participate to be one in purpose (Rothaermel & Sugiyama, 2001). Therefore, a sustained social interaction, shared attributes and values, and a delineated geographical space need to be in place for the community to function effectively and efficiently (Karp et al., 1977). However, a management scholar such as Lawrence (1995) suggests that it is membership rules not the geographical boundaries, which help sustain the community. These membership rules further suggest that the general perspectives and assumptions behind the organizational community building can be applicable to VC regardless of the geographically dispersed groups.

Since the concept of *virtual community* is relatively a new phenomenon, it is interesting to understand why it is formed and what it takes to form it. Furthermore, it is crucial to discover how this new form of informal community establishes their social network in order to build the social capitalthe central issue that is addressed in this chapter. It is stated by Stolterman, Agren, and Croon (1999) that *virtual community* is a concept to form some of the new social "life forms" surfacing from the Internet. In support to that, virtual community is defined as a social entity where a number of people relate to one another by the use of a specific technology (Rheingold, 1993; Jones, 1995; Lapachet, 1995; Schuler, 1996; Smith & Kollock, 1997). In addition, a virtual community is considered a source from which individuals seek social support using CMC (Walther & Boyd, 1997) and emerges from a surprising intersection of human needs and technology (Igbaria, 1999). Hiltz and Wellman (1997) state that there is a significant difference between communities' off-line and computer-supported communities, which defines a virtual community as normally more dispersed in space and time, but more closely knit. Members are more heterogeneous in their characteristics but with more homogeneous attitudes.

Before defining virtual community, the concept of *community* must first be defined. The community to the ordinary inhabitant is where he lives and probably works. It is associated with a place and a name in his thought (Nelson, Ramsey, & Verner, 1960). Community is where one goes to shop, to attend a show, to meet friends, or simply to loaf. The common-sense concept of community is that it involves an area, people, and the relationships among people (structure). The elements of structure in a community consist of groups, formal organizations, institutions, division of labor, values, social differentiation, and functions. Therefore, according to Nelson, Ramsey, and Verner (p. 24, 1960), community may be formally defined as: "... the structuring of elements and dimensions to solve problems which must be or can be solved within the local area."

Virtual communities emerge from a surprising intersection of human needs and technology. When the ubiquity of the telecommunications network is combined with the information structuring and storing capabilities of computers, a new communication medium becomes possible. Virtual community is a term commonly used to describe various forms of computer-mediated communication, particularly long-term, textually mediated conversations among large groups. It is a group of people who may or may not meet one another face-to-face, and who exchange words and ideas through the mediation of computer networks and bulletin boards (Igbaria, 1999).

This phenomenon is due to the rapid growth of a medium called the Internet or known as *cyberspace*. Virtual communities exist mainly in cyberspace. The word *cyberspace* was first used by science-fiction-author William Gibson in his 1984 book *Neuromancer*. According to Benedikt (1991), cyberspace is a virtual world, consisting of computer networks and different techniques for communication:

Cyberspace is a globally networked, computer-sustained, computer-accessed, and computer-generated, multidimensional, artificial, or "virtual reality." In this reality, to which every computer is a window, seen or heard objects are neither physical nor, necessarily, representations of physical objects but are, rather, in form, character and action, made up of data, of pure information. (p. 122)

The activities in cyberspace have grown in an explosive manner. Today it is very difficult to estimate how many have access to cyberspace, mainly due to the many definitions of the concept of cyberspace. There is reason to believe that the number of users will continue to grow during the coming years when computers and other equipment get less and less expensive and computer education becomes more common.

So, basically, a *virtual community* is a group of people trying to achieve collective goals by using new information technology as a means. Even though there have been discussions and forums, so far there are no good definitions of these new social structures emerging in cyberspace. It is of course difficult to come up with good definitions when the technology used is changing and developing all the time. That is why the study of virtual communities until now has largely been an explorative one. Therefore, virtual communities are conceptualized as an information technology-based system that supports the communication and social relationships between people whether individuals or groups of people.

In order to achieve a universally usable virtual communities and community networks, there are two challenges. First is to focus on developing technologies accessible to a wide-range of people on a variety of devices. Second is to ensure the software also supports the sociability, that is, effective social interaction online (Preece, 2000). Borrowing from the work of Robert Bellah (1986) in his book titled "Habits of the Heart," Kowch and Schwier (1997) introduced four types of virtual community with concomitant purposes such as: (1) virtual community of relationship, (2) virtual community of place, (3) virtual community of mind, and (4) virtual community of memory. In the same year, Hagel and Armstrong (1997) classified virtual community based on the basic human needs such as: (1) virtual community of interest which is similar to the virtual community of mind; (2) virtual community of relationship, (3) virtual community of fantasy which is similar to virtual community of place, and (4) virtual community of transaction. By combining both ideas, the following are illustrations of five types of virtual community: (1) virtual community of relationship, (2) virtual community of place, (3) virtual community of mind or interest, (4) virtual community of memory, and (5) virtual community of transaction.

Virtual Communities of Relationship

A virtual community of relationship is usually based on a collective concept where a group of people establish trust and form mutual bonds between them. In such a case, family members, friends, and close friends come together virtually to share their excitements, experiences, concerns or problems. For example, a social utility website such as 'Facebook,' people register and get connected with their friends from all parts of the world in which they exchange information about oneself. Not only that, they also use this platform to get to know other people. Consequently, establishing rapport and relationships, and sharing information become a common goal for this kind of virtual community. In essence, the key characteristic of this type of community is based on the relationships that each member builds during their course of action in cyberspace.

Virtual Communities of Place/Fantasy

A virtual community of place or fantasy is about individuals that value and share a common place or surroundings in cyberspace. Most of the time, virtual community of fantasy attempts to create an environment that is imaginary in nature where it replicates or mimics the real world phenomenon. Based on this environment, some key benefits gained by individuals are sense of belonging, camaraderie, unity, and heritage. An example of this type of virtual community is 'Everquest', a massively multiplayer online role playing game (MMORPG) where hundreds and thousands of people from all over the world gather in a virtual place to compete or collaborate with each other to defeat monsters and go on quests.

Virtual Communities of Mind/Interest

The main principle of virtual community of mind or interest is that they work as a collective mind based on the notion of being and doing. Individuals will enjoy sharing of ideas, interests, values and goals. One of the example for this type of community is related to hobbyists that engaged in join interests such as collecting stamps, old coins, antique furniture, or a group of owners' of a particular car. The difference between virtual community of fantasy and interest is that for virtual community of interest, people are connected by their pursuits or hobby. On the other hand, for virtual community of fantasy, they are bind together for entertainment, fun and games.

Virtual Communities of Memory

A virtual community of memory exists with the mark of an event or incident that took place in the past—whether it was a tragedy or enchantment. Most of the times, the historical events bring together all walks of people because the incidents do affect one's life deeply. Thus, people join virtual community for the purpose of sharing those moments by pouring their feelings of sadness, anxieties, anger, excitements, and joy that they hold on for so long regarding the event. In another word, such virtual community can also be considered as a central point where individuals can get help or support from other members that have gone through the same event in the past. Community can also provide ways to deal with the issues or problems and can gain knowledge by understanding the causes and effects of a tragedy. An example of this community is called 'World War Veterans' where people relate their experiences and share information on what had happened and lessons to learn in coping with war.

Virtual Communities of Transaction

People are normally engaged in activities such as selling and buying product and services in this type virtual community called transaction. In this community, buyers will also have opportunities to ask other buyers' opinions on the things that he or she wants to buy in a ICT platform such as discussion forums. For example, in 'eBay' it provides a place for transaction where people buy and sell unlimited goods and services. The system also allows people to understand and learn which seller is reliable or not based on their credibility rating. Sellers can also understand the consumer buying patterns by looking at their historical purchases. The organizers' of these types of communities does not need to be a vendor. They can be a third party that only provides a platform for a critical mass of buyers and sellers. What is important in this form of community is that people get together through purchases and selling they make.

Significance of Knowledge Sharing

The significant of knowledge sharing is evident in organizations. According to the theory of organizational knowledge creation (Nonaka, 1992; Nonaka & Takeuchi, 1995; Krogh et al., 2000), *knowledge* is generated through a process of interaction of tacit and explicit knowledge. Knowledge is either transformed within one single person or among a group of people. What matters most—knowledge is neither given nor pre-defined, but rather created through a process of individual interpretation and personal construction (Renzi, 2002).

There are two broad types of knowledge: explicit and tacit (Polyani, 1975; Nonaka & Takeuchi, 1995). Explicit knowledge is knowledge that can be expressed in words and numbers, and shared in the form of data, scientific formula, specifications, and manuals (Hossain, D'Eridita, & Wigand, 2002). Explicit knowledge is packaged, easily codified, communicable, and transferable. An example of explicit knowledge is knowledge included in manuals that accompanies the purchase of electrical goods, for example, the purchase of a microwave oven. On the other hand, tacit knowledge is knowledge that is highly personal, hard to formalized, and difficult to communicate or share with others (Hossain, D'Eridita, & Wigand, 2002). Subjective insights, intuitions, and hunches fall into this category of knowledge. Tacit knowledge is deeply rooted in an individual's actions and experience, as well as in the ideals, values, or emotions he or she embraces. An example of tacit knowledge is knowledge a chemistry professor may have on carrying out experiments of certain substance.

Tacit knowledge can be further broken down into two elements—cognitive and technical. According to Nonaka (1992), cognitive elements pertain to a person's mental model, which in turn comprises of beliefs, perceptions, viewpoints, and mental maps. On the other hand, the technical elements, comprise elements of definite know-how and skills that apply to specific situations.

In their research, Nonaka and Takeuchi (1995) also view knowledge as existing or created by an individual or in a group. They illustrate this briefly by stating that it is the intersection between tacit and explicit knowledge that creates learning. They also add that there is an infinite loop between the externalization and internalization of knowledge within an organization. The loop begins with the conversion of tacit individual knowledge to explicit knowledge through interaction. Then, the explicit knowledge is then combined or reproduced to create new knowledge. This new knowledge is then transferred to other individuals or groups. From here on, the whole process or loop begins all over again.

UNDERSTANDING THE FORMATION PROCESS OF SOCIAL CAPITAL

The use of Internet or other forms of information and communications technologies (ICT) is increasingly seen as a useful mode to share data, collaborate on research, and exchange messages for both the organizational and virtual community. In management research, VC is viewed to be very similar to organizational community. Both VC and organizational community research suggests that the importance of social interaction among its members using various Internet tools with a set of rules as a guiding principle for individuals to act or participate (Lawrence, 1995). The concept of VC evolved as a result of the implementation of electronic information exchange (EIES) systems for computerized conferencing in 1976 (Kitchin, 1998). A collective intelligence capability for decision making was cultivated through the implementation of EIES. To date, understanding how individuals interact and exchange information through the use of the Internet and its implications on the formation of social capital is limited. Social capital can be essentially viewed as a network of contacts of the individuals or participating organizations in an exchange.

It is important to note that social capital is becoming a core concept in business, political science, healthcare, and sociology. Social capital is a common framework for understanding the depth of a community's social connectedness. It refers to features of social organization such as networks, norms, and social trust that facilitate coordination and cooperation for mutual benefit (Putnam, 1995). The World Bank (1999) refers to social capital to the institutions, relationships, and norms that shape the quality and quantity of a society's social interactions. Increasing evidence shows that social cohesion is critical for societies to prosper economically and for development to be sustainable. Social capital is not just the sum of the institutions that underpin a society—it is the glue that holds them together (The World Bank, 1999). Another view of social capital presented by Cohen and Prusak (2001, p. 4) is that social capital consists of the stock of active connections among people: the trust, mutual understanding, and shared values and behaviors that bind the members of human networks and communities and make cooperative action possible.

The notion of social capital was first introduced by Lyda Judson Hanifan's discussions of rural school community centers (Hanifan 1916, 1920 cited in Smith, 2001). He used the term to describe "those tangible substances [that] count for most in the daily lives of people" (1916, p. 130). Hanifan was particularly concerned with the cultivation of good will, fellowship, sympathy and social intercourse among those that "make up a social unit."

It has taken some time during the years for the concept to come into extensive usage. Most recently, it has been the work of Robert D. Putnam (1990, 2000) that has initiated social capital as a focus for research and policy discussion. However, other prominent contributions have come from Jane Jacobs (1961) in relation to urban life and neighborliness. Pierre Bourdieu (1983) first used the term to refer to the advantages and opportu-

nities accruing to people through membership in certain communities with regard to social theory, and James Coleman (1988) in his discussions of the social context of education and also used it to describe a resource of individuals that emerges from their social ties. For Coleman, it differs from the financial capital found in bank accounts and the human capital inside people's heads; instead, social capital inheres in interpersonal relations. Social capital describes the durable networks that form social resources through which individuals and groups strive for mutual recognition. As such, social capital is the necessary infrastructure of civic and community life that generates "norms of reciprocity and civic engagement."

Adler and Kwon (2002) define social capital as the goodwill that is engendered by the fabric of social relations and that can be mobilized to facilitate action (p.17). Social capital at the firm level is created through the connectivity or relatedness between human resources of the firm and the creation of knowledge value sometimes termed as "intellectual capital" (Chaminade & Roberts, 2002). But social capital also is used to refer to the network of social relationships. The term social capital also has been picked up by the World Bank as a useful organizing idea. And we also have begun to see social capital as a focus for organizational maintenance and development (Cohen & Prusak, 2001).

Usually social capital is described as a community level attribute. Jacobs (1961) defines social capital as *neighborhood networks*. Networks are not merely the result of historical accident; they came about as individuals spend time and energy to connect with others. According to Putnam (1995), social capital represents features of social life— networks, norms, and trust that enable participants to act together more effectively to pursue shared objectives.

A SOCIOLOGICAL APPROACH FOR SOCIAL CAPITAL FORMATION

In their comprehensive review of the conceptual literature of social capital, Nahapiet and Ghoshal (1998) divide the concept into three dimensions (different from Putnam's dimensions): structure, cognitive, and relational. Structural social capital refers to the ways in which motivated recipients gain access to actors with desired sets of knowledge and intellectual capital. This dimension of social capital usually is studied using a network approach. In the network approach, the frequency of contact and resulting social distance among actors in a particular firm or organizational field are plotted to form a web-like diagram illustrating actor interaction patterns. Most of the objective of this type of research is to determine the central nodes of the network or the critical communicators, which is helpful in understanding communication patterns as well as organizational behaviors such as power positioning and knowledge flows (Brass & Burkhardt, 1992; Edelmen et al., 2002).

In contrast, cognitive social capital recognizes that exchange occurs within a social context that is both created and sustained through ongoing relationships (Nahapiet & Ghoshal, 1998). Similar to the notion of community of practice (Brown & Duguid, 1991) and some aspects of virtual community, cognitive social capital refers to the shared meanings that are created through stories and continual discussions within a specific, often clearly defined group. These shared meanings are self-reinforcing in that participation in the community is dependent upon a priori understanding of the context and continual contribution to the on-going dialogues.

Finally, the third dimension of social capital refers to the relational aspect. It is concerned with the underlying normative dimensions that guide exchange relationship behaviors. Norms exist when the socially defined right to control an action is not held by the individual actor, but instead is held by others (Coleman, 1990). Therefore, norms represent degrees of consensus and hence are powerful (Nahapiet & Ghoshal, 1998).

Apart from the above dimensions, two areas of research are of interest to this sociological approach for understanding the development process of social capital: (a) Elementary Theory of Social Structure by Willer and Anderson (1981) and (b) Social Exchange Theory by Thibault and Kelley (1952).

ELEMENTARY THEORY OF SOCIAL STRUCTURE (ET)

ET involves the understanding of the mechanics of exchange, conflict, coercive relations, and the hybrid combinations of the three (Willer & Anderson, 1981; Willer, 1999). These mechanics then are used to examine the formation of social capital through knowledge sharing practices in virtual communities.

ET is a modeling procedure that can be used to build models of properties inside the actor, like preferences and beliefs, and for properties outside the actor, like social relations, and social structures (Willer, 1999, p. 23). This approach is similar to Nahapiet's and Ghoshal's (1998) cognitive social capital dimension mentioned earlier.

The core of ET is the concept of *power exercise*. Power exercise is the movement of valued resources among agents, the control of one agent by another, or by both. In general, people who exercise power will gain more and will give less to people over whom power is exercised. Due to this, the direction of power and the amount exercised is an essential concern to people in society (Willer, 1999). Power consists of benefit and control. These two are interrelated. In illustrating who gets what, when, and how people interact, two kinds of events indicate that power is being exercised. First, A is exercising power over B when A *benefits* more than B. Second, A is exercising power over B when A *controls* B more than the contrary (Willer, 1999, p.16).

ET predicts exchange among agents from structure. For example, ET employs the experimentally validated predictor of *exclusion*. Exclusion refers to the level of exchange among agents within a network. Three types of networks are examined within the ET literature—equal power, strong power, and weak power. An equal power network represents a state of no exclusion, or a network of agents that face an equal probability of exclusion. Figure 1 shows two potential representations of equal power networks. One representation is the simple case of a dyad where two agents have an equal potential for exchange. The other is a more complex structure consisting of four agents where every agent is directly connected to every other agent. Assuming only one exchange can happen at a point in time, it can be seen that all agents have the same chance of being excluded during any given exchange.

A strong power network consists of one or more agents who are never excluded from an exchange and one or more agents who are potentially always excluded from an exchange. Figure 2 includes two examples of strong networks where the probability of an A-exchange is 100% and the probability for a B, C, or D-exclusion is 100%.

Weak power exists between the two extremes of equal power and strong power. That is, no single agent is necessarily any more powerful than any other agent in the network as all the agents have a—albeit unequal—probability of exclusion. This is best illustrated by showing how a strong power network can be changed into a weak power network. Figure 3 illustrates how allowing for the possibility of a B-D exchange can reduce the variability in the probabilities of exclusion.

Although a number of social structure theories are *reductionist*—which assumes that exchange is dependent upon rationality, habit, or emotion—it has been shown that exchange is more accurately predicted by variables such as exclusion (Willer, 1999). Thus, structure and other variables at the macro-level are a potentially more powerful determinant of exchange than characteristics of any one particular agent.

Willer (1999) further suggests that preference and beliefs of the actors in a social relation are built out of sanctions. A sanction is defined as "a social action transmitted by one actor and received by another, which alters the 'preference state' of the actor receiving the sanction." An act is a sanction if and only if it affects the preference state of the receiving actor. Figure 4 below suggests two types of sanctions. 4a is a positive sanction because B is willing to accept what A is offering while 4b is a negative sanction because B is not willing to accept what A is offering. All actors prefer positive sanctions to no sanction and no sanction to negative sanctions (Willer, 1999).

A social exchange exists when at least two sanctions are involved within a social relation. Figure 5 presents three examples of social exchanges—exchange, coercion, and conflict (Willer, 1999). Both sanctions are positive for exchange, both sanctions are negative for conflict, and one sanction is positive, and the other is negative for coercion.

Figure 1. Equal power networks

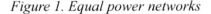

Figure 2. Strong power networks

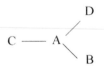

Figure 3. Strong power to weak power

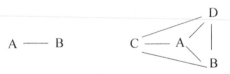

Figure 4. Types of sanctions

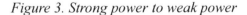
a. Positive Sanction

b. Negative Sanction

Specifically, exchange refers to situations involving economic exchanges (e.g., paying for the knowledge of another individual) or exchange involving a mutual *gift* (e.g., sharing knowledge freely with a trusted colleague). It is important to note that this chapter does not highlight the economic exchanges; instead it focuses more on the behavioral exchanges of knowledge that can further be illustrated by using social exchange theory.

Willer (1999) suggested there are three systems or models of social control and norm enforcement as illustrated in Figure 6. Each system is treated as having four actors—*a, b, c*, and *d*. There are two alternative forms of interaction possible for

Figure 5. A list of social relations

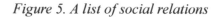

Figure 6. Systems of social control and norm enforcement

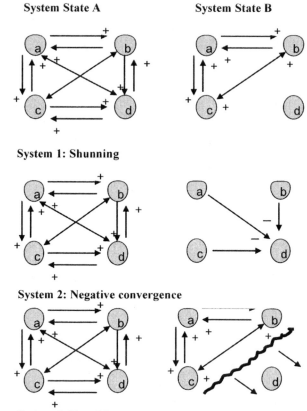

these members; (1) system states A, and (2) system states B. Each of these system states represent a norm that is being enforced. System state A in each case represents the sharing of goods and services among members, which involves positive sanctions, while system state B represents the response of *n*-1 actors to nonconformity by actor d. Nonconformity refers to the commission of act *x*, from the set *x*, which other members have an interest in prohibiting.

The first system of social control and norm enforcement is called *shunning*. In this system, actor *d* has committed act *x*, while actors *a*, *b*, and *c* may remain to transmit and receive positive sanctions. Actor d has not disrupted the network between *a*, *b*, and *c*, but it has been shunned by them as a result of its act. No other action has been implemented on *d*.

The second system is called *negative convergence*. This is when actor *d* has violated the norm by the commission of act *x*. In reaction, actors *a*, *b*, and *c* transmit negative sanctions, accusations, insults, or threats toward actor *d*. As a consequence, actor *d* is at the point of convergence toward these negatives. The third system is called *expulsion*. In this system, an infringement of a norm by actor d leads to the expulsion of d from the network by other actors. This type of norm enforcement usually involves physical as well as being thrown out from the group. Expulsion is a norm of enforcement that cannot stand alone since negative convergence acts as a backup if the deviant resists the attempt of being rejected.

The principle of ET suggests that agreements occur at the point of equal resistance for undifferentiated actors in full information systems (Willer, 1999). That is, agents make an exchange that will maximally benefit all the agents involved while minimizing the possibility of conflict. Most pertinent to this discussion is (1) ETs foundation in established social and economic theory, and (2) its applicability to knowledge sharing. In order to directly link ET to KS we must return to the concept of a sanction. Although sanctions can have positive or negative effects on the agents involved, they are not rewards or punishments. A sanction is an exchange of goods between agents. A good

in this sense can be best illustrated by contrasting it with a service. Although services can be exchanged among agents in a network, goods are what ultimately flow through a network.

A service might be delivered, but the service *per se* terminates upon the completion of its delivery. That is, one might gain some knowledge or information in receiving a service, but knowledge and information are the objects of study that are ultimately and repeatedly exchanged. In this sense, knowledge or information can be viewed as a good rather than a service. Knowledge is an object whose exchange is directly linked to a measurable act and whose effect can be directly linked to the observable behavior of the agents involved in the exchange.

This directly ties into the requirement that a sanction always links an objective—and therefore quantifiable—acts with a subjective—and therefore potentially quantifiable—effect. Again, this allows for the application of the experimentally grounded theory of ET to an organizational setting. Following from the discussion above, a service could be an objective act that represents an exchange of knowledge. The effect of this act can potentially be measured by using a combination of methods focused on gathering and analyzing data at both the individual and group levels. Additionally, the basic assumption that agents prefer positive sanctions suggests that further information about the flow of specific knowledge could potentially be used to further validate the findings at the individual and group levels. For example, knowledge that results in negative sanctions will potentially result in a different—perhaps, more abbreviated—pattern of exchange than knowledge resulting in positive sanctions.

SOCIAL EXCHANGE THEORY

The ET theory works from the premise that actors or participants of a community often times will exercises power over the three main social mechanics—exchanges, coercion, and conflicts. Even though this theory is well-established and able to predict the pattern of exchanges, or ties the sanctions with the actions to avoid conflicts, but it is difficult to determine the relationships in the environment where formal social structure is not evident, such as the VC. Thus, we look at another theory—social exchange, which has a more appropriate approach to understanding the dynamics of VC. Basically, this theory establishes that in order for exchanges of goods and behaviors to take place in an organization, there is a joint activity or transaction that would involve two or more actors when each of them has something the other would value (Thibault & Kelley, 1959; Homans, 1961; Emerson, 1972). Here, the assumption made is that actors face substantial degrees of uncertainty and ambiguity about what the potential partner values, the utility of different exchanges to them, and what exchanges are been made between others in the exchanged network (Molm &Cook, 1995).

Social exchange theory primarily deals with how actors react to these uncertainties and ambiguities, in which the actors based their expectations of rewards, cost, and punishments. Likewise, the actors also use this information to anticipate their future exchanges in terms of the rewards, cost, and punishments. In addition, this theory highlights the importance of cost and rewards in the formation of social relationship.

According to Thibault and Kelley (1959), exchange theory is based on the exchange of rewards and costs to quantify the values of outcomes from different situations for an individual. People strive to minimize costs and maximize rewards, and then base the likeliness of developing a relationship with someone on the perceived possible outcomes. For example, when a person perceives a greater outcome from another person, he or she intends to disclose or share the knowledge greater and thus develops a closer relationship with that person. Another important aspect of this theory is that people will establish a reciprocal relationship among themselves once these two main elements—cost and rewards—are fulfilled.

This theory is applicable to VC because it helps people to understand the crucial issue of *how can I best gain knowledge yet reduce the costs* through social network without emphasizing the power status of members in a society. Power seems not to be the main determinant to ensure effective knowledge sharing though there is an implication of the power element in reality. More profoundly, the establishment of social capital works on the premise of relationship. Since VC works in an informal setting, the empowerment element becomes more relevant, while the exercise of power is less salient.

PROPOSED CONCEPTUAL FRAMEWORK

A conceptual framework called *process of building social capital* is developed in the context of virtual community (refer to Figure 7). To note, this framework is adapted from an organizational context, and by integrating the ideas, in this section we attempt to explore and apply it in another context—the VC. Moreover, this framework is proposed as an integration and inclusion of both the above-mentioned theories that take into account the key social capital variables such as structure, trust, memberships, technology, volunteerism, reciprocity, and leadership.

First of all, this model begins with the first layer of the types of knowledge, tacit and explicit. A full understanding of these two types of knowledge will facilitate people to differentiate how knowledge is exchanged and shared among people in organizations. Then, the process of knowledge sharing introduced by MITRE Corporation (2002) is illustrated. Since knowledge is a mix of experience, values, contextual information, and expert insights, providing a framework for evaluating and incorporating new experiences and information is thus crucial. MITRE suggests that knowledge flows among people and collections in four ways: individuals or groups exchange it with others (knowledge exchange), record it or capture it (knowledge capture), reuse the recorded knowledge assets (knowledge reuse), and finally, generate new knowledge as they internalize learning into the way they think and know (knowledge internalization). These are the four types of knowledge sharing activities, which is similar to Nonaka and Takeuchi's concepts of externalization and inter-

Figure 7. A conceptual framework of the process of building social capital

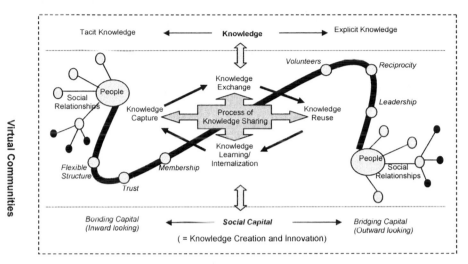

(Source: Adapted from MITRE, 2002; and Putnam, 1995)

nalization. These conceptions are also applied and adopted from MITRE to be used in virtual communities. Furthermore, Nonaka & Takeuchi (1995) and Sveiby (2001) assert that knowledge sharing involves a two-way process between two or more employees, and it is believed to develop the competency of the employees involved. Together these processes build a learning virtual community, equipped with skills such as creating, acquiring, transferring knowledge, and adapting actions to reflect new insight and innovation.

In line with the idea of structuration, Giddens (1984) integrates the concept of knowledge and social relationships. He states that a relationship between people is established as soon as they share knowledge with one another and that particular relationship between people consequently influences the way knowledge is being shared. Knowledge can be shared between people interacting face-to-face, or through technology either asynchronous or synchronous (which is known as virtual community). In the above model (refer to Figure 7), it is explicitly shown that *people* are linked to several nodes that indicate the networks based on the establishment of social exchanges of goods and behaviors. In this respect, they are assumed to have the reciprocal element when they determine the value of knowledge each of them has. The exchange of knowledge is further moderated

by the elements of power, control, and benefits by each exchanging party as highlighted in the elementary theory of the social structure.

In Figure 6, there is a dark line with several key nodes representing the *social capital* variables, which are directly connected to the people with their own social bonds, norms, and networks. It is hoped that these antecedents consisting of six key variables will, in turn, facilitate the final process—the knowledge sharing and creation of social networks and exchanges to build social capital in VC. Subsequently, this outcome, social capital, is framed as the last layer of the proposed conceptual framework where social capital can be seen as having two additional dimensions—bonding (or exclusive) and bridging (or inclusive). The former may be more inward-looking and have a tendency to reinforce exclusive identities and homogeneous groups. While the latter may be more outward-looking and encompass people across different social divides (Putnam, 2000, p. 22). Putnam goes on to explain that bonding capital is good for under girding specific reciprocity and mobilizing solidarity, while bridging networks, by contrast, is better for linkage to external assets and for information diffusion. Moreover, bridging social capital can generate broader identities and reciprocity, whereas, bonding social capital bolsters our narrower selves (p. 22-23). These are not *either-or* categories to which social networks can neatly be assigned but rather *more-or-less* dimensions in which comparisons can be made on the different forms of social capital (p. 23). In the next section, by using the above framework (see Figure 7), the six antecedents of building the social capital based on a sociological standpoint are discussed.

SOCIOLOGICAL IMPLICATIONS OF VIRTUAL COMMUNITIES

According to Nahapiet et al. (1998), the key idea behind social capital building is that networks of relationships involve a valuable resource for providing people with privilege access to information and opportunities. The interpersonal dynamics between individual networks are equally important as having the social network of individuals. Thus, the implication of positive interactions that take place between individuals in the network is significant because it leads to the success of building the social capital in both the organizational context as well as the VC (Lesser, 2000).

Creating social capital implies creating the opportunity, the motivation, and the ability for knowledge sharing in VC. Thus, the propositions have some complex implications in the sense that VC emerges as a new form of community that exists without a formal structure, and it transcends across space, time, and distance. It, therefore, frames these antecedents based on the organizational perspectives present and contributes a new outlook of the key idea of social capital building and social exchange network. More important, it helps to promote a better understanding of the process of building the social capital in the VCs.

Flexible Structures and Mobility

As mentioned, tacit knowledge is difficult to gain because it is not tangible or easily codified in a formal structure, yet it is most desirable in organizations today. In essence, the know-how (tacit) knowledge is expected to be able to tap more resourceful and intangible information from people. Thus, to promote a greater flow of this type of knowledge, Chaminade and Roberts (2002) suggest that organization needs to allow mobility and teamwork by removing all the traditional and hierarchical boundaries that exists in an organization, even at the managerial level. In support of that, Fairtlough (1994) states that when a high degree of innovation and speed is required, the elimination of job descriptions, enhanced flexibility and initiative, as well as, increased self-motivation would be the key success to effective organization.

Trustworthiness Among Members

Putnam (2000) promotes *trust* as the essential component of social capital. He further asserts that trust helps to increase cooperation. The greater the level of trust within the communities, the greater the likelihood of cooperation in which the end result all leads to enhanced trust among members. Nahapiet and Ghoshal (1998) emphasize that over time a culture of cooperation would surface among this trusted group of people that can be strengthened through social interactions. However, this social relationship can wither if it is not maintained. Thus, interaction is a precondition for the development and maintenance of social capital (Bourdieu, 1986).

Memberships

There is a significant relationship between trust and membership. Membership reflects the degree of civic engagement and the nature of horizontal relations between individuals as members that have established the necessary trust between them. Additionally, membership describes the element of cohesiveness that is expected to exist in any social relationship, which acts as a glue that bonds the members together. McGrail et al. (1998) stipulates that membership measures have not focused on memberships of national organizations such as environmental groups or unions because they are considered hierarchical and bureaucratic. In this structure, it does not generate much social capital as compared to a more flexible and lateral relationship that exists in virtual environment.

Table 1. Propositions to understand formation of social capital in virtual communities

Understanding the Formation of Social Capital in VC
Proposition 1: The flexible and mobile structure of VC allows better knowledge sharing and thus the ability to build successful social capital.
Proposition 2a: Trustworthiness and interactions among members are two quintessential elements for high cooperation among members of VC for knowledge sharing and social capital building.
Proposition 2b: A high level of trusting relationships and a cooperative spirit among VC members promotes lower transaction costs.
Proposition 3a: A non-hierarchical and informal structure of VC promotes cohesive membership in order to establish a strong social and trusting relationship in social capital building.
Proposition 3b: Greater cohesiveness in turn allows members to share greater knowledge in building social capital.
Proposition 4: An active role of volunteers helps to facilitate and support the organization of the knowledge-sharing activities in VC.
Proposition 5: In order to sustain the VC, the reciprocal element among members needs to exist sufficiently.
Proposition 6: The emergence of leadership roles in VC helps to integrate and distribute social capital among members through knowledge-sharing activities.

Volunteerism

The commitment to the community increases when people continue to volunteer (Ginsburg & Weisband, 2002). Volunteerism represents selfless actions that promote community spirit and civic participation; while at the same time, changes the volunteer's self-concept to promote further volunteerism (Omoto & Snyder, 2001). Active volunteers are those who are motivated because they perceive equitable and rewarding relationships and thus are more likely to continue their services (Pandey, 1979). Therefore, this act of volunteerism is a precondition to promote and sustain loyalty and commitment of the members.

Reciprocity

Reciprocity increases trust and refers to the simultaneous exchange of items of roughly equal value and continuous relationship of exchanges at any given time—repaid and balanced (Coleman,

1990; Putnam, 1993). Furthermore, Taylor (1982) (in Bullen & Oynx, 1998) highlights that social capital is a combination of short-term altruism and long-term self-interest as it does not only imply the immediate and formally accounted exchange of legal or business contract. The individual provides a service to others or acts for the benefit of others at a personal cost. Yet, based on general expectations of human nature, there is always a need for reciprocal acts where their kindness would be returned at some undefined time in the future. Normally, when a community has a strong reciprocal relationship, people express their care and interest for each other more often. In turn, this relationship encourages the knowledge sharing that forms the social capital.

Leadership

Only effective management and efficient roles played by a leader will reduce the costs and accelerate the developments of new products and services in an organization. Furthermore, organizations will need to react faster and use its resources more efficiently, in this case, particularly, its social capital in order to enhance knowledge sharing. Likewise, effective creation of knowledge sharing by the leader promotes efficient distribution of the social capital in an organization.

FUTURE DIRECTIONS AND CONCLUSION

This chapter attempts to propose that if the previously mentioned variables are the success factors in the organization, can the same variables be applied in the VC environment? It is suggested that the sociological perspective provides an interesting view to this new phenomenon of VC because several studies (though limited) have shown that community can exist in both the physical as well as virtual space. With rapid expansion of new communication and information technologies, more and more people are engaged in the community activities that take place on the Internet. They have learned to establish as well as enjoy friendships and relationships with hundreds and thousands of people across the globe without constraints such as time, distance, and geographical locations (Mohd Yusof, 2005). Therefore, it is useful to note that this chapter only provides a conceptual framework to explore and understand the dynamics of social network in VC. For empirical work, researchers can benefit from the six propositions presented in this chapter (see Table 1.0), which can lead to future research. In summary, some potential key research questions are:

- What is the impact of flexible structures and mobility on the formation of social capital in VC?
- How do members develop trust among themselves in order to facilitate the social capital formation?
- To what extent does membership promote knowledge sharing among VC?
- In what ways do volunteerisms facilitate knowledge-sharing activities in VC?

- How important is the reciprocal element in motivating knowledge sharing among VC?
- What is the role of emergent leadership in facilitating the formation of social capital in VC?

Additionally, there are other antecedents, causal factors, and moderating factors that can be explored apart from the six variables presented in this chapter. For example, the following variables also are as important, such as types of technologies used (asynchronous vs. synchronous), social presence, ease of use and usefulness of technology, organizational culture, cultural values, and so forth.

In a nutshell, there is no doubt that social capital is an important resource for the sustainable livelihoods of virtual communities. VC provides a new platform for people to understand the dynamics of interactions that take place in virtual space, and the process of social group formation by taking into consideration the antecedents that are expected to promote greater exchanges of knowledge and then translate as their fundamental assets—social capital. Social capital provides vast opportunities for societies to resolve collective problems more easily, as more synergistic values are added when people cooperate and commit with each other. By doing his or her part, this effort facilitates the community to advance smoothly, particularly when the members are bonded by trust and close relationships—consequently leading to a more intensified process of knowledge sharing among the members in the VC.

REFERENCES

Adler, P., & Kwan, S.W. (2002). Social capital: Prospects for a new concept. *Academy of Management Review, 27*(1), 17-40.

Bellah, R. N. (1985). *Habits of the heart: Individualism and commitment in American life*. New York: Harper Collins.

Benedikt, M. (Ed.) (1991). *Cyberspace: First steps*. Cambridge: MIT Press.

Boer, N. I., van Baalen, P. J., & Kumar, K. (2002, April 5-6). The implications of different models of social relations for understanding knowledge sharing. *3rd European Conference on Organizational Knowledge, Learning and Capabilities (OKLC),* Athens Laboratory of Business Administration, Athens, Greece.

Bourdieu, P. (1983) Forms of capital. In J.C. Richards (Ed.), *Handbook of theory and research for the sociology of education.* New York: Greenwood Press.

Brass, D. J., & Burkhardt, M. E. (1992). Centrality and power in organizations. In N. Nohria & R. G. Eccles (Eds.), *Networks and organizations: Structure, form and action.* Boston: Harvard Business School Press.

Brown, J. S., & Duguid, P. (1991). Organizational learning and communities of practice: Towards a unified view of working, learning, and innovation. *Organization Science, 2*(1), 40-57.

Bullen, P., & Onyx, J. (1998). *Measuring social capital in five communities in NSW.* [online]. Available: http://www.map1,com.au/A2.htm

Burnett, G. (2000). Information exchange in virtual communities: A typology. *Information Research, 5*(4), paper 82. Retrieved January 25, 2007, from http://informationr.net/ir/5-4/paper82.html

Chaminade, C., & Roberts, H. (2002, April 5-6). Social capital as a mechanism: Connecting knowledge within and across firms. *The 3rd European Conference on Organizational Knowledge, Learning and Capabilities (OKLC),* Athens Laboratory of Business Administration, Athens, Greece.

Cohen, D., & Prusak, L. (2001). *In good company. How social capital makes organizations work.* Boston: Harvard Business School Press.

Coleman, J. C. (1988). Social capital in the creation of human capital. *American Journal of Sociology, 94,* 95-120.

Coleman, J. C. (1990). *Foundations of social theory,* Cambridge, MA: Harvard University Press.

Edelman, L. F., Bresnen, M., Newell, S., Scarbrough, H., & Swan, J. (2002, April 5-6). The darker side of social capital. *3rd European Conference on Organizational Knowledge, Learning and Capabilities (OKLC),* Athens Laboratory of Business Administration, Athens, Greece.

Emerson, R. (1972). Exchange theory, part 1: A psychological basis for social exchange. In J. Berger, M. Zelditch, & B. Anderson (Eds.), *Sociological theories in progress,* 2. Boston: Houghton-Muffin.

Fernback, J., & Thompson, B. (1995). *Virtual communities: Abort, retry, failure?* Available http://www.well.com/user/hlr/texts/VCcivil.html

Giddens, A. (1984). *The constitution of society.* University of California Press.

Ginsburg, M., & Weisband, S. (2002). Social capital and volunteerism in virtual communities: The case of the Internet chess club. *Proceedings of the 35th Hawaii International Conference on System Sciences.*

Granovetter, M. S. (1982). The strength of weak ties: A network theory revisited. In P.V. Marsden & N. Lin (Eds.), *Social structure and network analysis* (pp. 105-130). Beverly Hills: Sage.

Hanifan, L. J. (1916). The rural school community center, *Annals of the American Academy of Political and Social Science, 67,* 130-138.

Hiltz, S. R., & Wellman, B. (1997). Asynchronous learning networks as virtual communities. *Communications of the ACM,* 44-49.

Homans, G. L. (1961). *Social behavior: Its elementary forms.* New York: Harcourt Brace Jovanovich.

Hossain, L., D'Eridita, M., & Wigand, R. (2002). Towards a product process dichotomy for understanding knowledge management, sharing and transfer systems in organizations. *Submitted to IBM Systems Journal,* New York.

Igbaria, M. (1999). The driving forces in the virtual society. *Communications of the ACM, 42*(12), 64-70.

Jacobs, J. (1961). *The death and life of great American cities.* New York: Random.

Jones, S. (Ed.) (1995). *Cybersociety: Computer-mediated communication and community.* Thousand Oaks: Sage.

Karp, D., Stone, G., & Yoels, W. (1977). *Being urban: A social psychological view of city life.* Lexington, MA: Heath and Company.

Kitchin R. (1998). *Cyberspace: The world in the wires.* Chichester, UK: John Wiley & Sons.

Kowch, e. & Schwier, R. (1997). Characteristics of technology-based virtual learning communities. In *Learning Comminities and Technology, University of Saskachewan,* 1-12.

Krogh, G. V., Ichijo, K., & Nonaka, I. (2000). *Enabling knowledge creation: How to unlock the mystery of tacit knowledge and release the power of innovation.* New York: Oxford University Press.

Lapachet, J. (1995). *Virtual communities: The 90's mind altering drug and facilitator of human interaction?* Master's thesis. School of Library and Information Studies, UCLA, Berkeley.

Lawrence, T. B. (1995). Power and resources in an organizational community, *Academy of Management Best Papers Proceedings* (pp. 251-255).

Lesser, E. (2000). Leveraging social capital in organizations. In E. Lesser (Ed.), *Knowledge and social capital.* Boston: Butterworth-Heinemann.

McGrail, K. M., Ostry, A., Salazar Thomas, V., & Sanmartin, C. (1998). Determinants of population health: A synthesis of the literature. *Health Canada.*

Mohd Yusof, S. A. (2005). *Rules of the game: The social world of EverQuest.* Unpublished dissertation, Syracuse University, NY.

Molm, L., & Cook, K. (1995). Social exchange and exchange networks. In K.S. Cook, G.A. Fine, & J.S. House (Eds.), *Sociological perspectives on social psychology* (pp. 209-235). Boston: Allyn & Bacon.

Nahapiet, J., & Ghoshal, S. (1998). Social capital, intellectual capital and the organizational advantage. *Academy of Management Review, 23*(2), 242-266.

Nelson, L., Ramsey, C. E., & Verner, C. (1960). *Community structure and change.* New York: The Macmillan Co.

Nonaka, I. (1992). A dynamic theory of organizational knowledge creation. In *Organization Science, 5,* 14-37.

Nonaka, I., & Takeuchi, H. (1995). *The knowledge-creating company.* New York: Oxford University Press, Inc.

Omoto, A. M., & Synder, M. (2001). *Basic research and practical problems: Volunteerism and the psychology of individual and collective action.* In W. Wonsinska et al. (Eds.). Mahwah: Lawrence Erlbaum.

Pandey, J. (1979). Social participation as a function of internal/external control of reinforcement. *Journal of Social Psychology, 107,* 284-285.

Polanyi, M. (1975). *Personal knowledge: Toward a post-critical philosophy.* Chicago: University of Chicago Press.

Putnam, R. D. (1990). The prosperous community: Social capital and public life. *American Prospect, 13,* 35-42.

Putnam, R. D. (1995). Bowling Alone: America's declining social capital. *Journal of Democracy, 6,* 65-78.

Putnam, R. D. (2000). *Bowling alone: The collapse and revival of American community.* New York: Simon and Schuster.

Preece, J. (2002). Supporting community and building social capital. *Communications of the ACM, 45*(4), 37-39.

Renzi, B. (2002, April 5-6). Facilitating knowledge sharing through inter-action research. *3rd European Conference on Organizational Knowledge, Learning and Capabilities (OKLC),* Athens Laboratory of Business Administration, Athens, Greece.

Rheingold, H. (1993) *Virtual communities*. London: Secker & Warburg.

Rothaermel, F.T., & Sugiyama, S. (2001). Virtual Internet communities and commercial success: Individual and community-level theory grounded in the atypical case of TimeZone.com. *Journal of Management, 27*(3), 297-312.

Schuler, D. (1996). *New community networks: Wired for change*. New York: Addison-Wesley.

Smith, M., & Kollock, P. (1997). *Communities in cyberspace: Perspectives on new forms of social organizations*. Los Angeles: University of California Press.

Smith, M. K. (2001). *Social Capital*. [online]. Available: Http://www.infed.org/bibliosocialcapital.htm

Stolterman, E., Agren, P.O., & Croon, A. (1999). *Virtual communities: Why and how are they studied*. [Online]. Available: http://www.vircom.com/virtualcommunities.html

Sveiby, K. (2001), A knowledge-based theory of the firm to guide in strategic formulation. *Journal of Intellectual Capital, 2*(4), 344-58.

The World Bank (1999).What is social capital? *PovertyNet*. Available: http://www.worldbank.org/poverty/scapital/whatsc.htm

Thibaut, J. W., & Kelly, H. H. (1959). *The social psychology of groups*. New York: Wiley.

Turoff, M. (1991). Computer-mediated communication requirements for group support. *Journal of Organizational Computing, 1*(1), 85-113.

Walther, J. B., & Boyd, S. (1997). Attraction to computer-mediated social support. *International Communication Association Meeting in Montreal*.

Wenger, E. (1998). *Communities of practice*. Cambridge: Cambridge University Press.

Willer, D. (1999). *Network exchange theory (Edited)*, Westport, Cr: Praeger.

Willer, D., & Anderson, B. (1981). *Network exchange, and connection*. New York: Elsevier.

ADDITIONAL READING

Ahuja, G. (2000). Collaboration networks, structural holes, and innovation: A longitudinal study. *Administrative Science Quarterly, 45*(3), 425-455.

Ahuja, M. K., & Galvin, J. E. (2003). Socialization in virtual groups. *Journal of Management, 29*, 161-185.

Anderson, A. H., McEwan, R., Bal, J., & Carletta, J. (2007). Virtual team meetings: An analysis of communication and context. *Computers in Human Behavior, 23*, 2558-2580.

Bagozzi, R. P., Dholakia, U. M., & Mookerjee, A. (2006). Individual and group bases of social influence in online environments. *Media Psychology, 8*, 95-126.

Baron, S., Field, J., & Schuller, T. (Eds.) (2000). *Social capital: Critical perspectives*. Oxford University Press.

Baum, F. (2000). Social capital, economic capital and power: Further issues for a public health agenda. *Journal of Epidemiological Community Health, 54*, 409-410.

Birchmeier, Z., Joinson, A. N., & Dietz-Uhler, B. (2005). Storming and forming a normative response to a deception revealed online. *Social Science Computer Review, 23*, 108-121.

Blaxter, M. Poland, F. Curran, M. (2001) *Measuring social capital: Qualitative study of how older people relate social capital to health*. Final Report to the Health Development Agency. London.

Borgatti, S., & Cross, R. (2003). A relational view of information seeking and learning in social networks. *Management Science, 49*, 432-445.

Borgida, E., Sullivan, J. L., Oxendine, A., Jackson, M. S., & Gangl, A. (2002). Civic culture meets the digital divide: The role of community electronic networks. *Journal of Social Issues, 58,* 125-14.

Brukman, A. (2006) Learning in online communities. In R.K. Sawyer (Ed.), *The Cambridge handbook of the learning sciences* (pp. 461-472). Boston: Cambridge University Press.

Bryant, C. A., & Norris, D. (2002). Measurement of social capital: Canadian experience. *International Cconference on Ssocial Ccapital Measurement,* London, OECD.

Cross, R., Borgatti, S., & Parker, A. (2002). Making invisible work visible: Using social network analysis to support human networks. *California Management Review, 44*(2), 25-46.

Cross, R., Nohria, N., & Parker, A. (2002). Six myths about informal networks-and how to overcome them. *Sloan Management Review, 43*(3), 67-76.

Cross, R., & Parker, A. (2004). *The hidden power of social networks: Understanding how work really gets done in organizations.* Boston: Harvard Business School Press.

Cross, R., Parker, A., Prusak, L., & Borgatti, S. (2001). Knowing what we know: Supporting knowledge creation and sharing in social networks. *Organizational Dynamics, 30*(2), 100-120.

Cummings, J. (2004). Work groups, structural diversity, and knowledge sharing in a global organization. *Management Science, 50*(3), 352-364.

Cummings, J., & Cross, R. (2003). Structural properties of work groups and their consequences for performance. *Social Networks, 25*(3), 197-210.

Fine, B. (2000). *Social capital versus social theory: Political economy and social science at the turn of the millennium.* London: Routledge.

Glosiene, A. (2006). Social capital and information technology. *Journal of Documentation, 62*(5), 635-640.

Hall, H. (2004). Creation and recreation: Motivating collaboration to generate knowledge capital in online communities. *International Journal of Information Management, 24*(3), 235-246.

Haidt, J. (2006). *The happiness hypothesis. Putting ancient wisdom and philosophy to the test of modern science.* London: Heinemann.

Hansen, M. (2002). Knowledge networks: Explaining effective knowledge sharing in multiunit companies. *Organization Science, 13*(3), 232-248.

Matei, S. (2004). The impact of state-level social capital on the emergence of virtual communities. *Journal of Broadcasting and Electronic Media, 48*(1), 23-40.

Michinov, N., & Primois, C. (2005). Improving productivity and creativity in online groups through social comparison process: New evidence for asynchronous electronic brainstorming. *Computers in Human Behavior, 21,* 11-28.

Nip, J. Y. M. (2004). The relationship between online and offline communities: The case of the Queer Sisters. *Media, Culture & Society, 26,* 409-428.

Norris, P. (2004). The bridging and bonding role of online communities. In P.N. Howard & S. Jones (Eds.), *Society online: The Internet in context* (pp. 31-41). Thousand Oaks, CA: Sage.

Offer, A. (2006). *The challenge of affluence. Self-control and well-being in the United States and Britain since 1950.* Oxford: Oxford University Press.

Parr, J., & Ward, L. (2006). Building on foundations: Creating an online community. *Journal of Technology and Teacher Education, 14,* 775-793.

Pretty, J. N., & Ward, H. (2001). *What is social capital? World Development, 29*(2), 209-227. University of Essex Web site.

Schuller, T. (2001). The complementary roles of human and social capital. *ISUMA Canadian Journal of Policy Research, 2*(1), 18-24.

Smith, R. O. (2005). Working with difference in online collaborative groups. *Adult Education Quarterly, 55,* 182-199.

Swan, K., & Shea, P. (2005). The development of virtual learning communities. In S.R. Hiltz

& R. Goldman (Eds.), *Learning together online: Research on asynchronous learning networks* (pp. 239-260). Mahwah, NJ: Erlbaum.

Timmerman, C. E., & Scott, C. R. (2006). Virtually working: Communicative and structural predictors of media use and key outcomes in virtual work teams. *Communication Monographs, 73,* 108-136.

Wang, S., & Lin, S. S. J. (2007). The effects of group composition of self-efficacy and collective efficacy on computer-supported collaborative learning. *Computers in Human Behavior, 23,* 2256-2268.

Widen-Wurlff, G. (2004). Explaining knowledge sharing in organizations through the dimensions of social capital. *Journal of Information Science, 30*(5), 448-458.

Woolcock, M. (2001). The place of social capital in understanding social and economic outcomes. *ISUMA Canadian Journal of Policy Research, 2*(1), 11-17.

Zrebiec, J. F. (2005). Internet communities: Do they improve coping with diabetes? *Diabetes Educator, 31,* 825-836.

Chapter VIII
Business & IT Alignment in a Multinational Company:
Issues and Approaches

A. J. Gilbert Silvius
Utrecht University of Applied Sciences, The Netherlands

ABSTRACT

This chapter explores the theory and practice of business & IT alignment in multinational companies. In the first part of the chapter an overview of the theory is presented. In this part, the familiar frameworks for business & IT alignment are put in perspective in an "alignment development model." The second part of the chapter presents the practical issues that are experienced in aligning IT to business in multinational companies. These issues and considerations resulted from a focused group discussion with IT managers and CIOs of medium-sized and large organizations in The Netherlands.

INTRODUCTION

In almost all industries, developments like new technologies, mergers and acquisitions, entrepreneurial initiatives, regulatory changes and strategic alliances create a dynamic business environment. A key success factor for a successful company in such a dynamic environment is an effective and efficient information technology (IT)-supporting business strategies and processes. The necessity and desirability of aligning business needs and IT capabilities is examined in numerous articles (Pyburn, 1983; Reich & Benbasat, 1996; Chan et al., 1997; Luftman & Brier, 1999: Maes et al., 2000; Sabherwal & Chan, 2001), and its importance is well-recognized (Cumps et al., 2006). The annual survey on top management concerns by the Society for Information Management (www.simnet.org) ranked "IT and Business alignment" as the No. 1 concern for 3 years in a row (Society of Information Management, 2003, 2004, 2005).

In a survey by Synstar, 78% of European IT managers indicate that their IT is not aligned with business strategy (Synstar, 2004). Another survey shows similar results (Winmark & BMC Software, 2004). Given the *buzz* around "business & IT alignment" BIA in recent years, these results should be surprising. BIA does not seem to live up to its promise (Bloem & Van Doorn, 2004).

This chapter explores the theory and practice of BIA in multinational companies and provides some insights into the difficulties of putting theory into practice. In the first part of the chapter, an overview of the theory is presented. In this part the familiar frameworks for BIA are put in perspective in an "Alignment development model." The second part of the chapter presents the practical issues that are experienced in aligning IT to business in multinational companies. The last part of the chapter presents an analysis of the practical approaches to BIA t that the CIOs and IT managers in the focus groups took.

RESEARCH DESIGN

The research into the specific issues with BIA in multinational companies is part of a research program that explores the differences of BIA in theory and in practice. With this knowledge the theory on BIA can be further developed.

The first step of the research consisted of a literature review on the topic. The literature review is reported in the first section of the chapter. It focused on the following questions.

- How is BIA defined and interpreted?
- Which theories are developed on BIA?
- What was the development path of BIA?

To explore the specific issues with and approaches to BIA in multinational companies, a focused group discussion was organized with IT managers and CIOs of medium-sized and large organizations in the Netherlands. In total, 12 participants from multinational trade, manufacturing and financial companies joined the discussions. The focused groups were aimed at exploring the following questions.

- Which issues are faced in aligning IT with business requirements in practice in multinational companies?
- Which actions are taken to align IT with business requirements in multinational companies?

The results of these discussions are reported in the latter sections of the chapter.

THE DEVELOPMENT OF BUSINESS & IT ALIGNMENT

Phase 1: Traditional IT Planning

The challenge of aligning IT with business requirements is not new. Together with the rise of information systems in organizations, the need for alignment of its use with business processes and strategy grew. As a response to this challenge, methodologies of IT planning and system development were developed. Amongst others: business systems planning (IBM Corporation, 1981), and information systems study, and information engineering (Martin, 1982). These methodologies can be regarded as the predecessors of the BIA theory. Since these methodologies were developed in the '70s and '80s of the last century, it is not surprising that the goal of these methodologies is building a foundation for the development of (large) bespoke information systems. The methodologies, therefore, focused heavily on the analysis and structure of the organizations' data. Table 1 shows an overview of the characteristics of the main methodologies.

The application of these methodologies in practice resulted, however, in extensive schemes

Table 1. Characteristics of the main IT planning methodologies

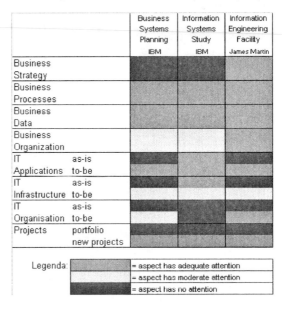

and reports, most of the time losing the (future) users of the systems along the way. IT planning, designed as a tool for business management, became a procedure by IT professionals for IT professionals (Pols, 2003). The rigid and structured nature of these methodologies, although theoretically sound, alienated the business and user side of organizations and their use faded.

Phase 2: Modern IT Planning

Since the traditional IT planning methodologies failed to provide a practical solution, the issue of aligning IT to business needs remained. In the '90s this led to another approach of IT planning (Pols, 2003). Less formalized, but more practical, this "modern IT planning" differs from traditional IT planning in the following aspects (Silvius, 2005).

- **Focus on strategy:** Where the traditional methodologies showed a strong focus on data analysis and structure, the modern methodologies for IT planning show a focus on the business strategy of the organization. IT is seen as an enabler for the goals and targets of the organization, and this is reflected in the process of IT planning. By working with (business) management to translate strategy into *smart* performance indicators, the relation between business goals and IT applications is strengthened.
- **Pragmatic vs. methodological:** The modern approach to IT planning is less formal in methodology. In order to gain acceptance for the results of the planning process, the project creating the IT plan is done *quick,* but also sometimes *dirty.* A sound analysis of the required data structures is quite often postponed to a *follow-up* project.
- **Results in system enhancement and/or selection projects:** Different from the traditional methodologies, is the modern approach to IT planning not primarily aimed at developing new (bespoke) information systems. Given the fact that today companies have more IT-legacy than in the ''70s and '80s, most results

from modern IT planning are enhancements to current systems. If, however, a new system should be developed, it makes more sense to select potential standard software packages, for example, regarding CRM, ERP and financial applications, than to develop bespoke systems.

- **Together with the business:** With the impact of IT on business shifting from an efficiency enhancing production factor toward a source of business innovation, the need for involvement of business professionals in the development of information systems became even more eminent. By clearly addressing the relation between business strategy, processes, and IT projects, modern IT planning succeeds in involving business professionals in the IT planning project, thereby building commitment for the IT plan.
- **Planning IT applications, infrastructure and organization:** In the traditional methodologies of IT planning, the IT infrastructure was a requirement, resulting from the IT applications to be developed. This approach, logical as it is, however, tends to underestimate the importance of the infrastructure as a company asset. In most organizations the IT infrastructure account for 30%-50% of the IT budget. Furthermore, its technology develops autonomously, separate from the applications. Modern IT planning, therefore, pays more attention to the IT infrastructure as a company asset that can be optimized by standardization and utilization of economies of scale. The same considerations apply to the organization of the IT processes.

Phase 3: Business & IT Alignment

The second half of the '90s saw the rise of business & IT alignment as a more logical, and also more fancy, label for the alignment process. Despite the apparent importance of aligning IT and business, the majority of publications are rather vague in terms of how to define or practice alignment (Maes et al., 2000). A first question seems to be how to define the word *alignment.* Other expressions used in this context are *fit* (Venkatraman, 1989), *harmony* (Luftman et al., 1993), *integration* (Weill & Broadbent, 1998), *linkage* (Henderson & Venkatraman, 1993), *bridge* (Ciborra, 1997), or *fusion* (Smaczny, 2001). A second question is whether IT aligns to business or business to IT? Or both? Wieringa et al. (2005) define BIA as "the problem of matching IT services with the requirements of the business," identifying business as leading. This logical, but also traditional, approach is opposed by Poels (2006) who states that BIA implies a "mutual influence" between business and IT.

Another question is whether BIA is a *state* or level that can be achieved or a *process* to get to a certain (higher?) state. The concept of BIA as a *state* is further developed by Luftman (2000), who assesses the BIA maturity level of organizations. Also Reich and Benbasat (1996) *measure* a degree or level of BIA. The process approach to BIA can be found in the methodologies of IT planning developed in the '70s and '80s (IBM Corporation, 1981; Martin, 1982). Also Weill and Broadbent (1998) support the process view when they state "Alignment is a journey, not an event."

In this jungle of questions and opinions, business & IT alignment delivers well over a million Google hits. Chan (2002) distinguishes two prevailing conceptualizations of the alignment problem. The first one focuses on planning and objectives integration and views alignment as the degree to which the business mission, objectives, and plans are supported by the ICT mission, objectives, and plans. This view can be found with Reich

and Benbasat (1996), Kearns and Lederer (2004) and Hirschheim and Sabherwal (2001). A more holistic conceptualization of BIA can be found with Henderson and Venkatraman (1993). Their widespread framework of alignment, known as the strategic alignment model, describes BIA along two dimensions (Figure 1). The dimension of strategic fit differentiates between external focus, directed toward the business environment, and internal focus, directed toward administrative structures. The other dimension of functional integration separates business and IT. Altogether, the model defines four domains that have been harmonized in order to achieve alignment. Each of these domains has its constituent components: scope, competencies, governance, infrastructure, processes, and skills. Henderson and Venkatraman pay extensive attention to the different approaches of achieving this alignment. In the model, this can be visualized by starting the process of alignment from any one of the four domains. Maes et al. (2000) refine the strategic alignment model by identifying three, instead of two, columns: business, information/communication and technology column, and three, instead of two, rows: strategy, structure and operations.

Other researchers added social elements of alignment to the formal methodological elements (Keen, 1991; Luftman et al., 1999; Reich & Benbasat, 2000; Chan, 2002).

In our study we define BIA as:

Business & IT alignment is the degree to which the IT applications, infrastructure and organization, the business strategy and processes enables and shapes, as well as the process to realize this.

In this definition, BIA can express both a *state*,' the degree of alignment, as a *process*, the activities or methodology to reach a certain state of alignment. The definition also implies that BIA covers not just the alignment process aimed at developing, selecting, or enhancing IT applications and infrastructure, but also the agreements regarding the management and maintenance of application and infrastructure services. In the strategic alignment model this is shown in the different levels

Figure 1. Strategic alignment model

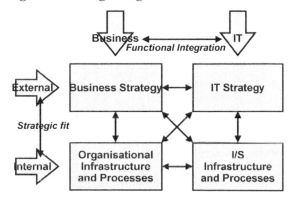

of alignment. The strategic level covers the alignment between business strategy and IT strategy, whereas, the operational level covers the alignment between business processes and organization, and IT infrastructure and organization.

In the definition, *business* is defined by business processes and business strategy and *IT* is defined as IT applications, infrastructure, and organization. This view finds support in the methodologies of IT planning mentioned earlier. The question whether IT aligns to business or the other way around is answered as *enables and shapes*. This indicates a two-way alignment.

The development of BIA can be summarized as shown in the alignment development model (Figure 2). This development reflects the shift in impact of IT on business. From an efficiency enhancing production factor, IT developed into a source of business innovation.

However, the impact of IT on business is not undisputed. In his famous article, "IT doesn't matter," Carr argues that IT, like electricity or railways, does not provide a strategic advantage anymore because of the fact that it is not unique and not scarce (Carr 2003). The fiery discussion that followed this publication is best summarized by Smith and Fingar (2003). For this chapter it is sufficient to conclude that for many organizations the use of IT is still of critical importance to their business. The challenge of aligning IT to business needs is, therefore, still relevant.

PRACTICAL ISSUES WITH BUSINESS AND IT ALIGNMENT

The message of BIA is logical and undisputed. IT should support the business, and this will be more successful if the IT resources are developed and organized with the business strategy and processes in mind. If this message is so clear, how can the results from the Synstar and Winmark-BMC research be explained? Earlier results of our research into the differences between the theory and practice of BIA provided the following considerations (Silvius 2007).

Figure 2. The development of BIA

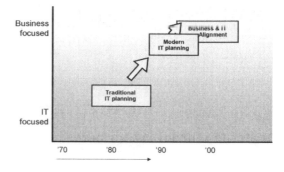

Alignment vs. Economies of Scale

The economic downturn of the last years forced many companies to cut back on IT costs. A widely used approach to cost savings was the utilization of economies of scale. Standardization of IT suppliers, systems, components, and configurations proved to be a practical way to save a significant percentage of the IT budget.

The first area of IT that was standardized was the IT infrastructure and the generic applications like e-mail, calendar, and the office suite. This area is not very specific to the business and could easily be standardized. The second wave of standardization hit the IT service management processes. The standardization of service levels and organization had, in some organizations, a relation with the business, which led to decentral additions to a central service level agreement.

The next step in IT standardization aimed at standardizing the configuration and versions of standard software packages in use (e.g., ERP and CRM). In this wave the effect on business was much stronger, since it hit the information systems supporting the core processes of the organization. In the urge for standardization, the ambition to align IT with business needs as best as possible loses from the ambition to realize cost savings.

The balance between optimally aligned (*unique*) and optimally standardized is a delicate one. Figure 3 illustrates this balance as found in the participating companies and shows that there is quite some variance in the *aligned zone*. The CIOs in the

Figure 3. The delicate balance between central IT standardisation and decentral uniqueness

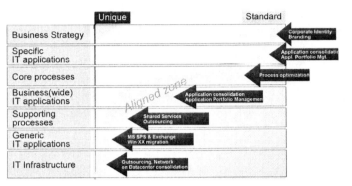

discussions agreed that the exact border between uniqueness and commonality was not always rationally deducted from the business requirements. Also aspects like history, culture, and balance of power are factors of influence.

Multiple Businesses

In most organizations that participated in the discussion groups the standardization of IT also included the centralization of IT resources. A practical issue in BIA for these CIOs was that the IT had to serve different business divisions with different businesses. The 1-to-1 relationship between IT and business that is suggested in the literature was in the practice of a multi-business-company an n-to-1 relationship. Each business division will have its own business requirements, but the IT requires standards to be cost-effective. In divisional organizations this situation is likely to occur. BIA than becomes the result of a negotiation process between divisional information managers and a centralized IT department.

Figure 4. BIA in a multi-business company

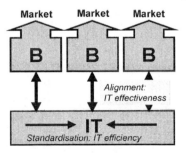

A Fuzzy Target

While trying to align IT with the business, many CIOs experienced a fuzzy target. With what *business* should IT align? According to the strategic alignment model, a first answer should be with the business strategy.

In practice, business strategy is unfortunately not often a clear target. An organization must be able to be responsive to developments in its environment. The company strategy is, therefore, not a destiny that is ever reached. In reality, strategy provides a direction, not a destiny.

On the second level of the strategic alignment model, the alignment is aimed at the business processes and organization. The organization provides only limited information about the business requirements. It is focused on hierarchical structure, but not on information content. An additional problem is that in many organizations the organization structure is not very stable. Departments and job titles change frequently. The business processes tend to be more stable. In the development of IT applications they provide an important basis for the analysis of the information requirements. A problem, however, is that there are multiple views of the business processes, all with different goals and different content. For example the process descriptions in the quality handbooks do not provide a sufficient basis for the IT analyst to work from because of lack of methodology, incompleteness and focus on activity. As a result of this most IT development projects will build their own process models according to their own modeling conventions.

SPECIFIC ISSUES WITH BUSINESS & IT ALIGNMENT IN MULTINATIONAL COMPANIES

To explore the specific issues with BIA in multinational companies, the participants of the focused group discussion were asked the following questions.

- Which issues are faced in aligning IT with business requirements in practice in multinational companies?
- Which actions are taken to align IT with business requirements in multinational companies?

Regarding the first question, specific issues with BIA in multinational companies, the participants recognized the issues mentioned above and added three specific considerations.

The Impact of Localization

Most multinational companies required an organizational structure that combined product or market divisions with country organizations. In almost all cases, some kind of matrix structure was inevitable. In cases of a medium-sized companies with only two subsidiaries abroad, the country organizations were completely autonomous regarding their IT, but in all other companies there were some form of central IT directives.

The issues arising from the matrix structure bear close resemblance to the practical issues with aligning business and IT in a multiple business company, as described above. Especially in Europe, different countries provide different market conditions and different legal requirements. These local conditions lead to local IT requirements.

In multinational companies with a strong standardization tendency these local requirements are often neglected resulting in *illegal* local solutions. These necessary, but uncontrolled, local solutions form an almost invisible legacy that slows down innovation and change. The CIO's agreed that localization of commonly used IT solutions was almost inevitable and should, therefore, be included in IT decision making.

The Role of the Corporate Center

Another consideration regarding BIA in multinational companies concerned the role of the corporate center. In corporate strategy literature the following roles are recognized (Table 2).

The participants of the discussion recognized the impact of the role of the corporate center in the approach to BIA in a multinational company.

- In a *financer* or *restructurer* type of center, aligning IT to business needs will be left to the country organizations and involvement of the corporate center will be null.
- In a *coordinator* type of center, however, BIA will be a more centralized process with all specific issues described above.

Figure 5. Business strategy is not a clear target

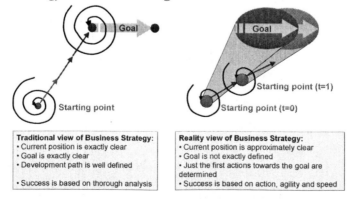

Table 2. Possible roles of the corporate center in a multinational company

Corporate center	
Role typology	*Main tasks*
Financer	- Supply of financial means (external/internal) - Allocating financial means - Controlling financial allocations
Restructurer	- Reorganizing companies to sell them and/or improve performance - Replace underperforming management
Supporter	- Provide supporting services (e.g. HRM, IT, logistics)
Coordinator	- Stimulate and realize cooperation withing the group (e.g. share knowledge, stimulate use of common facilities, etc.)
Strategist	- Visionair, searching for new possibilities - Provide guidance

- If the corporate center is the *supporter* type, the BIA process will have a strong country-by-country basis, but with central influences because of economies of scale.
- In the *strategist* type of center, its role in BIA depends on the importance of IT for the business of the company. If IT is an integrated part of the business, BIA will be a task of the corporate center. If IT is not part of the business, but merely a facilitator, IT will be left to the country organizations.

Of the companies involved in the discussions, the role of the center was assessed as shown in Table 3.

BUSINESS AND IT ALIGNMENT IN PRACTICE

Based on the second question to the discussion groups—Which actions are taken to align IT with business requirements?—the following list of BIA practices could be developed.

Create an Overview

A first action for all CIOs was to establish an overview of current IT applications, assets, budgets, and resources. For most CIOs, their starting situation was one of IT anarchy as a result of the uncontrolled

Table 3. Assessment of the corporate center roles of the participation companies

Corporate center	
Role typology	Participants assessment (n=12)
Financer	8
Restructurer	0
Supporter	12
Coordinator	10
Strategist	3

implementation of the personal computer as an important IT platform and the economic growth in the '90s. Providing an overview is a prerequisite for creating awareness about the cost of IT.

Create Buying Power

A quick-win for the CIOs was the centralization of IT procurement contracts in order to organize the organization's buying power. This action usually created an immediate visible return that brought the CIO the respect of senior management. Another practical benefit of centralized procurement contracts is that it helps the CIO to get and maintain the overview mentioned above.

Install a Project Authorization Process

A relatively simple action to increase the planning and control cycle of IT is the tightening of the project authorization process. By requiring clear business cases, the CIO could strengthen the involvement of business managers in the preparation of IT projects. The project authorization process provided the CIOs the opportunity to create an overview of projects, next to the earlier mentioned overviews of IT assets, resources, and applications.

Develop (Technical) Standards

With the increased quality of information provided by the CIO, the awareness of the actual IT situation grew with senior management. The fact that this actual situation, most of the time, was one of suboptimal solutions, lacking standards, overlapping projects, and huge numbers of applications, combined with the tighter budget constraints in recent years, built a foundation on which the CIO could act. Starting with the more technical side of IT, most CIOs developed a set of technical standards for hardware, network, server platforms, databases, development platforms, and so forth. These standards are a low-interest topic for business managers, but provide an opportunity for the CIO to create economies of scale and to gain control.

Rationalize the Application Portfolio

A next step for most CIOs and an actual challenge for the front-runners is the cleaning-up of the application portfolio. Most organizations use between 200 and 2,000 different software applications or versions. It is estimated that a rationalization of the portfolio could save between 10% and 35% of the IT budget for maintenance and enhancement. This action, however, relates very much to the business process, which makes it complex. The *aligned zone* in Figure 4 is, therefore, quite complex.

CONCLUSION

The input provided by the participants in the discussion groups made it clear that aligning IT to business needs in the practice of multinational companies is not a *by-the-book* process. Multinational companies provide specific challenges in which local requirements and the role of the corporate center determine the way in which BIT Alignment can be shaped. On one hand, BIA in multinational companies is not as straightforward as implied by the methodologies. On the other hand, the actions taken by the CIOs in order to align IT to business needs are quite pragmatic and sometimes even simplistic. The CIOs agreed that the success of BIA in their organizations probably depended more on the focus of the corporate strategy, the IT awareness of (senior) business management, and the IT management skills of the company, than on the methodology followed.

FUTURE RESEARCH DIRECTIONS

Given the complexity of strategic planning and decision making in multinational companies there still is much that we do not know. A first area of research in the field of strategic management is the effectiveness and efficiency of the different roles of the corporate center in a globalizing market. Given the increasing globalization and cross-border linkages, the question whether a just-financially involved corporate center is viable, becomes eminent.

Given the different roles of the corporate center, another interesting area of research would be to specify the BIA actions and practices for these roles. Each role would than imply a logical set of BIA actions and practices. Further research also could include testing the effectiveness and efficiency of these BIA actions and practices. This last research direction would not have to be limited to multinational companies. The effectiveness of BIA actions and practices is a worthwhile research area in itself.

REFERENCES

Bloem, J., & Doorn, M. van. (2004). Realisten aan het Roer, Naar een prestatiegerichte governance van IT' (in Dutch), Sogeti VINT.

Carr, N. G. (2003). IT doesn't matter. *Harvard Business Review*, May.

Chan, Y. E., Huff, S. L., Barclay, D. W., & Copeland, D. G. (1997). Business strategy orientation, information systems orientation and strategic alignment. *Information Systems Research, 8*(2), 125-150.

Chan, Y. E. (2002). Why haven't we mastered alignment? The importance of the informal organization structure. *MIS Quarterly Executive*, Vol. 1, No. 2.

Ciborra, C. U. (1997). De profundis? Deconstructing the concept of strategic alignment. *Scandinavian Journal of Information Systems, 9*(1), 67-82.

Cumps, B., Martens, D., De Backer, M., Haesen, R., Viaene, S., Dedene, G., et al. (2006). *Predicting business/ICT alignment with AntMiner+', KBI0708,* Research paper Department of Decision Sciences and Information Management (KBI). Catholic University of Leuven.

Henderson, J. C., & Venkatraman, N. (1993). Strategic alignment: Leveraging information technology for transforming organizations. *IBM Systems Journal, 32*(1).

Hirschheim R., & Sabherwal R. (2001). Detours in the path toward strategic information systems alignment: Paradoxical decisions, excessive transformations, and uncertain turnarounds. *California Management Review, 44*(1), 87-108.

IBM Corporation (1981). Business systems planning; information systems planning guide. *IBM Application Manual.*

Kearns, G.S., & Lederer, A. L. (2004). The impact of industry contextual factors on IT focus and the use of IT for competitive advantage. *Information & Management, 41*, 899-919.

Keen, P. (1991). Every manager's guide to information technology. *Harvard Business School Press,* Boston.

Luftman, J. N. (2000). Assessing business-IT alignment maturity. *Communications of the Association for Information Systems, 4*, Article 14.

Luftman, J. N., & Brier, T. (1999). Achieving and sustaining business-IT alignment. *California Management Review, 42*(1).

Luftman, J. N., Lewis, P. R., & Oldach, S. H. (1993). Transforming the enterprise: The alignment of business and information technology strategies. *IBM Systems Journal, 32*(1).

Luftman, J. N., Papp, R., & Brier, T. (1999). Enablers and inhibitors of business-IT alignment. *Communications of the Association for Information Systems, 1*, Article 11.

Maes, R., Rijsenbrij, D., Truijens, O., & Goedvolk, H. (2000). *Redefining business-IT alignment through a unified framework* (White Paper).Retrieved from http://imwww.fee.uva.nl/~maestro/PDF/2000-19.pdf

Martin, J. (1982). *Strategic data-planning methodologies.* Prentice Hall.

Poels, R. (2006). *Beïnvloeden en meten van business – IT alignment* (in Dutch). Dissertation Free University of Amsterdam, Amsterdam.

Pols, R. van der (2003). Nieuwe informatievoorziening; informatieplanning en ICT in de 21e eeuw (in Dutch). Academic Services, The Hague.

Pyburn, P. J. (1983). Linking the MIS plan with corporate strategy: An exploratory study. *MIS Quarterly, 7*(2), 1-14.

Reich, B. H., & Benbasat, I. (1996). Measuring the linkage between business and information technology objectives. *MIS Quarterly, 20*(1), 55-81.

Reich, B. H., & Benbasat, I. (2000). Factors that influence the social dimension of alignment between business and information technology objectives. *MIS Quarterly, 24*(1), 81.

Sabherwal, R., & Chan, Y. E. (2001). Alignment between business and IS strategies: A study of prospectors, analyzers, and defenders. *Information Systems Research, 12*(1), 11-33.

Silvius, A. J. G. (2005). Business & IT alignment in theory and practice. *Proceedings of the IMB 2005 Conference.*

Silvius, A. J. G. (2007). Business & IT alignment in theory and practice. *Proceedings of the HICCS 2007 Conference.*

Smaczny, T. (2001). Is an alignment between business and IT the appropriate paradigm to manage IT in today's organisation? *Management Decision, 39*(10).

Smith, H., & Fingar, P. (2003). *IT doesn't matter; business processes do.* Tampa, USA: Meghan-Kiffer Press.

Society of Information Management (2003, 2004, 2005). *Execs provide insight into top manage-*

ment concerns, technology developments in new SIM survey. Retrieved from http://www.simnet.org/Content/NavigationMenu/About/Press_Releases/PressReleases.htm

Synstar (2004). *The pressure point index: V.* Synstar.

Venkatraman, N. (1989). The concept of fit in strategy research. *Academy of Management Review, 14*(3).

Weill, P., & Broadbent, M. (1998). *Leveraging the new infrastructure: How market leaders capitalize on information technology*. Harvard Business School Press.

Wieringa, R., Gordijn, J., & Eck, P. van. (2005, August 29-30). Value-based business-IT alignment in networked constellations of enterprises. In *Proceedings of the 1st International Workshop on Requirements Engineering for Business Need and IT Alignment (REBNITA 2005)*. Paris.

Winmark, & BMC Software (2004). The Communication Gap: The Barrier to Aligning Business and IT.

ADDITIONAL READING

Chan, Y.E., Huff, S. L., Barclay, D. W., & Copeland, D. G. (1997). Business strategy orientation, information systems orientation and strategic alignment. *Information Systems Research, 8*(2), 125-150.

Cumps, B., Martens, D., De Backer, M., Haesen, R., Viaene, S., Dedene, G., et al. (2006). *Predicting business/ICT alignment with AntMiner+',* KBI0708. Research paper Department of Decision Sciences and Information Management (KBI). Catholic University of Leuven.

Henderson, J.C., & Venkatraman, N. (1993). Strategic alignment: Leveraging information technology for transforming organizations. *IBM Systems Journal, 32*(1).

Luftman, J. N. (2000). Assessing business-IT alignment maturity. *Communications of the Association for Information Systems, 4*, Article 14.

Luftman, J. N. (2003). *Competing in the information age: Align in the sand* (2nd ed.). Oxford University Press.

Luftman, J. N., Lewis, P.R., & Oldach, S. H. (1993). Transforming the enterprise: The alignment of business and information technology strategies. *IBM Systems Journal, 32*(1).

Luftman, J. N., Papp, R., & Brier, T. (1999). Enablers and inhibitors of business-IT alignment. *Communications of the Association for Information Systems, 1*, Article 11.

Maes, R., Rijsenbrij, D., Truijens, O., & Goedvolk, H. (2000). Redefining business-IT alignment through a unified framework. (White Paper). Retrieved from http://imwww.fee.uva.nl/~maestro/PDF/2000-19.pdf

Reich, B. H., & Benbasat, I. (1996). Measuring the linkage between business and information technology objectives. *MIS Quarterly, 20*(1), 55-81.

Weill, P., & Broadbent, M. (1998). *Leveraging the new infrastructure; how market leaders capitalize on information technology*. Harvard Business School Press.

Chapter IX
Intercultural Collaboration in the ICT Sector

Martina Maletzky
Technische Universität Berlin, Germany

ABSTRACT

In the context of global sourcing in, and internationalization of, the ICT sector, intercultural collaboration is for many ICT workers a daily affair. Especially in the field of software development, where the needs for communication are high, intercultural collaboration poses a particular challenge. Misunderstandings and an unproductive work atmosphere may result in hidden costs for the companies. This chapter highlights the different types of intercultural collaboration in the ICT sector, identifying the special challenges that occur and suggesting ways in which companies may minimize such challenges of intercultural collaboration.

INTRODUCTION

Intercultural collaboration is a necessity for many ICT workers since the ICT sector has become highly globalized. In the context of international market entries, mergers, network production, as well as near- and offshoring, three modes of intercultural collaboration take place: collaboration in multicultural teams, in dispersed teams and in the context of foreign assignment. If persons with different cultural backgrounds work together, challenges occur due to different value systems, work and communication styles. They join the general difficulties of internationalization and industrialization in the ICT sector and, thus, are often overlooked but may hold risks and provoke hidden costs. This chapter describes the challenges of intercultural collaboration and methods to con-

trol the risk of intercultural friction focusing on the particular modes of collaboration. Companies should include results of intercultural research into their selection of personnel strategies. Additionally a systematic intercultural personnel development by cross-cultural trainings and coaching helps the collaborators to handle culture differences and to establish a productive collaboration.

Due to advanced globalization, intercultural collaboration is becoming a necessity for employees of many sectors and, thus, of the ICT sector as well, because "information technology is largely now a global field, business, and industry" (Aspray, Mayadas, & Vardi, Moshe Y., 2006, p. 9). While the classical industries already had a boom of internationalization with regard of their production locations in the 1970s and 1980s, the ICT producing sector has become increasingly globalized in the last two decades (OECD, 2004). But, particular big companies, such as IBM, already built factories of production in the 1950s outside of the United States. In the 1980s and 1990s, the internationally distributed capacities of production have been integrated in a new model of organization: the network production or "wintelism," for which the IT Industry has become a paradigm (Ferguson & Morris, 1993). In the year 2004, the OECD states the ICT sector as a leader in the globalization of industry. Motives for expansion of the ICT firms are gaining market access, economies of scales, growth, and access to skills and technology. "Cross-border M&As are the most common form of ICT expansion, enabling faster build-up than greenfield investment" (OECD, 2004, p. 6). A recent development is international sourcing of IT- and ICT-enabled business services, or offshoring and nearshoring.[1] Off- and nearshoring refer to a total or partial transfer of functions to external enterprises or to dependent enterprises in lower-wage countries as, for example, subsidiary companies and joint ventures in lower-wage countries. The trend is reinforced by competition. Drives are the dynamics of digital delivery, the need to fill skill shortages, to cut costs, and to increase efficiency (OECD, 2004). Offshoring and outsourcing require a minimum degree of industrialization, what means a standardisation and decomposability of the production process in order to reach a reduction of the vertical integration. This means a challenge for implementation in the software industry and its employees, because their work often is associated with creativity, which is limited by this process (Boes & Trinks, 2006). Thus, having to handle technical challenges of internationalization and industrialization, soft factors, as for example, those related to cross-cultural collaboration, play a subordinated role regarding personnel development and organizational strategies in the ICT sector. But, they often influence the success of international projects and they may provoke hidden costs[2] (DB Research, 2006).

In the context of the internationalisation of the ICT industry, different modes of intercultural collaboration proceed: (a) multicultural teams, (b) virtual teams, and (c) foreign assignments.

a. **Multicultural teams:** In times of workforce shortages, which according to the economic theory seems to be a periodic phenomenon (López-Bassols, 2002), one often-practised solution is the inflow of foreign ICT workers, as it has occurred in Europe in a massive way from 1995 until the crisis of the new economy at the beginning of the new millennium in 2002, and especially 2003.[3] At the latest, since then, many countries developed special policies in order to ease the workflow (McLaughlan & Salt, 2002). The immigration of ICT workers provokes an international composition of working teams in the ICT sector. While in many European countries, as for example Germany, Ireland, and so forth, cultural diversity in highly skilled jobs in the ICT branch has not been common, in the USA and its melting pot, especially in the Silicon Valley where cultural diversity already has a long tradition. Thus, attention to diversity has grown exponentially in U.S. organizations in the 1980s (Ferdman & Brody, 1998), while in the European debate it does not show such a high presence. The same happens to personnel development strategies in the context of diversity at work.

b. **Dispersed teams:** In the context of saving costs, international network production and off- or nearshoring virtual teams are increasing (Martins, Gilson, & Maynard 2004; Davidson & Tay, 2002). Especially if a partial transfer of functions to low-wage countries takes place, the projects often are conducted in geographically dispersed cross-cultural teams. In the context of nearshoring, many companies hope that because of less culture differences dispersed collaboration will be eased (DB Research, 2006), which has not been evidenced yet.

c. **Sojourns:** In the context of M&As and founding of subsidiaries, intercultural collaboration normally takes place in the form of sojourns. Executives are sent abroad in order to co-ordinate offshore or nearshore centres, the process of merging and founding, or in terms of knowledge transfer.

All types of collaboration have particular challenges to overcome, but all have one thing in common: They have to deal with culture differences of the collaborators. According to the UNESCO, *culture* is defined as a "... set of distinctive spiritual, material, intellectual and emotional features of society or a social group, and that it encompasses, in addition to art and literature, lifestyles, ways of living together, value systems, traditions and beliefs" (UNESCO, 2002). Culture differences can be interpreted as differences in structures of social systems. They appear where individuals of one social system or culture show accumulations of behavior patterns, which are not observable in the same frequency in another cultural context. That means that the peculiarities of each culture exist in the form of a Gaussian distribution, but with a displacement of the average. The range of the overlap varies, known as the dimensions "difference" or "similarity" of both cultures (see Schroll-Machl, 1999, p. 343).

Intercultural interaction is influenced by three dimensions (Thomas, Hagemann, & Stumpf, 2003): culture differences, individual differences, and intercultural knowledge and experience (see Figure 1).

Culture differences influence the intensity, quality, and duration of problems related to cultural adjustment. Individual differences are shown in the ability to cope with cultural differences, while former intercultural experiences may have led to a development of a higher degree of intercultural competence, depending on the quality of former

contact with other cultures. Intercultural competence may be defined as the ability of perception, appreciation, respect, and productive utilisation of cultural conditions and their influences on perception, thinking, judging, feeling, and interaction. This should be given either by observing the own behavior or the behavior of other persons with different cultural backgrounds (see Thomas, 2003, p. 99).

In the following chapter, I describe general challenges of intercultural collaboration. In this context, I will focus then on the particular challenges of the three modes of intercultural collaboration. In the second part of the chapter, I point out possible methods reducing intercultural friction. This can be reached by selection of personnel, including intercultural research results and cross-cultural personnel development strategies, as there are cross-cultural trainings and coaching.

BACKGROUND: CHALLENGES OF INTERCULTURAL COLLABORATION

According to Moore and Brown (2004), 51% of CIOs perceive the greatest offshore outsourcing challenges overcoming cultural differences. Comparative, cultural studies have pointed out the high importance of culture influencing perception, cognition, motivation, emotion, and interpersonal behavior (Thomas, 2003; Hall, 1990; Hofstede, 1980, 1991, 1993, 1997, 2000). In the context of internationalization strategies, soft factors are essential, since the interaction has to take place, bridging culture differences, as they occur (e.g., in communication styles, work-related values, and working styles, etc.) (Stumpf, 2003, p. 309). Unfortunately they are often neglected (Bolten, 2002, p. 4). Even if a common language is spoken and historical ties are strong, as it is for example in the case between India and the UK, the culture distance may be high. DB research reports that 56% of British ICT companies mention culture differences as an obstacle for offshoring in India (p. 7). If there is no common mother tongue, *communication* for all, or at least some collaborators, takes place in a foreign language. That even may

Figure 1. Determinants of intercultural interaction

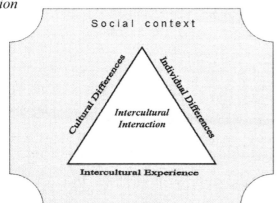

be a challenge if the *lingua franca* is dominated in an excellent way, because the way of coding and decoding a message and communication rules are culture-specific (Hall, 1990; Hofstede, 1980[4]; Demorgon, 1989). Even having the same mother tongue, linguistic mismatches may occur, as it happens frequently between Indian and American collaborators (Matloff, 2005). Additionally, the nonverbal communication is an important factor of interaction, but its interpretation varies over cultures, too. In Albania, accordance is expressed, for example, by sidewise-shaking of the head (DB Research, 2006).

Work and leadership styles may have a big range. In some cultures, strict super ordinates and high degree of control are desired. Leadership styles that work in one culture may cause problems in another culture. The disregard of stricter hierarchies may cause problems (Winter, 2006; Matloff, 2005; Hofstede, 1980) and unintentionally one may appear as rebellious. On the other hand, it also is possible that egalitarian leadership styles ask too much of the subordinates, which they are not used to handling with participative leadership styles. Thus, problems may occur, for example, faults may not be reported at the time and, therefore, provoke further problems that are difficult to be resolved (Maletzky, 2006).

Some investigations have been carried out in order to classify cultures by *dimensions*, to be able to understand and predict the behavior of persons with a differing cultural backgrounds and to ease the interactions. The highest impact was caused by the dimensions of Hofstede (1980[5]), Trompenaars (1993), Demorgon (1989) and Hall (1990). Nevertheless, it is not possible to predict all facets of culture, taking into account that cultures also vary insight and that, in times of globalization, fast changes occur (Giddens, 2001). Thus, it is more important to develop a general ability for culture learning (Furnham & Bochner, 1982, 1986). The condition for culture learning is intercultural competence, that enables to decipher underlying structures of the others behavior and, thus, to adapt more easily to a foreign culture.

Especially in the context of partial transfer of functions to low-wage countries as it is characteristic for ICT off- and nearshoring projects (Wieandt 2007), a lack of intercultural sensibility and competence may cause unpredictable problems, because correct match-fixing has to be done in order to assure that the final product made by foreign workers overseas really exhibits those characteristics that have been required and a frictionless implementation can take place. If this is not the case, additional costs could be the result because it will be necessary to change part of the products, so forth, and, therefore, cause a belated delivery of the final product to the clients.

M&A processes require an especially high degree of sensibility and intercultural competence because of an often unbalanced distribution of power, which leads to mistrust and avoids a integrative corporate identity. According to studies of Booz-Allen and Hamilton, Mc Kinsey, KPMG and A.T. Kearney, between 34% and 58% of takeovers are failures. Reasons are misunderstandings and coordination problems, as well as strict aspiration to reach a consensus (see Bolten, 2002).

Besides general challenges occurring when persons of different cultures collaborate, the above-described three modes of intercultural collaboration show special challenges, which I will highlight in the following.

Multicultural Teams

A team is multicultural if at least one team member has a different cultural background than the others. By employing multicultural teams, companies often make significant benefits in productivity (Townsend et al., 1998). Those teams predict a high potential of innovation and effectiveness in problem solving, including the variety of perspectives, skills, and personal attributes that multicultural team members contribute to an organization (Maznevski, 1997). They may generate more ideas of higher quality in brainstorming tasks (McLeod & Lobel, 1992), and outperform cultural homogeneous teams at identifying problems and generating solutions (Watson et al., 1993). But, a well-planned combination of workforce is of high importance, since cultural differences among team members can cause conflict, misunderstanding, and poor performance (Shenkar & Zeira, 1992).

Differences in social categories as nationality and ethnicity also may have an important impact on the group process as well as on its achievement (McGrath, Berdahl, & Arrow, 1995). Achievement of multicultural teams depends, in general, on the degree of diversity, the right composition of the team, and the way the team members handle the culture differences. That is influenced by culture-specific processes of socialization and the activation of national stereotypes (Stumpf, 2003, p. 341). Frictions can take place since the understanding of role-taking inside the team and working styles may vary. Since cohesion depends on perceived similarities, it is more difficult to reach, because of occurring differences in values and norms. At least a high identification with a common goal should be assured, which sub serves cohesion as well (Rosenstiel, 2004). Thus, according to Kopper (2003), we have to state: "The first commandment of effective multicultural teamwork is 'assume differences until similarities are proven.' Collaboration can be improved by merely understanding that differences exist and then trying to discover content of those differences" (p. 381).

In order to increase the productivity of cultural diverse teams, diversity trainings could take place, which focus on raising the awareness of culture differences and lowering discrimination between the collaborators in order to reach a high cohesion and identification with work.

Virtual Teams

Teams are defined as virtual teams if they predominately communicate via media and their workplaces are located in different places. The geographical distance between team members may exponentiate challenges that take part in intercultural collaboration in general. Carmel (2005) points out five major challenges that global software development teams have to face, working together over distance: (1) adjusting to geographical dispersion of IT personnel and users, (2) loss of communication richness with less face-to-face contact, (3) coordination breakdown in project management, (4) loss of teamness, and (5) dealing with culture differences.

Additionally, virtual teams have to face difficulties in communication and coordination arising from time zones, geographical locations, and culture (Edwards & Sridhar, 2002). The special problems in communication occur because of the usage of less rich channels as phone, fax, e-mail, electronic databases (see Davidson & Tay, 2002; Sharpe, 2001). Solutions of problems may take a longer time because of time dispersion of the other team members. Besides, camaraderie is difficult to reach because of seldom face-to-face contact, but at the same time it is an important fact for the productivity of a team (Rosenstiel, 2004). Team cohesion also is difficult to reach, because team members often belong to multiple teams. Social integration and cohesion in virtual teams are only produced by the constant use of technological-communication tools, also in order to support informal communication, maintenance of social relations, and discussion on working issues (see Edwards & Sridhar, 2002; Hynsell, 2000; Joisten, 2005).

Intercultural problems are the following ones: On the one hand the communication is handicapped by the *lingua franca* because the coding and decoding of a message is culturally influenced and, thus, may provoke misunderstandings. On the other hand the message is filtered by the communication media, which may undermine important context information that helps to understand a message, for example, the nonverbal language. Without the nonverbal language signs, an important framework of orientation lacks, which also provides the information whether the own behavior is appropriate or not. The communication may be difficult, especially between persons of a high-context culture and those of a low-context culture (Hall, 1990). High-context cultures tend to give indirect information that is only understandable if the context is known, while those of low-context cultures express all the necessary information in the verbal message. Thus, during the interaction between persons from these cultural backgrounds, the one of the low-context culture may annoy the one of a high-context culture because of verbalizing taboos. This may lead to an unfruitful work atmosphere. On the other hand, the person from a low-context culture possibly is not able to decipher the message in a correct way. One example would be the indirect expression of a negation in Latin American or many Asiatic countries. There "no" is seldom expressed explicitly. "Yes" may have the meaning of a "no" if there is a delay in pronouncing it or depending on the additional information given, as for example, the exact date of delivery, a "yes" may be understood as a "yes." In this case, nonverbal communication may give a further orientation. This possibility is missed by the usage of most communication media.

With few face-to-face contacts, trust is another element that is difficult to reach, but which, at the same time, is constitutive for the identification with a common goal (Davidson & Tay, 2002) and productive collaboration. Thus, it is necessary that the group members know each other at least in the context of a kick-off meeting (Hynsell, 2002) and stay in a continuous contact by temporary collocating them through site visits, and so forth (Davidson & Tay, 2002). The fluidity of communication must be assured, because even informal "coffee kitchen" communication is a very important part of collaboration. "Despite the multiple promises of dispersed, cross-functional teamwork, evidence suggests that accessing, combining, and applying knowledge in these teams may be inherently problematic" (Sole & Edmonson, 2002).

In order to bridge the geographical distance, the choice of the right communication medium is of a high importance. The preference of the usage of particular media is culture specific. Knowledge about the cultural background of the collaborators is an important factor of success. In cultures where personal aspects dominate the business-like aspects, media that favours a direct interaction, for example telephone and video conferences, seem to be favoured. The necessity of the transmission of the message context should be taken into account by doing the right choice.

According to Edward Hall's finding of the existence of low-context vs. high-context cultures we may suppose that persons of low-context cultures have fewer problems by communicating by e-mail than those of high-context cultures (see Figure 2). In high-context cultures, the intonation of an expression or the mimics may help to understand its meaning, in this context the use of high-context

media is not very helpful to transmit the holistic dimension of a message. Even if emoticons are used in order to enrich the communication, it is not possible to transmit all notions since the interpretation and writing of them also vary (Aoki, 1995 cited by Opdenakker, 2006). Thus, in order to assure a successful collaboration over distance, special communicative skills are necessary. Abstract processes, which before could be discussed face-to-face, with the possibility to show on the monitor about what one is talking, must be verbalized now. New challenges occur by virtual teamwork. It is not investigated yet if cultural differences tend to increase or to be less important in the case of virtual collaboration. Investigations taking into account these special premises lack, as well as the evaluation of the adequacy of tools, in the cross-cultural context. According to this, cross-cultural trainings especially designed for the challenges of intercultural, virtual collaboration with a scientific basis still do not exist.

Foreign Assignments

Foreign assignments are defined as the long term relocation of an employee to another country. Many companies send employees abroad in order to assure a frictionless working process, to introduce special techniques of production, organization of a new company, co-ordination and control, transferring know-how, or for the development of global management abilities (Götz & Bleher, 2000). As such, the expatriates, sent to a company's subsidiary overseas, have to adapt to the host culture. This process is called acculturation, which "refers to changes that occur as a result of continuous firsthand contact between individuals of differing cultural origins" (Redfield, Linton, & Herskovits, 1936 in Ward, 1996, p. 124). According to the host culture's requirements of adaptation, the acculturation process may vary (Berry, 1990). With Ward (1996), acculturation to a host culture is characterized by stress, disorientation, and learning deficits, which provoke changes in behavior and thinking. In all cultures, particular values and norms exist, which determine the interaction routines of members of a certain culture. They help to predict the interaction of the other members

Figure 2. Which technology for which kind of task?

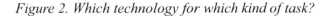

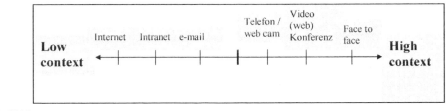

Source: Zaninelli 2003

of the same social system (Thomas, 2003). Thus, the interaction routines of members with different cultural backgrounds differ.

If someone interacts in an unexpected way and against the established norms, his behavior is sanctioned. Being a stranger, it is more likely to behave inappropriately and to perceive the other's behavior as unexpected and unpredictable, which may lead to a culture shock (Oberg, 1960). Culture shock is defined as an unpleasant feeling that may violate expectations of a new culture. Oberg mentions different aspects of culture shock: strain, a sense of loss, feelings of deprivation, rejection, role confusion, surprise, anxiety, disgust, indignation, feelings of impotence.[6] It is not surprising that the success of sojourns abroad is estimated by less than 30% (Trimpop & Meynhardt, 2000, p. 183). Unsuccessful sojourns provoke very high costs. Miller (1989) estimates them as 3 to 4 times as high as the normal expatriate's annual salary staying in the home company. But, "Whereas most measures of success and/or failure in expatriate assignments are based on the expatriate's early return to the home country, several other indications of failure exist" (Littrell et al., 2006, p. 357). The reasons for failure are mainly social and psychological ones: problems of adjustment by the expatriate or the spouse; personality and coping styles with the work overseas (Tung, 1987). Additionally the motivation to work overseas plays an important role for success, too.

Reasons for problems overseas may be, according to Hamill (1989), inadequate selection or recruitment criteria (technical skills rather than cultural empathy), inadequate pre-departure-training, poorly designed compensation packages, lack of advanced planning for repatriation, and loss of status or remoteness through working at periphery also cause discontentedness (Hamill, 1989).

As Stahl (1998) pointed out, problems of expatriates additionally are caused by the company structure, for example, reintegration in the company after the sojourn, the relations to the parent company, adequate treatment of personnel and leadership, amount of work and its contents, as well as role conflicts. Other problems have been identified in relation to the host culture. There we can list communicative problems, few contacts to persons of the host culture, quality of life, and different economic practices.

In all cases of intercultural collaboration, knowledge about culture peculiarities and a sensibility of the workers' cultural bias is important for avoiding misunderstandings. Companies should support their workers in applicating intercultural development of personnel and starting with an adequate selection of personnel and project staffing.

HOW TO PREVENT CHALLENGES OF INTERCULTURAL COLLABORATION?

Companies may reduce the potential of friction in intercultural collaboration by incorporating results of intercultural studies in their strategies of selection of personnel as a first step. Since a perfect applicant does not exist, a second step should be the training and coaching of the staff, working in an intercultural environment (see Table 1).

In the following, strategies and contents of intercultural selection of personnel will be highlighted. This contains different phases of international selection of personnel as well as personal skills, predicting effective collaboration across cultures, and should be measured in the process of intercultural personnel selection and needs assessment for cross-cultural trainings. Also, I describe two main methods of intercultural personnel development: cross-cultural trainings and coaching. Cross-cultural trainings are focused on two aspects: on overseas assignment and on developing domestic employees, working in multicultural teams or working contexts. Trainings differ in timing, theoretical framework, and methods depending on the employee's and company's needs.

Intercultural Selection Strategies of Personnel

In order to assure a productive intercultural collaboration, companies should begin with an adequate way of selection of personnel. In the context of sojourns, normally, a well-engineered selection process takes place primarily because of the high costs joining its failure and the high responsibility of the expatriates, and also the selection of a project leader and international team members should be well-structured.

Most of the current literature focuses on the finality of a foreign assignment, but it has a similar validity for the other types of intercultural collaboration. Particular skills predict effective collaboration across cultures. In the context of multicultural and virtual teams, especially the cross-cultural and partnership skills play an important role (for details, see below).

With Kealey (1996), there are seven situations that make the task of doing effective cross-cultural personnel selection difficult: (a) a lack of reliable tools, (b) poor analysis of the host environment, (c) an unintegrated selection process, (d) ignoring the role of the spouse and family, (e) no monitoring of field performance, (f) the multidimensional nature of intercultural effectiveness, and (g) the limitations of all individuals. But:

Table 1. Methods to reduce intercultural risks

	Method	Focus	Performance	Goal
Personnel selection	Sustainable intercultural personnel selection	• Sojourns • Multicultural teams • cross-cultural virtual teams	• Before, while and after recruitment	• Develop a profile of skills and knowledge • Define training needs • Develop an information pool including intercultural experiences • Redefine future soft skills required
Personnel development	Cross-cultural training (pre-departure, post-arrival and re-entry training)	• Sojourns	• Off the job	• Ease cross-cultural adjustment of sojourner • Increase (intercultural) performance
	Coaching	• Sojourns	• On the job	• Help to handle problems overseas
	Diversity training	• Multicultural teams	• Off the job	• Increase culture awareness, tolerance • Increase performance

Table 2. International selection of personnel: A three phase model

Goal	establishing the profile of skills and knowledge	planning and implementing the selection procedures	training and monitoring the overseas performance
Tasks	Job analysis Socio-cultural analysis Institutional analysis Counterpart screening	Pre-screening program (self assessment) Identify selection committee Administer selection instrument conduct selection interviews	Design training based on needs analysis Establish training contract with the individual Conduct training Monitor performance overseas
Outputs	Job objectives identified Scope of work, including job requirements and constraints Selection criteria from international personnel established	Personnel selected with best potential to succeed Training needs of international personnel identified	Trained personnel equipped with the knowledge and skills needed to succeed overseas.

Source: Kealey 1996, p. 101

Effective selecting tools themselves cannot guarantee that international personnel will adapt and perform effectively on the overseas assignment. For this reason, the development of the profile of skills and knowledge for each international position and linking of selection and training are important activities to undertake. (Kealey, 1996, p. 100)

Regarding this, Kealey has developed a three-phase model of international selection of personnel (see Table 2) based on three goals: (1) establishing the profile of skills and knowledge, (2) planning and implementing the selection procedures, (3) training and monitoring the overseas performance. Kealey's model is focused on sojourns, but also may be useful for intercultural collaboration in cultural diverse and virtual teams, only the training necessities vary. It gives an overview of a holistic personnel selection, which also integrates other than technical aspects. Unfortunately the daily selection practice is focused to a high degree on technical skills. Therefore, besides the analysis of job requirements, according to Kealey, cultural constraints and the host organization environment make up the general profile of the cross-cultural collaborator. Cultural toughness[7] and particularities should be taken into account, not all persons are suitable for all host cultures. The analysis of personnel needs should not be a one-sided process, the counterpart should be included into the development of the job profile and into the decision-making process.

The first goal is the basis for the other goals and should be modified by means of the experiences made with it and those experiences the expatriates make overseas.

Social skills play a crucial rule for successful cross-cultural collaboration. A higher emphasis on nontechnical requirements, such as adaptation skills, cross-cultural skills and partnership skills in the personnel selection process should take place. According to Kealey (1996, p. 86), they may be worked out in detail as shown in Table 3.

Adaptation skills are such characteristics that enable a person to adjust to a foreign environment. They are strongly related to cross-cultural skills, which help to understand the host cultural context and to honor its particularities. Partnership skills endorse these processes, because they ease the contact to strangers and thus to understand underlying structures of unfamiliar behavior by clarifying communication.

In the second phase of planning and implement-

Table 3. Nontechnical skills predicting effective collaboration across cultures

Adaptation Skills	Cross-Cultural Skills	Partnership Skills
Positive attitudes	Realism	Openness to others
Flexibility	Tolerance	Professional commitment
Stress tolerance	Involvement in culture	Perseverance
Patience		Initiative
	Political astuteness	
Marital / Family stability		Relationship building
	Cultural sensitivity	
Emotional maturity		Self-confidence
Inner security		Problem-solving

ing the selection procedures, the pre-screening program should give the candidates the chance to inform themselves about the job and to acquire more information about the country of posting in order to make the right decision in going abroad. Often the motivations and expectations are not adequately thought out and may cause problems ex post.

The more differing and multiple the sources of information one has on a particular candidate, the more reliable the resulting selection procedure. In this regard, "assessment center methodologies perhaps offer the most potential for effective international screening because they elicit a variety of responses, both verbal and behavioral, to the different situations presented to all candidates. (Kealey, 1996, 101)

Assessment centres normally are not common in the international selection process, because of the time needed and the high costs, never-the-less if it is not possible to applicate an assessment centre selection, Kealey (1996) recommends a combination of structured and open-ended interviews, paper and pencil tests, reference checks and behavioral assessment.

The third phase links the results of the first two phases with the pre-departure or pre-project training, and monitoring of the selected personnel. The performance overseas should be monitored and the results should be a basis for former profiles.

After the process of selection of personnel and recruitment, a continuous intercultural personnel development is of high importance in order to embitter the intercultural competence of the employees. In the following, we will highlight different methods, goals, and the different theoretical frameworks of intercultural personnel development and their pros and cons.

Intercultural Personnel Development

Intercultural personnel development is an important factor in order to diminish friction in intercultural collaboration. Finality of the intercultural personnel development is the amplification of intercultural competence. It takes place as cross-cultural training or coaching. Different types of cross-cultural trainings (CCT) exist, depending on their focus. "Whereas traditional CCT focuses on preparing individuals for overseas assignments, multicultural training is directed at improving the cultural awareness of domestic employees in the hopes of improving their ability to interact with individuals from diverse cultural backgrounds" (Littrell et al., 2006, p. 356).

Cross-cultural training may be divided in pre-departure training before the foreign assignment as well as post-departure training and re-entry training before the return of the sojourner. In multicultural teams or organizations *diversity training* is an instrument of personnel development in order to minimize racism and to create a more productive working atmosphere. In the last decades, diversity training has received growing attention in the United States, and, according to Lippman (1999), 36% of firms of all sizes are offering some diversity training (Ferdman & Brody, 1998; Robertson et al., 2003), in other countries it is still neglected. *Intercultural coaching* normally takes place on the job overseas and is also a recent trend, being an answer to the criticism of cross-cultural trainings that they cannot address to all problems that may occur overseas.

Personnel Development off the Job

Fruitful personnel development should be sustainable. In the case of sojourns, sustainability means that the support of the expatriate should not stop at the pre-departure or pre-project phase. According to this, Thomas, Kinast and Schroll-Machl (2000) developed a helix model of personnel development, which means that there is no end: former experiences should be included in further development strategies. The intercultural personnel development should start with the personnel selection according to experiences made with sojourns or intercultural collaboration. Then a pre-departure training should take place, which should include both, cultural-general and/or cultural-specific preparation depending on the type of intercultural collaboration. During the residence overseas, the expatriate should be accompanied and before the end of the sojourn re-entry training is necessary. After the return, the experiences made by the expatriates should be used in order to create a database with information about the subsidiaries overseas, culture-specific experiences, population data, political conditions, geographical particularities, and the social system.

In case of multicultural and cross-border virtual teams, coaching may help to decipher conflictive potential and to clarify misunderstandings during the collaboration process. After the project, a documentation phase also should be included in order to file the specific intercultural experiences and problems that have occurred. This data should be integrated in future trainings and mechanisms of personnel selection. In the following, different training types and coaching will be described in detail.

Cross-cultural trainings.[8] Goals of trainings differ from goals of education. According to Nadler (1970), trainings are designed to improve human performance on the job, while education is not linked to a special job. With Landis and Baghat (1996), cross-cultural "training in an increasingly shrinking, highly interdependent world is no longer a luxury, but a necessity that most organizations have to confront in a meaningful fashion" (p. 7). Thus, the market of cross-cultural trainings is booming but "the field of cross-cultural trainings has not yet achieved the status of a profession" (Paige & Martin, 1996), main critics are a gap of theoretical foundation of cross-cultural trainings (Gudykunst, Guzley, & Hammer, 1996). Consequently, discussions have been raised about the contents and ethics in cross-cultural trainings.

Ethical Principles of Cross-Cultural Trainings

In sum, the following ethical principles have been developed for training practice (see Paige & Martin, 1996, p. 39, according to Kagan, 1972; Nieto, 1992):

- Trainers should help learners to understand the dynamics of cultural intervention and change agentry.
- Trainers should promote learner awareness of culture-bound and unconscious behavior.
- Trainers should promote changes in the existing patterns of learner's behavior if they will be maladaptive in the new culture.
- Trainers should provide opportunities for learners to gain skills in identifying and helping others change their maladaptive behaviors.
- Trainers should provide opportunities for learners to become responsible for their own choices and to help others become responsible for theirs.

Another common point of criticism, according to a lack of professionalism of trainers, is that, in practice, many cross-cultural training programs show a lack of theoretical frameworks. Nevertheless, there many training programs that base on a theory, but they are not immune against criticism.

Theoretical Frameworks of Cross-Cultural Training

According to Littrell et al. (2006), cross-cultural trainings base mainly on four theoretical frameworks: the social learning theory, the U curve of adjustment theory, culture shock theory, and the sequential model of adjustment. Depending on the theoretical background, the assumptions for cross-cultural trainings differ. Table 4 provides an overview of the theoretical frameworks, their contents, and assumptions for cross-cultural trainings.

According to Bandura (1977), the *social learning theory* assumes that social learning is a process influenced by observation and experience. Applying this theory to cross-cultural trainings it is supposed that the expatriate may learn by observing appropriate and inappropriate host country behavior. By doing so, he will develop the necessary skills to interact appropriately in the host cultural context and develop a sensibility for inappropriate interactions. Critics may argue that one-sided cognitive learning is not appropriate for all persons and does not necessarily lead to competent interactions (Ferdman & Brody, 1998). Training contents would base on information about the host country, and using videos or texts showing appropriate and inappropriate behavior, with an explanation about what makes the behavior appropriate.

The *U-curve of adjustment* has been developed by Calvero Oberg. In 1960, he described different stages of adjustment to a host cultural context. It is a function of time and has the form of a U-curve. That means that at a beginning stage the expatriate feels euphoria and only perceives positive aspects of the foreign assignment and the host culture. Then follows a phase of friction, where misunderstandings occur and collision with the different norms and values takes place. In the next step, differences will be accepted and tried to

be understood until a broad understanding of the host cultural context takes place and the expatriates adapt to it. Assumptions for cross-cultural trainings are that understanding the process of cultural adjustment can reduce the anxiety associated with it. An awareness of these phases should be created as well as coping styles in order to stay the course. The U-curve theory has been criticized because of the fact that the order can vary and some steps may be skipped, as well as a lack of differentiation between distinct subgroups of sojourners and adaptation to quite different phenomena (Furnham, 1987). Training contents will be information retrieved from cultural studies to raise the awareness of the adjustment process and in order to show the expatriate that the different stages of adjustment are something normal.

Another theoretical approach is the *culture shock theory*. With Littrell et al. (2006), "Culture shock is defined as a normal process of transition, adaptation, and adjustment in which an individual who enters a foreign environment for an extended time period experiences cultural stress involving some degree of anxiety, confusion, disruption, helplessness, and irritability" (Befus, 1998; Church, 1982) (p. 366). Therefore, in order to lower the level of psychological distress, cross-cultural trainings should provide coping styles. As with the other theories, the culture shock theory also has been criticized. Furnham (1987, p.45) claims: "Nearly all users have suggested that the experience is negative—though this may not necessarily be the case."

The *theory of met expectations* assumes that an individual has expectations regarding the characteristics of a job before entering in an organization. According to Caligiuri et al. (2001) and Wanous et al. (1992), these former expectations are compared to the actual experiences. If they coincide with the reality of the job, the individual is more likely to be satisfied, committed, and adjusted. The assumption for cross-cultural trainings are the following: Having a more realistic idea about the conditions of the work overseas, there will be less illusion and, therefore, less dissatisfaction, and, as such, information about the host countries' living and working conditions become the most important aspects of trainings. A counter-argument could be that in a case of negative expectations, self-fulfilling prophecies may take place.

The sequential model is based on the viewpoint that training is a process and should not be a one-time event. Selmer et al. (2001) developed a training program according to that assumption, corresponding to the cycle of adjustment that an individual progresses through the adaptation process to a foreign environment.

The rationale behind the dynamics of adjustment suggests that the impact of training differs at the various phases of the foreign assignment, depending on the individual's psychological receptivity to the culture at the given stages. (Selmer et al., 2001; Littrell, 2006, p. 366)

According to Selmer and colleagues (2001), four phases of adjustment exist: the *ethnocentric phase, the culture-shocked phase, the conformist phase*, and the *adjusted phase*. The program of the cross-cultural training should correspond to each phase of adjustment. Pre-departure and post-arrival training should take place. The pre-departure training should address information about the host country and the adjustment phases. Post-arrival training, first, should stress cultural awareness in order to lower ethnocentrism. The next stage of cross-cultural training has to be structured so that the individual is instructed on how to learn about his or her environment, and the expatriates should be taught how to sort out the experiences they had gained. During the conformist phase "Training exercises should be designed so that the expatriate interacts with host nationals in structured or unstructured situations, and then the expatriate should be provided with immediate feedback on the appropriateness of the behavior exhibited during the interaction" (Littrell et al., 2006, p. 367). These assumptions overlap with those, which are made for coaching as well.

Many theoretical frameworks have been proposed for designing programs of cross-cultural training or explaining their effectivity. Nevertheless, not all are empirically tested and, therefore, should be used cautiously. Which theoretical framework seems to be adequate depends on the objective a cross-cultural training has.

Objectives of Cross-Cultural Trainings

According to Gudykunst, Guzley and Hammer 1996, the broad objectives of cross-cultural trainings have a wide range, they can be directed to help to adjust to new cultural environments, to interact effectively with members of other cultural groups in cultural diverse environments, or counsel members of other cultural groups. Cross-cultural trainings normally involve some changes in three areas: cognition, affect, and behavior. In the *cognitive area*, cross-cultural trainings help to stimulate a general reflection about how culture, as well as attitudes and stereotypes influence interaction with members of other cultures. In the *affective area*, cross-cultural trainings try to develop the ability to self-control when interacting with persons with another cultural background. In the *behavioural area*, cross-cultural trainings focus on abilities and methods in order to adapt own behavior patterns to the particular host culture.

Classifications of Cross-Cultural Trainings

The three areas may be trained by the following techniques, which can be categorized in two dimensions: the approaches (didactic, experiential) used in the trainings and their content (culture-general and culture-specific), which base on different assumptions.[9] The combination of these issues leads to four types of classifications of training types: didactic culture-general, didactic culture-specific, experiential culture-general, and experiential culture-specific, which have different contents (see Table 5).

According to Bolten (2000), all types of trainings have advantages and disadvantages. The *didactic culture-general* types have a high effect on cognitive learning in order to understand processes of intercultural communication. Disadvantages are that they normally take place in an academic way, which has been criticized by many executives as

Table 4. Theoretical frameworks as basis of cross-cultural training programs

Theoretical framework	Content	Assumption for the trainings
Social learning theory (Bandura 1977)	Social learning is a process influenced by observation and experience.	• Intercultural learning by observing approbiate and inappropriate host country behaviour. (Bhagat & Prien, 1996; Black & Mendenhall, 1990) • Sensibilizing for model behavior in the host country and thus more likely to reproduce that type of behavior (Bhagat & Prien, 1996).
U-curve of adjustment (Church 1982)	Adjustment process is characterized by ups and downs. A first phase of euphoria is replaced by frustration and in the last phase of adaptation the individual begins to recover.	• Expatriate has to be tailored to the different phases of adjustment and to get aware of all these stages in order to overcome the challenges which occur in the phase of frustration.
Culture shock theory (Oberg, 1960; Church, 1982; Befus, 1998).	Individual who enters a foreign environment for an extended time period experiences cultural stress involving some degree of anxiety, confusion, disruption, helplessness, and irritability	• By addressing the problems associated with culture shock, lower levels of psychological distress, and the expatriate will be provided with coping skills for dealing with physiological, behavioral, emotional, and intellectual effects of culture shock (Befus, 1998).
Theory of met expectations (Caligiuri et al., 2001; Wanous et al., 1992)	Met expectations lead to greater levels of job satisfaction, commitment, adjustment, and performance	• By transmitting realistic expectations satisfaction, commitment, adjustment and performance should be increased.
Sequential model (Selmer et al., 1998).	Four phases of adjustment exist: the ethnocentric phase, the culture-shocked phase, the conformist phase, and the adjusted phase	• Training should take place in the four phases with different contents corresponding to the particular needs. (Bennet et al., 2000; Forster, 2000; Kealey & Protheroe, 1996; Bennet et al., 2000; Rahim, 1983; Selmer, 2001,)

Source: Modified version of Littrell et al. (2006)

being very abstract. The *didactical culture-specific trainings* may lead to a deeper understanding of a specific cultural system. But, if they are only descriptive, referring to "do's and taboos," they may lead to a reinforcement of stereotypes. The *experiential culture general trainings* may help to experience interculturality in cultural diverse groups. Negative effects are that the situations are normally fictitious and many participants do not take them seriously. The *experiential culture-specific trainings* normally train behaviors of the economic context and do not focus enough on culture-specific knowledge in general.

Unfortunately, many companies do not invest in cross-cultural trainings or do it only in a very short-term way in a one-day briefing (Littrell et al., 2006). Reasons are, for example:

the short length of time between selection and expatriate departure; the belief that technical competence is the main factor in determining success; the opinion that managers who operate well will be effective regardless of location; and the costs associated with training have all been supplied as reasons for neglecting preparatory training on international assignments (Litrell et al., 2006, p. 359 citing Baumgarten, 1995; Black & Mendenhall, 1990; Deshpande & Viswesvaran, 1992; Kealey & Protheroe, 1996).

Table 5. Classifications of cross-cultural trainings and their contents*

	Didactic	Experiential
Culture- general	Transmission of general knowledge about culture, by videos, presentations, discussions and culture assimilators, case studies, presentations of theories of intercultural communication, cultural anthropology and culture-comparing-psychology, discourse analysis.	Active experiencing of in which way the own and foreign cultural background influence behaviour patterns and values, by workshops, simulations, exercises in order to reach self-assessment Role taking games, self assessment questionaires.
Culture- specific	Transmition of knowledge about the particular cultural background and country specific themes as e.g. cultural standards by cultural specific assimilators, language teaching, culture specific presentations about history, execute case studies .	Culture-specific exercises based on own experiences made by bicultural communication trainings, country specific simulations and interactional role playing games, sensitivity trainings.

*Own design, based on different sources (Bolten 2000, p.72; Götz/Bleher, 2000, p. 32ff)

An important factor of success is additionally the commitment of the management supporting the strategies of the human resource development.

While cross-cultural trainings try to minimize the problems of adjustment and to sensibilize for the cultural otherness before the assignment, intercultural coaching, taking place *on* the job overseas and thus may address to concrete problems, is an alternative, which in the last years has reached more and more impact in the literature but still is not very common in the companies. It has the advantage that particular problems may be reflected with the coach who should have a profound knowledge of both cultures. He or she may stimulate clarifying communication about the origin of the problems and possible solutions.

Aims of coaching are, according to Peuker, Schmal, and Götz (2002), to favour the integration of the expatriate in the host culture and his/her enhancement in case of problematic situations. In order to reach this, a trustful relationship between the coach and the expatriate is a premise, because sensible areas may be touched as, for example, the expatriate's leadership competence, and so forth. It should take place in terms of stimulating an independency after a certain time (see Peuker, Schmal, and Götz, 2002). The expatriate should learn techniques of coping with stress and of deciphering unfamiliar behavior of host nationals.

In many companies, intercultural coaching takes place in an informal way. Expatriates who already have been overseas for a long time would introduce those who are new in the host cultural and company context. This is perceived as a big help by the newcomers, but may provoke a reinforcement of stereotypes, which will be passed in an unreflected way and may contain ethnocentric viewpoints (Maletzky, 2006). Thus, coaching by specially qualified coaches should be assured in order to amplify the perspective and avoid misunderstandings. Disadvantages are the high costs and the fact that a coach may get insights in areas that often are confidential.

Intercultural re-entry trainings. In the context of foreign assignment, expatriates additionally should participate in re-entry training, because the phase of reintegration into the host company and culture shows similarities to the adaptation to foreign culture (see e.g., Gullahorn & Gullahorn, 1963). One's own culture could become strange over time. Some theories even emphasize that the return of a sojourn may also cause culture shock. In this context, it may be estimated that the difficulties of reintegration rise in proportion to the duration of the foreign assignment. But the process of intercultural re-entry is often neglected, which may provoke underestimated problems for the company, too. According to Gomez-Meija and Balkin (1987), "a large number of expatriates who are successful for the duration of their assignment decide to leave the organization within one year of returning to the home country" (see Littrell et al., 2006, p. 358).

Intercultural re-entry means, according to Adler (1981), the process of reintegration into primary home contexts after a sojourn. We can name six general areas of re-entry problems that should be taken into account by those trainings (see Martin & Harrel, 1996, p. 314:

- **Cultural adjustment:** For example, problems in order to adjust to the home cultural context and to the daily routines, social adjustment
- **Social adjustment:** For example, feeling of social alienation, superiority, and so forth.
- **Linguistic adjustment:** For example, problems to readopt to the home cultural way of speaking.
- **National or political adjustment:** For example, problems with changes in political conditions, and so forth.
- **Educational adjustment:** For example, absence of educational programs, and so forth.
- **Professional adjustments:** For example, resistance to changes by colleagues, too high expectations, and so forth.

They can vary according to the expatriate's personality, host- and home cultural background. A detailed evaluation of the necessities should take place, preparation.

The re-entry training should begin during the sojourn. The contact to the mother company should be maintained in order to be notified about changes and to assure a less problematic reintegration and to stay informed about professional requirements. In the *pre-re-entry phase*, professional briefings should take place, as well as information about possible changes in the political system, and so forth. During the *re-entry phase*, readjustment issues are of high importance as there are, for example, employment issues such as job searches, and so forth.

Cross-Cultural Personnel Development on the Job

Intercultural coaching. Analysing the intercultural problems that occur during the sojourn or international projects of expatriates, many of them do not decrease by the time. That shows, according to Bolten (2000, p. 65), that cross-cultural trainings before the sojourns are not enough in order to overcome intercultural problems. In the context of virtual and cultural diverse teams, we can make the same assumption. Thus, a high necessity of support during the sojourn and the projects may be stated. Many times a fruitful utilization of the potential inherited in the situation of cultural overlap (Bolten, 2000) does not take place. This may be additionally stimulated by intercultural coaching on the job. Companies often have to handle with multicultural workforce especially in times of workforce shortages, which predicts a high productivity if the team composition is well done and the team members are aware of the high potential of cultural diversity and are sensibilized for culture differences, if not friction may take place. A well done diversity training may help to establish a positive working atmosphere. Thus some aspects have to be considered, which will be highlighted below.

Diversity Training

Diversity training is a method to develop heterogeneous teams or workforces. Diversity may be defined in a wide-range, for example, as race, gender, age, and so forth. In this context, cultural diversity is of interest, and the overcoming of stereotypes and the creation of a fruitful team atmosphere are the objectives.

Diversity training can overlap greatly with intercultural communication training, in that it often incorporates the same goal. Moreover, many methods and tools included as components of diversity training are derived or adapted from cross-cultural training approaches. (Ferdman & Brody, 1998, p. 284)

According to Robertson et al. (2003), it may be distinguished between two main types of diversity training: *awareness training* and *the developing of skills.* "*Awareness training* primarily targets trainee's attitudes toward diversity (and) *skill-based training targets* behaviors rather than attitudes, focusing on communication skills and conflict management, or resolution strategies (Kerka, 1998) across diverse group identities" (Robertson et al., 2003, p. 152) (emphasis added). According to Ferdman and Brody (1998), different levels are targeted by diversity trainings: the individual, interpersonal, group, intergroup, organizational or societal level. Depending on the different levels, the training focus and methods vary (see Table 6).

All these targets and objectives want to decrease racism and raise efficiency of labor. They are related to different motivations introducing diversity trainings. Reasons for the implementation of diversity trainings may be legal or social pressure, a moral imperative, or business success. The more intrinsic the motivations are, the more success of training is predictable, because then a high commitment within the top management may be supposed, which is constitutive for its success. According to Ferdman and Brody (1998), the lower the commitment of the (top) management, the less is the success of the trainings in general, because less resources are available and the duration of the trainings are shorter. Furthermore, participants' motivation is more observable if the management encourages the trainings and points out its necessity. In order to reach organizational goals, as for example, to create an egalitarian atmosphere between workforce with different ethnic backgrounds, it is necessary to implement long-term trainings.

Just as cross-cultural trainings, in general, diversity trainings may take part by experiential or didactic learning. "The basic premise of the *didactic approach* is that interaction among people from different cultures will be more effective when there is a reciprocal understanding of the other's culture" (Ferdman & Brody, 1998, p. 295) (emphasis in original). The didactic approach involves frontal presentations and group discussions. It targets, primarily, knowledge objectives and awareness. "The *experimental approach* presumes that the best learning occurs through active engagement and participation" (Ferdman & Brody, 1998, p. 295) (emphasis in original). In this context, many diversity training programs include simulation and role-play activities. But also group discussions of individuals and collective experiences are usual in order to make aware of stereotypes and ways of thinking.

It is not easy to decide which training design is more effective. All have their advocates and antagonists. Awareness programs are, for example, accused of perpetuating stereotypes (Flynn, 1998).

Employees who lack the critical behavioural skills needed to avoid unlawful discrimination may learn little from a training program with an awareness focus. Those unhappy with the current organizational climate for diversity are likely to view awareness training as window dressing, for appearance's sake only, leading to resentment. (Robertson et al., 2004, p. 153)

Developing skills by role-playing games, and so forth, runs the risk of creating a scapegoat. Some trainers use confrontational methods, which may be problematic, especially if there is not enough time to create an atmosphere of trust, which is constitutional for the success of this method. According to Robertson et al. (2004, p. 153), first, it should be assessed: "What are employee attitudes toward diversity and how strongly are those attitudes held?" The commitment of the ideas influences the changing. Ideas with low commitment may be changed by the input of new information, while high commitment of the ideas makes them difficult to change and the best way is by an experiential design (Petty & Cacioppo, 1986). Some investigations argue that diversity trainings are more effective if they are closely linked to business strategy or organizational culture and sufficient leadership support (Sims & Sims, 1993; Wheeler, 1994; GilDeaneGroup, 1993 cited by Ferdman & Brody, 1998).

Table 6. Level, focus and peculiarities of accordant diversity trainings

Targeted levels	Focus of training program	Peculiarities
Individual	• changing attitudes and / or behavior	
Interpersonal	• Development of more effective communication patterns • Learning how to deal with problematic relationships	• Specific • Temporary • Do not require top management involvement • Housed in Human Resources or Training Department
Group	• Team building • Development of efficacy	
Intergroup	• Changes of patterns of relationships	• Part of a broader organizational process • Infused throughout all levels • More resources • Long term orientated • Require top management involvement
Organizational	• Make the organization as a whole more inclusive and effective	
Societal	• Diminish oppression	

Source: Ferdman and Brody (1998)

FUTURE TRENDS

Intercultural collaboration will increase in the future in many industrial sectors, including the ICT sector. But, unlike theories predicting a convergence of cultures, which state that the world will develop a uniform culture, probably dominated by western values (Ritzer & Stillmann 2003; Ritzer, 1996), it is more likely that new combinations of values create new cultural or regional differences, such as the theory of a "global melange" (Nederveen Pieterse, 2004).[10] That means, that challenges due to cultural differences will not decrease in the future and intercultural competence will still be a condition of successful internationalization processes.

In order to stay competitive, not only to increase internationalization, but doing it effectively will be of high importance. Newer approaches accentuate that competitive advantage may be established by utilizing cultural differences appropriately (Welge & Holtbrügge, 2003). At the same time, intercultural personnel selection and development will be indispensable for successful internationalization processes. Thus, delays and change of locations may be minimized, especially SMEs, which have not established extended networks over the world,

yet need knowledge about cultural particularities in order to negotiate successfully.

Dispersed teams are the most cost-saving form of collaboration over distance, and their presence will increase (Martins, Gilson, & Maynard, 2004). This may be predicted especially in the context of the software branch, where the product may be transported electronically and off- and nearshoring increase. Challenges for intercultural collaboration may rise because of a lack of face-to-face contact.

Intercultural coaching is a recent trend and will have an increasing impact because of the possibility to solve problems, when they occur. Computer-based coaching could be a cost-saving alternative to the common face-to-face coaching. It also has the advantage of anonymity, which would reduce the anxiety of losing face-to-face contact.

Continuous evaluation of the working atmosphere of multicultural teams onshore and offshore, or overseas will be important in order to assure a fruitful working atmosphere. In cultures that have a high tendency to lose face-to-face contact, this will be hardly reached by conventional evaluation techniques. Also, the anonymity, which may be reached in computer-based methods, should be used to create appropriate tools.

Only few computer-based cross-cultural trainings exist, but a future trend will be an increase of such training tools, because they have the advantage to be location-independent and cost-saving. Normally, they focus on culture-specific training methods, and it should be carefully evaluated that they do not reinforce stereotypic perception of the users, since there is no possibility of a clarifying exchange with a trainer.

CONCLUSION

Fruitful intercultural collaboration is of high importance in the context of internationalization. Being involved in general challenges of industrialization and internationalisation, that, especially for the software branch, does not have such a long tradition yet, soft factors tend to be neglected. Intercultural competence is part of the soft factors, which predicts less friction during the intercultural collaboration. Three frameworks for intercultural collaboration in the ICT sector have been pointed out: sojourns, multicultural teams, and dispersed teams. All provoke particular challenges. While during sojourns the expatriate's adequate adaptation to the host cultural context is of high importance for performance, multicultural teams depend on the right composition, mutual awareness, and a high degree of acceptance of the otherness. Virtual multicultural teams suffer a lack of trust and have to handle with a high risk of misunderstandings and a negative working atmosphere, because the face-to-face contact, which in many cultures gives a first orientation about appropriate behavior, drops out. Knowledge transfer issues are another challenge to overcome. Problems that may occur in the context of intercultural collaborations are difficult to anticipate and may cause hidden costs. Nevertheless, investigations have found that there are some personal skills that predict successful interactions across cultures. They can be subsumed in three categories: adaptation, cross-cultural, and partnership skills. They are typical for a high intercultural competence, which is required for successful intercultural interaction, independent of the type of intercultural collaboration in the ICT sector.

Sustainable personnel selection, which integrates conclusions of cross-cultural studies can help to identify appropriate applicants. That means that the profile of skills is worked out by a needs assessment, which, in case of overseas assignment, incorporates the needs of both company locations and focuses on technical as well as intercultural skills, and the experiences made by expatriates or collaborators in multicultural (dispersed) teams for further recruitment processes. Training needs also should be screened during the personnel selection, since the perfect applicant does not exist. Cross-cultural or diversity trainings should be designed according to the individual needs and the form of intercultural collaboration. While the preparation of future expatriates requires culture-general and culture-specific contents, virtual and multicultural teams, depending on their composition, should get general training raising cultural awareness and promoting tolerance. Coaching for all groups is an important measure in order to decipher misunderstandings and potential conflicts, even if it is mainly promoted in the context of cross-cultural trainings.

An often-neglected factor is the influence of the spouse or family in the context of foreign assignments. Sojourns are often terminated prematurely because of their family's inability to adjust. Thus, cross-cultural training and coaching programs designed for expatriates should also comprise the expatriate's family. Unfortunately many companies neglect trainings or invest only few resources. Often only short-term briefing sessions are held before the departure of an expatriate (Littrell et al., 2006) or the start of multicultural teamwork. Additionally, diversity trainings often lack the commitment of management and, correspondingly, are not very successful because then the participants become more resistant.

Failure of sojourns are mainly seen as failure of the expatriates' competences on a personal level, the group level often is not taken into account, but is also of high importance (Maletzky, 2006). Personnel development should include both parts, because, even if the expatriate is well-adapted, misinterpretations of his or her behavior by the collaborators overseas are influenced by stereotypic perceptions. This is a neglected aspect that may lead to an unfruitful collaboration (Maletzky, 2006). This is a surprising fact because we cannot assume that most of the collaborators overseas, especially those on a bottom level have been living in a foreign country or had close contact to foreigners before. We can only suppose that perceptions are strongly influenced by unreflected stereotypes and, therefore, may cause struggle. Accordingly, intercultural team development is a necessity in cultural diverse working teams in situ and overseas.

FUTURE RESEARCH DIRECTIONS

Intercultural collaboration in the ICT sector has, until now, been rarely addressed. This is especially relevant in the context of high-end sourcing, since, for example, the outsourcing of software architecture, product design, and so forth, require a high degree of communication, coordination, and control throughout the working process. In the context of global sourcing and internationalisation, this implies additional challenges, since different cultural backgrounds must be taken into account.

Quality management systems and standardisations are limited in not being culturally neutral. Different ways of understanding and exertion provoke problems. More research should be done in this field, including an examination of to what extent cultural differences and worldwide competition between ICT workers affect the collaboration, cohesion, and productivity of intercultural teams.

Collaboration in dispersed teams is especially problematic due to difficulties in assuring knowledge transfer and the use of poorer communication channels. International virtual teamwork is a special case of intercultural teamwork, due to the lack of face-to-face contact. These aspects have not yet been systematically researched, but will be of high interest for many practitioners as this form of collaboration increases. This aspect is not taken into account enough in cross-cultural training, which normally addresses conventional forms of intercultural collaboration. There is no literature focusing on the intercultural development of virtual teams. At the same time, in the context of a growing tendency to near- and offshoring and reducing costs, as well as embetterment of technical tools,

geographically dispersed intercultural teams will increase in the future.

Technical tools and media should be evaluated and developed focusing the usefulness for intercultural collaboration. It may be supposed that in the context of the use of messengers there may occur misunderstandings in decoding the messages. The interpretation schemes of symbols, which should transmit feelings, cannot be seen as universal. On the other hand, it also may be possible that using a media such as the Internet there occurs something like a culture-neutral space and cultural differences decrease because the otherness is not perceived as strong as it does face-to-face. Many channels of perception are limited and the language is in the foreground, thus the whole bandwidth of differences may not be perceived.

There is a large market of cross-cultural trainings, but only a few investigations analysing their effect exist (see Thomas, Kinast, & Schroll-Machl, 2000). Effective evaluation tools are still lacking. Professionalisation of the trainers should be a future aim in order to guarantee a better performance. Contents of diversity trainings are often derived from those of cross-cultural trainings preparing a sojourn. More investigation should take place on this special issue, because according to Littrell et al. (2006), "multicultural teams face their own unique set of challenges" (p. 363). Additionally, investigations about foreign assignment and trainings mainly are focused one-sided on the expatriate's situation overseas. In this context, studies that take into account both, the expatriate's perspective as well as the perspective of the host cultural collaborators, are rare, but may bring an important input to the practice because a one-sided perspective biases the results (Maletzky, 2006). Cross-cultural trainings should, in addition, be developed according to sector-specific needs. There is still a lack of research into which specific training contents would be needed, especially for the ICT sector.

REFERENCES

Adler, N. (1981). Reentry: Managing cross cultural transition. *Group and organization studies, 6*(3), 341-356.

Aoki, K. (1995). Synchronous multi-user textual communication in international tele-collaboration. *Electronic Journal of Communication, 5*(4). Retrieved, June, 5, 2006 from: http://www.cios.org/getfile\AOKI_V5N495

Aspray, W.; Mayadas, F., & Vardi, Moshe Y. (Eds.). (2006). Globalization and offshoring of software. A report of the ACM job migration task force. *The executive summary, findings and overview of a compehensive ACM report on offshoring of software worldwide.* Association for Computing. Retrieved March 15, 2006 from http://www.acm.org/globalizationreport/summary.htm

Bandura, A. (1977). *Social learning theory.* Oxford, UK: Prentice Hall.

Baumgarten, K. (1995). Training and development of international staff. In A.W. Harzing & J. Van Ruysseveldth (Eds.), *International human resource management* (pp. 205-228). London, Thousand Oaks, New Delhi: Sage.

Befus, C. P. (1988). A multilevel treatment approach for culture shock experience by sojourners. *International Journal of Intercultural Relations, 12,* 381-400.

Bennet, R., Aston, A., & Colquhoun, T. (2000). Cross-cultural training: A critical step in ensuring the success of international assignments. *Human Resource Management, 39,* 239-250.

Berry, J. W. (1990). Psychology of acculturation: Understanding individuals moving between cultures. In R.W. Brislin (Ed.), *Applied cross-cultural psychology* (pp. 232-253). Newbury Park, London, New Delhi: Sage.

Bhagat, R., & Prien, K. O. (1996). Cross-cultural training in organizational contexts. In D. Landis & R. S. Bhagat (Eds.), *Handbook of cross-cultural training* (2nd ed., pp. 216-230). Thousand Oaks, CA: Sage.

Black, J. S., & Mendenhall, M. E. (1990). Cross-cultural training effectiveness: A review and a theoretical framework for future research. *Academy of Management Review, 15,* 113-136.

Black, J. S., Morrison, A. J., & Gregersen, H. B. (1999). *Global explorers: The next generation of leaders.* New York: Routledge.

Boes, A., & Schwemmle, M. (2004) *Herausforderung Offshoring. Internationalisierung und Auslagerung von IT-Dienstleistungen.* Düsseldorf.

Boes, A., & Trinks, K. (2006). *Theoretisch bin ich frei. Interessenhandeln und Mitbestimmung in der IT-Industrie.* Berlin: Edition Sigma.

Bolten, J. (2000). Interkultureller Trainingsbedarf aus der Perspektive der Problemerfahrungen entsandter Führungskräfte. In K. Götz (Ed.), *Interkulturelles Lernen / Interkulturelles Training* (pp. 61-79). München, Mering.

Bolten, J. (2002). *Das Kommunikationsparadigma im internationalen M&A Prozess. Due Dilligence und Post-Merger-Management im Zeichen der zweiten Moderne. Interculture Online* 2/ 2002.

Caligiuri, P., Phillips, J., Lazarova, M., Tarique, I., & Bürgi, P. (2001). The theory of met expectations applied to expatriate adjustment: The role of cross-cultural training. *International Journal of Human Resource Management, 12,* 357-372.

Carmel, I. (1997). Thirteen assertions for globally dispersed software development research. In *Proceedings of the 3rd Hawaii International Conference on Systems Science.*

Carmel, E., & Tjia, P. (2005) *Offshoring information technology. Sourcing and outsourcing to a global workforce.* Cambridge: Cambridge Univ. Press.

Church, A. T. (1982). Sojourner adjustment. *Psychological Bulletin, 91,* 540-572.

Davidson, E. J., & Tay, A. S. M. (2002). *Studying teamwork in global IT support.* Retrieved June 23, 2006, from http://ieeexplore.ieee.org/iel5/8360/26341/ 01173663.pdf?tp=&arnumber=1173663&isnumber=26341

DB Research (2006). Offshoring an neuen Ufern. Nearshoring nach Mittel- und Osteuropa. Retrieved September 20, 2006, from http://www.

dbresearch.de/PROD/DBR_INTERNET_DE-PROD/PROD0000000000200245.pdf

Demorgon, J. (1989). *L'exploration interculturelle. Pour une pédagogie internationale.* Paris: Armand Colin.

Deshpande, S. P., & Viswesvaran, C. (1992). Is cross-cultural training of expatriate managers effective: A meta analysis. *International Journal of Intercultural Relations, 16,* 295-310.

Edwards, H., Keith & Sridhar, Varadharajan (2002). Analysis of the effectiveness of global virtual teams in software engineering projects. In *Proceedings of the 36th Hawaii International Conference on System Sciences (HICSS '03).*

Ferdman, B. M., & Brody, S. E. (1998). Models of diversity training. In D. Landis & R.S. Baghat, *Handbook of cross-cultural training,* (pp. 282-306). Thousand Oaks, London, New Delhi: Sage.

Ferguson, C. H., Morris, C. R. (1993). *Computer wars – How the West can win in a post-IBM world.* New York: Times Books.

Flynn, G. (1998). The harsh reality of diversity programs. *Workforce, 77*(12), 26-30.

Forster, N. (2000). Expatriates and the impact of cross-cultural training. *Human Resource Management Journal, 10,* 63-78.

Fowler, S. M., & Mumford, M. G. (Eds.). (1999). *Intercultural sourcebook: Cross cultural training methods.* Yarmouth: Intercultural Press.

Furnham, A., & Bochner, S. (1982). Social difficulty in a foreign culture. In S. Bochner (Ed.), *Cultures in contact* (pp. 161-98). Elmsford, NY: El Sevier.

Furnham, A. (1987). The adjustment of sojourners. In Y.Y. Kim & W.B. Gudykunst (Eds.), *Cross cultural adaptation. Current approaches. International and Intercultural Communication Annual, Vol. XI* (pp. 42-61). Newbury Park, Beverly Hills, London, New Delhi: Sage.

Furnham, A., Bochner, S. (1986). *Culture shock: Psychological reactions to unfamiliar environments.* London: Methuen.

Giddens, A. (2). *Entfesselte Welt, wie Globalisierung unser Leben verändert.* Frankfurt/Main: Suhtkamp.

GilDeane Group (1993). *Cross cultural and diversity trainers. Do they know what they are doing?* The complete report on the May 1993 survey conducted by cultural diversity at work. Seattle.

Gomez-Mejia, L., & Balkin, D. B. (1987). The determinants of managerial satisfaction with the expatriation and repatriation process. *Journal of Management Development, 6,* 7-17.

Götz, K., & Bleher, N. (2000). Unternehmenskultur und interkulturelles Training. In K. Götz (Ed.), *Interkulturelles Lernen / Interkulturelles Training* (pp. 11-61). München/Mering: Hampp.

Gudykunst, W. B., Guzley R. M., & Hammer, M. R. (1996). Designing intercultural. In D. Landis & R.S. Baghat (Eds.), *Handbook of cross-cultural training* (2nd ed. pp. 61-80). Thousand Oaks, London, New Delhi: Sage.

Gullahorn, J. T., & Gullahorn, J. E. (1963). An extension of the U-curve hypothesis. *Journal of Social Issues, 3,* 33- 47.

Hall, E. T., & Hall, M. R. (1990). *Understanding culture differences.* Yarmouth: ME.

Hamill (1989). Expatriate policies in British multinationals. *Journal of General Management, 4,* 18-33.

Hofstede, G. (1980). *Culture's consequences. International differences in work related values.* Beverly Hills, London: New Delhi: Sage.

Hofstede, G. (1991). *Cultures and organizations. Software of the mind.* Berkshire: Mc Grawhill Professional.

Hofstede, G. (1993). *Interkulturelle Zusammenarbeit: Kulturen – Organisationen – Zusammenarbeit.* Wiesbaden

Hofstede, G. (1997). *Lokales Denken und globales Handeln.* München.

Hofstede, G. (2000). Images of Europe. In C. Robertson-Wensauer (Ed.), *Aspekte einer angewandten Kulturwissenschaft* (pp. 233-254). Baden.

Hynsell, D. (2000). Global teamwork for a global resource. In *Professional Communication Conference, 2000. Proceedings of 2000 Joint IEEE International and 18th Annual Conference on Computer Documentation* (IPCC/SIGDOC 2000). Retrieved July 17, 2006, from http://ieeexplore.ieee.org/servlet/opac?punumber=7114

Joisten, M. (2005). Aneignung und Nutzung von Instant Messaging in Organisationen: Eine strukturationstheoretische Analyse. In C. Stary (Ed.), *Mensch und Computer 2005: Kunst und Wissenschaft – Grenzüberschreitung der interaktiven ART* (pp. 45-50). München: Oldenbourg Verlag.

Kagan, S. (1972). *Ethics and concepts of cultural therapy* (ERIC Document Reproduction Service No. ED 069379). Washington, DC.

Kealey, D. J. (1996). The challenge of international personnel selection. In Landis & Baghat (Eds.), *Handbook of cross-cultural training* (2nd ed., pp. 81-105). London, New Delhi.

Kealey, D. J., & Protheroe, D. R. (1996). The effectiveness of cross-cultural training for expatriates: An assessment of the literature on the issue. *International Journal of Intercultural Relations, 20,* 141-165.

Kealey, S., & Ruben, B.D. (1983). Cross-cultural personnel selection: Criteria, issues and methods. In D. Landis & R. Brislin (Eds.), *Handbook of intercultural training* (Vol.1, pp. 155-175). Elmsford, NY.

Kerka, S. (1998). Diversity training. *ERIC Clearinghouse on Adult, Career and Vocational Education Trends and Issues Alert.* Retrieved from http://ericacve.org/docs/diverse.htm

Kolb, H., Murteira, S., Peixoto, J., & Sabino, C. (2004). Recruitment and migration in the ICT sector. In M. Bommes, H. Kirsten, U. Hunger, & H. Kolb (Eds.), *Organisational recruitment and patterns of migration interdependencies in an integrating Europe* (pp. 147-179). Osnabrück: IMIS.

Kopper, E. (2003). Multicultural teams. In N. Bergemann & A.L.J. Sourisseaux (Eds.), *Interkulturelles management* (pp. 363-382). Berlin, Heidelberg, NY, Hong Kong, London, Mailand, Paris, Tokyo.

Landis, D., & Baghat, S. (1996). A model of intercultural behavior and training. In D. Landis & S. Baghat (Ed.). *Handbook of cross-cultural training* (2nd ed., pp. 1- 6). Thousand Oaks, London, New Delhi.

Lippman, H. (1999). Harnessing the power of diversity. *Business and Health, 17*(6), 40.

Littrell, L. N., Salas, E., Hess, K. P., Haley, M., & Riedel, S. (2006). Expatriate preparation: A critical analysis of 25 years of cross-cultural training research. *Human Resource Development Review,* September.

López-Bassols, V. (2002). *ICT skills and employment.* OECD Science and Technology. (Working Paper, 2002/10), OECD Publishing. (Publication No. 10.1787/110542373678).

Maletzky, M. (2006, September). Teamwork in a globalised context: Influencing factors on achievement in German Mexican collaboration. Conducted at the *10th International Workshop on Teamworking (IWOT 10)*, Groningen, Netherlands.

Martin, J., & Harrell, T. (1996). Reentry Training for Intercultural sojourners. In D. Landis & R. S. Baghat (Eds.), *Cross-cultural training* (2nd ed., pp. 307-326). Thousand Oaks, London, New Delhi.

Martins, L. L., Gilson, L. L., & Maynard, T. M. (2004). Virtual teams: What do we know and where do we go from here? *Journal of Management, 30*(6), 805-835.

Mattloff, N. (2005). Offshoring: What can go wrong? *IT Pro,* July/August.

Matveev, A. V., & Nelson, P. E. (2004). Cross cultural communication competence and multicultural team performance perceptions of American and Russian managers. *International Journal of Cross Cultural Management, 4*(2), 253-270.

Maznevski, M. L., & Peterson, M. F. (1997). Societal values, social interpretation, and multinational teams. In C.S. Granrose & S. Oskmap (Eds). *Cross-cultural work groups* (pp. 61-89). Thousand Oaks, CA: Sage.

McGrath, J. E., Berdahl, J. L., & Arrow, H. (1996). Traits, expectations, culture and clout. The dynamics of diversity in groups. In S.E. Jackson & M.N. Ruderman (Eds.), *Diversity in work teams. Research paradigms for a changing work place* (pp. 17-45). Washington, DC.

McLaughlan, G., & Salt, J. (2002). *Migration policies towards highly skilled foreign workers.* RDS. London. Retrieved June 15, 2006, from http://www.homeoffice.gov.uk/rds/pdfs2/migrationpolicies.pdf

McLeod, P. L., & Lobel, S. A. (1992). *The effects of ethnic diversity on idea generation in small groups.* Paper presented at the Academy of Management Meeting, Las Vegas.

Miller, E. L. (1989). Auslandseinsatz. In K. Macharzina & M.K. Welke (Eds.), *Handbuch Export und internationale Unternehmung* (pp. 73-83). Stuttgart.

Moore, S., & Brown, A. (2004). *Cultural challenges in offshore outsourcing.* Forrester Research Inc.

Nadler, L. (1970). *Developing human resources.* Houston.

Nederveen Pieterse, J. (1997). Globalization and hybridization. In M. Featherstone, S. Lash, & R. Robertson (Eds.), *Global modernities* (pp. 45-68). London, Thousand Oaks, New Delhi.

Nederveen Pieterse, J. (2002). Collective action and globalization. In P. Hamel, H. Lustiger-Thaler, J. Nederveen Pieterse, & S. Roseneil (Eds.), *Globalization and social movements* (pp. 21-40). Basingstoke.

Nederveen Pieterse, J (2003). Die Ausnahmestellung der Supermacht: Globalsierung auf amerikanisch. In U. Beck, N. Znaider, & R. Winter (Eds.), *Globales Amerika? Die kulturellen Folgen der Globalisierung* (pp. 93-132). Bielefeld.

Nederveen Pieterse, J. (2004). *Globalization and culture: global mélange.* Lanham.

Nieto, S. (1992). *Affirming diversity: The social political context of multicaultural education.* White Plains, NY.

Oberg, K. (1960) Cultural shock. Adjustment to new cultural environments. *Practical Anthropology, 7,* 177-182.

OECD (2004). *Highlights of the OECD information technology outlook.* Stand Retrieved August 25, 2006, from http://www.oecd.org/dataoecd/20/47/33951035.pdf

Opdenakker, R. (2006). *Advantages and disadvantages of four interview techniques in qualitative research.* Forum: Qualitative Social Research, 7(4) available at: http://www.qualitative-research.net/fqs-texte/4-06/06-4-11-e.htm

Paige, R., & Martin, J. N. (1996). Ethics in cross-cultural training. In D. Landis & S. Baghat (Eds.), *Handbook of cross-cultural training* (2nd ed., pp. 35-60). Thousand Oaks, London, New Delhi.

Petty, R., &Cacioppo, J. (1986). *Attitudes and persuasion: Central and peripheral routes to attitude change.* NY: Springer-Verlag.

Peuker, L., Schmal, A., & Götz, K. (2002). Interkulturelles Coaching für Expatriates im Ausland. Ein neues Betreuungskonzept soll Fach und Führungskräfte in ihrem Auslandseinsatz unterstützen (pp. 40-47). *Personalführung.*

Rahim, A. (1983). A model for developing key expatriate executives. *Personnel Journal, 62,* 312-317.

Redfield, R., Linton, R., & Herskovits, M. J. (1936). Memorandum for the study of acculturation. *American Anthropologist, 38,* 149-152.

Ritzer, G. (1996). *La Mc. Donaldización de la sociedad. Una análisis de la racionalización de la vida cotidiana.* Barcelona.

Ritzer, G., & Stillmann, T. (2003). McDonaldisierung, Amerikanisierung und Globalisierung: Eine vergleichende Analyse. In U. Beck, N. Znaider,

& R. Winter (Eds.), *Globales Amerika? Die kulturellen Folgen der Globalisierung* (pp. 44-68). Bielefeld.

Robertson, L., Kulik, C., Pepper, M. (2004). Using needs assessment to resolve controversies in diversity training design. *Group & Organization Management*, *28*(1), 148-174.

Rosenstiel, L. v. (2004). Kommunikation in Arbeitsgruppen. In *Lehrbuch Organisationspsychologie* (pp. 387-414). Bern, Göttingen, Toronto, Seattle.

Roy R., Henson, H., & Lavoie, C. (1996). *A primer on skill shortages in Canada*, R096-8E, Human Resources Development, Canada.

Scherf, Schütt & Partner, Beratungssozietät für effektives Ressourcenmanagement (2006). *Voraussetzungen für erfolgreiches Outsourcing von Software-Entcklungs-Projekten*, Bonn. Retrieved November 23, 2005, from www.sspberatung.de

Schroll-Machl, S. (1999). Länderkundliche / völkerkundliche Seminare. Bildungsziele und Programmodule. In H. Hahn (Ed.), *Kulturunterschiede. Interdisziplinäre Konzepte zu kollektiven Identitäten und Mentalitäten* (pp. 341-370). Frankfurt / Main.

Selmer, J. (2001). The preference for predeparture or postarrival cross-cultural training: An exploratory approach. *Journal of Managerial Psychology*, *16*, 50-58.

Sharpe, R. (2001). Globalization: The next tactic in the fifty-year struggle of labor and capital in software production. In R. Baldoz, C. Koeber, & P. Kraft (Eds.), *The critical study of work, labor, technology and global production*. Philadelphia: Temple University Press.

Shehkar, O., & Zeira, Y. (1992). Role conflict and role ambigity of chief executive officers in international joint ventures. *Journal of Business Studies, 23*(1), 55-75.

Sims, S. J., & Sims, R. R. (1993). Diversity and difference training in the United States. In R.R. Sims & F.F. Dennehy (Eds.), *Diversity and differ-*

ences in organizations: An agenda for answers and questions (pp. 73-92). Westport, CT.

Sole, D., & Edmonson, A. (2002). Situated knowledge and learning in dispersed teams. *British Journal of Management, 13*, 17-34.

Stahl, G. (1998). *Internationaler Einsatz von Führungskräften*. München/Wien.

Stumpf, S. (2003). Interkulturelles Management. In A. Thomas, E-U. Kinast, & S. Schroll-Machl (Eds.), *Handbuch interkulturelle Kooperation* (pp. 229-242). Göttingen.

Thomas, A. (1999). Handlungswirksamkeit von Kulturstandards. Beispiele aus der deutsch-amerikanischen und deutsch chinesischen Interaktion. In H. Hahn (Ed.), *Kulturunterschiede* (pp. 109-120). *Interdisziplinäre Konzepte zu kollektiven Identitäten und Mentalitäten*. Frankfurt / Main.

Thomas, A., Kinast, E.U., & Schroll-Machl, S. (2000). Entwicklung interkultureller Handlungskompetenz von international tätigen Fach und Führungskräften durch interkulturelle Trainings. In K. Götz (Ed.), *Interkulturelles Lernen / Interkulturelles Training* (pp. 97-122). Stuttgart.

Thomas, A. (2003). Psychologie interkulturellen Lernens und Handelns. In Thomas (Ed.), *Kulturvergleichende Psychologie*. Göttingen, Bern, Toronto, Seattle. (2. Auflage).

Thomas, A., Hagemann, K., & Stumpf, S. (n.d.). Training interkultureller Kompetenz. In N. Bergemann & A.L.J. Sourisseaux (Eds.), *Interkulturelles Management* (pp. 3-20). Berlin, Heidelberg, NY, Hong Kong, London, Mailand, Paris, Tokyo.

Townsend, A. M., DeMarie, S., & Hendrickson, A. R. (1998). Virtual teams: Technology and the workplace of the future. *The Academy of Management Executive, 12*(3), 29.

Trimpop, R. M., & Meynhardt, T. (2000). Interkulturelle Trainings und Einsätze: Psychische Konsequenzen und Wirkungsmessungen. In K. Götz (Ed.), *Interkulturelles Lernen / Interkulturelles Training* (pp. 183-211). München / Mering.

Trompenaars, F. (1993). *Riding the waves of culture. Understanding cultural diversity in business.* London.

Tung, R. (1987). Expatriate assignments: Enhancing success and minimizing failure. *Academy of Management Executive, 2,* 117-126.

UNESCO (2002). *Universal declaration on cultural diversity.* Retrieved June 23, 2006, from http://www.unesco.org/education/imld_2002/unversal_decla.shtml

Wanous, J. P., Poland, T. D., Premack, S. L., & Davis, K. S. (1992). The effects of met expectations on newcomer attitudes and behaviors: A review and meta-analysis. *Journal of Applied Psychology, 77,* 288-297.

Ward, C. (1996). Acculturation. In D. Landis & S. Baghat (Eds.), *Handbook of intercultural training* (2nd ed., pp. 124-147). Thousand Oaks, London, New Delhi.

Watson, W. E., Kumar, K., & Michaelson, L. K. (1993). Cultural diversity's impact on interaction process and performance: Comparing homogeneous and diverse task groups, *Academy of Management Journal, 36,* 590-602.

Welge, M. K., & Hottbrügge, D. (2003). Organisatorische Bedingungen des interkulturellen Managements. In N. Bergemann & A.L.J. Sourisseaux (Eds.), *Interkulturelles management* (pp. 3-20). Berlin, Heidelberg, NY, Hong Kong, London, Mailand, Paris, Tokyo.

Wheeler, M. (1994). *Diversity training: A research report.* (Report No. 1083-94). New York.

Wieandt, M. (2007, March). The development of knowledge transfer and collaboration in a nearshore software development project. Conducted at the *First Information Systems Workshop on Global Sourcing: Services, Knowledge and Innovation.* Val D'isére, France.

Winter, (2006). In Indien ticken die Uhren anders. Retrieved october 11, 2006 from http://www.computerwoche.de/it_strategien/outsourcing_offshoring/581724/index.html

Zaninelli, S. M. (2003). Der Mix macht's. Die Auswahl der passenden Kommunikationsmittel vermindert Reibungsverluste im Geschäftsablauf. Retrieved July 23, 2006 from http://www.culture-contact.com/pdf/der_mix_machts.pdf

ADDITIONAL READING

Agar, M. (1994). *Language shock. Understanding the culture of communication.* NY.

Ang, S., Van Dyne, L., Koh, C. (2006). Personality correlates of the four-factor model of cultural intelligence. *Group & Organization Management, 31*(1), 100-123.

Asante, M. K., Gudykusnt, W. B. (1989). *Handbook of international and intercultural communication.* Newbury Park.

Auer, P., Besse, G., & Méda, D. (Eds.). (n.d.). Offshoring and the internationalization of employment. A challenge for a fair globalization? (pp. 143-162). *Proceedings of the France ILO Symposium ILO.* Geneva.

Bhabha, H. (1994). *The location of culture.* NY.

Blommaert, J. (1991). How much culture is there in intercultural communication? In J. Blommaert & J. Verschueren (Eds.), *The pragmatics of intercultural and international communication* (pp. 13-31). Amsterdam/Philadelphia.

Berger, S., Kurz, C., Sturgeon, T., Voskamp U., & Wittke, V. (2001). Globalization, production networks, and national models of capitalism – On the possibilities of new productive systems and institutional diversity in an enlarging Europe. *SOFI-Mitteilungen, 29.* http://www.sofi-goettingen.de/fileadmin/SOFI-Mitteilungen/Nr._29/berger-kurz-ua.pdf

Brislin, R., Worthley, R., & MacNab, B. (2006). Cultural intelligence. Understanding behaviours that serve peoples goals. *Group & Organization Management, 31*(1), February, 40-55.

Brislin, R. W., Cushner, K., Craig, C., & Yong, M. (Eds.). (1986). *Intercultural interactions a practical guide*. Newberry Park, London, New Delhi.

Cali, A. P., Watson, M. B., & de V de Kock, G. (1997). *Identification and selection of successful future IT personnel in a changing technological and business environment*. Retrieved April, 17, 2007, from http://delivery.acm.org/10.1145/2700 00/268864/p31-calitz.pdf?key1=268864&key2=8 912286711&coll=portal&dl=ACM&CFID=15151 515&CFTOKEN=6184618

Chrobot-Mason, D. (2004). Managing racial differences. The role of mayority managers' ethnic identity development on minority employee perceptions of support. *Group & Organization Management, 29*(1), 5-31.

Faust, M. (2005). *Reorganization and relocation in the German fashion industry*. Paper prepared for the Conference Organisational Configurations and Locational Choices of Firms: Responses to Globalisation in Different Industry and Institutional Environments, University of Cambridge, Cambridge.

Faust, M., Voskamp, U., & Wittke, V. (2004). Globalization and the future of national systems: Exploring patterns of industrial reorganization and relocation in an enlarged Europe. In Faust, M., Voskamp, U., & Wittke, V. (Eds.), *European industrial restructuring in a global economy: Fragmentation and relocation of value chains* (pp. 19-81). Göttingen: SOFI.

Fenwick, M. (2004) On international assignment: Is expatriation the only way to go? *Asia Pacific Journal of Human Resources, 42*(3).

Fischer, R., Ferreira, M. C., Leal Assmar, E. M., Redford, P., & Harb, C. (2005). Organizational behaviour across cultures. *Theoretical and Methodological Issues for Developing Multi-level Frameworks Involving Culture, 5*(1), 27-48.

Frenkel, S., Orlitzky, M. (n.d.). Organizational trustworthiness and workplace labor productivity: Testing a new theory. *Asia Pacific Journal of Human Resources, 43*(1).

Garman, A., Corbett, J., & Benesh, J. (2005). Ready-to-use simulation. The hidden cost of employee turnover. *Simulation & Gaming*, June.

Glick, N. D. (2002). The relationship between cross cultural experience and training, and leader effectiveness in the US foreign service. *Journal of Cross Cultural Management, 2*(3), 339-356.

Janssens, M., & Brett, J. M. (2006). Cultural intelligence in global teams: A fusion model of collaboration. *Group Organization Management, 31*, 124-153.

Langille, B. A. (2006). Better governance of the internationalization of employment. In P. Auer, G. Besse & D. Méda (Eds.), Offshoring and the internationalization of employment. A challenge for a fair globalization? *Proceedings of the France ILO Symposium* (pp. 143-162). ILO: Geneva.

Lasser, S., & Heiss, M. (2005). Collaboration maturity and the offshoring cost barrier: The trade-off between flexibility in team composition and cross-site communication effort in geographically distributed development projects. In *Proceedings of the IEEE International Professional Communication Conference (IPCC 2005)* (pp. 718-728). Limerick, Ireland.

Meland, H., Waage, R. P., & Sein, M. K. (2005, April 14-16). The other side of turnover: Managing IT personnel strategically. *Proceedings of the 2005 ACM SIGMIS CPR Conference (SIGMIS CPR'05)*.

Narayanaswamy, R., & Henry, R. M. (2005, April 14-16). Effects of culture on control mechanisms in offshore outsourced IT projects. In *Proceedings of the 2005 SIGMIS-CPR'05*, Atlanta, Georgia, USA.

Nelson, R. E., & Gopalan, S. (2003). Do organizational cultures replicate national cultures? Isomorphism, rejection and reciprocal opposition in the corporate values of three countries. *Organization Studies, 24*(7), 1115-1151.

Raj Isar, Y. (2006). Tropes of "intercultural": Multiple perspectives. In N. Aalto & E. Reuter (Eds.), *Aspects of intercultural dialogue* (pp. 13-26). Köln.

Rundstrom Williams, T. (2005). Exploring the impact of study abroad on students' intercultural communication skills: Adaptability and sensitivity. *Journal of Studies in International Education*, *9*(4), 356-371.

Salo-Lee, L. (2006). Intercultural competence research and practice: Challenges of globalization for intercultural leadership and team work. In N. Aalto & E. Reuter (Eds.), *Aspects of intercultural dialogue* (pp. 79-94). Köln.

Starke-Meyerring, D., & Andrews, D. (2006). Building a virtual learning culture. An international classroom partnership. *Business Communication Quarterly*, *69*(1), 25-4.

Steinwachs, K. (2001). Information and culture: The impact of national culture on information processes. *Journal of Information Science*, *25*(3), 193-204.

Thomas, D. C. (2006). Domain and development of cultural intelligence. The importance of mindfulness. *Group & Organization Management*, *31*(1), 78-99.

Triandis, H. C. (2006). Cultural intelligence in organizations. *Group Organization Management*, *31*, 20-26.

Triandis, H. C. (2001). The study of cross cultural management and organization: The future. *International Journal of Cross Cultural Management*, *1*, 17-20.

Vallaster, C. (2005). Cultural diversity and its impact on social interactive processes. Implications from an empirical study. *International Journal of Cross Cultural Management*, *5*(2), 139-163.

Wong, M. M. L. (2005). Organizational learning via expatriate managers: Collective myopia as blocking mechanism. *Organization Studies*, *26*(3), 325-350.

Zander, L., & Romani, L. (2004). When nationality matters. A study of departmental, hierarchical, professional, gender and age-based employee groupings' leadership preferences across 15 countries. *International Journal of Cross Cultural Management*, *4*(3), 291-315.

ENDNOTES

[1] Offshoring means outsourcing or founding of spin offs in a geographical far located low-wage country, while nearshoring refers to the same process in a geographical nearer low-wage country. The distance is not specific, but often the distance of 1000 kms (ca.621 miles) is taken as demarcation. (Scherf, Schütt & Partner, 2005). For a detailed description of off- and nearshoring see the chapter "Offshoring in the ICT Sector in Europe" in this book.

[2] See chapter "Offshoring in Europe" in this book.

[3] For detailed description, see Kolb et al. (2004).

[4] See also Hofstede (1991, 1993, 2000).

[5] He first found the four dimensions: power distance, masculinity vs. femininity, uncertainty avoidance, and individualism vs. collectivism. The same dimensions are described also in Hofstede (1991, 1993, 2000) but a fifth dimension has been included: long-term orientation

[6] For a critical reflexion, see Furnham (1998).

[7] Cultural toughness pertains to the notion that it is more difficult to adjust to certain countries than to other countries.

[8] For detailed description of training methods and inventories, see Fowler (1999).

[9] For more detailed information see, Gudykunst/Guzley, Hammer (1996, p. 65f).

[10] For a critical reflection of convergence and hybridization, see also Nederveen Pieterse (1997, 2002, 2003).

Chapter X
Computer–Mediated Communication:
Enhancing Online Group Interactions

J. Michael Blocher
Northern Arizona University, USA

ABSTRACT

Advancements in information technology have transformed much in all aspects of today's society. In particular, synchronous and asynchronous electronic communication systems support countless interactions every day. However, these communication systems have specific limitations that can cause miscommunications as well. Because of that, computer-mediated communications (CMC) has been a robust research agenda in many disciplines. This is especially true of education, where online learning has become common place in all but a few universities, thus requiring learners to interact via CMC within virtual learning environments. This chapter will use educational CMC research as a lens to promote and support an understanding of how to better utilize and facilitate electronic communication, regardless of the field or endeavor.

BACKGROUND

Over a decade ago, Rheingold (1993) described how the Internet, specifically, synchronous and asynchronous electronic communication could create a non-linear and level environment that provides the conduit for human interaction that is culturally neutral—where members meet in virtual communities judged by ideas, thoughts, and contributions, rather than by race, gender, age, physical appearance, or national origin. In particular, CMC was described as a venue where participants could engage in discussions on bulletin boards and listservs with equal impunity and have the opportunity to create a cyber community. Due to the lack of visible and contextual cues, participants engaging in this, somewhat, anonymous form of communication were free from prejudice and able to speak their mind more freely and openly than in traditional face-to-face group interactions. However, this turned out be only somewhat correct, and the literature provides ample examples of how CMC group interactions follow similar patterns and styles that have been identified within traditional face-to-face group interactions.

Communication Style Differences

Communication style differences, particularly, gender-based differences have been identified as one area that has been investigated in more historic group interaction literature. Specifically, women tend to engage in group interactions with a style distinctly different than men. Eakins and Eakins (1978) in researching gender styles within group interactions discovered that women tend to be more engaged in developing intimacy and maintaining relationships than their male counterparts. In other words, women tend to be more interested in building relationships and developing closeness within their group than men do. For example, women are more apt to ask for another's opinion, desiring to engage others within the conversation. Men, on the other hand, tend to be more directive and less apt to draw out the interaction (Fishman, 1983). Perhaps this is because, in general, women are more interested in the social aspects of group interaction. For example, Carli (1984) reported that women are more social-oriented, while men are more task-oriented in their interactions. Furthermore, Briton and Hall (1995) reported that women tended to be better at using nonverbal cues, being more expressive, utilizing body language, eye contact, and gestures to send and receive subtle messages to promote and enhance communication in group interactions. Men, on the other hand, leaned toward competitiveness and dominance seemed more apt to be more competitive and less socially motivated in their group interactions—using fewer subtle nonverbal cues.

In terms of group interactions where productivity is at issue, Maguire (1999) reported that within studies of marketing executives women work more to build consensus while men tended to make faster decisions. One could argue that one style is better than the other at supporting communication in group interactions, as both have benefits and limitations. For example, being more direct could be seen as a way to improve communication by not clouding the issue with possibly vague nonverbal cues. On the other hand, by providing more information via other channels (e.g., body language, facial expressions, etc.), the verbal message might be further enhanced, with less chance of misunderstandings. Furthermore, by utilizing a communication style that seems competitive and dominating, issues of power may cloud or hinder the real message. Again, on the contrary, using less direct verbal communication could be seen to hinder one's ability to provide leadership. Which style makes a better communicator—one who builds community or consensus through social group interactions enhanced with non-verbal cues, or one who improves productivity with more directive style communication?

It could be argued that it might be better to try to understand these communication style differences, rather than trying to debate which might be more effective, as each has benefits and limitations. This is especially important within the CMC environment. As we will see in the next section, CMC group interactions have other issues based upon the various CMC media, which can greatly impact these more traditional communication style differences.

CMC Communication Style Differences

Of course, these gender differences are generalities. One's individual group communication style is just that, individual. However, these gender-related communication style differences seem to parallel a CMC environment as well. As in all social environments, membership within a CMC group environment can be dominated by more spirited individuals, and certain hierarchies can develop or emerge based upon the members' interactions within that virtual community. Of particular note,

Herring (1993) details that virtual communication spaces may not be the democratic spaces described earlier—primarily because of the communication style differences brought naturally to the environment by the various group members and the community ethos that the group develops. For example, her study reported that men generally made "strong assertions," engaged in "self-promotion," asked "rhetorical questions," came from an "authoritative orientation," provided "challenges and humor." Women, on the other hand, tended to ask "questions," provided "attenuated assertions," presented "apologies," had a "personal orientation" and provided "support" in their CMC. As discussed above, these two gender-based communication styles mirror those of the traditional research. Generally, women tend to foster consensus and community building, while men tend to demonstrate a communication style that is more directive in nature.

While this supports the argument that men are more apt to utilize a more directive CMC style, perhaps more interesting are specific investigations into chat (synchronous communications) that have detailed how gender communication style differences were power-based in particular. Soukup (1999) stated that in his study, "Masculine participants were aggressive, argumentative, and power oriented. While feminine participants sought relationships and intimacy, they were often dominated and overpowered by the aggressive discourse of the masculine members (p. 169)." Perhaps, even more disturbing, findings were reported by Herring (1999). She described male-dominated harassment of female participants in two case studies, stating: "Due perhaps to the youth and sexual preoccupations of the majority of its users, Internet relay chat (IRC) tends to sexualize female participants, and to involve them in flirtatious interactions. Accordingly, the ideal for female interactions in IRC appears to be cooperative flirtation, as it is also in many off-line recreational social realms" (p. 163).

One would think that this type of interaction might inhibit female members when engaging in online communication, perhaps making them more apt to adjust or change their online communication engagement; perhaps even hide or mask their gender identity in CMC environments to guard against this type of interaction. To answer that question, Jaffe, Lee, Huang, and Oshagan (1999) investigated how participants, when given opportunities, chose to select anonymous pseudonyms for their CMC. Some participants chose pseudonyms with same gender, others chose pseudonyms that were cross gender, and finally some chose pseudonyms that were gender neutral. Gender-neutral and cross-gender pseudonyms then collapsed into gender-masking, thus providing two categories as same-gender and gender-masking. They reported that, "Seventeen (81%) of the 21 male participants in the pseudonymous conference chose pseudonyms that retained their gender identification. In contrast, 13 (81%) of the 16 females in the pseudonymous conference chose pseudonyms that masked their gender identification" (1999, p. 227). This significant difference ($p < .001$) between men and women demonstrates a greater tendency, by women, to utilize a pseudonym that masked their gender. The authors of this study saw this as evidence of a direct strategy to level the playing field stating:

This finding is interpreted to reflect an effort to rectify an imbalance, felt by women, of social parity when interacting in mixed-gender situations. An especially pertinent example of previous gender-based naming practices provides historical justification for such sentiments. In anecdotal recollections within the scientific research profession, female authors were often referred to by first and last names, while only initials and last name identify males. (Jaffe, Lee, Huang, & Oshagan, 1999, p. 230)

The CMC literature provides examples where group interactions within CMC environments seem to exacerbate the communication style differences, perhaps making men aggressive and making women more engaged in building social relationships in their communication styles. However, it seems that if given the opportunity, women tend to mask their gender for strategic purposes.

Summary

Although the CMC technology does have the potential to provide a non-linear and level environment that provides the conduit for human interaction that is culturally neutral, it seems that it may not. Indeed, the studies described above strongly indicate that CMC may not be the level playing field that it was once thought to be. In particular, there are communication style differences within the CMC environment that parallel traditional communication styles, thus creating a group communication environment where the communicators interact in similar ways that they would in traditional face-to-face environments—where gender, power, and communication style may have a strong impact on one's communication within group interactions.

It is important to remember that these are general tendencies and that not all CMC group interactions are destined to exhibit the type of interactions described above. Rather these are tendencies that could impact one's experience engaging in CMC, which might be exacerbated by some of the unique communication issues that are specific to current text-based CMC. For example, often a message is sent that is totally benign. However, the message even when taken simply for the written text may be taken for a completely different meaning than originally intended, because the sender and recipient engaged in the communication at different times, locations, and states of mind. Being more knowledgeable about the tendencies and limitations of CMC could help limit more adversarial interactions that were based upon miscommunication due to CMC issues or communication styles. In particular, becoming aware of and monitoring one's personal communication style could help make the individual more thoughtful and strategic about their communiqués, thus reducing the tendencies for miscommunication to occur. The next section will discuss specific issues at work within the current CMC environments that might hamper communication and strategies that could be implemented to enhance more equitable and clear CMC engagement.

ISSUES

As described, gender, power, and communication style can impact one's personal communication interactions within a CMC environment. Although these elements parallel traditional face-to-face communication interactions, there are issues with CMC that are unique to that environment. In particular, the discussion will focus on current CMC issues in terms of how asynchronous and synchronous electronic communication tools limit the capacity of communication cues and meta-information as well as communication styles in terms of gender, and whether these issues can be influenced to help ameliorate those limitations.

Media Richness

Much of the CMC literature suggests that communicating within electronic messaging systems, which are primarily text based, limits communication because of the lack of other communication cues or components. Media richness theory (Daft & Lengel, 1986) defines communication media in terms of face-to-face communication elements. These elements include immediacy of feedback, non-verbal, and other cues that enrich communication. In other words, a medium is considered richer or thicker when it can support a greater number of cues to communicate a person's ideas (e.g., facial expressions, gestures, voice inflection, etc.). In light of media richness theory, current CMC is defined as being "lean" because much is asynchronous communication, lacks immediacy of feedback and generally lacks "multiplicity of cues."

In terms of immediacy of feedback, imagine a face-to-face interaction where participants give and receive concurrent and instant feedback while they monitor the message reception and consider its impact. Compare that to asynchronous CMC where interactions are often delayed by hours, if not days. Indeed, can a sender remember the exact meaning of a message or state of mind they were in upon sending a message when they receive the reply a day or two later? Even synchronous CMC (chat) lacks in immediacy, where there is a lag time of waiting for the individual to complete their typing. Furthermore, synchronous chat is dependent upon the individual's keyboarding skills.

In addition to the limitations of asynchronous communication, text-based CMC also does not include non-verbal cues, inflection, and other elements of face-to-face interactions. As most current CMC messages are text only, they are devoid of very rich communication cues that can cause miscommunication. These missing cues can impact CMC with possible miscommunications in several ways. For example, often in verbal communication of most languages inflection describes how the message is to be taken. English speakers often use inflection to relay whether something said is a statement or a question. Punctuation provides cues in the written language to account for this issue. However, many times in CMC group interactions, communicators use less than formal writing styles, which often can cause confusion. An additional example is sarcasm. While one might fully understand one's intent of a sarcastic statement in a verbal interaction, the message can very easily be mistaken in a written interaction.

Media Richness' Impact on Communication Style

Can media richness in CMC impact one's ability to communicate, depending upon an individual's communication style? In other words, if one's communication style utilizes communication cues that are missing in the leaner CMC media, will it create a less equal communication environment? To help answer that question Dennis, Kinney, and Hung (1999) investigated decision-making task performance in terms of media richness and gender differences. In particular, they attempted to answer questions of the impact of media richness on performance in terms of "decision time," "decision quality," "consensus change," and "communication satisfaction." The study investigated gender-based teams performing equivocal tasks both in synchronous chat and face-to-face. As women tend to better utilize and read non-verbal cues, which are missing in CMC, they were

especially interested in the results of the impact of gender on the performance tasks. Teams of all male, all female, and mixed gender were formed and compared performing equivocal decision-making tasks in both face-to-face and chat environments. The results indicated that only "decision time" was impacted by the use of CMC. Indeed, "decision quality," "consensus change," and "communication satisfaction" were not significantly impacted by the use of CMC. Interestingly, the all-female team took five times as long to complete an equivocal task of reaching a decision utilizing CMC than it did face-to-face. This supports the idea that CMC has a more profound impact on women than men due to the lack of cues that women tend to better utilize as they needed more time to complete the tasks. More interesting, however, is that the decision quality of the all-female team utilizing CMC was higher than the all-male and mixed-gender team; second only to the all-female face-to-face decision-making team. In other words, while missing the nonverbal cues, it took this team much longer to perform the task, but the female members still took the time to perform at a high level regardless of media—suggesting that they could, and did, modify their engagement to successfully complete the task.

This study provides evidence that media richness, or leanness of, in this case, does impact one's ability to engage in CMC group interactions. More specifically, since women tend to utilize nonverbal communication cues more often, a CMC medium that strips out those communication cues, can provide a distinct gender disadvantage. However, it is very important to remember here that these are tendencies. Indeed, anyone who utilizes a communication style that is supported by nonverbal communication cues and engages within a CMC group interaction where those cues are missing due to the medium's leanness is at a disadvantage—regardless of gender.

CMC Strategies

From the study detailed above it seems that the participants modified or enhanced their communication within the limited media in some way to better perform their tasks. While it is clear that various CMC media have limitations, users can and do use strategies that can help ameliorate the limitations of a particular media. There are specific examples of communicators modifying their communication to better fit a medium. As a case in point, text shortcuts, such as: btw = by the way, irl = in real life, cu ltr = see you later, and imho = in my humble opinion, have been developed and utilized within in CMC environments providing evidence of communicators utilizing new methods to speed up and facilitate their interaction. The practice of abbreviated-text messaging and instant messaging has become common place. Indeed, mobile phone text messaging has become a social phenomenon practiced by young people in many parts of the world. For example, Grinter and Eldridge, (2003) describe how British teenagers are similar to teenagers in other parts of the world in their use of a meta-language of shortened words to send text messages for a variety of purposes, including coordinating future communications within other media, generally phone calls. This trend suggests that these young communicators have developed an understanding and the strategic utilization of various media for a variety but connected purposes.

The above example shows modifying a simple communication method to be more strategically purposeful of the specific communication media. However, as discussed above, gender-based communication style is much more complex. Will one utilize CMC strategies to reduce the limitations of CMC media? Fahy (2003) investigated supportive CMC strategies within an online learning environment to see if participants utilized strategies that would increase interaction and reduce interpersonal distance within the leaner CMC media. Specific strategies were defined as supportive and were seen to replace or approximate "sociolinguistic devices and strategies, including nonverbal elements normally available in face-to-face interaction, (Ridley & Avery, 1979)" (Fahy, 2003. pg. 5). The results suggest that these participants were able to and took the time to utilize important CMC strategies. As Fahy states: "One-quarter (25.9 per cent) of all interaction in these conferences was classified as

supportive, a proportion which, though it must be tested against wider and larger conferencing samples, indicates the importance attached to the interpersonal in these online interactions" (Fahy, 2003, p. 11). Students who engaged in these online conferences did, in fact, utilize the CMC strategies that approximated the missing cues, thus enriching the lean medium that promoted a more supportive group interaction.

Gender-Based Communication Style Identification

While the CMC literature suggests that men and women tend to utilize different communication styles in CMC, one might ask: How strong are these tendencies and can the communication style give away the author's gender identity in an anonymous interactive environment? Can one judge the gender of a CMC author based on the CMC style without knowing the author or his/her gender? Does one's awareness of CMC styles provide a tool to distinctly judge an author's gender? In other words, is a person's gender given away by his or her communication style even in an anonymous CMC environment? Savicki, Kelley, and Oesterreich (1999) detail a series of studies where participants were grouped in male-only, female-only and mixed-gender groups for CMC interactions. Their anonymous messages were then provided to participants to be judged as to the author's gender based upon the communication style analysis. They analyzed messages that included a greater number of "I" statements, statements of personal opinion, self-disclosure, and coalition language. "Since this pattern of communication was related to high levels of satisfaction with the group process and high levels of group development, it was labeled the high group development communication style (HCS) and contrasted with the opposite style, low group development communication style (LCS)" (p. 187).

As might be predicted, participants were quite accurate in judging a LCS message authored by men (.708), while significantly less accurate (p < 0.001) in judging an HCS message authored by men (.395). In opposition to prediction, however, participants were significantly less accurate (p < 0.05) in judging HCS messages authored by women (.549) than LCS messages authored by women (.662). These results support the finding that participants were significantly more accurate when judging LCS messages than HCS messages, regardless of the gender of the author. In this study, if a message exhibited HCS it was more difficult to accurately judge the author's gender than messages that exhibited LCS. They also reported that the judge's gender or CMC experience did not seem to factor into the level of accuracy as no significant differences for these variables were found.

These mixed results suggest that, while gender identification may be possible, it is quite limited. In other words, if authors utilize HCS within their anonymous CMC messages, there is less likelihood of being identified as male or female. If one's communication style includes HCS in the CMC messages, they may well be taken for their information and not for their gender. This may have an impact on helping promote a more democratic communication environment based on gender inequities previously discussed.

Gender-Based Communication Style Training

Certainly, promoting more democratic CMC group interaction seems a prudent thing to try to achieve. However, can one be trained, and more importantly to become motivated, to utilize HCS to support participation, satisfaction, and group development within a CMC environment? Savicki, Kelley, and Ammon (2002) investigated that question by grouping participants in male only (MO), female only (FO), and mixed gender (MIX). They examined how HCS training would impact participation, satisfaction, and group development. The results were mixed, For example, while they reported that the FO groups scored higher on group development, it may have been due to the potential of gender-based communication style tendencies for that group of females rather than HCS training. However, HCS training for the MIX groups had a greater impact than the MO. The authors state that:

. . . the MIX groups responded somewhat more to the training than the MO groups. The combination of men and women in the same group seemed to change the norms toward more acceptance of HCS communication. Gender is an important variable influence communication in online groups (Savicki & Kelly, 2000). Gender communication norms seem to be quite strong and should be taken into account when selecting participants for virtual teams. (p. 267)

It seems logical to presume, and from the findings of this study, that it is possible to provide HCS training to impact user engagement. The MIX groups did provide some evidence of the success of the training. However, the HCS training MO groups had less success, according to the authors, because of previously established gender norms. Training individuals to change their communication style for group interactions, in terms of developing higher group development communication skills, may be more complex than first thought. For example, it may not be as simple as providing HCS training, as more social communication interaction norms are at play. However, this study also instigates a question. What interactions in the MIX groups promoted consensus or community building to change the communication norms of accepting increasing use of HCS communication more than the MO groups?

Summary

The studies described above detail some of the major issues of CMC. Specifically, current CMC systems tend to be lean media in terms of media richness theory, which can impact certain populations based upon their communication strengths. However, it also would seem that communicators believe it is important and take steps to ameliorate the limitations that the lean media present by utilizing communication methods and strategies that are supportive in nature. Interestingly, utilizing higher group development communication style (HCS) might limit the identification of the communicator, thus possibly providing a more level communication venue in terms of gender. More importantly, however, it seems that the studies above demonstrate that communication styles, although tend to be gender-based, may be a matter of choice. Furthermore, although it seems possible to provide training to support more HCS communication, the process may be quite complex. Indeed, higher group communication development may be greatly impacted by the membership of that group. Although this might seem logical and somewhat simplistic, it could have very complex implications. For example, in becoming knowledgeable about, and strategic in the use of their communication style, CMC users could become better more effective and thoughtful communicators by utilizing a style that is more engaging, supportive, and more likely to foster group development. However, they may not be motivated, or perhaps do not believe they have the permission to do so based upon the membership and communication norms of their virtual group.

RECOMMENDATIONS

From the review of the literature there are several issues that dominate the various common CMC systems and the participants who engage in group interactions within them. In particular, there are issues of media richness and communication style differences. In addition, there is the issue of a group's communication norms. These factors can impact the group's communication norms, which might be defined by: (A) the makeup of the group membership, (B) the purpose of the group, and (C) the media they employ to communicate. These issues can provide some challenges for CMC users. Drawing from distance or distributed learning theory will provide some recommendations to help support electronic communication by building online communities where group interaction is enhanced by developing membership within a community of practice. In addition, the literature suggests CMC strategies that might help communicators better their electronic communiqués, thus reducing miscommunications and more equitable group interactions. Finally, current CMC technologies generally provide for text-only communication. In particular, there is the issue of media richness with communication environments that utilize a suite of tools that include only the traditional text-based synchronous and asynchronous e-communication systems. Utilizing multimedia CMC systems that include audio and/or video in addition to the lean text-based synchronous and asynchronous systems can help thicken the communication media, thus alleviating some of the limitations and issues discussed above. All of these will be discussed in the next section.

Community Building

As discussed earlier in this chapter, Rheingold (1993) described virtual communities where members interact using CMC within a level social environment. Although this ideal may have been suggested prior to having a greater understanding of some of the media limitations and how group interactions are impacted by them, it does not mean that the idea should necessarily be abandoned. This is especially important as group communication norms can dictate the membership engagement of communication style. One only needs to look at the incredible growth in online tools like, MySpace (n.d.), Orkut (n.d.), and the plethora of blogs to see that people want to communicate and engage in CMC group interactions. For example, more advanced robust open-community CMC systems, such as BuddySpace, are being developed to provide the users with greater flexibility, in terms of connectivity with other platforms. In addition, BuddySpace provides the users' location, which can help group individuals who might have similar interests because of their locale. However, as with any community, online community members may not be as supportive to one another as they ultimately could, or perhaps should. Therefore, it would be wise to understand the elements of community building as it may impact CMC group interactions in online communities.

In a very well-established text, Kim (2000) provides details and recommendations of community-building strategies that are supported by three underlying design principles: (a) design for growth and change, (b) create and maintain feedback loops, and (c) empower members over time. These principles suggest that the placement of responsibility of community development begins with the designers or developers rather than members. However, it supports the cultivation of member ownership by its three design principles. For example, designing for growth and change, allows for the community to be molded by the feedback received from the members as they gain empowerment. With the empowerment of the members over time, the organizational ownership and responsibility of the community will be cultivated and be accepted by its members. That it not to say, however, that in an online community, the members cannot be the designers and or developers. Regardless, in Kim's recommendations the members will assume responsibility and ownership of the community.

Another example of community building is detailed in the work of Wenger (1998). In defining a "community of practice," he provides a detailed outline that identifies a more complex view of communities, stating:

A community of practice defines itself along three dimensions:

- **What it is about:** It's joint enterprise as understood and continually renegotiated by its members.
- **How it functions:** Mutual engagement that binds members together into a social entity.
- **What capability it has produced:** The shared repertoire of communal resources (routines, sensibilities, artifacts, vocabulary, styles, etc.) that members have developed over time. (p. 54)

Wenger's description of a community of practice suggests that "members bind together in a social entity" by sharing routines, sensibilities, artifacts, vocabulary, and style. Wenger goes on to say, "Even when a community's actions conform to an external mandate, it is the community—not the mandate—that produces the practice. In this sense, communities of practice are fundamentally self-organizing systems (p. 2)." The concepts outlined in Wenger's community of practice have very interesting implications in light of the HCS

training findings of Savicki et al. (2002). In that study, the mixed-gender groups moved toward building a community of practice by changing their norms to accept and use more HCS in their CMC within their group interactions. However, one also could argue that the male-only group members also moved toward building a community of practice by not changing their group's communication norms to accept and use the HCS communication strategies. The HCS training had little or no effect on the male-only group. On the contrary, the group maintained their communication style regardless of the training, perhaps because of the strong influence of the male group communication norms. The external mandate, as Wenger describes, could be seen as the training to change to HCS communication, which was not accepted by the male-only groups, but was more so by the mixed-gender groups. In this case, the CMC norms were developed and determined by the group. This supports the idea, in terms of online communities, that the ownership and responsibility for the practice of the community lays within the members of the community, not the administrators or developers of an online space.

To provide an example in practice, let us look at designing and developing an online course of study, which utilizes CMC systems to build communities of practice that support enhanced group interactions. It is important to remember that online course delivery has its roots in the distance learning model originally developed that utilized the traditional mail system to send materials to learners in remote locations in the early part of the 20th century. As technology developed, course material delivery moved to more advanced systems: radio, television, CD-ROM, and, eventually, to the Internet. As the delivery methods advanced, opportunities for learner interaction became greater because of the possibilities for group interactions using CMC. Distance learners were no longer limited to primarily one-way information dissemination for their learning experience.

Distributed learning is a term that has been used to replace distance learning by some. Dede (2004) defines distributed learning communities where learners engage collaboratively to develop knowledge as they interact within the various electronic communication and information delivery systems. In this concept of community building, group interactions are distributed via CMC and other more advanced electronic tools, to help members actively engage with one another for the specific purpose of learning. Here, learners within the distributed learning community utilize a variety of resources in a highly structured learning environment. Learning management systems, such as WebCT (n.d.) and BlackBoard (n.d.) include the tools to support this definition of distributed learning.

Although the use of the CMC systems will provide the opportunity for group interactions within a distributed learning environment, the members within the community are still responsible for their interaction and, thus, for their learning. Therefore, designing and developing an online course of study that utilizes distributed learning elements is more complex than using a system to make course materials and opportunities for group interaction available. The key to a distributed learning environment, accordingly, is building communities of practice through the utilization of multiple electronic communication systems that advances the opportunities for the members to engage, thus making CMC the vital means of group interaction.

In this example, the designer, developer, and/or the instructor begin by selecting the interactive communication systems to utilize. They also will need to design learning activities and assignments that will have the learners engage with the course materials and activities. Finally, they also provide guidelines for group interactions the learners will have with the instructor and their peers. Palloff and Pratt (1999) described effective strategies for building and the cultivation of an online learning community that fosters greater group interaction that augments online learning. They outline a framework for online instruction that provides for: (a) mutually negotiated guidelines, (b) focused outcomes, (c) active creation of knowledge and meaning, and (d) collaborative learning. Interestingly, these elements echo the communities of practice work of Wenger (1998) in terms of sharing the responsibility of community building and, in this case, learning throughout the membership of the community. All of the members, including learners and instructors, become responsible for developing the community of practice. For example, by promoting mutually negotiated guidelines, learners are given the opportunity to share ownership of the learning environment that will bind the members together in a joint enterprise. Learners utilize CMC to communicate with their peers and instructors to mutually produce the shared repertoire of communal resources and learning guidelines that will structure their social entity—the learning community. Through their collaborations they actively create knowledge and meaning based on the focused outcomes, as defined by the community. Designing an online learning environment with these four strategies will then support the members in building a community of practice for learning that utilizes the pedagogy and technology of distributed learning. Here members become responsible for and have the tools to *"bind together in a social entity" where they share routines, sensibilities, artifacts, vocabulary, and style.* As learners collaboratively build their learning community of practice through the construction of artifacts, vocabulary, routines, sensibilities, and style, they are building shared knowledge.

The idea of building shared knowledge is at the heart of the distributed cognition work of Hutchins (2000). Distributed cognition theory suggests that knowledge and knowledge acquisition go beyond the individual. Rather, knowledge is constructed through the social interactions, where individuals share and co-construct knowledge. In other words, knowledge is not constructed by the individual alone, but instead by the interacting members engaged in the learning process. This is an important characteristic of distributed learning that supports the concept of communities of practice producing a "shared repertoire of communal resources (routines, sensibilities, artifacts, vocabulary, styles, etc.) that members have developed over time" (p. 54). If the joint enterprise of that online group is that of learning, then membership within that community supports and fosters shared knowledge construction. This suggests that, in terms of community building, through their group interactions the social entity and its members build knowledge as they build community.

This section has focused on the elements of community building within online groups, emphasizing that through the development of an online community of practice where group interaction is enhanced by members negotiating the communication norms and behaviors and working collaboratively to build and distribute knowledge. In doing so, through enhanced group interactions the social entity builds community, shares elements and resources that support the individuals within that community. Therefore, to support the initial building of community, it is suggested that administrators and developers of those groups provide ample tools and, perhaps structure, but that it is ultimately the membership that makes the rules. This does not fully address issues of power, as individuals who tend to be more aggressive may still dominate discussions and communications. Although the CMC administrators of the online community could censure inappropriate individuals, and some communities may decide that some form of policing is appropriate, still, here, the membership should be responsible for the decision making of that policy. It is recommended that by building an online community of practice, inequities, and disagreements would be settled by the membership of that community, based upon that group's agreed-upon norms. The next section will outline various communication strategies that will help reduce miscommunications that can often be the cause for online disagreements.

Utilizing CMC Strategies

Building a community that shares and co-constructs knowledge could be enhanced by what has been learned about CMC strategies. Although, as has been argued above, the membership of an online community is responsible for setting the communication norms of their group, it still seems prudent to be aware of helpful communication strategies. For example, if the membership of the online community creates routines, sensibilities, artifacts, vocabulary, styles, as Wenger (1998) suggests, it would seem that communicators would benefit from understanding, being aware of, and utilizing CMC strategies within their messages that support more personal interactions. By doing so, there may be less miscommunication, which can often erupt into disagreements.

To better understand communication interactions, Fahy, Crawford, and Alley (2001) developed the transcription analysis tool (TAT), which provides five CMC interaction categories, three of which have subcategories.

T1 – Questioning
    T1 (a) vertical
    T1 (b) horizontal
T2 – Statements
    T2 (a) direct
    T2 (b) answers or comments
T3 – Reflections
T4 – Scaffolding
T5 – References, Authorities
    T5 (a) references, quotations, paraphrases
    T5 (b) citations or attributions

In a later study, Fahy (2003) utilized a specific subset of the categories from the TAT, listed above, to investigate participant use of supportive communication strategies. The supportive communication strategies investigated included:

- T1 (b) horizontal questions, which promote more discussion as this type of question does not presume one correct answer, but rather invites any plausible answer.
- T2 (b) referential statements, message statements that directly or indirectly refer to another's message, thus engaging more than just the author of the message.
- T4 scaffolding and engaging comments including:
  - **Acknowledgement:** Recognizing or acknowledging comments or statements from prior messages.
  - **Agreement:** Expressing agreement.
  - **Apology, or self-criticism:** Making an apologetic statement.
  - **Closing:** using some sort of summary or closing (e.g., later).
  - Emoticon: using emoticons (e.g., ;-)).
  - **Humor:** Using humor to lighten the mood.
  - **Invitations:** Statements that invite a response.

    ° **Rhetorical questions:** Posing a rhetorical question.
    ° **Salutation:** Using a greeting, especially with the individual's name.
    ° **Signature:** Using a signature or nickname.
    ° **Thanks:** Expressing thanks.

He found that participants believed that supportive CMC strategies were important and utilized them within an online learning environment in 25.9% of the interactions. In particular, he found that the most commonly used supportive communication strategies utilized by his participants included: (a) referential statements, (b) signatures, (c) greetings, and (d) horizontal questions.

Within a community of practice or learning, it is recommended that members become aware of and begin to utilize these strategies. While it might seem logical to use some of these strategies in group interactions, messages are often received that do not include any closing and, at times, not even something as important as the sender's name. In utilizing these strategies the CMC message will include more communication cues to help enrich the medium with more information. As described earlier, a lack of nonverbal cues can be a possible issue for female members of a community, and this simple strategy might better support a member's understanding of a particular message. Simply utilizing emoticons to replace the nonverbal cues (e.g., facial expressions) missing from CMC can provide more information to the recipient of the message. For example, utilizing the winking emoticon can provide information to the recipient that the statement was not meant to be taken seriously. Other more complex strategies, such as stating acknowledgement and agreement, provide the recipient with information that might replace a head nod or other gestures, not communicated in text-only CMC. Furthermore, apologies for miscommunications or other miscues provide "I" statements and self-disclosures that are associated with higher group development communication style (HCS). The use of horizontal questions, inviting responses, and providing referential statements of another's message support the notion of enhancing social interactions, which encourages additional participant engagement in group interaction. With the use of these more supportive CMC strategies, members will engage in richer CMC to better understand one another, and, thus, augment community building. Again, it is the membership of the community that decides upon the communication norms of that community. However, with more members of the online community being aware of and utilizing these communication strategies the membership is more apt to adopt them, making them a routine of their social entity's repertoire of vocabulary and style.

Although the various CMC strategies adopted and utilized by a community might improve text-based communication, advances in Internet technologies have brought about the development of multimedia CMC tools also could improve communication. The next section will deal with some of types of current multimedia tools that can better support the needs and predilection of the community.

Multimedia CMC Tools

Although computer desktop video conferencing and telephony have increased the media options for CMC, they still do not provide all of the rich aspects of face-to-face interaction. However, these multimedia technologies do add additional communication cues beyond the text-based communication strategies mentioned above. Therefore, it does seem prudent and is recommended to utilize advanced online multimedia communication technologies to the traditional tool set to thicken the communication conduit when possible and, perhaps more importantly, when appropriate.

By utilizing a video conferencing, for example, communication can be enhanced with facial expressions, hand gestures, voice inflection and other cues missing from text-only CMC. In addition, many of these tools provide interactive whiteboards for shared graphic demonstrations. These tools can be used to provide more graphic elements to enhance one's ideas or concepts. Furthermore, some of these tools also permit document or application sharing. This can be a valuable tool that can provide technical support and foster online collaboration.

Although these tools can provide the added communication support, they also can complicate the communication process. In terms of video conferencing, for example, some individuals may dislike being on display and this use may cause some discomfort. Also, utilizing the audio and video components, one must have a camera and microphone for each individual, which requires the users, to some extent, to be more technically proficient to set up and use these multimedia peripherals. In addition, high speed Internet connectivity for all parties interacting within the group communication is really a must. Although it is possible to utilize these tools with low bandwidth, it can become very stilted and, thus, very frustrating, perhaps negating the advantages. Furthermore, some of these multimedia CMC tools are open systems allowing one to communicate with anyone, while others are more closed to specific group membership. Because the various types of systems, it is important to know the strengths and weaknesses, and to understand their relative costs and benefits, as they have specific requirements and individual features—keeping in mind the purpose or objective of the group's communication. The multimedia CMC tools listed below were chosen to provide examples of the different types currently available and are not inclusive of all tools.

Skype

Skype™ (n.d.) is an Internet telephony service that utilizes a computer with Internet connectivity, primarily for audio, provides computer to computer Internet Telephony. Although it does provide a video option, it currently is in the beta version. However, once connected users also have a chat window available for synchronous messaging as well. Users can set up conference calls with up to four participants plus the host.

Skype client software includes all of the features one might expect in such a tool, such as an address book of contacts for organizational and ease of use purposes. Skype accounts also provide several services for various fees, such as SkypeIn, which provides the user a phone number much like a tradition phone including voicemail, and Skype-Out, which permits users to make phone calls to both land and cell phone lines, including SMS, a form of instant messaging. Requirements include a headset with microphone, which is used instead of a microphone and speakers to keep feedback from occurring. The easy-to-use client software can be downloaded for free. More importantly, is that computer-to-computer communication is free. There is a fee to utilize calls to and from land or cell phones; users need a pre-paid account. However, the costs are quite inexpensive, especially for international calls. Because this form of Internet Telephony primarily focuses on audio, Skype might be a good tool to consider when beginning utilizing multimedia CMC, as it only requires a headset and the easy-to-use free software to get started.

iVisit

iVisit (n.d.) combines a variety of CMC tools including, video conferencing, instant messaging, file sharing, and desktop sharing. Although server licenses are available, most users have to obtain access to the software application in the traditional server/client relationship, where iVisit provides the server access, and users download client software and sign up for one of two types of accounts, Light and Plus. The software includes several windows, including; the video feed with controls, an address book that lists both people and places (available conferences), and a chat window for both the individual and all chatting within a conference.

An iVisit Light is a free account that permits users to interact as guests in open or public conference rooms or invited into private conference rooms. iVisit Plus accounts are yearly subscriptions that permit the ability to host a conference room that can accommodate eight visitors, including the host. Although this can be increased to 16 simultaneous users for no extra fee, it is not recommended due to the complexity of managing that many in an online video conference. In addition to being able to host a conference, the iVisit Plus account provides greater audio quality and video resolution, plus other benefits. One rather interesting feature of iVisit is the ability to make recordings of participants audio and video feeds. Although the Light account only permits saving the file into an iVisit proprietary file format, the Plus account provides for QuickTime recordings. While using iVisit for multimedia, CMC provides greater cues that video provides, it also is more complex to setup, requiring a camera, microphone, and/or headset. Depending upon the technical sophistication and needs of the particular community, this tool may be worth the complexity.

Microsoft NetMeeting and Messenger

For quite a few versions, Microsoft Windows-based operating systems have provided multimedia CMC tools that include various features depending upon the particular version. The tools range from earlier versions of Microsoft NetMeeting (n.d.) to, most recently, Microsoft Live Messenger (n.d.). While Live Messenger is quite similar to Yahoo Messenger and focuses on instant messaging (IM), audio-video Internet telephony (somewhat like Skype), and file sharing, NetMeeting also includes application sharing. NetMeeting, will no longer be part of the new Windows Vista operating system. Instead, Microsoft will include a new suite of CMC tools called, Windows Meeting Space for home and home office users, Office Live Meeting Windows Meeting Space for small and medium business users, and Office Live Meeting Office Communications Server 2007 for large enterprises (Microsoft NetMeeting, n.d.). Each level of the application will work similarly to NetMeeting in that it will still support desktop, application, and file sharing across networks. One of the biggest changes from earlier versions of NetMeeting, however, will be the increase in the number of users that can connect simultaneously. One of the biggest advantages of the Microsoft multimedia CMC tool set is that it is readily available within one's operating system. However, with the newer versions, outlined on the Microsoft Web site, members within online communities will need to decide which tool best suits their needs and available resources.

Elluminate®

Elluminate® (n.d.) is a comprehensive online multimedia-conferencing tool that includes audio, chat, interactive whiteboard, application sharing, file transfer, and direct messaging. It truly goes beyond the tools previously listed, as its primary focus is to support group interactions. As such, Elluminate includes additional features designed to provide greater user interactivity, such as: (a) participant profiles to provide greater information (photo & bio) about the participants, (b) polling, which permits a moderator to get some feedback regarding an issue, question, or comment, and (c) breakout rooms, a great feature should users want to break up a large conference for smaller group discussions. One important feature is that it utilizes full duplex audio, meaning that more than one individual can speak at the same time. However, the tool also provides for moderator control, should that be desired. In addition, the tool is designed for assistive access with closed-caption transcript and key stroke configurability. Elluminate also provides for input from a Web cam, which provides video feed of the speaker, although this feature is not the primary focus as with iVisit.

Elluminate provides multimedia CMC on a much more enterprise scale, and, as such, the cost is commensurate. There are several versions available, each appropriately priced, including Lite, Academic, and Enterprise editions, depending upon the user's size and needs. Currently, Elluminate is being utilized by corporate trainers and universities. In addition, Elluminate has partnered with WebCT Vista, eCollege, Blackboard, and others to devise power links that permit Elluminate to work seamlessly within these course management systems. This multimedia CMC tool is designed for communities that want to focus on the synchronous interactive components that this tool provides. The software also provides for asynchronous delivery by including a session recording feature, which makes sessions available for later viewing. Although Web-delivered video via a Web cam is available, Elluminate does not focus on multiple, simultaneous video feeds such as iVisit. Depending upon need, this tool might provide users with a very interactive multimedia CMC tool, but as with any complex tool, deployment and implementation are a consideration. Again with this tool, users will be required to have a microphone, speakers, or headset to interact with the multimedia elements.

Multimedia CMC Uses for Support and Collaboration

The level of multimedia CMC tools available varies from those that are very simple to those that are much more comprehensive and quite very complex. As mentioned, it should be the membership of the community that selects the CMC tools. In addition to increasing the number of communication cues engaged users receive due to the addition of audio and video, there are further ways to utilize the multimedia CMC tools. In particular, the application-sharing feature of some multimedia CMC tools better support collaborations that enhance community building and augment the shared construction of knowledge. For example, one of the primary uses for Microsoft Application Sharing is to provide remote technical assistance. When individuals are having difficulties with a computer application they can be supported by sharing that application with a distant help agent. The user can watch and listen as the help agent provides instruction and demonstrates the application elements that caused confusion. In this way the utilization of a multimedia CMC tool for remote assistance can be used to help members by any more knowledgeable member within the community.

A more collaborative example of utilizing multimedia CMC tool to support a distributed learning environment is using the application sharing for group authorship. In this case, team members can schedule synchronous online meetings where they utilize application sharing to show and discuss Web resources. They also can use application sharing to work collaboratively on the same file to produce a shared Word document or presentation. In doing so, they are collaboratively engaging in the production of an artifact, thus, co-constructing knowledge.

Summary

This section provided recommendations that could enhance CMC group interactions. Specifically, it is recommended that the users of CMC consider fostering the building online communities of practice where members co-construct, hopefully, equitable communication norms in their online group interactions. It also is recommended that the members engaged in group interactions become aware of and utilize CMC strategies that enhance their interactions by fostering more clear communications. Finally, it is recommended that multimedia CMC tools be considered to enhance and enrich CMC when practical and appropriate.

FUTURE TRENDS

This chapter has discussed the issues and recommendations of current CMC group interactions. Over the past few years, incredible advances in communication technologies have become available and have been embraced by our society. So what does the future hold? In reviewing the literature of those who've studied aspects, issues, and elements of CMC group interaction, one observation is evident—electronic computer-mediated communication has expanded in use, sophistication, and reach. More people now use various types of computer-mediated communication than ever before to communicate with others in all parts of the world. However, the literature provides evidence that online group interactions can suffer the same issues as traditional face-to-face group interactions. With that in mind, one could predict that future trends in CMC group interaction will include the continued expanding use, advancement, and sophistication of CMC tools to an even more global scale than currently exists. With the expanding global reach, users' skills, in terms of more sophisticated tools and more strategic use, will need to increase as well. With more diverse users making use of the various CMC tools, communicators will need to become better accomplished CMC users to compensate for the limitations of the various CMC systems. In addition, they will need to be more knowledgeable about possible group interaction issues that pertain to newer systems. If that prediction holds true, future global CMC users would benefit from greater investigation of cultural communication differences and global CMC interactions as they relate to the various media that transmits their messages.

Expanding and Changing CMC Skills

Computer-mediated communication has become an important aspect of our society. However, as detailed in this chapter, there are issues that are embedded within CMC group interactions that may impact one's ability to clearly communicate via the various asynchronous and synchronous systems. It would seem that being aware of the strengths and limitations of the CMC tools and having skill using those strategies, would provide an advantage. For example, having knowledge of, monitoring, and then intentionally utilizing some of the communication strategies listed above may make one more apt to better communicate within a lean or limited CMC system. By utilizing some of the CMC text-based strategies listed above, regardless of gender, one could promote his or her higher group communication style (HCS), thus enhancing the message with richer, more engaging levels of communication. In other words, those individuals who are more CMC savvy, in terms of being able to more purposefully utilize communication strategies would be better able to foster and support persuasive arguments, promote agenda, and clearly share their ideas. Given knowledge of the specific strengths and weaknesses of various communication styles within specific CMC media would provide a powerful advantage to those who might strategically adjust their own communication style accordingly.

Parallel events are beginning to happen within the use of mobile phones for text messaging. For example, users are utilizing text messaging with their mobile phones or instant messaging on their computers for quicker, asynchronous communication when they cannot talk aloud or in lieu of e-mail or other slower CMC systems. When thinking about future possible trends, it seems logical to focus future practical efforts toward educating members of communities engaged in CMC to better understand the limitations of various CMC systems and how best to understand, monitor, and promote clear, concise, and perhaps strategic CMC style. This may become much more important as higher-speed Internet bandwidth becomes more widely available making multimedia CMC tools more common place.

Expanding Need for Global Understandings

This chapter has focused upon detailing specific issues of CMC style differences and media issues, and has provided some recommendations on building communities of practice within these CMC systems. For the most part, the discussion has focused on the research literature that discusses CMC style issues as they relate to group interaction differences and the various media available that might impact the communication cues available. As education, business, and industry extend their reach to more global markets, CMC will be utilized more extensively for interaction by members of various cultures and languages. While certain elements of CMC may better support these endeavors, there will be other issues that could compound good CMC group interaction. For example, asynchronous CMC better supports members in various time zones allowing for business to operate at their normally desired time. With more synchronous multimedia utilization globally, users will be required to interact 24/7. In addition, more global group interactions will require users to be sensitive to diversity in both language and culture. For example, an international student from China was concerned when his advisor sent him an e-mail where some of the text was colored red. He thought she was angry with him—when in truth, she simply was trying to emphasize a point by making it stand out. From her perspective, this was a very benign strategy. Because the color red has specific connotations within the Chinese culture, there was a pretty serious cultural miscommunication for this Chinese student. While no harm was intended by this communication strategy, its use created an unintended consequence of causing great alarm for the student.

Future research in CMC utilization will continue to include the issues of gender and communication style. However, these issues are bound to be expanded by cultural differences as CMC tools are used by members across a more global society trying to build communities of practice with various cultural differences. A very powerful example of building community within a multi-ethnic online discussion group is described in the work of Kadende-Kaiser (2000). She examined CMC interactions of members of Burundinet, a multiethnic discussion forum for Burundians in the Diaspora. Most of the discussion focused on the terrible ethnic violence between the Hutus and Tutsis by members that spoke Kirundi (the native language), French (the colonial language), and English. In addition to their language differences, members came from very different perspectives on a very divisive topic. In this example, social rules were changed to provide more equitable social interactions. "This would not be the case in Burundian social settings, where seniority and social status determine who can interact with whom, or who is even excluded in the interaction. . . . In internet communication, however, these cultural rules regarding turn-taking on the basis of age and social rank are irrelevant; any subscriber can play the role of social mediator" (p. 131). Indeed, the membership of Burundinet fashioned the rules as she states:

Mutual respect and politeness, on the one hand, and the freedom of expression, on the other, do not have to be mutually exclusive. Therefore, many Burundinet members seek to preserve individual subscriber rights to express their opinion, regardless of what views they have in mind. As one net member advised: 'It seems more wise that we try to preserve a minimum of formal politeness toward the others, and at the same time we need to allow every Burundinetter to express his/her opinion on Burndi, regardless of what this opinion is' (Author I, 1996). These statements and individual opinions serve as the foundation for message composition and they contribute to the establishment of the rules for interaction on Burundinet. (p. 134)

Although cultural differences, such as this, may cause issues when filtered through the lean medium of current CMC technologies within a more global community, the membership of Burundinet demonstrated how it established unique rules for CMC interaction within their virtual community to permit discussion regardless of their differences. This provides a very good example of how the CMC group interaction communication norms are established by the membership.

Summary

This section provided some ideas of what the future might hold for CMC group interactions. Certainly, we can presume that CMC usage will increase and become more complex and, perhaps, robust. CMC users will be required to become more technically proficient. A more important concern, however, will be that as the usage of CMC expands more globally, the communities that will better prosper will be those that trend toward the development of communities of practice, where members think about their responsibility in the development of their shared repertoire of communal resources in light of possible cultural differences. It will be vital for members engaged in CMC group interactions to be aware of, and provide consideration for, cultural differences. While the CMC strategies outlined above may work well for certain cultures, will they work well within a global community? Or, will they have unintended consequences?

Future Research Directions

There is a history of research that has investigated face-to-face group interaction that supersedes the CMC tools that are now employed. The findings from that earlier research seems to parallel research findings of those engaged in CMC group interactions. For example, gender-based CMC style differences can impact those engaged in online group interactions. However, there are strategies that users can and do employ to adjust their CMC group interactions in an attempt to replace missing nonverbal cues, thus supporting and fostering better communication. Therefore, future research that further investigates how users manipulate their CMC style strategically by employing CMC techniques and/or adjusting their CMC group interactions, based upon the medium, could prove very enlightening. Because members engaging in CMC group interactions can and do take responsibility for developing their community of practice, researchers also would be advised to study the process of defining and developing communication norms within an online community of practice.

As technologies continue to advance, richer media will become commonplace for CMC group interactions. Regardless of new, more advanced multimedia electronic communication systems, there still will be a filtering of sorts on communication cues within CMC systems. Future researchers would be advised to focus their investigations on how multimedia might hinder or enhance group interactions based upon gender, and perhaps more importantly, culture. In particular, it seems essential to investigate global CMC group interactions in light of cultural and language differences. For example, community systems like BuddySpace, that provide the users' location could provide cues to support those engaging in group interactions within that type of online community space.

Researchers should be encouraged to take advantage of the known CMC issues and focus their investigations on more global issues that are bound to emerge as communities expand. While gaining knowledge of how more robust, multimedia CMC might impact various individuals it vital, future research should go beyond and also focus on how to best educate members of global communities of practice to provide clear, concise communication within those more advanced electronic communication systems. With continued knowledge of the advanced CMC systems and the diverse cultural interactions that happen with them, this form of information technology will better serve the expanding global community.

Finally, instant messaging (IM) and text messaging has become widespread, globally. This form of asynchronous communication is novel in that it changes the type and, perhaps, the reason for a particular communiqué. For example, one might "text" or "IM" another because they are busy—working, in class, or talking with others—and cannot be interrupted with a traditional phone call or chat. Furthermore, this form of communication has developed its own lexicon and syntax. While people may have wanted to communicate in similar ways in the past, this technology has changed the way many communicate, as evidenced by its overwhelming use. Specifically, this technology has provided the opportunity for people to multitask in many areas of life, which brings up an

interesting question. How will this new form of communication impact or change more traditional forms of communication? With that in mind, an interesting opportunity for future research would be to investigate how technology advances have impacted or changed more historical forms of human communication and social interactions.

REFERENCES

BuddySpace (n.d.). Retrieved March 15, 2007, from http://www.buddyspace.org

Carli, L. L. (1984). Sex differences in task behaviors, social behaviors and influences as a function of sex composition of dyads and instructions to compete or cooperate. *Dissertation Abstracts International, 45*(1-B), 401.

Daft, R. L., & Lengel, R. H. (1986). Organizational information requirements, media richness and structural design. *Management Science, 32*(5), 554-571.

Dede, C. (2004). Enabling distributed learning communities via emerging technologies: Part I. *THE Journal, 32*(2), 12-22.

Dennis, A. R., Kinney, S. T., & Hung, Y. C. (1999). Gender differences in the effects of media richness. *Small Group Research, 30*(4), 405-437.

Eakins, B. W., & Eakins, R. G. (1978). *Sex differences in human communication.* Boston: Houghton Mifflin.

Elluminate (n.d.) Retrieved September 22, 2006, from http://elluminate.com

Fahy, P. J., Crawford, G., & Ally, M. (2001). Patterns of interaction in a computer conference transcript. *International Review of Research in Open and Distance Learning, 2*(1).

Fahy, P. J. (2003). Indicators of support in online interaction. *International Review of Research in Open and Distance Learning, 4*(1).

Fishman, P. M. (1983). Interaction: The work women do. In B. Thorne, C. Kramarae, & N. Henly

(Eds.), *Language, gender and society.* Rowley, MA: Newbury House.

Grinter, R. E., & Eldridge, M. (2003). Wan2tlk?: Everyday text messaging. In *Proceedings of ACM Conference on Human Factors in Computing System (CHI 2003)* (pp. 441-448).

Herring, S. (1993). Gender and democracy in computer-mediated communication. *Electronic Journal of Communication/La Revue Electronique de Communication* [On-line serial], *3*(2). Reprinted in R. Kling (Ed.). (1996). *Computerization and controversy* (2nd ed.). New York: Academic Press.

Herring, S. (1999). The rhetorical dynamics of gender harassment on-line. *The Information Society, 15,* 151-167.

Hutchins, E. (2000). The cognitive consequences of patterns of information flow. *Intellectica, 1*(30), 53-74.

iVisit (n.d.). Retrieved September 22, 2006, from http://ivisit.com

Jaffe, J. M., Lee, Y., Huang, L., & Oshagan, H. (1999). Gender identification, interdependence, and pseudonyms in CMC: Language patterns in an electronic conference. *Information Society, 15*(4), 221-234. (EJ602017)

Kadende-Kaiser, R. M. (2000). Interpreting language and cultural discourse: Internet communication among Burundians in the Diaspora. *Africa Today, 47*(2), 121-148.

Kim, A. J. (2000). *Community building on the web: Secret strategies for successful online communities.* Berkley, CA: Peachpit Press.

Maguire, T. (1999). Gender cues impact marketers. *American Demographics, 21*(1), 16.

Microsoft Live Messenger (n.d.). Retrieved October 25, 2006, from http://get.live.com/messenger

Microsoft NetMeeting (n.d.). Retrieved October 25, 2006, from http://www.microsoft.com/windows/NetMeeting

Orkut (n.d.). Retrieved March 15, 2007, from http://www.orkut.com

Palloff & Pratt (1999). *Building learning communities in cyberspace: Effective strategies for the online classroom.* San Francisco: Jossey-Bass.

MySpace (n.d.). Retrieved March 15, 2007, from http://www.myspace.com/

Rheingold, H. (1993). A slice of my virtual community. In L. M. Harasim (Ed.), *Global networks.* Cambridge, MA: MIT Press.

Savicki, V., Kelley, M., & Oesterreich, E. (1999). Judgments of gender in computer-mediated communication. *Computers in Human Behavior, 1*(2), 185-194.

Savicki, V., & Kelley, M. (2000). Computer mediated communication, gender and group composition. *CyberPsychology and Behavior, 3,* 817-826.

Savicki, V., Kelley, M., & Ammon, B. (2002). Effects of training on computer-mediated communication in single or mixed gender small task groups. *Computers in Human Behavior, 18,* 257-259.

Skype (n.d.). Retrieved September 22, 2006, from http://www.skype.com

Soukup, C. (1999). The gendered interactional patterns of computer-mediated chatrooms: A critical ethnographic study. *The Information Society, 15,* 169-176.

Wenger, E. (1998). *Communities of practice: Learning, meaning and identity.* New York: Cambridge University Press.

ADDITIONAL READING

Barnes, S. B. (2001). *Online connections: Internet interpersonal relationships.* Creskill, NJ: Hampton Press.

Barrett, M., & Davidson, M. J. (2006). *Gender and communication at work: Gender and organizational theory series.* Burlington, VT: Ashgate Publishing.

Collison, G., Elbaum, B., Haavind, S., & Tinker, R. (2000). *Facilitating online learning: Effective strategies for moderators.* Madison, WI: Atwood Publishing.

Day, P. (Ed.). (2004). *Community practice in the network society: Local action/global interaction.* New York: Routledge.

Ermann, M. D., & Shauf, M. S. (2003). *Computers, ethics, and society.* New York: Oxford Press.

Green, E. (2001). *Virtual gender: Technology consumption and identity matters.* New York: Routledge.

Jonassen, D. H., & Harris, P. (Eds.). (2004). *Handbook of research on educational communications and technology (A project of the Association for Educational Communications and Technology).* Mahway, NJ: Lawrence Erlbaum Associates, Inc.

Katz, J. E., & Rice, R. E. (2002). *Social consequences of Internet use: Access, involvement, and interaction.* Cambridge, MA: The MIT Press.

Kelly, T. B., Berman-Rossi, T., & Palombo, S. (Eds.). (2001). *Group work: Strategies for strengthening resiliency.* Binghamton, NY: The Haworth Press, Inc.

Kisielnicki, J. (Ed.). (2002). *Modern organizations in virtual communities.* Hershey, PA: IRM Press.

Krolokke, C., & Sorensen, C. A. (2006). *Gender communication theories & analyses: from silence to performance.* Thousand Oaks, CA: Sage Publications.

Lau, R. W. H., Li, Q., Cheung, R., & Liu, W. (Eds.). (2005, July 31-August 3). Advances in Web-based learning – ICWL 2005. *4th International Conference,* Hong Kong, China. Heidelberg, Germany: Springer-Verlag.

LeVine, P., & Scollon, R. (Eds.). (2004). *Discourse and technology: Multimodal discourse analysis.* Washington, DC: Georgetown University Press.

Moggridge, B. (2007). *Designing interactions.* Cambridge, MA: The MIT Press.

Palloff, R. M., & Pratt, K. (2005). *Collaborating online: Learning together in community.* San Francisco: Jossey-Bass.

Saint-Onge, H., & Wallace, D. (2003). *Leveraging communities of practice for strategic advantage.* Burlington, MA: Butterworth-Heinemann (an imprint of Elsevier Science).

Shane, P. M. (2004). *Democracy online: The prospects for political renewal through the Internet.* New York: Routledge.

Stangor, C. (2004). *Social groups in action and interaction.* New York: Psychology Press.

Sullivan, N.E., Mesbur, E.S., Lang, N.C., Goodman, D., & Mitchell, L. (Eds.). (2003). *Social work with groups: Social justice through personal, community and societal change.* Binghamton, NY: The Haworth Press, Inc.

Talbot, M. M. (1998). *Language and gender: An introduction.* Malden, MA: Blackwell Publishers Inc.

Tu, C. (2004). *Online collaborative learning communities: Twenty-one designs to building an online collaborative learning community.* Westport, CT: Libraries Unlimited (an imprint of Greenwood Publishing Group, Inc.).

Tubbs, S. (2004). *A systems approach to small group interaction (NAU).* New York: McGraw Hill.

Vestal, W. (2006). *Communities of practice and associations.* Houston, TX: APQC.

Wenger, E., McDermott, R., & Snyder, W. M. (2002). *Cultivating communities of practice.* Boston: Harvard Business School Publishing.

Wiberg, M. (Ed.). (2005). *The interaction society: Theories, practice and supportive technologies.* Hershey, PA: Information Science Publishing.

Chapter XI
The Dynamics and Rationality of Collective Behavior within a Global Information System

Jacek Unold
University of Economics, Wroclaw, Poland

ABSTRACT

The scope of interests in the area of information systems (IS) has focused mainly on technological aspects so far. If the human component were taken into account, it has been analyzed from the level of an individual. So have all new concepts of rationality. This chapter argues that collective behavior, which is a basic determinant of the global IS dynamics, does not proceed in a planned manner, but is adaptive and follows certain patterns found in nature. It follows that this behavior can be expressed in a model form, which enables to structure it. A model exemplification of a global information system is a modern, electronic, stock exchange. The identification of quantitative attributes of a social subsystem can provide substantial theoretical and methodological premises for the extension of the optimizing and individualistic notion of rationality by the social and adaptive aspects.

INTRODUCTION

General Perspective

One of the main issues, both in the theory and practice, of social and economic sciences is the question of integration, that is, how actions and interactions of individuals lead to the emergence of phenomena that characterize social entireties.

This topic acquires particular importance in light of the dynamic integration processes of societies, for example, the recent enlargement of the European Union, when, in 2004, 15 new member states joined this commonwealth. The integration processes, aided with the most recent achievements in information technology (IT), harmonize with globalization and virtualization of human activity, from social to political to a business one.

The outlined issue is the background of two basic research threads proposed in this chapter. The first part refers to the question of human behavior within an information system (IS). A fully integrated society of the future will make a fundamental, subjective element of a global information system. That global IS will be either a ubiquitous and wireless Internet, or some totally different, unknown yet, technological platform. And it is crucial that so far interests in the area of IS have concentrated mainly on technological aspects. The issue of human behavior within an IS has been generally omitted as one belonging to other disciplines. Admittedly, since the mid-1990s we have observed some growth of interest in the domain of social aspects of the IS development (Avison & Fitzgerald, 2003), but those interests have concentrated on the specificity of individual behavior. However, the nature of global phenomena and the features of dispersed collectivities denote a necessity of a new perspective on the society and organization. No longer can we perceive the human component of an IS as independent individuals. The users of local, regional and global telecommunications networks create a specific form of a *virtual crowd*, accessing the same sources of information and reacting to the same sets of stimuli. These users, through their interactions, compose the phenomenon of an IS dynamics. The dynamics not understood as one referring to the flow of energy (e.g., electrical impulses), but dynamics based on the collective information processes, reflected in collective actions. A phenomenon that was called by Simon (1955) "a collective mind."

And here we find the other research thread of this chapter: the issue of human rationality. The Western organizational culture still is based on three main determinants: individualism, competition, and a mechanistic-reductionist perspective. As a result, the essential body of scientific achievements in the area of human behavior concerns individuals (Nelson & Quick, 2005), and this is reflected in the paradigm of rationality. This depiction, known as rational choice theory (Alingham, 2006), assumes that individuals are perfectly rational, with clearly defined preferences, and optimizing their

behavior at all levels of a decision-making process. Reductionism, which is related to it, postulates that collective behavior is composed of the sum of rational behavior of all individuals. Since this *sum* is purely theoretical and abstract, it generally is accepted that all phenomena concerning a collectivity are exclusively qualitative and cannot be structured.

The deficiencies of the traditional, idealistic approach to rationality have been known and discussed for a long time. Admittedly, since Simon's idea of "bounded rationality" it has been allowed that human actions can be more "satisficing" than "optimizing," but all new concepts of rationality still refer only to individual behavior (Halpern & Stern, 1998). At the same time, it has been emphasized that there is a need for such a formulation of the rationality principle so that it can take into account the specificity of collective behavior, so different from the individual one.

This chapter tries to briefly explore the existing possibilities of an effective modeling of collective information processes, and of structuring this phenomenon through the identification of its quantitative dimension. The potential findings should help formulate a new, wider, approach to rationality, which could respond to the integration and globalization trends of modern societies.

Objectives

The main objective of this chapter is a presentation of an innovative approach to the analysis and modeling of collective information processes and the mechanisms of collective behavior within a model global IS. This is the first such attempt in relation to the above-mentioned social aspects of information systems. Extensive literature studies helped formulate the following research questions:

1. Are information processes of collectivity and the resulting collective behavior, which constitute the dynamics of an information system, phenomena of exclusively qualitative nature, impossible to structure?

2. Does irrationality or non-rationality, and unpredictability of individual actions determine irrationality and unpredictability of the whole social system within a Global IS?
3. Is there a research method allowing to identify and analyze a phenomenon of "social rationality," from its theoretical to methodological to empirical dimension?

These research questions produced the following theses:

1. Collective behavior, which is a basic determinant of the IS (global IS) dynamics, does not proceed in a planned and intended manner, but is adaptive and follows certain patterns found in the world of nature.
2. Collective behavior can be expressed in a model form, which enables to structure this phenomenon, otherwise considered purely qualitative so far.
3. The identification of quantitative attributes of collective behavior can provide substantial theoretical and methodological premises for the extension of the optimizing and individualistic notion of rationality by the social and adaptive aspects.

THEORETICAL BACKGROUND

Electronic Exchange as a Global Information System

The Notion of Information System (IS)

There are very many definitions of an information system. Some, such as the following example, emphasize the use of information and communication technology (ICT): "Any telecommunications and/or computer related equipment or interconnected system or subsystems of equipment that is used in the acquisition, storage, manipulation, management, movement, control, display, switching, interchange, transmission, or reception of voice and/or data, and includes software, firmware, and hardware" (National Information Systems Security Glossary, 1999, p. 31).

Others narrow it down to systems that support management decision making. This is typical for more recent approaches, which generally adopt a broader view. It goes well beyond the integration of hardware and software, and considers an information system to be any system that has collection, processing, dissemination, and use of information as a major component in terms of its purpose and the activities it carries out. Most modern information systems with any degree of complexity will, in practice, almost always incorporate ICT, but the technology is not the defining aspect. The significant issues are the generation, processing, and use of information.

For example, according to Vigden et al. (2002, p. 2), an information system is a set of interacting components—people, procedures, and technologies—that together collect, process, store, and distribute information to support control, decision making, and management in organizations. This definition stresses the mutual relation between an organization's management system and its information system.

Benson and Standing (2002, p. 5) identify the basic components of an information system: people, data/information, procedures, software, hardware, and communications.

Pearlson and Saunders (2004, p. 14), in turn, define an information system as the combination of people (the "who"), technology (the "what"), and processes (the "how") that an organization uses to produce and manage information. They also refer to information technology as the technical devices and tools used in the system.

The scope of this analysis makes one more definition of an IS especially useful for further considerations. Buckingham et al. (1987) define an information system as: "A system which assembles, stores, processes and delivers information relevant to an organization (or to society), in such a way that the information is accessible and useful to those who wish to use it, including managers, staff, clients and citizens. An information system is a human activity (social) system which may or may not involve the use of computer systems."

This definition is useful in that it emphasizes the human and organizational aspects of information systems. The definition also makes clear that not all information systems use information technology, and that an information system is in essence a human activity system situated in an organizational context—technology is important to information systems but must be considered jointly with human and organizational dimensions.

There are two clear examples of information systems, at somewhat different ends of the spectrum. A payroll system is an information system. This was one of the first applications to be computerized. Today, payroll systems are not simple, there exists a wealth of legislation with which the system has to cope and comply. A payroll system also must be flexible and maintainable, for almost every few days there are changes. It does not provide any competitive advantage to an organization, it is just a necessary system for an organization to have to enable it to be in business. It is what is termed, a mature application. There are many such mature systems in organizations, for example, invoicing systems, billing systems, order processing systems, inventory systems, and personnel systems.

The next example system is very different. It is an electronic auction house, such as eBay. It is relatively new (eBay started in 1995) and uses the World Wide Web as its user interface. Yet, essentially, it is just an information system. It matches buyers with sellers utilizing an auction concept. This concept is not new, there have been auctions for hundreds of years, but the electronic auction enables buyers and sellers to be geographically distributed across the world, whereas, the traditional auction required the buyers and sellers, and the product being auctioned, to be together in a particular place at a particular time. The electronic auction breaks the tradition in terms of both time and space. The auction house usually provides payment, insurance, delivery, security, and other services to its clients if required and, in general, provides an environment that enables people to participate easily and securely in an auction from the comfort of their home or workplace. So, the electronic auction is an information system, comprising people, rules, procedures, technology, software, communications and allied services.

IS Categories

There are different typologies and different levels of analysis within the area of information systems. Most generally, there are three basic categories of information systems:

- Simple manual (paper-and-pencil) IS
- Informal (word-of-mouth) IS
- Computer-based IS

Our concern in research today is with computer-based information systems. We must remember, however, that many information systems in organizations are informal—the office grapevine and conversations at the water-cooler are typical examples of these. Although the informal aspects of information systems are difficult to manage and are not amenable to an engineering approach, their influence should not be under-estimated.

This is consistent with the system's view presented by Thompson (1976, pp. 2-26) three decades ago. He argued that the organization consisted of two systems. The artificial system is the tool designed by the owner, managers, or both to accomplish a particular goal. The informal organization of social relationships constitutes a natural system whose goal is not entirely compatible with the artificial system's goal. The result is that the effectiveness of the artificial system is always limited by the natural one.

Thus, there are other forms of information systems. Organizations have always needed information systems, although the formal aspects of these information systems would have been implemented using paper-based filing systems (paper-and-pencil) in the pre-IT era.

One of the many ways to identify the development of IS/IT is using a three-era model (Ward & Peppard, 2002, p. 23). The prime objective of using IS/IT in the eras differs:

1. **Data processing:** To improve operational efficiency by automating information-based processes (from the 1960s onward—the DP era).
2. **Management information systems:** To increase management effectiveness by satisfying their information requirements for decision making (from the 1970s onward—the MIS era).
3. **Strategic information systems:** To improve competitiveness by changing the nature or conduct of business—from the 1980s onward (the SIS era).

Next, focusing, for example, on management information systems, they sit on the boundary between information and knowledge—MIS are really support tools providing management with the information needed to do the job. In essence, different kinds of information are able to be accessed and analyzed, and summarized reports produced. The reports are used at the highest levels of management to produce long-term strategic plans, and in middle management to improve the quality of service and employee efficiency, or for simple operational matters. MIS can be divided into five basic categories (Benson & Standing, 2002, p. 87):

- Management reporting systems (MRS)
- Decision support systems (DSS)
- Expert systems (ES)
- Executive information systems (EIS)
- Groupware

To conclude this brief overview of IS categories, let us concentrate on another important criterion. It is the range of applicability, and there are micro- and macro-economic information systems. In light of the dynamic growth of a global telecommunications network, we can complete this typology with a relatively new category of global information systems. Turban et al. (2005, p. 277) define global information systems as inter-organizational systems that connect companies located in two or more countries. There are three main categories of organizations

that use global information systems: multinational, international, and virtual organizations. Companies that have global operations usually use the Internet. The major benefits of global information systems for such organizations include:

1. Effective communication at a reasonable cost.
2. Effective collaboration to overcome differences in distance, time, language, and culture.
3. Access to databases of business partners and ability to work on the same projects while their members are in different locations.

Global systems involve multiple organizations in multiple countries. Examples include: airline reservation systems such as Travelocity (www.travelocity.com) or Expedia (www.expedia.com), police and immigration systems, electronic funds transfer (EFT) systems (including networks of ATMs), and many commercial and educational systems for international organizations such as the European Union (http://cordis.europa.eu).

Also, the electronic auction house, described earlier, belongs to this category. We may posit, then, that a modern, electronic exchange (stocks, commodities, currencies) also constitutes a good example of a certain category of global information systems. Besides, the performance of capital markets is a typical example of group (crowd) reactions (Plummer, 1998), which will be especially useful in further analysis.

Another important observation from this brief analysis points to a certain structural characteristic of an information system. Regardless of different definitions and approaches, people constitute the basic component of any information system. We may assume, then, that the most important element of each information system is its social subsystem, which complies with the basic categorization of IS, and with the notion that IS do not have to use modern technologies.

The social subsystem of an electronic and virtual stock exchange will be the subject of further analysis.

IS Dynamics

Dynamics (Latin: *dynamikos,* "strong," "possessing strength") according to *Webster's Unabridged Dictionary* (2005, p. 564), refers to "that branch of mechanics which treats of the motion of bodies (kinematics) and the action of forces in producing or changing their motion."

According to Eden and Spender (2003), the dynamics of an organization represents changes in the various types of knowledge, in the learning and unlearning processes. The basic determinants of this phenomenon are thus:

- Knowledge
- Learning
- Unlearning

Organizational learning is a metaphor indicating the way an organization adapts to the constantly changing environment. Organizational learning occurs as knowledge, acquired and developed by individual members, is embedded in *organizational memory.* At the same time, collective knowledge cannot be understood without paying attention to the communication processes going on among the group's members (Weick, 2000). It follows that information and decision processes flowing in the social subsystem of a given IS condition the phenomenon of the IS dynamics, and learning and unlearning are a specific category of these processes. Decision processes usually precede taken actions, therefore, collective behavior, as a consequence of collective information and decision processes, is the next determinant of the IS dynamics.

The IS dynamics, generally understood as the systems ability to act, refers directly to a phenomenon defined as the "activity system" (Eden & Spender, 2003). The notion of activity system, jointly with the notion of the *organization's culture* point to the next determinant of the IS dynamics. It is the *collective mind,* which can only be identified in the practice of the activity system, and for many analysts the terms organizational culture and collective mind are scarcely separable.

As early as 1895, Le Bon (2006) in his classic "The Crowd: A Study of the Popular Mind" posited that a crowd is primarily a *psychological* phenomenon rather than a physical one (although the two concepts are not necessarily mutually exclusive). He considered that any number of otherwise independent and spatially separate individuals could form a crowd, provided that the members had a *common cause.* This implies that *crowd-type* pressures can be found in a large range of groupings. We can identify the occurrence of this phenomenon during football games, manifestations, and revolutions, in schools (peer pressure) and religious cults. We also can find it in many organizations, especially those, where the identification of an employee with the company is very strong. Le Bon argued that "whoever be the individuals, the fact that they have been transformed into a crowd puts them in possession of a sort of collective mind" (2006, p. 53).

A crowd is, then, something other than the sum of its parts—in particular, a crowd has an effective mind of its own, and each individual's behavior is altered by membership of a crowd. Generally, this phenomenon reveals how strongly a group influences its members and is described more precisely by the "social laws" (Pring, 1993). According to these laws:

- A group of people, or "crowd," is subject to instincts that individuals acting on their own would never be.
- People involuntarily follow the impulses of the crowd, that is, they succumb to the herd instinct.
- Contagion and imitation of the minority make individuals susceptible to suggestion, commands, customs, and emotional appeals.
- When gathered as a group or crowd, people rarely reason but, instead, follow blindly and emotionally what is suggested or asserted to them.

Today, it is assumed that an organism does not even need a brain in order to be intelligent.

Intelligence is a property that emerges when a certain level of organization is reached that enables the system to process information. The greater the ability to process information, the greater the intelligence. If a system has the capacity to process information, to notice and respond, then that system possesses the quality of *intelligence* (Wheatley, 2005, p. 98). Any entity that has capacities for generating and absorbing information, for feedback, for self-regulation, possesses mind. This approach offers us a means to contemplate *organizational intelligence.*

The issue of human behavior within an information system is the most recent research trend in the area of information systems development (ISD). In 1994, Morita, the founder of Sony Corp., pointed to the constantly growing gap between the world of business, and generally a society, and the new world of information technology, and called it the "IT/business gap." Arguably, it was the first human aspect within the area of IS that was detected so clearly. The problem identified by Morita a decade ago concerned individual attitudes and actions. Today, the Internet revolution and an unprecedented growth of dispersed collectivities denote a necessity of a new perspective on the society and organization. No longer can we perceive the social subsystem of an IS as a set of independent individuals. The users of the global information system create a specific form of a *virtual crowd,* accessing the same sources of information and reacting to the same sets of stimuli.

The idea that behavior in financial markets is essentially a crowd phenomenon is the basis of this analysis. At one extreme, a self-aware individual is potentially unpredictable except within the very broadest of guidelines. However, at the other extreme, people as a group are predictable. This is the essence of the crowd phenomenon, and the main challenge is to find a quantitative measure of this phenomenon. It follows that the individualistic and optimizing approach to rationality has become insufficient in that new, virtual environment, and the next big challenge in the discussed area is an attempt to adapt the traditional paradigm of rationality to the new reality.

Rationality of Human Behavior

Traditional Approach to Rationality

Battram and Battram (2002, p. 94) argue that modern management thinking is underpinned by three myths. These are: the myth of the rational person, the myth of the economic person, and the myth of the scientific person.

The rational person is characterized by the property of perfect knowledge, and the ability to obtain and retain perfect information. Also it is assumed that people are always rational and logical, and all else being equal, decisions are always about selecting the best alternative. The myth of the economic person is that the market is perfect, free and open, and everyone behaves perfectly within it. Similarly, the myth of the scientific person tells us that our decisions are always logical, perfectly quantified, based on an understanding of cause and effect, and carried out in our mind, without any influence from emotions, and other distractions.

The key word of those three myths is "rationality." Rationality (Latin: *rationalis,* "reasonable"), according to *Webster's Unabridged Dictionary* (2005, p. 1193), refers to the "possession of," "agreeableness to," or "exercise of reason." Reason, in turn, is a "basis or cause;" or a "statement in justification or explanation of a belief or action" (2005, p. 1197).

Rational behaviors follow stable, consistent, and coherent beliefs or rules that enable individuals to understand what they are doing and why. The most clearly elucidated rules of rational behavior are based on self-interest. As early as the late 1800s, Edgeworth (1881/1974), in *Mathematical Psychics* asserted that the "first principle of Economics is that every agent is actuated only by self-interest." And so, Edgeworth's *first principle* of self-interest came to define the core of economic and political models.

Today, the notion of positive science is premised on a rational method, and social scientists have struggled continually with the concept of rationality, both in defending their methods and in describing human behavior. One side in the debate argues that the classical economists' model of rational decision making offers the best way to understand decision behavior. This model focuses on the value, or utility, of the decision outcome. And since the publication of Von Neumann and Morgenstern's (1944) seminal work, the concept of maximizing expected utility became synonymous with rationality. This axiomatic single-person decision theory considers only rational outcomes, those made based on maximization of expected utility, unencumbered by external pressures or cognitive limitations.

The second group of researchers, those concerned with decision processes, advocate identifying specific behaviors or concerns that characterize humans and incorporating their influences into the classical models.

A third approach to the debate advocates the inclusion of context, particularly social context, as an additional element influencing the decision maker (Halpern, 1997; Mele & Rawling, 2004). As this third, more recent, approach develops, it may either extend or repudiate the classic model.

Within economics a theory of rational choice developed, adding to the self-interest argument the notion of "revealed preferences" (Halpern & Stern, 1998). The theory assumes that people are capable of expressing both consistent preferences (evaluative judgments) and consistent beliefs (predictive judgments concerning cause and effect). This individual choice model combining self-interest with preference simplifies our understanding of decision making by offering maximization of expected utility as the sole criterion of a rational choice.

The economists' preference for investigating rationality in a vacuum emerged from their tendency to study an ideal market with perfect competition, which functions without prolonged human or social contact. As a result, the central assumptions of rational choice theory are powerful simplifications. Arrow (1990, p. 25), a Nobel-prize winning economist, argues that: "[The rationality assumptions] . . . imply an ability at information processing and calculation that is far beyond the feasible and that cannot well be justified as the result of learning and adaptation."

The critics of the classical rational choice structure, including anthropologists and some psychologists and sociologists, long have argued that decision making, even economic decision making, tends to occur in a social setting (e.g., Lichbach, 2003; Coleman, 1998). Recently, researchers, including some economists have agreed that rationality has a social component (e.g., Shi, 2002; Sato, 2006). The social context creates pressures of its own, influencing the decision process and outcome. Arrow (1990, p. 25) acknowledged the importance of context in this observation: "Rationality is not a property of the individual alone, although it is usually presented that way. Rather, it gathers not only its force but also its very meaning from the social context in which it is embedded." Recent laboratory work, based on these earlier empirical observations, suggests that the social context exerts its effects even when there is no communication between transactors (Halpern, 1997). This observation has a particular significance for further analysis, which concerns the rationality of collective behavior of investors taking actions in the virtual environment of present-day capital markets.

Alternative Notions of Rationality

The first response to Von Neumann and Morgenstern's formulation of rationality as maximization was Simon's (1955) idea of *satisficing*. Simon observed that human decision making is "boundedly rational": it is limited by our inability to process all the information that is available as well as by our inability to be consistent in our preferences. As a result, people tend to "satisfice" or use a variety of heuristics (shortcuts) in their decision-making process.

Simon's critique of the maximization principle was based on two issues. First, in order to maximize one has to have all the relevant information, and this usually is not the case. Second, people are limited in their ability to process information; hence, the chance that people would be able to maximize is rather small. According to this model, people select a subsample of the space of total relevant alternatives and search until they find a *good enough* alternative. Search is terminated when an alternative gets selected, and since the process does not continue to ensure the selection of the optimal alternative, it is defined as satisficing, which differs from maximizing.

Simon's analysis of bounded rationality treated individual and organizational decision making similarly. The development of behavioral decision theory over the last 30 years, however, has focused more on the individual level of analysis. Recent attempts have been made to link the two and over the last decade relationships between these two levels of analysis have been explored (e.g., Kahneman & Lovallo, 1993; Shapira, 2002).

In 1978 March proposed variants on the classical notion of rationality. In addition to the notion of *bounded rationality*, he suggested several alternatives. *Limited rationality*, describes the features of a process where decision makers try to simplify a decision problem because of problems associated with considering or anticipating all the alternatives and all the needed information. *Contextual rationality* highlights the effects of a social context where there are multiple other claims on decision makers' attention. *Game rationality* highlights the degree to which self-interests and calculation guide the behavior of a decision maker, while *process rationality* is the extent to which decision makers focus on the process of making choices, rather than on the decision outcomes. *Selected rationality* refers to the process of selection through survival or growth, while *posterior rationality* refers to the discovery of intentions after actions have been taken.

Last but not least, *adaptive rationality* was supposed to emphasize the experiential learning of individuals and the way experience affects learning. This was the first case of a usage of the term "adaptive rationality." This concept, however, related to individuals only and remained in the area of theoretical proposals. This chapter explores the possibilities of an extension of the notion of adaptive rationality to the whole social system within a given IS, and supports it with a practical case study.

In 1992, Mumby and Putnam unshackled rationality and expanded it to embrace emotionality. Their concept of *bounded emotionality* fuses the emotional foundations of the social phenomenon, rationality, with the currently reified perspectives. The boundedness stems from each party's mutual respect for the other's space and dignity (a choice that a person makes) rather than the boundedness of rationality that is treated as a constraint without choice. Originally, this approach was supposed to unite the concepts of *bounded rationality* and *emotionality*. The authors suggested acknowledging the *emotionality of rationality*, in order to create an appreciation of "intersubjective understanding, community, and shared interests" (1992, p. 480), recognizing not only the cognitive, instrumental dimensions, but also the social dimensions of human behavior, in which emotions play an important role.

Similarly to March's adaptive rationality, bounded emotionality still remains a theoretical concept, without any empirical achievements.

Finally, in 1998, the concept of *bonded rationality* was introduced (Halpern & Stern, 1998). Just as human cognitive limitations on our ability to process and use information lead us to have "bounded rationality," so also do our shared limitations on information processing and on our understanding of the evaluation of alternatives lead us to a "bonded rationality" based on our need to interact effectively with other people.

Bonded rationality is a model of human interaction that argues first, that we share ways of evaluating alternatives that may not be objectively optimal, and second, that we reason rationally about these shared evaluations. It follows that we should study evidence of suboptimal transaction behavior as elucidating shared ways of valuing alternatives rather than as evidence of nonrational reasoning.

Bonded rationality derives from the fact that our personalizations (individual acts of understanding alternatives) can be understood by others, and that we wish these personalizations to be understood by others. The decision maker who is bondedly rational usually is understood (although not necessarily agreed with) by peers because his or her personalized perceptions share common cognitive bounds and contextual references. Bonded rationality thus both derives from, and facilitates, social interaction.

What is important, bonded rationality argues that individuals reason rationally about alternatives as they personalize these alternatives, but this rational reasoning proceeds in terms of the axioms of rational choice theory. Nevertheless, the concept of bonded rationality explicitly adds social and cultural context to considerations of psychological influences in rational decision making. It is thus both more realistic than theories of rationality that ignore context, and a fertile source of research questions. By emphasizing the importance of how decision makers personalize alternatives, bonded rationality focuses attention on the influences of psychology, sociology, and anthropology on rational decision making.

This cursory survey of alternative notions of rationality shows that in spite of the development of diverse concepts, and a general consensus about the existence of many possible ways to describe rational behavior, still dominates the classic, single-person and optimizing, version of rationality. This creates a need to both continue research in the area of social and organizational aspects of rationality and search for empirical evidence for proposed theoretical concepts.

METHODOLOGICAL BACKGROUND

The Paradigm Shift

Most of today's organizations are designed and managed according to the assumptions taken from 17th century physics, from Newtonian mechanics. This machine imagery leads to the belief that studying the parts is the key to understanding the whole. These assumptions also are the base from which we do research in all of the social sciences. Intentionally, or not, we work from a world view that has been derived from the natural sciences. Even to this day, many scientists keep searching

for the "building blocks" of matter, the physical forms from which everything originates.

However, we need to expand our search for principles of organization to include what is presently known about the universe. Only this can help us explain how to create structures that move with change, that are flexible and adaptive, even boundaryless, that enable rather than constrain.

One of the first differences between new science and Newtonianism is a focus on holism rather than parts. Organizations are understood as whole systems, and attention is given to relationships within those networks. When we view systems from this perspective, we enter an entirely new field of connections, of phenomena that cannot be reduced to simple and linear cause and effect, or explained by studying the parts as isolated contributors. In this new land, it becomes critical to sense the constant working of dynamic processes, and then to notice how these processes materialize as visible behaviors and forms. The most recent trend even goes as far as assuming that a system is a set of processes that are made visible in temporary structures (Wheatley, 2005, p. 23).

The new science research referred to in this chapter comes from the disciplines of quantum physics, biology, chemistry, theories of evolution and co-evolution, theories of complexity and chaos. They span several disciplines, so the proposed research approach is, by definition, multidisciplinary, and interdisciplinary.

For example, in physics, the search for radically new models is characterized by the major discoveries in quantum mechanics. In the quantum world, relationship is the key determiner of everything. In a homologous process, described as *relational holism*, whole systems are created by the relationships among subatomic particles. Subatomic particles come into form and are observed only as they are in relationship to something else. Electrons are drawn into these intimate relations as they cross paths with one another, overlapping and merging; their own individual qualities become indistinguishable. There are no *building blocks*. Many physicist nowadays describe elementary particles as, in essence, a set of relationships that reach outward to other things.

A new understanding of change and disorder also has emerged from chaos theory. Work in this field has led to a new appreciation of the relationship between order and chaos. These two forces are now understood as mirror images, two states that contain the other. A system can descend into chaos and unpredictability, yet, within that state of chaos the system is held within boundaries that are well-ordered and predictable. Chaos is necessary to new creative ordering.

In chemistry, Prigogine's and Nicolis's (1977) work confirmed that disorder can be the source of new order. Prigogine coined the term "dissipative structures" for these newly discovered structures. In a dissipative structure, anything that disturbs the system plays a crucial role in helping self-organize into a new form of order. Whenever the environment offers new and different information, the system chooses whether to accept it and respond. If the system brings the information inside, the information grows and changes. If the information becomes such a large disturbance that the system can no longer ignore it, then real change is at hand. At this moment, far from equilibrium, the system will fall apart. In its current form, it cannot deal with the disturbance, so it dissolves. But this disintegration does not mean the end of the system. If a living system can maintain its identity, it can self-organize to a higher level of complexity.

In this way, dissipative structures demonstrate that *disorder* can be a source of new *order*, and that growth appears from disequilibrium, not balance. The things we try to avoid in organizations-disruption, confusion, chaos-are thus necessary to awaken creativity. And so, our concept of organizations is moving away from the mechanistic creations that were useful in the age of bureaucracy. We now speak of more fluid, organic structures, of boundaryless and seamless organizations. We are beginning to recognize organizations as whole systems, construing them as *learning organizations* or as *organic* and noticing that people possess self-organizing capacity. Most importantly, however, organizations are living systems, possessing the same capacity to adapt and grow that is common to all life. And fluctuation and change are essential to the process by which order is created.

Scientists of chaos study shapes in motion. Wholeness is revealed only as shapes, not facts. Systems reveal themselves as patterns, not as isolated incidents or data points. Wheatley (2005, p. 125) raises a question: "If we were to understand organizations in a similar way, what would constitute the shapes in motion of an organization?" This chapter makes an attempt at answering, at least partially, this question.

Collectivity of Investors as a Complex Aadaptive System

The flow of collective information processes determines organizational learning, which is a useful metaphor describing the way an organization, including a virtual and global one, adapts to its environment. The research on collective mind and collective behavior can be conducted within a social subsystem of an electronic stock exchange, which was recognized as a model representation of a global information system. The performance of capital markets is a typical example of crowd reactions. After the memorable crash of world financial markets in August 1998, Alan Greenspan, chair of the U.S. Federal Reserve Bank, affirmed that "markets are an expression of the deepest truths about the human nature" (Ramo, 1999).

Financial markets are fast-moving, continually oscillating, reflections of the processes of transformation and change. Unlike any other crowd, the behavior of financial market crowds is clearly reflected in simple, and specific, indicators. These are the price movements themselves, and certain mechanical indexes of the underlying activity and energy of the crowd, such as trading volumes. Financial markets are, therefore, an ideal source of information about all crowd behavior.

The introductory analysis shows that the social subsystem of an electronic and virtual stock exchange reveals at least four characteristics of a nonlinear, complex adaptive system. Turniansky and Hare (1998, p. 106), analyzing the issue of self-organization, identify the main characteristics of a complex adaptive system. Such a system:

- Consists of a network of agents acting in a self-managed way without centralized control.
- The environment in which the agents find themselves is constantly changing and evolving since it is produced by the interactions with other agents.
- Organized patterns of behavior arise from competition and cooperation among agents producing structures arising from interactions and interdependencies.

The processes in a complex adaptive system are those of mutual adjustment and self-regulation. Each self-organizing structure is responsive to disequilibrium, is open to the environment for the exchange of information and energy, and is able to process information and energy. They are decentralized systems having a bottom-up direction from combining actions rather that top-down centralized control. The structure that emerges is not simply an aggregation of individual actions, but rather has unique properties not possessed by individuals alone.

Self-organization cannot be imposed from outside, but operates from within the system itself. Organization is not designed into the parts, but is generated by the interaction of those parts as a whole. The self-organizing form has implications for organizational learning. Self-organizing or self-renewing systems are characterized by system resiliency, rather than stability. When the systems have to deal with new information they recognize themselves in the ways needed to do so. Its form and function engage in a fluid process where the system may maintain itself in its present form or evolve to a new order. The system possesses the capacity for spontaneously emerging structures, depending on what is required. It is not locked into any one best form but, instead, is capable of organizing information in the structure that suits the present need. In other words, instead of making information fit the existing structure, structure is made to fit the information.

In a seemingly paradoxical way, openness to the environment, to information from outside, leads to higher levels of system autonomy and identification. Some fluctuations will always break through, but what comes to dominate the system over time is not environmental influences, but rather the self-organizing dynamics of the system itself. In response to environmental disturbances that signal the need for change, the system changes in a way that remains consistent with itself in that environment. The system is autopoietic, focusing its activities on what is required to maintain its own integrity and self-renewal (Cooper, 2006). As it changes, it does so by referring to itself; whatever future form it takes will be consistent with its already established identity.

Each element in the system influences other elements directly, indirectly, or both. The relationships are mutually determining and determined. As each agent (here: investor) tries to adapt to the others, it changes the environment of the others as well. Freedom and order coexist and support each other in autonomous systems. Wheatley (2005, p. 95) argues that "self-organization succeeds when the system supports the independent activity of its members by giving them a strong frame of reference. When it does this, the global system achieves even greater levels of autonomy and integrity."

Effective self-organization is supported by two critical elements: a clear sense of identity, and freedom. In organizations, if people are free to make their own decisions, guided by a clear organizational identity for them to reference, the whole system develops greater coherence and strength. The organization is less controlling, but more orderly. Jantsh (1980, p. 40) argues that "the natural dynamics of simple dissipative structures teach the optimistic principle of which we tend to despair in the human world: the more freedom in self-organization, the more order." This is precisely the case with the electronic stock exchange. The social subsystem of a modern stock exchange:

1. Consists of a network of investors (agents) acting in a self-managed way without centralized control.
2. The environment in which the investors operate changes and evolves constantly, which

is the result of continuous fluctuations in the economy and market situation, but also is produced by the interactions among the investors.

3. Competition among the investors leads to a consensus, reflected by a current market trend.

4. This trend suggests the hidden existence of organized patterns of collective behavior, which is the result of the emergence of a natural dynamic structure of this social system.

The classification of the analyzed social system as a complex adaptive systems allows for the application of the most recent findings of many disciplines, considered to have no relations with the science of management and organization. For example, complexity theory can offer a range of new insights into the behavior of social and economic systems. The idea of self-organization and emergence can be used to identify and explain the dynamics of individual and collective behavior on the stock market. Thousands of independent and difficult to observe transactions, carried out by individual participants of the market, generate the emergence of specific and *predictable* patterns of collective behavior. These phenomena can only be identified on the higher, collective, not individual, level of social organization. Kauffman's (1996) famous phrase "order for free" describes that the process of "crystallization," also known as the emergence of complexity in complex adaptive systems. The fundamental challenge of such defined research would be to find a quantitative measure of that emergence.

Chaos theory, a sub-discipline of complexity theory, identifies, and analyzes the dynamics of nonlinear systems. In nonlinear systems, iteration helps small differences grow into powerful effects. In complex ways, the systems feeds back on itself, magnifying slight variances, communicating throughout its networks, becoming disturbed and unstable. Iteration launches a system on a journey that visits both chaos and order. The most visible consequence of iteration is found in the creation of

fractals. The process of fractal creation suggests some ways organizations can work with the paradox that greater openness is the path to greater order. A fractal reveals its complex shape through continuous self-reference to a simple initial pattern.

To see how chaotic processes reveal the order inherent in a system requires that we shift our vision from the parts to the whole. Wholeness is what rushes in under the guise of chaos whenever we try to separate and measure dynamical systems as if they were composed of parts. For example, *strange attractors* are not the shape of chaos, but the shape of wholeness. When we concentrate on individual actions of individual investors, we see only chaos, emotions, and lack of rationality. But when we stand back and look at what is taking shape on the market, we see order. Order always displays itself as *patterns* that develop over time. Thus, the shape of the entire system is predictable or predetermined, which will be showed later on in this chapter.

There is a difference between *fractals* and *strange attractors*. Strange attractors are self-portraits drawn by a chaotic system. They are always fractal in nature, being deeply patterned, but they are a special category of mathematical object. Estimates are that there are only about two dozen different strange attractors (Posamantier & Lehman, 2007). In contrast, fractals describe any object or form created from repeating patterns evident at many levels of scale. There are infinite number of fractals, both natural and human-made. Fractals are everywhere around us, in the patterns by which nature organizes clouds, rivers, mountains, plants, our bodies. We live in a universe of fractal forms. Everywhere in this fractal landscape, there is self-similarity. There is pattern within pattern within pattern. There is no end to them, no scale small enough that these shapes cease to form.

Many disciplines have seized upon fractals, testing whether self-similar phenomena occur at different levels of scale in both natural and human-made systems. From architects who explain the beauty of building and towns as the repetition of harmonious patterns, to business forecasters who have observed a fractal quality in market behaviors. Fractals also have direct application for how we should understand organizations. All organizations are, in fact, fractal in nature. Each organization is deeply patterned with self-similar behaviors evident everywhere. These recurring patterns of behavior are what many call the culture of the organization. The organizational culture, as was noted before, is often identified directly with collective mind. Hence, if we could identify a specific fractal in the market behavior, we would be allowed to affirm that there is a sort of *collective mind* on the market. This, in turn, would indicate that there is a certain form of *collective,* or *social,* rationality, most likely quite different from the individual one.

Research Method

Three-Element Ecological Model

The idea of self-organization bears the notion of an "open system," contrary to the Newtonian "closed system." It also allows for the full utilization of the concept of "entropy" in social sciences. More than two decades ago Capra (1984, p. 32) argued that the new paradigm of rationality should take into account the fact that "an economy is a living system, and one of many aspects of a large ecological and social structure." And so, to model and structure the behavior of our complex adaptive system, we can use the elements of environmental economics—one of the most trendy areas in economics (e.g., Callan & Thomas, 2006). The general methodological concept proposed in this chapter is based on a three-element system, *society-economy-nature,* and it replaces the two-element system, *economy-nature,* which has been applied in economics since the 1960s. This will allow for the identification of the dependencies in its two-element subsystem, *society-nature.* This, in turn, will help identify and describe phenomena, which are observed in the surrounding world of nature and, to the same extent, are expected to regulate behavior of the crowd. This should be the actual, as opposed to only formal and declared, introduc-

tion of the ideas of open system and entropy to economic and social sciences.

Generally, the research method consists of the following stages:

identification-analysis-synthesis-exemplification-verification-interpretation-discussion

More accurately these stages are:

- Identification of the research area.
- Identification of the mechanism of collective behavior.
- Analysis of the identified mechanism.
- Synthesis, a mathematical description of the mechanism.
- Exemplification and verification of the mechanism.
- Interpretation and discussion: a new approach to rationality.

Next is a brief description of the main stages of the research method applied in this chapter.

Identification of the Research Area

The collectivity of investors composes a non-linear complex adaptive system. Each crowd can be defined in terms of its processes rather than its physical characteristics. The basic catalyst for the formation of a crowd is a condition of non-equilibrium. The presence of two crowds in a financial market (*bulls* and *bears*), ensures that a state of conflict of interest exists within the rules of the investment game. Such a condition creates stress and competition, and provides the purpose for the creation of a crowd. In order to achieve its objectives, a crowd must be open to the environment for the exchange of both energy and information. Crowd members of the financial market are in a constant state of expectant attention and are, therefore, vulnerable to suggestion. Moods, feelings, and ideas in such an environment are very contagious and they spread rapidly. Modern Internet communications ensure that the same effects can be quickly achieved even if the crowd is not assembled in one place. Crowd behavior ensures that a price movement triggers an emotional response among members of opposing crowds, and, thereby, ensures that the most recent movement in prices is continued into the future.

In this sense, change and progress within the analyzed system come about as a result of a dynamic interplay, both between individuals and the crowd to which they belong, and between a crowd and its environment. Independent fluctuations in the environment itself can lead to a number of different responses by a crowd. Ultimately, however, the crowd will always adapt to permanent changes in the environment. And all price movements are part of a very simple pattern, which is the response to information shocks, and prices oscillate rhythmically in response to the metabolic fluctuations of the crowd.

Identification of the Mechanism of Collective Behavior

The important feature of any self-organizing system, whether it be a crowd or a living organism, is that it *oscillates* during the transfer of energy and information. In fact, the presence of continuous fluctuations can be taken as a *prima facie* evidence of the presence of "mental activity." Once a crowd with common values and a common objective has

been established, it will then respond positively to the input of new items of information from the environment. There is a great partnering that exists between the system and its environment. The theory of co-evolution relies on the fact that the relevant feedback loops generate stable fluctuations between a particular system and a higher-order system (Brand, 2006). Mathematicians call these stable fluctuations *limit cycles*. A limit cycle is defined as the isolated periodic oscillation between two variables, and is represented graphically by an isolated closed non-linear path (King et al., 2006). If the limit cycle is stable, the oscillations will spiral on to the solution path from a wide range of initial states. If, on the other hand, the cycle is unstable, a disturbance will cause the oscillations to spiral away from that solution path. It follows that co-evolving systems utilize stable limit cycles.

Figure 1 represents an idealized stable limit cycle. Within the context of this analysis, the *x*-axis on this figure represents an index of crowd behavior and the *y*-axis represents an index of environmental change. In reality, the two-dimensional limit cycle relating *x* and *y* (or the crowd and the environment) actually unfolds through *time*. For this part of the analysis, however, this factor can be omitted.

According to chaos theory, a limit cycle is one of the three possible forms of an attractor (Feudel

Figure 1. Idealized stable limit cycle

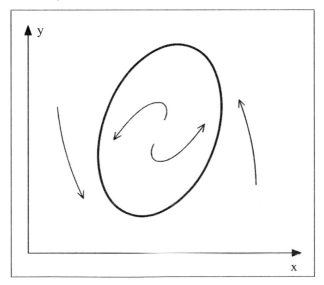

et al., 2006). This observation is critical for further analysis and discussion.

Analysis of the Identified Mechanism

The viability and resiliency of a self-organizing system comes from its great capacity to adapt as needed, to create structures that fit the moment. Neither form nor function alone dictates how the system is organized. Instead, they are *process structures*, reorganizing into different forms in order to maintain their identity. The system may maintain itself in its present form or evolve to a new order, depending on what is required. It is not locked into any one structure; it is capable of organizing into whatever form it determines best suits the present situation.

Whenever a self-organizing system experiences any amplification process, change is at hand. If the amplifications increase to the level where they destabilize the system, the system can no longer remain as it is. At this moment, the system is at a crossroads, standing posed between death and transformation. In chaos theory, it is known technically as a bifurcation point. For the investors, it is either a moment of great fear (at the very bottom of a bear market) or great euphoria (at the end of a bull market). Abandoning its present form, the system is free to seek out a new form in response to the changed environment.

According to this analysis, the price-sentiment limit cycle operating in a financial market is also integrated with limit cycles relating that market to the wider economic, social, and political environment. Although limit cycles are the main mechanism whereby a self-organizing system copes with fluctuations in its environment, they do not fully represent the adjustment processes that are involved. In reality, bits of information become available only in discontinuous or discrete time intervals. The adjustment process depends on whether or not the recipient system is prepared for the information. If the information is unexpected, then the information impacts as a *shock*, and the system may have to change its dynamic structure in order to cope (Plummer, 2006, p. 50). Shocks occur because of a sudden divergence between current price movements and expected price movements, and may derive from two sources: first, they may be triggered by an unexpected movement in prices themselves; second, they may be precipitated by unexpected changes in the social, political, or economic development.

In practice, shocks are delivered to systems that already are oscillating in a limit cycle pattern

Figure 2. Information shock and "jump" from the cycle path (Source: Based on Plummer, 2006)

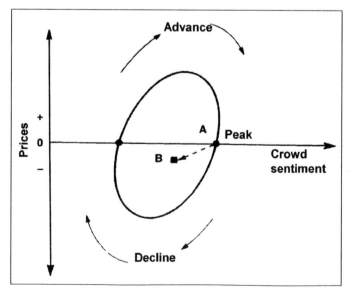

with their niche in the environment. Divergences between lower-level cycles and higher-level cycles are rectified by those shocks, and the fluctuations will continue at least until the limit cycle of the next higher degree is able to reassert control. When an information shock appears, the process of adjustment begins (see Figure 2).

In this analysis, the limit cycle is biased to the right. This reflects a fact that sentiment usually turns prior to price reversals. Hence, prior to market peaks, sentiment will begin to deteriorate as the percentage increase in prices falls. On the other hand, just prior to market troughs, sentiment begins to improve and the percentage fall in prices decreases.

Whatever the source of the shock, the response of the market is essentially the same. The shock is represented here by a "jump" inward from the path of the limit cycle as the change in prices moves across the zero percent change line. Hence, in the case where a market is moving from bullish to bearish, the position on the phase plane will jump from point A to point B as the price moves into negative territory. There will be both a fall in prices and a drop in crowd sentiment (see Figure 2).

Since the limit cycle is essentially stable, it follows that behavior will try to return to the solution path. Technically it means that the fall in prices begins to slow and lower prices encourage a return of "bulls." This, in turn, causes prices to rise and stimulates a reversal in sentiment. Eventually, however, higher prices encourage some profit taking or reducing the previous losses, and prices begin to slip again. The subsequent price collapse is very deep and painful, but it brings prices back to the solution path of the limit cycle, and this phenomenon is expressed by a spiral of the adaptation process of collectivity (see Figure 3).

The key question is: Since there are several different spiral movements what kind of a spiral represents these phenomena? The answer is found in the world, or even the Universe, surrounding us, because a *collectivity is also a natural system* (Frost & Prechter, 2001). And this is the stage when we can utilize the three-element system, *society-economy-nature*, and look for analogies between its two natural subsystems, *society* and *nature*.

Synthesis: A Mathematical Description of the Mechanism

Contemplating the beauty and form of all the wonders of nature and giving further thought to the achievements of man in many fields, we learn that

Figure 3. Formation mechanism of a spiral of the adaptation process of collectivity (Source: Author's research based on Plummer, 2006)

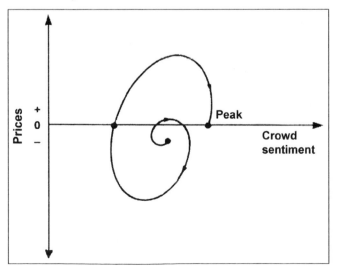

all of these have one thing in common—the *Fibonacci Summation Series* (Posamentier & Lehman, 2007). Long ago, Thomas of Aquinas described one of the basic rules of aesthetics—man's senses enjoy objects that are properly proportioned. He referred to the direct relationship between beauty and mathematics, which is often measurable and can be found in nature. Man instinctively reacts positively to clear geometrical forms, in both his natural environment and in objects created by him. Thomas of Aquinas was referring to the same principle that was a little earlier described by the 13th century mathematician, Fibonacci. He developed the summation series:

1,1,2,3,5,8,13,21,34,55,89,144, . . .

This mathematical series develops when, beginning with 1,1, the next number is formed from the sum of the previous two numbers. If each number in the series is divided by its preceding value (e.g., 21:13), the result is a ratio that oscillates around the irrational 1.618033988. . ., being higher one time and lower the next. But never in eternity can the precise ratio be known to the last digit, therefore, for the sake of brevity, it is referred to as 1.618. Algebraically it generally is designated by the Greek letter phi (ϕ=1.618).

This ratio is known as the Divine Proportion, the Golden Section, or the Golden Mean. Kepler called the ratio, one of the jewels in geometry." Many people have tried to penetrate the secrets of the Pyramid of Gizeh, which is different from the other Egyptian pyramids. More detailed observations give a clue that the pyramid was designed to incorporate the phi proportion of 1.618. The same phenomenon is found in the Mexican pyramids. A different representation of Fibonacci numbers is found in the number of axils on the stem of a plant as it develops (Fisher, 2001).

The Greek mathematician Euclid related the Golden Section to a straight line (see Figure 4).

The line AB of length L is divided into two segments by point C. If C is such a point that L: AC equals AC:BC, then C is the Golden Section AB. In other words, the point C divides the line AB into two parts in such a way that the ratios of those parts is 1.618 and 0.618 (1:1.618).

The Golden Section occurs throughout nature. In fact, the human body is a tapestry of Golden Sections in everything from outer dimensions to facial arrangement.

Another common occurrence of the Divine Proportion can be observed in the Golden Rectangle, which sides are in the proportion of 1.618 to 1 (see Figure 5).

According to Pythagorean theorem:

$CG = \sqrt{5} + 1$; $FG = 2$;
$CG : FG = (\sqrt{5} + 1) : 2 = (2,236 + 1) : 2 = 3,236 : 2 = 1,618$.
$DG = \sqrt{5} - 1$; $FG = 2$;
$DG : FG = (\sqrt{5} - 1) : 2 = (2,236 - 1) : 2 = 1,236 : 2 = 1,618$.

Works of arts have been greatly enhanced with the knowledge of the Golden Rectangle. Fascination with its value and use was particularly strong in ancient Egypt and Greece and during the Renaissance, all high points of civilization. But the value of it is hardly limited to its beauty, it serves function as well. Among numerous examples, the most striking is that the double helix of DNA

Figure 5. Construction of the Golden Rectangle

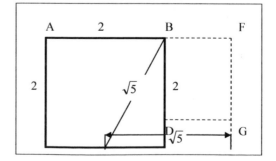

Figure 4. Golden section of a line

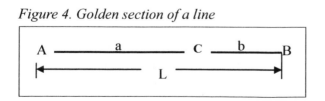

Figure 6. Geometry of the Golden Spiral (Source: Author's research based on Frost and Prechter, 2001)

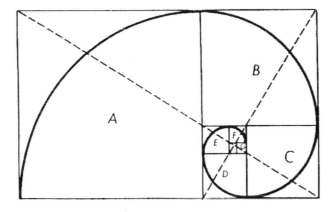

itself creates precise Golden Sections at regular intervals of its twists.

While the Golden Section and the Golden Rectangle represent static pieces of natural and man-made aesthetic beauty and function, the representation of an aesthetically pleasing dynamism, an orderly progression of growth or progress, can be made only by one of the most remarkable forms in the Universe, the Golden Spiral.

To construct a Golden Spiral a Golden Rectangle can be used. Any Golden Rectangle can be divided into a square and a smaller Golden Rectangle. This process then, theoretically, can be continued to infinity. The resulting squares, which have been drawn, appear to be whirling inward. A spiral can be drawn by connecting the points of intersection for each whirling square, in order of increasing size. As the squares whirl inward or outward, their connecting points trace out a Golden Spiral (see Figure 6).

At any point in the evolution of the Golden Spiral, the ratio of the length of the arc to its diameter is 1.618 and the diameter is related to the larger radius just as the larger radius is to the smaller radius, by 1.618, as illustrated in Figure 7.

The Golden Spiral, which is a type of logarithmic or equiangular spiral, has no boundaries and is a constant shape. From any point on it, one can travel infinitely in either the outward or inward direction. The center is never met and the outward reach is unlimited.

Now, the tail of a comet curves away from the sun in a logarithmic spiral. A spider spins its web into a logarithmic spiral. Bacteria grow at an accelerating rate that can be plotted along a logarithmic spiral. Meteorites, when they rupture the surface of the Earth, cause depressions that correspond to

Figure 7. Constant proportions in the Golden Spiral (Source: Author's research based on Frost & Prechter, 2001)

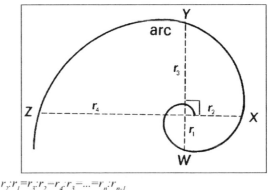

$$r_2 : r_1 = r_3 : r_2 = r_4 : r_3 = \ldots = r_n : r_{n-1}$$
$$d_2 : d_1 = d_3 : d_2 = \ldots = d_n : d_{n-1}$$
$$(d_1 = r_1 + r_3,\ d_2 = r_2 + r_4,\ etc.)$$

233

a logarithmic spiral. Pine cones, sea horses, snail shells, ocean waves, ferns, animal horns, and the arrangement of seed curves on sunflowers and daises all form logarithmic spirals. Hurricane clouds and the galaxies of outer space swirl in logarithmic spirals. Even the human finger, which is composed of three bones in Golden Section to one another, takes the spiral shape (Fisher, 2001). Everywhere, the design is the same: a 1.618 ratio, perhaps the primary law governing dynamic natural phenomena.

PRACTICAL VERIFICATION

Application of the Logarithmic Spiral on the Index Chart

According to the three-element model, this natural law, permeating the universe and described by the Fibonacci ratio $\phi = 1.618$, should refer to the dynamics of collective behavior as well. Since adaptations to the exchange of information spiral and financial markets reflect psychology and the dynamics of the crowd, the spiral identified in price formations also should be logarithmic.

All technical approaches to understanding the stock market depend on the basic principle of order and form. No matter how minute or how large the form, the basic design remains constant. And the stock market has the very same mathematical base

as do all those natural phenomena. It appears that the top of each successive wave of higher degree is the touch point of the logarithmic expansion. The spiral form of market action is repeatedly shown to be governed by the Golden Ratio, and even the Fibonacci numbers themselves appear in market statistics more often than mere chance would allow. Any point on the spiral represents the optimum price-time relationship.

The most challenging part of the spiral is to see it work in extreme market situations, when behavioral patterns are strongest. With the correct center and starting point chosen, the spiral can identify turning points in the markets with accuracy never seen before.

Examples from an Emerging Market

One of the examples of how to use the concept of the spiral to predict the basic market moves is shown in Figure 8. It represents a chart of the Warsaw Stock Exchange index.

The stock market in Poland was reopened in 1991 after more than half a century. The x-axis on the chart represents the dates of consecutive trading days, and the y-axis represents the value of the index in a logarithmic scale (albeit the scale can also be arithmetic).

A logarithmic spiral has been applied, with the center and starting point in the middle of an almost two-year base, preceding the sharp move

Figure 8. Four spiral rings defining the Warsaw Stock Exchange bull market

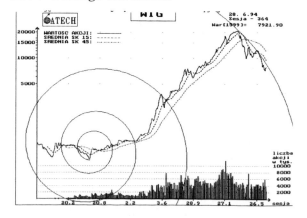

Figure 9. The fourth spiral ring as the ultimate destination of the bear market

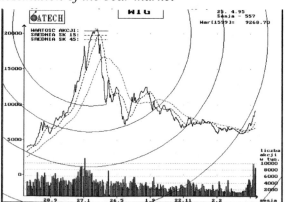

upward. On the second ring of the curve, we can locate a point that approximately ends the long period of basing, on the third ring there is the end of the first wave of enormous gains, and a sharp and painful correction takes place (first days of June 1993). The fourth ring is the ultimate target of the bull market, and the beginning of a long and devastating bear market in March 1994.

The center of the spiral can be placed either in the middle of the market or at one of the extreme points (highs or lows). The spiral itself can be turned either clockwise or counterclockwise. The next important factor is the swing size, that is, the distance between the center and the starting point (Fisher, 2001). Once those parameters have been set, we can begin working with the curve. And the most important factor is the meaning of consecutive spiral rings. At this time no rules have been offered for investing when the first spiral ring is penetrated. Usually we may wait some important moments, when ring number two is reached. It is not often that the third ring of the spiral is penetrated in the same direction as the major trend. But when it happens a significant trend change should follow, as it took place in Warsaw in June 1993. A penetration of the fourth ring in the continuing trend direction must occur even less than any other ring penetration. But, it does happen, and it should indicate a dramatic trend change. These are moves such as the stock market collapse of October 1987 in New York, or March 1994 in

Warsaw (see Figures 8 and 9). The fourth ring is the ultimate price target. When it is penetrated, the point of penetration can be used as an entry signal. There is no need to wait for a confirmation. Another good example of the importance of the four rings of the spiral is presented in Figure 9 on an arithmetic scale.

A long and painful bear market in Warsaw has its major turning points on the four rings of the spiral. On the second ring a dynamic and upward correction wave begins. The third ring points to the beginning of a consolidation phase, preceding the final shake-out. The fourth ring is the end of the bear market.

Figure 10 presents how the logarithmic spiral applies to the next stages of the development of Polish emerging stock market. The spiral embraces all the vital turning points of the index chart, starting at the peak of the first wave of the bull period in March 1994, through a year-long bear market in 1994 and 1995, the next, very extensive, bull market, to the end of the next corrective wave in July 1999.

Examples from Developed Markets

In the next step, the observations from one of the emerging markets should be confirmed at a few much more developed exchanges. And indeed, in all the following examples the development of the market trend proceeds according to the logarithmic extension.

Figure 10. Logarithmic spiral on the Warsaw Stock Exchange index chart

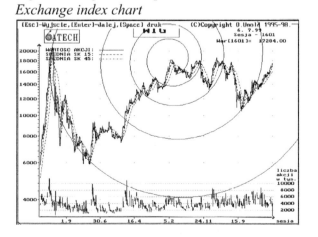

Figure 11. Logarithmic spiral on German DAX

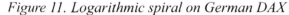
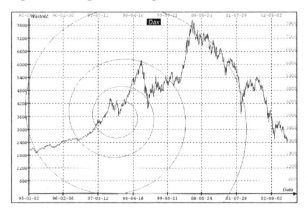

The next figure confirms the logarithmic extension of German DAX index, charted from January 2005 to March 2003 (see Figure 11).

Yet another one reveals a similar pattern at French CAC40, from January 1995 to March 2003 (see Figure 12).

Last but not least, the Hangseng index of the Hong Kong stock exchange, analyzed in the time frame June 1987-April 1999, follows the logarithmic expansion (see Figure 13).

The above examples, taken from a few of the world's best developed markets, confirm the universality of the analyzed mechanisms of collective behavior in complex adaptive systems.

CONCLUSION: INTERPRETATION AND DISCUSSION

The most general conclusion drawn from this chapter is that the same law that shapes the spiraling galaxies mold the spirit and attitudes of men en masse. It shows up so clearly in the market because the stock market is the finest reflector of mass psychology. It is a nearly perfect recording of man's social psychological states and trends, reflecting the fluctuating valuation of his own productive enterprise and making manifest its

very real patterns of progress and regress. What is more, the empirical evidence is available for study and observation. It seems that these parallels are too great to be dismissed. On the balance of probabilities, we may come to the conclusion that there is a principle, everywhere present, giving shape to social affairs. The stock market is no exception, as mass behavior is undeniably linked to a law that can be studied and defined. The briefest way to express this principle is by a simple mathematical statement: the 1.618 ratio.

The logarithmic spiral identified within the analyzed information system is self-similar and isomorphic. It follows that information processes of collectivity also are isomorphic. The identification of isomorphism and self-similarity in the analyzed system is of great importance in the proposed research procedure. The spiral in Figure 3 represents a new, modified form of the attractor presented in Figure 1. This spiral is a metaphorical equivalent of a fractal attractor (strange attractor). This metaphor has deep theoretical grounds, as a logarithmic spiral actually is a fractal.

The identification of a fractal attractor (strange attractor) in a social subsystem of a model global information system carries far-reaching theoretical and methodological consequences. It implies self-similarity and recurrence of system behavior.

Figure 12. Logarithmic spiral on French CAC40

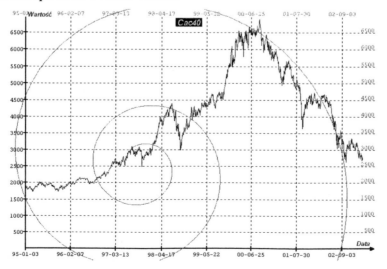

Figure 13. Logarithmic spiral on Hangseng index chart in Hong Kong

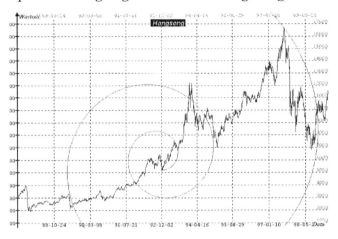

Recurring patterns of behavior in an organization are called organizational culture, and the notion of "organizational culture" is used interchangeably with the concept of "collective mind" (Eden & Spender, 2003). Thus, the identification of a fractal attractor in the analyzed social system suggests, on the grounds of chaos theory, the occurrence of rationality of collective behavior and defines the model representation of the adaptability of collective behavior a spiral movement.

It is worth emphasizing that the concepts of *collective mind* and *organizational intelligence* add a crucial qualitative dimension to information systems analysis. They add the missing internal social dimension to the technical or mechanistic dimension, which is, generally, the focus of the classical theory of systems and organizations.

Another research thread that can be used to theoretically explain the identified phenomena and justify the method applied in this chapter is Heisenberg's uncertainty principle, with the example of the dual nature of electrons, that is, unpredictability of behavior on the individual level versus predictability on the collective level of an "electron cloud" (Heisenberg, 2000). The decision-making process of collectivity within a model global information system is adaptive and follows specific patterns found in nature. Therefore, unlike the decision-making process of an individual, this process can be expressed mathematically and,

under certain conditions, ought to be predictable. In other words, individual behavior, which is often irrational and unpredictable, is expected to compose an adaptive, spiral, and thus, predictable process of collective decision making.

The main potential scientific result of the proposed research approach could be a new formulation of the rationality paradigm. In the era of globalization and virtualization, we shift our interest from traditionally perceived *physical collectivities* to a *dispersed, virtual crowd*, which is a totally new social phenomenon. The observations included in this chapter should allow us to identify the theoretical grounds of a new paradigm, which will refer to the behavior of crowd and the notion of adaptation as a more natural reaction to information stimuli than optimization. Moreover, adaptation would not exclude traditional optimization. Optimization would remain a specific case of adaptation, applicable to strictly deterministic decision situations.

The importance of the adaptation issue has been recognized in organizational sciences for a long time. The organization theorist Barnard held that adaptation was the central problem of organization. Barnard was concerned with cooperative adaptation, hereafter referred to as adaptation (C), which was accomplished in an intentional way. Formal organization, especially hierarchy, was the instrument through which the "conscious, deliberate, purposeful" cooperation was accomplished (Barnard, 1938, p. 4). Barnard's insights have had a lasting effect on organization theory.

A different approach to adaptation was presented by the economist Hayek, who emphasized autonomous adaptation of a spontaneous kind. He maintained that adaptation was the main problem of economic organization, and argued that it was realized spontaneously through the price system. Changes in the demand or supply of a commodity give rise to price changes, whereupon "individual participants . . . [are] able to take the right action" (Hayek, 1945, p. 527). Such price-induced adaptations by individual actors are referred to as adaptations (A), where (A) denotes autonomy. The conclusions of this chapter directly refer to Hayek's notion of adaptation, providing theoretical, methodological, and empirical framework for further research in this area.

This way, the above conclusions could contribute to an increased understanding of mutual interactions between societies and individuals in the era of birth and growth of the Global Information Society. These findings might help examine and structure the unique influence that social processes exert on the decision-making processes of an individual. In this sense, we would be able to speak of *system rationality*, which should not depend on the rationality or irrationality of the system's components.

FUTURE RESEARCH DIRECTIONS

The research method proposed in this chapter is interdisciplinary and intersectorial. It combines the theoretical and methodological principles of Information Systems with the most recent achievements in such new and progressive disciplines as chaos theory and environmental economics. On the level of theory, further research should look for deeper references between the behavior of dispersed collectivities in a model global IS and the principles of chaos theory. The identification of a fractal attractor in a model of collective behavior is just an initial step in this direction. This could

overlap with methodology, when a more sophisticated mathematical apparatus would be used to describe these exciting phenomena.

The next step in the practical verification procedure could include other areas of collective activity. The global IS epitomized in this chapter is a modern, electronic, stock market. However, Fonseca (1989) already proved that a logarithmic expansion regulates the natural development of the urban populations, as well. The next case could analyze, for example, the behavior of social systems in medium and large size companies. The initial challenge here would be to find the proper indicators, which, in the case of a stock market, were the historic value of the index, represented by an index chart, or the volume of trading. Other areas of collective actions could include voting groups, but taken internationally and along a model dividing lines, for example, conservatives versus liberals. This case might be easier to structure, because of the well-known political marketing methods, and a well-developed research regarding the influence of modern IT on human behavior.

A very important research thread is the influence the global IT exerts on human behavior. While individual behavior already is pretty well described in the literature, the collective behavior still is mostly unknown. This issue could be related to the one of social rationality. For years, academics have been trying to formulate a new paradigm of rationality. All of these attempts, however, are highly theoretical and lack any practical verification. The notion of adaptive rationality, introduced in this chapter, could help construct a new approach to rationality, going well beyond the overused notion of bounded rationality, and being supported by a solid practical verification.

REFERENCES

Alingham, M. (2006). *Rational choice theory: Critical concepts in the social sciences*. Oxford, UK: Routledge.

Arrow, K. (1990). Economic theory and the hypothesis of rationality. In J. Eatwell (Ed.), *A dictionary of economics: Utility and probability.* New York: W. W. Norton.

Avison, D., & Fitzgerald, G. (2003). *Information systems development: Methodologies, techniques and tools.* New York: Mc-Graw Hill.

Barnard, C. (1968). *The functions of the executive.* Cambridge, MA: Harvard University Press.

Battram, A., & Battram, A. (2002). *Navigating complexity: The essential guide to complexity theory in business and management.* London: Spiro Press.

Benson, S., & Standing, C. (2002). *Information systems: A business approach.* Sydney, Australia: John Wiley & Sons.

Brand, R. (2006). *Synchronizing science and technology with human behavior: The co-evolution of sustainable infrastructures.* London: Earthscan.

Buckingham, R. A., Hirschheim, R. A., Land, F. F., & Tully, C. J. (1987). *Information systems curriculum: A basis for course design, Information Systems Education: Recommendations and implementation.* Cambridge, UK: Cambridge University Press.

Callan, S. J., & Thomas, J. M. (2006). *Environmental economics and management: Theory, policy and applications.* Cincinnati, OH: South-Western College Publications.

Capra, F. (1984). *The turning point: Science, society, and the rising culture.* New York: Bantam.

Coleman, J. S. (1998). *The foundations of social theory.* Cambridge, MA: Belknap Press.

Cooper, R. (2006). *Organizational identity and self-transformation: An autopoietic perspective.* London: Ashgate Publishing.

Eden, C., & Spender J. C. (2003). *Managerial and organizational cognition: Theory, methods and research.* London: Sage Publications.

Edgeworth, F. (1881/1974). *Mathematical physics.* London: Kegan Paul.

Feudel, U., Kuznetsov, S., & Pikovsky, A. (2006). *Strange nonchaotic attractors: Dynamics between order and chaos in quasiperiodically forced systems.* Hackensack, NJ: World Scientific Publishing Company.

Fisher, R. (2001). *The new Fibonacci trader workbook: Step-by-step exercises to help you master the new Fibonacci trader.* New York: Wiley Trading Series.

Frost, A. J., & Prechter R. (2001). *Elliot wave principle.* New York: John Wiley & Sons.

Halpern, J., & Stern R. (1998). *Debating rationality: Nonrational aspects of organizational decision making.* London: Cornell University Press.

Halpern, J. (1997). The transaction index: A method for standardizing comparison of transaction characteristics across different contexts. *Group Decision and Negotiation, 6,* 557-572.

Hayek, F. (1945). The price system as a mechanism for using knowledge. *American Economic Review 9.*

Heisenberg, W. (2000). *Physics and philosophy* (Penguin Modern Classics). London: Penguin Books Ltd.

Jantsch, E. (1980). *The self-organizing universe.* Oxford, UK: Pergamon Press.

Kahneman, D., & Lovallo, D. (1993). Timid choices and bold forecasts: A cognitive perspective on risk taking. *Management Science, 39,* 17-31.

Kaufmann, S. (1996). *At home in the universe.* Oxford, UK: Oxford University Press.

King, A. C., Billingham, J., & Otto S. R. (2006). *Differential equations: Linear, nonlinear, ordinary, partial.* Cambridge, UK: Cambridge University Press.

Le Bon, G. (2006). *The crowd: A study of the popular mind (1896 reprint).* Whitefish, MT: Kessinger Publishing.

Lichbach, M. I. (2003). *Is rational choice theory all of social science?* Ann Arbor: University of Michigan Press.

March, J. G. (1978). *Bounded rationality, ambiguity, and the engineering of choice.* Bergen, Norway: Universitetsforlaget.

Mele, A. R., & Rawling, P. (2004). *The Oxford handbook of rationality (Oxford Handbooks).* Oxford, UK: Oxford University Press.

Morita, A. (1994). *Made in Japan: Akio Morita and Sony.* London: HarperCollins.

Mumby, D. K., & Putnam, L. L. (1992). The politics of emotion: A feminist reading of bounded rationality. *Academy of Management Review, 17,* 465-486.

National Information Systems Security (INFOSEC) Glossary. (1999). *NSTISSI 4009.* Ft Meade, MD: Author.

Nelson, D. L., & Quick, J. C. (2005). *Study guide for Nelson/Quick's organizational behavior: Foundations, reality and challenges.* Cincinnati, OH: South-Western College Publications.

Nicolis, G., & Prigogine, I. (1977). *Self-organization in nonequilibrium systems: From dissipative structures to order through fluctuations.* New York: John Wiley & Sons.

Pearlson, K. E., & Saunders, C. S. (2004). *Managing and using information systems: A strategic approach.* Hoboken, NJ: John Wiley & Sons,

Plummer, T. (2006). *Forecasting financial markets: The psychology of successful investing.* London: Kogan Page.

Posamentier, A. S., & Lehman, I. (2007). *The fabulous Fibonacci numbers.* Amherst, NY: Prometheus Books.

Pring, M. (1993). *Investment psychology explained.* New York: John Wiley & Sons.

Ramo, J. C. (1999). *The three marketeers.* Time, February 15.

Sato, Y. (2006). *Intentional social change: A rational choice theory: Stratification and inequality.* Rosanna, Australia: Trans Pacific Press.

Shapira, Z. (2002). *Organizational decision making.* Cambridge, UK: Cambridge University Press.

Shi, Y. (2002). *The economics of scientific knowledge: A rational choice institutionalist theory of science.* Northampton, MA: Edward Elgar Publishing.

Simon, H. (1955). A behavioral model of rational choice. *Quarterly Journal of Economics, 69,* 99-118.

Thompson, V. (1976). *Bureaucracy and the modern world.* Morristown, NJ: General Learning Press.

Turban, E., Rainer, R. K. Jr., & Potter, R. E. (2005). *Introduction to information technology.* New York: John Wiley & Sons.

Turniansky, B., & Hare, A. P. (1998). *Individuals and groups in organizations.* London: Sage Publications Ltd.

Von Neumann, J., & Morgenstern, O. (1944). *Theory of games and economics behavior.* Princeton, NJ: Princeton University Press.

Ward, J., & Peppard, J. (2002). *Strategic planning for information systems.* Etobicoke, Canada: John Wiley & Sons.

Webster's Encyclopedic Unabridged Dictionary (deluxe ed.). (2005). London: Random House.

Weick, K. E. (2000). *Making sense of the organization.* New York: Blackwell Publications.

Wheatley, M. (2005). *Finding our way: Leadership for an uncertain time.* San Francisco: Berrett-Koehler.

ADDITIONAL READING

Arnold, V. I. (2004). *Catastrophe theory, Chapter 1: Singularities, bifurcations, and catastrophes.* Springer.

Becker J., & Niehaves, B. (2007). Epistemological perspectives on IS research: A framework for analysing and systematizing epistemological assumptions. In D. Avison & G. Fitzgerald (Eds.), *Information Systems Journal, 17*(2), 197-214.

Chudoba, K. M., Wynn, E., Lu, M., & Watson-Manheim, M. B. (2005) How virtual are we? Measuring virtuality and understanding its impact in a global organization. In D. Avison & G. Fitzgerald (Eds.), *Information Systems Journal, 15*(4), 279-306.

Cilliers, P. (2005). *Complexity and postmodernism: Understanding complex systems, Chapter 6: Self organization in complex systems and Chapter 7: Complexity and postmodernism.* Routledge.

Davidson, D. (2004). *Problems of Rationality.* Oxford University Press.

Fonseca, J. W. (1989). *Urban rank size hierarchy: A mathematical interpretation.* In Institute of Mathematical Geography, Ohio University. Retrieved April 21, 2007 from http://www.zanesville.ohiou.edu/geography/urbanrank/index.htm

Foss, N.J. (2003). Bounded rationality and tacit knowledge in the organizational capabilities approach: an assessment and a re-evaluation. In J. Chytry (Ed.), *Industrial and Corporate Change (Oxford Journals), 12*(2), 185-201.

From ICT Research to Innovation. In Europe's information society thematic portal. Retrieved April 21, 2007, from http://ec.europa.eu/information_society/research/innov/index_en.htm

Grossman, S. J., & Stiglitz, J.E. (1980). On the impossibility of informationally efficient markets. In *The American Economic Review, 70*, 393-408.

Hanna, R. (2006). *Rationality and Logic, Chapter 5: The psychology of reasoning.* The MIT Press.

Hui, P.M., Kwong Y. R., Cheung P., & Johnson, N.F. (1999). In P.M. Todd (Ed.), *Global Behavior in a Population of Adaptive Competitive Agents. Vol 7*, Iss. 3/4.

Information and Communication Technologies (ICTs). *In: Research: 7ᵗʰ framework programme.* Retrieved April 21, 2007, from http://ec.europa.eu/research/fp7/index_en.cfm?pg=info

Kirkpatrick, C. D., & Dahlquist, J. R. (2006). *Technical analysis: The complete resource for financial market technicians.* FT Press.

Lee, M. E. (2005). From enlightenment to chaos: Toward nonmodern social theory. In R. Eve (Ed.), *Chaos, complexity, and sociology: Myths, models, and theories.* Sage Publications.

Logarithmic Spirals (see the links). Retrieved April 21, 2007, from http://www.notam02.no/~oyvindha/loga.html

Lovett, F. (2006). Rational choice theory and explanation. In D. D. Heckathorn (Ed.), *Rationality and Society, 18*, 237-272.

Lucas, C. (2007). *Complex adaptive systems—Webs of delight.* In The complexity & artificial life research concept for self-organizing systems. Retrieved April 21, 2007, from http://www.calresco.org/lucas/cas.htm

Mastering ICTs to Promote Innovation. In: *Europe's information society thematic portal.* Retrieved April 21, 2007, from http://ec.europa.eu/information_society/research/index_en.htm

Medina, L. F. (2005). The comparative statics of collective action: A pragmatic approach to games with multiple. In D.D. Heckathorn (Ed.), *Rationality and Society, 17*, 423-452.

Ogata, K. (2003). *System dynamics.* Prentice Hall.

Palmer, K. D. (2007). Self-adaptation, self-organization and special systems theory. In K. Palmer (Ed.), *Journal of Autopoietic Theory.* Retrieved April 21, 2007 from http://autopoietic.net/

Parisi, D. (2006). Complexity and cognition. In A. Carseti (Ed.), *Functional models of cognition: Self-organizing dynamics and semantic structures in cognitive systems.* Springer.

Peitgen, H. O., Jurgens, H., & Saupe, J. (2004). *Chaos and Fractals, Chapter 6: The chaos game: how randomness creates deterministic shapes.* Springer.

Rich, E. A. (2007). *Automata, computability and complexity: Theory and applications.* Prentice Hall.

Searle, J. R. (2003). *Rationality in action (Jean Nicod Lectures), Chapter 1: The classical model of rationality and its weaknesses.* The MIT Press.

Smith, L. (2007). *Chaos: A very short introduction.* Oxford University Press.

Smith, T. S. (2005). Nonlinear dynamics and the micro-macro bridge. In R. Eve (Ed.), Chaos, *complexity, and sociology: Myths, models, and theories.* Sage Publications.

Technical Analysis, In Investopedia. Retrieved April 21, 2007, from http://www.investopedia.com/terms/t/technicalanalysis.asp

The Global Information Society Project. Retrieved April 21, 2007, from http://global-info-society.org/

Trippi, R. L. (1994). *Chaos theory in the financial markets.* McGraw-Hill.

Truex, D., Holmstrom, J., & Keil, M. (2006). Theorizing in information systems research: A reflexive analysis of the adaptation of theory in information systems research. In K. Lyytien (Ed.), *Journal of the Association for Information Systems, 7*(12).

Vives, X (1995). The speed of information revelation in a financial market. In A. Lizzeri & K. Shell (Eds.), *Journal of Economic Theory, 67,* 178-204.

What Is Global Information Technology? In: *IS-World Net.* Retrieved April 21, 2007, from http://www.american.edu/MOGIT/git/define.htm

Chapter XII
Group Decision Making in Computer–Mediated Communication as Networked Communication:
Understanding the Technology and Implications

Bolanle A. Olaniran
Texas Tech University, USA

ABSTRACT

Networked communication is proliferating our world. The fact that global information communication technologies (ICTs) are becoming increasingly available is facilitating human computer interaction, which permeates the use of computer-mediated communication (CMC) in various organizations, groups, and interpersonal contexts. As a result, the issue facing today's organizations is not whether to use global information technologies (GITs) in networked communication, but rather how to use them for effective functioning and as efficient coordination tool; especially how to incorporate GITs into the decision-making process. Consequently, this chapter examines the issues in designing CMC into group interactions and decision-making processes.

INTRODUCTION

The shift toward globalization in organizations necessitates increase reliance on information communication technologies (ICTs). However, the nature of ICTs required is not the stand alone, but rather networked ICTs. The growth in networked ICTs such as e-mail, computer conferencing, desktop conferencing, and videoconferencing emanates from the need for speed in decision making and the general ability to coordinate activities of geographically dispersed workers, or to facilitate learning beyond certain geographical boundaries. The networked communication process and the accompanying decision-making processes are made possible by the Internet.

BACKGROUND

Many organizations and business executives continue to realize the role of employee participation in the decision-making process and organizational productivity for survival. Thus, organizations continue to develop ways to actively engage their members in teams either in co-located or distributed virtual groups. Networked global information technologies (GITs) especially benefits geographically dispersed groups to engage in decision-making process virtually. However, the literature addressing GITs and computer-mediated communication (CMC) focus on comparative features of the technologies over face-to-face (FtF) or traditional communication media instead of looking at the decision-making process occurring over these media as instances of networked communication. There is a potential benefit in examining decision making as networked communication. This approach allows one to ask questions about what technology to use, or why use a particular technology, and when to use a given communication technology? Therefore, the goal of this chapter is to offer insights about the decision-making process in ICTs by looking at some key factors that must be addressed, while offering some recommendations regarding the effective decision-making process when using GITs. First, however, the next section identifies and discusses factors in networked communication decision making as a way to address issues and problems in the networked communication.

ISSUES, CONTROVERSIES, AND PROBLEMS

Although the group decision-making process is made possible in networked communication, the tendency to succeed or fail hinges on attention to some key issues. For instance, there is a greater need to adapt communication technology and communicative behaviors to accommodate the decision-making process across different geographical boundaries and social contexts (Olaniran, 2004). The decision-making process where group members are located across different geographical boundaries and time zones necessitates the need to attend to culture. Attending to different cultural needs is not only necessary, but also is increasingly essential for an effective decision-making process to occur. It has been suggested, that success in organizations at large has less to do with market forces than it does with the cultures and the values existing within cultures (Alas & Vadi, 2003; Cameron & Quinn, 1999). There are specific instances of the culture factor in networked communication and the decision-making process. A case study identified that the East Asian culture and its social structure showed cultural differences through the suppression of e-mail use when subordinates are interacting with superiors. More specifically, subordinates are reported to refrain from the use of e-mail in communicating with supervisors in a team process (Lee, 2002). Consequently, the East Asian culture exhibits different tendencies from the Western culture when it comes to accounting for power structure. Western culture, however, does not see anything wrong in subordinates' usage of e-mail with superiors. This is not an isolated incident, as a similar difference was found with the Dutch who showed greater preferences for a more structured decision-making process than their American counterparts (Kiser, 1999; Gezo, Oliverson, & Zick, 2000).

Attention to the issue of culture is important in networked communication for two reasons. One, culture preferences may affect the choice of GIT or communication medium for interaction. Two, the need to realize that technology (i.e., networked ICTs) may not necessarily overcome some deeply held traditional beliefs that underlie how individuals communicate.

Culture is also important in networked communication because it interferes with interactions of groups in organizational decision-making processes. For instance, people in co-located groups have greater access to multiple communication media and, thus, have the benefit of using multiple channels, which in turn permits a broader range of messages, cues, and feedback immediacy (Olaniran, 2004). This is not the case in networked group decision-making processes. Even when individuals have access to other communication media, their usage may be impossible due to geographical distance, and thus, clarification that facilitates message comprehension may be hindered with delayed feedback (Olaniran, 1995). For example, Armstrong and Cole (2002) found that remote sites in virtual teams often fell off radar screens and usually were ignored during telephone and videoconferences. In addition, in videoconferencing, unless the system has cascading capacity, the most visible locations participants are able to see are restricted to two (i.e., picture in picture). Furthermore, time zone differences also create some sense of psychological distance along with the problem of finding a time that works for all group members.

Similarly, the temporary nature and short history of many geographically dispersed teams has become the center of attention in development and sustenance of the relationship among members in CMC decision-making groups (Poole & DeSanctis, 1992). For example, consensus building is one such area in decision making. It is argued, that when mediated group members in dispersed groups have limited time, they often fail to seek adequate social and contextual information to support their attributions (Crampton, 2002; Olaniran, 1994; Walther, 2002). This may result in dire consequences for participants in maintaining relationships or developing cohesion in dispersed CMC groups. Without a shared frame of reference that is developed through frequent and previous interactions, participants encounter problems in decision-making groups. Accuracy in interpreting group members' messages becomes difficult (Olaniran, 2004). The problem is expected to occur in unitary organizations operating under the same cultural norms, while it is expected to be height-

ened or exacerbated in distributed networks and in organizations that are geographically dispersed (Kelly & Jones, 2001; Olaniran, 2004).

It is important to examine some of the reasons why decision making over GITs is attractive to organizations that are committed to it and why others are clamoring to explore it. The next section looks at the key benefits of computer-mediated communication and other GITs.

Some Key Benefits of CMC

Freedom to Participate

CMC has been touted as the means to bring about freedom of participation and increased interaction in groups (McComb, 1994; Olaniran, Stalcup, & Jensen, 2000). CMC discussions offer greater freedom and opportunities to participate than face-to-face (FtF) meetings (Phillips & Santoro, 1989; Olaniran, 2004). In general, the greater participation in CMC (e.g., e-mail or computer conferencing) is attributed to the concurrency of the communication medium. Concurrency is the ability of a communication medium to allow different individuals to simultaneously contribute to the decision process in network communication (Valacich, Paranka, George, & Nunamaker, 1993). In other words, group participants do not have to wait until a group member completes a thought or yields the floor before they can add their comments. Thus, participants can input their comments at the same time without interfering with other members' messages especially in synchronous interaction. In an asynchronous interaction, the technology still allows members to participate in the decision process at their convenience by allowing individuals to work around different schedules and time zone differences. This is not the case with FtF. Participation in the decision process through FtF occurs with the requirement that all group members be in attendance to contribute their ideas. Also, FtF interaction requires members to take turns in order to have meaningful interactions.

Equalized/Democratic Participation

Another benefit of the freedom to participate or increased participation enhanced by CMC is the possible equalized or democratic participation. Some scholars have argued that CMC increases the democratic decision-making process (Dubrovsky, Kiesler, & Sethna, 1991; Phillips & Santoro, 1989). This is the area where characteristics and features (tools) designed into different GITs come into play. For instance, certain decision-making tools, such as voting and analyses tools, are offered in some decision support systems that allow groups to reach consensus on decisions (Poole & DeSanctis, 1992). In addition, videoconferencing, through the ability to see co-communicators improves participation and interpersonal interaction as a whole (Badenhorst & Axmann, 2002). However, one must not forget the fact that it is the choices that people make about GIT features regarding their appropriation or use that will determine the final outcomes such as facilitating democratic decision-making process or equalized participation. For example, Poole and DeSanctis (1992) found that the choices people make in using CMC systems often counter the intent of the system designer. In other words, CMC features are designed to accomplish the spirit, which is a particular purpose, but those features, are applied in unintended ways. More specifically, groups appropriate systems from, not only the structural features of the technology but also from other relevant institutions, such as the environment and from group characteristics (Poole & DeSanctis, 1992). Furthermore, user knowledge affects the way tasks are approached in CMC. For example, it has been shown that inexperienced users are more interested in task accomplishment, while more experienced users are interested in efficient application of ICTs (Trumbly, Arnett, & Johnson, 1994). The former stressed learning the minimum requirements for task performance, while the latter put greater emphasis on comprehension of technological features. Consequently, the resulting outcomes in one group over another may vary to a certain degree. The next section will address conditions for which to use ICTs and how to use them successfully.

SOLUTIONS AND RECOMMENDATIONS

Given some of the possible contextual variations in decision making and communication outcomes in networked communication, it is useful to address conditions when certain GITs can be used to foster effectiveness and efficiency. First, effectiveness, in a general sense refers to the idea of process or usage leading to accomplishment of group goals. Second, effectiveness, in a specific sense, refers to the opportunity that GIT offers to improve what is possible under the traditional method (e.g., FtF). Efficiency, on the other hand, focuses on factors such as the speed or cost at which access to information is attainable. Therefore, deciding what technology to use and when to use it is possible by focusing on these two factors.

In light of contextual variations in technology use, there are certain conditions under which equality may result from CMC interactions. For instance, it should be noted that anonymity usually neutralizes any status effect and, thus, allows participants to contribute freely to discussion. Individual identity is protected, and participants do not have to worry about how their messages will be received (i.e., evaluative apprehension) by other participants (Olaniran, 1994). However, the challenge with anonymity is that even when organizations attempt to safeguard members' anonymity in the decision-making process within CMC, users still may be apprehensive about their contributions. Furthermore, while anonymity is available under experimental conditions, most organizational use of CMC is devoid of anonymity. Yet, a certain degree of equal participation still may be achieved in such settings. For instance, when the communication setting surrounding the problem solving and decision making is informal (e.g., when participants, organizational, and group members are on a first-name basis), interactions that overlook status are possible, enhancing freedom to voice opinions and increase the level of attention paid to opinions and suggestions. In other words, organizations should pay attention to developing open communication climates that would carry over into interaction over technology communication networks.

The need to facilitate an open communication climate and increase participation in group interactions also involves attention to the social norms that guide communication, the structure, and rules, or organizational cultures that guide acceptable communicative behaviors. This argument is in line with the finding that when GIT is used in conditions where group norms are salient, members tend to exhibit behaviors that conform to accepted group norms (Lea & Spears, 1992). Thus, it is necessary to note how social contexts like rules and norms may take precedence over medium effects.

Furthermore, unlike dyadic relationships, group interaction focuses attention away from independent users (i.e., sender and receiver of messages) toward interdependent relationships. Therefore, if a group member selectively discards someone's message in CMC, others can re-introduce the message during the discussion. This is something that might be too threatening in FtF, especially when the decision process involves interaction between high- and low-status individuals. In essence, CMC has the capacity to mask cues attributable to power and status differences, and therefore, increases the freedom to exchange information (Siegel, Dubrovsky, Kiesler, & McGuire, 1986).

Consequently, CMC holds an advantage over traditional FtF interaction in reducing negative impacts of selective message processing or redistributing power among group members. This argument is consistent with the network paradigm presented by Rice (1990), which emphasizes principles of convergence, where attention is redirected from individuals as independent senders and receivers to one where an individual is an actor in a network characterized by interdependent relationships in social settings. To this end, Kelly and Jones (2001) contend that managers and organizational decision makers pay as much attention to the underlying development and the social communication structure as they do to GIT infrastructure.

The role that social cues play in decision making and communication interaction needs to be addressed. The degree with which GITs allow social cues in interaction differs depending on the type. A general criticism of text-based GIT is that it is lacking in nonverbal cues. For instance, research on relational communication argues that nonverbal codes are relationally warm and fulfilling while arguing that verbal codes are best at satisfying the content or task function (Walther, 2002). Notwithstanding, the lack of nonverbal cues in certain technologies, GITs, have been shown to encourage participation by masking status effect that is likely in FtF discussion. Furthermore, the lack of nonverbal cues in CMC does not equate an absence of social cues from the communication process. For example, different forms of social cues have been found in CMC: Paralinguistic cues that involve textual manipulation to add context and considerable socio-emotional content to messages (Lea & Spears, 1992; Rice & Love, 1987). Others consist of lexical surrogates and icons used to produce codes or symbols that convey expressions similar to nonverbal facial expressions such as the smiley. More recent examples include sophisticated emotions with audio capability like the ones employed in the Yahoo instant messengers and other computer conferencing. Furthermore, paralinguistic codes such as capitalization, parenthetical notes, and exclamation marks are used to express emotion and meaning (Lea & Spears, 1992).

There also is empirical evidence that confirms text-based CMC groups demonstrate socio-emotional tone from the moment of initial interaction (Walther, 1997). At the same time, advances in computing capability, graphical emoticons are improving how social information is conveyed in CMC.

Making Networked Communication Work

The choice and selection of GITs must be based on the overarching goal of the group. The two-stage model of the group decision-making process may be used to offer some guide (Olaniran, 1994, 2004). The two-stage model consists of the idea generation and idea evaluation. The idea generation stage involves groups attempt to analyze problem, determine goals, and generate possible solutions for a given task. The idea evaluation, on the other hand, focuses on developing criteria for evaluating possible solutions, and discussions of implications of possible decisions and the eventual consensus on selection of solution to the task.

The need for member creativity is particularly important during the idea generation stage of the decision-making process. In order to accommodate creativity, interaction procedures that maximize participants' participation as alluded to earlier are important (Olaniran, 1994, 1995). Consequently, GITs that nurture individual creativity while reducing evaluation apprehension would be the most productive. It would appear that any GIT would do, provided the organizational culture and interaction norms stress informality. However, when, this is not the case, organizations and groups should strive to use text-based CMC with special attention to protect participants' anonymity. In this case, networked communication that utilizes central bulletin board or discussion list where ideas are less likely to be traced back to individual contributors. This way, group members are able to participate without fear of reprisals. Furthermore, they will not be participating as in FtF where nonverbal cues can negatively influence group member's level of participation. Specifically, Olaniran (1994) found that anonymous CMC groups generated more than three times as many ideas as FtF groups and almost two times as many ideas than other CMC groups when group members do not have to worry about their identity being revealed.

The decision to select either synchronous or asynchronous CMC should be determined by the amount of lead time a group has to complete the task, as it would seem to have no effect on the idea generation stage. However, the need to offer anonymous participation holds certain implications for the degree to which e-mail, intra-organizational instant messengers, teleconferencing and video-conferencing can be used in the idea generation stage of the decision model. These communication media clearly reveal the user's identity in networked

communication. The way around this problem, it seems, is to have in place organizational and group climate that stresses informal structure.

The *idea evaluation stage*, contrary to the *idea generation stage*, focuses on the role of critical thinking in the process of enhancing decision quality. Thus, the need for group members to freely discuss the pros and cons of each possible solution is crucial. At the same time, the need to develop social interaction and bond (i.e., cohesion) with other group members is important and best nurtured during the idea evaluation stage.

Therefore, communication media that can facilitate critical analyses of ideas while helping in addressing relational and social needs of group members are needed during idea evaluation stage. The development of a lasting relationship while reaching high quality decision making is best accomplished in a group when the social structure such as breaking down cultural barriers, removal of perceived distance, and utilization of GIT media that can appeal to different senses are in place. For example, Waldir Arevoedo (a research analyst at Gartner Inc.) argues that the more CMC interactions involve multiple media that can support cues such as voice, text, and audio, the more the barriers of time, distance, and culture can be overcome (Solomon, 2001). Therefore, ICTs such as videoconferencing and audio teleconferencing offer the most cues for accomplishing relational goals in the decision-making process and networked communication.

An alternative, is to provide multiple communication media or ICTs that allows participants to take control of how they chose to participate in the decision-making process. Thus, when group members need social relations they can select the medium that best accomplishes the desired goal. However, at times, these communication media are not accessible (Olaniran, 2004). When access to multiple communication media, or those providing nonverbal cues, are not the case, attempts must be made to manipulate text-based CMC to meet the need of group members. One method offered for developing social relations is to allow members to work in ongoing groups where group members are able to continue to negotiate and renegotiate their relationships over different tasks (Olaniran, 2004). This suggestion may also help foster critical thinking needed in idea evaluation of the decision making by allowing members to refrain from free riding or lurking activity.

As in the idea generation stage, the decision to use synchronous or asynchronous networked communication should depend on the amount of time a group has. Notwithstanding, synchronous networked communication fosters increased immediacy and feedback, such that clarification of ideas and answers to group member concerns are instantaneous. Similarly, synchronous networked communication allows the decision-making process to flow more smoothly than in asynchronous interactions. On the other hand, idea evaluation in asynchronous networked communication offers group members more time to reflect over ideas before composing a response.

FUTURE TRENDS

One of the major hindrances to adoption and usage of global information systems in organizations' decision-making processes around the globe, involves the propensity to transfer and use communication technology. The propensity to transfer and use communication technology involves the degree to which global and multinational corporations are willing to allow their technologies to become accessible to their joint venture partners in another country or world region. The problem with propensity to transfer and use technologies has even far greater consequences for the less economically developed countries (LEDCs) where infrastructure and cultural values are different. In essence, the propensity to use global information systems begins with access to technology and the willingness to use it. For the most part, the lack of adequate access to certain global information systems, creates a digital divide between individuals from economically developed and those from the less economically developed countries.

Bozeman (2000) argues that technology transfer is based on cost and benefits, and usually the transfer

exists only when benefits outweigh the cost. This is significant in the race to use GIT and in bridging the digital divide between economically developed countries (EDCs) and LEDCs. Major information technology advances occur in developed countries, to the detriment of LEDCs, such that affordability becomes a critical issue. Along the same line of reasoning, Ya'u (2004) argues that LEDCs are primarily consumers of global information systems and technologies. As consumers of GITs, LEDCs face knowledge deficiency that also could affect creative use of technologies. Furthermore, there is different motivation regarding the propensity to transfer technologies. While the United Nation's Commission on Science and Technology for Development wants to use ICT to bridge the digital divide by creating human development initiatives in LEDCs, World Trade Organizations (WTO) and traditional organizations are in it for profit motives in what has been described as another attempt to re-colonize LEDCs in the new global order (Ya'u, 2004). Consequently, the motivation to transfer technologies is not aimed at bridging the digital divide, but, instead, it is driven by conglomerates' needs to access other markets in response to their home markets, which are increasingly inadequate for sustaining required corporate growth due to saturation of the developed countries' markets (Ya'u, 2004).

Furthermore, Ishemo (2004) claims that new information and communication technologies are invented in the framework of capitalism development. Consequently, foreign direct investment and critical technology transfer goes to profitable markets rather than markets where there is the need to promote universal access by subsidizing access to global information systems These strategies perpetuate the divide rather than actually bridging it. For instance, it was found that international firm, large host country, and recently established affiliates correlate highly with technology transfer. Grosse (1996) stresses the profit motive behind technology transfer when indicating that technology transfer is greater when the cost of carrying out the transfer is low and when the resulting benefits of technology transfer were higher. Similarly, host countries' local government regulations that govern partnerships and joint venture programs and political instability in LEDCs creates additional risks for technology transfer, which some companies are not willing take. Organizations fear that, unless the revenue potential is substantial in a given market, their investment in the country may be short-lived.

At the same time, when technology is available, the propensity or motivation to use it is an internal one. There has to be a willingness or motivation on the part of potential users to want to try or use them (Storck & Hill, 2000). The motivation to use a particular technology is linked to the cultural norms in place. Some cultures resist technology or adopt technology only as long as it does not conflict with their cultural norms (e.g., Heaton, 2001). The example of Cuba's application of the Internet illustrates this point. Also, older generations have the tendency to resist new technology because of complacency with old ways of doing things (Wheeler, 2001). At a specific level of culture is the issue of language, where over 87% of Internet content is in English (Wilborn, 1999; Van Dam & Rogers, 2003). Non-English-speaking individuals may feel that technology has nothing to offer them. It stands to reason that people in poor nations or rural communities would be motivated to learn and use technology when it helps them access information tailored to their specific needs (see Sassi, 2005).

Certainly, realization of benefits offered by any global information system, depends on the ability of the users to explore and experience proposed benefits on their own. Forced usage would result in resistance and rejection of the technology as a whole and, more specifically, it would create failure to achieve successful incorporation into the decision-making process.

Implications and Recommendations

The driving factor in decision-making processes (networked or otherwise) is the need to attain a level of trust that is essential for group members to reach consensus and effectively make a decision. Schein (1992) argues that decision makers must value and develop relationships that would facilitate joint problem solving and solution implementation. The goal in decision-making groups is to foster adaptability, creativity, and flexibility in group interactions, which have direct impact on organization learning. In connection with learning, it has been suggested that a focused task-oriented culture is crucial to cope with the external environment, while a relational-oriented culture is crucial for accomplishing internal integration (Alas & Vadi, 2003). However, developing organizational learning also demands the ability to work together as teams (Alas & Vadi, 2003; Senge, 1997). Thus, a sense of common identity is developed when each group member serves as reference point for one another. Group participants' dependence on one another for socio-emotional, as well as task support, enhances relational development that indirectly influences commitment and overcomes barriers to learning.

The information provided in this chapter suggests that the issue facing modern organizations is not whether to use ICT or CMC in the decision-making process. Rather, the challenge is how to adapt communication technology in group collaboration and the decision-making process effectively and in a way that fosters task and relational goals respectively. In order to accomplish such a complex task, attention must be paid to certain environmental factors. First, organizations embarking on implementing networked communication in its group decision-making process would need to realize that there are social obstacles that technology or CMC is unable to overcome. For instance, technology can be used to facilitate relationships within organizations provided individuals seek out such relations. Otherwise, technology in and of itself would not create trust, creativity, and adaptability needed for success in group decision-making processes. Second, the decision to use GIT in a group process need not be based on the idea of "everyone is using it," rather, it must be evaluated based on the fact that its deployment will help accomplish goals that are central to organizations' core practices. Third, the social context in which GITs are being deployed is just as important as the task for which they are deployed to accomplish. Differences in outcomes from research in GIT and group decision processes are significantly influenced by how individuals adapt technology, which is often different than GIT designers' intent.

Organizations' need to recognize that GIT and other groupware provides a part of the overall communication environment (Kelly & Jones, 2001). It is important to understand that GIT and other decision support are available to supplement face-to-face and other traditional media and not replace them. It is also recommended that software designers need to help organizations overcome some of the challenges in GIT. One is the issue of bandwidth, which prevents against implementing more sophisticated GIT applications, such as those allowing audio and video channel cues, the likes of computer videoconferencing and IPTV. Along the same line, designers need to create third-party software that offers multiple cues that are easy to deploy in the context of group decision making, and are easy to access across the globe.

Networked communication media designers are encouraged to keep in mind criteria involved in the decision-making process by paying attention to the stages, goals, and social needs of organizations and users. One way to bring this about is to create GIT architecture in a way that adheres to the "analytic hierarchy process" (AHP) of decision making at the minimum. The AHP involves decision-making communication protocols that conform to real-world problems (Ghinea, Magoulas, & Siamitros, 2005; Saaty, 1980). The AHP approach is similar to the two-stage model of decision making by emphasizing that a networked communication media allows users to be able to generate sets of alternatives, prioritize those alternatives, address issues of resource allocations, and predict possible outcomes while resolving conflicts. The capacity to address subjective criteria in the decision-making process also is considered as paramount in any systems design. The AHP should be taken as minimum criteria upon which other features can be incorporated into GITs.

Along the same line, Olaniran (2004) recommends a combined media in virtual or networked

groups. He suggests that the combination of both FtF and CMC media in decision making offers an approach that gradually introduces group members to GITs and also creates an approach where GIT users do not feel like they are completely giving up face-to-face interaction for electronically mediated communication. Finally, the need to address the needs of GIT users is important to the decision-making process as much as the decision outcomes from the use of these technologies.

FUTURE RESEARCH DIRECTION

Future research on global information technology (GIT) must begin to explore communication technologies not as "either or" when compared with traditional FtF medium. Rather the unique characteristics of each communication technologies should be assessed and then effort should be made to identify how these characteristics can complement established and effective communication interaction and decision-making processes. Furthermore, it is essential that new research focuses on cultural implications of communication technologies. For instance, questions such as: How different communication technologies reinforce or disrupt clearly established cultural patterns of communication across the globe? What effects do dimensions of cultural variability have on organizations' struggles with communication media selection and usage? These questions are essential in the globalization age where product and service standardization along with market differentiation (i.e., globalization) is the norm.

Along a similar trail of thought is the need for researchers to explore how best to use new and modern CITs to reinforce existing organization culture. It has been found that CITs do not excel when used to change organizational cultures, but instead, they help promote existing cultural norms (e.g., Canessa & Riolo, 2006).

Future research also needs to focus on the use of certain CITs (e.g., videoconferencing and synchronous CMCs). While these CITs are purported to add immediacy and in a videoconferencing case, geographical distances in terms of different international datelines may render them useless. Similarly, it would help to examine the impacts of these synchronous CITs on actual member participation in the decision-making process and as communication media of choice by organizational members. The issue of anonymity or perception of anonymity makes using asynchronous CITs attractive to people for participation in the decision-making process. Thus, there is the need for future research to explore implications of synchronous interactions over CITs when anonymity is removed especially within different cultures.

Taken together, addressing these areas would add significant information to the body of literature in GIT. At the same time, it will help researchers on theory development. As for organizations and their members, the information would be invaluable in identifying what works and how to effectively incorporate CITs into the decision-making process.

CONCLUSION

Finally it is essential that as executives in their respective organizations attempt to deploy or incorporate GITs into their decision-making processes, it would help for them to pay attention to how users in different cultures react to these technologies. Additional impetus could come from researchers who would be able to evaluate meaningfully the role of different cultures in GIT deployment. For instance, while the idea of democratic participation and freedom to contribute in the decision-making process is welcome in the Western culture; would individuals in power distant culture (where status is cherished as the cultural norm) welcome this approach? In other words, there are several cultural factors, including the exercise of power, in terms of who has it, and how they guard it, that may hinder effective implementation of global information technologies in decision-making processes that are beyond the scope of this chapter. However, this chapter offers a potentially successful platform for executives to adapt and modify as situations demand.

REFERENCES

Alas, R., & Vadi, M. (2003). The impact of organizational culture on organizational learning at six Estonian hospitals. *Trames, 7*(2), 83-98.

Armstrong, D. J., & Cole, P. (2002). Managing distances and differences in geographically distributed work groups. In P. Hinds & S. Kiesler (Eds.), *Distributed work* (pp. 167- 186).

Badenhorst, Z., & Axmann, M. (2002). The educational use of videoconferencing in the arts faculty: Shedding a new light on puppetry. *British Journal of Educational Technology, 33*(3), 291-299.

Bozeman, B. (2000). Technology transfer and public policy: A review of research and theory, *Research Policy, 29*, 627-655.

Cameron, K. S., & Quinn, R. E. (1999). *Diagnosing and changing organizational culture based on the competing values framework.* Boston: Addison-Wesley.

Canessa. E., & Riolo, R. L. (2006). An agent-based model of the impact of computer-mediated communication on organizational culture and performance: An example of the application of complex systems analysis tools to the study of CIS. *Journal of Information Technology, 21*, 272-283.

Crampton, C. D. (2002). Attribution in distributed work groups. In P. Hinds & S. Kiesler (Eds.), Distributed work (pp. 191-212).

Dubrovsky, V. J., Kiesler, S., & Sethna, B. N. (1991). The equalization phenomenon: Status effect in computer-mediated communication and face-to-face decision making groups. *Human-Computer Interaction, 6*, 119-146.

Ghinea, G., Magoulas, D., & Siamitros, C. (2005). Multicriteria decision making for enhanced perception-based multicriteria communication. *IEEE Transactions on Systems, Man and Cybernetics-Part A: Systems and Humans, 35*(6), 855-866.

Gezo, T., Oliverson, M., & Zick, M. (2000). Managing global projects with virtual teams. *Hydrocarbon Processing, 79*, 112c-112i.

Grosse, R. (1996). International technology transfer in services. *Journal of International Business Studies, 27*(4), 781-800.

Heaton, L. (2001). Preserving communication context: Virtual workspace and interpersonal space in Japanese CSCW. In C. Ess & F. Sudweeks (Eds.), *Cultural attitudes towards communication and technology* (pp. 163-186). Australia: University of Sydney.

Ishemo, S. L. (2004). Culture and historical knowledge in Africa: A Cabralian approach. *Review of African Political Economy, 31*(99), 65-82.

Kelly, S., & Jones, M. (2001). Groupware and the social infrastructure of communication. *Communication of the ACM, 44*(12), 77- 80.

Kiser, K. (1999, March). *Working on world time. Training, 36*(3), 28-34.

Lea, M., & Spears, R. (1992). Paralanguage and social perception in computer-mediated communication. *Journal of Organizational Computing, 2,* 321-341.

Lee, O. (2002). Cultural differences in email use of virtual teams a critical social theory perspective. *Cyberpsychology & Behavior, 5*(3), 227-232.

McComb, M. (1994). Benefits of computer-mediated communication in college courses. *Communication Education, 43,* 159-170.

Olaniran, B. A. (2004). Computer-mediated communication in cross-cultural virtual groups. In G.M. Chen & W.J. Starosta (Eds.), *Dialogue among diversities* (pp. 142-166). Washington, DC: National Communication Association.

Olaniran, B. A. (1994). Group performance in computer-mediated and face-to-face communication media. *Management Communication Quarterly, 7,* 256-281.

Olaniran, B. A. (1995). Perceived communication outcomes in computer-mediated communication: An analysis of three systems among new users. *Information Processing & Management, 31,* 525-541.

Olaniran, B. A., Stalcup, K., & Jensen, K. (2000). Incorporating computer-mediated technology to strategically serve pedagogy. *Communication Teacher, 15,* 1-4.

Phillips, G. M., & Santoro, G. M. (1989). Teaching group discussion via computer-mediated communication. *Communication Education, 38,* 151-161.

Poole, M.S., & DeSanctis, G. (1992). Microlevel structuration in computer-supported group decision making. *Human Communication Research, 19,* 5-49.

Rice, R. E. (1990). Computer-mediated communication system network data: Theoretical concerns and empirical examples. *International Journal of Man-Machine Studies, 32,* 627-647.

Rice, R. E., & Love, G. (1987). Electronic emotion: Socioemotional content in a computer-mediated network. *Communication Research, 14,* 85-108.

Saaty, T. L. (1980). Analytic hierarchy process. New York: McGraw Hill.

Sassi, S. (2005). Cultural differentiation or social segregation? Four approaches to the digital divide. *New Media & Society, 7*(5), 684-700.

Schein, E. (1992). *Organizational culture and leadership.* New York: Jossey Bass.

Senge, P. M. (1997). *The fifth discipline: The art and practice of the learning organization.* New York: Century Business.

Siegel, J., Dubrovsky, V., Kiesler, S., & McGuire, T. W. (1986). Group processes in computer-mediated communication. *Organizational Behavior and Human Processes, 37,* 157-187.

Solomon, C. M. (2001). *Managing virtual teams. Workforce, 80*(6), 60-65.

Storck, J., and Hill, P. A. (2000). Knowledge diffusion through strategic communities, *Sloan Management Review, 41*(2), 63-74.

Trumbly, J. E., Arnett, K. P., & Johnson, P. C. (1994). Productivity via an adaptive user interface:

An empirical analysis. *International Journal of Human-Computer Studies, 40,* 63-81.

Valacich, J. S., Paranka, D., George, J. F., & Nunamaker, Jr. (1993). Communication concurrency and the new media: A new dimension for media richness. *Communication Research, 20,* 249-276.

Van Dam, N., & Rogers, F. (2002, May). E-Learning cultures around the world: Make your globalized strategy transparent. *Elearning,* 28-33.

Walther. J. B. (2002). Time effects in computer-mediated groups: Past, present, and future. In P. Hinds & S. Kiesler (Eds.), *Distributed work* (pp. 235-257).

Walther, J. B. (1997). Group and interpersonal effects in international computer-mediated collaboration, *Human Communication Research, 23,* 342-369.

Wheeler, D. (2001). New technologies, old culture: A look at women, gender, and Internet in Kuwait. In C. Ess (Ed.), *Culture, technology, communication: Towards an intercultural global village* (pp. 187-212). Albany: State University of New York Press.

Wilborn, J. (1999). The Internet: An out-group perspective. *Communication, 25*(1 and 2), 53-57.

Ya'u, Y. Z. (2004). The new imperialism & Africa in the global electronic village. *Review of the African Political Economy, 99,* 11-29.

ADDITIONAL READING

Alge, B. J., Wiethoff, Klein, H. (2003). When does medium matter: Knowledge-building experiences and opportunities. Organizational Behavior and Human Decision Processes, 91, 26-37.

Avgerou, C. (2002) Information systems and global diversity. Oxford: Oxford University Press.

Borghoff, U. M., & Pareschi, R. (1998). *Information technology for knowledge management.* Berlin, Germany: Springer.

Chi, L. & Holsapple, C. W. (2005).Understanding computer-mediated interorganizational collaboration: A model and framework. *Journal of Knowledge Management, 9(*1), 53-75.

Galliers, R. D., & Leidner, D. E. (Eds.) (2003) *Strategic information management:Challenges and strategies in managing information systems.* Oxford: Butterworth-Heinemann.

Gasker, J. A., & Cascio, T. (2001). Empowering women through computer-mediated class participation. *Affilia: Journal of Women & Social Work, 16*(3), 295-313.

Hague, B. N., & Loader, B. (1999). *Digital democracy: Discourse and decision making in the information age.* New York: Routledge.

Hara, N., Bonk, C. J., & Angeli, C. (2000). Content analysis of an on-line discussion in an applied educational psychology course. *Instructional Science, 28,* 115-152.

Kameda, T., Ohtsubo, Y., & Takezawa, M. (1997). Centrality in socio-cognitive networks and social influence: An illustration in a group decision making context. *Journal of Personality and Social Psychology, 73,* 296-309.

Kayworth & Leidner (2002). The global virtual manager: A prescription for success. *European Management Journal, 18*(2), 183-194.

Lipnack, J., & Stamps, J. (2000). *Virtual teams: People working across boundaries with technology (2nd ed.).* New York: John Wiley & Sons.

Majchrzak, A., Rice, R. E., King, N., Malhotra, A., & Ba, S. (2000). Computer-mediated inter-organizational knowledge-sharing: Insights from a virtual team innovating using a collaborative tool. *Information Resource Management Journal, 13,* 44-53.

Majchrzak, A., Rice, R. E., Malhotra, A., King, N., & Ba, S. (2000). Technology adaptation: The case of a computer-supported inter-organizational virtual team. *MIS Quarterly, 24,* 569-600.

Malone, T. W. (1997). Is empowerment just a fad? Control, decision-making, and information technology. *Sloan Management Review, 38*(2), 28-35.

Martins, L. L., Gilson, L., & Maynard, M. T. (2004). Virtual teams: What do we know and where do we go from here? *Journal of Management, 30*(6), 805-835.

Massey, A. P., Montoya-Weiss, M. M., & Hung, Y. (2003). Because time matters: Temporal coordination in global virtual project teams. *Journal of Management Information Systems, 19*, 129-155.

May, A., & Carter, C. (2001). A case study of virtual team working in the European automotive industry. *International Journal of Industrial Ergonomics, 27*(3), 171-186.

Maznevski, M. L., & Chudoba, K. M. (2000). Bridging space over time: Global virtual team dynamics and effectiveness. *Organization Science, 11*, 473-492.

McGrath, J. E. (1991). Time, interaction, and performance (TIP): A theory of groups. *Small Group Research, 22*, 147-174.

Montoya-Weiss, M., Massey, A. P., & Song, M. (in press). Getting it together: Temporal coordination and conflict management in global virtual teams. *Academy of Management Journal, 44*(6), 1251-1262.

Mortensen, M., & Hinds, P. (2001) Conflict and shared identity in geographically distributed teams. *The International Journal of Conflict Management, 12*(3), 212-238.

Olaniran, B. A. (2001). The effects of computer-mediated communication on transculturalism. In V. Milhouse, M. Asante, & P. Nwosu (Eds.), *Transcultural realities* (pp. 83-105). Thousand Oaks, CA: Sage.

Olaniran, B. A. (2004). *Computer-mediated communication as an instructional Learning tool: Course Evaluation with communication students.* In P. Comeaux (Ed.), Assessing online teaching & learning (pp. 144-158). PA: Anker Publishers.

Olaniran, B. A. (2006a). Applying synchronous computer-mediated communication into course design: Some considerations and practical guides. Campus-Wide Information Systems. *The International Journal of Information & Learning Technology, 23*(3), 210-220.

Olaniran, B. (2006b). Challenges to implementing e-learning and lesser developed countries. In A. L. Edmundson (Ed.), *Globalized elearning cultural challenges* (pp. 18-34). Hershey, PA: Idea Group Inc.

Olaniran, B. A. (2007). Culture and communication challenges in virtual workspaces. In K. StAmant (Ed.), *Linguistic and cultural online communication issues in the global age* (pp. 79-92). PA: Information Science Reference.

Pauleen, D. J. (2003). Lessons learned crossing boundaries in an ICT-supported distributed team. *Journal of Global Information Management, 11*(4), 1-19.

Pauleen, D., & Yoong, P. (2001b). Relationship building and the use of ICT in boundary-crossing virtual teams: A facilitator's perspective. *Journal of Information Technology, 16*, 205-220.

Poole, M. S., & DeSanctis, G. (1990). Understanding the use of group decision support systems: The theory of adaptive structuration. In J. Fulk & C. Steinfield (Eds.), *Organizations and communication technology* (pp. 175-195). Newbury Park, CA: Sage.

Potter, R., & Balthazard, P. (2002). Virtual team interaction styles: assessment and effects. *International Journal for Human-Computer Studies, 56*, 423-443.

Powell, A., Picolli, G., & Ives, B. (2004). *Virtual teams: A review of current literature and directions for future research.* The Data Base for Advances in Information Systems, 1(winter).

Rosen, B., Furst, S., & Blackburn, R. (2006). Training for virtual teams: An investigation of current practices and future needs. *Human Resource Management, 45*(2), 229-247.

Rutkowski, A. F., Vogel, D. R., Genuchten, M. V., Bemelmans, T. M., & Favier, M. (2002). E-collaboration: The reality of virtuality. *IEEE Transactions on Professional Communication, 45*(4), 219-229.

Saidon, H. J., & Sitharan, R. (2004). The use of Internet for an international collaborative project. *Leonarno Electronic Almanac, 12*(8). Retrieved from http://mitpress2.mit.edu/e-journals/LEA/Text/Vol_12_n08.txt

Shekhar, S. (2006). Understanding the virtuality of virtual organizations. *Leadership and Organization Development Journal, 27*(6), 465-483

Tomassello, M., Kruger, A., & Ratner, H. (1993). Cultural learning. *Behavioral and Brain Sciences, 16*, 495-552.

Yoo, Y., & Alavi, M. (2001). Media and group cohesion: Relative influences on social presence, task participation, and group consensus. *MIS Quarterly, 25*(3), 371-390.

Chapter XIII
Understanding Global Information Technology and Outsourcing Dynamics:
A Multi-Lens Model

Robert C. Yoder
Siena College, USA

Vera Eccarius-Kelly
Siena College, USA

Suvarna Cherukuri
Siena College, USA

ABSTRACT

This chapter provides information technology (IT) project leaders, call center management, researchers, and educators with an analytical tool to examine current concerns and anticipate future trends related to globalization and information technology. The authors propose to use a multi-lens analysis as a framework for evaluating outsourcing opportunities. This approach offers a valuable and effective full-circle methodology for assessing technological, political, organizational, economic, legal, educational, and cultural considerations that encourage a fuller understanding of the issues, problems, and opportunities that globalization and technological innovation creates. An understanding of these factors related to outsourcing and other technical collaborative projects can avoid costly miscalculations, reduce misunderstandings, and promote mutually beneficial results. Outsourcing is part of a larger socio-political and cultural process, and extends beyond the narrow parameters of economic and technological considerations. The discussion of the various lenses is supported by relevant material from case studies and qualitative interview data collected by the authors in Germany and India from IT experts, call center managers, and call center agents.

INTRODUCTION

In this chapter, the authors propose the multi-lens model as an analytical tool offering a systematic view of the forces and trends that influence outsourcing decisions. This tool provides a framework that encourages a multi-pronged assessment of the outsourcing phenomenon. Recognizing that the rapid development and diffusion of information and communications technologies is a major driver of globalization, the authors present a group of factors that we believe impact the outsourcing process. It is simplistic to look at outsourcing as purely an economic or technical decision–it is important to recognize that outsourcing contains social, legal, and political aspects as well, and to understand their interrelationships.

This model is presented in the context of outsourcing and offshoring—pertinent and pervasive issues that many organizations confront in order to continue their success in today's global, interdependent business environment. The authors believe that a broad understanding of globalization and its effects upon knowledge-based professions will benefit call center supervisors, their team leaders, and information and communication technology (ICT) managers by encouraging them to innovate

and adapt continually to new opportunities created by globalization. Thus, companies will need to train and deploy their staff in new ways to maintain flexibility and competitiveness. This includes effective use of technology for supporting the collaboration of work processes and increasing cultural awareness to enhance team building across geographic and organizational boundaries.

Using lenses is not a new idea. Andersen and Dawes (1991) presented four lenses, or perspectives, to explore the political, organizational, economic, and technological aspects of information management. Here the authors have enlarged the scope of these perspectives and added additional legal, cultural, and educational lenses (Figure 1) to reflect categories immanent in recent globalization literature, such as The Lexus and the Olive Tree (Friedman, 1999), In Defense of Globalization (Bhagwati, 2004) and Globalization and Its Discontents (Stiglitz, 2003). Globalization is a force that significantly influences all lenses of the model. Note that there is flexibility in which lenses to use for a specific situation, and the relative importance of each lens will vary. Our goal is not to present a detailed discussion of every possible lens, but to show that understanding globalization issues is naturally multidisciplinary. As Manfred Steger

Figure 1. Multi-lens model

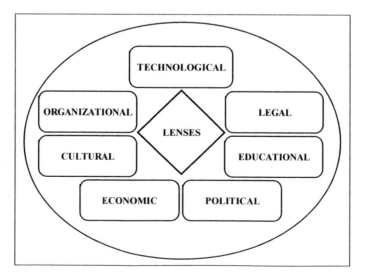

writes, "The greatest challenge facing today's globalization researcher lies, therefore, in connecting and synthesizing the various strands of knowledge in a way that does justice to the increasingly fluid and interdependent nature of our postmodern world" (Steger, 2003).

Outsourcing, Offshoring, and Nearsourcing

Often located in industrialized countries, many corporate IT and call center managers consider the practice of outsourcing as a panacea to rising operating costs and at-risk revenue in expensive North American and Western European facilities. It is common for managers to argue that additional financial benefits arise from aggressive international direct marketing and sales strategies. However, outsourcing IT departments and call center services often creates a host of multi-faceted problems. This chapter encourages corporate leaders and decision-makers to think beyond the immediate financial benefits and to consider key factors that determine success or failure following an outsourcing decision. Commonly ignored predicaments include sudden political instability in emerging democracies or repressive regimes, and inadequate employee training that leads to stress, absenteeism, and poor customer service. Excessive centralization of organizational operations also undermines teamwork and empowerment of employees. Managers must think creatively about how they can build a successful relationship with facilities abroad. To ensure that an outsourcing decision leads to reduced operating costs and improved customer satisfaction, it is imperative that managers first engage in the research necessary to achieve clearly defined and articulated goals. The Multi-Lens model assists managers in creating successful business plans and execution strategies that involve outsourcing.

The authors use the more general term outsourcing to indicate any task or business processes performed by another company, regardless of where that company is based. Traditionally this process most strongly affected the manufacturing sector

(cars, furniture, textiles, etc.). Historically, most U.S. manufacturing has taken place in low-cost assembly operations in countries like China, Taiwan, and Mexico, where "over a million Mexican citizens work in more than 3000 maquiladora plants, carrying out assembly operations for U.S. companies" (NASSCOM, 2004, p. 78).

In the 1980s, it became commonplace for U.S. businesses to outsource professional information technology support tasks to other U.S. companies like Electronic Data Systems (EDS) and IBM with large multi-year contracts. For example, "Dow has systematically outsourced its information technology needs over the past decade. In 1994, it outsourced a 10-year IT contract to EDS. In 1997, it outsourced help-desk operations to Compaq under a 3-year deal. In 2000, it signed a 7-year $1.4 billion contract with EDS for building and maintaining a converged voice-data network. In 2001, it entered into a five-year agreement with IBM for an end-to-end Web hosting service" (NASSCOM, 2004, p. 79). As the demand for IT workers outstripped supply, companies increasingly imported talented, yet lower-cost foreign workers.

The term offshoring (offshore outsourcing) refers to discrete business components that typically are performed in a lower-wage country to take advantage of reduced cost structures for labor expenditures, building rents, tax rates, etc. Foreign workers in the IT sector tend to be highly educated and motivated individuals who provide sophisticated services to U.S. customers in such sectors as finance, banking, pharmaceuticals, and healthcare.

Network and data center management tasks also are increasingly outsourced. Such tasks are handled by separate companies abroad that specialize in particular and often narrowly focused services, and are located in societies that are perceived as future power-houses of innovation, including India and China. U.S. corporations became early adopters of the business process outsourcing (BPO) and call center industry in the early 1980s, however, less than a decade later most large corporations headquartered in other industrialized countries also began offshoring jobs related to call center services, payroll, and software application development. Some multinational companies including General Electric, Hewlett Packard, and Deutsche Bank created their own "captive" organizations in developing countries. Thus, some offshore work is not necessarily outsourced. In another significant development, Hindustan Computers Limited (HCL), previously owned by Deutsche Bank and now one of India's leading IT and technology companies, initiated a process now called reverse-outsourcing by establishing call centers in Northern Ireland to obtain language skills and infrastructure advantages.

Nearsourcing is a relatively new term indicating a tendency to re-assess the original enthusiasm for outsourcing business components to developing countries far away from corporate headquarters. Some European and U.S. corporate leaders find it easier to employ teams with closer "cultural proximity" and ideally reach their sub-contracted facilities within a short 3-4 hour flight. European Union (EU) member states have developed a strong interest in highly capable Eastern European IT and call center operations, specifically those located in Poland, Slovakia, or Hungary since they are now an integral part of the enlarged EU. Their universities have a tradition for excellence in the technical sciences, producing graduates strong in mathematics and computer science while salaries are only about half of those in Western Europe (Woodard, 2007).

Leveraging language skills can play a significant role in such choices as many Polish and Hungarian employees speak German, English, and other languages. But Western European businesses also go beyond E.U. borders by seeking out IT experts in Ukraine and Russia. U.S. businesses nearsource to Canada and also throughout Latin America, where there appears to be a particular interest in Central American Free Trade Agreement (CAFTA) countries, including the Dominican Republic.

High-speed Internet connections make outsourcing, offshoring, and nearsourcing a reality anywhere in the world, yet companies prefer to set up in politically stable (and not necessarily democratic) environments to establish sub-contracting partnerships. Clearly, this allows companies to compete more easily with businesses on a global level by collaborating with foreign companies or opening subsidiaries abroad. Recently, outsourcing structures have become more complex as offshore companies in places such as India and Eastern Europe accept sophisticated design tasks, and, in turn, outsource to companies located in even lower-wage countries, such as Indonesia or Vietnam. This "ladder" effect for comparative advantage encourages industrialized countries to specialize in "high-end" capital- and knowledge-intensive activities to attract "inshoring" foreign investment that utilizes a skilled workforce (Neuhaus & Kunze, 2006).

As the offshoring market matures and becomes more sophisticated, cost alone will not be the determining factor for selecting business partners. Offshoring has evolved from shifting commodity work to low-wage countries to a web of "complex, multishore arrangements with more nuanced and strategic goals" to create a synergistic relationship between skill sets, location and cost (Brandel, 2007).

THE BASICS OF GLOBALIZATION

Outsourcing should be understood in the context of the larger globalization debate because of its impact on societies. According to the World Bank:

... globalization—the growing integration of economies and societies around the world—has been one of the most hotly-debated topics in international economics over the past few years. Rapid growth and poverty reduction in China, India, and other countries that were poor 20 years ago, has been a positive aspect of globalization. But globalization has also generated significant international opposition over concerns that it has increased inequality and environmental degradation. (The World Bank, 2007)

Technology has been driving the globalization process throughout history. Warfare, the most primitive form of globalization, has spread technological inventions, caused cultural diffusion, and forced the migration of millions of people. While the perspective of economists on the nature and timing of globalization tends to represent a more short-term (post-1970s) emphasis on corporations and technology, political scientists and sociologists analyze globalization trends from the perspective of the rise of modern capitalism as it emerged in the 16th century (Pieterse, 2004, p. 17). Historians and anthropologists, in contrast, take a much more long-term approach to examining social forms of interactions (Pieterse, 2004). Pointing to the Middle Ages when people traded with each other, historians suggest that global trade crossed great geographic distances. The famous Silk Route provides a convincing example to illustrate the long-standing exchange of goods between European and Asian traders.

The Economic and Social Research Council (2007), an independent British research institution, proposed a categorization of the globalization phenomenon into four sub-categories including (a) economic globalization (the expansion of financial capital and markets), (b) political and military globalization (the increase of global interdependence and of political actors), (c) social and cultural globalization (the movement of ideas, values and people), and (d) environmental globalization (the long-distance transport of often harmful substances, etc.).

For the purpose of this chapter, the authors broadly define globalization as an economic, political, and social process that fundamentally changes the way in which the international economy is organized. Globalization means that instant telecommunications and modern forms of transportation now prevail over economic barriers and political boundaries that once tended to insulate countries from each other's influence and economic pressures in the past (Mittelman, 1997). The effect has been powerful. People and organizations around the globe now interact in ways that challenge the established post-war order within the economic, social, political, cultural, and ideological realms.

Social scientists disagree about how governments should respond to the displacement of workers as a consequence of globalization, and to what extent the middle class in high-wage countries will shrink in the coming decades. In the highly industrialized, technologically advanced world, workers who are currently excluded from the workforce will require specialized job training programs if they hope to re-enter the job market. New and young entrants into the global job market require entirely different preparation to be able to compete in the future. As a result, the European Union re-launched its Lisbon Plan in 2005 for sustained growth and new employment opportunities, hoping to position its member states as knowledge-based economies rather than competing with inexpensive labor or exploiting natural resources. In the developing world, the discussions are less lofty but have focused on the need to increase educational opportunities for young people who may otherwise become permanently excluded from entering the global workforce.

Cognizant of this reality, knowledge workers and managers alike require a clear understanding of the political, socio-economic, and ideological discord that exists as a result of the impact of globalization on different societies. A lack of attention to such issues will lead to poor decision making—causing long-term damage to corporate interests abroad.

DISCUSSION OF LENSES

Global IT is taking us into uncharted territory, which is transforming our cultures, politics, legal systems, and economic systems. Any discussion on offshore outsourcing will be incomplete without taking into consideration various factors that influence decision-making processes. When technology relocates, it does not do so in a vacuum. It relocates along with capital and labor in multiple contexts of culture, economy, and politics. Therefore, we provide the multi-lens model, which we hope will enable a holistic understanding of offshore outsourcing. The multi-lens model diagram (Figure 1) incorporates a variety of perspectives and ideas that researchers and corporate decision-makers might not consider in order to gain insight into the complexities of the globalization debate today. The proposed set of lenses (technological, political, organizational, economic, legal, educational, and cultural) encourages analytical thinking about how a variety of countries, corporations, social groups, and individuals perceive both threats and opportunities presented by the outsourcing phenomena. Within each lens, the unit of analysis can be at the international, national, or organizational level. The reader will encounter many examples of cross-connections between the lenses, where topics could just as easily be presented in other lenses. This is a natural result of using our approach—recognizing interrelationships reinforces a holistic understanding of globalization in general and outsourcing in particular.

The Technological Lens

In *Strategic Outsourcing*, Benn and Pearcy (2002) highlight technology as the leading catalyst in the present wave of outsourcing. The emergence of global communications systems has driven globalization to new levels. Internet bandwidth is plentiful and inexpensive due to an over-investment during the dot-com boom in the U.S. The Internet, as an interoperable "network of networks," provides seamless global communication regardless of the computer system used or the geographic location of the user. Since the Internet reduces transaction costs to almost zero, newly industrialized countries can quickly become producers of information products, using the Internet as a delivery mechanism. This increases competition since geographic distance can be overcome with a simple click of a mouse. Decision-making power becomes diffused because consumers can now search for the lowest available price. Although the Internet facilitates entry into global markets to challenge established and large companies, continuous innovation, personal contacts, and cultural understanding will be required to maintain a competitive advantage.

The Internet permits instantaneous interconnectedness and an easy way to disseminate information and products. New "time-compression" forces have been unleashed to speed up product development cycles. Products become obsolete or commoditized quickly, and trends happen quicker. Information gathering and distribution happens at little cost to individuals enabled by cell phones/cameras, Web sites, and blogs. The Internet tends to break up information monopolies leading to state agencies and companies to lose absolute control of the flow of information. Organizations are adopting e-commerce and other sophisticated global information systems to integrate with suppliers, customers, distributors, and other stakeholders to cut costs and provide the best value for their customers.

The open-source movement uses global collaboration to create excellent software at no cost, giving individuals and companies in newly industrialized countries the basic and necessary software components such as operating systems [Linux] and Web servers [Apache] to launch their own e-commerce sites. The cost dynamic between Linux and Windows may change due to the emerging pool of low-cost Linux developers and system administrators in India, China, and elsewhere (Fishman, 2005).

Workflow technology that automates and monitors complex business processes has been instrumental in increasing the efficiency of call centers and other BPO organizations. Companies like the American National Insurance Company use workflow software to provide their call center agents with instant access to customer information and to enforce business rules (Worthen, 2004). Similarly, European call centers have invested in automatic call distributor (ACD) devices to handle heavy flows of incoming calls. ACD systems route incoming calls based on a set of instructions that determine the best available employee for a specific type of incoming call. The routing instructions are often linked to regional language specializations, accents, or other variables that are taken into account to determine why the customer contacted a call center. ACD systems consist of hardware for terminals and software for the routing strategy. An additional function for these external routing applications relates to computer telephone integration (CTI) technology. CTI allows call center agents to be highly efficient as the routed customer call pulls up data that informs the agent on the PC about the customer's prior history of calls, the number of complaints filed, or purchases completed. The agent can then quickly assess how to deal with the customer and even decide to re-route him/her to someone better prepared to respond to a specific inquiry based on available data. Management can easily monitor calls and track workflow statistics.

Workflow extends to manufacturing as well. Some companies, like Dell computer, have moved from mass production to mass customization, a demand-pull rather than supply-push model, which means that a Dell computer is not assembled until a customer configures and orders it over the Internet. Sophisticated supply chains like Wal-Mart will order a replacement item as soon as it is scanned at the checkout register. The use of extranets (secured access into an information database) as a way to link a company with suppliers, distributors, and other stakeholders is becoming commonplace. Similarly, supply chain management offers a strategic advantage for many companies, and represents the manifestation of globalization as the physical Internet of products flowing from country to country. However, some flexibility may be required for maintaining continuous operation in politically sensitive or disaster-prone areas of the world. Companies are discovering that different supply chains may be needed for different products, and instant communication is required to keep "just in time" inventory costs down and to avoid the whiplash effect of variances in demand being amplified within the supply chain (The Economist, 2006). The worldwide sourcing of components is evolving into a supply web that is constantly changing. The use of radio frequency identification (RFID) tags to continually track the location of goods throughout the supply chain is becoming commonplace. These tags, along with tag readers and software allow an unprecedented level of real-time visibility into the supply chain. Sophisticated RFID tags can detect temperature changes or the impact of dropped goods. An emerging global concern is that the radio frequencies assigned to such devices has not yet been standardized among countries.

Videoconferencing, voice over IP (VoIP), and the availability of other computer-mediated communication between workers at any location increases collaboration and productivity, and makes offshoring of complex projects possible. While occasional face-to-face meetings contribute to building trust among team members and can be critical for promoting understanding, most projects can be kept on track through the complementary use of e-mail, videoconferencing, source code version control software, and other technological innovations such as wiki that enables the creation of collaborative Web content and project documentation. The "Wikipedia" is an example of this technology. Sophisticated Internet-based multiplayer computer games such as World of WarCraft utilizing 3D-simulated worlds are being developed around the world. Some companies are using this game technology for training and team building (Jana, 2007).

All of these collaborative technologies depend on a robust and secure Internet; the global supply of customers and potential partners also includes a global supply of hackers. Providing secure network connections continues to be a challenge. The rapid global adoption of the Internet and creation of new products that communicate using the Internet protocol (IP) is leading to a shortfall of unique network addresses. In a way, the Internet is a victim of its own success. The version of IP commonly in use (version 4) was not designed for such expansion and uses a 32-bit network address mechanism that does not efficiently allocate all 32 bits. Many countries already use a technical work-around called network address translation to share IP addresses. A global transition to IP version 6 that provides 128-bit network addresses and improved security features will be necessary in the near future (Hain et al.). China already has embarked on the China Next Generation Internet (CNGI) project to use IP version 6 to support its computer infrastructure and its burgeoning population of mobile data networking users, who access Internet services.

Cell phone technology allows emerging countries to leapfrog the traditional wired telephone network and go directly to advanced communications services. Competition among cell phone manufacturers is increasing as China enters the market. The potential for cell phone games and as a mechanism for mobile commerce—the buying and selling of goods and services through wireless devices—is driving innovative, high-end applications. The use of cell phones for commerce is still in the experimental stages, but prototypes for vending machines that dispense soda in response to a customer calling a number posted on the machine already exist in South Korea, Japan, and Europe. The charge shows up on the customer's phone bill. Other approaches include using the cell phone as a charge card. Purchases are captured by a radio transmitter in the cell phone and a special receiver at the point-of-sale terminal (Baltzan & Phillips, 2008).

It is clear that, in the past, technology was merely a business tool. Today it drives the direction of businesses as one of the most powerful competitive advantages outsourcing firms can have over their rivals in the fast moving economic landscape.

The Political Lens

The political lens is an important one because understanding the nature of politics in the globalized world lessens the risks of conducting international business and better prepares outsourcing managers for political events that may hinder business process outsourcing opportunities. Yahoo's travails are a striking reminder that even if the Internet reduces the distance between two points, politics will always matter. The study on human organ selling in China was self-censored by Yahoo on its China Web site, because Chinese officials had been implicated in the scandal, though the article received substantial attention on its U.S. Web site. Yahoo decided it was better to censor itself rather than risk offending Chinese authorities (Wild, Wild, and Han, 2005).

The political lens may be understood at multiple levels:

a. Political risk.
b. Situations of insurgency, terrorism, and regional instability.
c. Immigration laws, anti-immigration sentiments, and movement of labor.
d. Acceptance of foreign capital.
e. Governmental intervention.

Managers must be aware of how political risk can affect their companies. In a broad sense, macro political risk threatens all companies regardless of industry. Among political factors that concern U.S. corporate management during a decision to outsource to a particular location will include foreign governments' attempts to control the flow of information, the potential for corporate espionage, sudden regional instability, and terrorism. The growing practice of abducting engineering and IT staff for ransom in Nigeria and Mexico now worries U.S. and European managers, as regionally based violence and the potential for acts of terrorism deter investment. In the Philippines, a preferred location for offshore IT operations, a militant Muslim group called Abu Sayyaf engaged in a series of bombings, abductions, and murders. The group currently operates in the southern part of the country (Mindanao) and is accused of past collaboration with Ramzi Youssef, who was involved in the 1993 World Trade Center bombings. Unanticipated political events can cause sudden and severe interruptions to regular business operations. The recent military coup targeting the elected prime minister of Thailand, or the violent protests in Hungary as a response to the ruling government's misleading information about the state of the economy, are typical examples. It is impossible to prepare for all contingencies, but business managers must be aware of potentially disruptive political developments, and implement plans that position the corporation with flexible and possibly redundant business capabilities.

Immigration policies and movement of labor across countries has been critical to the outsourcing debate. In the U.S., outsourcing became an issue in the 2004 U.S. presidential election. From 2001-2003, 180,000 new foreign IT workers had been contracted in the U.S. Growing political pressure from displaced technology workers culminated in Congress lowering the number of H1-B visas to

65,000. This level was reached very quickly, even though Congress approved 20,000 extra visas in 2004 (Francis, 2004). H-1B visas allow workers to reside in the U.S. for up to six years and require paying comparable U.S. wages. Although companies must certify that bringing in these "specialty" workers won't eliminate U.S. jobs, some U.S. labor unions claim that H1-B visas were designed for short-term niche labor shortages and are being misused for long-term IT positions that have the effect of driving down wages in the U.S. for the benefit of businesses by substantially increasing the size of the labor pool. However, the growth of offshoring tends to reduce the immigration of technology experts, since they can now find jobs that allow them to enjoy a high standard of living in their own countries.

In reaction to an intensification of the anti-immigration mood in the U.S., some politicians proposed stricter tax policies on companies that relied substantially on offshoring, while others criticized state agencies, including Indiana's department of labor, for outsourcing IT work (Ribeiro, 2003). Following the dot-com bust in 2001 with immense pressure on companies to reduce expenditures, the number of outsourcing contracts increased and employees of multinational companies were transferred to the U.S. on L-1 visas that do not require salaries comparable to standard U.S. wages. The L-1 visa, which is an intra-company transfer of employees from a foreign company to a U.S. company, has no ceiling. During the last few years the U.S. issued approximately 320,000 L-1 entry visas each year (NASSCOM, 2004).

In addition to the introduction of anti-outsourcing bills in the U.S., there is a rising political awareness of the effects of outsourcing and immigration in the European parliament and other related institutions. According to Kabayashi-Hillary (2002), the European Trade Union Congress has started to take the view that corporate restructuring related to outsourced services may be for short–term profit at the cost of long-term sustainable development. An issue of concern is the fact that IT experts from Eastern Europe, Ukraine, and Russia temporarily work in Western European facilities. They receive

training for particular projects prior to their return to their respective home countries where they lead specialized software development teams. Germany, in particular, pursues this nearsourcing approach since many of the foreign IT workers speak both German and English fluently. German IT experts interviewed for this chapter complained that such arrangements lead to a reduction of overall wages, lower traditional benefits packages, and weaken both development and control over software development projects.

On the global level, lower-wage countries are spurring investment by fostering transparent government with less corruption, free markets, and convertible currency. Other factors include having an autonomous legal system, tax laws that protect foreign investment, and a sound transportation and information infrastructure. Equitable privacy and intellectual property policies also are critical success factors. A recent A.T. Kearney report in Foreign Policy (2005) ranked countries by their "globalization index." The index based on four general areas includes: Economic Integration (trade and foreign investment), Technological Connectivity (number of internet users and hosts, network infrastructure), Personal Contact (travel and tourism, telephone traffic, compensation and other transfers), and Political Engagement (membership in international organizations, treaties signed, UN presence). The highest ranked countries in the report were Singapore, Ireland, Switzerland, the United States, and the Netherlands. The report also found a "strong relationship between globalization and political freedom" and that "globalized countries have lower levels of perceived corruption" (p. 59).

Positive political will toward foreign capital is another factor of which companies should be well aware. Governments can hinder smooth business operations through tariffs, quotas, embargoes, local content requirements, administrative delays, and currency controls. Managers of companies that intend to outsource should do a thorough analysis of political and governmental policies. A clear example of positive political engagement relates to China's decision to join the World Trade

Organization (WTO) in 2001. All WTO members comply with the same tariff regulations and must allow arbitration for trade disputes. Although some Chinese companies are subject to foreign competition, a number of industries in China remain protected, forcing foreign companies to form alliances with Chinese manufacturing and distribution firms. Political tensions between mainland China and Taiwan, and growing trade disputes continue to present the main threats to developing more efficient U.S.-China relations. For example, the China Currency Act of 2005 (HR 1498) specifically targets the undervaluation of the Yuan as "both a subsidy for exports from the People's Republic of China and a non-tariff barrier against imports into China, to the serious detriment of the United States manufacturing industry." China also has been criticized for maintaining import tariffs in some industries and shutting out foreign firms from government contracts (Magnusson, 2004).

The future of world organizations setting global standards for trade agreements, the management of financial markets, and concerns related to social justice is uncertain. The 2006 WTO Doha round failed to consider the specific needs of poor and less-developed countries as trade ministers from highly industrialized nations protected their own interests. The U.S. called for liberalization of markets while protecting its agricultural subsidies for cotton, rice, and soybeans. The EU and India criticized farm subsidies but were unwilling to cut their own farm and industrial tariffs (The Economist, 2006a).

Although multilateral trade agreements reduce the complexity and level the playing field for smaller, impoverished, and less technologically advanced countries, most successful trade agreements now occur on a bilateral level or take place between politically aligned trading blocs.

Stiglitz (2003) heaps criticism on the International Monetary Fund because the IMF did not take into account how people would be affected by its cookie cutter solutions to economic crises. Some of the IMF's policies for developing countries included implementing strict budgetary controls and preferred payback to creditor banks. This resulted in massive unemployment, artificially high exchange rates, and rapid privatization of industries and natural resources, often at bargain prices for buyers linked to corrupt governments. In addition, ensuing one-sided trade liberalization policies opened up developing countries' markets to goods from developed countries without granting similar access to markets in Europe and the United States.

The Organizational (Management) Lens

The most immediate and obvious implication of outsourcing for U.S. and Western European companies relates to the replacement of internal jobs with hires abroad. The advantages of lower labor costs, cheaper real estate, and related support staff expenses must be weighed against the loss of valuable employee knowledge and experience. In addition, negative effects on company morale can increase turnover, create inefficiencies among insecure teams, and even encourage acts of sabotage. Other concerns include loss of control of IT projects, especially if subcontracting occurs, and the need to acquire expertise in negotiating outsourcing contracts. Effective management of remote teams becomes more complex and can create a feeling of disconnect between the corporate mission and the teams abroad. Scheduling work becomes more complicated because of different (and more frequent) holidays in Europe and by weekends that start on Thursdays in Israel. High turnover rates in India and elsewhere among programmers and call center technicians lead to project delays, quality concerns, and uncontrolled dissemination of proprietary information.

The potential advantages of outsourcing are considerable. Companies can quickly acquire technology expertise utilizing best practices, gain increased flexibility for variable demand for IT services, and free up internal staff for higher-value, strategic projects. Many companies take advantage of time zone differences to operate 24x7. Off-hours call centers and IBM's "Java Around the Clock" programming teams are examples. Sometimes, mainframe and other computing resources can be used more effectively by staggering the workload over the entire day.

Outsourcing and offshoring can be thought of as organizational innovations in response to the availability of a large pool of talented and inexpensive labor along with an abundance of network bandwidth and networking infrastructure in developing countries. This is different from internal process improvements, such as total quality management and continuous improvement that were developed in Japan and other countries in the 1980s that mostly targeted manufacturing jobs. Today, outsourcing primarily affects professional, knowledge-based jobs. Businesses outsource "any activity where we can digitize and decompose the value chain" (Friedman, 2005a), and "activities comprising a job that does not require physical proximity, local knowledge, and complex interactions" (Magnusson, 2004). Software development, IT services, banking, and insurance sectors are particularly susceptible to outsourcing, while customer-facing service jobs are less amenable to outsourcing (McKinsey, 2005).

Globalization exerts pressure on businesses to compete in the global market and take advantage of offshore talent through innovative ways to "fragment complex management processes and reintegrate them into the whole" (Pralahad, 2005). Companies are learning how to outsource and how to determine what level of outsourcing works for them. Many begin this transition by "transaction outsourcing" that outsources only "well-defined processes that have clear business rules" (Overby, 2005). Transaction outsourcing does not require protracted contract negotiations or extensive hands-on management. This work is readily extractible from the value chain, and non-core as it does not have significant strategic value. Most companies choose to retain control over strategic, proprietary processes and methodologies, so that they can distinguish their brand in order to charge a premium.

Successful companies adapt quickly to new market conditions and seek competitive advantage through technology. These "virtual firms" use networks to create and link dynamic workgroups without being limited by traditional organizational structures or geography. IBM has implemented this idea globally by creating a human supply chain that tracks the skill set of its technical staff and optimizes the creation of teams worldwide to work on specific tasks. Engineers track world news events and weather patterns in command centers to anticipate problems. IBM has increased its presence in India from about 9,000 employees in 2003 to over 43,000 in 2006. Other staffing increases took place in China, Brazil, and Eastern Europe to give IBM flexibility to perform work at many locations using the most appropriate people for the job (Hamm, 2006).

A related organizational innovation, virtual integration (also known as insourcing), combines separate organizations to operate as a single entity as far as the customer is concerned. An example of this is Toshiba and UPS. Broken Toshiba laptop computers are sent via UPS to their repair center staffed by specially trained UPS employees (Bowman, 2005).

Innovation is becoming the most important strategic advantage. Former outsourcing companies are now developing their own electronic designs and software to compete with their former trade partners. Businesses focus on controlling leading-edge technologies and products to attain the best profit margin, otherwise they risk becoming a low-profit *commodity* supplier. Another approach for fostering innovation in organizations is deploying Business Intelligence technology so that employees at all levels and all departments can make better and faster decisions. This is done by loading information from a variety of organizational and external databases into an enterprise data warehouse, and providing users with intuitive reporting and analytic tools to mine the warehouse for patterns and trends so that the company can quickly respond to changing business conditions and opportunities. Some organizations have been able to sell information from their data warehouse as a value-added product, turning a former cost center into a revenue stream.

Increased competition from efficient firms around the world increases the importance of becoming a "learning organization" by "creating new business knowledge, disseminating it widely throughout the company, and quickly building the new knowledge into their products and services" while encouraging new ideas and calculated risk-taking (O'Brien & Marakas, 2006). A successful business strategy emphasizes creating value for the consumer. That, however, can only be achieved once human resources—and not just financial capital—are categorized as essential. Training, coaching, and ongoing performance evaluations encourage staff to feel valued and appreciated by the company. In particular, it is essential for IT teams abroad and call center supervisors and their team managers to perceive themselves as empowered decision-makers within the organizational structures. Effective team building takes place in less rigidly organized environments that encourage staff members to feel empowered to pursue solutions that satisfy customer needs. Organizational structures that encourage continuous learning, team-oriented attitudes, and independent decision-making capacities on all levels of the company succeed at satisfying customer needs at a much higher level.

The Economic Lens

The economic lens reveals a very important dynamic that continues to drive the outsourcing movement. An increase in trade opportunities along with greater access to information has allowed millions of consumers in newly industrializing countries to consider global goods and services. At the same time, access to new markets also has created large cohorts of knowledge workers ready to compete for jobs in finance, information technology, insurance, and many other service areas. By 2004, the effects of globalization were swift and stunning—the market research company, "International Data Corporation (IDC) valued the annual global business process outsourcing (BPO) market at \$382.5 billion, a 10.8% jump over 2003. IDC estimates that by 2009, the market will hit

\$641.2 billion. GE has gained significantly by offshoring of business services to India over the last 6 years. It has invested close to \$400 million in India. Annual revenues are at about \$1 billion and the company saves \$300 million every year" (Couto & Divakaran, 2006, p. 2). Also, estimates exist that in the areas of application development, integration, and maintenance, offshore IT services providers have already reached a 17% market share, increasing to a 24% share by 2008 (Gens, 2004) and that finance and accounting outsourcing will exceed \$47 billion by 2008.

A study by Forrester Research indicates that over 3 million professional and service jobs will move out of the U.S. by 2015 (McCarthy, 2002). Economic theory predicts that work and production of goods will move to regions that permit cost-structure efficiency. Outsourcing work not only frees up capital, it also allows employees to do different, more sophisticated work, resulting in a cheaper and better final product. However, the expanding labor market exerts tremendous downward pressure on labor costs. Overseas firms offer high-quality work at much lower costs in comparison with Western European and U.S.-based companies, often by paying workers 75% less. Attendant support costs, such as health benefits, taxes, and workplace and environmental regulatory requirements also can be much lower offshore. The lack of unions and organized labor in developing countries contributes to this trend, although that will be changing in a number of newly industrialized countries including Mexico, China, and India.

The emerging middle class in India is pushing up wages and benefits, prompting Indian companies to outsource work to even lower-wage countries. Call centers, once known for driving the Indian high-tech revolution, are becoming a commodity. The Indian trade organization NASSCOM estimates that call centers account for only 35% of the business process outsourcing industry as compared to 85% in 2000 (Kripalani, 2006). Indian companies are taking on call center tasks only in conjunction with high-margin software development and data center management contracts, prompting some companies to consider building call centers in lower-cost areas in the U.S. or Canada. More and more frequently now, European companies are opening up call centers closer to their own operations, preferring Eastern Europe and Ireland at the moment.

Although offshoring drains jobs from high-wage countries, workers and companies in newly industrialized countries can now afford to buy products from highly industrialized countries, resulting in a much larger market for goods and services. The growth of the middle class in India and China has raised literacy rates and the standard of living while enabling more women to enter the workforce, resulting in reduced birth rates and child mortality (Friedman, 2005a).

The Legal Lens

The legal lens allows for an examination of corporate preparedness on the international, national, and local organizational levels. It is important for organizations to understand the legal environment in which they operate. Some countries have enacted laws that restrict trans-border flow of data or require the data to reside on a server within the country of origin. In addition, negotiating outsourcing contracts to ensure that proper safeguards are included is a complex process and requires expert advice. Successful contracts require the outsourcing company to perform background screening of their employees and to hold them responsible for any actions that break contract agreements (non-compete agreements and intellectual property clauses, for example). It also is important to build flexibility into the contract to allow for changing business conditions. In addition, the contracting company needs to verify network security and to ensure that test data does not identify actual customers (Fitzgerald, 2003).

In countries where the legal framework provides for portable health care insurance, pension benefits, and continued training, displaced workers have the opportunity to move to new jobs in a new industry (Friedman, 2005c). Increasing numbers of labor activists in the U.S. push for the creation of legislation that provides government benefits for retraining, healthcare, and relocation expenses

for displaced IT workers by expanding the Trade Adjustment Assistance act (Thibodeau, 2006). In Western Europe, such rights have been guaranteed through the Lisbon Accords.

Since offshoring jobs are predominantly knowledge-based today, the enforcement of intellectual property laws abroad has become crucial to protect patents and copyrights. Several high-profile cases have alerted corporate managers to this growing problem. The lack of a police response to a stolen source code in India (Vijayan, 2004), and Indian call-center staff members who used passwords from banking customers to transfer funds to their own accounts are just two examples (Puliyenthuruthel, 2005). In June 2006, an HSBC employee was charged with stealing confidential data of the bank's customers in the UK to illegally transfer their money. Working for HSBC in Bangalore, India, the employee accessed personal security information leading to an estimated loss of 233,000 British pounds. A similar case was reported from MphasiS BFL, New Delhi. Several employees of this firm were involved in a scam that targeted Citibank trying to steal approximately $350,000. Such instances are common in the corporate world. However, it is complicated when fraudulent cases involve cross-border legalities. Similarly, China's lax enforcement of software, music, and movie piracy are a major concern as well. It is estimated that over 90% of Chinese computers run on pirated or unlicensed software, contributing to the ability of Chinese companies to underbid U.S. rivals (Magnusson, 2004).

A related issue is the lack of environmental and labor/workplace regulations that allow countries to create below-market prices for goods and services. This so-called "China price" reflects exploitation that ultimately damages both trading partners in the long run. Trade agreements must deal with this unfair arrangement to address the treatment and living conditions of labor. It should be noted, however, that an increasing number of countries recognize offshoring as a strategic imperative for their economic well-being and have taken dramatic steps to rectify some of these problems. Of interest to corporate managers are the Global Sullivan Principles, developed by the Leon H. Sullivan

Foundation, that promote a holistic approach to economic, social, and political justice for corporate relationships with local communities. The principles support human rights, equal opportunity, racial and gender diversity on decision-making committees, and serve to improve the quality of life in communities important to the economic success of corporations. Collaborative agreements and economic partnerships between companies that outsource projects and communities abroad can lead to more profitable outcomes and reduced legal costs.

With knowledge as an evermore valuable asset and increasing access to instantaneous global communication, it is important to ensure that the legal contract defines how knowledge related to an outsourcing relationship should be treated. Kobayashi-Hillary (2002) remarks that:

International clients, particularly U.S. companies, tend to throw in their standard intellectual property clause and assume that U.S. law would govern. That is not the case if another country's laws apply; special requirements for assignment need to be fulfilled for the client to own the intellectual property. International clients also need to ensure that the dispute resolution mechanism specified in the contract can be enforced, for example, a U.S. court judgment cannot be enforced in all countries. (p. 202)

The U.S. Department of Commerce recommends that businesses create contracts containing very clear terms for payment and performance standards when dealing with Chinese firms. It is important to be specific about when events happen and which currencies will be used. The mechanism for contract disputes should be stipulated in the contract. Usually the first approach to invoke is simple negotiation; Chinese government-recognized arbitrators may be used if negotiations fail. Furthermore, all agreements should be in compliance with WTO rules (U.S. Department of Commerce, 2003).

The Educational Lens

Outsourcing has exacerbated the global competition for brain power or intellectual capital. In the past, the best and brightest students dreamed of going to the U.S. for graduate school or to obtain a professional job. That has changed, however. Today, offshoring can provide high quality jobs in newly industrialized countries and does not require extended stays in either the U.S. or in Europe. Excellent universities in China and India (University of Science and Technology of China, Indian Institute of Technology, and Indian Institute for Management) are attracting top-quality students. The United States attempts to attract students by creating 20,000 visas for foreign workers who hold graduate degrees from U.S. universities. A National Academy of Science report recommends "granting automatic 1-year visa extensions to foreign students in the U.S. who receive doctorates in science, engineering, or math so they can seek employment here" (Friedman, 2005b). Although post-9/11 immigration restrictions remain a barrier for some foreign students wishing to study in the U.S., many American universities have established partnerships with foreign institutions to expand research collaboration, increase their international stature, and to facilitate student and faculty exchanges.

The sheer number of foreign graduates is staggering. Some 70,000 new accounting grads emerge from Indian universities each year and many start their careers at a pay rate of about $100/month. India has some 22 million graduates (6 million science graduates, 1.2 million engineering graduates, and 600,000 doctors). China had more than 2 million students graduating from its universities in 2003 (600,000 engineering degrees, 200,000 science degrees, and 100,000 medical degrees) (Wharton School, 2005). However, companies should ensure that the degree-granting institutions represent the quality education they officially claim.

The percentage of students that graduate with engineering, math, or science degrees in Asia (Japan: 66%, China: 59%) is substantially higher than in the U.S. (32%) (Friedman, 2005a). Meanwhile, the number of U.S. college freshmen planning to major in computer science dropped to 1.4% in 2004, down from 3.4% in 1998 (Denning, 2005). In the U.S. 12th graders scored below the national average of 21 other countries in math and science, identifying a growing weakness within the educational system (Friedman, 2005b). Requiring sciences and mathematics in every year in high school and substantial efforts to encourage women and minorities to study engineering could increase U.S. competitiveness in the coming decades.

An article published in the New York Times (2005) outlined the economic risks linked to faltering governmental and private support that at one time could be counted on to spur invention and scientific research. Now the long-term outlook required for breakthrough research results, often gives way to short-term commercial interests because immediate returns on incremental improvements have been preferred in the U.S. The need for increased funding for basic scientific research is becoming a more and more serious issue as the U.S. trails many Asian countries in research and development funding as well as the number of doctoral degrees awarded in science and engineering. An interesting indicator for this shift is that the number of U.S. patents awarded to foreign residents has grown to about 50 percent of the total (O'Brien, 2005).

To address this issue, two important shifts need to be taken into consideration with regard to education. There is an alarming lack of new U.S. scientists, especially among women and minorities, and there is woefully insufficient funding for basic research in engineering and the physical sciences. If these developments are not reversed, the U.S. will lose both its technological and innovative edge within the coming generation. Recent calls for educational reform are reminiscent of the United States' response to the Soviet Union's launching of the Sputnik satellite in 1957. By 1958, the U.S. had passed the National Defense Education Act in response to the challenge. In effect, this nationalized the education system to meet the needs of Cold War competition by adopting more formal methods of instruction, and providing economic and other incentives for private and state universities to

perform federally supported research. While the U.S. government expressed a willingness to invest heavily in education, innovation, and research at that time, that is no longer the case today.

It also is interesting to note that both Russia and Japan have backed away from state-mandated curricula and exam-driven assessments as the U.S. continues to broaden the use of standardized examinations as exemplified by the No Child Left Behind Act.

The downturn in the Japanese economy in the 1990s fueled educational changes to respond more effectively to the pressures of globalization. Japan determined that its educational system needed to de-emphasize uniformity and promote innovation by decentralizing control of schools, to allow more parental involvement, and increase intellectual diversity. A Japanese educational report stated that "people in the world are linked directly, information is instantly shared, and the globalization of the economy is progressing. The structure and aspects of society have been changing on a global scale, and complexities have emerged which are difficult to cope with given existing organizations and systems. ... The traditional education system is lagging behind the current of the times" (Spring, 2006, p. 217). Clearly, the U.S. Department of Education ought to take studies and trends in the international educational arena into account to prepare future generations of U.S. students for an increasingly globalized market.

Businesses need to take increased interest in training their knowledge workers to maintain their competitive edge. EDS is a leading example by "providing 20,000 of its 87,000 technical workers with updated business and technology skills . . . by enrolling in one or more of the 718 training courses it has set up for 2005" (Hoffman, 2005). Some analysts stress that people skills and verbal communication skills are equally important as technical skills to develop future leaders with the ability to synthesize and integrate knowledge across many disciplines. The E.U.'s educational policy uses regionalism to cope with global economic competition by encouraging students to learn two additional languages beside their own, while emphasizing sciences and mathematics. The "Lisbon strategy" includes improving education and teacher training, and developing skills for a knowledge-based society by improving access to IT, increasing recruitment in scientific and technical studies, and an emphasis on lifelong training. Several European countries have initiated apprenticeship programs to train call center operators able to respond effectively to customer needs in multiple languages. Their training consists of effective e-mail responses to customer inquiries, problem-solving, and technical training. One company, Techovate, has hired young, adventurous European workers for their call centers in India. These workers receive the prevailing Indian pay, live quite well locally, and gain valuable international experience that often leads to management positions after several years abroad (Overdorf, 2005).

The U.S. faces a politically charged problem with regard to language studies. Cultural conservatives support English-only instruction to enhance national unity and economic strength, which also is enforced by the No Child Left Behind Act. Some politicians believe that it is unnecessary to learn other languages since the U.S. dominates the world economic scene, but others are realizing that "gaps in our national language capabilities have undermined cross-cultural communication and understanding at home and abroad" (Spring, 2006, p. 249). An article in Education Week reports that "national-security experts have warned that U.S. foreign-language capabilities are insufficient to meet the demands for translators, analysts, and other critical positions in government and business" (cited in Spring, 2006, p. 249). This shortage has prompted the U.S. Department of Defense to open foreign language centers.

The Cultural Lens

Cultural understanding and cross-cultural communication is a significant driver for offshore outsourcing. It is also one of the most neglected issues often causing consternation among corporate managers. At the outset, culture does not seem to be a factor in the cost-cutting equation of outsourcing, but it is important for enhancing communication

and for the development of strong client-vendor relationships. Prahalad and Lieberthal (1998) raise some pertinent questions: "How many of today's multinationals are prepared to accommodate 30 % or 40 % of their top team of 200 coming from China, India and Brazil? How will that cultural mix influence decision making, risk taking, and team building? Diversity will put an enormous burden on top-level managers to articulate clearly the values and behaviors expected of senior managers, and it will demand large investments in training and socialization..." (cited in Deal, 2000).

Cultural sensitivity or rather the lack of ethnocentrism plays a pivotal role in international business. Inter-cultural communication between clients and vendors across the globe will require cultural literacy in terms of understanding the other culture to function effectively within it. Managers in the outsourcing business should be aware that different cultures have different attitudes towards work and time. People in Latin America, Mediterranean and South Asian cultures are casual about their use of time, while Americans and Japanese are typically punctual. Notable cultural differences exist in leadership styles, too. Large American firms developed leadership in terms of professional management and its capital is obtained from the capital markets rather than from private family fortunes. Therefore, their leadership styles are responsive to boards of directors and to Wall Street (Quinn, 2005). Other cultures may have a high prevalence of family based leadership styles. Quinn (2005) notes that European and Japanese chief executives are the most consensus-oriented, and Chinese and American top executives are more likely to make decisions based on their own sense of accountability.

When a company is hiring a vendor for outsourced work, it should acquaint itself with local leadership styles and work ethic. Organizations hoping to operate successfully on a global level must be cognizant of both language and cultural traditions in order to promote their goods effectively in the global marketplace, particularly when collaborating with offshore companies. In addition, social pressures among workers in newly-industrialized countries, who earn a higher than average income in comparison with workers in other sectors, can quickly reject traditional arrangements of communally-oriented decision making, which often creates intergenerational or communal conflict.

A host of cultural challenges for new and established business ventures can be found in every country, and even in specific regions within each country. Corporate managers interested in serving the best interest of their company, and keen on satisfying both the needs of their customers and employees, need to display clear signs of cultural competency and sensitivity. Managers must now be astute observers of political and social conditions, and attain the ability to acquire superb local support networks, including language experts.

Operating a supply chain in China, for example, can create obstacles that are unfamiliar to many U.S. and European managers. The Chinese government regularly interferes with international trade regulations complicated by the fact that laws are not uniformly enforced. The practice of bribing, although officially classified as a crime in China as in the U.S. and Europe, is a reality in China and can become necessary to accomplish specific trans-actions. Personal relationships—*guanxi*—play an important role in Chinese business, leading many Western companies to hire Chinese import/export companies to utilize their regional contacts in order to expedite customs clearances and facilitate other transportation issues (Koch, 2005). A collaborative relationship with local experts, not just expatriates who have long-standing experience in a country, creates a network that allows for rapid assessments of emerging cultural conflicts and can reduce disputes over the interpretation of contractual terms.

The Internet and other commercial forces have spread pop culture through music, movies, and fashion, but the underlying ideas and values expressed through pop culture often cause the most intense cultural disagreements around the world. The Internet as a medium for cultural exchange has prompted some to protect their regions from perceived threats of Western influence. Negative public reactions to the dissemination of Western commercial and media images, and the availability of certain products have caused disruptions, particularly in countries where cultural taboos, religious beliefs, and social conservatism are in direct conflict with more liberal traditions in the West. This leads to restrictive import laws in several Islamic countries such as Pakistan, Iran, and the Gulf States including Saudi Arabia where sexuality and women's roles in society are formalized, controlled, and restricted. The Wahhabi reform movement, which originally emerged within Saudi Arabia, introduced limits on the use of alcohol and tobacco, and imposed a far stricter enforcement of rules related to the segregation of the sexes. Over the past decades Saudi Arabia spent substantial amounts of money on religious and social projects in other Muslim countries that are dependent on financial support from wealthy oil countries in the Gulf region. As a consequence, a growing number of religious institutions have made a reactionary shift towards conservative ideas and values.

Managers must be fully aware that the impact of globalization, including the spread of ideas, customs, and commercial ventures, has been highly controversial in many countries. While an increasing amount of web pages in languages other than English will eventually cause a back-feed of ideas and practices from East to West and from South to North, the current dominance of English and Western concepts of commercialism often threaten local cultures. Supporters of globalization argue that the spread of ideas such as democracy and capitalism will lead to eventual improvements in standards of living worldwide. They propose that free markets will allow people in less developed countries to gain economic opportunities that they did not enjoy before. Opponents of globalization, however, assert that free markets provide multi-national corporations with the ability to ignore labor, cultural, human rights, and environmental standards to increase their profits. In turn, those profits are utilized, critics suggest, to continue to marginalize or exclude local enterprises and cultural peculiarities. This translates into a growing gap between the wealthy and the poor, some of whom remain permanently excluded from the benefits of globalization. Stiglitz (2003) warns that rapid globalization can have a devastating impact on the environment, and also inhibits cultural adaptation to market changes, resulting in increased crime, migration, and other effects of social dissolution.

The widespread use of English in business and media is driving a process of cultural homogenization, albeit to varying degrees. International aid organizations, such as the World Bank, the Asian Development Bank, the Association of Southeast Asian Nations (ASEAN), the International Monetary Fund (IMF), the United Nations (UN) and other non-governmental organizations use English as one of their predominant working languages. English has become a vehicle for participation in the global economy and has taken on a utilitarian, commercial purpose. English, however, also represents a different legacy. It is one of the languages of colonization, used to train the native elite to implement repressive laws on behalf of the colonizers and to protect colonial structures. The dominance of English today creates new global boundaries based on emerging post-modern social and economic class structures. The lack of specific language skills can create insurmountable barriers, prohibiting people from contributing their knowledge and experience to conversations about their own country's future, and its political, economic, and socio-cultural direction. Elite schools that teach English in developing countries often exacerbate economic inequalities that contribute to strong anti-western feelings. After several devastating terror attacks in Africa, Europe, Australia, and the U.S. it has become quite obvious that studying English and having a sense of familiarity with Western education and culture may not necessarily lead to the adoption or acceptance of those value systems, but instead can contribute to a process of extreme alienation and rejection.

In the case of India, it is clear that the country enjoys a language advantage in comparison with other newly industrialized nations such as Mexico. India's English-speaking workforce, its strong cultural bias towards education and self-improvement opens up vast opportunities for the current generation of young and educated workers. But some language difficulties continue to persist. For example, Dell closed a customer support center in India because customer satisfaction plummeted after callers failed to understand accents or terminology used by call center staff (Castro, 2003). However, there are many successful help desk operations and call centers in India who provide their employees with specific language training in American, British, and Canadian accents to facilitate communication and improve customer service. Most call center respondents interviewed for this chapter in Bangalore have gone through "accent neutralization" courses. Call center agents are expected to speak without a heavy accent. It is interesting to find "call center colleges" and training institutes that initiate the young workforce into the outsourcing culture.

In India, English language skills can raise an individual's income from about $80/month to over $200/month within a call center environment and in data entry related employment. This represents a dramatic rise in social status. Call center work is much more respected in emerging countries than in highly developed countries. A call center college principal in Bangalore interviewed for this study remarks: "The training program goes on for 4-5 weeks. We assure them placement on the successful completion of the training. The idea is to get into an international call center because of the higher pay-scale…Some companies have higher demands. For example, IBM wants royally excellent people."

Some Asian countries, including Japan and China, maintain their strong national identity while focusing on English language instruction. Japan promotes English at all levels of school, and encourages overseas study. China highlighted its growing competency in English by competing for and winning the bid to host the 2008 Olympics. Many countries emphasize the utility of English as the common commercial language yet support regional and national languages in schools and at home. Local dialects and expressions are often helpful for creating effective advertising campaigns although the pervasiveness of international consumer brand names regularly contributes to the adoption of foreign phrases, symbols, and terminology. Many transnational corporations have successfully adapted to local tastes while maintaining their brand identity.

FUTURE RESEARCH DIRECTIONS: GENDER, HEALTH, AND ENVIRONMENT

We propose gender, health, and environment as three additional areas that merit attention for future research directions. The increasing and evolving role of women in IT and outsourcing makes it imperative for future research agendas to do a systematic analysis of gender issues. In addition, health and environment directly impact employees' levels of stress, absenteeism, and customer service. Managers will need to assess the conditions under which employees work prior to undertaking outsourcing initiatives.

The BPO industry is witnessing an overwhelming entry of women into the hi-tech workforce in countries like India, Israel, and Turkey. However, in developing countries, "women are concentrated in routine jobs at lower levels and lower salaries than men. For example, women constitute a disproportionately high number of employees in call center services, data entry, and programming, but there are very few women at the managerial levels" (World Bank, 2006). This reality must be taken into consideration. Hafkin and Taggart (2001) argue that, in order to retain and build upon the employment gains associated with globalization and information technology, women also need to have the opportunity to move into more technical, higher-level, and better-paying jobs. It is essential to note that global information technology and offshore outsourcing does not simply have an impact on technical aspects of a society, but also influences social aspects. This is nowhere more evident than in the discussion of gender. When women enter technological spaces, they are also promoting social and cultural changes. Increased employment opportunities allow women to control their earnings and strengthen their status within the household. Over time women become

empowered as wage earners and eventually gain a political voice in countries where they have not mobilized traditionally. Just as technology is often accompanied with social change—Jansen (1989) aptly remarks "technological designs are social designs" (p. 196)—gender has a similar impact. Many outsourcing stakeholders are increasingly realizing the importance of gender issues and capability building among women (Brennan, 2004).

In countries like India, where women would have ordinarily worked in a typical 9-5 job or stayed at home, they are breaking conventional barriers by working at odd hours, usually the night shift. They are making use of multiple domain expertise like banking, insurance, investment, and information technology. The ratio of Indian women software professionals in information technology is rising steadily and is likely to be 65 (men):35 (women) by the end of 2007 (Padmanabhan, 2006).

In contrast to the Indian scenario, a recent study conducted by the Information Technology Association of America shows a large decline in women's workforce in IT (it was 41% in 1996 and fell to 32.5% in 2004). This reduction in the percentage of women in the IT workforce primarily targeted women holding administrative positions (Bakshi, 2005).

Besides India and China, Israel is another big player in the BPO space. Additional countries where a growing number of women work in call centers include South Africa, Northern Ireland, Ireland, the Philippines, the Czech Republic, Poland, Hungary, and Russia. In 2004, the proportion of male versus female workers in IT services was 76:24, while in contrast, the ratio stood at 31:69 in the BPO industry. Such developments make it obvious that an understanding of gender issues becomes imperative for managers who lead BPO and call center operations in countries where growing numbers of women are employed. Successful managers are expected to be sensitive to gender-specific concerns and to take appropriate action to protect female employees from sexual harassment, a hostile work environment, and outright violence.

One issue that often intersects with gender is that of safety of women employees—an issue not to be ignored by managers developing an outsourcing blueprint. The most pressing issues regarding women who work in BPO firms in India deals with their physical safety following the end of their shifts. With close to 40% of women in BPO's working during the night shift, the possibility of physical assaults and violence against them is high. In a particularly notorious case, a young woman working for HCL's call center in Bangalore was brutally raped and murdered in 2005. As a result of public pressure, companies increased security and offered female employees guarded transportation that drops them at home. The ability and willingness of corporations to protect their female employees from violence will determine the future role women play in the BPO industry in many markets.

Mainstream research on offshore outsourcing has often ignored the issues of employee wellness and health. It is interesting to note that employee health and wellness have been incorporated in western organizational philosophies. However, when such companies outsource their work to some of the cost-effective locations these issue are often compromised. In a post-modern organizational culture, wherein capital and labor are witnessing cross-border travel, so should the philosophies of health and wellness. Considerations related to the working environment ought to be of particular interest to managers keen on working with a highly motivated and energetic workforce.

Managers must be concerned with social and ethical implications of outsourcing. Workers who experience inhumane working conditions such as poor air quality, a lack of air circulation and excessive heat, the absence of proper sanitary facilities and potable water will eventually commit acts of sabotage or direct their anger at someone within call center operations. As Weincek (2004) remarks, "one current ethical question with which managers must deal with is determining what should be the company's responsibility for outside workers, their work environment, and their community?…Should the outsourcing company ensure that the workers are treated fairly by the company's standards? Should the outsourcing company be responsible for employee safety and working conditions?" (p. 149)

Qualitative data collected for this research—primarily in the form of interviews from call-center employees—brought the health issue to the forefront of the outsourcing debate. The criticality of health as an emerging consideration was one of the central themes generated by our respondents. One of the respondents for this study rightly remarks:

Surely health problems. Your biological system is changed. You are awake at a time when your system is used to sleep. I have acidity problems and problems related to digestion. We skip many meals or eat them at odd times. That does not go well with the body clock.

Managers need to ponder such employee concerns since motivated and loyal employees who work in a healthy atmosphere are crucial to maintain a long-term sustainable advantage. Several factors contribute to the lack of attention to environmental and labor issues in IT outsourcing. The first is a narrow understanding of IT outsourcing in developing countries, with a specific focus on core capabilities. Mitchell (2004) argues that outsourcing brokers, client representatives and third party project managers in the IT and BPO outsourcing arena do not wish to risk alienating their clients, colleagues and counterparts by raising issues of environmental responsibility and fair labor practices offshore.

Industrial companies in India have opened software development and call center divisions to take advantage of the tax holidays provided to firms with export-oriented IT divisions. These tax holidays are being used to declare income from polluting industrial activities as having been derived from IT operations. An industrial firm with an IT division can avoid high Indian tax rates on non-IT income by routing that income through a firm's IT division. (Mitchell, 2004: 1)

In response to such developments, social justice non-profit organizations propose ongoing training and education seminars for employees as a vehicle to empower workers to become leaders within their own societies. The aim is to protect not only labor standards, but also to improve environmental standards and conserve land and resources for future generations. Global environmental issues are very real and growing: a study released by environmental groups in China found that nearly two hundred of China's largest cities had dangerously high pollution levels (Fishman, 2005). In countries with a high percentage of indigenous populations such as Guatemala for example, it is important to establish a flow of communication with local community leaders and activists to support the preservation of indigenous peoples' traditional knowledge and to show respect for their relationship to their region's natural resources (Spring, 2006).

CONCLUSION

Assessing political, organizational, economic, technological, educational, legal, and cultural considerations can turn a disappointing outsourcing experience into a successful partnership. Companies need to encourage their project managers to become intellectually curious about issues beyond the immediate technological and bottom-line questions at hand in order to maintain a high level of competitiveness in a globalized market.

Many aspects of programming and accounting work are becoming a commodity. Flexibility and continued innovation are needed to "create value through leadership, relationships, and creativity." Special attention should be paid to the dynamic of adding value with higher-end customer services such as systems analysis or financial services rather than routine tasks (Kearney, 2005).

In this era of globalization, BPO managers and executives need to prepare employees to develop skills that encourage team-building, cultural sensitivity, and political literacy. To be competitive in the modern workplace, decision-makers need to develop a holistic approach to analyzing future opportunities, or they will find themselves ill-prepared to deal with unanticipated or surprising events.

The multi-lens model provides managers with a tool that helps them anticipate potential obstacles to a successful outsourcing experience in newly industrialized countries. Decision-makers can utilize the lenses to gain valuable perspectives and insights into a world less familiar to them, and develop a holistic appreciation for the confluence of different, but tangential global dynamics that shape our lives and, inevitably, our future.

REFERENCES

Andersen, D., & Dawes, S. (1991). *Government information management: A primer and casebook.* Upper Saddle River, NJ: Prentice-Hall.

Baltzan, P., & Phillips, A. (2008). B*usiness driven information systems.* McGraw-Hill.

Benn, I., & Pearcy J. (2003). *Strategic outsourcing.* Oxon, UK: Hodder & Stoughton.

Bowman, R. (2005, March). *Thinking strategically about outsourcing: 3PLs can do much more than cut costs.* Retrieved August 12, 2006, from http://www.supplychainbrain.com

Bhagwati, J. (2004). In defense of globalization. London: Oxford University Press.

Brandel, M. (2007, March 12). *Outsourcing 2.0: The business rationale for exporting your job.* Computerworld.

Brennan, L., & Johnson, V. (2004). *Social, ethical, and policy implications of information technology.* London: Information Science Publishing.

Castro, A. (2003, November 24). *Amid complaints, Dell closes overseas call centers, USA Today.* Retrieved April 27, 2007, from http://www.usatoday.com/tech/news/2003-11-24-dell-support-home_x.htm

Couto, V., & Divakaran, A. (2006). *How to be an outsourcing virtuoso.* Strategy + Business. Retrieved September 10, 2006, from http://www.Strategy-business.com/resilience/rr00036

Deal, T., & Kennedy, A. (2000). *The new corporate culture.* Cambridge, MA: Perseus Books.

Denning, P. J., & McGettrick, A. (2005, November). Recentering computer science. *Communications of the ACM, 48*, 15.

ESRC (Economic and Social Research Council). Retrieved April 12, 2007, from http://www.esrc. ac.uk/ESRCInfoCentre/about/CI/CP/Our_Society_Today/globalisation/GloExp.aspx?ComponentId=15223&SourcePageId=16965

Fishman, T. (2005). *China, Inc.* New York: Scribner.

Fitzgerald, M. (2003, November). At risk offshore. *CIO Magazine, 17*(4).

Francis, D. (2004, October 14). Endangered species: US programmers. *Christian Science Monitor, 17*.

Friedman, T. (2000). *The Lexus and the olive tree: Understanding globalization.* New York, NY: Anchor.

Friedman, T. (2005a). *The world is flat.* New York: Farrar, Straus and Giroux.

Friedman, T. (2005b, October 14). *Science needs to top national conversation.* The Times Union.

Friedman, T. (2005c, May 31), *Globalization 3.0.* Blueprint Magazine. Retrieved May 10, 2006, from http://www.dlc.org

Gens, F. (2004, October). *Offshoring U.S. IT services: It's less and more than you may think.* Retrieved July 10, 2006, from http://www.idc.com

Hain, T., et al. (n.d.). *e-Nations, The Internet for all.* Retrieved April 10, 2007, from http://www.nav6tf.org/documents/e-Nations-Internet-For-All.pdf

Hamm, S. (2006, June 5). *IBM wakes ip to India's skills.* Business Week.

Hoffman, T. (2005, March 7). *EDS pushing massive IT retraining effort.* Computerworld.

Jana, R. (2007, March 12, p. 2). *Inside innovation: Custom corporate games.* BusinessWeek.

Kearney, A. T. (2005, May/June). Measuring globalization, Foreign Policy, 52-59.

Kobayashi-Hillary, M. (2005). *Outsourcing to India: The offshore advantage.* New York: Springer.

Koch, C. (2005, October). Making it in China. *CIO Magazine, 19*(2).

Kripalani, M. (2006, August 7). Call center? That's so 2004. Business Week.

Mittelman, J. H. (Ed.). (1996). *Globalization: Critical reflections.* Boulder, CO: Lynne Rienner Publishers.

Magnusson, P. (2004, December 6). How to level the playing field. *BusinessWeek.*

McCarthy, J. (2002, November). *3.3 million US services jobs to go offshore.* Forrester Research. Retrieved on July 10, 2006, from http://www.forrester.com

McKinsey Global Institute (2005). *The emerging global labor market.* Retrieved July 24, 2006, from http://www.mckinsey.com/knowledge/mgi

Mitchell, A. (2004). *Offshore environment, labor practices challenged.* In E-Commerce Times, Retrieved April 12, 2007, from http://www.technewsworld.com/story/37586.html

Mitchell, A. (2004). Environmental impacts of outsourcing. In *E-Commerce Times.* Retrieved April 12, 2007, from the World Wide Web http://www.technewsworld.com/story/37421.html

Neuhaus, M., & Kunze, F. (2006). *Inshoring to Germany: Global networking is not a one-way street.* Deutsche Bank Research. Retrieved on April 5, 2007, from http://www.dbresearch.com

O'Brien, J., & Marakas, G. (2006). *Management information systems.* Columbus, OH: McGraw-Hill.

O'Brien, T. (2005, November 13). Not invented here. *New York Times,* p. 21.

Overby, S. (2005, October). Secrets of the outsourcing masters. *CIO Magazine, 19*(1).

Overdorf, J. (January-February, 2005). Outsourcing jobs to … Europeans? *Business 2.0, 6*(1), 32.

Padmanabhan, P. (2006, March). *Women and IT: Perfectly matched.* CIOL. Retrieved September 10, 2006, from http://www.ciol.com/content/search/showarticle1.asp?artid=81488

Pieterse, J. N. (2004). *Globalization and culture: Global mélange.* New York: Rowman and Littlefield Publishers.

Pralahad, C. K. (2005, June 8). The art of outsourcing. *The Wall Street Journal* p. A14.

Puliyenthuruthel, J. (2005, April 25). The soft underbelly of outsourcing. *Business Week.*

Ribeiro, J. (2003, December 1). *India hits back on outsourcing job fears.* InfoWorld. Retrieved April 28, 2007, from http://www.infoworld.com/article/03/12/01/HNindiahitsback_1.html

Spring, J. (2006). *The rise of the educational security state.* Mahwah, NJ: Lawrence Erlbaum.

Steger, M. (2003). *Globalization: A very short introduction.* New York: Oxford University Press.

Stiglitz, J. (2003). *Globalization and its discontents.* New York: W.W. Norton and Company.

Strategic Review 2004. *The IT industry in India.* New Delhi: NASSCOM.

The Economist. (2006, June 17). The physical Internet: *A survey of logistics*, pp. 1-20.

The Economist. (2006a, July 29). *The future of globalization*, p. 11.

Thibodeau, P. (2006, April 24). IT inion head opposes H-1B increase, seeks aid for workers hit by offshoring. *Computerworld*, p. 20.

U.S. Department of Commerce. (2003). *Dispute avoidance and dispute resolution.* Retrieved April 29, 2007, from http://www.export.gov/china/exporting_to_china/disputeavoidanceandresolution.pdf

Vijayan, J. (2004, August 30). A painfully slow process. *Computerworld.* Wharton School. What's driving India's rise as an R & D hub?

Knowledge @ Wharton. Retrieved September 10, 2006, from http://knowledge.wharton.upenn.edu/index.cfm?fa=viewArticle&id=1274&specialId=40

Wiencek, D. (2004). Ethical challenges of information systems: The carnage of outsourcing and other technology–Enabled organizational imperatives. In L. Brennan & V. Johnson (Eds.), *Social, ethical, and policy implications of information technology.* London: Information Science Publishing.

Wild, J., Wild, K., & Han, J. (2005). *International business-The challenges of globalization.* Upper Saddle River, NJ: Prentice Hall.

Woodard, C. (2007, March 9). *Eastern Europe's silicon rush.* The Chronicle of Higher Education.

World Bank Group. Retrieved April 12, 2007, from http://www1.worldbank.org/economicpolicy/globalization/index.html

World Bank. (2006). *Information and communication technologies (ICT's) women's enterprises and labor force participation.*

Worthen, B. (2004, November 15). A new glue or the old soft shoe? *CIO Magazine, 18*(4).

ADDITIONAL READINGS

Castells, M. (1996-1998). *The information age: Economy, society, and culture.* Oxford: Blackwell.

Crothers, L. (2007). *Globalization and American pop culture.* New York: Rowman and Littlefield Publishers.

Giddens, A. (1999). *Runaway world: How globalization is reshaping our lives.* London: Profile Books.

Hafkin, N., & Taggart, N. (2001). *Gender, information technology, and developing countries:* An analytic study, for the Office of Women in Development Bureau for Global Programs, Field Support and Research, United States Agency for International Development (USAID). Retrieved

April 12, 2007, from http://www.usaid.gov/wid/pubs/hafnoph.pdf

Hall, E. T., & Hall, M. R. (1990) *Understanding cultural differences*. Yarmouth, ME: Intercultural Press.

Hawkesworth, M. E. (2006). *Globalization and feminist activism*. New York: Rowman and Littlefield Publishers.

Krieger, J. (Ed.) (2006). *Globalization and state power*. New York: Pearson Longman Publishers.

Lechner, F., & Boli, J. (Eds.). (2000). *The globalization reader*. Malden, MA: Blackwell Publishing.

O'Meara, P., Mehlinger, H., & Krain, M. (Eds.). (2000) *Globalization and the challenges of the new century: A reader*. Bloomington, IN: Indiana University Press.

Veseth, M. (2005). *Globaloney: Unraveling the myths of globalization*. New York: Roman and Littlefield Publishers.

Chapter XIV
Global IT Outsourcing:
Current Trends, Risks, and Cultural Issues

Subhankar Dhar
San Jose State University, USA

ABSTRACT

Enterprises inside and outside the IT industry have long used offshore developments and outsourcing methods to reduce information system development and maintenance costs and as a source of specialized, low-wage workers. In the last decade, there has been a spur of activities in offshore outsourcing, which is driven by the e-business revolution and a worldwide demand for IT skills. This contributed to the growth of IT-related industries in countries such as Ireland and India. Meanwhile, vendors from the Philippines, Russia, Hungary, China, Taiwan, Mexico, and other countries entered the market; and in some cases, adapted business models established by Indian firms that have dominated the services sector in the past decade. The emergence of new offshore centers has been marked by new approaches and skill sets, adding to the services and value propositions that define the offshore sector today. In this paper, we will identify the main risk factors and best practices in global IT outsourcing. In addition, we will delve into some important issues on IT outsourcing, particularly the challenges as well as the benefits. Finally, we will present case studies of two Global 200 organizations and validate some of the claims made by previous researchers on IT outsourcing. This study will help management to identify risk factors and take the necessary remedial steps.

INTRODUCTION

In today's global economy, outsourcing has become a very common phenomenon. Many large organizations have outsourced some or all of their IT functions. Factors like lower costs, improved productivity, higher quality, higher customer satisfaction, time to market, and ability to focus on core areas are some of the benefits of outsourcing. However, there are many challenges and risks associated with IT outsourcing (Alvares et al., 1995; Beamish et al., 1995; Feeny et al., 1995; Lacity and Willcocks; 1995, Cross, 1995; Nam et al., 1996; Bahli and Rivard, 2003; Lee et al., 2003; Rothman, 2003; Sabherwal, 2003; Adeleye et al., 2004; Dibbern and Goles, 2004).

IT outsourcing is as an act of delegating or transferring some or all of the IT related decision making rights, business processes, internal activities, and services to external providers, who develop, manage, and administer these activities in accordance with agreed upon deliverables, performance standards and outputs, as set forth in the contractual agreement (Dhar et al., 2004).

Whenever there is an outsourcing decision, there is an inherent risk associated with it. In addition, in any outsourcing deal, there are some hidden costs, unexpected outcomes, diminishing service levels, to name a few (Earl 1996; Lacity & Hirschheim, 1993; Antonucci et al., 1998; Aubert et al., 2001; Clark et al., 1995; King et al., 2000).

There are four major aspects of the proposed research that are summarized by the following questions:

1.   What are the objectives of outsourcing?
2.   What are the major factors that contribute to risk in global offshore IT outsourcing? How do we minimize the risk in IT outsourcing projects?
3.   What are best practices for outsourcing?
4.   How do we validate some of the assumptions made by prior research?

Although there are quite a number of studies that address the risk factors and hidden costs in outsourcing, we found out that there is no single study that takes a comprehensive approach to analyzing the issues like risks, benefits, challenges, and best practices in the context of global outsourcing. In addition, many of the important risk factors that are quite important to global outsourcing are not properly analyzed. Of particular interest to us are the effects of risk assessment factors like geographical location, political, cultural, quality standards, legal contracts and intellectual property, as many of these were not well studied or well documented before. These are some of the motivating factors behind this study, where we address not only the risks and benefits, but also the challenges and best practices, two case studies, and to validate some of the claims made by previous researchers on IT outsourcing. Hence, this research fills the gap in the current literature with regards to risk assessment factors in offshore outsourcing in a global context.

This paper discusses current trends in IS outsourcing, cross cultural issues and presents case studies of two Global 200 organizations and validates some of the claims made by previous research on IT outsourcing. Our main contribution in this paper is to identify sixteen different risk assessment factors that are quite sensitive to global IT outsourcing. In addition, we also analyzed two large organizations (FIRM-1 and FIRM-2) that are currently outsourcing their IT functions and identify the objectives, key benefits, important risk factors, challenges and best practices. We also found how transaction cost theory has played an important factor in the decision making process for outsourcing. This research is unique in the sense that it analyzes two multinational organizations FIRM -1 and FIRM-2 that have been involved in outsourcing for quite sometime. The outsourcing work is done on remote offshore locations in India, China and some other countries in Asia. Hence, this study is truly global in nature as both the organizations conduct business in various parts of the world including the Americas, Europe, Asia, and Australia and in some parts of Africa. In addition, FIRM-1 is one of the suppliers of FIRM-2. Thus both organizations have common goals of making their global supply chain successful, and maximizing the overall profitability. Finally, we do a comparison of each of these factors for both the organizations. Hence, this study is timely and relevant from both an academic and a practitioner's perspective.

CURRENT TRENDS IN GLOBAL IT OUTSOURCING

In recent years, with globalization and improved communication infrastructure, there has been a spur of activities in global outsourcing also known as offshore outsourcing. Offshore outsourcing had been considered as an irreversible mega trend, in view of such factors as lower domestic economic growths during the years 2001-2003, increased domestic wage rates during the years 1998-2000, and ability of the offshore vendor to offer lower wage rates. Also, in view of the domestic economic recovery (Chabrow, 2003) almost competitive lower rates offered by domestic IT services companies, and increasing feedback on outsourced offshore software projects in year 2002-2003 (Overby, 2003; Koch, 2003), as being made available, will throw some light on the earlier assumptions of offshore outsourcing being considered as an irreversible mega trend. Further, some state governments are taking steps to reduce offshore IT outsourcing under domestic and political pressures. The current trends in global IT outsourcing, as per Drew Robb (2002) and Gartner (Morello, 2003) can be summarized as follows:

a. **More software related work will be outsourced overseas in the coming years.** According to Forrester Research, the demand for offshore outsourcing will account for 28% of IT budgets in Europe and the U.S. within two years. Further, the number of offshore IT workers worldwide (software developers working overseas on projects for Western firms) will go from 360,000 today to more than 1 million by the end of the decade.

b. **Some of the major corporations are opening dedicated offshore development centers.** While many small and medium-sized enterprises started offshore outsourcing with small projects, larger enterprises started to invest large amounts of money by setting up huge dedicated development centers in their countries of choice. For example, several years ago, Microsoft, Oracle, Intel, Hewlett-Packard and GE had already built campuses in India. Over the past couple of years, though, Intel, Boeing and Motorola have preferred Russia as the best place for dedicated centers. Intel has 400 workers at one Russian center working on wireless LAN and modem projects. It plans to ramp this up to more than 1,000 staff over the next couple of years.

c. **The standardization and protection of intellectual property (IP).** One of the biggest challenges the enterprises are facing today is protection of the intellectual property. Some

enterprises are quite reluctant to outsource information systems development in countries where piracy is abundant and IP protection law is still in its infancy. Enterprises are particularly concerned about these issues with countries like China and Russia where governments are receptive to changes in the law that will protect IP. But with leading global corporations now heavily involved in Russia and India, the legislative picture is changing.

d. **Global outsourcing moves up the value chain.** In the early stages of outsourcing, low-end jobs, back office operations, and call centers were outsourced. Once the vendors delivered services successfully and gained high confidence level from the enterprises, they began to outsource high-end jobs like design and development. This trend is going to continue in the coming years.

e. **Stratification of offshore countries based on cost and skill sets.** Countries like India and Ireland offer a very attractive destination for outsourcing because of lower cost and an available skilled talent pool. However, the wages are also rising in these countries as more and more enterprises are outsourcing their work there. In addition, there are also some hidden costs associated with outsourcing that diminishes the cost advantage factor. Ireland, for example, can no longer compete on price with most countries. And India now finds itself sub-contracting work to China and Malaysia in an effort to stay competitive. To survive, these countries must move up the value chain while others take their place as the place to go to find an abundance of highly skilled programmers at low rates.

f. **Outsourcer and the vendor are forming long-term strategic partnerships.** The outsourcing vendors are becoming strategic partners of the enterprises for whom they are doing the outsourcing job. This partnership is based on long-term commitments and mutual trust from both the parties. After all, trust is one of the most significant successes in an outsourcing deal.

g. **Application on demand enabled by application service provider (ASP) is becoming popular (Lee et al., 2002).** One of the most promising business models that have emerged is the application service provider (ASP), which is based on the utility computing model and is enabled by the Internet (Lee et al., 2003). The ASP model offers the deployment and management of various IT functions over the World Wide Web or private network. The revenue model is based per-user fee or monthly fee. ASP offers low cost alternatives to huge IT investments, access to highly complex packaged software products, and faster deployment of IT solutions managed by a third party. Although there are some tangible benefits of ASP, there are some potential drawbacks. Since ASP's provide packaged software solutions, sometimes they may not be able to provide customizations that are required for each individual business processes.

CULTURAL ISSUES IN OFFSHORE OUTSOURCING

a. **Cultural awareness:** Cultural issues have significant impact on the success or failure of global IT outsourcing. There are many challenges that arise from offshore outsourcing when people from two (or more) different cultures work on a project. Managers need to understand that cultural barriers and resistance to change have adverse effects, which have to be dealt with an exceptional ability to blend the culture of the partnering organization and corporate departments. Executives should review their own company's culture and that of the outsourcing organization and understand them both. This will provide valuable insights during the process of outsourcing.

b. **Cross-cultural communications:** Problems can arise between the outsourcing partners where native languages of the people involved are different. There is evidence that

Norwegian companies who outsource their work prefer Russian counterparts for an outsourcing partner to Asian partners because of physical proximity, cultural affinity towards a European mindset, and the relative ease with which the Russians learn the Norwegian language (Krishna et al., 2004).

c. **Relationship management:** Relationship management is another important aspect related to cultural issues in outsourcing. When selecting a provider, companies must set up a worst-case scenario and use the best people to manage the deal. Some believe that with the onset of ASPs and globalization, outsourcing will become a critical strategy placing a burden on the formation of a successful partnership. Executives generally believe that retaining and developing employees is critical for success. They also contend that culture is the heart of the company and management must retain the best people and focus on the basics.

People development is an essential management skill and never more needed than in the context of the changes required during the process of outsourcing. It is worth remembering that technical changes concerning systems and processes can be made relatively rapidly with the right kind of technical expertise. But the changes in attitudes and behaviors that are essential to sustain the new culture in any outsourcing arrangement can only be achieved at a human pace. One approach to alleviate cultural barriers is to work with teams of compatible cultural background and form strategic partnerships for long term relationship.

THEORETICAL CONCEPTS BEHIND OUTSOURCING

There are various theoretical justifications for outsourcing. The most popular ones are transaction cost theory (TCT) (Williamson, 1995; Ang & Straub, 1998), agency theory (Bahli & Rivert, 2003), and coordination theory (Sabherwal, 2003) to name a few. We have chosen TCT over the other theories in this research because a careful analysis of the two cases revealed that TCT was the basis for their outsourcing decision.

Transactional Cost Theory

A goal of the organization is to reduce cost and to achieve cost efficiency (Aubert et al., 2001; Diromualdo et al., 1998). Keeping that in mind, Williamson developed the transactional cost theory (TCT). Transaction costs are related to the effort, time, and costs associated with searching, creating, negotiating, monitoring, and enforcing a service contract between buyers and suppliers. As per Williamson, there are two types of costs involved for any service—production costs, and coordination cost. Production cost is the cost incurred to make the product or to provide the service. It includes the cost of labor, material, and capital. Coordination costs include monitoring, controlling and managing the work internally. If the job is handed over to an external vendor, the coordination costs are called transaction costs. As per (author's first name needed) Williamson (1985), transaction cost theory depends on the following parameters:

- **Cost:** There are two types of costs associated with any service or product: (1) production cost and (2) transaction cost. Williamson argues externally outsourcing of work results in lower production costs than doing it internally due to economies of scale. But in such a case the transaction cost is high because vendors need to be managed and monitored. In an in-house arrangement, production cost is high because it is difficult to achieve economies of scale. But at the same time, the transaction cost is low because of low coordination costs.
- **Asset specificity:** It is defined as the degree of customization of the transaction. It could be site specificity, physical asset specificity, or human asset specificity. High asset specificity results in high transaction. Also the production cost goes up with high asset specificity because specific assets have limited utility in other markets (Hirschheim & Lacity, 1993).

- **Opportunism threat:** When the work is given to an external vendor, coordination costs increase because quite possibly the vendor may be opportunistic. Hence, managing and monitoring the vendor becomes more difficult. But when the work is done internally coordination costs are low because the workers may be less opportunistic. Vendors also become opportunistic when there is competition in the market, and when there are a less number of vendors (Hirschheim & Lacity, 1993). When there are only a few vendors in the market, organizations looking for such vendors cannot bargain much. Organization may not save much by outsourcing because the vendor may charge excess or may not perform as promised. All these lead to a high transaction cost.
- **Uncertainty:** Williamson outlines that uncertainty increases the transaction cost. Transaction cost goes up especially for asset-specific investments, under uncertain conditions (Hirschheim & Lacity, 1993).

Thus, all these parameters should be weighed well to make a decision. A detailed analysis and trade-off study should be carried out before making an outsourcing decision.

RISKS DEFINED

Risk and risk management have been widely studied in various contexts, such as finance, economics, insurance, healthcare, operations research, and engineering. Each discipline has its own way of analyzing and interpreting risks. This section elaborates the main issues of risks and presents our perspectives on issues related to risks.

Risk as an undesirable event. According to Levine and Schneider (1997, pg. 38), risk is "...*events that, if they occur, represent a material threat to an entity's fortune.*" Using this approach, risk can be interpreted as an occurrence of undesirable events.

a. **Risk as a probability function:** In some disciplines, risk is defined as the probability of an event. *It is the chance of a serious, adverse outcome* (Bahli & Rivard, 2003).

b. **Risk as a variance:** In finance, risk is calculated as the variance of the distribution of outcomes.

c. **Risk as expected loss:** In some disciplines such as casualty insurance, risk is interpreted as expected loss, which is the product of a loss function and a probability function (Bowers et al., 1986).

RISK FACTORS

Many researchers have studied the risk factors that are common in IT outsourcing (Jurison, 1995; Earl, 1996; Overby, 2003; Dhar et al., 2004). We summarize their work on risk factors:

We found that some studies have addressed many risks factors associated with IT outsourcing. We decided to focus specifically on risk factors that are quite common, important and sensitive to global IT outsourcing, and later validate those using case studies. Of particular interest to us are the effects of risk factors like geographical location, political, cultural, quality standards, legal contracts and intellectual property, security, etc.

In the past, information security is often not properly handled in outsourcing arrangements. Recent studies have addressed security concerns in the context of IT outsourcing (Khalfan, 2004). Information security is a combination of three things: integrity, availability and confidentiality. Integrity refers to gathering and maintaining accurate information and discarding outdated information. Availability means making the data available whenever needed. Confidentiality means taking appropriate measures (both software- and hardware-wise) so that unauthorized disclosure of data do not take place. Security services have also been outsourced as noted by Vijayan (2001) and (Schneier 2002). The potential risks are significant and choosing a wrong outsourcer will lead to undesirable consequences.

The important risk factors for our study are summarized as follows, (see Table 2).

Table 1. IT outsourcing risk exposure

Undesirable outcomes	Factors leading to outcome
Unexpected transition and management costs (Cross, 1995; Earl, 1996; Nelson et al, 1996)	• Lack of experience and expertise to the client with the activity (Earl, 1996; Lacity et al., 1995) • Lack of experience of the client with outsourcing (Earl, 1996) • Uncertainty about the legal environment
Switching costs (including lock-in, and repatriation and transfer to another supplier) (O'Leary, 1990)	• Asset specificity (Williamson, 1985) • Small number of suppliers (Nam et al., 1996) • Scope • Interdependence of activities
Costly contractual amendments (Earl, 1996)	• Uncertainty (Alchian & Demsetz, 1972; Barzel, 1982) • Technological Discontinuity (Lacity et al., 1995) • Task complexity
Disputes and litigation (Aubert et al., 1997; Lacity & Hirschheim, 1993)	• Measurement problems (Alchian & Demsetz, 1972; Barzel, 1982) • Lack of experience and expertise of the client and/or of the supplier with outsourcing contracts (Earl, 1996; Lacity et al., 1995) • Uncertainty about the legal environment • Poor cultural fit
Service debasement (Lacity & Hirschheim, 1993)	• Interdependence of activities (Aubert et al., 1997; Langonis &Robertson, 1992) • Lack of experience and expertise of the supplier with activity (Earl, 1996) • Supplier size (Earl, 1996) • Supplier financial stability (Earl, 1996) • Measurement problems (Alchian & Demsetz, 1972; Barzel, 1982) • Task complexity
Cost escalation (Lacity & Hirschheim, 1993; Lacity et al., 1995)	• Lack of experience and expertise of the client with contract management (Earl, 1996; Lacity et al., 1995) • Measurement problems (Alchian &Demsetz, 1972; Barzel, 1982) • Lack of experience and expertise of the supplier with activity (Earl, 1996)

Continued on following page

Table 1. continued

Undesirable outcomes	Factors leading to outcome
Loss of organizational competencies (Earl, 1996; Lacity et al., 1995)	• Scope • Proximity of the core competencies (Hamel & Prahalad, 1990) • Interdependence of activities
Hidden service costs (Lacity & Hirschheim, 1993)	• Complexity of the activities • Measurement problems (Alchian & Demsetz, 1972) • Uncertainty (Barzel, 1982)
Cost of delayed delivery / non-delivery	• Vendor fails to deliver as per contract (Bahli & Rivard, 2003) • Delayed delivery due to unexpected change in the requirements
Poor quality and reliability	• Inability to control vendor's technical quality (Sabherwal, 2003) • Loss of control over vendor's technical quality
Damages due to security breach	• Security requirements practices (Adeleye et al., 2004) • Intellectual property protection • Privacy concerns
Loss due to disasters and recovery costs	• Loss of control over disaster recovery (Dibbern & Goles, 2004) • Loss of data and information
Loss due to vendor's opportunism, including loss in future revenue	• Vendor becomes competitor • Vendor takes advantages of contractual gap and charges additional amount for services (Wang, 2002)
Vendor lock-in	• Long term contractual agreement (Dibbern & Goles, 2004) • Few vendors leads to limited options (Bahli & Rivard, 2003)
Lack of trust	• Uncertainty (Barzel, 1982; Wang, 2002; Adeleye et al, 2004)
Business uncertainties	• Uncertainty (Barzel, 1982; Dibbern &Goles, 2004))

RESEARCH METHOD

In order to investigate our research problems, we did a thorough analysis of two large organizations that are involved in outsourcing. We have chosen these two organizations for various reasons. Both organizations have been doing IT outsourcing globally for several years. In fact, outsourcing has become a part of their business strategy. Their experience in dealing with offshore vendors coupled with efficient project management expertise helped them coordinate business processes over globally distributed teams. In addition, they had already dealt with multi-cultural teams, diverse geographic and political environments, and varying quality and intellectual property standards in different countries, to name a few. Hence, we came to the conclusion that these two organizations are good candidates for our research studies. We conducted in-depth interviews with key personnel, who were carefully chosen based on their roles, responsibilities and experience in dealing with outsourcing projects. Although we interviewed a handful of people, they represent large divisions within their organizations and are actively involved in the outsourcing strategies for their respective organizations. Hence, the data we collected is reliable and truly represents the outsourcing process of their organizations. Our approach is based on positivist case research as proposed in the case research literature (Dube & Parc, 2003), where we focus on qualitative analysis of the results rather than rigorous quantitative and analytical methods. The data was collected during the year 2003. In order to gain insightful information and perspectives on offshore outsourcing, respondents were given a detailed questionnaire to collect data and outsourcing related information. The participants were assured confidentiality of their personal and organizational information.

We analyzed the data by summarizing the interviews and questionnaire completed by each participant from each case. After analyzing the responses from each participant, we again contacted them if necessary for further clarification and explanation. This process of analysis clarified lots of complex issues that they had to deal with and helped us gain further insights in outsourcing.

Table 2. Risk assessment factors

Risk assessment factor	Description	Implications for Global Outsourcing
People	The people risk emerges from the experience level, training, and human resource deployment policies of the vendor. In addition, redeployment of existing IT staff of the customer is also a risk assessment factor (Gilbert, 2001).	Globally distributed teams with different skills and experience contribute to risk
Knowledge (Functional, Technological, Managerial)	Functional knowledge is the expertise, understanding, and experience in the given functional area of the activity. Technological knowledge is associated with the expertise in the areas of technology selection, analysis, architecture, design, development, integration, and maintenance support. Managerial knowledge is associated with the project management, risk management, resource management, and developing and administrating management processes to carry out the activities.	The level of functional, technological, and managerial knowledge contributes to risk in offshore outsourcing. Managerial knowledge is extremely important in a global context.
Cultural	Cultural risks arise from the dominant culture prevalent with the vendor, such as the attitudes, communication skills, language, selection policies, performance motivation, team spirit, level of cohesiveness, autonomy, participatory decision making, work ethics, management style, customer-orientation, and related organizational behavioral factors that shape the culture.	Country specific cultures can add risk in global outsourcing. Language and work ethics vary from country to country and that may contribute to risk.
Political	Political risks arise out of trading restrictions imposed by the sovereign, permissible ownership rights, nationalistic aspirations, type of government, and political and economical stability.	Political instability is a major concern for global outsourcing as the government rules and regulations may have adverse effects on outsourcing.
Financial	Financial risks arise out of project accounting standards, cash flow, asset base, and currency stability.	Accounting standards and variation in currency exchange rate contribute to risk.
Quality Standards	The software capability maturity model (CMM) and ISO 9000 compliance are hallmarks of quality standards. The ability to prepare test plans and performance standards are seen favorably while assessing the risks due to quality standards.	Quality standards vary from one country to another and contribute to risk.
Measurement	Performance measurement standards, benchmarking, and assurance of the performance are key elements in evaluating measurement risks.	Performance measurement standards vary from country to country which contributes to risk.
Scope, Cost, and Time Estimates	Ability to formulate the scope of the project, accurate cost and time estimation poses the risk.	It is quite difficult to accurately determine scope, cost, and time estimates in global outsourcing. This contributes to risk.
Company Specific Risks	Company specific risks are largely due to the outsourcer's financial strength, area of core competence, management, relationships and alliances with other major organizations, and (potential) acquisitions and mergers activities.	Different companies in foreign countries have different management and core competencies. These contribute to risk.
Legal Contracts and Intellectual Property	Intellectual property rights and their legal status in the country, brand protection, contractual bindings, and arbitration policies of the outsourcer constitute risk.	IP standards and law vary from one country to another and contribute to risk.
Security	Access control, authentication, usage of secure protocols, encryption, and security policies adopted by the outsourcer constitute risk.	Security is also a major concern in global outsourcing as protection and control of data pose a problem.
Disaster Recovery	Ability to protect software code, and related data, level of replication, redundancy, and back-up and recovery policies are the main factors in deciding the risks due to disasters.	Loss of control over disaster recovery contributes to risk.
Contract Management	Contract management involves formulating contracts, schedule planning, activity planning, sending and accepting deliveries, disputing resolution, and signing off. Inability to properly formulate or execute the contracts constitutes risk.	Contract management in global outsourcing is a risky business as monitoring the project activities becomes a challenge.
Relationships and Alliances	Ability to formulate customer-vendor interface at executive and working levels, customer relationship management, and developing long term alliances offers synergy at an organizational level.	Inability to manage relationships and alliances constitutes the risk in global outsourcing.

Continued on following page

Table 2. continued

Risk assessment factor	Description	Implications for Global Outsourcing
Geographic Location	The country, province, and city may be in different time zones, which require working at odd hours for the customer or outsourcer. The communication infrastructure, distance, industrial peace and stability in the region, availability of supporting infrastructure, social-economical-political stability constitutes the risk.	Vendor's geographic location poses some risks. Communication infrastructure failure in offshore projects incurs significant loss.
Multi-vendor Arrangements	Synchronization of development efforts, data format exchange standardizations, complexities due to multi-layer architecture dependencies or non-contagious independent parts constitute the risk with ability to work with multi-vendor arrangements.	In global outsourcing with multi-vendor arrangements, coordination has to be efficient. Otherwise execution becomes a problem and contributes to risk.

These case studies also reflect the global nature of outsourcing as some of the projects were done offshore. Hence, we tried to capture the global perspective and practices of outsourcing when we developed the cases. In addition, we tried to understand the theoretical perspectives and arguments that each participant put forward in the decision making process. In order to provide deeper insight into our qualitative analysis, we also included some comments from participants. We also did a comparison of the objectives, key benefits, major risk factors, challenges and best practices for the two cases and explained their implications from the Transaction Cost Theory.

CASE STUDY FORMAT

In order to understand the objectives, benefits, risks, challenges and best practices of outsourcing, case studies were done for two Global 200 organizations. All the participants joining discussions were involved in outsourcing projects and helped develop the case studies. We conducted a focus group survey of information technology executives and managers from both organizations who were involved in outsourcing information technology projects. Survey participants answered a detailed questionnaire, followed by an interview. The participants were offered choice to mention any other objectives, benefits, best practices, and any risk assessment factors not listed in the questionnaire. The participants were assured confidentiality of

their personal, organizational, and professional role information. The participant also shared their own experience in dealing with outsourcing projects and gave us valuable information about some of the best practices and challenges.

Each case has the following five sections:

I. **Background:** The background section provides a brief description of the organization studied.

II. **Introduction:** The purpose of the introduction section is to introduce the individuals, from each organization, that participated in the study. These individuals were actively involved in the outsourcing decisions of the firms.

III. **Outsourcing decision:** This section outlines the motivations, challenges, risks, and benefits associated with outsourcing decisions that each of these organizations faced.

IV. **Case conclusion:** The purpose of the case study conclusion is to summarize the interview results. It also highlights some deviations in the ratings by the participants of both of the firms.

V. **Anonymity:** Anonymity was deemed necessary to protect the identities of all the participants as well as the name of the organization. Both organizations are referred to as 'FIRM-1' and 'FIRM-2'. As per the requests of the participants, the names of the outsourcing partners are also kept confidential.

CASE STUDY: FIRM-1

Background

FIRM-1 is a large multi-national organization with more than 20,000 employees and 100 offices worldwide. It wants to be the leading provider of semiconductor-based solutions for consumer and communications applications and medical systems. Its annual revenue of approximately US$5-10 billion. It is one of the world's top semiconductor suppliers, with manufacturing facilities and partners in diverse geographic areas. It has 14 manufacturing and assembly sites, 20 design centers, four system labs, and more than 100 offices. The manufacturing facilities are located in the USA, the Far East and Europe serving customers worldwide. It also participates in its customers' business-to-business supply chain extranet. This enables FIRM-1 to get a visibility of demand for the customer's products, which in turn drives FIRM-1's production plan.

FIRM-1 believes that delivering these services and applications depends on the right business model, the right partners, and the right technologies. FIRM-1 is dedicated to semiconductor and related technologies and is customer focused. FIRM-1 provides its partners with scalable, versatile technologies and a world-wide manufacturing base.

Introduction

Three individuals from FIRM-1 were interviewed. Due to anonymity reasons, their names are not disclosed; they are referred to as 'Person 1,' 'Person 2,' and 'Person 3.' The names of the outsourcing partners are also kept confidential.

Outsourcing Decision

FIRM-1's management believes that if a business function is not its core competency, and better value is found externally, it is an ideal candidate for outsourcing. The core competency of FIRM-1 is semiconductor technology, and related R&D activities, which are kept in-house. Also it believes that the knowledge of knowing the customers' needs and providing those solutions faster to customers is another key to their success.

Many enterprise resource planning (ERP) and supply chain functions like manufacturing, fabrication, packaging, warehousing, and shipping and handling are outsourced. For more than 10 years, FIRM-1 has also outsourced some of its IT functions, which have changed over time.

FIRM-1 is in the process of changing its strategy on IT outsourcing. It is a global organization and has looked at its IT outsourcing globally. It used to have a more distributed outsourcing strategy, but now it is more centralized from a division standpoint.

The top management outlined the IT outsourcing strategy first. It then evaluated the approach not just from the overall organization's standpoint but also from a division standpoint. They picked potential suppliers by type of service, or technology that was required and divided those suppliers by divisions. Divisions then ran pilot projects with these outsourcing vendors for years. The results from these pilot projects were collected, which helped FIRM-1 to decide major outsourcing partners commonly for all divisions. So it took FIRM-1 almost twelve months of activity to get organized for IT outsourcing. But the strategy was always to keep a part of all these functions, especially controlling them, in-house.

When asked about how IT outsourcing decision has helped to reduce the supply chain costs (namely, core costs, non-coordination costs and transactional costs), one manager replied:

We are able to treat each application and its development as a variable cost and make very quick decisions based on ROI if we should even build it. Because the development costs are external, we incur no cost unless the initial business case justification (BCJ) process dictates that positive ROI will result. We always build contingency over-run costs into each project as a part of the BCJ process.

FIRM-1 has primarily two IT outsourcing vendors and also some niche players. It has divided the

Table 3. FIRM-1 participants

PARTICIPANTS	JOB TITLE	RESPONSIBILITY
Person 1	Senior manager, IT	Responsible for identification of outsourcing opportunities
Person 2	E-business director	Responsible for vendor selection, budget management, and monitoring the delivery of applications to requirements
Person 3	Project manager	Vendor management, execution and delivery of the projects

work between the two vendors in order to leverage their strengths. It describes the relationship with the vendors as strategic partners. When asked about their relationship with their outsourcing partner, one of the managers told us:

It is very positive. Our outsourcing partner has program management personnel in the US and act as members of our team. They understand how our company works and as such, this helps with the software applications that they build for us.

The outsourcing partners have their program management personnel on-site, i.e., personnel from the outsourcing partner are located within FIRM-1's campus and understand the business processes of FIRM-1. As such, this helps with the software applications and other services they provide to FIRM-1. It has a dedicated staff to manage the vendor relationship. In the past, FIRM-1 had some failures in terms of managing vendor relationships because of inadequate staffing and a poor contractual agreement. After they realized their mistakes, well-defined contracts were framed and signed by both parties. Also, weekly status meetings and monthly progress meetings were held to monitor the performance of the vendors.

Based on the responses of the participants, an effort is made to analyze and understand the focus areas like objectives, benefits, risks, and challenges involved in the IT outsourcing decisions in FIRM-1.

IT outsourcing practices: FIRM-1 keeps the project management functions in-house. It does not outsource project management responsibilities and complete project management control to its vendors. That was mainly a reaction of a bad experience from one of its earlier outsourced projects. However, there are multiple projects in which the roles and responsibilities are generally shared but control of the responsibilities of the projects themselves are never delegated. User acceptance and timelines are always controlled in-house, and never outsourced.

There has been a participative association with vendors in formulating design specifications. FIRM-1 partners with some key vendors to develop design specifications. These vendors are more key suppliers of software solutions and not pure 'IT outsourcing partners.' FIRM-1 also evaluates their vendors from time-to-time and if there are any value-added services or products that the IT outsourcing vendors have to offer, and if that product or service is beneficial, they definitely take a close look at it.

Another strong driver for FIRM-1 to outsource some portions of its IT is to focus on its core competency. In order to rapidly deploy their breakthrough projects, it takes its best and brightest resources to put on these projects. Therefore, these resources cannot do more repetitive and stable jobs. FIRM-1 tries to free up these core competent people to focus on its core processes, and to improve its competitive advantage.

FIRM-1 tries to outsource its 'non-critical' jobs to vendors. With the help of pilot projects, FIRM-1 has identified a couple of IT competencies, which it has in-house. The demand for these competencies is quite variable. So instead of maintaining it in-house, FIRM-1 decided to acquire those competencies through outsourcing partners. Moreover, these jobs are non-critical and are not related to FIRM-1's core business, its business creation initiatives or its ERP and supply chain management initiatives.

Objectives: For FIRM-1, cost reduction, focus on core activities, and professional services are the main objectives for outsourcing its IT to an external vendor. Building a competitive advantage, quality and reliability, access to state-of-the-art technology, and customer satisfaction are also some important objectives for IT outsourcing in FIRM-1. Knowledge about consumers' needs and providing solutions for those needs are very important to FIRM-1. So participants said that increased flexibility to meet the changing demands and market environment, and reduced time to market are other key objectives for outsourcing IT activities to their vendors.

Based on the participants' responses, a histogram is plotted, which is shown in Figure 1. While two respondents think that new technology can be an advantage, one respondent thinks that unproven/untested new technology can pose a risk to outsourcing and hence disagrees with the others.

Benefits: Participants from FIRM-1 emphasized that the main benefits achieved by outsourcing IT are reduction in costs, and optimal allocation and utilization of internal resources. FIRM-1 outsourced its IT function to low-cost and competent vendors in different countries, thus saving money. By outsourcing some functions of its IT, the management could identify and allocate its key resources, and utilize them efficiently to build a competitive advantage. Reduced time to market

and reduced delays, improved flexibility to respond to the changing demand and business environment, predictable outcomes, and a higher degree of success are some other benefits that FIRM-1 realized by IT outsourcing projects. Quality and reliability was also one of the benefits achieved by FIRM-1.

Each of the benefits was rated on a scale of 0-10. Based on the participants' responses a histogram is plotted, which is shown in Figure 2.

Risk factors: Knowledge being the core competency for FIRM-1, is the main risk factor for the firm. A careful planning of what knowledge to keep in-house and what to outsource is required. FIRM-1 wants to protect the core knowledge because it is afraid that outsourcing core knowledge will make them very much dependant on the vendors. This will put the vendors in an advantageous position in the outsourcing deal. Formulating scope and deciding the budget and schedule estimates is another critical risk factor. In the past FIRM-1 missed some schedules and the cost exceeded the budget. Also, the vendor did not provide the optimal service, because the scope was not clear. FIRM-1 learnt from its failures. And because ultimately it is FIRM-1 who is answerable to the consumers, a clear understanding of the requirements, finalizing the scope, and an agreement of both parties are very important to FIRM-1, along with budget and schedule. Apart from these, quality standards, financial stability of the vendor, its disaster recovery

Figure 1. Histogram for objectives for IT outsourcing (FIRM-1)

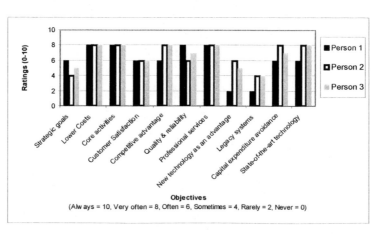

Figure 2. Histogram for benefits of IT outsourcing (FIRM-1)

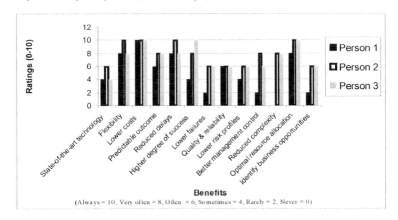

Figure 3. Histogram for risk factors of IT outsourcing IT (FIRM-1)

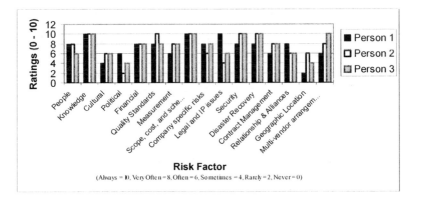

plans, and security are some of the important risk factors to FIRM-1.

When asked what risks their customers and suppliers may have faced from their decision of outsourcing, one of the managers told us:

We have had very difficult and costly outsourcing. We outsourced not only applications development and management of applications but also outsourced most of the staff. We outsourced too much of our core knowledge. And also under estimated what it takes to manage a vendor relationship at that price, and we didn't manage it well. As a result it became very advantageous to suppliers and disadvantageous to our customers. Very high costs and high stakes are involved here.

People, contract management, and performance measurement are some other important risk factors for FIRM-1. Legal contract and intellectual property protection is another risk factor for FIRM-1. Though FIRM-1 has a very efficient legal department to take care of the penalties and other legal issues of the contract, it believes that brand protection and intellectual property rights protection are key risk factors.

Figure 3 shows a histogram based on the responses of FIRM-1 participants.

Challenges: The main challenges for FIRM-1 in outsourcing IT projects are: (a) deciding what jobs to keep in-house and what to outsource, (b) ongoing vendor relationship management, and (c) setting up a governance model.

Selecting the right vendor is very challenging for FIRM-1. But since it has a cross divisional strategy, it has the option of partnering with alternative vendors. And that makes the ongoing management of vendor relationships one of their biggest challenges. Another challenge for FIRM-1 is the continuous commitment to the spirit of partnership

Cultural barriers and designing a contract do not pose a challenge for FIRM-1. Since FIRM-1 has a global presence, and has operations in many countries world wide, one of its strategies is to provide training, from time-to-time, to all its employees to deal with various cultures. Also designing a contract, especially the legal issues, is well taken care of by its legal department.

Figure 4 shows a histogram based on the responses of FIRM-1 participants.

Best practices: One of top best practices for FIRM-1 is the stakeholders' buy-in. This has helped FIRM-1 to deal with internal resistance and to carry out change management effectively. It also holds frequent informal meetings to review the progress of their projects. FIRM-1 has the policy of 'First Things First.' It prioritizes the action items as per their priority.

Other practices like empowerment and formation of steering committees and joint review boards are also important in FIRM-1's opinion and it practices them on a regular basis.

Based on the responses of FIRM-1 participants, a histogram, as shown in Figure 5, was plotted.

Case Conclusion

By outsourcing some portion of IT, FIRM-1 is able to efficiently manage its information systems. Some other measures that FIRM-1 has taken to tightly integrate its supply chain management with information systems are partnering with multiple vendors, penalties for non-performance, and well defined and dedicated management roles.

The management has explained the firm's strategy to all its employees, and it has tied this strategy to the current business environment. The employees are trained in newer technology, and from time-to-time they are also sent to such educational seminars and training programs. From an organizational standpoint, most of the organizations

Figure 4. Histogram for challenges of IT outsourcing (FIRM-1)

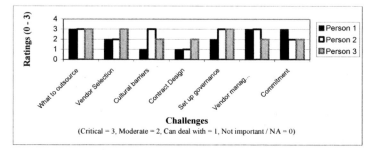

Figure 5. Histogram for best practices in IT outsourcing (FIRM-1)

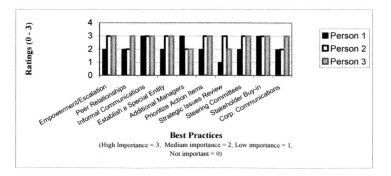

go in search of low-cost and competent services. And that's what FIRM-1 has been doing.

FIRM-1 believes that there will be 50% cost reduction if all but management and control are outsourced; 25% if only part of the activity is outsourced.

From the analysis, it is observed that cost reduction along with competent services is the main driving factor behind IT outsourcing decision. Costs are mainly related to development of a service or an IT application. By lowering costs, FIRM-1 was able to save money in a stringent budget situation, which is a driving factor for outsourcing. Focus on core activities, professional services, and reduced time to market are some other motivations and benefits.

Cost and loss of critical skills are the most important risks associated with IT outsourcing decision for FIRM-1. Deciding what jobs to outsource, ongoing vendor relationship management, and continuous commitment to the spirit of partnership pose challenges for FIRM-1 in making IT outsourcing decisions.

Apart from these, some other observations are noted in each of the focus areas. The participants said that it is a good strategy to outsource legacy systems, and that has been the trend for most of the organizations. FIRM-1 did outsource legacy systems in the past but are not doing it currently as it experienced some unsatisfactory outcomes in the past. So currently it is in the process of removing a bunch of legacy systems and has decided not to outsource them at the end of their life cycle. FIRM-1 believes that letting an external vendor replace the internal staff or anything in-house is definitely very complex. In the past, it had some failures. It had to continuously coordinate and monitor the outsourcing partner, which was not simple. So for FIRM-1, reduced complexity is not a benefit at all. In the risk category, geographical location is not a big risk factor for FIRM-1 to outsource their projects. Currently, the trend is to move to the Asia-Pacific region, especially India, for outsourcing jobs. This is mainly because of low cost and competent service. But participants were of the opinion that in another 5-7 years, China may also become one of the choices; it may also

offer similar services. So the trend would again change. Hence, FIRM-1 does not have any preference for any geographical location. It is also worth mentioning that FIRM-1 does not worry about contractual amendment costs, as those are well taken care of by its very efficient legal department. It has never experienced loss due to outsourcer's opportunism because of the type of business it is in. It believes such risks are mostly applicable to smaller organizations, start-ups, and software organizations. Since FIRM-1 does not market its software, it does not have this risk. They did face the risk of lack of trust but as soon as they realized it, they got ended their relationship with that particular outsourcing vendor. The participants stated if the partnering relationship is not 'win-win' or satisfactory to both parties, FIRM-1 won't plan to continue with the relationship. Hence, FIRM-1 evaluates its vendors quite meticulously because primarily if there is no trust between them, FIRM-1 does not want to do business with those vendors. To summarize, high competency, low cost, and non-core business functions are the key drivers of the outsourcing deals.

Applying transaction cost theory in our analysis, it is apparent that reducing transaction costs played an important role in the decision making process. Also, threat from opportunism and uncertainty is a risk for outsourcing.

CASE STUDY: FIRM-2

Background

FIRM-2 is a major, multi-national networking organization with annual revenues over US$20 billion. It provides the broadest line of networking solutions to most of the corporate, education, and government centers. Their hardware, software, and service offerings are used to create Internet solutions that allow individuals and enterprises to increase productivity, improve customer satisfaction and strengthen competitive advantage. It conducts most of its business over the Internet, and is recognized as the leader in this area.

FIRM-2 outsources much of its production. Customers visit the website to configure, price, route and place orders directly to FIRM-2. More than half of the orders are directly transmitted to the suppliers. Once the product is manufactured, it is shipped directly to the customer. As a result the order to delivery cycle time is reduced from approximately eight weeks to less than three weeks. Moreover, this helped FIRM-2 and its suppliers to manufacture based on actual orders and not on projection, lowering inventory costs for both FIRM-2 and its suppliers, while making customers happy with the speed of fulfillment of the orders.

Additionally, 85% of customer queries are handled through FIRM-2's website. It has established a business-to-business supply chain extranet for its manufacturers and suppliers. This online exchange is used to purchase supplies, make reports, and submit forecast and inventory information. With the help of this common platform, it has been possible for both FIRM-2 and its suppliers to reduce inventories by 45%.

FIRM-2 uses Internet extensively in every department of the organization. It also makes extensive use of intranet for its employees. Its employees use it to enroll in organizational benefits, and file expenses. More than 50 percent of technical training is provided online, saving the organization employee time and travel money while enabling employees to receive more training. Even peer reviews, collection of market information, and monitoring sales are all done online. It has also established a business-to-business supply chain extranet for its manufacturing partners and suppliers. With their Internet-based financial ap-plications, they are able to continuously monitor their sales data and are able to close their books within a short period of time.

Introduction

Five individuals, from various divisions at FIRM-2, were interviewed. Table 3 below shows their role and responsibilities.

FIRM-2 has outsourced its IT functions for the last 5 years. It has outsourced only portions of IT such as design, development, bug fixes, enhancements and customer support. FIRM-2 first identified those activities, which could be sent outside to finish faster. The core activities were kept in-house and the context activities were given out. Overall for FIRM-2, there is a central program office, which manages the relationship with the vendors and all the rates are negotiated centrally. FIRM-2 outsources its IT activities with five outsourcing vendors. It describes its relation with the vendors as very collaborative, focused on the success of the business client. During the outsourcing operations, the IT managers meet with Offshore Development Center (ODC) managers on regular basis. On site account managers ensure that critical issues are handled appropriately and provide oversight for the entire operation.

Outsourcing Decision

FIRM-2 is recognized as an innovator in conducting business over the Internet. It says that partnership is one of the pillars for the growth of

Table 4. FIRM-2 participants

PARTICIPANTS	JOB TITLE / ROLE	RESPONSIBILITY
Person 4	Lower management	Manage day-to-day IT activities with the regression facility at the outsourcing partner's facility in India; ensure that process is followed and reset / redesign process, if needed.
Person 5	IT manager (Middle management)	Responsible for managing team of IT professionals.
Person 6	Manager	Part of the group responsible for setting up the relationship with offshore outsourcing organizations.
Person 7	Senior manager	Responsible for outsourcing order-to-cash processes and systems, and for making outsourcing decisions.
Person 8	Senior manager	Responsible for defining business requirements, and prioritizing the outsourced tasks.

the organization and such strategic partnerships have helped and contributed significantly to the customer's, partner's and FIRM-2's bottom line. These strategic partnerships help FIRM-2 to focus on its core activities, and have helped FIRM-2 to reduce time to market. With these strategic alliances, it is possible for FIRM-2 to render quality services, and solutions to its customers. FIRM-2 tries to strike a partnership with such organizations that are leaders in their respective markets.

FIRM-2 outsources many supply chain activities like manufacturing, product design, product development, engineering, and shipping and handling activities to various partners. Since Internet plays a significant role in optimizing the supply chain of FIRM-2, information technology plays a very important role in the supply chain of FIRM-2. With the growth in information technology, enabled by the Internet, it is possible for all the partners in the value chain to work together more closely and effectively than before, making the whole supply chain more effective.

Based on the responses of the participants, an effort is made to analyze and understand the focus areas of IT outsourcing decisions in FIRM-2.

IT outsourcing practices: FIRM-2 keeps complete project management control within, when the vendor supplies project expertise, technical knowledge, and manpower. FIRM-2 also encourages participative association of vendor in formulating design specifications. But FIRM-2 does not enjoy

any access to attractive financing options from the vendor. Some other IT outsourcing practices that are followed by FIRM-2 are as follows:

a. Management of outsourcing vendors has become a core competency. So a centrally managed ODC project management office (PMO) is established that ensures common standards, governance policies and operating procedures across all vendors.

b. Quarterly reviews are conducted to evaluate performance and to optimize business processes. By optimizing the business processes, FIRM-2 is able to optimize its overall supply chain. It also reviews areas of improvements, changes, and defects periodically.

When asked about how they manage the relationship with their vendors, one manager told us:

IT managers meet with Offshore Development Center (ODC) managers on a regular basis. On site account managers ensure that critical issues are handled appropriately and provide oversight of the entire operation.

Objectives: For FIRM-2, cost reduction, and focus on core activities are the main objectives for outsourcing its IT to external vendors. Building a competitive advantage, the organization's strategic goals, quality and reliability, professional services, and customer satisfaction are also some important

Figure 6. Histogram for objectives for IT outsourcing (FIRM-2)

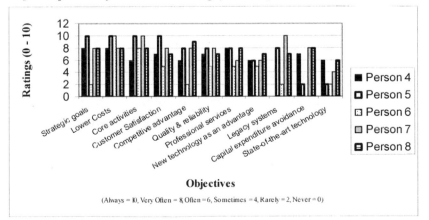

objectives for IT outsourcing in FIRM-2.

Apart from the options mentioned in the questionnaire, maximum coverage for support related activities (context activities), decreased IT costs for non-critical projects, tap into wider talent pool, and reduced time to market are some other primary objectives for FIRM-2 to outsource its IT.

Based on the responses from the participants of FIRM-2, a histogram is plotted, which is shown in Figure 6.

Benefits: The major benefits for FIRM-2 in outsourcing its IT are lower costs, optimal allocation and utilization of internal resources, and flexibility to respond quickly to changing demands and business environments. Predictable outcome, a higher degree of success, and higher quality and

reliability are some other benefits that FIRM-2 realized by IT outsourcing projects.

Based on the FIRM-2 participants' responses, a histogram is plotted, which is shown in Figure 7.

Risk factors: Most important risk factors for FIRM-2 are:

a. Knowledge/expertise
b. Quality standards
c. Scope, cost and time estimates
d. Measurement of performance

Participants from FIRM-2 believe that scope and requirements of the outsourced projects must be finalized, properly documented and stick to the specifications. Otherwise, if the requirements

Figure 7. Histogram for benefits of IT outsourcing (FIRM-2)

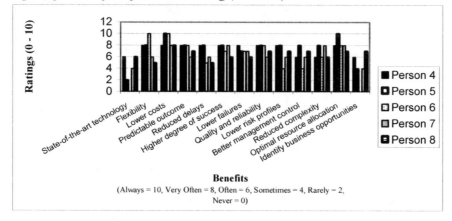

Figure 8. Histogram for risk assessment factors in IT outsourcing (FIRM-2)

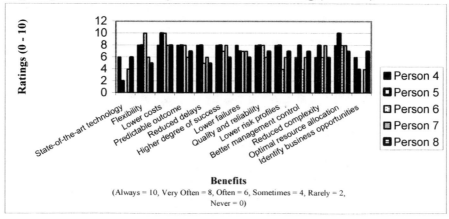

change continuously it would be difficult for both FIRM-2 and its vendors to do the job. This would then result in budget over run, and schedule slip, along with performance. A multi-vendor arrangement is another risk factor, as it involves more coordination efforts and demands a closely-knit governance model. People are another risk factor faced by FIRM-2. Cultural factors added to this risk.

We also noticed that FIRM-2 takes a qualitative approach to measure the risks. When asked about how risk is measured, one manager told us:

We assess the loss of business or lack of customer satisfaction with late delivery of projects. We assess this quarterly via surveys and business-balanced scorecards. We also assess risks associated with projects coming in over budget due to lack of clarity in requirements and scope.

When asked what risks their customers and suppliers may have faced from their decision of outsourcing, one of the managers commented:

Heavily outsourced operations where vendors have significant knowledge of business process have significant risk to customers. If customers are directly dealing with outsourced vendors without having local IT counterparts in the loop, this will result into IT losing its core competence.

Based on the responses from the participants of FIRM-2, a histogram is plotted, which is shown in Figure 8.

Challenges: All the challenges asked in the questionnaire are important for FIRM-2. But cultural barriers and selecting the right vendor are the most critical challenges for FIRM-2 in outsourcing IT projects. Deciding what jobs to keep in-house and what to outsource, setting up a governance model, ongoing vendor relationship management, and continuous commitment to the spirit of partnership are also some important challenges for FIRM-2. Designing a contract was well taken care by the PMO of FIRM-2.

Based on the responses from the participants of FIRM-2, a histogram is plotted, which is shown in Figure 9.

Best Practices:

1. Empowerment and escalation
2. Frequent informal communications
3. Key strategic issues review meetings are the most important best practices in FIRM-2

Peer relationships and stakeholder buy-in are also important practices that FIRM-2 follows. Prioritizing the action items is also another best practice followed there.

Figure 9. Histogram for challenges of IT outsourcing (FIRM-2)

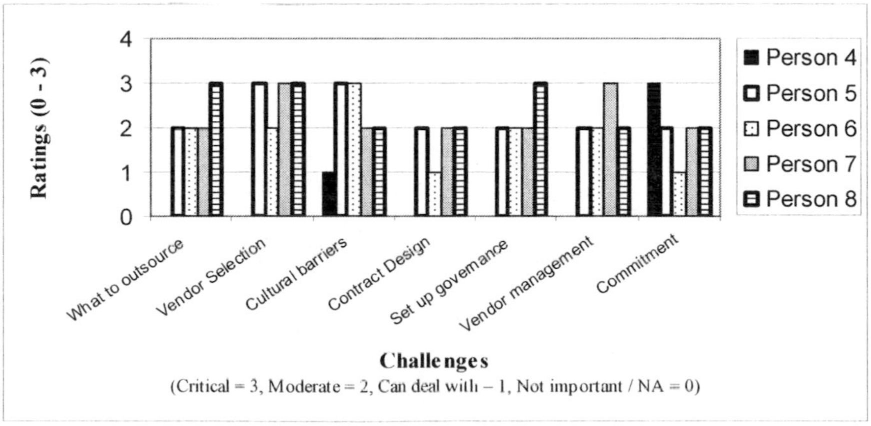

Figure 10. Histogram for best practices in IT outsourcing (FIRM-2)

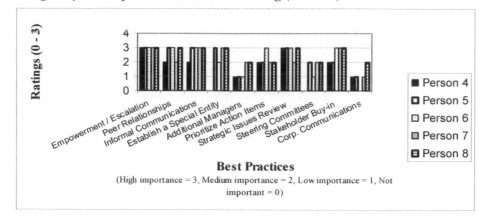

Another practice that is followed in FIRM-2 is the creation of Program Management Office (PMO). A central program management office is created to manage the outsourcing relationships. However, establishing a special entity, like a joint review board or corporate media communications are not very popular practices in FIRM-2.

Figure 10 shows the histogram for the best practices followed in FIRM-2.

Case Conclusion

By outsourcing, FIRM-2 is able to better manage the available resources to focus on core activities. Some other measures that FIRM-2 has taken to ensure its supply chain success are the following:

- Establish standards, governance, and guidelines for working with offshore outsource vendors.
- Manage projects locally, but distribute the work globally.
- Measure the performance and optimize the process.

The management is making all efforts to educate the employees in the concept of core and support activities. Building the 'one team' atmosphere is very helpful in this area. Both the onsite and offshore teams work collaboratively as a single team to help achieve the overall success. Also providing training, job rotation, and new career opportunities are some important steps towards dealing with the backlash against outsourcing.

FIRM-2 did not disclose its actual costs savings. However, an approximate estimate projected by the participants of FIRM-2 is slightly more than 50% cost savings on a per person basis.

From the analysis, it is observed that cost reduction is one of the main motivations behind IT outsourcing decisions in FIRM-2. Focus on core activities, and professional services are some other motivations and benefits. Cost and loss of critical skills are the most important risks associated with IT outsourcing decisions for FIRM-2. Cultural barriers and selecting the right vendors are most challenging for FIRM-2 in making their IT outsourcing decisions.

Apart from these, some observations are noted in each of the focus areas, which are described here. Some participants rated major capital expenditure avoidance and access to state-of-the-art technology as very low. They reasoned that IT outsourcing had actually caused their divisions a major capital expenditure, mostly in capital equipments, to set up their offshore development centers. Moreover, they were of the opinion that they certainly do not go offshore to access state-of-the-art technology. The outsourcing partners are providing FIRM-2 skilled resources, or state-of-the-art programmers, and not state-of-the-art technology. One of the persons had the opinion that IT outsourcing did not have much impact on the organization's strategic goals and competitive advantage, and his team did not have anything to do with reducing the burden of legacy systems.

As far as benefits are concerned, access to state-of-the-art technology is rated very low. This is because by outsourcing IT, FIRM-2 gets access to state-of-the-art programmers and resources. 'Better ability to identify possible business opportunities and threats so as to evaluate and manage them in the strategic perspective' is not an important factor for FIRM-2. It believes that going offshore does not decrease management's attention to the outsourced tasks. It still takes a lot of management overhead to run those outsourced tasks right.

Though financial, political factors and geographical locations are some other risk factors, FIRM-2 deals with five vendors, which are well established, competent and financially stable. Also these vendors are located in countries where the political situation is quite stable. So those risk factors are not very alarming. FIRM-2 has rarely faced risks like contractual amendment costs, disputes and litigation costs, vendor sub-contracting the job, and loss due to outsourcer's opportunism. All these are well taken care of and explicitly mentioned in the contract. Penalties for such unhealthy situations and non-performance are also clearly spelt out in the contract. This saves FIRM-2 from these risks, but makes the job of designing a contract very challenging.

Applying transaction cost theory in our analysis, it is apparent that reducing transaction costs played an important role in the decision making process. Also, threat from opportunism and uncertainty is a risk for outsourcing.

ANALYSIS OF THE CASES

After conducting the case analyses, it was clear that transaction cost theory was the theoretical foundation behind IT outsourcing decisions for both firms. As proposed by Williamson in the transaction cost theory, outsourcing work results in lower production or service costs than doing it internally due to economies of scale. The same argument is also true in the two cases that we analyzed. Another interesting point noticed from the analysis is that

FIRM-1 is one of the suppliers for FIRM-2. Thus they both have common goals of making their supply chain successful and maximizing the overall profitability. Both the firms described their relation with the IT outsourcing partners as very collaborative and healthy. The outsourcing relationship is managed using a combination of performance metrics, periodic discussions regarding timely delivery, budget and schedule. From the focused group interviews of participants from the firms, the following results and conclusions for each key area were drawn.

Objectives: It is observed that the top three important reasons for IT outsourcing, in both the firms, are lower costs, focus on core activities, and professional services. Almost 75% of the respondents were of the opinion that lower costs, professional services, quality and reliability are most often the motivations for IT outsourcing projects. 63% of the respondents said that focus on core activities is another motivation for IT outsourcing.

Benefits: It is clear that for both the firms, the main benefit of IT outsourcing is reduction in costs. Also management is able to allocate and utilize the resources optimally. Flexibility to respond to changing demands is the third ranked benefits, which both the firms achieved by IT outsourcing. Almost 63% of the respondents said that reduction in costs is always the benefit of IT outsourcing. Seventy-five percent of the participants said that predictable outcome is another key benefit of IT outsourcing. Sixty-three percent of the respondents said that a higher degree of success and optimal allocation and utilization of resources are most often achieved benefits of IT outsourcing. And 50% of the participants said that increased flexibility is also a key benefit of IT outsourcing.

Risk factors: The main risk factor observed for both the firms is knowledge. Both organizations felt that knowledge transfer needs to be carried out meticulously. The organizations as well as their outsourcing partners should follow proper methodology for knowledge transfer and information sharing. Secondly, both firms felt that there should be project scope, cost, and time estimates for such outsourcing projects. It is observed that 75% of the respondents said that knowledge is the most critical and always a risk factor in IT outsourcing. Fifty percent of the participants said that scope, cost and time estimates is another critical risk factor. Sixty-three percent of the participants said that monitoring and measurement of performance is a most often a risk factor. And more than 50% of the participants were of the opinion that quality standards are another risk factor in IT outsourcing.

Challenges: The biggest challenge for both firms is selecting the right vendor and deciding what to outsource and what to keep in-house. Since both firms have a good legal department and a program management office, they have not faced the challenge of designing a contract very often. Setting up a governance model, ongoing management of the vendor relationship, and continuous commitment to the spirit of partnership are some very important challenges for both the firms. It is

clear that 50% of the participants said that selecting the right vendor, and deciding what to outsource and what to keep in-house are the most critical challenges while 63% said that continuous commitment to the spirit of partnership is a moderate challenge faced in IT outsourcing projects. Fifty percent of the participants said that setting up a governance model, ongoing management of the vendor, and designing a contract were some of the challenges.

Other factors contributing to risk: Apart from the risk factors described earlier, there are other factors that also directly or indirectly contribute to risks in outsourcing. Transition and management cost is one of the top priority risk, followed by cost escalation risks. There are also some hidden costs involved in outsourcing like cost of retention/lay-offs, and the cost of ramping up. In addition, loss of critical skills, switching costs, and poor quality and reliability are the other very important risks involved in outsourcing. From the interviews, we

Table 5. Summary of the case studies

Category	FIRM-1	FIRM-2	Implications from Transaction Cost Theory
Objectives	Cost reduction, focus on core activities, professional services, building a competitive advantage, quality and reliability, access to state-of-the-art technology, and higher customer satisfaction.	Cost reduction, focus on core activities building a competitive advantage to enable the organization's strategic goals, quality and reliability, professional services, higher customer satisfaction, maximum coverage for support related activities (context activities), decreased IT costs for non-critical projects, tap into wider talent pool, and reduced time to market	Reduce overall transaction cost
Key Benefits	Cost reduction, optimal allocation and utilization of internal resources. Reduced time to market, improved flexibility to respond to the changing demand and business environment, predictable outcomes, higher degrees of success, and higher quality and reliability.	Lower costs, optimal allocation and utilization of internal resources, flexibility to respond quickly to changing demands and business environments. Predictable outcomes, higher degrees of success, and higher quality and reliability.	Reduce overall transaction cost
Important Risk Factors	Knowledge, people, contract management, performance measurement, formulating scope and deciding the budget and schedule estimates.	Knowledge/expertise, quality standards, scope, cost and time estimates, measurement of performance, multi-vendor arrangements, cross culture.	Threat from opportunism and uncertainty
Challenges	Deciding what jobs to keep in-house and what to outsource, ongoing vendor-relation management, setting up a governance model, selecting the right outsourcing partner.	Cultural barriers, selecting the right vendor, deciding what jobs to keep in-house and what to outsource, setting up a governance model, ongoing vendor management, and continuous commitment to the spirit of partnership.	Threat from opportunism
Best Practices	Stakeholders' buy-in, frequent informal meetings, prioritizes the action items as per their importance.	Empowerment and escalation, frequent informal communications, key strategic issues review meetings, peer relationships and stakeholder buy-in, prioritizing the action items, creation of PMO.	Reduce overall transaction cost

found that 63% of the respondents said that the most critical risks are unexpected transition and management costs, and other hidden costs. Almost 50% said that cost escalation, and poor quality and reliability are another critical or moderate risk. Seventy-five percent said that switching costs is another moderate risk.

Best practices: Empowerment and escalation are the top priorities for the two firms. Also both organizations hold informal communication sessions frequently to update the management and the employees about the outsourced projects. Stakeholder buy-in was the next important practice that both firms followed. It is observed that more than 87% of the respondents said empowerment and escalation, and frequent informal communications are the most important practices followed in their firms. Seventy-five percent said that stakeholder buy-in is another best practice followed in their organization.

Apart from the results observed in each key area, the following observations were noticed for both firms:

Both firms felt that there are other risks involved in outsourcing. Transition and management cost is the top priority risk, followed by cost escalation

risk. Hidden costs, like the cost of retention and lay-offs and the cost of ramping up, is the third import risk. Loss of critical skills, switching costs, and poor quality and reliability are the other very important risks involved in outsourcing. It is seen that 63% of the respondents said that most critical risks are unexpected transition and management costs, and other hidden costs. Almost 50% said that cost escalation, and poor quality and reliability are another critical or moderate risk. 75% said that switching costs is another moderate risk.

For risk reduction, there are several methods that both organizations follow. We combined all the responses from all of the persons interviewed from both organizations and listed them in Table 5. Let us also mention here that the first three responses (Person 1, Person 2 and Person 3) are from FIRM-1 and that rest of the responses (Person 4 through Person 8) are from FIRM-2.

CONCLUSION AND FUTURE RESEARCH DIRECTIONS

In many large organizations, IT outsourcing is being considered as a viable cost reduction alternative. Other than cost reduction, a short-term

Table 6. Summary of risk reduction practices

Risk Reduction Practices in IT Outsourcing	Person 1	Person 2	Person 3	Person 4	Person 5	Person 6	Person 7	Person 8
Round the clock project management over globally distributed teams	☒	☑	☑	☑	☒	☒	☑	N/A
Complete project management control with the vendor, over project initiation, planning, and execution for the outsourced project	☒	☒	☒	☒	☒	☒	☒	☑
Complete project management control with the organization, where the vendor supplies project expert technical knowledge, manpower, and other intellectual resources	☑	☑	☑	☑	☑	☑	☑	☑
Participative association of vendor in formulating design specifications	☑	☑	☑	☒	☑	☑	☑	☑
Complete outsourcing of projects, except design specifications, to vendors located at offshore locations inside and outside the country	☒	☒	☒	☑	☒	☑	☑	☑
Access to value added products from the vendor	☑	☑	☑	☑	☒	☒	☑	☑
Access to attractive financing options for the outsourcing deal from the vendor	☒	☑	☑	N/A	☒	☒	☒	☒

requirement of highly skilled resources is another objective for firms to outsource IT. The top management of both firms are convinced of the benefits of outsourcing and supports outsourcing decisions. More than anything, support of the top management is key towards the success of IT outsourcing for both firms.

Risks in outsourcing can be managed through proper contractual agreement and quality standards. This has also been described in the work of McFarlan and others (McFarlan et al., 1995). In addition, continuous monitoring of projects can also reduce risks. Both organizations have risk contingency plans. Broadly, risk is measured on performance metrics over time. Risk factors are weighed to reflect financial implications as well. The metrics to measure the effectiveness of an outsourcing arrangement are checked frequently, and are brought up during the quarterly review meetings. If a risk is time bound, risk mitigation plans are created and executed. If there are repeated and multiple failures to meet the service level agreements (SLA) goals, then alternative vendors may be identified for part or rest to complete the rest of the work. If the business processes and QA methodology are very robust, well thought and the project management is done properly, risks will be reduced in global outsourcing.

Other than effective project management, and participative association of vendors in formulating design specifications, it is very important to have planned and periodic reviews to improve the communication with the team members. The concept of 'one-team' should be strengthened. Also quality management programs and metrics should be followed. It is again a good practice to have an out-clause and penalty for not meeting the SLAs.

Selecting the right outsourcing partner is an important factor in a successful outsourcing project. Another interesting observation is that the organization and the outsourcing vendor are forming partnerships, which is based on mutual trust and long-term commitment. This trend has also been observed in the work of Lee and other researchers (Lee et al., 2003).

FUTURE RESEARCH DIRECTIONS

As IT outsourcing matures, its implications, issues and challenges are also evolving. We discuss a number of issues and future directions of research, which appear to be important. Further research will be necessary to determine the potential benefits and impact.

- **Focus on core competencies:** In order to gain efficiency and time to market products and services rapidly, many enterprises are outsourcing certain parts of their IT to free up management and IT personnel and valuable resources (Halvey et al., 1996). As global outsourcing moves up the value chain, management needs to focus on their core competencies and outsource some high-end work for high quality and a reduction in development time. However, there are some hidden costs associated with outsourcing that need to be studied in detail.

- **The growth in alliances and partnerships:** New strategic partnerships and alliances are being formed between multiple companies, which offer synergistic skills with a focus on target markets. However, the long term merits and success of these partnerships are yet to be determined.

- **Equity holding deals:** As new partnerships are forming, equity-holding deals are also on the rise. Many vendors are taking stake in the outsourcing client and clients taking stake in their outsourcing vendors. Further research is necessary to see if the new wave of outsourcing arrangements and deals offer value to both the vendor and client that were not present earlier.

- **Offshoring:** Due to the high-skilled labor shortages in the U.S. and in many developed nations, offshore outsourcing is growing as many companies look offshore for better quality IT services in shorter turn-around times and at lower costs. Future research can potentially address some of the important characteristics related to the cultural differences, work ethics and best practices of both the vendor and the client in trying to develop good working relationships as they engage in long term costly and often risky projects of offshore outsourcing. These issues become quite important and challenging particularly in multi-vendor arrangements.

- **Insourcing:** With rising, hidden costs of outsourcing coupled with growing concerns about job loss in developed nations, many are in favor of insourcing. Many organizations that made large scale outsourcing operations hoping for a better return on investments found out later that the tangible benefits were not fully attained through the outsourcing arrangements as planned (Hirschheim & Lacity, 2000). They also hoped for better service levels and superior customer satisfaction. However, in some cases it was just the opposite and some outsourcing contracts were terminated due to this. More studies are required in this area to explore the pitfalls of outsourcing.

- **The rise of ASP:** Application on demand enabled by ASP is becoming popular (Lee et al., 2002). Although there are some tangible benefits of ASP, there are some potential drawbacks. Since ASP's provide packaged software solutions, sometimes they may not be able to provide customizations that are required for each individual business process. Further research is required to prove the merits and ROI of ASP.

- **Security and protection of intellectual property (IP):** Security is one of the biggest concerns today for outsourcing deals, as the sensitive data needs to be protected from fraudulent practices. In addition, intellectual property laws vary from country to country. Because of varying IP standards are not properly implemented in various countries, we anticipate many disputes and lawsuits in the future.

NOTE

This research is funded by the Lucas Fellowship award.

REFERENCES

Adeleye, B. C., Annansingh, F., & Nunes, M. B. (2004). Risk management practices in IS outsourcing: An investigation into commercial banks in Nigeria, International *Journal of Information Management*, (24), 167-180.

Alchian, A.A., & Demsetz. H. (1972). Production, information cost and economic Organization. *American Economic Review*, (62), 777-795.

Alvares, K., Chapman, T., Comerford, J., Hovey, V., Kovner, A. R., Peisch, R., Pisano, G. P. & Puryear, R. (1995). When outsourcing goes awry. *Harvard Business Review, 73*(3), 24-37.

Ang, S. & Straub, D.W. (1998). Production and transaction economies and IS outsourcing: A study of the U.S. banking industry. *MIS Quarterly, 22*(4).

Antonucci, Y.L., Lordi, F.C. & Tucker, J.J III (1998). The pros and cons of IT outsourcing. *Journal of Accountancy, 185*(6), 26-30.

Aubert, B.A., Patry, M., Rivard, S., & Smith, H. (2001, January). IT outsourcing risk management at British Petroleum. In *Proceedings of the 34th Hawaii International Conference on Systems Sciences.*

Aubert, B.A., Patry, M., & Rivard, S. (1997). *A tale of two outsourcing contracts.* Cahier du GreSI (97-05).

Bahli, B., & Rivard, S. (2003). The information technology outsourcing risk: A transaction cost and agency theory-based perspective. *Journal of Information Technology, 18*(3), 211-221.

Barzel, Y. (1982). Measurement cost and the organization of markets. *Journal of Law and Economics*, (25), 27-48.

Beamish, P., Marcolin, B., & Mclellan, K. (1995). Financial and strategic motivations behind IS outsourcing. *Journal of Information Technology, 10*(4), 299-321.

Bowers, L.N., Gerber, U.H., Hickman, C.J., Jones, A.D., & Nesbit, J.VC. (1986). *Actuarial mathematics, The Society of Actuaries.*

Chabrow, E. (2003). *Tech buying fuels strong GDP growth.* InformationWeek, November 3.

Clark, T.D. Jr., McCray, G.E., & Zmud, R.W. (1995). The outsourcing of information services: Transforming the nature of business in the information industry. *Journal of Information Technology, 10*(4), 221-237.

Cross, J. (1995). IT outsourcing: British petroleum's competitive approach. *Harvard Business Review, 73*(3), 94-109.

Dhar, S., Gangurde, R., & Sridar, R. (2004). Global information technology outsourcing: From a risk management perspective. In *Proceedings of the 5th Annual Global Information Technology World Conference, San Diego, CA.*

Dibbern, J., & Goles, T. (2004). Information systems outsourcing: A survey and analysis of the literature. *The DATA BASE for Advances in Information Systems, 35*(4).

Diromualdo, A., & Gurbaxani, V. (1998). Strategic intent for IT outsourcing. *Sloan Management Review, 39*(4), 67-80.

Dube, L., & Pare, G. (2003). Rigor in information systems positivist case research: Current practices, trends and recommendations. *MIS Quarterly, 27*(4), 597-635.

Earl, M.J. (1996). The risks of outsourcing IT. *Sloan Management Review, 37*(3), 26-32.

Feeny, D.F., Lacity, M.C., & Willcocks, L.P. (1995). IT outsourcing: Maximize flexibility and control. *Harvard Business Review, 73*(3), 84-93.

Hamel, G., & Prahalad, C. K. (1990). *The core competence of the corporation.* Harvard Business Review.

Hirschheim, R., & Lacity, M.C. (1993). The information systems outsourcing bandwagon. *Sloan Management Review, 35*(1), 73-86.

Jurison, J. (1995). The role of risk and return in information technology outsourcing decisions. *Journal of Information Technology, 10*(4), 239-247.

Lacity, M.C., & Willcocks, L.P. (1995). Information systems outsourcing in theory and practice. Journal of Information Technology, 10(4), 203-207.

Lee, J., Huynh, M.Q., Kwok, R. C., & Pi, S. (2003). IT outsourcing evolution—Past, present, and future. *Communications of the ACM, 46*(5), 84-89.

Levine, M., & Schneider, M. (1997). Making the distinction: risk management, risk exposure. *Risk Management*, August, 36-42.

Khalfan, A. M. (2004). Information security considerations in IS/IT outsourcing projects: A descriptive case Study of two sectors. *International Journal of Information Management, 24*, 29-42.

King, W.R., & Malhotra, Y. (2000). Developing a framework for analyzing IS sourcing. *Information & Management, 37*, 323-334.

Koch, C. (2003). Outsourcing backlash. CIO, September 1.

Krishna, S., Sahay, S., & Walsham, G. (2004). Managing cross-cultural issues in global software outsourcing. *Human-computer Etiquette, 47*(4), 62-66.

McFarlan, F.W., & Nolan, R.L. (1995). How to manage an IT outsourcing alliance. *Sloan Management Review, 36*(2), 9-23.

Morello, D. (2003). *U.S. offshore outsourcing leads to structural changes and big impact.* Gartner, July.

Nam, K., Rajagopalan, S., Rao, H.R., & Chaudhury, A. (1996). A two-level Investigation of information systems outsourcing. *Communications of the ACM, 39*(7), 37-44.

Nelson, P., Richmond, W., & Seidman, A. (1996). Two dimensions of software acquisition. *Communications of the ACM, 39*(7), 29-35.

O'Leary, M. (1990). The mainstream doesn't work here anymore. *CIO, 6*(6), 77-79.

Overby, C. S., et. al. (2002). *US outsourcing decelerates, TechStrategy*. Forrester Research, March.

Overby, S. (2003). The hidden costs of offshore outsourcing. *CIO*, 60-66.

Robb, D. (2002). *5 top trends in offshore outsourcing. Datamation*, December.

Rothman, J. (2003). *11 Steps to successful outsourcing: A contrarian's view*. Computerworld, September.

Sabherwal, R. (2003). The evolution of coordination in outsourced software development projects: A comparison of client and vendor perspectives. *Information and Organization, 13*, 153-202.

Schneier, B. (2002). The case for outsourcing security. *Computer, 35*(4), 20-26.

Vijayan, J. (2001). Outsourcers rush to meet security demand. *Computerworld, 35*(9), 34.

Wang, E.T.G. (2002). Transaction attributes and software outsourcing success: An empirical investigation of transaction costs theory. *Information Systems Journal, 12*, 121-152.

Williamson, O.E. (1985). *The economic institutions of capitalism*. New York: Free Press.

ADDITIONAL READING

Dibbern, J., Goles, T., Hirschheim, R., & Jayatilaka (2004). Information systems outsourcing: A survey and analysis of the literature. *The Data Base for Advances in Information Systems, 35*(4), 6-102.

Hall, J. A., & Liedtka, S. L. (2007). The Sarbanes-Oxley Act: Implications for large-scale IT outsourcing. *Communications of the ACM, 50*(3).

Goo, J., & Nam, K. (2007, January). Contract as a source of trust—Commitment in successful IT outsourcing relationship: An empirical study. In *Proceedings of the 40th Annual Hawaii International Conference on System Sciences (HICSS).*

Kinnula, M., Seppanen, Y., Warsta, J., & Vilminko, S. (2007, January). The formation and management of a software outsourcing partnership process, In *Proceedings of the 40th Annual Hawaii International Conference on System Sciences (HICSS).*

Nyrhinen, M., & Dahlberg, T. (2007, January). Is transaction cost economics theory able to explain contracts used for and success of firm-wide it-infrastructure outsourcing? In *Proceedings of the 40th Annual Hawaii International Conference on System Sciences (HICSS).*

Sakthivel, S. (2007). Managing risk in offshore systems development. *Communications of the ACM 50*(4), 69-75.

Sargent, A. Jr. (2006). Outsourcing relationship literature: An examination and implications for future research. In *Proceedings of the 2006 ACM SIGMIS CPR conference on computer personnel research: Forty-four years of computer personnel research: achievements, challenges & the future SIGMIS CPR '06.*

Shao, B., & David, J. S. (2007). The impact of offshore outsourcing on IT workers in developed countries. *Communications of the ACM, 50*(2).

Taylor, H. (2006). Critical risks in outsourced IT projects: The intractable and the unforeseen. *Communications of the ACM, 49*(11).

Wu, F., Liu, C., & Li, P. P. (2006, June). *Management system of outsourcing: Protection of core competence perspective*. In SOLI '06. IEEE International Conference on Service Operations and Logistics, and Informatics (pp. 740-745).

Appendix

QUESTIONNAIRE ON IT OUTSOURCING PROJECTS

Purpose:
The purpose of this survey is to determine the objectives, practices, benefits, risk assessment factors, risk measurement, and risk mitigation methods of outsourced information technology projects. Your feedback of this survey is extremely important to us and will be very much appreciated.

1. Participant's Name: _____
2. Organization: _____
3. Please give a brief description about your role in outsourced IT projects.

4. Who is your IT outsourcing partner?
5. Do you wish to keep the above information confidential? Yes / No: _____ (please specify)
6. How do you describe your relationship with your outsourcing partner?
7. How do you manage the relationship?
8. Does your organization achieve the following objectives by outsourcing IT? Please score each of the objectives, on a scale of 0-10 (Always = 10, Very often = 8, Often =6, Sometimes = 4, Rarely = 2, Never = 0)

Sl.No.	Objective	Score (0-10)
1.	Company's strategic goals	
2.	Lower costs	
3.	Focus on core activities	
4.	Customer satisfaction	
5.	Competitive advantage	
6.	Quality and reliability	
7.	Professional services	
8.	Making new technology work to the advantage of the company	
9.	Reducing the burden of legacy systems	
10.	Allows major capital expenditure avoidance	
11.	Access to state-of-the-art technology	

9. Please list any other objectives you consider for outsourced IT projects? Also please score them on a scale of 0-10.
10. Which of the common practices / risk reduction practices utilized in your outsourced IT projects?

Sl.No.	IT Outsourcing practices / Risk reduction practices	Yes / No (please specify)
1.	Round the clock project management over globally distributed teams	
2.	Complete project management control with the vendor, over project initiation, planning, and execution for the outsourced project	
3.	Complete project management control with the organization, where the vendor supplies project expert technical knowledge, manpower, and other intellectual resources	
4.	Participative association of vendor in formulating design specifications	
5.	Complete outsourcing of projects, except design specifications, to vendor located at some offshore locations, within the country and out side	
6.	Access to value added products from the vendor	
7.	Access to attractive financing options for the outsourcing deal from the vendor	

11.   Please list any other practices you consider in your outsourced IT projects? Describe briefly.

12.   Does your organization achieve the following benefits by outsourcing IT? Please score each of the benefits, on a scale of 0-10 (Always = 10, Very often = 8, Often =6, Sometimes = 4, Rarely = 2, Never = 0)

Sl.No.	Benefits	Score (0-10)
1.	Access to state-of-the-art technology	
2.	Flexibility to respond quickly to changing demands and business environment	
3.	Lower costs	
4.	Predictable outcome	
5.	Reduced delays	
6.	Higher degree of success	
7.	Lower failures in service or products	
8.	Higher quality and reliability	
9.	Lower risk profiles	
10.	Better management control	
11.	Reduced complexity	
12.	Optimal allocation and utilization of resources	
13.	Better ability to identify possible business opportunities and threats so as to evaluate and manage them in the strategic perspective	

13.   Please list and score any other benefits that you consider for outsourced IT projects?

14.   Please list any major benefits that your customers and suppliers have realized out of the outsourced IT projects.

15.   Do you consider the following risk assessment factors to determine the risks associated with the outsourced IT projects? Please refer to Appendix for explanations of these risk factors. Please score each of the risk assessment factor, on a scale of 0-10 (Always = 10, Very often = 8, Often =6, Sometimes = 4, Rarely = 2, Never = 0)

Sl.No.	Risk Assessment Factor	Score (0-10)
1.	People	
2.	Knowledge	
3.	Cultural	
4.	Political	
5.	Financial	
6.	Quality Standards	
7.	Measurement	
8.	Scope, cost, and time estimates	
9.	Company specific risks	
10.	Legal contracts and intellectual property protection	
11.	Security	
12.	Disaster Recovery	
13.	Contract Management	
14.	Relationship & Alliances	
15.	Geographic Location	
16.	Multi-vendor arrangements	

16. Please list and score any other risk assessment factors you consider in your outsourced IT projects.

17. Following are some of the unfavorable outcomes in determining the risks associated with the outsourced IT projects? How critical are each one of them. Please rate each one of them, on a scale of 0-3 (Critical = 3, Moderate = 2, Low = 1, Not critical = 0).

Sl.No.	Unfavorable Outcome	Score (0-3)
1.	Hidden Costs	
2.	Unexpected transition and management costs	
3.	Switching costs	
4.	Contractual amendments costs	
5.	Cost escalation	
6.	Disputes and litigation costs	
7.	Service debasement	
8.	Cost of delayed delivery / non-delivery	
9.	Loss of organizational competencies / critical skills	
10.	Loss of autonomy and company's control over IT decisions	
11.	Loss of control over disaster recovery	
12.	Poor quality and reliability	
13.	Damages due to security breach	
14.	Loss due to disasters and recovery costs	
15.	Loss due to outsourcer's opportunism, including loss in future revenue, if outsourcer becomes competitor.	
16	Loss of innovative capacity	
17.	Vendor lock-in	
18.	Lack of trust	
19.	Vendor sub-contracting the job	
20.	Business uncertainties	
21.	Endemic uncertainties	
22.	Technological indivisibility	
	Irreversibility of the outsourcing decisions	

18. Please list and score any unfavorable outcomes you consider in your outsourced IT projects.

19. Do you prepare risk contingency plans? Yes / No: _____
20. How do you measure risk? Describe briefly.

21. Describe briefly your contingency plan, if outsourcing IT does not work as estimated?

22. Please list any risks that your customers and suppliers may have faced from your decision of outsourcing IT?

23. Information is the key driver for the success of a supply chain? By outsourcing IT, how have you achieved this success?

24. What were the measures taken to ensure this success?

25. How has IT outsourcing helped to reduce the supply chain costs (namely, core costs, non-coordination costs and transactional costs) in your organization?

26. Did your organization face the following challenges, while outsourcing IT? Please rate each one of them on a scale of 0-3 (Critical = 3, Moderate = 2, Can deal with = 1, Not important = 0)

Sl.No.	Challenges	Yes / No; Score (0-3)
1.	Deciding what jobs to keep in-house and what to outsource	
2.	Selecting the right vendor / partner	
3.	Cultural barriers	
4.	Designing a contract	
5.	Setting up a governance model to monitor the vendor and its services	
6.	Ongoing management of the vendor relationship	
7.	Continuous commitment to the spirit of partnership	

27. Please list and rate any other challenges that you faced in your outsourced IT projects?

28. Do you follow the best practices, listed below, in managing the outsourcing relationships? Please rate each one of them, on a scale of 0-3 (3 = High importance, 2 = Medium importance, 1 = Low importance, 0 = Not important)

Sl.No.	Best Practice	Yes / No; Score (0-3)
1.	Empowerment and Escalation	
2.	Peer Relationships	
3.	Frequent Informal Communications	
4.	Establish a Special Entity, like Joint Review Board, User involvement committee, Technology Review Board, Regional Governance Board	
5.	Appoint Additional Managers when implementing New Objectives	
6.	Prioritize Action Items	
7.	Key Strategic Issues Review Meeting	
8.	Steering Committees	
9.	Stakeholder Buy-in	
10.	Corporate Media Communications, as a means of mass communication for all employees	

29. Please list and rate any other best practices that you consider in your outsourced IT projects?

30. How are you dealing with the backlash on moving jobs out of this country, due to outsourcing projects?

THANK YOU FOR YOUR PARTICIPATION

Chapter XV
Quality Standardization Patterns in ICT Offshore

Esther Ruiz Ben
Technische Universität Berlin, Germany

ABSTRACT

In recent years, the ICT branch has experienced new internationalization impulses through the improvement of offshore practices. Particularly the development of modularization and standardization of some production processes have crucially contributed to enabling offshoring in globalized areas of ICT. Competencies as well as innovation sources have increasingly fragmented; resting upon cooperation and trust principles. Quality standards play a crucial role to satisfy and optimize these coordination and regulation needs so to warrant quality outcomes. In this chapter, I will give an overview of the development of quality standards related to offshore projects, focusing particularly on recent practices in Europe. To illustrate the importance of quality standards and quality management for ICT off- and nearshore projects, and moreover for the internationalization of the ICT branch, I present some preliminary results of my work in progress. From the perspective of project managers in large ICT firms, quality standards play a very important role as the internal controlling instrument of working and communication processes; as well as an external mechanism beyond the ICT network in order to get market advantages.

INTRODUCTION

During the late 1990s and particularly in 2000, the ICT sector has shown an enormous expansion, especially influenced by the development of the Internet, extended application areas and the former favorable economic situation. The commercialization and expansion of the Internet as a working basis, particularly in the 1990s, played in this phase a crucial role to begin enabling compatibilities in cross-national working practices; as well as creating a basis to build common knowledge exchange arenas that are fundamental for the further internationalization of the ICT branch. Thus, the use of the internet as an exchange working platform represented one of the first enabling steps toward the organization of work in global contexts in the sector, overcoming time and space barriers in working processes (Castells, 2001) (Editor note: Castells is not listed in the references section.)

Whereas organization control during the early 1990s concentrated on core firms that operated with local outsourcing companies to compete in an increasingly dynamic environment, involving new actors and customers around the world. In the late 1990s, the new diffusion and communication basis, supported by the Internet, contributed to the development of a new organizational paradigm known as network organization. Competencies, as well as innovation sources, have increasingly fragmented; resting upon cooperation and trust principles. Nonetheless, networks need to coordinate their operation activities and their innovation expectancies to guarantee the quality of their working processes, their staff and their customer-focused outcomes. And moreover, they are often bound to national and international regulations of working and production practices.

Network organizations must find a consensus regarding customer groups, innovation, quality and performance goals. Once these goals, as well as coordinative and regulative standards, are integrated within quality management systems, they serve as a legitimate basis for network performance.

Particularly in recent years, the ICT branch has experienced new internationalization impulses through the improvement of task delegation to foreign organizations, or in other words, offshore practices. The development of modularization and standardization of these production processes have crucially contributed to enabling offshoring in globalized areas of ICT.

Offshore tasks and production segments in the ICT sector are part of the internationalization of the sector and must be understood in the context of the globalization of the whole economy (Ruiz Ben & Wieandt, 2006). In the last few years, offshoring has expanded in the ICT sector due to the maturity of the branch in terms of standardization and consolidation of certain segments of the sector, mostly within the production part and related to the development of standard products. Some authors argue that offshoring constitutes a "prelude to software automation and mechanization," taking for example the automation of labor-intensive tasks in data centers, software customization, translation, website hosting and reuse of code that is currently

taking place in software service companies (Carmel & Tjia, 2005, p. 7). Although, this argument is still far away from the present situation. Particularly important in the adoption of international quality standards by the current impulse towards internationalization and the increasing global competition in the ICT sector. Thus, even if resistance towards the adoption of international quality standards exists in ICT organizations, due to the additional work it represents for the employees by way of documentation pressure, particularly large ICT organizations adopt them in order to accomplish the perceived expectations in the sector (Boiral, 2006). Another way to accomplish such market expectations is for the organization to develop particular quality management systems on the basis of internationally recognized quality standards (Ruiz Ben, 2007). However, the speed of innovation in the ICT sector is often too fast and the documentation of software development process needed in quality management systems is often neglected due to time pressure or lack of habitualization among employees (Ruiz Ben, 2005). In the context of the internationalization of the ICT sector, the adoption and adaptation of quality standards and documentation practices are not yet very well researched. Questions such as the existence of quality management systems in organizations or of the dynamics brought about in organizations when new quality standards are implemented to address qualification development, task definition and performance in international settings are still unexplored. In this chapter, I will give an overview of the development of quality standards and management mechanisms related to offshore projects, focusing particularly on recent practices in Europe and especially in the German ICT branch. I will present definitions of offshoring in ICT, explanations about quality standards in this field and discuss the institutions involved in the development of international standards. Moreover, I will present some of the results of my research regarding the transformation of tasks and qualifications in the internationalization process of the ICT branch, focusing on the importance of quality standards and management systems.

BACKGROUND

Quality Management and the Current Internationalization Process of the ICT Sector

The increasing development and introduction of quality standards in management systems experienced an important impulse during past years due to the expansion of ICT offshore practices. Quality standards support the foundation of tasks and work processes and represent a common communication base for international teamwork. Quality initiatives such as Six Sigma serve as a tool to implement existing quality standards, defined by organizations such as ISO, using data and statistical analysis to measure business processes, recruiting and outcomes. Principally, Six Sigma represents the practical realization of the total quality management (TQM) approach. The main philosophy of this tool is to define and identify defects as failures in relation to the customers' demands. Moreover, from the perspective of the market, quality standards are important for competing in a very dynamic environment. Particularly, quality standards are becoming a crucial role for the orientation of customers, but also for ICT enterprises, in order to better choose their partners in the framework of a globalized economy and international ICT industry.

In India for instance, managers in major ICT firms have developed their own teams to identify customers' needs and have designed various pathways towards TQM. Nevertheless, the transfer of knowledge and technology also becomes necessary for emerging smaller ICT firms that play a very important role in consolidating the market (Dutka & Sekhar, 2004). Thus, the establishment of interaction and learning platforms among ICT firms are very important for industry improvement (Crevoisier, 1999). Moreover, the national environment in which the firm is embedded plays an important role to establish a competitive ICT industry in the country and also the regional conditions of the country, which we can especially observe in the case of the EU. The political environment from a national, regional and international perspective influences offshoring and also standardization

processes regarding quality management in aspects related to working practice regulations.

At the same time, as (author's first name needed) Jakobs (2005) remarks, standardization politics change and national interests can become more important. Thus, Jacobs (2005, p. 25) comments, "…governments now have a vested interest in pushing such standards to support domestic firms. These firms, in turn, will look to standards setting for several reasons which are typically, though not necessarily, related to their own economic well-being." Therefore, standardization can be considered, according to this author, as an arena in which technical and non-technical (e.g., economic, organizational, or social) issues concur due to the importance of social interactions between diverse stakeholders (e.g., vendors, service providers, users, consumers, administrations, etc.) and technical experts who develop the standards. The gap between the needs and perspectives of the standard developers in the organization and the users who abide by the standards often leads to ad hoc solutions that do not always bring an effective and timely output. Especially for examining quality standardization patterns in relation to ICT offshore projects, it is important to take into account the actors interacting in the standardization process of quality systems and how they legitimate the establishment of standard settings in organizations. Intercultural aspects, as well as national regulations and rules, must also be considered in the analysis of this process; not to mention the financial aspects and embedded risks in offshoring practices that ICT organizations have to confront and that standardization may sometimes even veil.

Quality Standards in the Context of the ICT Branch in Europe

According to the British Standard Institution, a quality standard in accordance with ISO (2001, p.2000) provides an organization "with a set of processes that ensure a common sense approach to the management." Moreover, "the system should ensure consistency and improvement of working practices, which in turn should provide products and services that meet customer's requirements. ISO 9000 is the most commonly used international standard that provides a framework for an effective quality management system."[1] ISO Standards are widely used in the ICT branch and represent a very important basis for the development of management systems in organizations.

The ISO 9000 series of quality system standards have been applied to industrial practices for a long time (Van der Wiel, van Iwaarden, Williams, & Dale, 2004). By origin, they were developed on the basis of military standards (e.g., AQAP) and the British Standards (BS 5750) and were first published in 1987. Since then, two upgrades have followed in 1994 and 2000.

Following these authors, the initial aim of the ISO 9000 series was to build a trust basis for suppliers and manufacturers practicing business-to-business transactions. Tummala and Tang (1996) explain that the basic concept behind ISO 9000 is the notion that a set of characteristics of quality systems can be standardized and yield benefits both for organizations, as well as for their suppliers, due to the common certainty that they both should meet certain requirements.

ISO 9000 standards help ensure that organizations follow well-documented procedures in the production process, as well as in the delivery of their products or services. These procedures aim to guarantee that the products or services of an organization comply with customer specifications, but are still basic recommendations that must be further adapted to the special situation of the organization, its environment and its production scope.

Thus, the tension between the quests for universality embedded in ISO standards and the need to take into account the various stages of technological and commercial development are reflected in the adaptation of new quality management systems; especially in its implementation.

Nonetheless, ISO is not the only existing standard used to develop quality management systems in the ICT branch. Standards in this branch are very heterogeneous. Several classifications have been suggested. For instance, the one suggested by Blind (2004) distinguishes among product standards, control standards and process standards. Regarding the way standards are produced, Blind talks about three additional categories: standards that are set through the market (such as IBM's systems network architecture [SNA] and Microsoft Windows); standards that are set by government, through a regulatory process (mandatory standards); and standards that are negotiated through a voluntary consensus process (formal public standards developed by a publicly recognized standardization organization such as ISO, IEC and ITU) (2004).

Moreover, standards can also be defined in relation to their use: mandatory by law for every product concerned (for example when safety considerations have prompted regulations); those requested by a vendor or system integrator; or those including numerous instances where the application of a standard is mandatory for public procurement (as in the case of the European Handbook for Open Systems according to a decision of the European Council).

Therefore, considering this complexity regarding standard types, the definition of a typology of standards is still not totally satisfactory (OECD, 2001).

Regarding the motivation to implement formal standardization in organizations, some authors point out that the focus tends either to be on the reduction of transaction costs, especially related to information, or it is associated with network externalities (Schmidt & Werle, 1998). Standards can also be associated with reducing uncertainty or with enhancing competition by clearly defining the information required to serve a market. Mansell (1995) refers to the use of standardization for the facilitation of scale economies, either for suppliers or for influencing the distribution of cost and benefits related to the building and operating of large, complex technical systems.

Moreover, in order to develop themselves in new markets while protecting established ones, companies utilize standardization so to prevent compatibility and avoid the participation of competitors in the market. Thus, as some authors remark, companies use standards as strategic tools to consolidate a market position and gain advantage over competitors (Cargill, 1989; Bonino & Spring, 1991).

Particularly regarding quality standards, Van der Wiele, van Iwaarden, Williams, and Dale (2004) remark on the basis of a literature review that there is evidence of a positive impact created by ISO standards in some business countries and sectors. Heras (2002) points out that most of the studies conducted on the benefits of ISO standards are mainly anecdotal, case study based, and report descriptive statistics (Van der Wiele, van Iwaarden, Williams, & Dale, 2004).

Van der Wiele, van Iwaarden, Williams, and Dale (2004) report a positive impact of ISO 9000 on companies in The Netherlands and in the UK. Nevertheless, it is important to consider that the implementation of ISO needed changes in the organizations, especially when the last version of ISO 9000 was used. The participation of auditors in the process was also very important in the implementation of the quality recommendations.

Especially the participation of external and internal consulting in ICT offshoring plays a crucial role to legitimate the consequent organizational change (Ruiz Ben & Claus, 2005; Ruiz Ben & Wieandt, 2006; Wieandt, 2006; Ruiz Ben, 2006). Thus, as we mention elsewhere (Ruiz Ben, Wieandt, & Maletzky, 2008) in offshore processes, the selection of the providers in host offshore countries involves legal and consulting costs, and contracting issues (Morales, 2005). When organizations do not have experience with ICT offshoring, they usually work with benchmarking companies, utilizing consultants that provide an overview and evaluation of the specific chances and risks of ICT offshoring for the company (Amberg & Wiener, 2004).

Thus, from my point of view, to analyze quality standardization patterns in ICT offshore processes, it is important to consider the actors involved in the development of quality standards and the embedded environments of ICT organizations and networks, especially regarding legal, social and financial issues. Moreover, at the organizational level, we must take into account in which way the workers adopt or resist the introduction of quality standards in their working routines, particularly when they work on international projects.

In the next section, I will focus on the actors involved in the development of quality standards, considering the particular situation in Europe and especially the framework of the European Union after previously explaining the role of standards in ICT offshoring.

QUALITY STANDARDIZATION PATTERNS IN ICT OFFSHORE

Standards play a particularly important role as a 'selection mechanism', especially in the case of ICT networks in which alliances are often based upon trust and efficiency and in which narrowing diversity can benefit internal cohesiveness and support stability against external threats. Particularly in ICT offshoring processes, the standardization of working processes through methodologies such as CMM has played a crucial role in some offshore countries. These formal processes explain, in part, the tremendous success of the offshore industry in India (Carmel & Tjia, 2005). Nonetheless, particularly regarding quality standards, the Indian ICT Branch has played a very important role in developing new settings. A significant number of major Indian ICT companies have adopted a central measure for achieving quality, particularly Six Sigma methodology and/or its multivariate branches like TQM, supply chain management (SCM), and customer relationship management (CRM). Also, ITIL recommendations aligns with the international standards of ISO 20000 and represents a customizable framework that defines how service management is applied within an organization and how it plays an important role in the development of off- and nearshore projects.

Regarding production standards, already in the previous phases of the Internet expansion, the Directive on ICT Standardization of 1996 formulated by the Expert Group of the OECD represents an important milestone in the establishment of ICT standards. In order to assess the implications of emerging globalization and the consequent need for standardization in the ICT, the OECD sought the advice of a group of experts, who were responsible for the standardization of ICT in their respective companies. This group formulated several recommendations regarding the development of ICT standards, their coordination, management, tasks distribution, participation of the users, standardization ethics, etc. Particularly relevant in the recommendations is the role assigned to official standardization agencies, which shall be referred to below as "Standards Development Organizations," or "SDOs." The question is, how do these organizations define standards and how do they support their stability and diffusion? Werle and Iversen (2006) examined in a recent article the legitimacy of committee standardization in comparison to market processes of the technical standardization of ICT. Responsible for the development of a significant number of standards in the ICT branch are SDOs, in which agents of firms represent the majority of participants, due to the fact that enrollment in standardization development constitutes a time-consuming and resource-intensive activity requiring technical expertise (Werle & Iversen, 2006). Thus, these authors remark on the bias existing in SDOs towards industry interest representation. Blind (2005) also refers to the requirement of qualified personnel for the participation in standard development in SDOs (2005). Therefore, the chances for the enrollment of persons from developing countries or even from small- and medium-sized enterprises (SMEs) are rather limited (Jackobs, 2005). Taking into account the composition of the ICT branch in Europe that in its majority is represented by SMEs, also in Europe such bias is something important to consider. Nevertheless, in the framework of the EU, where the exchange of services and goods is free, due to recent regulations (OECD, 2004), European ICT companies can develop a self-reinforcing dynamic, gaining cost or quality advantages through offshoring (OECD, 2005; see also Aspray, Mayadas, & Vardi, 2006). At this point, it is very important to consider labor and employment rights, as well as issues related to privacy and data transfer, that are related to ICT offshoring processes in Europe.

Regarding data privacy laws, the European Union Data Privacy Directive adopted in 1995, applies to companies collecting or processing data within the EU or reciving data from the EU and is implemented by the respective EU countries through their national legislation (Eisner, 2005). Eisner (2005) points out that EU-approved transfer contract clauses are the most efficient way to handle data transfer in ICT offshoring processes in the EU. These clauses consist of an agreement between the transferring parties about a set of contracted provisions consistent with data privacy laws, allowing enforcement by EU authorities.

Another important issue related to EU regulations in the context of ICT offshoring is the EU Acquired Rights Directive, approved in 1977, that gives employees protection in the event of a business transfer[2]. This means that transferred employees must maintain the same working conditions that they had before the transfer took place. In the case of replacement, employees must be informed and consulted about related measures and sometimes be awarded a particular payment (Eisner, 2005).

These regulations are very important in the development of ICT offshoring in the EU context. Nevertheless, at the level of the implementation of working policies in organizations, and particularly regarding the employer's representation in the decision processes of the companies, there are many differences among the European Member States. Especially the differences between the former EU15 and new European Member States are very significant.

Because of the political divide in Europe before 1989, we can show specific conditions in regards to off- and onshoring. The former division led to the establishment of a highly developed and well performing western part (the Europe-15 Member States, Norway, and Switzerland) and a transforming, but well qualified and low regulated eastern part (the new member states Bulgaria and Romania). Thus, in Europe, even both home and host countries using offshoring practices occur in one market area regulated by the European Union. According to specific historical, political and socio-cultural conditions, and also in regard to the particular economic and industrial situation, as well as to the special position in the global ICT branch, each country has developed specific strategies to confront innovation demands and to cope with high qualified labor shortages and skill mismatches.

ICT companies, each depending on their size and market scope, had to react very fast to innovation pressures developing special internal training measures as well as hiring foreign workforces.

Particularly important for the adoption of quality standards in an organization is the speed of change. At the international, as well as the European level, some measures have been developed to confront this problem. Egeydi (2001, p. 39) comments the following:

According to the ISO/IEC Directives, 7 years were needed to take a standard from start to Draft International Standard in 1989, while in the Directives of 1992 this period had been reduced to 3 years.

... the approval time of recommendations in the ITU-T has been reduced from 4 years in 1988 to a maximum of 9 months in 2000 (ITU-T, 2000).

This represents an improvement in standardization processes; however, ICT networks often adopt their own quality standards embedded in more general management systems, such as Six Sigma. At the regulative level, Egeydi (2001, p. 44) remarks that formal standards constitute an important point of reference for European regulation: "The European Commission requires a degree of democratic accountability if it is to refer to such standards in a regulatory context. However, in the field of ICT standards have emerged with a high market relevance, standards that stem from standards consortia."

Egydi (2001) points out, however, that in the field of ICT, standards will seldom be part of regulation. Thus, this author pleads for more clarity from European regulators about what type of democracy is needed and for what purpose. Additionally, Egydi remarks that a systematical monitoring of democratic requirements by 'democratic' standards by developing organizations should be considered.

In sum, especially for ICT offshoring practices, this kind of monitoring would be positive and would establish clear cooperation environments among the EU15 countries and the new European Member States. However, the rapid dynamics in the ICT sector and the need to develop quality standards in line with the velocity of change lead to an internal adaptation of quality standards in organizations on the basis of internationally recognized standards. Adding to the problem of high dynamic changes in the ICT sector, increasing internationalization of the sector means that intercultural problems can emerge among project networks that use quality management systems established in home enterprises (Ruiz Ben, 2006). Thus, it is crucial to consider emerging expertise in international teamwork and prevent the overemphasizing of focusing on narrowed, organizational quality management standards and systems. The awareness of network interactions in projects and beyond them of emerging expertise and knowledge creation is crucial to developing effective quality management systems in internationalized ICT organizations. In the next section I will focus on this issue, presenting some results of our work in progress regarding the transformation of tasks and qualifications related to ICT off- and nearshoring.

Preliminary empirical results: Quality standards and quality management systems in the internationalization of the German ICT branch

In our current research about the transformation of tasks and qualifications in the framework of the internationalization of the German IT sector (INITAK), we have conducted interviews with personnel and quality managers in several IT enterprises (see description above and in appendix) that expand their activities in foreign countries and especially in Eastern Europe. The preliminary analysis regarding qualification and expertise requirements are related to one of our case studies in a large software development enterprise (F3). This enterprise is an affiliated company of a large, multinational enterprise with many establishments all around the world. Academically acknowledged persons founded the German establishment in the early 1980s. During the 1980s and 1990s, the enterprise expanded and founded six further locations in Germany, Switzerland and recently in Eastern Europe. The enterprise has an academic origin which still remains, as it is reflected for instance in the links to academicallybased professional federations (GI – Gesellschaft für Informatik). The motivation for off- and nearshore is basically to reduce costs, but also to expand the firm market scope and moreover to remain innovative in the rapidly internationalizing environment of the ICT sector.

Particularly the German establishment of F3, where we conducted our interviews in 2006 has itself experience with nearshore since 2004 in Eastern Europe. In the first phases of this nearshore project, the enterprise used the platforms of the multinational enterprise they belong to, which brings advantages regarding the availability of adequate personnel and infrastructure and the knowledge management of the enterprise. Nearly 50 employees are working in the nearshore establishment of F3. The standard integration procedure for these individuals is a visit in Germany for a training period of one year, in which they learn the project and quality standards of the enterprise.

Regarding the tasks that the F3 firm keeps in Germany during its current internationalization, the first specification phases of software development projects, during which the contact with customers is very intensive, remain in the German headquarters. However, some nearshore workers participate sometimes in the discussions with the customers, as a part of their integration training. The architecture phase also remains in Germany, whereas the developers in the nearshore center conduct the detailed design of the architecture. Therefore, the recruitment strategy of the firm F3 in its nearshore center is oriented towards hiring both very young university graduates and also experienced personnel that can rapidly adapt to the growing present project demands, as well as train and help to integrate young newcomers. The long-term internationalization perspective of F3 in the nearshore location is to expand their market opportunities in the country, building an increasingly autonomous center with high-qualified personnel. Apart from the high qualification requirements in computer science, one of the prerequisites for recruitment is high communication skills and an ability to speak in German.

For coordinating international teamwork between German and the software developers in the nearshore center due to the differences in work habits in Germany and in the nearshore country perceived by personnel managers, firm F3 uses as a common background the German institutionalized sense of professionalism and an especially strong hierarchical quality management system that goes beyond the firm through to the core, multinational owner enterprise. This system has been developed and institutionalized in the enterprise through the years, taking internationally recognized quality standards as a basis and functions as the internal control system for the whole, teamwork-oriented organization. Although the software developers who took part in our interviews were satisfied with the quality systems in the organization, a quality manager in firm F3 argues that this kind of system sometimes makes the organization "self-blind" if it does not permit acting in a reflexive way from the ground floor to reflect the typical, workday problems within projects. Thus, according to the quality manager, communication and social skills are especially important for two main reasons: first, to understand the problems of the software developers, as well as the technical and management problems within a project and second, to solve these problems according to three basic quality principles, or in the words of a quality manager, "the magical triangle for decision making: budget, timing and quality."

The quality manager in firm F3 emphasizes the importance of the "social component" in teamwork to reach high quality in production. Thus, in contrast to offshore projects in India, nearshore projects in Eastern Europe, as the quality manager points out, are easier to coordinate because the team members and the quality and project managers know each other and can more easily establish a communication basis:

We need the social component. We have observed this precisely in our nearshore center; the nearshore center people were first here and thus we could build a social relationship. You know each other, you get out together for a drink and then, when we telephone it is like as if he were in the neighbor room.

However, the firm plans to expand in the nearshore center country market, so that the autonomy requirements for software developers in the nearshore country will grow and they will have to act as mediators between different cultural backgrounds. Taking into account that the nearshore experience of the firm F3 beginning 2004 is still very short, I cannot yet give a clear picture about the teamwork culture in this international software development environment. However, it is important to note that although the German based corporate professionalism dominate the expectations of the personnel managers, due to some reported misunderstandings in teamwork practices between nearshore center and German software developers, the firm F3 has reacted initiating the design of common "corporate rules" for the nearshore projects that sometimes are developed "ad hoc" within the project, but takes also international quality standards as a basis. In which way the German based corporate professionalism will prevail or coexist with local habits in the international software development environment of the firm F3 or in other words, how expertise in both locations will be institutionalized is yet an open question that we will seek to answer in the next phases of our research.

The second firm about which I report in this paper, F1a, is an operation segment of a multinational company operating in the telecommunication and software areas of the ICT branch. F1a was recently established as operation segment and has since its origins experience with off- and nearshoring in India and Eastern Europe. As a part of a multinational company, F1a is tied to the cultural identity of its owner and particularly rooted in the tradition of the German industrial culture with a strong "Beamtentum" influence.

The experiences with off- and nearshore of F1a remain linked to the long internationalization tradition of the core owner company. This means a good starting basis for projects, since F1a can use the existing recruitment pool with experience in the company in base countries. Moreover, some team workers and specially the team coordinators often travel to the home or host locations of the nearshore projects to maintain face to face contacts, which is high valued to improve the communication and interaction of the team members. Particularly F1a has currently nearshore projects in Poland, Romania, and Slovakia. The programming phases of ICT projects have been delivered to these countries. The consequences for the organization of work processes are that tasks, work modules and deliveries must be clearly defined as well as the interfaces between work modules. This strong definition requirement in off- and nearshore projects is the main difference to local focused projects in the opinion of a project manager. This means a stronger standardization of processes and documentation practice as it was the case in

the past and a rapid adaptation to current needs selecting just some aspects of past documented processes. Documentation represents at this point a double-edged sword, since at the one hand it is needed to identify possible process failures and to find solutions as well as to check the processes with quality standards, but on the other hand it retards the working process and moreover, it is sometimes not clear what is relevant to be documented. As a project manager in the enterprise F1a remarks, definition of modules and tasks, documentation and process adaptation run parallel in successive constant iteration moments. In the words of the project manager:

The whole experience stored since an eternity resides somehow inside documentation and we cannot adopt just as it is. We look at what makes more sense and what makes less, in order to bring it to an extension that we can use in the project. Otherwise we lose too much time. We make everything parallel, we begin to define everything, to document and then the processes are adapted. And it is a kind of iterative process in which everything size by size puzzles together.

Quality management systems live and develop together within this process and they are extremely important for the improvement of the working process in internationalized software development environments. However, such systems did not exist in the past years or they were only available on the call, and were moreover not documented. Currently, in the enterprise F1a, documentation plays a crucial role in relation to quality systems and particularly in relation to offshore, since the teams work within an integrated global environment and structure in which the communication of work steps and developments, but specially the secure run of the process must be guaranteed and arbitrated. As the project manager puts it:

(...) looking back to the past, regarding the configuration system, there were no quality criteria or only few ones just on the call and not documented. And here due to this ongoing structure that we have set up, and taking into account the conjunction and succession of work process parts, we must of course lay down on something and we must document. Specially because with such an ongoing

system, in which we say to sales and marketing department: work with it, they can in fact work with it in the whole world just with the push of a button and in a critical moment they can also risk lots of money.

Particularly risks in the interfaces among several modules in home and host locations in off- and nearshore projects represent a difficult problem, which has sometimes lead to relocating offshore projects to nearer host destinations. As a controlling instance, consulting firms play a crucial role.

In the case of Fla, the supervision of the projects is conducted by an external consulting enterprise, which in the particular case of the project to which the interviewed project manager belongs, is extremely important due to its huge volume and complexity. As the consultant working in this project comments, quality standards are crucial in off- and nearshore projects, both for coordination and also as a basis to find solutions in case of work process problems. Quality standards are important for the external consultant also as a legitimating basis for possible changes in work processes that the consultant has to achieve and implement in the "client" enterprise, to which somehow he plays a twofold role as a external worker and also interacting in the day to day practice of the project with the employees "clients" as a colleague and supporter within the project. Thus, quality standards are the instrument to legitimate decisions in the work processes. The knowledge of such standards and also of the quality management systems of the company is also important for the team workers, since they have to implement them in the day to day project life. Thus, quality standards, as well as quality management, becomes more and more institutionalized in the company, which is reflected in the increasing number of courses that the company offers to the employees. Moreover, employees can only learn about quality standards and their implementation as well as about quality management within the company, since, first, it is not usual to get training in these issues at the universities and second, even if the employees have some knowledge having studied informatics or mathematics, they do not have the particular knowledge of their implementation in

such a complex environment of a multinational company. As the project manager puts it:

What we make here you cannot learn at the university. Either I know it from my studies, if I learn informatics or mathematics and there also especially software development and I know what a docmentation and a test as a whole means or I do not know. And even if I know it, I have never known it in such an environment like this.

Thus, internal continuous training in quality standards and in quality management is crucial for the employees working in off- and nearshore projects. And this means both in home and host countries. Nevertheless, quality standards must be also developed in line with the different internal improvement of quality management systems in different companies, which means that training about quality issues remains within the organization. This training should attend to the needs of the organization including its foreign locations, in which differing qualification and working habits exist and also different interpretations of the recommendations included in quality management systems. Thus, as quality managers in our two case studies remark, quality standards and management systems represent a double-edged sword making the organization blind about day-to-day problems among project workers in international teams. A balance between the recommendations included in quality management systems and the day-to-day expertise emerging in different projects and locations is needed in order to integrate working experiences into future projects and to establish an organizational knowledge basis. In other words, quality standardization as coordination tool for off- and nearshore projects should both establish a common working basis for different organizational settings and represent a dynamic process of self-reflection on working experiences. In off- and nearshore projects distance play a crucial role that is very often underestimated. At the organizational level the participation of project workers from different locations in the development of quality standards could represent a chance to establish more realistic working and communication patterns in international ICT organizations. Moreover, the cooperation of ICT organizations with educational institutions for the integration of quality standard and management issues in educational curricula in computer science or other related studies could support a common basis for the implementation of ICT qualifications in different national settings. In the next section I comment some future trends regarding quality standardization patterns in offshore in Europe.

FUTURE TRENDS

Taking into account the development in the European ICT Branch regarding offshoring (Ruiz Ben & Wieandt 2006; Ruiz Ben, Wieandt, & Maletzky, 2006), quality standardization will gain importance, first as coordination instruments in the development of the ICT branch in new geographical areas of the European Union. Due to this increasing significance of quality standards in the region, there will be a growing need for professionals with skills needed to engage in both standard setting activities in ICT companies and in Standard Setting Organizations. This represents an additional challenge for the educational institutions in the respective countries of the European Union that sum to the long-discussed problem of qualification mismatch in the ICT branch (Ruiz Ben & Claus, 2005; Ruiz Ben, 2003; Dostal, 2004). Educational institutions should more intensively cooperate with companies to prevent qualification mismatch in quality management, but also in project management issues. Internships about quality management should be established as a part of the curricula.

Intercultural aspects will gain also importance in the development of quality standards. The need to address these issues is crucial, in order to ensure equal access and opportunity for all European countries. From a global perspective, the World Summit on the Information Society represents an example for creating a discussion forum for these kinds of issues. Global SDOs like the ITU are also assigning growing focusing to equity aspects.

Considering the future trend towards increasing standardization, German companies seem to play in an advantage position, since as Tate (2001, p. 472) remarks:

In Germany, firms have been world leaders at creating a transnational infrastructure for standards, transferring their routine national standards work to the European and international levels which in turn remain closely integrated with more specialized national standards capable of supporting diversified quality strategies.

Nevertheless, as Tate further remarks, national varieties in standard settings in Europe are being compressed, but not eliminated. In the case of Germany, firms need "a comprehensive standards infrastructure capable of supporting high level product engineering" (2001, p. 472). Particularly at the process level, it is very important that standards develop in the line of process innovation rhythms. Therefore, firms will probably increasingly use international standard setting organizations for establishing their own standards in trans-national arenas. Particularly in Europe, this trend will be enhanced with the participation of the EU as harmonization, for instance. This could be a chance to better involve small and medium enterprises and also the new European Member States in the development of quality standards in the ICT branch.

CONCLUSION

In this chapter, I have shown which role quality standards play in the current internationalization process of the ICT branch focusing in the situation in Europe and particularly in Germany presenting some preliminary results of my work in progress.

First, I have given an overview of the importance of quality standards for the development of ICT off- and nearshore processes, as well as the role of the main actors in standards setting processes. Firms very often adopt ad hoc solutions in order to try to timely bring production outputs in line with the innovation rhythm of the market, due to the gap between the needs and perspectives of the standard developer, the organizations and the users of the standards. However, such solutions are very often ineffective. ICT companies practicing off- and nearshore mostly use quality standards as an instrument to reduce transaction costs, especially related to information and communication efforts among home and host centers, or as a basis to confront network externalities related to market competition. Thus, we can distinguish two main aspects of the adoption of quality standards in relation to off- and nearshore processes: an internal controlling aspect of working and communication processes and an external one beyond the network in order to get market advantages. Such advantages are mostly dominated by large enterprises playing the mayor role in the process of standards setting in SDOs and moreover due to their time and personnel resources to implement and adapt quality management systems in their network environments and to continually train their employees in order to implement quality standards in their day to day working practices.

In order to improve more democratic processes for the development of quality standards, the EU could adopt a harmonization entity role in the European context of the ICT branch. At the national level, a more intensive cooperation among small, medium and large enterprises with educational institutions and especially with universities could serve as a basis to reduce the particular disadvantages mentioned above and reduce possible qualification mismatches.

FUTURE RESEARCH DIRECTIONS

The research on quality standardization patterns in ICT off- and nearshore projects has been mainly focused on the level of the institutional support and composition development of quality standards. Also, management issues have been an important focus of research (Boiral, 2006; Tate, 2001; Carmel & Tjia 2005; Tummala & Tang, 1996). From the point of view of the day-to-day working practices, the question about how quality standardization patterns influence the working habitus of ICT professionals at different levels of the organiza-

tions is still open. Also, the transformation of tasks profiles in off- and nearshore projects and the related importance of quality managers for the implementation of international ICT projects are not yet fully researched. Aspects such as the balance between standardization of working processes and the emerging expertise of off- and nearshore projects in quality management systems are in some cases internally considered in organizations and represent an important problem in off- and nearshore projects. Here it is important to investigate which interaction and communication models between home and host organizations are best suited and how different actors in participating organizations can integrate their working experiences in the development of quality management systems. Moreover, the relation between innovation and implementation of quality standards in ICT organizations from an international perspective is another important issue for research. The question at this point is how quality standards contribute to the development of product and working process or on the contrary, they hindering dynamics of innovation. Particularly the adaptation of host organizations in off- and nearshore locations to quality standards implemented in home organization countries represents interpretation risks that can constitute a communication and creativity obstacle. Furthermore, the acceptance of imported quality management systems in host organizations should be better investigated in order to confront conflicts among workers in international ICT projects.

From an institutional perspective, the integration of quality standardization and quality management issues in university curricula is an important theme for research in order to confront the persisting mismatch between ICT educational and industrial development. At this point, it is important to investigate which models of institutional knowledge transfered in different regional settings have more successfully contributed to establishing learning patterns between educational institutions and ICT organizations. The chances and challenges for transferring such models to other contexts should be furthermore researched.

REFERENCES

Boiral, O. (2006). La certification ISO 14001: une perspective néoinstitutionnelle. *Management International, 10*(3), 67-79.

Carmel, E., & Tjia, P. (2005). *Offshoring information technology.* Sourcing and outsourcing to a global workforce. Cambridge: Cambridge University Press.

Crevoisier, O. (1999). Innovation and the city. In E. J. Malecki & P. Oinas (Eds.), *Making connections: Technological learning and regional economic change.* UK: Ashgate Publishing Company.

Dutka, D., & Sekhar, A. (2004, April 27-28). *Major Indian ICT firms and their approaches towards achieving quality.* Paper presented at an International Conference to Mark 20 Years of ASARC, University House, Australian National University.

Eisner, R. (2005). Offshore legal issues. In E. Carmel & P. Tjia (2005). *Offshoring information technology. Sourcing and outsourcing to a global workforce* (pp. 112-129). Cambridge: Cambridge University Press.

OECD. (2002a). *Technology outlook: ICTs and the information economy.* OECD & Dev.

OECD. (2002b). *Reviewing the ICT sector definition: Issues for discussion.* Paper DSTI/ICCP/IIS(2002)2. Retrieved August 25, 2006, from http://www.oecd.org/dataoecd/3/8/20627293.pdf

OECD (2002c). *Measuring the information economy.* Retrieved August 25, 2006, from http://www.oecd.org/dataoecd/16/14/1835738.pdf

Ruiz Ben, E., & Claus, R. (2004). Offshoring in der deutschen IT Branche. Eine neue Herausforderung für die Informatik. *Informatik Spektrum,* (4), 1-6.

Ruiz Ben, E., & Wieandt, M. (2006). *Growing East:* Nearshoring und die neuen ICT Arbeitsmärkte in Europa. FifF-Ko, (3). (forthcoming)

Tate, J. (2001). National varieties of standardization. In P. A. Hall & D. Soskice (Ed.), *Varieties of capitalism* (pp. 442-474). Oxford: Oxford University Press.

Tummala, V.M.R., & Tang, C.L. (1996). Strategic quality management. Malcolm Baldrige and European Quality Awards and ISO 9000 certification: Core concepts and comparative analysis. *International Journal of Quality and Reliability Management, 13*(4), 8-38.

van der Wiele, T., van Iwaarden, J., Williams, R., & Dale, B. (2004). *Perceptions about the ISO 9000 (2000) quality system standard revision and its value: The Dutch experience. ERIM Report Series ERS-2004-081-ORG (Organizational behavior and HRM).* Rotterdam: Erasmus Research Institute of Management.

ADDITIONAL READINGS

Adam, E.E. Jr., Corbett, L.M., Flores, B.E., Harrison, N.J., Lee, T.S., Rho, B., Ribera, J., Samson, D., & Westbrook, R. (1997). An international study of quality improvement approach and firm performance. *International Journal of Operations and Production Management, 17*(9), 842-73.

Askey, J.M., & Dale, B.G. (1994). From ISO 9000 series registration to total quality management, an examination, *Quality Management Journal,* July, 67-76.

Binney, G. (1992). *Making quality work: Lessons from Europe's leading companies.* The Economist Intelligence Unit, London. Special Report No. P655.

Blind, K. (2001). *Standardisation, R&D and export activities: Empirical evidence at firm level.* Proceedings of the Third Interdisciplinary Workshop on Standardization Research at the University of the German Federal Armed Forces (pp. 165-186). Hamburg, Germany: Univ. der Bundeswehr.

Bradley, M. (1994). Starting total quality management from ISO 9000. *The TQM Magazine, 6*(1), 50-4. Brecka, J. (1994). Survey of registrars for ISO 9000: Prices down, success rate up. Quality Progress, February, 20-1.

Brown, A., & Wiele, A. van der (1996). A typology of approaches to ISO certification and TQM. *Australian Journal of Management, 21*(1), 57-72.

Brown, A., Loughton, K., & Wiele, A. van der (1998). Smaller enterprises' experiences with ISO 9000. *International Journal of Quality and Reliability Management, 15*(3), 273-85.

Buttle, F. (1997). ISO 9000: Marketing motivations and benefits. *International Journal of Quality and Reliability Management, 14*(9), 939-47.

Corrigan, J. (1994). *Is ISO 9000 the path to TQM?* Quality Progress, May, 33-6.

Ebrahimpour, M., Withers, B.E., & Hikmet, N. (1997). Experiences of US- and foreign-owned firms: A new perspective on ISO 9000 implementation. *International Journal of Production Research, 35*(2), 569-76.

Flynn, B.B., Schroeder, R.G., & Sakakibara, S. (1995). The impact of quality management practices on performance and competitive advantage. *Decision Sciences, 26*(5), 659-92.

Forker, L.B., Vickery, S.K., & Droge, C.L. (1996). The contribution of quality to business performance. *International Journal of Operations and Production Management, 16*(8), 44-62.

Gotzamani, K.D., & Tsiotras, G.D. (2001). An empirical study of the ISO 9000 Standards' contribution towards total quality management. *International Journal of Operations & Production Management, 21*(10), 1326-42.

Heras, I., Casadesus, M., & Dick, G.P.M. (2002). ISO 9000 certification and the bottom line: A comparative study of the profitability of Basque companies. *Managerial Auditing Journal, 17*(1/2), 72-8.

Institute of Quality Assurance. (1993). *Survey on the use and implementation of BS5750.* London: Institute of Quality Assurance.

Hawkins, R. (2000). *Study of the standards-related information requirements of users in the information society.* Final report to CEN/ISSS. Retrieved February 14, 2000, from www.cenorm.be/isss

International Organisation for Standardization (ISO) (2004). *The ISO survey of ISO 9000 and ISO 14000 Certificates (Twelfth Cycle).* International Organisation for Standardisation, Geneva.

Jacobson, R., & Aaker, D. (1987). The strategic role of product quality. *Journal of Marketing, 51*(4), 31-44.

Johannsen, C.G. (1995). Application of the ISO 9000 standards of quality management in professional services: An information sector case. *Total Quality Management, 6*(3), 231-42.

Jones, R., Arndt, G., & Kustin, R. (1997). ISO 9000 among Australian companies: Impact of time and reasons for seeking certification on perceptions of benefits received. *International Journal of Quality and Reliability Management, 14* (7), 650-60.

Kanji, G.K. (1998). An innovative approach to make ISO 9000 standards more effective. *Total Quality Management, 9*(1), 67-78.

Kochan, A. (1993). ISO 9000: Creating a global standardisation process. Quality, October, 26-34.

Lee, T. (1995). The experience of implementing ISO 9000 in Hong Kong. *Asia Pacific Journal of Quality Management, 4*(4), 6-16.

Llopis, J., & Tarí, J.J. (2003). The importance of internal aspects in quality improvement. *International Journal of Quality and Reliability Management, 20*(3), 304-24

McAdam, R., & McKeown, M. (1999). Life after ISO 9000: An analysis of the impact of ISO 9000 and total quality management on small businesses in Northern Ireland. *Total Quality Management, 10*(2), 229-41.

Meegan, S.T., & Taylor, W.A. (1997). Factors influencing a successful transition from ISO 9000 to TQM: The influence of understanding and motivation. *International Journal of Quality & Reliability Management, 14*(2), 100-17.

Meeus, M.T.II., Faber, J., & Ocrlcmans, L.A.G. (2002). *Why do firms participate in standardization?* An empirical exploration of the relation between isomorphism and institutional dynamics in standardization. Working Paper Department of Innovation Studies, Utrecht: University of Utrecht.

Phillips, L.W., Chang, D.R., & Buzzel, R.D. (1983). Product quality, cost position, and business performance: A test of key hypotheses. *Journal of Marketing, 37*(1), 26-43.

Quazi, H.A., & Padibjo, S.R. (1998). A journey towards total quality management through ISO 9000 certification. A study of small and medium sized enterprises in Singapore. *International Journal of Quality & Reliability Management, 15*(5), 364-71.

Rada, R. (1998). Corporate shortcut to standardisation. *Communications of the ACM, 41*(1), 11-15.

Rada, R. (2000). Consensus versus speed. In K. Jakobs (Ed.), *IT standards and standardisation: A global perspective* (pp. 19-34). Hershey, PA: Idea Group Publishing.

Rust, R.T., Zahorik, A.J., & Keiningham, T.I. (1994). Return on quality (ROQ): Making service quality financially accountable. *Journal of Marketing, 59*(2), 58-70.

Seddon, J. (1997). Ten arguments against ISO 9000. *Managing Service Quality, 7*(4), 162-8.

Singles, J., Ruel, G., & Van de Water, H. (2001). ISO 9000 series—Certification and performance. *International Journal of Quality and Reliability Management, 18*(1), 62-75.

Stephens, K.S. (1994). ISO 9000 and total quality. *Quality Management Journal, 2*(1), 57-71.

Taylor, W.A. (1995). Senior executives and ISO 9000. *The International Journal of Quality and Reliability Management, 12*(4), 40-57.

Terziovski, M., Samson, D., & Dow, D. (1997). The business value of quality management systems certification: Evidence from Australia and New Zealand. *Journal of Operations Management, 15*(1), 1-18.

Terziovski, M., Power, D., & Sohal, A.S. (2003). The longitudinal effects of the ISO 9000 certification process on business performance. *European Journal of Operational Research, 146*(3), 580-95.

Tsiotras, G., & Gotzamani, K. (1996). ISO 9000 as an entry key to TQM: The case of the Greek industry. *International Journal of Quality and Reliability Management, 13*(4), 64-76.

Tummala, V.M.R., & Tang, C.L. (1996). Strategic quality management, Malcolm Baldrige and European Quality Awards and ISO 9000 certification: Core concepts and comparative analysis. *International Journal of Quality and Reliability Management, 13*(4), 8-38.

Weiss, M., & Cargill, C. (1992). Consortia in the standards development process. *Journal of the American Society for Information Science, 43*(8), 559-565.

Weiss, M.B.H., & Sirbu, M. (1990). Technological choice in voluntary standards committees: An empirical analysis. *Economics of Innovation and New Technology, 1*, 111-133.

Wiele, A. van der, Dale, B.G. & Williams, A.R.T. (1997). ISO 9000 series registration to total quality management: The transformation journey. *International Journal of Quality Science, 2*(4), 236-52.

Williams, N. (1997). ISO 9000 as a route to TQM in small to medium sized enterprises: Snake or ladder? *The TQM Magazine, 9*(1), 8-13.

Yahya, S., & Goh, W.K. (2001). The implementation of an ISO 9000 quality System. *International Journal of Quality and Reliability Management, 18*(9), 941-66.

ENDNOTES

[1] http://www.bsi-emea.com/Quality/Overview/WhatisaQMS.xalter (Retrieved August 20, 2006)

[2] The following example illustrates the use of the EU Acquired Rights Directive for ICT offshoring: "*When multinational companies are applying 'global sourcing' strategies, suppliers can be played off against one*

another and as a result, they can either win or lose a contract. In the case of long-term contracts for service delivery, staff can be transferred together with their jobs to do the same work for their new boss. This is necessary to ensure the continuity and quality of the service delivery. Such transfer of employees from one service provider to another requires special attention to maintaining the acquired working conditions. Recently, Siemens Business Services (SBS) took over a contract of Electronic Data Systems (EDS) to supply business services to the Coca-Cola Company. SBS agreed with the EDS on the transfer of a number of dedicated employees from the latter to the former in certain countries. These transfers were carried out within the EU Acquired Rights Directive that regulates the transfer of working conditions." Accessed August 29, 2006, from http://www.union-network.org/Uniindep. nsf/f73728e0eb1f5ca5c125700e003ccdbb/ $FILE/MOOSNewsletter3.pdf#search=%2 2acquired%20rights%20directive%20eu% 20offshoring%22

Chapter XVI
Offshoring in the ICT Sector in Europe:
Trends and Scenario Analysis

Esther Ruiz Ben
Technische Universtät Berlin, Germany

Michaela Wieandt
Technische Universtät Berlin, Germany

Martina Maletzky
Technische Universtät Berlin, Germany

ABSTRACT

In the context of globalization and internationalization, offshoring processes in the ICT Industry have increased considerably in the software and service sector in recent years due to the cost saving strategies and market entry policies of ICT organizations. Through the heterogeneity of the European ICT sector a regionalization trend regarding host country selection for ICT offshore is, nevertheless, observable. Historical and cultural ties between host and home countries as well as related national stereotypes play an important role in the regionalization process. Moreover, due to favorable EU policies and regulations, off- and nearshoring within the European Union acquire an additional attractive character for some major European producers, such as, for example, Germany. Thus the Eastern European Member States, which already build out certain sectoral specialization in regard to ICT service provision, have benefited from direct foreign investments. Off- and nearshoring also imply risks and hidden costs linked to structural aspects in host countries as well as to the overestimation of cultural and historical nearness. In our chapter we discuss the trends of the internationalization process in the European ICT sector taking into account related risks in off- and nearshore processes. We argue, furthermore, that long-term cooperation and intercultural training, with the support of local and European institutions, should be considered to confrontin a better way the challenges of the internationalization of ICT in Europe.

INTRODUCTION

During recent years and particularly in the period following the dot.com crisis, offshoring processes in the ICT sector experienced a very important increment primarily due to the pressure to cut costs. The acute labor shortage in the sector prior to the crisis decreased and the maturity of the technological and organizational developments of the late nineties facilitated the increasing standardization of some working processes permitting the delegation of tasks to foreign countries with cheaper labor costs. Thus, the perspective of many ICT organizations changed from attracting foreign workers to a relocation of tasks to foreign destinations.

Focusing on the situation in Europe, since 1995 there has been a rapid growth of foreign workers in the ICT sector in western European countries. According to Kolb et al. (2004):

In the UK the numbers of foreign workers in the ICT sector rose by 64.3% (from 55,501 to 91,184), the increase in Switzerland was 59.6% (from 6,986 to 11,149) and in Germany 54% (from 10,725 to 16,514). Also, The Netherlands display a 21.4% increase (from 28,000 to 34,000) in that period. There are, however, a number of differences in the occupational categories used in data collection, so that the validity of this data should not be exaggerated. The indicated trend, however, is unmistakable.[1] (p. 157)

Until 2003 this growth trend in the international immigration of high-qualified workers in EU countries focused especially on the ICT sector remained. Due to the labor shortage prior to the dot.com crisis foreign workers already working in Europe or in the USA played an important role in the early phases of ICT offshoring (Aspray, Mayadas, & Vardi, 2006, p. 17), so we can consider the policies of acquiring ICT foreign specialists since the late 90s the basis for an early development of the IT offshoring processes and for the long term internationalization of the ICT industry.

Educational policies play an important role in this process in the European Union not only at the tertiary level, but also regarding official training programs for continuous education mostly conceived within the framework of the information society concept of the EU. Because the EU cannot be viewed as a unified, homogeneous market, in the following pages we focus on ICT near- and offshore processes in the following European countries: United Kingdom, France and Germany as home

countries sending work and Ireland, Poland, Czech Republic and Hungary as host countries acquiring work. Furthermore, we look closely at the importance of particularly large ICT organizations as major players in the professionalization processes within the ICT sector. First, we will show the main features of internationalization of the European ICT sector defining the meaning of ICT near- and offshoring in the following section. The main thrust of our paper focuses on the situation of near- and offshore processes in the EU with special attention to the new Eastern European Member States. Then we will explain the hidden costs as well as the risks involved in near- and offshore projects. This will lead us to possible solutions and recommendations and, finally, to the scope of future trends and further research directions.

BACKGROUND: THE EVOLUTION AND INTERNATIONALIZATION OF THE EUROPEAN ICT SECTOR

The European ICT sector includes a broad variety of products and activities. Due to unclear production areas because many companies are engaged in different segments of the sector and due to country-specific measurements and data collection, a consistent and overall definition is still missing.[2] In its definition of the ICT sector, EITO (2006, p. 251) distinguishes between, first, information technology (IT), including hardware production (office machines, data processing equipment and data communication equipment), software, and services (including IT consulting); and second, telecommunications (TLC), referring to carrier service, communication devices, and network equipment. However, the growth of ICT services as well as innovation in hardware production indicates the important role of the software sector.

In a German study based on 920 interviews, the software sector is broken into two segments (GfK, IESE, ISI, 2000): the primary segment of the sector includes data processing services and computer producers while the secondary segment includes enterprises for machine production, electronics, automobile production, telecommunications and financial services. While in the primary segment software is a separate product, in the secondary it is embedded in other products or represents a service product. In the secondary segment of the software sector within the ICT branch the demand for innovative software products and services is specially important. Examples of the demand for services demand in the secondary segment in the case of Germany are especially the automobile, chemical or finance industry. They represent the main source of innovation for the software sector since the software boom of the late nineties.

In keeping with the emergence of the Internet and the dot.com-economy the European ICT industry boomed at the end of the 1990s providing high growth rates in IT production and services as well as high rates of employment. Due to the high demand of skilled workers during the boom phase and the related labor shortage in the ICT sector, particularly at the end of the nineties, European countries developed several strategies to attract highly skilled foreign IT workers (López-Basolls, 2002). An example is the Green-card- initiative in Germany enhancing immigration of highly skilled workers (Dostal, 2004). The UK, Ireland, France, The Netherlands, and Italy developed policies easing the inward flow of foreign ICT workers using specific work permits. In the Nordic countries, tax incentives should attract a foreign work force (Mc Laughlan & Salt, 2002). Another common strategy was that of reducing the length of time taken for work permit approval, although the time efficiency differed from one country to another. As an example, work permit provisions in the UK had a faster response rate than anywhere else.

At the beginning of the new millennium the sector was hit by the burst of the Internet bubble leading to a sharp decline in demand, prices and employment. Thus, since 2001 the inflow of foreign workers has decreased (OECD, 2004) and at the EU political level, long-term strategies have been designed to increase the competitiveness of Member States.

In the following years, European ICT companies sought new possibilities for cost reduction, access to specialists and technology when needed, and for economies in scales by standardization and the formalization of working processes. Offshoring and nearshoring seemed to provide a beneficial solution, offering international expansion, access to new markets and growth (OECD, 2004, 2005). While manufacturers of ICT started to outsource in cheaper locations many years ago, providing business support and IT related services has been enabled recently by rapid development in IT systems and broadband communication as well as by the liberalization in trading services (OECD, 2005).

The evolution of off- and nearshoring is closely related to the industrialization of the ICT sector. Boes and Trinks (2006) interpret offshoring as a new phase of industrialization in the ICT sector fostered by the emergence of an international, highly flexible and qualified ICT labor force as well as by an increasingly developing globalized collective economic area. Moreover, offshoring is enhanced through increased competition, trade deregulation and the liberalization of services. Due to recent regulations in the EU, where the exchange of services and goods is free, ICT companies may develop a self-reinforcing dynamic to gain cost or quality advantages through offshoring (OECD, 2004, 2005; Aspray, Mayadas, & Vardi, 2006). Thus, we assume that driving factors for offshoring must be understood in the framework of globalization and of the industrialization trend in the software sector. Both the financial and the dot.com crisis at the beginning of the new millenium acted as a catalyst in cost reduction in the ICT branch and led to a new phase in internationalization as a way to confront costs pressure while expanding in the new markets.

EU policies and regulations play an important role in the internationalization of the ICT branch because they influence offshoring plans in ICT networks and contribute to shaping institutional configurations and trajectories of the ICT branch. Labor and employment rights as well as issues related to privacy and data transfer have a special relevance for ICT offshoring. Data privacy laws, the European Union Data Privacy Directive adopted in 1995, apply to companies collecting or processing data within the EU or receiving data from the EU. They are implemented by the respective EU countries through national legislation (Eisner, 2005). Eisner (2005) points out that EU-approved transfer contract clauses are the most efficient way to handle data transfer in ICT offshoring processes in the EU. These clauses consist of an agreement between the transferring parties about a set of contract provisions consistent with data privacy laws. Once these clauses are effected by the transferring parties enforcement by the EU authorities is allowed.

Another important issue related to EU regulations in ICT offshoring is the EU Acquired Rights Directive approved in 1977 giving employees protection in the event of a business transfer.[3] This means employees must be transferred under the same working conditions they had before the transfer took place. In the case of replacement, employees must be informed and advised about related measures and are sometimes awarded a particular payment (Eisner, 2005). In the implementation of working policies in organizations, particularly regarding employees' representation in companies' decision making processes, there are many differences among the European Member States, the most significant between the former EU15 and the new European Member States. These differences are particularly important for those European companies focusing on nearshoring in Eastern Europe, as do many German firms. In contrast, other European players, such as many UK enterprises, have concentrated on offshore destinations, e.g., the well researched case of India. Thus, the internationalization of the European ICT sector does not show an homogeneous picture emerging in a clear direction. The specific focuses of different countries are related to historical and cultural ties as well as to the influence of particular national industrial specialization and the particular regional presence and interest of the major producers in the European ICT sector (UK, Germany, France, and Ireland).

To understand the regional orientation of the delivering and host countries of ICT work in Europe properly we will explain in the next section the meaning of both offshore and nearshore in their several variations.

The Meaning of ICT Off- and Nearshoring

As we explain elsewhere (Ruiz Ben & Wieandt, 2006), the terms off- and nearshoring refer to outsourcing practices, or the founding of subsidiary firms, in lower-wage countries (Aspray, Mayadas, & Vardi, 2006). The main motivation for ICT offshoring is to cut costs. Additionally, the expansion of market scope represents an important factor in offshore ICT production areas.

Offshoring refers to the outsourcing to, or the founding of, a subsidiary in a lower-wage country s far[4] from the home country. From the European point of view this could be China or India. The term nearshoring is used for activities closer to the homeland.[5] From a Western European point of view this could be Eastern Europe or Russia. To characterize the direction of sourcing, the country sending work is called the home country; the country receiving work, the host country (Aspray, Mayadas, & Vardi, 2006).

Off- and nearshoring appear in various forms: The term, "external offshore-outsourcing," refers to the partial or total transfer of functions to external enterprises in lower-wagecountries. This form applies best to back-officeprocesses without customer contact (?) and handled via the Internet. The term, "internal offshore-outsourcing," is used for the founding of a subsidiary or a joint venture[6] characterizing by partial or total transfer of functions to dependent enterprises in lower-wagecountries (OECD 2005; Riedl & Kepler, 2003; Boes & Schwemmle, 2004). According to Amberg and Wiener (2004c), subsidiaries and joint ventures are the prefered form of offshore-outsourcing because they may still be controlled via capital shares and, therefore, risks are considerably low. Because of the need for high investments in the foundingphase they are of interesting mainly to big companies (Boes & Schwemmle, 2004; OECD, 2005).

If offshoring is a substitute for a company's domestic capacity it usually implies a cutback of production and, therefore, job loss in the homeland although expanding offshoring may increase a company's performance in building up capacities abroad while keeping production output at home stable (Boes & Schwemmle, 2004). Expansive offshoring usually takes place through building international teams able to perform complex activities requiring adjustment or customer contact, minimizing coordination costs (Boes & Schwemmle, 2004). Staff members at home need to qualify in regard to co-ordination, project management and intercultural competences.

The shifting abroad of performances in the ICT sector may refer basically to all sub-sectors, all phases of the production process or overall activities of an enterprise (Amberg & Wiener, 2004b; Boes & Schwemmle, 2004).

a. On the level of a company's infrastructure, off- or nearshoring apply to the outsourcing of the physical production of hardware components, such as semiconductors, computer components and computers. Here, we find external offshoring to service providers as well as shared service centers in the form of joint ventures to keep control (Amberg & Wiener, 2004c).

b. On the level of applications and development, they affect the development of individual software or applications with tasks requiring lower qualifications, such as programming, software-testing and software maintainance (applications management), but also high-end services, such as IT research, software-architecture, product design, project management, IT consulting and business strategy.[7] Offshoring of applications and development in particular refers to a company's expansion

through providing access to cheap specialists and production capacities. Due to close collaboration with the customer in software production and applications management, the home company's workforce is still required.

c. On the process level, offshoring is designed as business process outsourcing, i.e., accounting, bookkeeping, digitalization of engineering drawings or desktop publishing implemented to substitute capacities (Amberg & Wiener, 2005; Aspray, Mayadas, & Vardi, 2006). That often leads to classical offshoring-outsourcing to external providers.

Figure 1 summarizes forms of offshoring used for such business activities.

In many cases, ICT companies combine or alternate forms of offshoring which may occur as either internal or external offshore-outsourcing. For example, a broadly adopted strategy is to start a small pilot project as expansion, later widened if the results are positive, while capacities in the home organizations may be cut down. On the other hand, an offshore project conceptualized as substitution may lead to the enhancement of the home organizations' overall performance. In that case so downsizing doesn't make sense; an expansion of the home organization may even be useful. Looking at the internal and external forms of offshoring we observe that companies start with an external provider which, with further development, is bought and integrated into the home organization. Thus, external offshoring may become internal expansion. In some casest a subsidiary turns into

Figure 1. Business activities, forms of offshoring and control

	Internal offshore-outsourcing	External offshore-outsourcing
Expansive offshoring	Application management and software development	Application management and software development
Substitutive offshoring	IT Infrastructure, hardware production, business processes	IT Infrastructure, hardware production, business processes
Level of control by home company	Comparatively high	Comparatively low

a buy-out or spin-off that still collaborates with the former motherorganization transforming internal to external offshore-outsourcing.

Saving costs primarily motivate off- and near-shoring. In this regard, a widely held view is that the profitability of offshoring is linked to certain budget, personnel, and time. According to our own research (Ruiz Ben, Wieandt, & Maletzky, 2007), offshoring is financially rewarding if projects encompass more than ten ICT workers abroad, a budget of a minimum of one million Euros, and a project duration of at least one year. Considering the offshoring activities of large companies, a long-term conceptualizaion is usually intended, leading to the funding of subsidiary software programming, development centres, or joint ventures.

Looking at European nearshore destinations, salaries in the new European Member States are still low and represent a clear advantage for ICT companies. Moreover, the qualification level in these new Member States and the high unemployment in some of them, especially Eastern European countries, represent additional advantages linked to the employees´ motivation and willingness to work, engagement and readiness for continuous learning, both indispensable in the ICT sector. Thus, they are attractive nearshore destinations for Western European companies, as we will show in the next section.

In the main thrust of our chapter we will show first an overview of the situation in the major home and host countries of ICT off- and nearshore projects in the EU to understand the regional orientation of the involved countries better. We will thenclassify the factors influencing the relationship between home and host countries as well as those affecting the performance of near- and offshore projects. This classification will lead to an explanation of transactions and hidden costs as well as the risks involved in near- and offshore projects.

MAIN THRUST: COUNTRY SPECIFIC ANALYSIS

Looking at the European countries in particular, the size and structure of ICT sectors differ among them. As Table 1 shows, Germany and the UK have the largest sectors with a collective market share of 41.6% in 2005 (EITO, 2006).

The historical and political divisions of Europe before 1989 led to the establishment of a highly developed and well performing western section (the Europe-15 Member States, Norway, and Switzerland) and a transforming but well qualified, and less regulated eastern section (the New Member States, Bulgaria, and Romania).

Germanys' ICT sector, the third largest in the world (Friedewald, 2004), in 2005 held a market share of 21.2% in Europe followed by the UK (20.4%) and France (16.9%). In the ICT sectors of the three countries, software and service were the largest sections (Bitkom, 2006; OECD, 2002c). Considering off- and nearshore expenditures, Great Britain and Ireland have the highest among the European Member States, amounting to 72%, followed by German-speaking countries (Germany, Austria, and Switzerland), accounting for 9% and France with a share of 8% (DB Research, 2006).

Table 1. European ICT market leaders and offshore expenditures. (Source: Eito 2006, DB Research 2006).

Country	Maket share of the European ICT market in percent, 2005	Share of Offshore expenditures in Europe in percent, 2005
Germany	21.2	9[1]
United Kingdom	20.4[3]	72[2]
France	16.9	8

Notes: 1 This number contains offshore expenditures of the German speaking countries (Germany, Austria, Switzerland). 2 This number contains offshore expenditures of Great Britain and Ireland. 3 This number does not include Ireland.

Within the new European Member States, the largest ICT markets are those of the Czech Republic, Poland, and Hungary, with high growth rates in the ICT area (EITO, 2006) and in ICT exports (DB Research, 2006). Moreover, the increasing globalization of the ICT sector implies interdependencies among ICT organizations with the development trends of the ICT sector in the EU approximating those in North America (EITO, 2006).

In Europe, both home and host countries of off- and nearshoring compete in one market area regulated by the European Union. Analyzing off- and nearshore strategies of the European market leaders, some ambivalences appear, leading to the conclusion that the enhancement of off- and nearshore strategies by hard factors such as tax incentives, a highly skilled workforce or a good technological infrastructure are impeded by soft factors, such as historical relationships and/or cultural pecularities, whichmay be considered critical. To analyze off- and nearshore strategies we distinguish hard and soft factors, as used in the literature (see, i.e., AT Kearney, 2004; DB Research, 2006).

Hard factors include direct measurable categories used to evaluate a country's performance as an investment location, such as cost levelss (wages, compensation costs for relevant positions, tax rate, costs of corruption and fluctuating exchange rates); peoples' skills (including language skills); availability of personnel, and business environment (infrastructure, government support, security of intellectual property and country environment (AT Kearney, 2004, p. 5); and geographical closeness. Another factor enhancing investment in the New European Member States is the funding policy of the EU that provides a broad array of programs to enhance investment and economic relationships of member countries (DIHK, 2004). The influence of these programs for the establishment of nearshore relationships has not yet been analyzed, but is considered important.

Soft factors may be defined as factors influencing the success of ICT near- and offshore projects[8] not quantifiable in an objective way. Soft factors include historical relationships between home and host countries as well as cultural pecularities,

with individuals socialized, e.g., the individual's sense-making attitudes and interpretationpatterns as linked, for example, to certain stereotypes. Thus, communication and working styles may differ among collaborators of different countries provoking friction, misinterpretations or misunderstandings (Hall, 1990; Hofstede, 1980; Hui, 1990; Thomas, 1999). Additionally the working climate may be influenced subliminally[9]with either negative or positive impact on commitment and team cohesion—important factors for effective work (Maletzky, 2006). However, literature on off- and nearshoring (see DB Research, 2006; AT Kearney, 2004), produced mostly by consulting firms, tends to evaluate soft factors in a predominantly positive way,assuming they enhance cross-national collaboration. Thus, for example, it is assumed that cultural nearness is a criterion for German companies in choosing Poland or the Czech Republic as a nearshore location. However, there is still discussion on the way historical relationships between Germany and Eastern European countries such as Poland or the Czech Republic, influenced not only by the former iron curtain but also by World War II's displacement processes[9] and border disputes,[10] remain as stereotypes and even build prejudices that negatively influence intercultural working teams.

In the case of English and French companies, that prefer offshoring to former colonies, the colonial past has to be taken into account, because it strongly impacts relationships between countries. For example, the UK and India have close relationships in regard to an array of political issues and areas (British High Commission, 2006). Considering individuals, a colonial past might have egative impact because feelings of superiority and inferiority may be part of the game. Thus, soft factors must be viewed very carefully and their impact (estimated on the basis of cultural pecularities and historical relationships) considered negative rather than positive.

In order to analyze off- and nearshoring strategies in Europe, we will take soft and hard factors into account while looking more closely at European ICT market leaders with Germany, the UK, and France representing home countries.[11] Ireland, as both home and host country, is introduced as well. We will also provide an overview of the New Member States characterized as host countries. The nearshore market leaders, Poland, Czech Republic, and Hungary, are described more intensively.

Offshoring Trends of Companies Representing Selected European Countries

The *English* companies opted mainly for offshoring in India, principally due to India's economical attractiveness as well as language advantages. India is associated with the UK especially through its colonial past and through the usage of English as its official language. Thus, UK companies shore off software and service work to India[12] in particular because it offers some advantages: India provides an attractive regulatory environment with low infrastructure costs and taxes, and a cheap, large and highly qualified workforce with technological and mathematical skills, combined with cultural experiences resulting from Indian information technlogy workers having worked or studied in the UK. According to the long tradition of offshoring services in India,[13] Indian enterprises are experienced in discovering new market demands, contracting, and trust building (Aspray, Mayadas, & Vardi, 2006). Another reason for English companies' activities in India is their comparatively long offshore tradition: they started offshoring activities before 1989 when the opening of Eastern European markets started. Now, relationships are institutionalized (Aspray, Mayadas, & Vardi, 2006). The common history of India and the UK is assumed to have a positive impact because members of one culture may know those of the other.

Despite the advantages of offshoring to Indi, most *German* ICT companies prefer Eastern European nearshore destinations for a couple of reasons: a sizeable number of highly qualified ICT workers have German language skills because they studied in Germany or chose German as their second language. Moreover, cultural closeness is assumed by the companies, although its impact is not analysed in detail yet. The short distance to Eastern European countries—Poland and the Czech Republic are neighboring countries of Germany—also permits personal contact between the nearshore provider and home organizations so more complex processes might be outsourced (Ruiz Ben & Wieandt, 2006; DB Research, 2006; AT Kearney, 2004). Moreover, Poland and the Czech republic offer labor cost and tax advantages. Large German firms with global practices, such as Siemens or SAP, are moving rapidly to build their offshore capabilities in Eastern Europe as well as in China and India, where they also look for market entry possibilities. They also have a global production network which they expand while middle- and small-size enterprises hesitate before starting nearshore production (Aspray, Mayadas, & Vardi, 2006).

Similar to the UK, some offshoring-strategies of *French* ICT companies are linked to the country's colonial history. Preferred offshore destinations are, therefore, former colonies such as Morrocco and Tunisia where French is spoken as the official language and which are geographically close to France. Moreover, these counties also offer highly qualified IT workers, low wages, and low taxes (Kleinhans, 2005). It could be assumed that Morroccan and Tunisian workers may also have experienced working or studying in France and have cultural knowlegde. French companies are also active in nearshoring business to Romania, considered a nearshore destination because of a well-qualified work force with French language skills (DB Research, 2006; Amberg & Wiener, 2004a).

Ireland has a special position as an offshore destination and home country at the same time (Carmel & Abott, 2006). The Irish ICT sector is fairly developed and experienced economic growth because it attracted US-based firms particularly, providing outsourcing services and software development. Ireland was one of the first countries to develop software industries primarily for export rather than for domestic purposes (Aspray, Mayadas, & Vardi, 2006). It has significantly increased its share of the export of computer and information services (OECD, 2004, p. 6) and offers shared service centres for large companies, including IBM, Microsoft and Intel (AT Kearney, 2004). Offering a secure business environment and a highly educated work force as advantages, negative factors are high compensation costs and a small work force. All in all, Ireland provides a "secure business environment, leadership in software industry and educated workforce." (AT Kearney, 2004, p. 21). Looking at the home country perspective, Irish ICT companies started offshoring to India because of costs, the highly qualified and experienced labor force, and language advantages (DB Research, 2006). Another factor might be that Irish ICT companies set up relationships with Indian subsidiaries of their U.S.- or UK-based customers. An Indian presence would then ease the processes of adjustment in more complex IT projects.

Among the new European Member States, *Poland, Hungary,* and the *Czech Republic* can be characterized as nearshore host countries. Providing the largest IT markets in Eastern Europe (EITO, 2006; Ruiz Ben & Wieandt, 2006), the Czech Republic, Poland, and Hungary offer low costs, good language skills, solid technical capabilities and infrastructre, and minimal regulatory problems for all western European firms (AT Kearney 2004, p. 8). However, because of the high share of workers with German language skills and to geographical closeness, they are particularly attractive for German companies (DB Research, 2006).

The *Czech Republic* attracts international companies by providing a well developed infrastructure, a stable business environment, and a particularly strong educational system. The Czech ICT sector is dominated by foreign companies and high FDIs (financial direct investment) that stimulate the growth of its ICT market (Ruiz Ben & Wieandt, 2006). In contrast, Poland and Hungary have similar educational systems, offer cost advantages, but "are perceived to have slightly inferior business environments, infrastructure and IP security" (At Kearney, 2004a, p. 10).

Poland's ICT sector made a small contribution to the country's GDP in 2003 (Gaspar 2004), but, due to growth in hardware production and software service delivery, the sector provided high growth rates in 2005 (EITO, 2006). While the majority of the main players in the Polish software market are domestic, Poland is seen as a location for business

process outsourcing, delivering to global players such as PP, IBM or Capgemini (Ruiz Ben & Wieandt, 2006).

In *Hungary* the situation in the ICT sector is rather different. The Hungarian ICT sector, similar to the Czech Republic, was dominated by foreign firms in all sections exept the software sector (Ruiz Ben & Wieandt, 2006) and accounted for 7% of the Hungarian GDP in 2003 (Gaspar, 2004). Offering low costs and and an average business environment, Hungary is an attractive destination county, attracting mainly German companies (AT Kearney, 2004; Auswaertiges Amt, 2006).

With small ICT sectors contributing from 1.2% to 2.4% to the national GDP, the Baltic countries are associated mainly with their neighbors. Estonia attracts foreign direct investment mainly from Sweden and Finland (Püss et al., 2004) while Lithuania is oriented towards the former Soviet Union (FSu), Russia (Lithuanian Free Market Institute, 2004), and Latvia towards the Baltic markets (Karnite, Kalva, & Karnitis, 2004). *Slovenia* and *Slovakia* offer stable business environments, attractive tax rates and a highly qualified work force, attracting German companies in particular (Stare, Kmet, & Bučar, 2004; Sirak, Salner, & Druga, 2004). Slovenia's ICT sector amounts to 7.5% of the GPD, quite large compared to Slovakia's share of 2% (Gaspar, 2004). Slovenia's software sector is dominated by a large number of small domestic firms seeking to serve to niche markets in banking, wholesaling and geographic information systems (Stare, Kmet, & Bučar, 2004). However, in Slovakia foreign global companies rule the market for IT services, operating substantial services to support their European customers. Regarding the accession countries, *Bulgaria* and *Romania*, that will join the EU, presumably in 2007, their ICT sectors are comparatively small, but developing quickly (EITO, 2006). The Bulgarian software market is dominated by domestic firms that export mainly their services, seeking to strenghten their position abroad while focusing on serving small and medium enterprises as customers, particularly in Germany (Yonkova-Hristova, 2004). Dominated by foreign investors from China, East Asia, and Europe, the *Romanian* ICT sector experienced significant growth throughout the nineties but still has little relevance for the economy (Gaspar 2004). French ICT companies in particular seek to exploit low labor cost advantages. Recently the situation has started to change in regard to the utilization of the skilled labor force in the production of software and Internet-based IT services (Carageea, Gheorghiu, & Turlea, 2003).

Summing up, hard factors have higher impact than soft factors determining which off- or nearshore location will be chosen. Soft factors often play an unconscious role. Costs, skilled labor force, stable business environments, and language advantages seem to have high positive influence on off- and nearshoring. Nevertheless, supposed cultural similarity is often related to the hope of minimizing hidden costs. The focus of the main players of the European ICT market on certain offshore- or nearshore destinations may be characterized a "regional" orientation based on hard factors. This trend is observable in all countries with large ICT markets. In the case of nearshoring, lower geographical and cultural distances facilitate personal contact as well as communication and, therefore, may faciliate the sourcing of more complex tasks and processes with higher value.

Considering country reports, we observe a tendency toward specialization beginning with regard to the secondary segment of the software sector (definition above). This means ICT companies focus particularly on demand from companies that are not primarily software producers themselves, but require the integration of software products and services. In the case of Slovenian ICT firms are, for instance, specialized in adapting standard software products for the banking and insurance sector as well as for the health sector.

Nevertheless, although specialization related to ICT offshoring may contribute to establishing working processes and knowledge transfer, in an increasingly globalized ICT sector, offshoring also involves costs and risks sometimes not predictable. In the next section we give an overview of hidden costs and risks involved in offshoring processes in Europe, that may be transferable to other regions.

Figure 2. Transaction and hidden costs and risks in ICT off- and nearshore projects

Transaction and Hidden costs		Risks	
Dimensions	Related costs' factors	Dimensions	Related costs' factors
Selection of Providers (Related to the country specific socio-cultural, historical and institutional factors of off- and nearshoring)	• Research • Consulting • Legal and contracting issues • Traveling • Benchmarking • Coordination and synchronisation policies	Cultural distance (Related to the country specific socio-cultural, historical and institutional factors of off- and nearshoring)	• Technological supporting tools • Intercultural training • Traveling
Restructuration	• Qualification and Experience of the potential working force. • Quality and project management	Intellectual Property	• Loss of property knowledge • Contractual costs
Knowledge Transfer	• Controlling systems and processes. • Continous training • Traveling		
Governance and risk mitigation	• Monitoring • Recovery in case of project failure		

Hidden Costs and Risks of Offshoring

One of the main motivations for ICT organizations' offshoring is cutting costs. Other related factors are access to knowledge, availability of labor force, and corporate restructuring, including concentration on core business and activities (Huws et al., 2004, 16). Experiences in recent years, particularly after the first years of 2000, when offshoring in ICT contexts in Europe expanded, show that ICT offshore processes involve many hidden costs as well as risks that managers did not previously consider. Thus, hidden costs and risks linked to offshoring processes experiences indicate that a situation may emerge in which total offshore costs, for instance, are higher than those before its implementation. For analytical reasons, following Carmel and Tjia (2005, 36), a distinction is made between ICT offshoring risks as to predictable implications of ICT offshoring, and transaction and hidden costs related to transactional practices.. ICT organizations find most transaction costs for offshoring at the process level. The following table shows the main dimensions and factors related to transaction and hidden costs as well as to risks in off- and nearshore projects.

Figure 2 shows the classification of transaction and hidden costs and of risks in off- and nearshore projects with their respective dimensions and related costs factors. As mentioned in the previous section, soft (cultural and historical) factors and hard (institutional and location) factors influence the delivering country's orientation as well as the performance of near- and offshore projects. Regarding transaction and hidden costs, these factors especially affect the selection of providers, while in relation to the risks in off- and nearshore projects, soft and hard factors are linked to cultural dimensions of near- and offshore projects.

Transaction costs in ICT offshoring are those related to the identification of suppliers in foreign countries, and negotiation and contracting with those suppliers. Once a supplier repertoire exists, concrete policies for coordination and synchronization oriented towards particular quality standards must be established. The establishment of coor-

dination and synchronization policies represents possible costs as well. Coordination and synchronization policies must also be negotiated and implemented in cooperating organizations, often causing conflict with existing rules and norms the employees use in day-to-day practices.

Regarding hidden costs, the selection of providers in host offshore countries is considered before the initation of the ICT offshore process. Selection costs include research, consulting costs, legal and contracting issue costs, as well as related traveling for contract negotiations (Morales, 2005). When organizations do not have experience with ICT offshoring, they usually work with benchmarking companies that provide an overview and an evaluation on specific chances and risks. Benchmarking represents, thus, another cost related to ICT offshoring.

Regarding restructuring, two major factors related to the human capital of the organizations and to their social environment must be taken into account: qualification and experience of the personnel available in the home country as well as in the host offshore country. In some EU countries, past strategies to hire high skilled foreign personnel, such as the "green-card" measure in Germany, represent an advantage to integrating off- and nearshore teams into the organizational culture, because employees with experience in German ICT companies help bridge qualification gaps. In home countries with strong cultural differences, personnel selection strategies, e.g., assessment contents, are not transferable (Lonner, 1990) and may cause additional costs for hiring local agencies specializing in this. Also there may be time loss due to a greater need to control personnel selection offshore (Matloff, 2005), and also onshore (Kealey, 1996). The qualifications and experience of the personnel are basic dimensions for the success of ICT offshore where national and international educational development play a crucial role. At the national level in the EU, the problem of synchronization between official qualification standards and the demands of knowledge and skills development in ICT organizations persist (regarding Germany s. Dostal, 2006). The increasing globalization of knowledge transfer and qualification differences in international arenas represent additional challenges confronting Europe in recent years through increasing standardization of qualifications (see Bologna process), the development of standard corporate certifications by ICT multinationals, sometimes in co-operation with local universities, and the increasing enrolment for consulting firms in the evaluation of qualifications and skills needs. However, regarding the situation in the New European Member and Candidate States in Eastern Europe the rapid restructuring of their educational systems shows some limitations in convergence with the qualification demands of the global ICT labor market. This is, for instance, the case in Bulgaria, where, although universities emphasize computer science education, specialization in programming skills without training in ICT networks has led to a shortage of personnel with knowledge in the area (Mroczkowski et al., 2001, 49). Important at this point is also the employees' awareness of quality standards and of integrating management systems with international scope. Meeting internationally recognized quality standards represents one of the crucial factors in deciding on restructuring measures in ICT organizations because it constitutes the basis for competing with other companies and establishing long-term customer relationships.

Organizational knowledge transfer, however, is managed internally within ICT networks and must be established and controlled. Both the establishment of a controlling system for knowledge management in ICT offshore projects and the controlling process itself bring additional hidden costs. Carmel and Tjia (2005, p. 38) point out that redundancy built into an offshore project in its early phases may represent the largest costs. These authors illustrate this assessment in the following terms:

A typical scenario takes place when several offshore developers need to travel to the client site for KT (knowledge transfer) early in the project life cycle (...). At these early stages the client firm is paying for double staffing for the same work, for its current and the offshore employees. (Carmel/Tjia, 2005, p. 38)

Travel costs for offshore developers have to be considered (Ruiz Ben & Claus, 2005).

Furthermore, in addition to the hidden costs involved in knowledge transfer, translation costs related to collaboration with offshore partners without a common language background may also emerge. Confrontation with these kinds of hidden costs in the EU differs according to historical and cultural factors in the various countries and regions. Thus, for example, the orientation of Germany is focused a great deal on Eastern Europe while the UK shows a longer offshore tradition in India. In Germany particularly, the recent enrolment of the most developed Eastern European countries, Hungary, Poland, and the Czech Republic, brings important impulses for offshore development for both.

Other hidden costs of ICT offshoring are related to governance and risk mitigation factors. Consulting groups report costs between 5% and 10% of an offshoring contract related to governance practices (Forrester, 2003; Koch, 2004). Such costs include new positions to communicate with providers and to monitor the providers' work. Regarding the mitigation of offshoring risks, ICT organizations must also consider costs related to possible recovery in case of project failure.

According to estimations by Forrester (2004), the total amount of hidden costs for ICT offshore projects can vary between 12% and 52% of an overall offshore contract. Nonetheless, such hidden costs represent those that are now, after past offshore experiences, relatively foreseeable. ICT offshoring also involves risks, or surprises, previously very difficult to identify and calculate.

Risks of ICT offshoring are, for example, related to cultural differences among team members (Maletzky, 2006; Ruiz Ben, 2006; Ruiz Ben & Wieandt, 2006). Thus, according to Edwards and Sidhar (2002, p. 2), problems of collaboration with offshore organization are mainly due to linguistic and cultural differences, different working and leadership styles (Hui, 1990), understandings of role-taking and national stereotypes, all influencing collaboration (Stumpf, 2003). Different communication patterns, e.g., low and high context communication, may also lead to misunderstandings

(Hall, 1990). In high context cultures communication takes place in an indirect way. In some Asiatic cultures, "yes," is the answer to a question even if, "no," is meant. The interpretation of the answer must take into account contextual information, for example, the time until the, "yes," was expressed. If the word, "yes", is hesitateda "no" must be understood. If the, "yes," was expressed immediately it represents an affirmation. Persons with a low contextual cultural background verbalize all the information. Contextual information is not necessary for understanding the message. Between persons of different cultural backgrounds different communication styles may provoke an unfruitful working atmosphere. Persons with high context communication style may be perceived by those with low context communication style as deceitful or dishonest, while the way around persons with low context communication may be perceived as aggressive and rude.

In the EU, with the differences in regional orientation of home countries mentioned above and the cultural and language diversity, coordinating different cultural backgrounds and languages represents another risk. Thus, for instance, according to Huws et al. (2004, 11), Germany is losing 0.20 of each Euro of corporate spending by moving to India or Eastern Europe, while the U.S. gains in contrast US$1.12-1.14. This losis due to differences in language and culture, according to these authors.

Research on virtual teamwork provides some indications of the challenges of teamwork over long distances which apply to these costs as well (Hynsell, 2000; Edwards & Sidhar, 2002). Team cohesion and trust are hard to acquire, but important factors for productivity. Communication between the teams onshore and offshore, via technical communication tools like e-mail, telephone, video conference or instant messaging, does not substitute for, and often does not even sustain, personal contact (Sharpe, 2001). Social integration and cohesion in virtual teams are produced only by the use of technological communication tools, if the tools are used constantly to support informal communication, maintenance of social relations, and discussions on working issues (see Edwards &

Sridhar, 2002; Hysell, 2000; Joisten, 2005). Thus, employees have to support offshoring by actively changing their work habits.

According to Hynsell (2002), to avoid misunderstandings a kick-offmeeting at the beginning of the project is indispensable to plan the project, to specify terminology, and to establish contact. Additional traveling costs must be considered in that case. Moreover, onshore as well as offshore organization should use the same project documents (Hynsell, 2000). Standardization of processes in the onshore organization eases the integration of the results of outsourced processes finished abroad (Boes & Schwemmle, 2004; Krcmar et al., 2005). Summarizing, collaboration with the offshore organization changes working processes and resuluts in some challenges to the project teams.

Additional risks regarding ICT offshoring are concerned with intellectual property (Campoy, 2004) or with loss of property knowledgeThe long-term risk related to the uncontrolled migration of information from one organization to another may even involve data security risks (Carmel/ Tjia, 2005, p. 47). According to DB research, the poorer the country, the higher the institutional risks (DB Research 2006). These issues are dependent on the situation in both the home and the host. Contractual or infrastructure risks in different countries may also be related effects. In Europe new regulations, related to the integration of the new East European Member States, represent a solid basis for the development of infrastructure demands for ICT offshore. Because of Germany's geographical and supposed cultural nearness to the new European Member States, the development of infrastructures in these countries is very important for its ICT market expansion and as a complement to direct investment in the region (see, i.e., Brynda et al., 2003; Garamvolgyi et al., 2004; Piatkowski, 2004). But it should be taken into account that apparent cultural nearness may also lead to underestimations and misunderstandings. Thus, the lack of closer consideration of cultural differences also holds hidden risks for ICT offshoring (see Barmeyer, 1999).

Nonetheless, infrastructure development is not the only solution needed for success in ICT offshore projects in Europea. In the next section an overview of possible solutions and recommendations to the above discussed risks of ICT offshore is given.

Solutions and Recommendations

Figure 3 shows three main factors that, in our opinion, should be considered to overcome the above-mentioned transaction and hidden costs, as well as ,risks, related to the practice of near- and offshoring.

Time (in other words, long-term organizational plans) represents a crucial factor in reducing costs and controlling risks because organizations can learn from their experiences how to manage knowledge transfer and how to organize structural and organizational learning. Internal benchmarking is essential in this process. Sometimes counseling from external firms may be necessary to learn from the ICT offshore experiences of other organizations. Time is also needed to establish cross-cultural teamwork environments with long-term scope. Large multinational firms with experience in globalized arenas have advantages related to the special availability of central bases in offshore host countries. Thus, the co-operation of medium-sized enterprises with larger companies is often a strategy used to develop ICT offshore by the former. Initial face-to-face contacts among geographical dispersed team workers in the early phases help to establish team cohesion and to reach a common work culture based on personal trust (Davidson & Tay, 2002). Previous adequate intercultural personnel selection and development strategies are essential in this context.[14] Furthermore standardization plays an important regulating role at this point that, however, should not be overemphasized, to maintain a positive climate for creativity and to enable innovation commitment.

In order to cope with risks evolving from the low commitment of employees in the implementation (Wieandt, 2006) of offshoring may be aided by a change manager who considers psychological and emotional factors.

At the governance level of ICT offshoring, several direct and indirect measures to manage service quality may be considered to control ICT offshoring risks. A service quality measuring system frequently used is the service level agreement (SLA). It includes the definition of service levels as standard aspects such as quality, speed, timeliness, etc. to measure the performance of providers. Specific measures are defined by the contracting parties. Moreover, customer rights and solutions in case of the failure of objectives are also provided. Regarding governance, time plays a crucial role in solutions, because all the methods (i.e., CMM, ISO) and supporting tools (i.e., ITIL, Six Sigma, BS 7799, balance scorecard) related to SLAs or similar governance systems focus on the completion of deliverables on time (Carmel & Beulen, p. 142). Thus, in the race for innovation in ICT offshoring, those enterprises with flexible timing and stability in knowledge development and transfer and with better work cooperation will have an adavantage in managing the internationalization process of in Europe.

Centralization and standardization of working processes needed for offshore production are seen as signs of maturity in the ICT-industry (Boes & Trinks, 2006). Thus, off- and nearshoring are interpreted as attempts to foster internationalization by building a global production network. As strategy they serve to optimise the value-chain through standardization and formalization (Boes, 2005; Ruiz Ben & Claus, 2004; Slama & Kaefer, 2005). In this discussion countries are represented as lo-

Figure 3. Solutions and recommendations to confront transaction and hidden costs and risks

	Transaction and Hidden costs. Risks
Solutions and Recommendations	• Long term cooperation with ICT organisations in host countries. • Long term exchange with local universities and educational institutions in host countries. • Avoiding overemphasizing of standard methods

cations for the ICT industry, serving as resources for production and seeking to attract industry to creatie work and wealth for their people: "Driven by the global rationalization of production, countries have specialised in smaller ranges of products and services, and in the 2001-02 downturn, countries specialised in the ICTs became more specialised, while those that were not became less so" (OECD, 2004, p. 6). So, at the country level, strategies of specialization developed by the collaboration of companies and governments are observed.

To overcome synchronization problems and the early need for highly skilled workers within the EU, national policies were designed to acquire foreign ICT workers (OECD, 2001), focusing primarily on facilitating the immigration processes. Thus, some EU Member States, Germany, UK, The Netherlands, and Italy, developed special policies, such as specific work permits. A common strategy was that of reducing the length of time taken for work permit approval, although the efficiency differed from one country to another. For example, work permit provisions in the UK provided a faster response rate than anywhere else.

Nevertheless, these measures represent concrete short-term solutions with no guarantee about their adaptation to future developments and no consideration of the transformation of the ICT labor market[15]. Thus, since 2001 the inflow of foreign workers has decreased (OECD, 2004) and, at the EU political level, long-term strategies have been designed to increase the competitiveness of the Member States. These policies have contributed to facilitating the incorporation of new offshore workers from outside the EU because work permit approvals now take less time and are less complicated. Inside the EU these exchanges are no problem.

Moreover, in the framework of the Lissabon agenda, in the plan of action of the year 2001 the European Commission demanded easier acceptance of professional qualifications and as well as those acquired on the job, lifelong learning, and improvement of educational systems. One of the concrete measures included in the Lissabon framework is the Bologna process of European educational standards. The goal is to unify the European university educational system along

the lines of the American model of bachelors and masters degrees. Standardization of the sequencing of degree programs is sought. Additionally, the Bologna initiative has stimulated new interdisciplinary and specialized studies in computing within European Universities, such as bioinformatics, media-informatics and so on (Aspray, Mayadas, & Vardi, 2006).

As an answer to the challenges of work force shortage at the organizational level, companies are working more closely with the educational system. This may be in terms of agreements with Universities offering internships to university students, campus recruiting, and so on. More and more public-private partnerships are arising, as observed in Germany, for instance, where ICT companies like SAP or the Telekom co-operate with Universities in joint education programs.

FUTURE TRENDS

As mentioned, the combination of hard and soft factors, and the consideration of risks related to offshoring determine the decision about the selection of host countries for ICT projects. There is a trend towards regional preference of German ICT nearshore projects for the area of the new European Member States, Poland, Czech Republic, or Hungary. On the other hand, the UK tends to deliver ICT offshore projects mostly to India because of the closer relationship between the countries and language advantages. A similar trend occurs in France with their past colonial areas of northern Africa.

Currently, the main players in the European ICT sector have made several experiments in different locations with off- and nearshore partners helping to develop a basis for establishing certain regional specialization. From the perspective of the host countries, specialization in certain working areas involves long-term risks in development, but also provides the chance for developing one's own strong ICT industry, as is the case in India or in Ireland.

Focusing on the situation in Europe, further integration of the New Member States will be most advantageous to the German ICT sector, because the basis for futur expansion already exists in those countries. Within the European nearshore host countries, governments support this expansion particularly by improving ICT educational programs, but also indirectly by maintaining financial incentives for the entry of foreign capital. Moreover, due to high competition, companies specialize in regard to a certain group of customers as, for example, the case of Bulgarian software firms seeking to acquire German SME customers (Yonkova-Hristova et al., 2003).

Another example of increasing specialization in a regional area of the New European Member States is the Slovakian SME specialization in medical software, banking and insurance, and customs and government support of multinationals. The trend towards specialization is deeply linked to qualification policies in the different countries, and they are connected to broader EU educational policies and constitute a crucial factor in establishing long-term near- and offshore links among countries (Aspray, Mayadas, & Vardi, 2006, p. 29).

Intensive cooperation between universities and corporations in Western and in Eastern Europe based upon their trend to specialization in the different New European Member States may cause a strong dependency on the development of the home ICT companies and that, in turn, might result in a downturn of both ICT qualifications and the ICT industry in European nearshore host countries in coming innovation and internationalization phases. Particularly if salaries rise in the new European Member States and a new crisis situation emerges in the ICT sector, home companies will move further away, seeking cheaper offshore target countries. Unemployment risks for the work force and the closing down of many dependent companies might be consequences.

Another trend in regard to specialization is the focus on branches. We observe ICT companies founding subsidiaries in nearshore countries, imitating their own customers who outsource their production. Examples are provided by the automobile industry where production is outsourced out for example to Slovakia and followed by firms like T-systems. The specialization of ICT companies to serve industries of the above defined secondary sector may be characterized as a mo-

tor of innovation for the primary ICT producing branch which seek to develop targeted solutions for individual customers but at the same time have to rely on economies of scale in order to increase their competitiveness. A solution to this problem is to focus on clients of the same industry. Therefore, the secondary sector bridges the innovation-gap creating the need for innovation.

Due to the above mentioned increasing differentiation and specialization of the ICT sector in regard to certain industries, branches, working areas, coordination and control are increasingly demanded in the branch. These tasks are in the particular competence area of specialized IT consultants, who are gaining influence in the internationalization process of the ICT branch. Moreover, tasks in the ICT service segment of the branch such as accounting, call center tasks or those related to help desks emerge also in the near- and offshore countries (EITO, 2006). Encompassing knowledge on business and information technology, IT consultants are assigned to advice in regard to IT strategy as well as to process implementation. Therefore, they are important promoter of IT offshoring and nearshoring and on the process level often seen as facilitators. The growth of IT consulting is also due to the increasing standardization in the software sector, which is needed to perform off- and nearshoring. With their expertise and experience, consultants assist the implementation of process standards and management systems which is for them a new niche in the consulting market.[16] Large ICT companies who can afford the costs basically assign IT counsultants. The chambers of foreign trade particularly advise small and medium sized enterprises. They have a key function in the process of internationalization as well, since they provide information about market entries, market information and juridical particularities. The national chambers of commerce also organize advanced training and help to establish business relations among companies and support intercultural exchanges. Thus, ICT consultancy, as well as the national chambers of commerce, plays a very important role in the development of specialization, regionalization and internationalization of the ICT industry while consultants influence future paths in the sector. Taking into account that the ICT sector in Europe is mostly composed of small and medium enterprises (EITO, 2006; Fraunhofer 2001), the role of the national chambers of commerce is to stabalize and equilibrate to some extent the competence of the multinationals in the European Union is very important and will be crucial to palliate possible future crisis situations through the support of network relations among small and medium ICT enterprises or for example by supporting international training exchanges.

Nevertheless, the transformation of tasks and qualification demands in the ICT sector are very difficult to forecast. Particularly the speed difference between knowledge development in the ICT branch at the organization level and in the official educational institutions. As a result, professionalization of expertise areas in the ICT sector are hindered (Ruiz Ben, 2006). Moreover, it is difficult to predict which tasks will remain stable in the sector and which will disappear in the next innovation cycle. The growth of IT services in nearshore countries that provide services like accounting, call center or help desks are very important and the related demand of skilled workforce is also growing. However, it is difficult to predict how long this trend will remain and how effective and rapidly the qualification of new personnel will occur. On the one hand, according to DB research, the pool of formal well qualified workers in the off- and nearshore destinations is large. But, not all of the workers are well prepared for the work in an international company, because not all universities fulfill the standards required in Western Europe (DB Research, 2006). In the Czech Republic, Hungary, and Poland the percentage of well qualified workforce is only about 50%, which relativises the absolute numbers of workforce. On the other hand, the percentage of graduates in ICT relevant studies is decreasing. In Western Europe and the U.S., the rate is below average. In the Middle Eastern European countries, which have traditionally had high percentages of highly skilled graduates in technical, mathematical programs of studies and in natural sciences, the interest in those studies is also slowing down. In 2003, less than 2% of graduates in the new EU

Member States have studied computer science. In India, the percentage was estimated at about 5.7%. A shortage of specialists is feared to slow down the boom in the Indian IT industry (DB Research, 2006). Due to this workforce shortage and taking into account the predicted demographic development in Europe, ICT multinationals began to develop programs to retain their older workers. At the same time, several EU policies aim to attract young people to technical studies. How these measures will develop and which effect they will have is still yet to be determined. However, due to the future retention of older workers with lower salaries in these organizations, a stagnation of offshore practices could occur and may create a backward trend against project decentralization.

Considering the forcasted growth and further establishment of offshoring as a part of the companies' IT service delivery strategy (EITO, 2006), offshoring may be interpreted as a way into the global market and international production networks (Powell, 2001). In the long run, which is the goal of the Lissbon contract, the salaries in the Middle Eastern European countries will grow as transformation and unification in the European economic area. EU subventions enforcing the goal of unification will attract many less developed countries as off- and nearshore locations, but many European Member States will become too expensive as nearshore destinations, as will soon be the case in Spain. If these countries develop their own capacities in the ICT sector and establish a solid and dynamic education system rapidly enough and in line with the innovation rhythm, they could follow the example of Ireland and play a dual role as offshore destination and home country for off- and nearshoring. Here, the question arises, which model will the New European Member States adopt as orientation for their curricula, particularly in technical areas? On the one hand, an intensive cooperation between universities and the industry would bring advantages for the adaptation in innovation cycles. On the other hand, it involves dependency risks that might be extended to a certain orientation of the universities towards a particular country with the aim of enabling market entrance for home enterprises, since highly qualified work force could serve as marked openers of the eastern european market in general. However, the initial concept of the extended workbench seems to be the subject of an transformation process itself, which doesn't work as easy if highly skilled young staff is highered to do low skilled jobs at the bottom of the value chain.

The aim to create a unified European Union has also been highlighted from a cultural perpective, stimulating youth exchanges, university cooperations, country cooperations. This requires a high sensibility, however, especially if the historically grown relationships are not as positive as the case in the German-Polish relationship, which was complicated by displacements, borderline conflicts and negative stereotypes. This historical background may influence the working athmosphere and the success of collaboration in a subtle way. An open question at this point is how the increasing interaction among European countries will contribute to new ties and a consolidated European ICT sector.

CONCLUSION

In this chapter, we have shown the current and future trends of offshoring projects in the European ICT sector with a special focus on the New European Member States. We have contextualized off- and nearshoring in the European Union, assuming that they are a part of the globalilization process and the onward going industrialization of the ICT sector. Particularly the fast development in IT systems and the broadband communication as well as the increasing liberalization of trade in services stimulated by high cost pressures, especially after the sharp decline of demand, prices and employment as result of the burst of the internet bubble facilitated the ongoing industrialization and internationalization of the ICT sector.

In our chapter we have also shown that a homogeneous picture emerging through a clear development direction is not visible in the process of internalizing the European ICT sector. The main producers within the European Union, UK, Germany, France, and Ireland show differ-

ent country-specific focuses related to historical and cultural ties. Also, the respective national industrial specialization influences the particular regional presence and interest focus of each country. While UK and France mainly shore off in their former colonies, improving language advantages, historical grown relationships and the economic attractiveness, German companies seem to prefer doing nearshoring in the Eastern European countries because of language, cultural, geographic, economic and strategic reasons. Ireland follows up the matter of established relationships while it has been offshore destination of U.S. companies and shores itself off in India, now. Thus, we have argumented that a trend towards a regionalization of the ICT sector in the EU is currently taking place and it is supported by particular EU policies and measures.

As we have mentioned, EU policies and regulations such as labor and employment rights and issues related to privacy and data transfer play an important role in the decision to do off- or nearshoring within the EU. Especially some of the new Member States, such as the Czech Republic, Poland, and Hungary, which show high growth rates, low costs, good language skills, solid technical capabilities and infrastructre and minimal regulatory problems in the internationalization process of the European ICT sector. However, they are not free from risks such as dependence of off- and nearshore home enterprises or a too extreme qualification and production specialization (OECD, 2004, p. 6). Additionally, Slovakia, Slovenia, Romania, and Bulgaria are off- and nearshore destinations, which try to establish market niches in accordance to the relationships with ICT home countries.

Particularly the combination of soft and hard factors in the decisions to off- and/or nearshore ICT tasks and work processes influence the specialization trend in the European host countries. As we have shown in our paper, since cost saving is the main motive for doing near- or offshoring, hard factors such as tax incentives, a highly skilled workforce or a good technological infrastructure play a crucial rule in the selection process of near- and offshore host countries. Nevertheless, soft factors such as cultural ties among countries have also had an impact on the success of off- and nearshoreprojects, even if they are often understimated or ignored. Such factors constitute hidden costs and constitute risks in ICT off- and nearshore projects that could even lead to a repatriation of delegated tasks.

We have shown that a previous period of cooperation with local firms and contacts with local universities are important to prevent transaction and hidden costs related to the selection of providers, but also to reduce risks related to knowledge transfers and governance. Moreover, the establishment of training exchanges workers in both home and host ICT off- or nearshore countries can serve as a basis to reduce fluctuation risks. These exchanges should also include intercultural training in order to reduce risks that are related to the cultural distance between the host and home countries and their implications for successful collaboration and a fruitfull working athmosphere. Time constitutes at this point a crucial ressource for the success of off- and nearshore projects, but also regarding innovation, qualification and skills adaptation as well as knowledge transfer. Thus, organizations have to decide between short or long time benefits related to their internationalization plans. In order to reduce qualification mismatch and especialization risks, cooperation with educational institutions at both home and host countries is important. In our opinion, it is more important for EU education policies to take into account the risks of qualification mismatches related to the internationalization of the ICT sector from a long-term perspective and trying to prevent specialization risks for the working force.

FURTHER RESEARCH DIRECTIONS

International curricula in engineering and ICT-related studies, as well as continuous training programs, should be designed in cooperation with ICT enterprises and universitites promoting international exchanges. Nonetheless, it is difficult to define the scope of cooperation and international exchanges beyond the EU context. Further research should be done to analyze the impact of off- and nearshoring

on professionalization processes in the ICT branch in order to support an adaptation to the market needs by the universities and educational institutions, trying to avoid new skill mismatches.

This article is limited to the European ICT market and has only shown impacts on the European main producers and their off—and nearshore destinations. In this context, we have focused on the new European Member States as emerging countries in the European internationalization process. India and other offshore destinations haven't been highlighted in detail, because they are not in Europe or are, in the case of the relationship between the UK and India, have already been well researched.

Nonetheless, although many investigations about offshoring have been conducted, especially by consulting companies, the results of this kind of research should be carefully considered, since the main interest of consulting companies focuses on producing resemblance between their own and their clients' interests (Bloomfield & Danieli, 1995). In order to win clients, consulting firms promote certain trends and offer the related consulting services at the same time (see, i.e., Ernst & Kieser, 2003). This ambigous double role is also reflected in the consultants' literature on offshoring, which highlights cost advantages as well as risks, which will require the consultants' support. Depending on their assignment, consultants may have an important role in offshoring processes since they provide knowlegde on the implementation of standardization and quality management procedures, knowledge on off- and nearshore-countries and contacts. In the implementation process, they may have a legitimating and persuading function (see Wieandt, in this volume). To shed more light on their role in different organizational and cultural contexts, further investigation is also required.

Taking into account the increasing rate of virtual teams, a particular focus of research should be on intercultural cross-border activities within ICT off- and nearshore projects, which have yet to be sufficiently investigated sufficiently.

Also, the impact of soft factors on the working conditions in off- and nearshore projects to which we have referred are not yet well studied. The historical relationships among countries and their cultural distances seem to be influencing factors. But to what degree are the contextual factors favoring and slowing down successful collaborations in this sector have yet to be investigated. Therefore, qualitative studies will need to consider both perspectives: those of the collaborators in the offshore home and host countries, taking into account the dimensions of time, and the frequency of contacts and their impacts on stereotypes, fruitful collaborations and changeability, as well as (collective) emotions.

REFERENCES

Amberg, M., & Wiener, M. (2004a). *Projektmanagement im Rahmen des IT-Offshoring: Planungsphase.* Working paper No. 10, Friedrich-Alexander-Universität Erlangen-Nürnberg, Lehrstuhl für Betriebswirtschaftslehre, Wirtschaftsinformatik III.

Amberg, M., & Wiener, M. (2004b). *Eignungskriterien für IT Offshoring.* Working paper No. 2, Friedrich-Alexander-Universität Erlangen-Nürnberg, Lehrstuhl für Betriebswirtschaftslehre, Wirtschaftsinformatik III.

Amberg, M., & Wiener, M. (2004c). *Formen des IT Offshoring, Working paper No. 2,* Friedrich-Alexander-Universität Erlangen-Nürnberg, Lehrstuhl für Betriebswirtschaftslehre, Wirtschaftsinformatik III.

Amberg, M., & Wiener, M. (2005). *Kritische Erfolgsfaktoren für Offshore-Softwareentwicklungsprojekte.* Eine explorative Studie. Retrieved March 29, 2006, from http://www.wi3.uni-erlangen.de/OSE/Studie_KritischeErfolgsfaktorenOffshoreSoftwareentwicklungsprojekte_Amberg+Wiener.pdf

Amberg, M., Herold, G., Kodes, R., Kraus, R., & Wiener, M. (2005). *IT-offshoring – A cost-oriented Analysis.* Retrieved March 25, 2006, from http://www.wi3.uni-erlangen.de/index.php?id=45

Aspray, W., Mayadas, F., & Vardi, M. Y. (Eds.) (2006). *Globalization and offshoring of software.* A Report of the ACM Job Migration Task Force.

The executive Summary, Findingsm and Overoew of a compehensive ACM report on offshoring of software worldwide. Association for Computing. Retrieved March 15, 2006, from http://www.acm.org/globalizationreport/summary.htm

Auswärtiges Amt (2006). *Beziehungen zwischen Ungarn und Deutschland.* Auswärtiges Amt. Retrieved September 28, 2006 from, http://www.auswaertiges-amt.de/diplo/de/Laenderinformationen/Ungarn/Bilateral.html

Barmeyer, C. I. (1999). Landeskundliche und interkulturelle Kompetenzen im deutsch-französischen Training. In H. Hahn (Ed.), *Kulturunterschiede. Interdisziplinäre Konzepte zu kollektiven Identitäten und Mentalitäten* (pp. 371-387). Frankfurt/Main.

Baker, J., & Ivancevich, J. (1971). The assignment of American executives abroad: Systematic, haphazard, or chaotic? *California Management Review, 13,* 39-44.

Bitkom (2006). *Kennzahlen zur ITK-Branchenentwicklung.* Frühjahr 2006. Retrieved July 7, 2006, from http://www.bitkom.de/files/documents/ITK-Marktzahlen_Kurzfassung_Fruehjahr_2006.pdf

Bingen, D. (2001). Deutsch-polnische Beziehungen. In. Bundeszentrale fuer politische Bildung (Ed.), Polen. *Informationen zur politischen Bildung No. 273.* Retrieved September 28, 2006, from http://www.bpb.de/publikationen/0117168222480146228467126 6039564.html

Boes, A., & Schwemmle, M. (2004). *Herausforderung Offshoring.* Internationalisierung und Auslagerung von IT-Dienstleistungen. Düsseldorf: Edition Hans Böckler Stiftung.

Boes, A., & Trinks, K. (2006). *Theoretisch bin ich frei!* Interessenhandeln und Mitbestimmung in der IT-Industrie. Berlin: Edition Sigma.

Borowski, P. (1998). Die DDR zwischen Moskau und Bonn. In. Bundeszentrale fuer politische Bildung (Ed.), *Zeiten des Wandels.* Deutschland zwischen 1961-1974. Informationen zur politischen Bildung No.258. Retrieved September 28, 2006, from http://www.bpb.de/publikationen/03089068607234028765148366824753. html

British High Commission (2006). *UK and India: Global partners*. British High Commission. Retrieved September 28, 2006, from http://www. britishhighcommission.gov.uk/servlet/Front?pag ename=OpenMarket/Xcelerate/ShowPage&c=P age&cid=1017170902405

Brynda, P., Hofmanová, L., Držková, K., Fuchsová, D., Mejstřík, K., Holická, K., & Merkner, T. (2003). *Factors and impacts in the information society. A prospective analysis in the candidate countires. Report on the Czech Republic*, Institute for Prospective Technology Studies, European Commission, Technical Report EUR 21277 EN, Spain.

Campoy, A. (2004, September 27). Think locally: Indian outsourcing companies have finally begun to crack the European market. *Wall Street Journal*.

Caragea, A., Gheorghiu, R., & Turlea, G. (2003). *Factors and impacts in the information society. A prospective analysis in the candidate countires.* Report on Romania, Institute for Prospective Technological Studies (Publication No. EUR 21279 EN). Spain.

Carmel, E., & Tjia, P. (2005). *Offshoring information technology.* Sourcing and outsourcing to a global workforce. Cambridge: Cambridge University Press.

Copeland, L., & Griggs, L. (1985). *Going international*. New York: Random House.

Davidson, E.J., & Tay, A.S.M. (2002). *Studying teamwork in global IT support.* IEEE. Retrieved June 23, 2006, from http://ieeexplore.ieee.org/iel5/8360/26341/01173663.pdf?tp=&arnumber=1 173663&isnumber=26341

DB Research (2006). *Offshoring an neuen Ufern.* Nearshoring nach Mittel- und Osteuropa. Retrieved September 20, 2006, from http://www. dbresearch.de/PROD/DBR_INTERNET_DE-PROD/PROD0000000000200245.pdf

Deutsche Indurstie- und Handelskammern (DIHK) (2004). Merkblatt. *Fördermittel für Investitionen in den neuen EU-Mitgliedstaaten und den Beitrittskandiaten.* Retrieved September, 28, 2006, from http://www.dihk.de/oio/downloads/merk blatt_foerderprogramme.pdf

Edwards, H. K., & Sridhar, V. (2002). Analysis of the effectiveness of global virtual teams in software engineering projects. In *Proceedings of the 36th Hawaii International Conference on System Sciences* (HICSS '03).

Ernst, B., & Kieser, A. (2003). In search of explanations for the consulting explosion. In K. Sahlin-Andersson & L. Engwall (Eds.), *The expansion of management knowledge: Carriers, flows, and sources* (pp. 47-73). Stanford: Stanford University Press.

Eisner, R. (2005). Offshore legal issues. In E. Carmel & P. Tjia (Eds.), *Offshoring information technology. Sourcing and outsourcing to a global workforce* (pp. 112-129). Cambridge: Cambridge University Press.

EITO (2006). *Report 2006.* European Information Technology Observatory.

Forrester cons. (2003) *Unlocking the savings in Offshore.* Research Report. February.

Friedewald, M., et al. (2001). Softwareentwicklung in Deutschland. Eine Bestandaufnahme. *In Informatik-Spektrum, 24*(2), 81-90.

Friedewald, M. (2004). *Benchmarking national and regional policies in support of the competitiveness of the ICT sector in the EU.* Interim report, prepared for European Commission, Directorate-General Enterprises, D4 under Contract FIF 20030871.

Garamvölgyi, M., Gáspár, P., Halász, A., & Jaksa, R. (2004). *Factors and impacts in the information society. A prospective analysis in the candidate countries. Report on Hungary.* International Centre for Economic Growth (publication No. EUR 21408 EN). European Centre, Hungary.

Hall, E.T., & Hall, M.R. (1990). *Understanding cultural differences.* Yarmouth / ME.

Hönicke, I. (2006). *Deutschland gehen die Spezialisten aus.* Retrieved August 8, 2006, from http://www.computerwoche.de/job_karriere/arbeitsmarkt/579884/ index.html

Hofstede, G. (1980). *Culture's consequences.* International differences in work related values. Beverly Hills: London.

Hysell, D. (2000). Global teamwork for a global resource. In Professional Communication Conference, 2000. In *Proceedings of 2000 Joint IEEE International and 18th Annual Conference on Computer Documentation (IPCC/SIGDOC 2000).* Retrieved July 17, 2006, from http://ieeexplore.ieee.org/servlet/opac?punumber=7114

Hui, H.C. (1990). Work attitudes, leadership styles, and managerial behaviors in different cultures. In R.W. Brislin (Ed.), *Applied cross cultural psychology (pp. 186-208).* Newbury Park; London; New Delhi: Sage.

Joisten, M. (2005). Aneignung und Nutzung von Instant Messaging in Organizationen: Eine strukturationstheoretische Analyse. In C. Stary (Ed.), *Mensch und Computer 2005: Kunst und Wissenschaft – Grenzüberschreitung der interaktiven ART (pp. 45-50).* München: Oldenbourg Verlag.

Karnite, R., Klava, M., & Karnites, K. (2004). *Factors and impacts in the information society.* A prospective analysis in the candidate countries. Report on Latvia, Institute for Prospective Technology Studies, Spain, EUR 21283 EN.

Kearney, A.T. (2004a). *Making offshore decisions.* A.T. Kearney's 2004 Offshore Location Attractiveness Index. Retrieved February 22, 2006, from http://www.atkearney.de/content/misc/wrapper.php/id/49103/name/pdf_making_offshore_s_1081956080c0df.pdf

Kinast, E.U., & Schroll-Machl, S. (2002). Ansätze für eine Strategie interkulturellen Handelns. *Personalführung, 11*, 32-39.

Kremar, H., Böhmann, T., & Walter, S. (2005). Wissensmanagement im Kontext der IT Infrastructure Library (ITIL). In N. Gronau, P. Pawlowski, T. Schildhauer, & P. Schütt (Eds.), *KnowTech 2005. 7.* Konferenz zum Einsatz von Knowledge Management in Wirtschaft und Verwaltung (pp. 491-499). München: Universitätsverlag, forthcoming.

Koch, C. (2004, March 1). Bursting the CMM hype. *CIO Magazine.*

Kucera, J., & Segert, D. (2002). Beziehungen zu Beutschland. In Bundeszentrale fuer politische Bildung (Ed.). *Tschechien. Informationen zur politischen Bildung No. 276.* Retrieved September 28, 2006, from http://www.bpb.de/publikationen/AMSJPB.html

Lonner, J.W. (1990). An overview of cross-cultural testing and assessment. In R.W. Brislin (Ed.), *Applied cross-cultural psychology.* Newbury Park; London; New Delhi: Sage.

Maletzky, M. (2006). *Teamwork in a globalised context—Influencing factors on achievement in German Mexican collaboration.* Conducted at the 10th International Workshop on Team-working in September, 2006, (IWOT 10). Groningen, The Netherlands.

Mattloff, N. (2005, July-August). *Offshoring: What can go wrong?* IT Pro.

Morales, A.W. (2004). *Has this trend sprung a leak?* Software Development Management. Retrieved January 20, 2004, from www.sdmagazine.com

McLaughlan, G., & Salt, J. (2002). *Migration policies towards highly skilled foreign workers.* RDS. London. Retrieved June 15, 2006, from http://www.homeoffice.gov.uk/rds/pdfs2/migrationpolicies.pdf

Lithuanian Free Market Institute (2004). *Factors and impacts in the information society.* A prospective analysis in Lithuniana. Working Paper No. 24 (Publication No. EUR 21281 EN). Vilnius.

López-Bassols, V. (2002). *ICT skills and employment.* OECD Science, Technology and Industry Working Papers No. 10.

OECD (2002a). *Technology outlook: ICTs and the information economy.* OECD & Dev.

OECD (2002b). *Reviewing the ICT Sector Definition: Issues for Discussion, Paper DSTI/ICCP/IIS(2002)2.* Retrieved August 25, 2006, from http://www.oecd.org/dataoecd/3/8/20627293.pdf

OECD (2002c). *Measuring the Information Economy, on-line source.* Retrieved August 25, 2006, from http://www.oecd.org/dataoecd/16/14/1835738.pdf

OECD (2004). *Highlights of the OECD Information Technology Outlook.* Retrieved November 14, 2005, from http://www.oecd.org/dataoecd/20/47/33951035.pdf

OECD (2005). *Potential Offshoring of ICT-Intensive Using Occupations, Paper DSTI/ICCP/IE(2004)19/FINAL.* Retrieved November 14, 2005, from http://www.oecd.org/dataoecd/35/11/34682317.pdf#search=%22DSTI%2FICCP%2FIE(2004)19%2FFINAL%22

Piatkowski, M. (2004). *Factors and impacts in the information society. A prospective analysis in the candidate countries. Report on Poland.* TIGER, Transformation, Integration and Globalization Economic Research, Leon Kozmizski Academy of Entrepreneurship and Management (Publication No. EUR 21276 EN). Warschau.

Powell, W. (2001). The capitalist firm in the 21st century: Emerging patterns. In P. DiMaggio (Ed.), *The twentyfirst century firm* (pp. 34-68). Princeton: Princeton University Press.

Püss, T., Rajasalu, T., Venesaar, U., & Viies, M. (2004). *Factors and impacts in the information society. A prospective analysis in Estonia,* Working Paper No. 25 (Publication No EUR 21284 EN). Estonian Institute of Economics at Tallinn University of Technology, Estonia.

Ruiz Ben, E., & Claus, R. (2004). Offshoring in der deutschen IT Branche. Eine neue Herausforderung für die Informatik. *Informatik Spektrum, 4,* 1-6.

Ruiz Ben, E., & Wieandt, M. (2006). *Growing East.* Nearshoring und die neuen ICT Arbeitsmärkte in Europa, forthcoming in FifF-Ko No. 3.

Scherf, S., & Partner, Beratungsozietät für effektives Ressourcenmanagement (2006). *Voraussetzungen für erfolgreiches Outsourcing von Software-Entccklungs-Projekten, Bonn.* Retrieved November 23, 2005, from www.ssp-beratung.de

Seemann, A. (2000). *Deutsche Führungskräfte in Frankreich.* St. Ingberg

Sharpe, R. (2001). "Globalization": The next tactic in the fifty-year struggle of labor and capital in software production. In R. Baldoz, C. Koeber, & P. Kraft (Ed.), *The critical study of work, labor, technology and global production.* Philadelphia: Temple University Press.

Sirák, A., Druga, P., & Salner, A. (2004). *Factors and impacts in the information society: A prospective analysis of the candidate countries.* Report on Slovakia. Slovak Governanxe Institute, Bratislava, Slovakia (Publication No. EUR 21285 EN).

Slama, D., & Kaefer, W. (2005). *Model driven offshoring.* Retrieved on November 29, 2005, from http://www.sigp.de/publications/os/2005/06/kaefer_slama_OS_06_05.pdf

Stare, M., Kmet, R., & Bučar, M. (2004). *Factors and impacts in the information society.* A prospective analysis in the candidate countries. Report on Slovenia. Working Papers No. 26 (Publication No. EUR 21278 EN). Institute of Maroeconomic Analysis and Development Ljubljana, Slovenia.

Stumpf, S. (2003). Interkulturelles Management. In A. Thomas, E-U. Kinast, & S. Schroll-Machl (Eds.), *Handbuch interkulturelle Kooperation* (pp. 229-242). Göttingen.

Süddeutsche Zeitung (2006, September 4). *Premier kritisier Köhlers Auftritt bei Vertriebenen, in Süddeutsche Zeitung online.* Retrieved September 28, 2006, from http://www.sueddeutsche.de/ausland/artikel/292/84208/

Thomas, A. (1999). *Handlungswirksamkeit von Kulturstandards.* Beispiele aus der deutsch-amerikanischen und deutsch chinesischen Interaktion. In H. Hahn (Ed.),Kulturunterschiede. Interdisziplinäre Konzepte zu kollektiven Identitäten und Mentalitäten. (pp. 109-120). Frankfurt / Main.

Trimpop, R.M., & Meynhardt, T. (2002). Interkulturelle Trainings und Einsätze: Psychische Konsequenzen und Wirkungsmessungen. In K. Götz (Ed.), *Interkulturelles Lernen / Interkulturelles Training* (pp. 183-211). München / Mering.

Tung, R. (1982). Selection and training procedure of U.S.: European and Japanese multinationals. *California Managemet Review, 1,* 51-71

Xuereb, M. (2004). *Factors and impacts in the information society: A prospective analysis in the candidate countries.* Report on Malta. Institute for Prospective Technology Studies (Publication No. EUR 21280 EN). Spain.

Yonkova-Hristova, A., Stanchev, K., Bogdanov, L., Dimitrov, M., Angelov, G., Stoev, G., Kostadinova, S., & Marinova, E. (2003). *Factors and impacts in the information society: A prospective analysis in the candidate countries.* Report on Bulgaria. Institute for Prospective Technology Studies (Publication No. EUR 21282 EN). Spain.

ADDITIONAL READINGS

Abbott, P. (2007, March 13-15). *What do we know about distance in offshore outsourcing?* The First Information Systems Workshop on Global Sourcing: Services, Knowledge and Innovation Val d'Isère, France, JIT 06-228

Abbott, P. Y., & Jones, M. R. (2002). The importance of being nearest: Nearshore software outsourcing and globalization discourse. In E. A. Wynn, E. A. Whitley, M. D. Myers, & J. I. DeGross (Eds.), *IFIP TC8/WG 8.2 Working Conference on Global and Organizational Discourse about Information Technology* (pp. 375-397). Barcelona, Spain: Kluwer Academic Publishers.

Aken, A., & Michalisin, M D. (2007, April 19-21). *The impact of the skills gap on the recruitment of MIS graduates.* Proceedings of the 2007 ACM SIGMIS CPR conference on 2007 computer personnel doctoral consortium and research conference: The global information technology workforce 2007, St. Louis, Missouri. Retrieved April 22, 2007, from http://portal.acm.org/toc.cfm?id=1235000&coll=GUIDE&dl=GUIDE&type=proceeding&idx=SERIES303&part=Proceedings&WantType=Proceedings&title=Special%20Interest%20Group%20on%20Computer%20Personnel%20Research%20Annual%20Conference&CFID=17154900&CFTOKEN=49213597

Ardichvili, A., Page, V., & Wentling, T. (2003). Motivation and barriers to participation in virtual knowledge-sharing communities of practice. *Journal of Knowlegde Management, 7*(1), 64-77.

Barr, A., & Tessler, S. (1996). *Good programmers are hard to find: An alternative perspective on the immigration of engineers.* Stanford Computer Industry Project, Research Note. October.

Barr, A., & Tessler, S. (1996). *The US domination of worldwide product sales increased in 1995.* Stanford Computer Industry Project, Research Note. October.

Benamati, J.S. (2007, April 19-21). *Current and future entry-level IT workforce needs in organizations.* Proceedings of the 2007 ACM SIGMIS CPR conference on 2007 computer personnel doctoral consortium and research conference: The global information technology workforce 2007, St. Louis, Missouri. Retrieved April 22, 2007, from http://portal.acm.org/toc.cfm?id=1235000&coll=GUIDE&dl=GUIDE&type=proceeding&idx=SERIES303&part=Proceedings&WantType=Proceedings&title=Special%20Interest%20Group%20on%20Computer%20Personnel%20Research%20Annual%20Conference&CFID=17154900&CFTOKEN=49213597

Bresnahan, T., Gambardella, A., & Saxenian, A. (Eds.). (2004). *Building high tech clusters.* Cambridge: Cambridge University Press.

Business Week (2004). Forget India, let's go to Bulgaria. *Business Week,* Issue March 1, 2004.

Carley, M. (2004). *Industrial relations in the EU, Japan and USA, 2002.* Retrieved June 12, 2006, from http://www.eiro.eurofound.eu.int/print/2004/01/feature/tn0401101f.html

Carmel, E., & Abbott, P. (2006). *Configurations of global software development: Offshore versus near-shore.* Paper presented at GSC 2006, May 23, Shanghai, China. Retrieved July 17, 2006, from http://delivery.acm.org/10.1145/1140000/1138509/p3-carmel.pdf?key1=1138509&key2=581029761

1&coll=&dl=acm&CFID=15151515&CFTOKE
N=6184618

Carmel, E. (2006). Building your information systems from the other side of the world: How Infosys manages time differences. *MIS Quarterly Executive, 5*(1).

Carmel, E. (1997). Thirteen assertions for globally dispersed software development research. In *Proceedings of the 30th Hawaii International Conference on Systems Science.*

Casale, G. (1997). Recent trends and issues in industrial relations in Central Europe. In J. Brady (Ed.), *CEE Industrial Relations and the market economy*, vol. 8 of the Official Proceedings of the Fifth IIRA Congress. Dublin Oak Tree Press.

Clarke, L., Cremers, J., & Janssen, J. (2003). *EU enlargement—Construction labor relations as a pilot.* London: Reed Business Information.

Cramton, C. D. (2001). The mutual knowledge problem and its consequences for dispersed collaboration. *Organization Science, 12*(3), 346-377.

DB Research (2007). *Offshoring work, not jobs.* Retrieved April 23, 2007, from http://www.dbresearch.de/PROD/DBR_INTERNET_DE-PROD/PROD0000000000209059.pdf

Dyer, J.H., & Nobeoka, K. (2000). Creating and managing a high-performance knowledge-shairng network: The Toyota case. *Strategic Management Journal, 21*, 345-367.

Empson, L. (2001). Fear of exploitation and fear of contamination: Impediments to knowledge transfer in mergers between professional service firms. *Human Relations 54*(7), 839-862.

Espinosa, A., & Carmel, E. (2004). The impact of time separation on coordination in global software teams: A conceptual foundation. *Journal of Software Process Improvement and Practice, 8*(4).

Fazekas, K. (2004). *Low participation and regional inequalities—Interrelated features of the Hungarian labor market.* Case Study, in: Zeitschrift für Arbeitsmarktforschung 2004, Nr. 4, S. 375-392.

Fenema, P.C., Tiwari, V., & Vlaar, P.W.L. (2007, March 13-15). *Requirements analysis in offshore is development. Bridging differences in understanding.* Proceedings of the First Information Systems Workshop on Global Sourcing: Services, Knowledge and Innovation Val d'Isère, France, JIT 06-210.

Gáspár, P. (2004). *Factors and impacts in the information society: A prospective analysis in the new member states and candidate countries in the EU.* Synthesis Report, Technical Report No. EUR 21572 EN of the European Commission and the Institute for Prospective Technological Studies. Retrieved April 25, 2006, from http://www.jrc.es

Ghemawat, P. (2001). Distance still matters. *Harvard Business Review, 79*(8), 137-147.

Golinowska, S. (2004). Labor market and social policy development in Poland. *Zeitschrift für Arbeitsmarktforschung, 2004*(4), 346-374.

Huang, H. & Trath, E.M. (2007, April 19-21). *Cultural influences and globally distributed information systems development: experiences from Chinese IT professionals.* Proceedings of the 2007 ACM SIGMIS CPR conference on 2007 computer personnel doctoral consortium and research conference: The global information technology workforce 2007, St. Louis, Missouri. Retrieved April 22, 2007, from http://portal.acm.org/toc.cfm?id=1235000&coll=GUIDE&dl=GUIDE&type=proceeding&idx=SERIES303&part=Proceedings&WantType=Proceedings&title=Special%20Interest%20Group%20on%20Computer%20Personnel%20Research%20Annual%20Conference&CFID=17154900&CFTOKEN=49213597

Kiesler, S., & Cummings, J. (2002). What do we know about proximity and distance in work groups? A legacy of research. In P. Hinds & S. Kielser (Eds.), *Distributed work* (pp. 57-82). Cambridge, MA: MIT Press.

Lasser, S., & Heiss, M. (2005, July 10-13). Collaboration maturity and the offshoring cost barrier: The trade-off between flexibility in team composition and cross-site communication effort in geographically distributed development projects.

In *Proceedings of 2005 IEEE International Professional Communication Conference, at Vienna.*

Markus, M. L. (2004). Technochange management: Using IT to drive organizational change. *Journal of Information Technology, 19,* 3-19.

Martins, LL., Gilson, L., & Maynard, T.M. (2004). Virtual teams: What do we know and where do we go from here? *Journal of Management, 30*(6), 805-835.

Narayanaswamy, R., & Henry, R.M. (2005). *Effects of culture on control mechanisms in offshore outsourced IT projects.* Proceedings of the 2005 ACM SIGMIS CPR Conference on Computer Personnel Research, Atlanta, Georgia. Retrieved Nov 12, 2005, from http://delivery.acm.org/10.1145/1060000/1056 004/p139-narayanaswamy.pdf?key1=1056004&key 2=1829337711&coll=GUIDE&dl=GUIDE&CFID= 17154208&CFTOKEN=74491686

Newell, S., Bresnen, M., Edelmann, L., Scarbrough, H., & Swan, J. (2006). Sharing knowledge across projects. *Management Learning, 37*(2), 167-185.

Oshri, I., van Fenema, P., & Kotlarsky, J. (2006). Knowledge transfer in globally distributed teams: The role of transactive memory. Accepted for publication in: *Information Systems Journal* (09-23-06).

Radkevitc, U. (2005). Belarus attempts to become the Eastern European bangalore. *Outsourcing Journal,* March.

Ruiz Ben, E. (2008). Global expertise and quality standards in ICT offshore projects: Time and institutionalization aspects. In L. Wilcocks & M. Lacity (Eds.), *Technology and globalization. London: Palgrave.* (forthcoming)

Ruiz Ben, E. (2006, September 7-8). Expertise, time and institutionalization of team work in international software development environments. In IWOT X. *International Workshop on Teamwork. University of Groningen.*

Saxenian, A. (1994). *Regional advantage.* Cambridge, MA: Harvard University Press.

Steinwachs, K. (1999). Information and culture—The impact of national culture on information processes. *Journal of Information Science, 25*(3), 193-204.

Stobbe, A. (2006, November 13). Getting the balance right: The economic benefits of offshoring. In *Proceedings of the Think tank of Deutsche Bank Group.* London. Retrieved April 23, 2007, from http://www.dbresearch.com/PROD/DBR_INTERNET_EN-PROD/PROD0000000000209059.pdf

Thissen, M.R., Page, J.M., Bharathi, M.C., & Austin, T.L. (2007) *Communication tools for distributed software development teams.* Proceedings of the 2005 ACM SIGMIS CPR Conference on Computer Personnel Research, Atlanta, Georgia. Retrieved November 12, 2005, from http://delivery.acm.org /10.1145/1060000/1056004/p139-narayanaswamy. pdf?key1=1056004&key2=1829337711&coll=GU IDE&dl=GUIDE&CFID=17154208&CFTOKEN =74491686

Weiler, A. (2005). *Annual Review of Working Conditions in the EU: 2004-2005.* European Foundation for Improvement of Living and Working Conditions. Luxembourg: Office for Official Publication of the European Communities.

Wieandt, M. (2006, September 6-8). *Teamwork when implementing off-shoring: Exploring the German ICT sector.* Paper presented at the IWOT X Workshop in Groningen, The Netherlands.

Wieandt, M. (2008). Knowledge transfer and collaboration in a nearshore software development project. In L. Wilcocks & M. Lacity (Eds.), *Technology and globalization.* London: Palgrave.

Wiener, M. (2006). *Critical success factors of offshore software development projects.* Wiesbaden.

Yan, J., & Hunt, J.G. (2005). A cross cultural perspective on perceived leadership effectiveness. *International Journal of Cross Cultural Management, 5*(1), 49-66.

Yavas, F., & Rezayat, F. (2003). The impact of culture on managerial perceptions of quality. *International Journal of Cross Cultural Management, 3*(2), 213-234.

Zhu, Y., Nel, P., & Bhat, R. (2006). A cross cultural study of communication strategies for building business relationships. *International Journal of Cross Cultural Management, 6*(3), 319-3411.

ENDNOTES

1   Kolb, H., Murteira, S., Peixoto, J., & Sabino, C. (2004). Recruitment and migration in the ICT sector. In M. Bommes, K. Hoesch, U. Hunger, & H. Kolb (Eds.), *Organizational recruitment and patterns of migration inter- dependencies in an integrating Europe* (pp. 147-179). Osnabrück: IMIS.

2   For a broad discussion see OECD (2002b)

3   The following example illustrates the use of the EU Acquired Rights Directive for ICT offshoring: *"When multinational companies are applying 'global sourcing' strategies, suppliers can be played off against one an- other and as a result they can either win or lose a contract. In case of long-term contracts for service delivery, staff can be transferred together with the jobs to do the same work for the new boss. This is necessary to ensure the continuity and the quality of the service delivery. Such transfer of employees from one service provider to another requires special attention for the maintaining of the acquired working conditions. Recently, Siemens Business Services (SBS) has taken over a contract of Electronic Data Systems (EDS) to supply business services to the Coca-Cola Company. SBS has agreed with EDS on the transfer of a number of dedicated employees from the latter to the former in certain countries. These transfers are carried out within the EU Acquired Rights Directive that regulates the transfer of working con- ditions."* Retrieved August 29, 2006, from http://www.union-network.org/Uniindep. nsf/f73728e0eb1f5ca5c125700e003ccdbb/ $FILE/MOOSNewsletter3.pdf#search=%2 2acquired%20rights%20directive%20eu% 20offshoring%22

4   The distance is not specific. Scherf, Schütt, and Partner (2005) set the limit of 1000Km (ca. 621miles) to define it.

5   To use a broader definition independent of the location of the outsourcing company OECD (2004, p. 6) one may refer to the term, "international sourcing." Aspray, Mayadas, and Vardi (2006, p.16) define "offshoring" geographically and link it to the existence of water between home and host country. According to a manager of an IT consulting firm conducted in our own research project, off- and nearshoring are defined on the basis of a mixture of costs and distance (Interview UNB 3)

6   For example as a shared-servicesenter (SSC) serving other companies and thus increasing sales volume (Amberg & Wiener, 2004c: 15).

7   As we know from our own research project on IT offshoring, this is true for big outsourcing companies such as Accenture and Capgemini who habe Indian consultants working on projects with their European colleagues.

8   A.T. Kearney's location attractiveness index also encompasses "cultural adaptabilty" (AT Kearney, 2004, p. 5) but does not take into account cultural differences or historically grown relationships as we do here. Another model to analyse soft factors is provided by McKinsey and includes shared values, strategy, structure, systems, staff, style and skills (12Manage, 2006) measured by ques- tionnaires.

9   Issues of displacement are still discussed in the involved countries (see, i.e., Süddeutsche Zeitung 04.09. 2006) For a broad overview on the influence of displacement on German- Polish relantions see Bingen (2001).

10   Despite officially co-operative relations between the former eastern part of Ger- many, the German Democratic Republic (GDR), and Poland and the Czech Republic, relationships were impeded by mistrust and differences due to the relationships between Poland and the Czech Republic to Western Germany as well as due to ideological reasons

(Borowsky, 1998; Bingen, 2001; Kucera & Segert, 2002)

[11] ICT sectors and markets of the Nordic Countries Sweden, Finland, Norway, and Denmark as well as of the southern countries, like Spain, Italy, or Greece, are rather small (EITO, 2006)

[12] Market presence in Eastern Europe and the New Member States is due to customers'demands and market entry strategies rather than to low cost production. According to the country reports, large English companies such as Vodafon have their settlements in Eastern European Countries (see, i.e., Sirak, Salner & Druga, 2004; Stare, Kmet, & Bučar, 2004, or Gaspar, 2004), but this is mainly due to the safeguarding of market entry and to customer care strategies. Particularly in Malta, UK firms dominate the domestic telecommunications, software, and IT-related service market (Xuereb, 2004).

[13] According to Aspray, Mayadas, and Vardi (2006), the first US-based offshore activities with a destination of India started in 1972.

[14] See chapter "Intercultural Collaboration in the ICT Sector" in this book.

[15] Nonetheless, as we mentioned before regarding the case of Germnay, the green card programme to hire foreign highly qualified ICT workers at the beginning of the new millenium, represented a first platform to make offshore practices available.

[16] At the same time, they are main promoters of management systems and standardization issues seeking to prove their importance in rising debate on offshoring-maturity, see, i.e., Kearney (2004) what to move offshore http://www.atkearney.com/shared_res/pdf/What_To_Move_Offshore_S.pdf#search=%22offshoring%20%2B%20maturity%22, Sourcing Interests group (2003). Offshore-outsourcing Part 2: Implementation, retrieved October 5, 2006 from http://www.neoit.com/pdfs/whitepapers/Oct-03-OffshoreOutsourcingPart-2.pdf#search=%22%22offshoring%20maturity%22%22

Chapter XVII
Information Technology Consulting in Global Information Technology

Michaela Wieandt
Technische Universität Berlin, Germany

ABSTRACT

In general terms, IT consulting is the service provided by an IT consulting agency when a company implements a new IT system, that is, a system with which companies store, retrieve, disseminate, and use information (FEACO, 2006). Parallel to the internationalization of the IT sector in globalizing economies, the field of IT consulting has grown and diversified significantly during the last ten years, comprising at present a wide range of business areas, technologies, and services. Due to the fact that information technology is increasingly seen as linked to business strategy, the borders of management consulting are becoming more difficult to discern. This chapter covers the various aspects of IT consultants' work to enable a more detailed exploration of their practices and their influence in organizations around the globe in the future. It gives an overview of the latest developments in IT consulting, identifying the main characteristics and discussing current research on the roles of IT consultants in broad economic and specific organizational contexts, providing a conceptual framework for further analysis.

INTRODUCTION

In globalizing economies, the implementation of information and communication technologies in organizations is believed to play a crucial role in making business processes more effective, in saving costs and in increasing a company's competitiveness (i.e., Kennedy Information, 2004a, 2004b, 2004c). The business processes of companies are becoming increasingly embedded in systems, the control of which managers must oversee, and which can structure procedures and processes (Newell et al., 2006; Walsham, 2002; Breitenlechner & Buchta, 2001). Because the ICT sector develops very quickly, managers and decision makers find it difficult to keep up constantly with recent developments and to decide whether to extend or to change existing IT systems. This is one of the reasons why they look for the advice of qualified IT consultants (Bloomfield & Danieli, 1995; Sturdy, 1997). Moreover, IT consultancy firms provide IT services ranging from application management to programming. Consequently, IT consulting is a field exhibiting high growth rates all over the world (EITO, 2006).

However, research on IT consulting is rare and fragmentary, and definitions vary across scientific disciplines such as sociology, economics, and information science. The exploration of consulting in sociology and economics focuses particularly on management consulting in Europe and the U.S. and its impact on managerial decision making (i.e., Fincham & Clark, 2002), neglecting IT consulting because it is considered mostly the sale of software products or IT systems (Jackson, 1996). Information management research, also addresses the social side of IT implementation (see Jasperson et al., 2002), covering specific problems, and highlighting the technical side of software and systems implementation (see Krcmar et al., 2005; Markus, 2004; Amberg & Wiener, 2004). IT consulting is barely addressed here, although it is an important field of practice for information system managers (Cameron, Knight, & Semmer, 2005).

IT consultancy covers a broad variety of aspects that should be addressed analytically. Given the growing importance of information technology for the set-up and operation of business processes, IT consulting is increasingly believed to provide an exchange of knowledge between management and information technology. IT consultants seek to present themselves as the link between the two worlds of business and technology (Bloomfield & Danieli, 1995) and, because of their presence in several organizations, they may also be seen as agents of information technology implementation, fostering new IT applications or practices.[1] Because strategy also influences IT consultancy, it might be characterized as a form of management consulting (Bloomfield & Danieli, 1995). On the other hand, IT consultants are involved in the design, building and implementation of IT systems linked to the operational business process level. Depending on the scope of the IT project (Markus, 2004), it may be associated with organizational change, possibly including elements of change management[2]. Another aspect is the provision of IT services associated with programming, applications management and software maintenance, covering various tasks and requiring different skills. Moreover, the context of IT outsourcing implies the issue of innovation, which may be influenced by IT consultants as well (Ruiz Ben, 2007).

The chapter will cover this variety, providing a first step by mapping the field and providing a conceptual framework for studying various sectors and dimensions of IT consulting. First, the background illustrates the growing relevance of IT consultancy, giving an overview of the scope of the field in reference to the IT services market development. The main body of this chapter will discuss the principal characteristics of (management and IT) consultancy and information technology to show the blurring borders and to outline some overlaps. In particular, a critical approach on consulting provides useful insights regarding the implementation of IT. Bringing these characteristics together, the solution section suggests a conceptual framework to reconcile different perspectives on consultancy to enrich the perspectives of IT consultancy research. The future trends show possible developments in the field and the conclusions sum up the suggestions made. Future research suggestions will allude to potential opportunities and directions.

BACKGROUND: THE WORLDWIDE MARKET DEVELOPMENT OF IT CONSULTING

IT consultancy is understood broadly as a service provided by an independent, professional IT consultant in interaction with a client for the purpose of giving advice on information technology, be it a product or the development of a system or software for a complex business-related problem (Becker, 2005; Bloomfield & Danieli, 1995).

Measuring the scope and distribution of IT consulting, we face some difficulties in data collection because of the lack of a homogenous definition. In public data collection such as EITO (2006) and OECD (2002a; 2002c; 2004), IT consulting is seen as an aspect of IT services, including consulting on software, technological equipment, systems development and integration as well as service support and operations management. EITO also includes outsourcing and offshoring services (EITO, 2006, pp. 46-50). More detailed but limited publicly available data is provided by private institutions such as Kennedy Information in the U.S. or Luenendonk in Germany (Kennedy Information, 2004a, 2004b, 2004c, 2004d; Luenendonk, 2006a, 2006b), with information on sections of the ICT sector characterized as belonging to IT consultancy because they encompass advisory functions such as IT strategy and systems development. According to these data sources, four sections of IT consulting are identifiable: (1) IT strategy and planning, (2) systems development and integration, (3) software and hardware consulting, and (4) IT outsourcing and offshoring.

Another restriction to data analysis is that many large global players offering a wide range of ICT products and services do not break down their data into product groups or market segments (Luenendonk, 2006a). As a result, the data available permit only a general and rather broad overview of the development and scope of IT consulting in the U.S., Europe and Asian countries. In regard to Asia, most of the data available is on Japan and India, Asia's main players in regard to ICT and IT services.

Connecting business and technology, IT consulting evolved with the growing complexity of ICT products, solutions and technologies during the 1990s. The constant development of IT consultancy is already mirrored in the blurring borders of the field and is becoming increasingly difficult to define because IT consulting encompasses the implementation of ICT and consulting.

Table 1. Worldwide leading IT-consulting firms, countries of origin and business. (Source: Kennedy Information, 2005b; OECD 2004)

Company	Country	Main business
Accenture	USA	IT-consulting, Outsourcing
Atos Origin	France	IT company
Bearing Point	USA	Consulting
Capgemini	France	Consulting, IT outsourcing
Cognizant Technologies	USA	Software
CGI Group	Canada	Information management
CSC	USA	Software
Deloitte	USA	Consulting
EDS	USA	Outsourcing
Fujitsu	Japan	Hardware
Hewlett-Packard (HP)	USA	Hardware
Hitachi	Japan	Hardware
IBM Business Consulting Services	USA	Hardware
LogicaCMG	United Kingdom	System integration business
SAP	Germany	Software
Siemens Business Services	Germany	IT-consulting
Tata Consultancy Services	India	Software, IT-consulting
Unisys	USA	Hardware
Wipro Technologies	India	Software

The IT sector experienced sustainable growth during the 1990's due to the diffusion of information technology and computing throughout all industrial sectors and the convergence of information technology and the telecommunications sector worldwide (OECD, 2002a). Considering the development of worldwide ICT consulting, the main actors in the field of IT consulting are characterized by software and hardware companies that are enlarging their portfolios to meet demands for assisting and implementing technological solutions as well as maintaining and upgrading their level of competitiveness. System vendors offer consulting on systems integration and outsourcing. Consulting firms integrate information technology in strategy and process consulting alike (Kennedy Information, 2004a, 2005b, OECD, 2004; Luenendonk, 2006a). Table 1 shows, in alphabetical order, the leading IT consulting firms, their country of origin and their main business activities[3].

According to OECD (2004), the top 10 companies[4] with offices in most developed and developing countries dominate the IT consulting market, accounting for one-third of total sales in 2003 (OECD, 2004)[5]. As Table 1 shows, among the leading companies U.S.-based firms dominate. Exceptions include one Canadian firm, some European players from France, Germany, and the UK as well as companies from Japan and India.

In the consulting sector, management consultants increasingly integrated the need for consulting on IT products and services because of the growing importance of information technology for the support of business processes, i.e., in the financial and health care sectors (Kennedy Information, 2004a; Breitenlechner & Buchta, 2001) leading to a further blurring of the borders of IT consulting (Bloomfield & Danieli, 1995). Among the top ten management consulting firms (OECD, 2004), it is true of PricewaterhouseCoopers, Bearing Point, Deloitte Consulting and McKinsey & Company, among others. AT Kearney, independent of EDC after a management buy-out in January 2006, may also be added (AT Kearney, 2006).

In most parts of the world, the market development of IT consulting is closely linked to the development of the ICT sector (Kennedy Information,

2004b). On the one hand, the rising demand for information technology goods increases demand for IT consulting services. During the boom in the late 1990s, demand for ICT goods grew, as did growth rates of IT services and consulting (OECD, 2002c; Kennedy Information, 2004b), turning consulting into an important segment of the ICT sector (Luenendonk, 2006a). With the economic crisis and the burst of the Internet bubble in 2001-02, demand for ICT goods and for IT services dropped. According to Kennedy Information (2004b), competition among IT consulting firms, particularly in the systems integration section, rose due to low-cost offshore firms putting pressure on prices. Similarly, hardware and software firms expanded into the IT consulting market to meet market saturation tendencies in their core sectors. The number of IT consulting suppliers increased because firms in the hardware and software sector seek to expand their offers in times of stagnation or recession. At the same time, the number of customers decreased.

With recent market consolidation, the rates for IT service grew again, although moderately, due to price stabilization in 2005 (Rothberg, 2006). The data on rates varies, ranging from annual growth rates of 1.9% (Kennedy Information, 2004b) to 5.2% leading up to 2010 (Rothberg, 2006).

Considering the four sections of IT consulting the IT strategy and planning section is characterized by high rates of growth with an annual growth rate of 8% from 2003 to 2007, which, considering its market share of 6% in the worldwide consulting market, is a rather small fraction (Kennedy Information, 2004a). According to Kennedy Information (2004a), "this desire for more return on investment is a direct response to the 'dot-com' boom spending on systems and applications that didn't always provide the expected return on investment." In this view, stronger coordination and planning of IT investments help optimize IT projects. IT consultants help select the best solution for the company. Moreover, the diversification of IT products is seen as responsible for the requirement of developing a strategy in regard to information technology systems, particularly for large companies in the sectors of healthcare, financial services and the public sector (Kennedy Information, 2004a). Similarly, it is relevant for connecting information technology and management, because IT is seen as having a strategic impact, combining know-how on technology as well as on business strategy (Armbrüster & Kipping, 2003).

IT outsourcing services are "one of the strongest areas of growth" (Rothberg, 2006). Kennedy Information forecasts worldwide annual growth rates of 6% (Kennedy Information, 2005a), particularly due to the focus on smaller outsourcing contracts (EITO, 2006; Kennedy Information, 2005a).

Considering regions, the size of the IT service sector differs among countries, with the U.S. providing the largest IT service sector followed by Europe and Japan (EITO, 2006).

North America is the largest market on both the supply and demand side (Aspray, Mayadas, & Vardi, 2006; Kennedy Information, 2004a). U.S. companies spent the most money on consulting services, amounting to US$170 billion in 2000 (OECD, 2004). Considering data from EITO, it may be assumed that IT consulting has a major share in the U.S. consulting market because the IT service sector in the U.S. accounted for 151.7 billion € in 2005, a share of almost one-third (27.8%) of the total ICT sector. It is forecasted to grow at 0.97% up to 169.3 billion € in 2007. According to OECD (2004), the major actors in the IT consulting market are in the U.S., among consulting firms as well as among IT companies (OECD, 2004).

Considering the sections of IT consulting, the worldwide market share of North American companies, offering consulting on IT strategy and planning, amounts to 45% (Kennedy Information, 2004a). The outsourcing market of the USA is expected to increase with growth rates of 8% until 2008 (Kennedy Information, 2005a). According to ACM, the dominance of the U.S. in the software and service sector is due to "a number of factors, including a legacy of government funding of R&D, computer science research in the open U.S. higher education system, early adoption by sophisticated users, the world's largest economy and market, and leading semiconductor and data storage industries that helped spread the use of computing" (Aspray, Mayadas, & Vardi, 2006, p. 21).

Europe is the second largest market in the world, with a turnover of 36 billion EUR in the field of management consulting in 2003 (OECD, 2004). In the world market of IT strategy and planning consulting, Europe has a market share of around one-third in 2004 (Kennedy Information, 2004a), derived from the largest markets, specifically Germany and the UK (OECD, 2004)[6]. Looking at concentration tendencies, market concentration in the field of IT services, defined as market share of the top ten vendors, ranges from 6.2% (France) to 15.3% (Spain) (EITO, 2006). This is a low degree of concentration compared to the market dominance particularly of US-based internationalized companies in the consulting market with market shares ranging from 50% in Germany in 2001 (BDU, 2001)[7] to 60% in the UK in 2000 (OECD, 2004). Due to the trends of outsourcing and downsizing there are many thousands of smaller consulting firms in Europe concentrating on IT outsourcing and serving specialised niches for certain customers (Rudolph & Okech, 2004; OECD, 2004). According to EITO (2006), in 2005 the IT service sector accounted for 20% of the whole ICT sector in Europe amounting to 124 million € including an annual growth rate of 4.3%.

Considering the sections of IT consulting, EITO (2006) stated that IT consulting on software and technological equipment as well as services in systems integration and development "have had difficulties in the last few years" (EITO, 2006, p. 64) because market development in the ICT sector experienced a decline during the crisis years (Kennedy Information, 2004b). According to EITO (2006), their long-term outlook will be positive, with positive growth rates in 2005 and 2006 because they are "strategic in nature" (EITO, 2006, p. 64). Due to low growth rates in general, the ICT service sector suffered price pressure, for which IT outsourcing is partly responsible, as well as customers being extremely price-conscious (EITO, 2006). Because European companies seek to reduce costs, the overall value of the service market will "inevitably decrease in the long run" (EITO, 2006, p. 64), IT consulting in global information technology, may be compensated for by further growth, if the general economic situation recovers, providing secure growth and, the capacity to invest in ICT products and services as well (EITO, 2006).

A market segment of considerable growth in the market of IT consulting is IT outsourcing and IT offshoring. According to EITO (2006, p. 44), "outsourcing services will continue to ensure high levels of growth in the service market," making them "be the main protagonists of market growth" (EITO, 2006, p. 64). Within Europe, the trend suggests geographical variation with more contract activity in Northern Europe than in Central or Southern Europe where low overall economic performance impedes investment in ICT services and products (see also chapter XVI). EITO forecasts that European companies will "continue to concentrate on small budget projects focused on the replacement of aging equipment and the implementation of network and integrations services." To reduce costs further, IT offshoring is said to be an important element of European IT services delivery in the next two years and will therefore grow as well (EITO, 2006, p. 64).

In regard to the ICT sector, Asia's main players are Japan and India. India, China, Malaysia, Singapore, and the Philippines were attractive outsourcing and offshoring regions, exporting software and IT services to the U.S. and Europe in particular (AT Kearney, 2004; TPI, 2004)[8]. Therefore, the worldwide market share of IT consulting is comparatively lower because IT consulting is provided mainly in the home countries of companies who buy IT services offshore. Nevertheless, Asian countries provide consulting services in the Asian market (Kennedy Information, 2005b). Asia Pacific's worldwide markets' share of consulting on strategy and planning account for about 20% (Kennedy Information, 2004a).

Japan's ICT sector, with a total market value of 287 billion € and a global market share of 14.3% in 2006, is the third largest market in the world after Europe. In Asia it is, therefore, the biggest player. The IT Service section is comparatively small, with a market share of 16.9% in 2005 (EITO, 2006). Nevertheless, growth of 1.3% for 2007 is forecasted. The service sector in Japan is quite low in market shares compared to other industrialized nations (Takada, 2003). Despite its being one of the world's leading economies, Japan has a short tradition of management consulting, which was barely institutionalized in the Japanese economy during the 1980s (Faust, 2000). Although a few American consultants tried to enhance the spread of management concepts, the Japanese in their own style translated these ideas, discovering them as new management concepts a few years later. Consequently, there are few Japanese IT consulting companies being established internationally (Takada, 2003).

India is known to be the most attractive country for offshore service delivery (AT Kearney, 2004; Kennedy Information, 2004d). India's software services represent the largest share of Indian exports (Aspray, Mayadas, & Vardi, 2006) and have a comparatively long tradition, starting in 1974 (Aspray, Mayadas, & Vardi, 2006). Considering that India produces mainly software and related services, IT consulting is assumed to have a small market share. According to Aspray, Mayadas, and Vardi (2006), India is moving up the value chain, providing higher value jobs in software and related services. As a result, a possible trajectory is the expansion of more complex and larger projects in the systems integration and design section, also requiring IT consulting skills. "In order to grow, the Indian industry will have to shift to more complex activities by securing larger projects, undertaking engineering services, integrating and managing services, or bidding on projects that include transforming a client's entire work process" (Aspray, Mayadas, & Vardi, 2006, p. 22).

Therefore, the development and growth of IT consulting has to be seen in relation to the development of the ICT sector worldwide, but it must also be said that more detailed data on the international development would be necessary to give a better evaluation of developments. As the data presented here reveal, world market leaders in IT consulting are usually technology firms who offer consulting services to expand their competitiveness. On the other hand, large management consultancy firms seek to broaden their competencies by offering IT consulting services. Therefore, a conceptual framework should consider research strands from both sides, as I will now demonstrate.

IT CONSULTANCY: A CONCEPTUAL FRAMEWORK

The Scope of IT Consulting: Research Strands

According to mentioned data sources, four sections of IT consulting are identifiable: (1) IT strategy and planning, (2) systems development and integration, (3) software and hardware consulting, and (4) IT outsourcing and offshoring, which refers more to advising whether or not, if, and how to use outsourcing or offshoring, rather than to the provision of outsourcing services. Within these sections, two levels of consultancy are distinguishable conforming to the main strands of consultancy research: (a) management advice, related to an organization's (IT) strategy and long-term planning, and (b) the process level, referring to the practical implementation of changes in business processes while collaborating with employees on project teams. Management advice is analysed by a critical consulting approach which is related to the strategy and planning level, analysing consultants' impact on organizations and managerial decision making (Fincham & Clark, 2002). A well studied issue is the relationship between consulting and the occurrence of management fashions (Abrahamson, 1996; Abrahamson & Fairchild, 1999)[9]. The issue of IT strategy and planning is relevant here (see also Armbrüster & Kipping, 2003), posing the question as to whether or not to use outsourcing or offshoring. On the process level, analysis and implementation of change is combined with the consultant accompanying the implementation process. Concentrating on the consulting process and process attendance, process level attendence is also offered by specialists aiming to restructure organizations comprehensively using scientific methods (for an overview, see Gebert, 2004; Fratzer, 2005; Argyris, 1999; Argyris & Schön, 1974). This second level of consultancy is associated particularly with systems development and integration, software and hardware consulting as well as IT outsourcing and off-shoring on the level of implementation.

Research on management consulting suggests that management consulting firms tend to integrate methods drawn from the organization development approach in regard to the sustainable implementation of restructuring measures (Fincham & Clark, 2002; Ernst & Kieser, 2003; Schnelle, 2005; Kühl, 2005; Seidensticker, 2005)[10]. Although, in practice, management consulting is intermingled with process-related consulting, focusing on the implementation of change, the two levels have to be analytically distinguished, given that the practice of strategic- and process-related consultancy is related to different tasks and positions within an organization. Based on the existing literature I will first analyse the role of IT consultants working on the level of long-term strategic managerial advice and then contrast this with the process level of IT consulting.

The Long-Term Advice: (Management) Consulting on IT Strategy and Planning

According to the critical consulting approach (Fincham & Clark, 2002; Ernst & Kieser, 2003), the expansion of management consulting is due to the various functions of consultants as well as to the ability of consulting firms to create demand by defining new problem areas in need of expertise. Employed by a company's top management, management consultants analyse processes and give advice on strategy. They are "supra experts" who have an overview of management techniques and recent trends, and who "are called in by managers in order to provide help in regaining control of the perceived complexity that is [...] caused by functional differentiation" (Ernst & Kieser, 2003, p. 51; see also Faust, 2000). Ernst and Kieser (2003) explain the growth of consulting by pointing to the increasing complexity and dynamism of business environments, referring to developments such as globalization, new technologies, the development of information technology, the de-regulation of markets and the intensification of competition. Referring to Luhmann (1980), they argue that the growth of consulting is due to "functional differentiation" which "implies that complexity is increased through efforts aiming at its reduction" (Ernst & Kieser, 2003, p. 49). In this view, experts on certain problems generate solutions by breaking down problems into various aspects, creating new problems that were non-existent formerly. Converted into IT consultants as specialists in information technology they develop, store, and transmit specialized knowledge on information technology. As supra experts they draw and judge on previously autonomous knowledge generated by experts in subsystems (in this case the subsystem of information technology development) to develop a comprehensive view of a company's problems.[11] They also extract knowledge from successful companies and apply it to their clients' organizations (Bloomfield & Danieli, 1995). Called to provide orientation in a complex environment, consultants "are bound to contribute to its increase [in complexity] as management becomes aware of the possibilities that the field of management consulting has to offer" (Ernst & Kieser, 2003, p. 52). This also applies to IT consulting as shown by Bloomfield and Danieli (1995). IT consultants present themselves as intermediaries between business and technology: "they seek to portray themselves as obligatory passage points" (Bloomfield & Danieli, 1995, p. 28)—a necessary institution to be consulted if information technology is introduced. According to Bloomfield and Danieli (1995), this applies especially to management consultants who specialize in IT-based projects but belong to general management consultancy firms, because they are able "to claim that IT is not just a technical issue but an organizational one as well, and that they have expertise in both areas" (Bloomfield & Danieli, 1995, p. 24). Therefore, the link between organizational change and IT applies especially to management consultants specializing in IT. In contrast, IT consultants from software firms or equipment suppliers may be bound more to issues of implementation, which have a smaller scope within the organization. It may be the case also that consulting firms collaborate or that two consultancy firms are employed (Armbrüster & Kipping, 2003; Mang, 2006).

To attract more clients and to improve their marketing through the use of branding, consulting firms seek to develop "package approaches" (Ernst & Kieser, 2003, p. 53) and to standardize problems and solutions, which are claimed to be targeted at the client's special case in order to avoid the impression of offering an off-the-shelf solution. According to OECD (2004), this applies particularly to international IT consulting companies. This is supported by Gabriel and Lohnert (2001), describing SAP standard software implementation as a major task for IT consultants who specialize in a certain software and seek to implement long-term solutions to which customers are then bound for years. This also accounts for IT-based or IT-producing cross-company collaboration, which applies to outsourcing and offshoring relations (Willcocks & Lacity, 2006). IT consultants are also responsible for the design of working processes and contracts (such as SLAs), adjusting generally acknowledged quality and process standards to shape work relationships and distributed work arrangements (Amberg & Wiener, 2004; Boes & Schwemmle, 2004; Wieandt, 2006; Ruiz Ben, 2007).

Furthermore, following Ernst and Kieser (2003), consultants are interested in knowledge production because this creates a further need for orientation and, as a result, a source of demand. To intensify demand, consultants actively take part in the set-up of management fashions (Ernst & Kieser, 2003) often related to certain technologies or software tools, i.e., customer relations management, business process re-engineering or quality management (Breitenlechner & Buchta, 2001; Bloomfield & Vurdubakis, 2002; Schmutte, 2003). Therefore, "consultants not only instrumentalize existing complexity, they also attempt to intensify managers' perception of overall complexity" (Ernst & Kieser, 2003, p. 52) to produce demand. IT consultants promote certain technology solutions, and, in the words of Bloomfield and Danieli (1995), therefore also "seek to create a niche and persuade clients that they are within it" (Bloomfield & Danieli, 1995, p. 28).

To secure demand, consulting firms have to explore new areas of business. This applies especially to IT consultants who suffered economic decline throughout 2000-02 and, because of the entry of new actors to the market, experienced a constant growth in competition. Ernst and Kieser suggest three mechanisms for creating demand which apply also to the IT consultant market and similarly serve the spread of information technology: (1) the acquisition of new clients in the public sector and non-profit organizations as well as small and medium sized enterprises. IT consulting firms especially seek to expand into new regions, following their clients as described above. (2) The expansion of the scope of the services is observable in the whole IT sector due to the crisis in 2001-02, as the examination of the IT consulting market has shown. Nonetheless, IT consulting firms seek to widen their scope within the information technology area in regard to new technologies and services such as offshoring and outsourcing as well as to specialize in certain branches like banking/insurance, education or automobile production (see also chapter XVI, in this volume). Considering the market development described above, we can state that IT consulting is a method of ensuring that a customer stays with an ICT company. In offering consulting services, firms provide an overall presence in regard to information technology strategy, selection of products and implementation of technological solutions. An indication of this is that many IT consulting firms seek to expand into the regions of their larger clients in order to support them locally (Kennedy Information, 2005b).

(3) Management fashions, or popular trends in the world of management, are created particularly by management consultants, but also by other actors such as business mass media publications, business schools and management gurus who create texts and publications mainly read by managers and speedily gain large shares in the public management discourse (Abrahamson, 1996; Abrahamson & Fairchild, 1999; Jackson, 2002). According to Ernst and Kieser (2003), this strategy is highly effective in terms of market volume and turnover, as shown by Jackson (1996), for business re-engineering projects. In regard to IT consulting, this applies, for example, to the trends of e-business (Bloomfield & Vurdubakis, 2002), IT outsourcing and IT offshoring (Boes & Schwemmle, 2004). The success of management fashions is linked to their

adoption by organizations. "The more companies that are reported as having achieved competitive advantages through the implementation of a management concept—and the consultancies are eager to spread success stories—the higher the propensity of nonadopters to get onto the bandwagon" (Ernst & Kieser, 2003, p. 60; see also Jackson, 2002). According to Dimaggio and Powell (2004), the tendency of managers to adopt strategies promising success used by other organizations is due to institutional isomorphism, which reduces uncertainty, complexity and information overload.

The Process Level Perspective: Roles of IT Consultants

In contrast, in order to implement change, consultants specializing in process implementation have to have a detailed knowledge of the company's organizational structure and workflow as well as of special fields of business processes such as personnel, administration or marketing strategies. To give a more detailed picture of what IT consulting comprises on the process level, it is necessary to take a short look at IT projects and their implementation (see also Chapter XVIII in this volume). According to Markus (2004), IT projects are characterized by a life cycle encompassing at least four phases: (1) the planning phase, when the project is assessed, funded, and planned, (2) the design phase, when the technological solution is developed and built, (3) the implementation phase with the roll-out and operation of the new solution within the organization, and (4) the benefit capture phase when the project is evaluated. IT consultants have key functions in the first three phases of an IT project, being involved in the planning process, which relies on issues of IT strategy. They accompany the implementation of projects and give advice regarding the building and design process, defining user requirements. During this phase they are usually part of the project team and collaborate with an organization's employees. In the roll-out phase they may attend to the change management process, conceptualize some training or educational units for users, and do some system adjustments. This process level perspective can be associated mainly with the implementation of organizational change (Argyris & Schön, 1974; Schein, 2004). Some theories of organizational change can be identified in the aspects of information technology implementation, i.e., addressing the organization in total, pointing to the emergence of learning processes, or involving as many actors as possible. For example, the technochange conception (Markus, 2004) addresses organizations in total, encouraging the participation of users and referring to prototyping as a learning approach rather than an implementation approach, in which users have to accept what the IT department offers them. Additionally, Gillard (2005) refers to communication models when addressing the solution of communication problems in technology implementation. Moreover, there is an awareness occurring of the relevance of group processes and teamwork for project work, which influences IT implementation (Gillard, 2005).

Considering these approaches, there are some more important functions IT consultants have on the process level. According to Ernst & Kieser (2003), they provide temporary management capacity to overcome shortcomings or carry out certain tasks, i.e., project management of offshoring projects (Wieandt, 2006) or programming capacities (Ruiz Ben, 2007). Additionally, to collaborate with employees of different levels and departments, they need to develop strategies of persuasion and impression management, to gain trust and acceptance, and to cope with conflict (Loose, 2001; Sosik & Jung, 2003; Muhr, 2004; Schnell, 2005; Wieandt, 2006; Chapter XVIII in this volume). Considering customer scepticism regarding information technology solutions since the dot-com crisis (Kennedy Information, 2004a), an IT consultant's ability to persuade actors within the organization is becoming increasingly valuable. They also need these skills when pushing through changes in working processes, such as formalization and standardization, particularly necessary in the context of outsourcing and offshoring (Wieandt, 2006).

Moreover, they provide weapons for intra-organization politics, and can offer ideas, e.g., for the solution of misfit problems, as addressed by Markus (2004). They find models and words of orientation and they interpret, simplify or reassure

when necessary (Ernst & Kieser, 2003). Providing technological and managerial knowledge, IT consultants seem to provide a link between managers and technicians, enabling the exchange of knowledge by translating it from one world to another (Boes & Trinks, 2006). According to Bloomfield and Danieli (1995), this identity is an important instrument for maintaining one's status as an expert throughout the implementation process. They interpret the issue of IT strategy as a resource "which serves as a symbolic means of establishing identities: those experts in devising strategies and those organizations in need of strategic advice" (Bloomfield & Danieli, 1995).

Accordingly, within the organization consultants serve to legitimize the decisions of management, being "certifiers of rationality" who can guarantee "expert knowledge is being applied to all functions and all levels of an organization" (Ernst & Kieser, 2003, p. 55). In this regard, IT consultants justify the implementation of a certain technology or strategy, for example, IT offshoring (see Boes & Schwemmle, 2004).[12]

A specific characteristic of IT consulting is the aspect of technology. According to Bloomfield and Danieli (1995), mutual understanding between client and consultant is needed during the consulting process so the client is able to accept the advice of the consultant. This "depends on their discursively negotiated identities, normative assertions about what should be done, who significant others are, what they stand for or represent, crucially, what is technical and what is social" (Bloomfield & Danieli, 1995, p. 29). The distinction between what is technical and what is social is important in the IT consulting-client relationships because it defines responsibilities and authority and is thus subject to power. Moreover, the difference between management consulting and IT consulting refers to the nature and life cycle of IT projects, as explained above. IT consultants may also be involved in process implementation, that is, in the design and building of an IT system, as well as in its implementation (Markus, 2004).

Summing up, there is a lot of resemblance between management and IT consulting, which may be due to the nature of consulting as such.

Special characteristics of IT consulting include the construction of the technical and the social as well as one's involvement in IT project implementation. The long-term level and process level of IT consulting are important dimensions for further analytical work. Based on this distinction, I will develop a conceptual framework in the following section.

Solutions: A Conceptual Framework

Although Jackson (1996) identified IT consulting as selling software products or outsourcing services, and therefore excluded it from analysis, today the link between IT consulting and management strategies is emphasised. Breitenlechner and Buchta (2001, p. 117) state that IT consulting goes beyond the sale of IT products or services because IT consultants have to analyse complex working processes regarding relevant requirements and the demands of the company's employees to determine whether software or IT solutions would be useful in supporting the company's workflow.[13] Characterized as services in the field of information technology,[14] the introduction of new technological equipment and software,[15] as well as IT system development and integration, form part of the strategic decision-making of companies in regard to the implementation of customer relations-management, e-business or process management (Breitenlechner & Buchta, 2001; Bloomfield & Danieli, 1995). In this realm, IT consulting supports business processes by providing technological know-how to implement new management strategies (see also Scheer & Köppen, 2001; Ernst & Kieser, 2003; FEACO, 2006; Niedereichholz & Niedereichholz, 2006; Grimme, 2006; EITO, 2006).

According to FEACO (2006a), the field of IT consulting may be divided into three main sections. IT consulting refers to (1) technological equipment or software as well as to (2) IT systems development and integration. IT consulting may also include (3) consulting on IT outsourcing or IT offshoring services, for instance, shared service centres, business process outsourcing or application service provision. The definition provided by EITO (2006, p. 258)[17] includes these sections, but also specifies "planning and design activities that assist clients in making IT-related decisions on business direction or information technology" to emphasize the link between IT consulting and strategy and planning as well as process implementation, which also refers to training and education (see also Kennedy Information, 2004b). An analogue definition is provided by the German BDU (2004) classifying IT consulting and services as the analysis of suppliers and the selection, analysis and implementation of hard- and software systems, including training. Summing up, we can suggest that the field of IT consulting is divisible into (1) IT strategy and planning, (2) systems development and integration, (3) software and hardware consulting, and (4) IT outsourcing and offshoring.

Consequently, referring to the distinction between management- and process-related consulting as described above, IT-consulting first encompasses elements of process-related consulting because it comprises the implementation of IT systems, which involves tasks of process supervision. Second, it refers to consulting on IT strategy and planning as shown by Bloomfield and Danieli (1995). What they described ten years ago can still be considered up-to-date when looking at the developments in IT and management consulting. Therefore, IT consulting crosses the border into management consulting, which is even vaguer than ten years ago, taking into account that IT consulting on strategy is also done by hardware providers such as IBM. Considering that IT consulting is defined as being limited to IT-related consulting, the linkage to strategy is strongest in this section.

Although consulting on equipment and software applies to the dimension of product venturing as mentioned by Jackson (1996), it is also part of the process level because it serves basically to support business processes. Following Bloomfield and Danieli (1995), IT consultants try to distinguish themselves from systems hardware or software vendors by referring to their status as neutral and independent experts. Nevertheless, they are expected to give advice concerning the decision in favour of a certain IT product, be it SAP- or Oracle-based, because this is why they were hired

(Greiner, 1989; Ortmann et al., 1990). The difference is that they consider a range of possibilities and that their advice is believed to be based on an objective analysis of the situation—an impression they try to enhance by using a certain methodology or scientific methods of analysis when doing an assessment (Bloomfield & Danieli, 1995). According to Grimme (2006), implementing a new IT system or integrating IT systems may be an expression of a new strategy of management, but she sees the work of the IT consultant as the introduction of IT at the level of work processes and the daily routines of employees. Considering examples involving customer relations, management systems or bundling processes through software-supported process re-engineering (Niedereichholz & Niedereichholz, 2006; Hans & Köppen, 2001), it can be suggested that the main tasks of implementation are related more to technology than to management techniques. Nevertheless, considering a company's strategy and business goals is a part of IT-consulting as well, because technology is installed to reach economic targets.

However, consulting on IT outsourcing and IT offshoring[18] is a special case because IT outsourcing and offshoring are basically strategies used to enhance the internationalization of production, to provide market entry, to increase efficiency, or to ensure that enterprises remain focused on their core competences (OECD, 2004; Aspray, Mayadas & Vardi 2006; Ruiz Ben & Claus, 2005; Boes, 2005; Amberg & Wiener, 2004). Therefore, the borders of IT and management consulting are crossed again, at least because, in practice, both management consulting firms and IT consulting firms offer consulting on outsourcing, while the providision of services is relevant to the dimension of IT services. Although implementation work is associated with technological issues at the level of working processes (i.e. see Krcmar, et al., 2005), outsourcing is related to strategy issues as well as to IT services. According to Grimme (2006), to provide high quality work, consulting on IT outsourcing must be limited to technological support of management consulting.

Suggesting a conceptual framework, I distinguish between the dimension of IT services and that of consulting in IT consultancy work, comprising both contracts and Service Level Agreements. This distinction is in some ways associated with the analytical difference between the process and the long-term planning level. Combining both enables

Figure 1. Dimensions and sections of IT-consulting

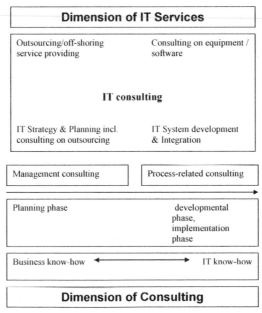

the detailed analysis of more strategic consultancy and more process-related implementation work. Figure 1 provides an overview of the sections and dimensions of IT consulting.

In its centre IT consulting focuses on advising on information technology issues in regard to IT equipment, systems development and integration, outsourcing and IT strategy and planning. While IT consulting on the selection of equipment and software leads to the promotion of a certain product and therefore to sales, IT consulting on systems development and integration, as well as on IT strategy and planning, is more relevant to management consulting (see also Bloomfield & Vuldubakis, 2002). Consulting on IT outsourcing involves IT strategy and planning, while outsourcing as a provision of services can be characterized as the selling of services. This conception also refers to the life cycle of an IT project by linking the planning phase, in most cases actually initiated by managers who call in IT consultants, to the management consulting dimension and the development and implementation phase to the process consulting dimension, as they consist mainly of process accompaniment. In regard to knowledge, we can state that advising the management side will require more business knowledge while consulting on the side of technological implementation relies on technological knowledge. Of course, this has to be combined with the specific organizational and process background (Wieandt, 2007b).

In the practice of IT consulting, the borders of management consulting are crossed by both sides: IT firms offer management consulting services (Ernst & Kieser, 2003, p. 58) and management consulting firms increasingly integrate IT services in their portfolios due to market developments. Given that information technology gains strategic importance in line with technological support and optimization of business processes (Breitenlechner & Buchta, 2001), IT consulting as a means of supporting management strategies, by providing technological knowledge and infrastructure, becomes an increasingly central market segment in the field of consulting as well as in the ICT sector. Therefore, a conceptual framework able to cover all of these aspects may provide an analytical basis for further exploration of the dimensions of IT consulting in regard to new market developments, pointed out in the next section.

FUTURE TRENDS IN IT CONSULTING

We can find some future trends in IT consulting on the supply as well as on the demand side.

Looking at the supply side of IT consulting, we observe that the building of alliances and partnerships of market leaders leads to a network of close collaboration to maintain leadership of the market and to set standards of technology use and distribution (Kennedy Information, 2004b, 2005b; Armbrüster & Kipping, 2003; Mang, 2006). According to Luenendonk (2006a), an overall development is the occurrence of "Business Innovation / Transformation Partners," mainly big ICT companies in the hardware and software sectors or management consulting firms offering management consulting, IT consulting and service providing, all from one source. Examples include companies such as Accenture or Capgemini, that offer not only consultancy but also programming capabilities worldwide. An example of a partnership between management consultancy and IT is the alliance of Arthur D. Little and ALTRAN, where Arthur D. Little provides management knowledge and ALTRAN, IT know-how. This development serves market concentration in the form of acquisitions and mergers of big companies as well as alliances (Kennedy Information, 2004c). Therefore, market concentration may also increase the specialization of IT consultancies. Moreover, IT consulting firms seek to expand to support their key clients locally. According to Kennedy Information, a trend within the IT consulting and systems integration market is to expand regionally and to enter new markets in the USA, Asia, and Europe (Kennedy Information, 2005b). Thus it seems probable that networks among consultants involving the collaboration of different consultancy firms on one project and supporting trends of specialization and concentration will gain further importance (Mang, 2006).

Specialization in certain branches is also seen as a means of concentrating know-how and expanding in a certain sector at the same time to target specific industries, such as banking, insurance or education, mainly through business process outsourcing and shared services such as "one-to-many-solutions," that is, one solution that can be used by many companies (Kennedy Information, 2005a; Armbrüster & Kipping, 2003). This is supported by the trend of new interdisciplinary and specialized studies in computing such as bio-informatics or media-informatics, particularly as set up by European universities, delivering analogous know-how (see Aspray, Mayadas & Vardi, 2006, p. 30).

Considering the development of the overall internationalization of production and the specialization of firms and networks (see Powell, 2001), we can assume that offshoring and outsourcing will be important future trends in consulting, serving both cost reduction as well as the improvement of IT processes and alliances in business process innovation. According to Kennedy Information (2005a), offshoring is driven by business process outsourcing as mentioned above: "As Western companies seek ways to reduce costs and low-cost countries are offering white-collar skills at a fraction of Western costs, an irresistible trend towards moving business processes offshore is emerging" (Kennedy Information, 2004d). EITO forecasts offshoring as an "important element of IT services delivery in the next two years." According to EITO, the use of offshore resources will become a standard element of IT services, with a positive effect beccause it allows providers "to deliver high-quality services at an attractive price and potentially filling any skills gaps which may occur due to the diminished attractiveness of IT as a career path following the turmoil of the last few years." (EITO, 2006, p. 64). Therefore, Europe's service market will experience an increase in offshore service spending, as it already has throughout 2005 and 2006. Regarding offshoring, business process outsourcing also indicates a stronger contribution of consultancies to the innovation of client firms, which may serve as a unique selling proposition. Moreover, the trend of advancing or improving the client firm is important, considering the stronger competition among IT consultancies. Therefore, on the one hand, successful outsourcing allows the client to free resources by outsourcing less important tasks, so the client may use available

resources for core functions and concentrate on more innovative procedures. On the other hand, the outsourcer, as an expert in IT, may increase the efficiency of IT as well. Accordingly, the implementation of quality and process standards furthers process advancement but, by producing a tendency towards worldwide consistency standards, it also results in more compatible processes, which will ease clients' collaboration and may lower their competiveness.

Considering regions, due to the trend towards IT offshoring and outsourcing, new markets and transforming countries will gain importance. Considering market concentration in the field of IT consulting, the expansion of large consulting providers in these countries will continue, leading to mergers and the acquisition of small- and medium-sized local firms (Kennedy Information, 2004b).

Looking at market trends on the customer side, an example of a new trend in IT consulting is the implementation of service oriented architectures (SOA), which will make application management easier and alter IT landscapes within the next years.

On the customer side, business process outsourcing will cause organizational change combined with a close collaboration with the outsourcer and/or IT consultants. This may lead to new business models as well as to innovation cycles. Accordingly, the use of software tools to automate processes in the field of customer relations (i.e., help desk systems) or e-business plays a major role in process design, but also in enhancing communication between working groups.

CONCLUSION

In order to map the field of IT consulting, this chapter provided (1) an overview of recent market developments and (2) an outline of the role of IT consultants in modern economies and organizations, as well as (3) a suggestion for a conceptual framework for further analysis.

The worldwide consultancy market, with the US, Europe and Asia as the largest markets, pointed to two major tendencies: (1) a market concentration on a few globally-acting IT consulting firms originating in the sector of ICT and management consulting, and (2) a moderate growth of IT consulting related to IT strategy and planning, as well as to outsourcing services. Looking at the explanations for these trends, we can apply a demand-creating mechanism to market concentration, closely connected to the role of IT consultants in economies and organizations. To expand their scope of services, necessary due to the general economic decline, ICT companies and management consulting firms established IT services to develop a new market. Of course, in creating more complexity, technological development serves as a precondition of that development. The growing importance of IT consulting is due to market growth, but also correlates with the functions of IT consultants by attracting client companies, because consultants provide knowledge on techniques and processes, orientation in a complex world, legitimization of decisions, and support in implementing organizational change. This development further blurred the border between management and IT consulting as well as among IT consulting, IT software and hardware vendors, and service providers. Regarding the practice of IT consulting, I have shown some parallels to management consulting, possibly due to the nature of consulting as such. However some special characteristics of IT consulting include the identification of matters as either technical or social, as well as the involvement of consulting in IT project implementation, which is related to the process dimension of consulting as well as to IT projects.

The market overview as well as the analysis of the role of IT consultants was approached conceptually, distinguishing four sections of IT consulting: (1) IT strategy and planning, (2) systems development and integration, (3) software and hardware consulting, and (4) IT outsourcing and offshoring. These sections, belonging to the IT service dimension as well as to the consulting dimension, have to be differentiated further into a process-related and a management-related aspect. These two aspects correspond to the life cycle of IT projects, with the planning phase related to management consulting, encompassing particu-

larly business knowledge, and the development and implementation phase, related to the consultant's attending to a process relying on technological knowledge. Therefore, IT consulting is understood as consulting on information technology issues, including equipment, software, IT systems and development, IT strategy and planning, and IT outsourcing, which also includes IT offshoring. Encompassing IT services as well as consulting in regard to advising companies professionally and independently, information technology consulting is related to consulting and problem solution as well as to management consulting regarding IT strategy. To show how to apply this conceptual framework to further research, the next section points out possible future research directions.

FUTURE RESEARCH DIRECTIONS

To provide a deeper understanding of the role of IT consultants in modern economies, we need more detailed (publicly available) data on the sections and dimensions of the IT consultancy market, encouraging further in-depth research on consulting traditions and practices in the different parts of the world. This may shed more light on the role of IT consultants in the dissemination of technology and creation of "technology fashions". We may also observe the consequences of market concentration within IT consulting companies and how they could alter their practices. Networks among consultants will gain further importance in regard to the assignment of consultants to certain projects. Another issue might be the consequences of professionalization and virtual teamwork among IT consultants, already practiced in large companies such as Accenture, with large customers spatially dispersed. An interesting field of study might be the interaction among IT consultants of different cultural backgrounds and cultural diversity regarding assignments, perceptions of clients, and interactions among IT consultants and clients within organizations as well as across dispersed organizational units.

Consequently, a very important issue is the process level of IT consulting in regard to the implementation of new software, systems integration, and outsourcing. The question of process attendance needs to be addressed, as well as the question of user education and further services. This applies also to business process outsourcing tendencies, where a specific mixture of IT consultancy and process attendance emerges when an organization is prepared to outsource processes and IT-related services. This includes the close collaboration of external IT consultants and internal IT developers (Niedereichholz, 2000). This trend is accompanied by the use of software tools to automate processes in the field of customer relations (i.e., help desk systems) or e-business, as well as to enhance communication between working groups. An interesting field of research might be the exploration of the trend of standardizing certain processes and the analysis of the consequences regarding organizational structure and working processes as well as employees' reactions and strategies.

Another field of study might be the offshoring of software development and services which has been done for years by US-firms but discovered only recently by European firms (Aspray, Mayadas & Vardi, 2006; see also chapter XVI in this volume). IT consultants are involved in the planning process, in the decision of what is and what is not to be offshored because it is they who mainly do the assessment of the company's processes regarding performance and profitability (see Amberg & Wiener, 2004) in the implementation process, which is linked to the introduction of centralization, standardization, and quality management processes as well as to the set-up of the organization offshore (Wieandt, 2006). In this regard, the IT consultants' role in process-related innovation may be interesting to observe.

REFERENCES

Abrahamson, E. (1996). Management fashion. *Academy of Management Review, 21*(3), 254-285.

Abrahamson, E. & Fairchild, G. (1999, December 4). Management fashion: Lifecycles, triggers, and collective learning processes. *Administrative Science Quarterly, 44*, 708-740.

Amberg, M., & Wiener, M. (2004). *Projektmanagement im Rahmen des IT-Offshoring: Planungsphase.* Working Paper No. 10 of Lehrstuhl für Betriebswirtschaftslehre, Wirtschaftsinformatik III, Friedrich-Alexander-Universität Erlangen-Nürnberg, Erlangen.

Argyris, C. (1999). *On organizational learning.* Oxford: Blackwell.

Argyris, C. & Schön, D.A. (1974). *Theory in practice.* Increasing Professional Effectiveness. San Francisco: Jossey-Bass.

Armbruster, T., & Kipping, M. (2003). Strategy consulting at crossroads. Technical change and shifting market conditions for top-level advice. *International Studies of Management and Organization 32*(4), 19-42.

Aspray, W., Mayadas, F. & Vardi, M. Y. (Eds.), (2006). *Globalization and offshoring of software.* A Report of the ACM Job Migration Task Force. The executive Summary, Findings and Overview of a compehensive ACM report on offshoring of software worldwide, Association for Computing. Retrieved March 15, 2006 from,: http://www.acm.org/globalizationreport/summary.htm.

Kearney, A.T. (2004). *Making offshore decisions.* A.T. Kearney's 2004 Offshore Location Attractiveness Index, Retrieved February 22, 2006 from, http://www.atkearney.de/content/misc/wrapper.php/id/49103/name/pdf_making_offshore_s_1081956080c0df.pdf.

Kearney, A.T. (2006). *A.T. Kearney: Management Buy-out von EDS erfolgreich abgeschlossen. A.T. Kearney wieder unabhängig—Anteile zu 100 Prozent im Besitz des eigenen Managements, press release January, 24 2006, Düsseldorf, Germany.* Retrieved January 26, 2006 from, http://www.atkearney.de/content/presse/pressemitteilungen_archiv_detail.php/id/49576/year/2006

Becker, A. (2004). Wirtschaftswissenschaften und Beratung. In. F. Nestmann, F. Engel, U. Sickendiek (Eds.), *Das Handbuch der Beratung, Band 1:*

Disziplinen und Zugänge (p. 193-205). Tübingen, Germany: DGVT.

Bloomfield, B. P. & Vurdubakis, T. (2002). The vision yhing: Constructing technology and the future in management advice. In. R. Fincham & T. Clark (Eds.), Critical consulting. *New Perspectives on the Management Advice Industry* (p. 115-129). Oxford: Blackwell.

Bloomfield, B. P. & Danieli, A. (1995). The role of management consultants in the development of information technology: The indissoluble nature of socio-political and technical skills. *Journal of Management Studies, 32*(1), 23-46.

Boes, Andreas. (2005). Auf dem Weg in die Sackgasse? Internationalisierung im feld software und IT-services. In. A. Boes & M. Schwemmle (Eds.), *Bangalore statt Böblingen? Offshoring und Internationalisierung im IT-Sektor* (pp. 13-65). Hamburg, Germany: VSA-Verlag.

Boes, Andreas & Schwemmle, Michael (2004). *Herausforderung Offshoring.* Internationalisierung und Auslagerung von IT-Dienstleistungen. Düsseldorf: Edition Hans Böckler Stiftung.

Boes, Andreas & Trinks, Katrin. (2006).*Theoretisch bin ich frei*! Interessenhandeln und Mitbestimmung in der IT-Industrie, Berlin: Edition Sigma.

Bohler, K. F. & Kellner, H. (2003). *Auf der Suche nach Effizienz. Die Arbeitsweisen von Beratern in der modernen Wirtschaft*, New York/Frankfurt am Main: Campus.

Breitenlechner, J. & Buchta, D. (2001). Strategie und Umsetzung: Ein Überblick. In. A.-W. Scheer & A. Köppen (Ed.), *Consulting. Wissen für die Strategie-, Prozess- und IT-Beratung* (p. 115-134), Berlin, Heidelberg & New York: Springer Verlag.

Bund Deutscher Unternehmensberater (BDU) (2001). *Facts and Figures zum Beratermarkt 2001.* Retrieved November 23, 2005 from, http://www.bdu.de/downloads/BDU_Studie_Facts%20and%20Figures2001.pdf

Bund Deutscher Unternehmensberater (BDU) (2004). *Facts and Figures zum Beratermarkt 2004.* Retrieved November 11, 2005 from, http.//www.bdu.de/downloads/Presse/Pressemitteilungen/FF%202004.pdf

Cameron, B.H., Knight, S. C. & Semmer, J.F. (2005, October 20-22). *The IT consulting model: Innovative methods for industry partnerships.* Paper presented at SIGITE 2005, Newark, New Jersey, USA.

Capgemini (2005). Veränderungen erfolgreich gestalten. *Change Management. Bedeutung, Strategien, Trends.* Brochure. Retrieved September 22, 2006 from, http://www.de.capgemini.com/m/de/tl/Change_Management_2005.pdf

DiMaggio, P. J. & Powell, W. W. (1983/2004). *The Iron cage tevisited: Institutional isomorphism and collective rationality in organizational fields.* In. F. Dobbin (Ed.), The New Economic Sociology: A reader (pp. 111-134). Princeton: Princeton University Press.

Ernst, B. & Kieser, A. (2003). In Search of Explanations for the Consulting Explosion. In. K. Sahlin-Andersson & L. Engwall (Eds.), *The expansion of management knowledge: Carriers, flows, and sources* (pp. 47-73). Stanford: Stanford University Press.

European Information Technology Observatory Group (EITO). (2006). *European Information Technology Observatory 2006.* Berlin.

Faust, M. (2000). Warum boomt die Managementberatung? *Und warum nicht zu allen Zeiten und überall, SOFI_Mitteilungen, 28*(2), 59-85.

FEACO (European Federation of Management Consultancy Associations) (2006). *Consulting services, online source.* Retrieved April 26, 2006 from, http://www.feaco.org/images/downloads/Anlagen/Anlage%20Market%20Overview%202004.pdf.

Fincham, R. & Clark, T. (2002) (ed.), *Critical consulting.* New Perspectives on the Management Advice Industry. Oxford: Blackwell.

Fratzer, Gerhard (2005). Organisationsentwicklung. In. F. Nestmann, F. Engel, U. Sickendiek (Ed.), *Das Handbuch der Beratung, Band 1: Disziplinen und Zugänge* (pp. 419-433). Tübingen, Germany: DGVT.

Gebert, D. (2004). Organisationsentwicklung, in: Schuler, H. (Hg.). *Lehrbuch Organisationspsychologie*, Bern / Göttingen: Hans Huber Verlag, S. 601-616.

Gillard, S. (2005). Managing IT-projects: Communication pitfalls and bridges. *Journal of Information Science, 31*(1), 37-43.

Greiner, T. (1989). Unternehmensberatung und Managementstrategien am Beispiel der Einführung von Produktionsplanungs- und Steuerungssystemen. In. Ortman, G. & Windeler, A. (Ed.), *Umkämpftes Terrain*. Managementperspetiven und Betriebsratspolitik bei der Einführung von Computer-Systemen. Opladen, Germany: Westdeutscher Verlag.

Grimme, K. (2006). *Der IT-Dienstleister als Helfer, nicht Treiber*. Die Implikationen des Transformational Outsourcing. CIO- Retrieved February 6, 2006 from, http://www.cio.de/knowledgecenter/outsourcing/822172/index1.html.

Hans, S. & Köppen, A. (2001). Problemlösung in der Beratung. In: A.-W. Scheer & A. Köppen (2001) (Eds.), *Consulting*. Wissens für die Strategie-, Prozess- und IT Beratung (pp.115-134). Berlin, Heidelberg, New York: Springer.

Iding, H. (2000). *Hinter de Kulissen der Organisationsberatung*. Qualitative Fallstudien von Beratungsprozessen im Krankenhaus. Opladen: Leske und Budrich.

Jackson, B. G. (1996). Re-engineering the sense of the self: the manager and the management guru. *Journal of Management Studies, 33*(5), 571-589.

Jackson, B. (2002). A fantasy Theme Analysis of three Guru-led management fashions. In. R. Fincham & T. Clark (Eds.), *Critical consulting*. New Perspectives on the Management Advice Industry (pp. 172-188). Oxford: Blackwell.

Jasperson, J., Carte, T., Saunders, C.S., Butler, B.S., Croes, H., & Zheng, W. (2002). Review: Power and information research: A metatriangulation review. *MIS Quarterly, 24*(4), 397-459.

Kennedy Information (2004a). *IT strategy and planning: The market for high value IT-consulting*. Executive Summary, Peterborough, NH USA: Kennedy Information.

Kennedy Information (2004b). *The Systems Integration Marketplace: Key data, forecasts & trends worldwide, executive summary*. Peterborough, NH USA: Kennedy Information.

Kennedy Information (2004c). *Alliances in consulting, IT, and business services: Strategy execution, and profiles, executive summary*. Peterborough, NH USA: Kennedy Information.

Kennedy Information (2004d). *The offshore services market: Key industry trends in India and beyond. Executive Summary*. Peterborough, NH USA: Kennedy Information.

Kennedy Information (2005a). *The global outsourcing market place: Key data, forecasts & trends. Report Summary*. Peterborough, NH USA: Kennedy Information.

Kennedy Information (2005b). *IT-consulting & systems integration leaders: Profiles and key firm data. Report Summary*. Peterborough, NH USA: Kennedy Information.

Krcmar, H., Böhmann, T. & Walter, S. (2005). Wissensmanagement im kontext der IT infrastructure Library (ITIL). In. N. Gronau, P. Pawlowski, T. Schildhauer, P. Schütt (Ed.), *KnowTech 2005. 7. Konferenz zum Einsatz von Knowledge Management in Wirtschaft und Verwaltung* (pp. 491-499), München.

Kühl, S. (2005). *Organisation, Intervention, Reflexivität: Auf der Suche nach einem Beratungsparadigma jenseits von zeckrationaler betriebswirtschaftlicher Beratung und systemischer Prozessberatung*. In: D. Seidl, W. Kirsch & M. Linder (Ed.), Grenzen der Strategieberatung. Eine Gegenüberstellung der Perspektiven von Wissenschaft, Beratung und Klienten (pp. 343-365), Bern/Stuttgart/Wien: Haupt Verlag.

Loose, Achim (2001). Netzwerkberatung und Beratungsnetzwerke—Strategischer Wandel durch externe Reflexion reflexiver Strukturation. In: G. Ortmann & J. Sydow (Eds.), *Strategie und Strukturation. Strategisches Management von Unternehmen, Netzwerken und Konzernen* (pp. 235-270), Wiesbaden: Gabler.

Luenendonk (2006). *IT-consulting und Services in Deutschland, Frankreich und Großbritannien: Lünendonk stellt Trendstudie 2006 vor. press release of January 26 2006, online source.* Retrieved June 2, 2006 from, http://www.luenendonk. de/presse_detail.php?ID=138&SFILTER=

Luenendonk (2006a). *Luenendonk-Liste 2006: Führende IT-Service-Unternehmen in Deutschland, Luenendonk company: Bad Wörishofen.* Retrieved June 2, 2006 from, http://www.luenendonk. de/download/LUE_ITS_2006_f300606.pdf.

Luenendonk (2006b). *Luenendonk-Liste 2006: Die Top 25 IT-Beratungs- und Systemintegrationsunternehmen in Deutschland, Luenendonk company: Bad Wörishofen, online-source.* Retrieved June 2, 2006 from, http://www.luenendonk.de/download/ LUE_ITB_2006_f240506.pdf.

Luhmann, N. (1980). *Gesellschaftsstruktur und Semantik.* Studien zur Wissenssoziologie der modernen Gesellschaft. Frankfurt am Main: Suhrkamp.

Markus, M. L. (2004). Technochange management: unsing IT to drive organizational change. *Journal of Information Technology, 2004*(19), 3-19.

Muhr, T. (2004). B*eratung und Macht. Mikropolitische Fallstudie einer Organisationsberatung, Dissertation Thesis.* Bielefeld: Germany. Retrieved May 10, 2006 from, http://deposit.ddb.de/cgi-bin/ dokserv?idn=975390678.

Newell, S.; Bresnen, M.; Edelmann, L.; Scarbrough, H. & Swan, J. (2006). Sharing knowlegde across projects. *Management Learning, 37*(2), 167-185.

Niedereichholz, C. (2000). Internes consuting. Grundlagen, Praxisbeispiele, Spezialthemen. München / Wien: Öldenbourg.

Niedereichholz, C. & Niedereichholz, J. (2006). Consulting Insight, München/Wien: Oldenbourg.

Organization for Economic Co-operation and Development (OECD) (2002a). *Technology outlook: ICTs and the information economy,* OECD & Dev.

OECD (2002b). *Reviewing the ICT Sector Definition: Issues for Discussion, Paper DSTI/ICCP/ IIS(2002)2.* Retrieved August 25, 2006 from, http:// www.oecd.org/dataoecd/3/8/20627293.pdf.

OECD (2002c). *Measuring the Information Economy.* Retrieved August 25, 2006 from, http://www. oecd.org/dataoecd/16/14/1835738.pdf.

OECD (2004). *Digital delivery of business services, unclassified.* Retrieved August 22, 2006 from, http://www.oecd.org/dataoecd/40/5/31818723. pdf.

Ortmann, G., Windeler, A., Becker, A. & Schulz, H.-J. (1990). *Computer und Macht in Organisationen.* Mikropolitische Analysen. Opladen, Germany: Westdeutscher Verlag.

Powell, W. (2001). The Capitalist Firm in the 21st century: Emerging Patterns. In: DiMaggio, P. (Ed.), *The twenty-first century firm (pp. 34-68),* Princeton: Princeton University Press.

Rothberg, D. (2006). *IT-consulting services hit a growth spurt.* In e-week enterprise news & reviews. Retrieved June 3, 2006 from, http://www.eweek. com/article2/0,1759,1950788,00.asp

Rudolph, H. & Okech, J. (2004). W*er andern einen Rat erteilt....* Wettbewerbstrategien und Personalpolitik von Unternehmensberatungen in Deutschland, Berlin: Edition Sigma.

Ruiz Ben, E. (2007). *Global expertise and quality Sstandards in ICT offshore projects: Time and institutionalization aspects.* Paper presented at the 1st. Information Systems Workshop on Global Sourcing: Services, Knowledge and Innovation,

Val d'Isère, France, 13-15 March 2007. Retrieved April, 17, 2007 from, http://globalsourcing.org. uk/papers/JIT06-183.pdf

Ruiz Ben, E. & Claus, R. (2004). Offshoring in der deutschen IT Branche. Eine neue Herausforderung für die Informatik. In: *Informatik Spektrum, 27*(4), 1-6.

Ruiz Ben, E., Wieandt, M. & Maletzky, M. (2007). Offshoring in the ICT sector in Europe: Trends and scenario analysis. In. Raisinghani, M. (Ed.), *Handbook of Research on Global Information Technology*. Hershey, USA: IGI Global, forthcoming.

Scheer, A.-W. & Köppen, A. (2001) (Ed.), *Consulting*. Wissens für die Strategie-, Prozess- und IT Beratung, Berlin, Heidelberg, New York: Springer.

Schein, E. H. (2004). *Organizational Culture and Leadership*. San Francisco: Jossey-Bass.

Schmutte, A. M. (2003). Six Sigma im Business Excellence Prozess—Wertorientierte Unternehmensführung mit Balanced Scorecard, EFQM und Six Sigma bei Siemens. In: A. Töpfer (Ed.) *Six Sigma*. Konzeption und Erfolgsbeispiele für praktizierte Null-Fehler-Qualität (pp. 377-386), Berlin, Heidelberg, New York: Springer.

Schnelle, T. (2005). Durchsetzen von Strategien durch diskursive Beratung Anschlussfähigkeit in der Umsetzung von Strategien. In: D. Seidl, W. Kirsch & M. Linder (Eds.). *Grenzen der Strategieberatung. Eine Gegenüberstellung der Perspektiven von Wissenschaft, Beratung und Klienten* (pp. 451-462). Bern/Stuttgart/Wien: Haupt Verlag.

Seidensticker, J. (2005). Über gewohnte Grenzen hinaus Strategieberatung zwischen Analyse und Umsetzung. In: D. Seidl, W. Kirsch & M. Linder (Eds.). *Grenzen der Strategieberatung. Eine Gegenüberstellung der Perspektiven von Wissenschaft, Beratung und Klienten* (pp. 419-429). Bern/Stuttgart/Wien: Haupt Verlag.

Sosik, J. & Jung, D.I. (2003). Impression management and performance in information technology consulting. The role of self-other rating agreement

on charismatic leadership. *Management Communication Quarterly, 17*(2), 233-268.

Sturdy, A. (1997). The consultancy process: An insecure business? *Journal of Management Studies, 34*(3), 389-413.

Takada, N. (2003). *Service Sector Innovation and Policy Issues in Japan*. Paper presented at the AT 10 Research Conference, February 20-21, Retrieved August 28, 2006 from, http://www.tcf.or.jp/data/20030220-21_Nobuaki_TAKADA.pdf#search=%22IT%20service%20sector%20%2B%20Japan%22.

Technology Partners International (TPI) (2004). *White Paper: Asia Pacific—Distinct and Dynamic Outsourcing Region*. Technology Partners International, Retrieved August 28, 2006 from, http://www.tpi.net/pdf/WhitePaper_AP_Distinct-dynamic%20FINAL_Intl.pdf.

Werr, A., Stjernberg, T. & Docherty, P. (1997). The functions of methods of change in management consulting. *Journal of Organizational Change Management, 10*(4), 288-307.

Wieandt, M. (2006, September 7-8). *Teamwork when implementing offshoring: Exploring the German ICT sector*. Paper presented at the IWOT X Workshop, Groningen, Netherlands.

Wieandt, M. (2007a). IT consulting and information technology implementation. In. Raisinghani, M. (Ed.), *Handbook of Research on Global Information Technology*. Hershey, USA: IGI Global, forthcoming.

Wieandt, M. (2007b). The Development of Knowledge Transfer and Collaboration in a Nearshore Software Development Project, *Paper presented at the 1ˢᵗ Information Systems Workshop on Global Sourcing: Services, Knowledge and Innovation, Val d'Isère, France, 13-15 March 2007*, Retrieved April 17, 2007 from, http://globalsourcing.org. uk/papers/JIT06-186.pdf

Willcocks, L.P., & Lacity, M. (2006). *Global sourcing of business IT services*. London: Palgrave Macmillan.

ADDITIONAL READINGS

Argyris, C. (1990). *Overcoming organizational defenses: Facilitating organizational learning.* New Jersey: Prentice Hall.

Argyris, C. (1993). *Knowledge for action: A guide to overcoming barriers to organizational change.* San Franciso: Jossey-Bass.

Argyris, C. (2006). *Reasons and rationalizations: The limits to organizational knowlegde.* Oxford: Oxford University Press.

Armbrüster, Th. & Kipping, M. (2002). Types of Knowledge and the Client-Consultant Interaction, In Sahlin-Andersson, K./Engwall, L. (Eds.), *The Expansion of Management Knowledge: Carriers, Flows and Sources, Stanford, CA.* Stanford University Press, S. (pp. 96-110).

Armbrüster, T. and Schmolze, R. (1999, February), 'Milk Rounds, Case Studies, and the Aftermath. Recruitment practices in management consulting in their consequences'. *Paper presented at the 2nd International Conference on Consultancy Work, King's College London.*

Benders, J. and van Veen, K. (2001). What is in a fashion: Interpretative viability and management fashions. *Organization, 8*(1), 33-53.

Benders, J., van den Berg, R.-J. & van Bijsterveld, M. (1998). Hitch-hiking on a hype: Dutch consultants engineering re-engineering. *Journal of Organizational Change Management, 11*(3), 201-215.

Burt, R. S. (1999, November), The Social capital of opinion leaders. *The ANNALS of the American Academy of Political and Social Science, 566,*37-54.

Byrne, J. A., J. Muller & W. Zellner (2002). Inside McKinsey, *Business Week, 3790,*66-73.

Byrkjeflot, H. (1998). Management as a system of knowledge and authority. In Alvarez, J. L. (Ed.), *The Diffusion and Consumption of Business Knowledge* (pp. 58-80). London: Macmillan.

Clark, T. & Greatbatch, D. (2002a). Collaborative relationships in the creation and fashioning of management ideas: Gurus, editors, and managers. In. Kipping, M. & Engwall, L. (Eds.), *Management Consulting: Emergence and Dynamics of a Knowledge Industry* (pp. 129- 145). Oxford: Oxford University Press.

Clark, T. & Greatbatch, D. (2002b). Knowledge legitimation and audience affiliation through storytelling: The example of management gurus. In Clark, T. & Fincham, R. (Eds.), *Critical Consulting. New Perspectives on the Management Advice Industry* (pp. 152-171), Oxford: Blackwell.

Clark, T. & Salaman, G. (1996a). Telling tales: Management consultancy as the art of Story telling. In. Grant, D. & Oswick, C. (Eds.), *Metaphor and Organizations* (pp. 167-184). London: Sage.

Clark, T. & Salaman, G. (1996b). The management guru as organizational witchdoctor. *Organization* (3), 85-107.

Czarniawska, B. & Joerges, B. (1996). Travel of ideas. In Czarniawska, B. & Sevón, G. (Eds.), *Translating Organizational Change* (pp. 13-48), Berlin, New York: deGruyter.

Czarniawska-Joerges, B. (1990). Merchants of Meaning: Management in the Swedish Public Sector. In Turner, B. (Ed.), *Organizational Symbolism* (pp. 139-150), Berlin, New York: de Gruyter.

Crainer, S. (1997). *The Tom Peters phenomenon: Corporate man to corporate skunk.* Oxford: Capstone.

Crucini, C. & Kipping, M. (2001). Management consultancies as global change agents? Evidence from Italy, *Journal of Organizational Change Management, 14*(6), 570-589.

Davis, G. F., Diekmann, K. A. & Tinsley, C. H. (1994). The decline and fall of the conglomerate firm in the 1980s: The deinstitutionalization of an organizational form. *American Sociological Review, 59,*547-70.

Dezalay, Y. (1993). Professional competition and the social construction of transnational regulatory expertise. In McCahery, J., Picciotto, S. & Scott, C. (Eds.), *Corporate Control and Accountability. Changing Structures and the Dynamics of Regulation* (pp. 203-215). Oxford: Clarendon

Djelic, M.L. (1998). *Exporting the american model.* Oxford: Oxford University Press.

Dyas, G. P. & Thanheiser, H. T. (1976). *The emerging European enterprise: Strategy and structure in French and German Industry.* London: Macmillan.

Faust, M. (2005). Consultants. In Beckert, J. & Zafirovski, M. (Eds.), *International Encyclopedia of Economic Sociology* (pp. 95-98). London: Routledge.

Fincham, R. (2002). Charisma versus technique: Differentiating the expertise of management gurus and management consultants. In Clark, T. & Fincham, R. (Eds.), *Critical Consulting. New Perspectives on the Management Advice Industry* (pp. 191-205). Oxford: Blackwell.

Furusten, S. (1995). *The managerial discourse—A study of the creation and diffusion of popular management knowledge.* Uppsala: Uppsala University, Department of Business Studies.

Guillén, M. F. (1994). *Models of management: Work, authority, and organization in a comparative perspective.* Chicago: The University of Chicago Press.

Heusinkveld, S. (2004). *Surges and sediments: Organizaton concepts between transience and continuity.* PhD thesis, University of Nijmegen, Nijmegen.

Heusinkveld, S. & Benders, J. (2002). Between professional dedication and corporate design: Exploring forms of new concept development in consultancies. *International Studies on Management and Organization, 32,*104-122.

Heusinkveld, S., Benders, J. & Koch, Ch. (2000, July 2-4). Dispersed discourse? Defining the shape of BPR in Denmark and The Netherlands. *Paper submitted to sub-theme 14 at the 16th EGOS Colloquium, Helsinki.*

Hirsch, P.M. (1972). Processing fads and fashions: An organization set analysis of cultural industry systems. *American Journal of Sociology, 77,* 639-659.

Jackall, R. (1988). *Moral mazes: The world of corporate managers.* New York: Oxford University Press.

Kieser, A. (2002a). On communication barriers between management science, consultancies and business organizations. In Clark, T. & Fincham, R. (Eds.), *Critical Consulting. New Perspectives on the Management Advice Industry* (pp. 206-227), London: Blackwell.

Kipping, M. (2002). Trapped in their wave: The evolution of management consultancies. In Clark, T. & Fincham, R. (Eds.), *Critical Consulting. New Perspectives on the Management Advice Industry* (pp. 28-49), London: Blackwell.

Kipping, M. (2000). Consultancy and conflicts: Bedaux at Lukens Steel and the Anglo-Iranian oil company. *Entreprises et Histoire, 25,*9-25.

Kipping, M. (1999a). American management consulting companies in Western Europe, 1920 to 1990: Products, reputation and relationships. *Business History Review 73*(2),193-222.

Kipping, M. (1999b), British economic decline: Blame it on the consultants? *Contemporary British History, 13*(3),23-38.

Kipping, M. (1998). The hidden business schools. Management training in Germany Since 1945. In Engwall, L. & Zamagni, V. (Eds.), *Management Education in Historical Perspective* (pp. 95-110). Manchester: Manchester University Press.

Kipping, M. (1997/98). Bridging the gap? Management consultants and their role in France. *The University of Reading, Discussion Papers in Economics and Management,* Series A, Vol. X, No. 375.

Kipping, M. (1997). Consultancies, institutions and the diffusion of taylorism in Britain, Germany and France, 1920s to 1950s'. *Business History, 39*(4),67-83.

Kipping, M. (1996a). Management consultancies in Germany, Britain and France, 1900-60: An evolutionary and institutional perspective. *Discussion Papers in Economics and Management*, Series A, Vol. X (1996/97), University of Reading, Department of Economics.

Kipping, M. (1996b). The U.S. Influence on the evolution of management consultancies in Britain, France and Germany Since 1945. *Business and Economic History*, 25 (1), pp. 112-23.

Kipping, M. & Amorim, C. (1999/2000). Consultancies as management schools. *The University of Reading, Discussion Papers in Economics and Management*, Series A, Vol. XII, No. 409.

Kipping, M. & Armbrüster, T. (Eds.), (1999). The consultancy field in Western Europe. *The Creation of European Management Practice (CEMP)* Report No. 6, The University of Reading.

Kipping, M. & Bjarnar, O. (1998). *The Americanisation of European Business*. London: Routledge.

Kipping, M. & Sauviat, C. (1996). Global management consultancies: Their evolution and structure. *Discussion Papers in International Investment and Business Studies*, Series B, Vol. IX (1996/1997), University of Reading, Department of Economics.

Kipping, M., Furusten, S. & Gammelsæter, H. (1998/99). Converging towards American dominance? Developments and structures of the consultancy fields in Europe. *The University of Reading, Discussion Paper in Economics and Management*, Series A, Vol. XI, No. 398.

Kogut, B. & Parkinson, D. (1993). The diffusion of American organizing principles to Europe. In Kogut, B. (Ed.), *Country Competitiveness* (pp. 179-202). Oxford: Oxford University Press.

Mazza, C. (1998). The popularization of business knowledge diffusion: From academic knowledge to popular culture? In Alvarez, J.L. (Ed.), *The Diffusion and Consumption of Business Knowledge* (pp. 164-181). London: Macmillan.

McKenna, C. D. (2001). *The youngest profession: Management consulting*. PhD dissertation Baltimore, MD: Johns-Hopkins University.

McKenna, C. D. (1997). The American challenge: McKinsey & Company's role in the transfer of decentralization to Europe, 1957-1975. *Academy of Management Best Paper Proceedings,* (pp. 226-31).

McKenna, C.D. (1996, May). Le Défi Américain: Management Consultants and the Transfer of American Organizational Models to Europe, 1957-1975. *Paper presented at the History Graduate Student Conference, University of Bielefeld - The John Hopkins University, University of Bielefeld.*

McKenna, C. D. (1995). The origins of modern management consulting. *Business and Economic History*, 24(1),51-58.

McKenna, C. D., Djelic, M.L. & Ainamo, A. (2003). Message and medium—The role of consulting firms in globalization and its local interpretation. In Djelic, M.-L. & Quack, S. (Eds.), *Globalization and Institutions* (pp. 83-107), Cheltenham: Edward Elgar.

Meyer, J. W. (1996). Otherhood: The promulgation and transmission of ideas in the modern organizational environment. In Czarniawska, B. & Sevón, G. (Eds.), *Translating Organizational Change* (pp. 241-252). Berlin: de Gruyter.

Meyer, J. W. & Rowan, B. (1977). Institutional organizations: Formal structure as myth and ceremony. *American Journal of Sociology, 83*,340-63.

Meyer, J. W. & Scott, W. R. (1992). *Organizational environments, ritual and rationality* (2nd ed.). London: Sage.

Micklethwaite, J. & Wooldridge, A. (1996). *The witch doctors: What the management gurus are saying, why it matters and how to make sense of it*. London: Heinemann.

Nystrom, P. C. & Starbuck, W. H. (1984). Managing beliefs in organizations. *Journal of Applied Behavioral Science, 20*,277-287.

O'Shea, J. & Madigan, C. (1997). Dangerous vompany. *The consulting powerhouses and the businesses they save and ruin.* London: Nicholas Brealey.

Røvik, K.A. (2003). The secrets of the winners: Management ideas that flow. In. Sahlin-Andersson, K. & Engwall, L. (Eds.), *The Expansion of Management Knowledge: Carriers, Ideas, and Sources.* Stanford: Stanford University Press.

Røvik, K.A. (1996). Deinstitutionalization and the logic of fashion. In. Czarniawska, B. & Sevón, G. (Eds.), *Translating Organizational Change* (pp. 139-172). Berlin, New York: deGruyter.

Sahlin-Andersson, K. (1996). Imitating by editing success: The construction of organizational fields. In Czarniawska, B. & Sevón, G. (Eds.), *Translating Organizational Change* (pp. 69-92). Berlin, New York: deGruyter.

Schein, E. H. (1988). *Process consultation. Vol. I: Its role in organization development.* Reading, MA: Addision Wesley.

Shapiro, E. (1996). *Fad surfing in the boardroom: Managing in the age of instant answers.* Reading, MA: Addison-Wesley.

Starbuck, W. H. (1993). Keeping a butterfly and an elephant in a house of cards: The elements of exceptional success. *Journal of Management Studies, 30,*885-921.

Sturdy, A. (2002). Front-line diffusion: The production and negotiation of knowledge through training interaction. In Clark, T. & Fincham (Eds.), *Critical Consulting* (pp. 130-151). Oxford: Blackwell.

Tisdall, P. (1982). *Agents of Change: The Development and Practice of Management Consultancy.* London: Heinemann.

Watson, T.J. (1994). Management "flavors of the month": Their role in managers' lives. *The International Journal of Human Resource Management, 5,*893-909.

Werr, A. (1999). *The language of change—The roles of methods in the work of management consultants.* Stockholm: Stockholm School of Economics.

Wooldridge, A. (1997, March 22), The advice business, *The Economist,* 3-5.

Zbaracki, M. J. (1998). The rhetoric and reality of total quality management. *Administrative Science Quarterly, 43,*602-36.

ENDNOTES

1. For example, Boes and Schwemmle (2004) assume that IT consultants have played a major role in the dissemination of IT offshoring.

2. Interestingly, some big IT consultancies address the issue of change management in their brochures (see, i.e., Capgemini, 2005).

3. Due to the policies of some firms, they do not publicise detailed data on their business activities so there is no data available on revenues of the IT consulting segment (Luenendonk, 2006a).

4. According to OECD (2004), in 2003 Microsoft, Oracle and Computer Association (software), IBM, Hewlett Packard, Hitachi and Sun Microsystems (hardware), EDS, CSC, Accenture and Capgemini (consulting) were leading companies.

5. Kennedy Information (2005b) numbers the market share of 17 leading companies up to 34.5% of the global consulting and systems integration market.

6. The market share of IT consulting in Germany amounted 40% in 2001 and about 28% in 2004 (BDU, 2001). According to OECD (2004), market share of IT consulting in the UK accounted ca. 28%.

7. This is still the case (see BDU, 2004). Luenendonk (2006b) enumerates the market share of the top 25 IT consulting and system integration companies 44% for 2005 which is an increase of 2% compared to 2004.

8. China provides mainly software and IT-related service for Japan (TPI, 2004; Aspray, Mayadas, & Vardi, 2006). Considering China's ICT sector, China's IT service sector "does not currently have a major impact on

[9] the world economy" (Aspray, Mayadas, & Vardi, 2006, p. 22).

[9] A management fashion is defined as "a relatively transitory collective belief, disseminated by management fashion setters, that a management technique leads to rational process" (Abrahamson, 1996, p. 257).

[10] Exponents of the organization development approach deny that management consulting firms' concepts are organization development because of the negligence of the basic assumptions (see Fratzer, 2005).

[11] The term "knowledge" may include (1) values, "visions," general approaches or philosophies, (2) procedures, (3) tools, and (4) knowledge on individual projects documented in information systems (Werr et al., 1997). Of course, there is a considerable body of research concerning the nature of knowledge differentiating implicit, situated and explicit, codified knowledge (see Wieandt, 2007b). Here, both sides are addressed

[12] This is particularly true for IT consultants relying on a high reputation which applies to almost all big consulting firms (Ernst & Kieser, 2003). Considered from the consultant's perspective, reputation is an important feature to receive assignments and consulting firms strive to gain reputation by publishing in important journals and by setting trends (Bloomfield and Danieli, 1995).

[13] Ernst and Kieser (2003, p. 58) also point out that firms "that were formerly concentrating in selling software [...] now try to address all aspects of the organisation including strategic issues."

[14] EITO defines IT consulting as "IT-related planning and design activities that assist clients in making IT-related decisions on business direction or information technology. IT-related business consulting includes corporate strategy assistance, process improvement, capacity planning, best practices, business process reengineering, and change-management services for business. Not included are consulting involving tax, audit, benefits, financial, and/or engineering issues. IT consulting includes information systems strategy assistance, information system and network planning, architectural and supplier assessments, product consulting and technical designs for information technology, and maintenance planning. [...] Implementation services also include all activities involved with custom application development and work performed on packaged applications. Training and education is also included in this segment." (EITO, 2006, p. 258).

[15] IT offshoring is understood here as outsourcing practice or founding of a subsidiary in lower-wage-countries which are far away (for further discussion see Boes & Schwemmle, 2004; Aspray, Mayadas & Vardi, 2006).

Chapter XVIII
Information Technology Consulting and the Implementation of Information Technology

Michaela Wieandt
Technische Universität Berlin, Germany

ABSTRACT

IT consulting seems to be of growing importance within organizations. The tendency towards complex large-scale IT consulting projects requires a more detailed exploration of the implementation process on the organizational level. Given that these projects contribute to or create organizational change (i.e. Markus, 2004), power relationships are assumed to influence the implementation of information technology. This paper examines the collaboration between IT consultants, employees and project managers within IT consulting projects, considering aspects of power negotiation and power politics within organizations. Based on the literature on IT consulting and IT project implementation, major risks and challenges of the implementation process as well as possible solutions will be identified and analyzed. Following Giddens' theoretical framework of structuration theory (Giddens, 1984), an actor's access to authoritative and allocative resources as well as his position and strategies in relation to power are explored. It will be shown that IT consultants may have a central position within the constellation of an IT project, depending on their strategies of impression management and charismatic leadership (Sosik & Jung, 2003).

INTRODUCTION

Throughout the recent market consolidation of the ICT sector since 2002, IT consulting grew within the segment of IT services due to the stabilization of prices in 2005 (Rothberg, 2006; see also chapter XVII in this volume). The data on rates vary and range from annual growth rates to 2010 of 1.9 % (Kennedy Information, 2004) to 5.2 % (Rothberg, 2006). However, IT consulting is expected to grow in future years (EITO, 2006, p. 64). The market growth of IT consulting, therefore, seems to indicate its increasing importance in regard to the implementation of information technology and large-scale IT projects in organizations.

While there exists a lot of research on the issue of IT implementation in organizations (for an overview see Jasperson et al., 2002; recent works include Gillard, 2005; Constantinidis & Barrett, 2006; Markus, 2004; Symon & Clegg, 2005), the role of external IT consultants in the process of implementation has been barely explored. Given their key positions as project leaders, their position within organizations and levels of collaboration with managers and employees on the organizational level throughout the implementation process require further exploration.

In contrasting the perspectives of organizations and consultants, this article aims to explore the collaboration of IT consultants with the project team within the organization (usually consisting of a project manager and team members in departments involved in, or affected by, the new technology) during the implementation process. Based on the structuration theory approach in organization theory (see Giddens, 1984; Ortmann, Windeler & Sydow, 1997), I will show the major challenges of IT implementation based on the nature of the project (i.e. time and budget constraints, embeddedness, knowledge transfer and teamwork; see Sydow et al., 2004), the nature of external consulting services within organizations, and power relationships.

Following Giddens (1984), power is conceptualized as closely related to action and provides access to allocative and authoritative resources. It is seen as a major instrument in the alteration of structures (i.e., of an organization), particularly as perceived by actors.

IT implementation will be analyzed in its social and organizational environment, structured by a certain organizational culture, the work habits and the power relationships of the people involved (Bloomfield & Danieli, 1995; Markus, 2004; Clegg & Simon, 2005). Following the distinction provided by Markus (2004), the focus will be on IT projects which imply a "technochange," i.e., a technological change which leading to an alteration of "organization behaviour and outcomes" (Markus, 2004, p. 6) and thus of power relationships within the organization (Orlikowsky, 1992; Ortmann et al., 1990; Friedberg,

1995, McKinlay, 2002). These IT projects are large-scale, meaning they affect many departments or even the whole organization, and last one year or more. They require the appropriate identification of user requirements, demand a definition of "users" or "user representatives," reflect or influence power interests and the strategies used by actors (Symon & Clegg, 2005). The level of communication between users and developers (Gillard, 2005) may affect the power loss or gain of certain actors because it often results in the resistance of employees; for example their non- or misuse of the new system. Precise communication is important in avoiding what Markus (2004) calls cultural and incentive misfits (or incompatibilities) within the technological solution. This demonstrates that the collaboration between the project team and its co-workers is structured by power politics and power relationships, which in turn are structured by resources available to the actors and the actors' strategies themselves (Friedberg, 1995).

In this context, IT consultants are believed to fill the gap between users and developers, providing both with an adequate technological solution for the organizations' performance improvement as well as the "right" translation and analysis of the users' needs during the process of implementation (Bloomfield & Danieli, 1995). On the other hand, as Ernst and Kieser (2003) point out, IT consultants follow their own interests in looking out for career prospects and taking care of their client potential, on which they depend. For example, the importance of organizations having an IT strategy is particularly promoted by management consultants such as McKinsey (Marwaha & Willmott, 2006; Craig & Tinaikar, 2006). As claimed by Bloomfield and Danieli (1995), the aim of IT consultants' strategies is to "create a niche and persuade clients that they are in it" and to "portray themselves as obligatory passage points" (Bloomfield & Danieli, 1995, p. 28, see also Bloomfield & Vurdubakis, 2002).

The article is organized as follows. The background will provide definitions of power, resources and strategies based on Giddens' concept and an extension of the ideas of Ortman, Sydow and Windeler (1997), as well as IT project-related issues involving IT consultants. In the main body I will examine some of the challenges involved in

IT implementation, which gain a special dynamic when IT consultants are employed. Secondly, some solutions and recommendations will be proposed. The next section will provide some future trends of IT consulting concerning the internationalization and virtualization of IT consulting services. Finally, some conclusions will be drawn and outlines for further research given.

PROCESSES OF IT IMPLEMENTATION IN ORGANIZATIONS AND IT CONSULTING

Organizations, Power, and IT Projects

To explore IT consulting more deeply, it is necessary to consider certain dimensions of IT projects in organizations supported by IT consultants. I define projects as temporary systems in which "groups comprising a mix of different specialists' competences (…) have to achieve a certain goal or carry out a specific task within limits set as to costs and time" (Sydow et al., 2004, p. 1480). Considering that defining the scope of a project can be challenging (Engwall, 1998), I will also describe IT projects here as encompassing the design, development and implementation of a new IT-system within an organization (Markus, 2004).

In this chapter, IT projects are assumed to be carried out within organizations, which themselves are understood sociologically as systems of organized activity reproduced by organizational actors (Ortmann, Sydow, & Windeler, 1997). According to Giddens (1984), the actors of an organization function within the organization's structures. These structures are formed by the internal rules of an organization and institutionalized by continuous, recursive[1] reproduction over time and space in the form of the actors' day-to-day social activity and routine and are therefore transformable by human action. In this sense, the idea of structure implies the normative and sense-making aspects of rules (that is, how the rules are perceived), which can be conceptualized as "normative elements and codes of signification" (p. xxxi). Structure, therefore, exists in

the actors' minds as "memory traces" (Giddens, 1984, p. 25). Following Giddens, because the "structural properties of social systems are both medium and outcome of the practices they recursively organize" (Giddens, 1984, p. 25), structures are in their nature both constraining and enabling, in that they define both the limits and the possibilities of an individual's action. Therefore, the organization's actors' freedom of choice is constituted by their perception and interpretation of the organization's structures and rules from which they derive the possibilities for action (Friedberg, 1995). Furthermore, this action can be constrained or enabled by the amount of power an actor possesses,[2] power, if we follow Giddens, being measured by the level of access to and use of allocative and authoritative resources in the sense of "structured properties of social systems, drawn upon and reproduced by knowledgeable agents in the course of interaction" that an actor may have (Giddens, 1984, p. 15). Therefore, authoritative resources are derived from the power one has to co-ordinate human agent activity, that is, the capacity to give instructions and lead people. Allocative resources refer to the amount of control one has over material products (Giddens, 1984), including budgets, allocation of personnel etc. According to Ortmann et al. (1990), power in organizations is exerted as well by the use of interpretation-patterns (or ways in which actors interpret rules, relations and circumstances), knowledge and norms, which can be defined as non-material allocative resources. This also applies to external actors who have a direct impact on the organization, such as consultants. Therefore, power is exerted within organizations through dominance within a hierarchy in terms of one's authority to issue instructions as well as by positively or negatively sanctioning social behavior, patterns of interpretation and suitable rules, such as those reflecting the culture of an organization (Schreyögg, 2000; Ortmann et al., 1990). For example, impression management strategies may be an important means of exerting power (Sosik & Jung, 2003) based mainly on the concept "that one must be more cooperative, and often more cautious, with those in a position of power." (Gillard, 2005, p. 40). In this context, a definition of what is technical and what is social is also reflected in power negotiations, being linked to the one who can exercise specific responsibilities and control resources (Bloomfield & Danieli, 1995). Thus, IT systems encompass both sorts of resources. in setting up business procedures and structuring operations they necessitate authoritative resources and may provide certain instruments for control (Markus, 2004). Being used by the organization to achieve an improved position of power, an IT system could also be considered an allocative resource (Gillard, 2005).

According to Giddens (1984), the exertion of power also requires the consensus of subordinate employees, for in most cases sanctions permit various forms of resistance of the new system by those involved. In this sense, all actors possess a degree of power and control of certain resources but due to the asymmetrical distribution of resources by the organization's hierarchy, the expectations connected with different posts and responsibilities and the organization's operational structure, some individuals have more power and act more autonomously than others.. According to Ortmann et al. (1990) and Friedberg (1995), the exertion of power is deeply linked to the personal interests and goals of an actor, whose actions are the expression of a strategy designed to reach his or her individual aims. The actor possesses the ability to make choices and select certain actions, which will function effectively within the power structures and relations of the organization.

In analysing IT projects, one must therefore consider that they are carried out within organizations whose specific structures can enable or constrain the action of certain actors. This reflects the results of Orlikowski's study (1992, p. 362), where "people's cognitions or mental models about technology and their work, and the structural properties of the organization such as policies, norms, and reward systems" are decisive variables in regard to whether and how the implementation of technologies may alter the nature of the work and the patterns of social interaction. The environment of an IT project is therefore an amalgamation of the individuals' perception (which depends on their cognitions and feelings), goals and interests as well as the organization's structure.

When looking at the project environment concretely, according to Sydow et al. (2004), it is important to consider whether a project is carried out in a functional or business-oriented organization, because the project relies on the resources and expertise of certain specializations and complexities, that may differ depending on the context of the organization. Large-scale IT projects are implemented within some functional (that is, administrative) organizations because they are assumed to improve the performance of the company. However, technology is also sought to connect businesses and establish common data bases (i.e., examples in Markus, 2004; Constantinidis & Barrett, 2005). Smaller IT projects are limited to a certain unit or department.

The type of organization seems to be influential as well. According to Sydow et (2004), the differentiation between mechanistic (centralized) and organic (decentralised) organizations (Burns & Stalker, 1961) suggests that the distinct context of an organization affects the management of a project in terms of the culture of an organization, its hierarchy and co-ordination as well as the level of access to resources possessed by IT project managers, IT consultants and employees. Similarly, Minssen (2005) distinguishes two styles of co-ordination which are linked to certain organizational cultures. Co-ordination by hierarchy reflects the exercise of authoritative resources such as the authority to issue instructions and is therefore associated with structured (or mechanistic) organizations in which power is mainly linked to positions and functions. Working tasks are highly structured and collaboration is based on following instructions, providing a low grade of autonomy on the individual level. Contrastingly, co-ordination by discourse is found in decentralized (or in terms of Burns and Stalker (1961), organic) organizations. In this case, power is indirectly exerted by patterns of interpretation and the orientation of the employees regarding market demands as well as their level of commitment and rationality and their convictions. Collaboration within such organizations is based on the autonomy of the employees who are seen as experts that can solve problems through cooperation among themselves. This collaboration, therefore, is characterized by discourse and intensive communication (Minssen, 2005). Labor is mainly organized in the form of teamwork.

Another important dimension of an organization's structure is whether organizations are project-based, i.e., organizing most of their internal and external activities in projects, or project-led, with projects being part of their operations, but with primary activity volume-based or operations-oriented (Sydow et al., 2004; Mickler & Kalkowski, 2002). In project-led organizations, line organization (the hierarchical structure of an organization) and project organization often compete for resources, challenging the project management in terms of meeting budget and time constraints (Mickler & Kalkowski, 2002).

In short, IT projects have differing organizational environments which in turn influence the project team's access to allocative and authoritative resources, collaboration with other departments and power relations, all of which may affect the implementation of IT. Gillard (2005) argues that, in order to implement large-scale IT projects many organizations have established matrix or grid structures, organized in a cross-functional matrix form to permit the close collaboration of individuals from different functional units within a project. This applies more to project-based organizations, for in them both structures (line and project) compete (Engwall, 1998; Mickler & Kalkowski, 2002; Soederlund, 2004). Therefore, IT projects are usually organized across business units but the basic environment can be either decentralized/organic or centralized/mechanic.

According to Mickler and Kalkowski (2002), who explored several IT-related projects, the access to authoritative resources such as the authority to issue instructions outside of the line organization depends on the priority of the project and is, therefore, dependent on power negotiations. Nevertheless, the integration of the various aspects of the project within an organization's command and control routines and co-ordination efforts points to the issue of embeddedness (Sydow et al., 2004) and remains difficult, especially in project-led organizations where the structure exists alongside a line organization. In that case, project team members have to reconcile both forms of organization in terms of different authorities and instructions they have to follow (Mickler & Kalkowski, 2002; Sydow et al., 2004). Here, the question of knowledge transfer from the IT project to the organization can be understood in two dimensions: Firstly, proper use of the new technology requires the training and education of the users (Markus, 2004). Secondly, there is some knowledge transfer and communication between the project team and

those departments of the organization are affected by the new technology to ensure that the project meets the needs of the business.

The question of to which resources the IT project team is given access depends on whether or not there are IT consultants involved. IT consultants are expensive. Their presence often indicates a high priority of the project because they are believed to catalyze project development by providing manpower or management capacity and/or through the legitimization of the project which, in turn, should encourage greater acceptance of the management's aims (Ernst & Kieser, 2003; Wieandt, 2006).

The next part sheds more light on the issue of IT consulting within an organizational context, depicting the IT consultants' positions and practices. I will explore the role of IT consultants in the IT implementation processes with respect to the distinction between an IT project and the technochange situation described by Markus (2004).

Information Technology Implementation and IT Consulting within Organizations

IT consultancy is understood broadly as a service provided by an external, independent, professional IT consultant. It aims to design a technology-based solution for a business- or management-related problem in collaboration with the client organization. Goals of IT implementation are usually cost saving, increased efficiency and improved organizational performance (Markus, 2004). If the client demands, a solution is developed and implemented by the IT consultant. This process may also involve the IT department of the organization as well as other departments, affected by, or expected to use, the new technology (Becker, 2005; Bloomfield & Danieli, 1995).

IT consulting implies advising organizations both in the public and in the private sector. Differences may lie in the distinct operational and organizational cultures of the two, but the goals of IT implementation (i.e., cost cutting and increased efficiency) are likely to be the same (Bloomfield & Danieli, 1995; Sturdy, 1997).

Therefore, IT consulting requires knowledge of business processes as well as of technology. IT consultants must be able to adapt to organizational cultures and routines to develop a solution that can be used in the intended way by the user group within the client organization (Markus, 2004). Moreover, IT consultants have to consider different organizational settings and types of organizations because these provide the conditions and context for the project through their power relationships, hierarchies, cultures and mentalities. For example, in project-led organizations there is a tendency to harmonize hierarchical structures with the line organization on the one hand and, on the other hand, the project organization, whose actors seek to gain resources and power to the disadvantage of others (Mickler & Kalkowski, 2002). Being external actors, IT consultants may be pulled into these struggles because they will be assigned to certain positions based either on their status within the hierarchy and/or on the experiences actors in the involved organization have with consultants (Muhr, 2004; Iding, 2000; Mingers, 1997)[3]. Moreover, their position within the hierarchy is linked to certain allocative and authoritative resources to which they do or do not have access and on which they can or cannot rely while completing the project. These resources define their scope of action to a large extent, because, in regard to day-to-day work, their ability to give instructions or their need to rely on the organization's project manager can affect their work, as can their ability to exchange project team members and so on. Thus, these resources are important variables in regard to project size, duration, and budget. An external consultant's interaction within an organization and his or her access to allocative and authoritative resources usually depends on the power relationships within the organization and on the organization's culture.

IT consulting refers to the following aspects of **information technology:** (1) equipment/hardware, (2) software, (3) IT systems and development and (4) IT planning and strategy (including IT outsourcing and IT offshoring), as I point out elsewhere (see chapter XVII in this volume). In order to define the scope of an IT project within an organization it is useful to look at the degree to which the IT implementation affects an organization's structure and operations as well as its working processes. Markus (2004) differentiates among IT projects themselves, technochange situations and organizational change programs[4]. IT projects refer to the performance of

technology, its reliability, cost of operation, and/or maintenance. They are usually conducted by the IT department and "do not require much effort on the part of IT 'users'" (p. 3), i.e., the upgrade of a departmental web-server. IT consultants are involved either to give advice related to products and/or processes, meaning they work within the project team in the IT department as external advisors.

Technochange situations, on the other hand, refer to new IT applications involving complementary organizational change or restructuring of work procedures or operations, i.e. a centralized ERP system to change operations in more or less all departments. IT consultants may be involved on all levels of the project and play a key role in the planning, development and implementation phases (Markus, 2004; Wieandt, 2006).

Organizational change programs are set up to improve an organization's culture and/or performance. Such interventions are focused on the people as well as on the structure and culture of an organization and applied through the use of information technology. Because these projects do not focus on the implementation of technology but rather on the development of an organization, they are omitted here in order to put emphasis on the former two (for an overview of technology in Organization Development practice, see Church et al., 2002).

Considering the various aspects of **IT consulting**, one can conclude that IT consulting on equipment and/or hardware is mainly related to IT projects whereas IT system development and integration as well as IT outsourcing and offshoring are linked to technochange management because these forms affect an organization's operational and working processes to a greater extent. Figure 1 demonstrates the relationship between various dimensions of IT consulting and the characterization of IT projects.

According to Markus (2004), the character of a project is linked to the above with respect to the degree of change. The target outcome of IT projects is mainly dependent on the performance of technology, the system's reliability and the cost of operation and/or maintenance within the project schedule and budget. Therefore, solutions refer more or less to the implementation of new IT, be it software or hardware, such as a new system or server. The basic approach is a project-related method (Sydow et al.,

2004). This suggests that an IT project is performed within a temporary organizational structure led by a project manager who is responsible for an outcome to meet stated specifications on time and budget. As such projects are usually performed within an organization's IT department, the IT project team consists mainly of IT specialists who work with IT vendors and, perhaps, IT consultants; for instance, when the IT department is too small to manage the project alone. Project duration is rather short, taking a few months or half a year.

Technochange situations aim to improve the organization's performance in general. The solution is therefore more broadly conceptualized in the form of new IT applications that require the alteration of organizational procedures and day-to-day routines, e.g. in the case of a new accounting system or data warehouse system. Because various departments may be affected, the team may encompass various specialists from the entire organization including user representatives, managers, and employees (Sydow et al. 2004; Markus, 2004; Gillard, 2005; Koch, 2004). The question of teambuilding depends on time and the intensity of collaboration (Sydow et al., 2004). IT consultants may play key roles here, attending the project manager or fulfilling project management tasks. Project duration is comparatively long, a year or even more (Markus, 2004).

According to Markus (2004), the life cycle of a technochange project encompasses a planning phase when "the technochange idea is proposed, approved, and funded" within the organization (Markus, 2004, p. 9), a project phase when the technological solution is designed, developed, tested and ready to start, and an implementation phase "during which the organization starts operating in a new way" (Markus, 2004, p. 9) in order to obtain the benefits derived from the new operations. Here, I will concentrate on the first three stages, as IT consultants are involved in these. Usually, they leave after having attended the implementation phase (Bloomfield & Danieli, 1995), having provided some training and education as well as performing adjustment tasks (Markus, 2004).

In the following section I will depict the major challenges of IT implementation in regard to IT consultants as well as organizations on the basis of Markus' (2004) distinction and, secondly, offer some solutions and recommendations.

IT CONSULTANCY AS AN IMPLEMENTATION OF CHANGE: CHALLENGES AND SOLUTIONS

The Major Challenges of IT Consultancy in Technochange Projects

Situations involving technochange are a specific case of IT implementation because they require

Figure 1. Technochange versus IT projects and dimensions of IT consulting (Source: Markus, 2004, p. 5; Wieandt in this volume)

Project character	IT project	Technochange
IT consulting dimension	Consulting on equipment / Software	IT System development & integration; outsourcing/off-shoring service providing; IT Strategy & Planning
Target outcome	Technology performance, reliability, cost of operation and/or maintenance, within project schedule and budget parameters	Improvement in organizational performance
Solution	New IT	New IT applications, often in conjunction with complementary organizational change and/or new IT; Restructuring of IT landscape, new division of tasks and processes through IT outsourcing / offshoring
Basic approach	The project	Organizational or business restructuring, followed by an IT project
Involved actors	IT specialists, IT consultants, managers, technology vendors	IT specialists, managers, IT consultants, internal staff specialists, technology vendors; outsourcing/offshoring provider

interaction between IT specialists and users in various departments. The constellation analyzed here is even more complex because IT consultants must mediate among management, IT specialists in the IT department, and specialist employees and/or users, so termed because they are assigned by, instructed by, and have to report to, management. They are, however, also project members interacting with IT department specialists and specialists of various organizational units. Figure 2 illustrates this constellation:

Communication and collaboration efforts as well as the communication partners of IT consultants change during the life cycle of a project. To shed more light on the role of IT consultants, I will concentrate on the phases of the project in which they are mainly involved, namely the planning phase, the project phase, and the implementation phase (Markus, 2004).

The Planning Phase

Before the project begins, IT consultants have to make a "sales pitch" (Bloomfield & Danieli, 1995). They must persuade management that they are trustworthy suppliers of "objective business advice" (Bloomfield & Danieli, 1995, p. 31) as well as specialists in organizational behaviour,

and that the issue on which advice is to be given requires knowledge and technology and business skills and, therefore, they can develop the "right" solution (ibid.). During the beginning phase of project planning, IT consultants communicate mainly with managers as well as with IT specialists in the organization to assess a project's targets, time and budget. Here, disagreements regarding cost and project scope may provoke pressure from IT consultants who might prefer a more expensive solution (to increase their own profit) and/or from managers who prefer a different approach, as well as from other specialists involved (Markus, 2004). This stage is characterized by the power negotiations employed by the involved actors.

A major challenge in this phase of the project is the adequate analysis of the project requirements that, if not properly identified, will cause serious problems both in the project phase and in the implementation phase (Markus, 2004). IT consultants who are mainly in charge of this assessment (Amberg & Wiener, 2004) have to ensure that they receive all the relevant information (see also Armbrüster & Kipping, 2003). On the other hand, results of this analysis may be used for the legitimation of certain requirements either by consultants or managers within the organization (Ernst & Kieser, 2003).

Figure 2. Actors' constellation of technochange situations

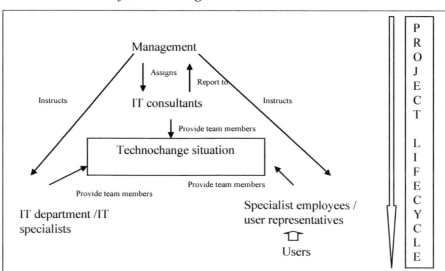

Particularly at the beginning of the communication and collaboration process with IT specialists, IT consultants must establish themselves as technology experts to be accepted, because acceptance forms a basis for trust in work relationships between consultants and employees (Bloomfield & Danieli, 1995; Bohler & Kellner, 2003). A challenge here is the emergence of competition, because a consultant's intervention may be interpreted as offensive by internal specialists, suggesting that the latter's performance is not sufficient to perform the project alone and/or that IT consultants have been assigned to control their work (see, i.e., Constantinidis & Barrett, 2005). According to Niedereichholz (2000), internal IT department members may be characterized as internal IT consultants because they give advice regarding questions of information technology and create small-scale internal solutions for certain problems. Thus, internal IT specialists may criticize external IT consultants and question their knowledge to defend their position as the only IT experts within the organization and to protect their scope of power. Therefore, IT consultants are often confronted with scepticism or criticism at the beginning and may have to persuade the organization's IT department members that collaboration with them will be to their advantage.

Whether IT consultants are perceived as competitors within an organization depends on the organizational culture and on employee interpretation patterns regarding stereotypes, experience and collaboration with consultants (Bohler & Kellner, 2003; Iding, 2000). Moreover, it depends on the concrete situation as well as on the point in time when IT consultants are assigned (Muhr, 2004). For example, a competitive situation is likely to emerge if consultants are assigned to "save" an ongoing project that has several problems.

The Project Phase

In the project phase, the IT solution is developed and built so that, at the end of the phase, the technology is brought to life (Markus, 2004). During this phase, adequate resources for the development process are required. Their provision depends on the organization's embeddedness and the back-

ground of the project. Additionally, IT consultants interact with the project team; So, main challenges are related to communication and problems in teamwork.

According to Markus, a major challenge in the project phase is the problem of inadequate resources (Markus, 2004, p. 9). Following the analytical perspective provided above, we can link this both to allocative and to authoritative resources to which project management and IT consultants have access. This encompasses for instance technological support, technical skills and the number of full-time employees available for the project, as well as the authority to issue instructions and to demand the fulfilment of certain tasks and/or information from operating units.

An IT project team that is supposed to develop a technochange solution often involves team members from various departments and with various backgrounds. In regard to communication with users or user representatives, Gillard (2005) describes three major pitfalls for both IT consultants and IT specialists. Firstly, they may use a language differing from that of employees in regard to the use of technical terms. Secondly, there may be different forms of sense-making between clients and consultants, that is, ways of interpreting things, creating different perceptions leading to confusion. In the case of a large-scale IT project affecting various departments. Thirdly, a major challenge for IT consultants is to address people with different backgrounds and perspectives speaking different occupational languages and to integrate or translate these views into a technological solution. Therefore, one major challenge is to adequately define user requirements and to consider that these may change during the process of development, especially if the project is of a perennial kind (Constantinidis & Barrett, 2005; Markus, 2004). Because they are members of both the technological as well as the business world, this translation is a task pertaining mainly to IT consultants. A second challenge is to design and to deliver an adequate solution (Gillard, 2005). IT consultants are expected to bridge communication problems because they are believed to have experiences in various business areas and to combine their knowledge of technology and business issues. In this sense, according to Bloomfield and Danieli (1995, p. 29), the IT consultant's "discursively negotiated identity" as a technology and business expert has to be maintained throughout the implementation process so that his or her advice is accepted and believed to be legitimate. Their status as experts must be acknowledged by all involved partiesso people trust in their judgement and opinion.

The third challenge addressed by Gillard (2005) touches the above-mentioned issue of power politics. Because a technochange IT project usually changes power relationships, leading to a power gain by one party or individual at the expense of others, a new IT system may encounter opposition. In the case of powerful opponents (i.e. members of the organization's top-management), an IT project may suffer budget cuts, schedule changes, or even—in the worst cas—project cancellation. Therefore, during the project phase, working conditions are subject to organizational change in terms of technological, financial and human resources and are closely linked to the development of organizational structures and leading units.

During the phase of project design and development, these issues may lead to a lack of important information that may cause problems when the system is fully implemented (Markus, 2004). Another issue may be that actors might try to sway project development in a certain direction or impede changes to the system that might place more control on their work. In this sense, system development could turn into a battleground of power negotiations and IT consultants have to be aware of the power positions, interests, and strategies of their co-workers to make sure that the project stays on track. Moreover, Gillard (2005) points out that IT managers may be reluctant to report negative information due to fear of embarrassment or retaliation. This may lead to the postponement of completion dates and the concealment of negative developments that might cause trust issues with superiors. This is especially the case if the projects' outcomes are coupled with the career advancements of IT managers. IT consultants may therefore have to find means of controlling the organization's IT managers in order to impede such developments and at the same time to encourage a

trusting relationship to make sure they are aware of all recent project developments.

In regard to the work of the project team, another issue discussed throughout the research literature on teams and of great importance for the project's outcome, is that of motivation and commitment (see Guzzo & Dickson, 1996; Minssen, 2005; von Rosenstiehl, 2004). Because IT project teams are composed of people with different personalities, various knowledge levels and various skill backgrounds employing a diverse range of technical terminologies, they may have to cope with the issue of creating cohesion within a team and nurturing a climate to enhance motivation and commitment (Koch, 2004). Furthermore, team cohesion depends on the intensity of collaboration (that is, whether there is a lot of collaboration or whether team members fulfil different tasks coordinated by the project manager) and the relationships between team members as well as factors like trust, commitment and motivation (Guzzo & Dickson, 1996). Another important variable is group size which may have negative effects if the group is too big (von Rosenstiehl, 2004). In order to enhance the project and meet required aims, IT consultants have an interest in motivating the project team members (Ernst & Kieser, 2003) and because of the ability attributed to them of overcoming resistance they are believed to have positive effects on the work of the team (Ernst & Kieser, 2003). Moreover, the development of a proper IT solution requires strong commitment from the people involved (Constantinidis & Barrett. 2005), especially if they do this work in addition to their routine job. This may be of more importance if the project is of long duration and is time-consuming (Markus, 2004). The task of enhancing commitment and motivation is more or less handed over to IT consultants if the organization's project manager does not have the ability to or have an interest in, stimulating the team members. Thus, IT consultants may have to develop strategies to motivate their fellow team members and to keep them on the project even if problems arise.

The issue of motivation and commitment may be of even greater importance if it comes to spatially dispersed team work. It may be difficult to create team cohesion due to the lack of face-to-face contact, linked to the out of sight, out of mind problem (see Sapsed & Salter, 2004: Edward & Sidhar, 2002: Hynsell, 2000). Moreover, the risk of free riding increases in virtual teams (ibid.).

If the targets of the project threaten the positions of team members, it may result in resistance within the team. In the case of a project involving IT outsourcing or offshoring which leads in many cases to involuntary reassignment or even job loss, the consequences of the project's goal could obviously threaten a team member's position. That is why the implementation of IT-offshoring is often accompanied by the resistance of employees (Boes, 2005). According to Wedde (2005), employees often use a strategy of direct resistance by employing where it is available and powerful, a shop committee council (Wedde, 2005; Killer & Kruse, 2005). Moreover, team members' strategies of delaying tasks, avoiding work while remaining passive as well as presenting themselves as unready for change (Wieandt, 2006) may require certain actions from project managers and IT consultants. Especially in this context, IT consultants have to cope with the above mentioned strategy of questioning their diagnoses and suggestions, which may be in the form of finding refutations in order to legitimize their practices and routines (Loose, 2001).

Other challenges mentioned by Markus (2004) include the effects of distance and time. Focusing on a certain problem or outcome can be a disadvantage because it may mean that you may "care less or not at all about things outside the project," and "being autonomous means the project team forms a 'knowledge silo' not available to others" (Sydow et al., 2004, p. 1481). According to Markus (2004, p. 10), this problem may arise if the project phase takes a long time, "during which the project team members are organizationally and psychologically distant from the ongoing operations of the organization." This is even the case if specialists from target departments are within the team (see also Symon & Clegg, 2005). Assigned as experts with experience from different organizations, IT consultants could be assumed to be able to solve this problem, however the involved IT consultants will also face this problem if they do not keep in touch with the operations of an organization's target departments. Linked to this issue of time is the problem of possible

changes within the business leading to alterations to the project's targets that could extend a project's duration if major changes are necessary (Markus, 2004).

Moreover, the longer a project takes, the more it loses management's attention and is likely to be terminated before it is finished. The pressure of time is, therefore, assumed to be high in IT projects, and even more so if the organization's top management sets a high priority on it.

Time pressure is also higher when IT consultants are assigned because they cost a lot of money (Iding, 2000). Management, therefore, may use its presence in order to hasten the project team, resulting in pressure on the project team which may have either positive or negative effects. Because time pressure is one of the key characteristics of work in ICT (see i.e. Latniack & Gerstmaier, 2006), IT workers and IT consultants are used to it and have often developed strategies to cope with time constraints, which could be viewed as motivating. (Kratzer, 2003; Latniak & Gerstmaier, 2006). However if time pressure is too high it may have negative consequences, such as a decrease in the motivation and commitment of team members (Latniack & Gerstmaier, 2006; Boes & Trinks, 2006). Another problem may be the different perceptions of deadlines by team members, leading to different work tempos and creating problems in meeting deadlines (Gevers, 2004).

A related downside of time pressure is that there is little time to reflect on and document the process and the knowledge gained (Sydow et al., 2004). In the case of IT projects, this "tyranny of projects" (Koch, 2004) may be a disadvantage in regard to further developments of the system after the first implementation, which may require a detailed documentation of what has been done before to prevent the "wheel" from being "reinvented over and over again" (Sydow et al., 2004, p. 1481; see also Newell et al., 2006).

The Implementation Phase

During the phase of implementation, the organization starts operating with the new technology and "troubleshoots problems associated with technology and new processes" (Markus, 2004, p. 9). Challenges reported here are connected to the use (or lack of use) of the new technology, which are, in turn, related to issues of resistance and misfits or incompatabilities.

In the implementation phase, a major challenge is that of problems arising during the project phase not recognized as problems at the time, either because of the communication issues mentioned above or due to schedule or budget pressures leading to cuts in important features of a project's scope (Markus, 2004). They may be related to the risk of new technology or procedures not working as expected because of problems such as bugged software. Implementation also requires training the userssufficiently in regard to intensity, skill level and relevance to work practice (Markus, 2004; Gillard, 2005).

An important challenge regarding the implementation of technology is the resistance of users or business units affected by the changes in the form of nonuse or misuse of the new system, backlash, and/or pressure to keep old systems and procedures (Markus, 2004). According to Markus (2004), resistance is mainly due to "misfits," defined as "misalignments between a technology or a technochange solution and important dimensions of the organizational setting in which it is used" (Markus, 2004, p. 14). She distinguishes between task or business process misfits, cultural misfits, and incentive misfits. The first relates to a business solution that is "technically adequate but still does not fit the ways people work in particular settings" (Markus, 2004, p. 14). Examples include knowledge bases designed for professionals but also used by novices, or ERP-systems not designed in relation to the area of production in which they are to be applied. Cultural misfits are associated with an organization's culture, portrayed in the words "the way we do things around here" (Markus, 2004, p. 14), as, for example, a system designed to enhance teamwork among workers who are used to working alone. They are also linked to certain aspects of national culture. According to Markus (2004, p. 14), a geographical information system was not accepted in India because the country hasn't got a "map culture", for example. Incentive misfits are closely related to an organization's set of hierarchical and power relationships because

they are linked to authority and reward systems. This applies to systems that do not offer rewards when additional work is required or systems allowing superiors more control or increased ability to interfere, resulting in a decrease of power and autonomy among the workers, e.g., in systems applied to standardize work processes or to set up quality management systems (Boes & Trinks, 2006; Krcmar et al., 2005). Thus, technological or business misfits may be remedied by changes to the system but cultural and incentive misfits, however, are more difficult to resolve, requiring extensive changes to the system or even a new phase of development in the case of cultural misfits, or the establishment of a new incentive structure in the case of incentive misfits. According to Friedberg (1995), all IT-systems will imply new dynamics of power and new asymmetries. These may be reduced but are not disposible.

These challenges may be applied to technochange projects in general. IT consultants are especially concerned because they portray themselves as experts in business, technology and organizational change (Bloomfield & Danieli, 1995), and such challenges should not occur within the technochange or large-scale IT projects they attend. When these problems do occur, IT consultants find themselves in an awkward position as their reputations may suffer, making it hard for them to gain further assignments in other organizations (Ernst & Kieser, 2003; Fincham & Clark, 2002; Faust, 2000).

Summary

In conclusion, a technochange project presents certain risks, involving issues related to one's relationships with members of the organization, communication and teamwork challenges, power politics and the influence of distance and time, any of which may occur throughout the planning, project and/or implementation phases of a project's life cycle. Figure 3 provides an overview.

During a project, IT consultants are forced to deal with issues arising from their relationships with other organizational actors. A main challenge is to overcome mistrust, skepticism and criticism and to avoid competition with the IT department.

IT consultants must be sure they have complete information on every process in order to make a complete and sufficient assessment. Given that the implementation of information technology is an issue of organizational power politics, IT consultants will also have to deal with power challenges throughout the whole process. Issues related to teamwork occur mainly in the project phase where teamwork is necessary. Certain challenges are interrelated; for example, problems of distance and time may lead to task or business misfits or cultural misfits in the form of communication problems.

The following section will provide some recommendations and solutions to the above–mentioned challenges.

Recommendations and Solutions

A major challenge for IT consultants at the beginning of technochange projects is to win the ac-

ceptance and trust of others as a basis for further collaboration. They achieve this mainly through displays of competence, knowledge and an amiable personality. Bloomfield and Danieli (1995) identify five main stratagems used by IT consultants to make themselves indispensable to clients as well as to maintain their identity as technology and business experts throughout the project. These stratagems rely on the knowledge and competence of the consultant, as well as their being able to classify problems as either of a social or technical nature, and referring to the example of significant others (that is, other organizations) in order to convince a client of the necessity of a certain IT strategy for the advancement of the organization. The first stratagem is to present themselves as representatives of technology and therefore "obligatory passage points" (Bloomfield & Danieli, 1995, p. 28), so that an organization will then perceive that the selection and implementation of an IT system or a new IT strategy requires the service of IT consultants. In order to present themselves as trustworthy, they claim to be independent experts on technology and

Figure 3. Challenges related to IT implementation and IT consultancy

	IT consultant's relations to actors	communication	teamwork	Power politics	Distance and time effects
Planning	• Non-acceptance, scepticism, criticism of managers, IT specialists and employees • Situation of competition • Mistrust • Lack of information in assessment	• Semantics: different technical languages • Sense-making • Adequate definition of user requirements		• Position of consultants within the organization • Access to allocative and authoritative resources • Interests of actors within the organization • Budget and time constraints of the project	
Project	• Resistance within the team	• Design a proper solution • Semantics: different technical languages • Sense-making • Adequate definition of user requirements	• Insufficient motivation & commitment • Resistance within team (avoidance, delay, refutation, passiveness, free riding) • Virtuality	• Attempts to push the project in certain directions • Budget and time cuts • Conciliation of negative developments	• Ongoing developments within the organization – change of business needs • Time pressure
implementation	• Resistance within the operational units	• Deliver a proper solution • Task or business misfits • Cultural misfits	• Deliver inadequate training and support of users	• Incentive misfits	

"stress that their own interests in terms of securing further work are best served by working closely with the user organization in developing a system which is tailored to the specific needs of that organization." (Bloomfield & Danieli, 1995, p. 29). Clients must be convinced that IT consultants provide objective technology and business advice and therefore IT consultants must persuade their clients that they are tackling real problems when diagnosing certain aspects of technology to be optimized and that their strategies and solutions are genuinely required by the client organization. The reciprocal process of identity construction is important here, as consultants must work side by side with members of the client organization, and as both sides will form opinions about the other, it is important that the IT consultant make himself accepted through such stratagems in order to carry out his work and achieve his goals. IT consultants might also allude to an organization's competitors in order to influence the client in a positive or negative way:

Positively, by persuading clients of what can be achieved by using an IT system (with the consultants' instrumental role in this achievement obviously being highlighted); and negatively, in terms of the client organization's need to increase effectiveness in the light of competitors' achievements. (Bloomfield & Danieli, 1995, p. 30).

Although these previously identified stratagems apply mainly to a consultant's relationships with management which must be convinced to hire the IT consultant in the first place, studies regarding consultants' leadership abilities in project teams are also relevant. In order to overcome situations of competition with IT department members as well as resistance within the team and to enhance commitment and motivation, IT consultants use certain strategies of impression management. Sosik and Jung (2003) discovered that IT consultants, in order to present themselves as charismatic leaders, employ of a set of five strategies, namely:

(a) exemplification to present oneself as a worthy role model, (b) ingratiation to make oneself more attractive or likable to others, (c) self-promotion

to present oneself as highly competent with regard to certain skills or abilities, (d) intimidation to present oneself as a dangerous and potent person who is willing to hurt or challenge others, and (e) supplication to appear needy with the purpose of soliciting aid from others. (Sosik & Jung, 2003, p. 239)

In order to gain the influence of superiors, IT consultants also use ingratiation strategies such as flattery or friendliness (Sosik & Jung, 2003). The strategies used to co-ordinate subordinate people depend on context as well as on personality. IT consultants who are more self-aware are more likely to use positive strategies to co-ordinate others, indicating a more communicative style. During my research based on in-depth interviews with IT consultants (Wieandt, 2006), I discovered three further strategies which can be linked to a positive attitude, namely:

- **The strategy of involvement:** Through frequent information and feedback, the IT consultant makes a person feel involved in the project.
- **The strategy of communication:** IT consultants use informal communication channels to build trust and alleviate fears.
- **The strategy of motivation:** Consultants try to motivate team members by promoting the possibility of career advancement through job enrichment and experience gained in the carrying out of management and coordination tasks.

According to Sosik and Jung (2003), IT consultants use different strategies depending on the target audience (see also Wieandt, 2006). The consultants in my study reported that they first analyze the responsibilities and authority of the people within an organization, classifying them as either "important" or "negligible," and then decide which strategy they should use in order to convince employees and managers to collaborate or to enhance motivation among employees. This requires the ability to adjust to certain characters and personalities as well as empathy and intuition in order to successfully employ these strategies successfully. There is also some indication that IT consultants use these strategies as a substitution for authoritative resources to which they usually do not have access in organizations (Wieandt, 2006). Therefore, these strategies may also be used as a means through which to cope with issues of power politics. However the strategies used are limited to an extent because at a certain point IT consultants require the authority and support of project managers and top-managers in order to overcome resistance (Wieandt, 2006). Therefore, to call upon authority can be considered another strategy.

In the context of teamwork, the creation of team cohesion, a team identity, and a common goal may be useful. This therefore requires the ability to be a charismatic leader. In regard to problems arising from virtual teamwork, solutions include fostering face-to-face meetings (mainly in the kick-off phase) (Hynsell, 2000), as well as enhancing the effectiveness of electronic communication tools (Joisten, 2005) and providing feedback (Geister, Konradt & Hertel, 2006).

Reflecting on the challenges posed by communication issues, Gillard (2005) suggests some solutions aimed at improving the communication skills of project managers and IT consultants. For instance, they should either avoid technical terminology or explain things in a way that the receiver can understand, restate complex information or things that were not understood and ask for feedback in the communication process. Moreover, IT consultants and the project manager must develop the ability to "glean accurate and sufficient information from the customer as well as the ability to efficiently transmit ideas, knowledge, images, and other information to the customer" (Gillard, 2005, p. 40) in order to avoid communication problems. This is achieved mainly by asking adequate questions, a method requiring the ability to put oneself into the position of the user. Furthermore, Gillard (2005) suggests the use of models developed to achieve effective communication, such as the Precision Model by McMaster and Grinder (Bostrom, 1989) or the communication model suggested by Cronan (1984). In order to analyze communication patterns and difficulties, the communication model by Schulz von Thun (2006) may also be used.

In regard to power politics, IT consultants use the above-described strategies to achieve the acceptance of their proposed solutions. Being viewed as advisors and experts, they are usually not given any access to authoritative resources during a project, therefore they must particularly rely on the project manager's competency as a leader and his or her ability to issue instructions and co-ordinate employees (Wieandt, 2006). These strategies therefore are very important instruments of influence during the process of implementation. In order to limit an IT consultant's influence, the IT project manager must be aware of these strategies and be prepared to exercise his or her own power and authority. A good strategy for both parties would be to develop common goals and collaborate, their objective being the enhancement of the project as their objective. Thus, IT consultants and project managers could become a powerful coalition in regard to preventing budget cuts and further time constraints during the project phase which may be forced on the project by the top-management.

The management of distance and time issues is very important when it comes to the success of IT projects and the prevention of task, business or cultural misfits. A strategy suggested by Markus (2004) and Gillard (2005) is prototyping, referring to a strong involvement of the user by developing a small simulation or prototype of a system to be implemented and tested by users. In order to avoid time and distance hindrances, preference is given to a series of short projects to deliver measurable organizational benefits. Moreover, during test implementation phases users may be involved via feedback processes (Krcmar et al., 2005). This requires close collaboration between users and IT specialists and consultants as well as intensive communication. The advantages of prototyping include, according to Markus (2004), the minimization of the risk of failure due to the smaller project sizes which, nevertheless, bring significant results. Moreover, results may motivate users to undertake additional change as they experience success.

Furthermore, the strategy of prototyping may prevent incentive misfits, since features of the new IT system that prove incompatible with the organization's existing reward system will be identified throughout the incrementally-organized development of the project and incongruities can be adjusted before they cause serious problems.

Summing up, there are numerous strategies IT consultants and organizations can employ to respond to challenges. The strategies used by IT consultants to compensate for their lack of access to authority in organizations may be used to exert power in political contexts, to overcome skepticism and resistance or to win trust and acceptance. To enhance the commitment and motivation of the project team by strategies of impression management, feedback and, in the case of virtual communication, an enhanced use of electronic communication tools may be used. In order to avoid misunderstanding between IT specialists and users, a precise mode of communication is needed and may be achieved through the use of communication models as well as the communication skills of IT consultants and specialists.

All solutions discussed here are limited by the will of the involved parties. For instance, powerful actors may have the ability to set up insurmountable obstacles to the implementation process, such as the withdrawal of the budget, which might result in the cancellation of the project despite all strategies of conviction. Therefore, the successful implementation of information technology depends on the employment of allocative resources such as budget, personnel and time as well as on the strategies and abilities of concerned parties. The importance of large-scale IT projects intended to improve an organization's performance is likely to increase if the strategic use of IT is further promoted. Moreover, IT may be used to connect spatially dispersed organizations and can thus be linked to the future of the global development of business and economics. In the next section I will introduce future trends of IT consulting associated with these developments.

FUTURE TRENDS

Due to the fact that the IT market is growing and a rising number of software and hardware suppliers will also be offering consultancy services, we will face an increased complexity in consulting environments and relationships among organizations. With the frequency of mergers and acquisitions in the IT consulting market escalating and the tendency for IT vendors to offer more extensive consulting services, the identity of IT consultants and IT vendors will be blurred more and more. As a result, it will become increasingly difficult for IT consultants to portray themselves as objective and neutral, both characteristics very important for their identity as experts. Consequently, one of the aims of IT consultancy firms might be to create a more distinguishable service for clients. In this context, the tendency to offer IT outsourcing and offshoring services could provide a chance for IT consultants to take on several tasks regarding the (re)structuring of processes, including the setup of the organization offshore and the administration of standardization and other change processes within the home organization (Boes & Schwemmle, 2004). For example, one can observe that big IT consultancy firms such as Accenture or Capgemini offer software development, system development, integration and maintenance services for their clients, produced in low cost locations all over the world. Consequently, IT consultants have to develop communication skills, not only in order to function effectively when working with client organizations but also within their own organization, because they are confronted with colleagues from other countries with whom they must collaborate.

The development of IT consultancy is closely linked to the development of IT strategy. Because the need for an IT strategy fosters the assignment of IT consultants; therefore consultants have an interest in promoting this issue. Moreover, the issue of IT strategy is closely related to innovation. The strategic use of information technology is believed to improve an organization's performance in terms of the optimization of business processes and operations. As a result, the design of an IT system is becoming more and more linked to the business side of an organization. Therefore, IT consultants are likely to specialize in certain branches or sub-branches, as well as dedicating themselves to certain technologies in order to deliver sophisticated and well-developed solutions.

In brief, to facilitate the sustainable implementation of information technology, IT consultants have to be aware of the social and political environment in which they work. The use of change management approaches and the consideration of psychological factors could be useful in overcoming resistance from employees in a positive way and fostering further motivation and commitment within an organization.

CONCLUSION

The collaboration of IT consultants and the success of a project depend on a broad range of factors as demonstrated in the previous sections. The organizational setting determineing hierarchical and organizational structures is a decisive factor in regard to the project team and the IT consultant's access to allocative and authoritative resources. Other decisive factors include whether or not the organization is project-based, with a homogeneous structure, or is project-led, with both a line and project organization competing with each other to produce different modes of co-ordination. At the same time, access to these resources is subject to power politics within the organization linked to the interests and strategies of organizational actors in regard to the new information technology system. Thus, the implementation of information technology is a very complex process comprising various groups of actors with different interests and strategies that vary depending on the scope of the project. Considering the phases of a project, specifically the planning, project and implementation phases, IT consultants may be confronted with problems of non-acceptance, mistrust, competition, scepticism and criticism which may lead to a lack of information sharing during the assessment as well as a lack of collaboration among co-workers within the team. Consequently, at the beginning of project they must establish themselves as trustworthy, knowledgeable and friendly technology and business experts within the organization. Being the linking element between business and technology,

they are mainly responsible for facilitating communication between IT users and IT specialists. As such, they have to overcome differences in occupational languages, reconcile different perspectives and define user requirements properly using communication models. They must alsoclearly explain concepts, ask for feedback, attain usable and accurate information from users and transmit ideas to users. Moreover, in supporting the project manager they have to enhance team commitment and motivation and may have to overcome resistance issues within the team that may occur during the project phase. In order to cope with challenges concerning relations and communication, IT consultants develop certain strategies and stratagems which assist them in overcoming resistance, convincing people and creating motivation. They present themselves as obligatory passage points on the way to an adequate technological solution, as independent and objective experts who are devisors of strategy and advisors to clients in need. In this context, an organization's competitors are used as comparison points to identify problems within the client organization, so that the consultant can seem valuable when providing the solution. In order to exert power and to persuade employees and project managers, IT consultants use positive strategies of impression management such as exemplification, ingratiation, self-promotion, supplication, involvement, communication and motivation as well as negative strategies such as intimidation. To avoid incentive, cultural and task or business misfits of the new system and to overcome distance and time issues, the model of prototyping is recommended in literature, comprising a step-by-step "hands-on"-approach (Gillard, 2005, p. 41) and a high involvement of users, splitting large-scale projects into several smaller ones, with significant results (Markus, 2004).

FUTURE RESEARCH DIRECTIONS

In view of the research on IT consultancy, there are still a lot of open questions. A primary issue is that of researching how the relationships between IT consultants and organizations differ, and how the processes used differ in the implementation process depending on the size of the organization, how it functions and other factors of its background. Furthermore, the question of an organization's structure needs to be addressed, because structural factors are assumed to make a difference in project environments. In this regard, a comparison of consultancy processes in different organizational and structural settings might show how these factors are affected by the organizational environment. The impact of variables such as the client organization's size, type or branch should be clarified. Possible differences in the projection methods of organizations functioning within various economic sectors may lead to specific types of organizational cultures linked to specific market conditions or mental characteristics of an occupation. Another interesting question addresses collaboration between internal and external consultants, since there exists little research on internal IT consultants (see Niedereichholz, 2000) up until now. Considering the relevance of IT consultants' strategies of impression management, it would be useful to examine and compare IT consultancy processes across countries and branches to find possible differences in strategies. Analysing the different dimensions of teamwork, collaboration and coordination in the context of power structures and actors' strategies would be very interesting and enlightening in regard to the implementation process and the issues of misuse and non-use. In this respect, the question of the place of emotion in the workplace should be investigated as well (Hochschild, 2003; Rastetter, 2001), as it addresses coping strategies of IT consultants. Adequate methods would include qualitative case studies (Yin, 2004).

The influence of the size, type or culture of the consultancy firm (i.e. whether it specializes in IT consultancy or whether it offers these services among others as do management consultancy firms) could also be the focus of further research projects. For example, it might be suggested that career models within consultancy firms play an important role in regard to the strategies consultants use, because they create specific rationalisms, perceptions and pressures.

An exploration of IT consulting focused on organizations might also provide more information on the role of IT consultants regarding innovation and organizational change. Given that the implementation of information technology is subject to power politics, far more research needs to done in regard to micro-politics and IT consulting processes in organizations. In this context an interesting question might be that of exploring what happens after the IT consultants have left an organization (see Sturdy, 1997). Moreover, the question of the evaluation of consultancy services is important, including an exploration of criteria such as customer satisfaction, the functioning or use of the system, or monetary outcome.

In order to increase our basic understanding of IT consultancy, a glance at the different aspects or fields of consultancy work discussed in this chapter might be useful for collecting empirical information by identifying differences such as process duration or strategies used. In this realm, the question as to whether and how a specific technology or system with different requirements and scopes leads to certain specific outcomes might be posed as well.

Bearing in mind recent economic developments, the issue of globalization should be considered in its various dimensions. For example, in IT off- and nearshoring processes IT consultants often mediate between onsite and offshore locations, structuring working processes, collaboration, knowledge transfer and coordination. Their work is also affected by the worldwide issue of quality standards. Moreover, it is observable that network relations between client and consultancy companies can arise, comprising several client firms and two or more consultancy firms in one joint venture project.

REFERENCES

Amberg, M. & Wiener, M. (2004). *Projektmanagement im Rahmen des IT-Offshoring: Planungsphase*. Working Paper No. 10, Friedrich-Alexander-Universität Erlangen-Nürnberg, Lehrstuhl für Betriebswirtschaftslehre, Wirtschaftsinformatik III.

Armbrüster, T. & Kipping, M. (2003). Types of Knowledge and the Client-Consultant Interaction. In. K. Sahlin-Andersson & L. Engwall (Eds.), *The Expansion of Management Knowledge: Carriers, Flows, and sources* (pp. 96-110). Stanford: Stanford University Press.

Becker, A. (2004). Wirtschaftswissenschaften und Beratung. In. F. Nestmann, F. Engel, & U. Sickendiek (Eds.), *Das Handbuch der Beratung, Band 1: Disziplinen und Zugänge* (pp. 193-205), Tübingen, Germany: DGVT.

Bloomfield, B. P. & Danieli, A. (1995). The Role of Management Consultants in the Development of Information Technology: The indissoluble Nature of socio-political and technical skills. *Journal of Management Studies, 32*(1), pp. 23-46.

Bloomfield, B. P. & Vurdubakis, T. (2002). The Vision Thing: Constructing Technology and the Future in Management Advice. In. R. Fincham & T. Clark (Eds.), *Critical Consulting. New Perspectives on the Management Advice Industry* (p. 115-129), Oxford: Blackwell.

Boes, A. (2005). Auf dem Weg in die Sackgasse? Internationalisierung im Feld Software und IT-Services. In. A. Boes & M. Schwemmle (Eds.), *Bangalore statt Böblingen? Offshoring und Internationalisierung im IT-Sektor* (pp. 13-65). Hamburg, Germany: VSA-Verlag.

Boes, A. & Schwemmle, M. (2004). *Herausforderung Offshoring.* Internationalisierung und Auslagerung von IT-Dienstleistungen. Düsseldorf: Edition Hans Böckler Stiftung.

Boes, A. & Trinks, K. (2006). *Theoretisch bin ich frei!* Interessenhandeln und Mitbestimmung in der IT-Industrie, Berlin: Edition Sigma.

Bostrom, R. (1989). Successful application of communication techniques to improve the systems development process. *North Holland Information & Management, 17*(1989), 275-295.

Bohler, K. F. & Kellner, H. (2003). *Auf der Suche nach Effizienz. Die Arbeitsweisen von Beratern in der modernen Wirtschaft.* New York/Frankfurt am Main: Campus.

Burns, T. & Stalker, G.M. (1961). *The Management of Innovation.* London: Routledge Kegan & Paul.

Church, A. H., Gilbert, M., Oliver, D. H., Paquet, K. & Surface, C. (2002). The role of technology in organization development and change. *Advances in Developing Human Resources, 4*(4), 493-511.

Constantinidis, P. & Barrett, M. (2006). Large-scale ICT innovation, power, and organizational change. The case of a regional health information network. *The Journal of Applied Sciences, 42*(1), 76-90.

Craig, D. & Tinaikar, R. (2006). Divide and conquer: Rethinking IT strategy. *McKinsey Quarterly 12*(1), 4-13.

Cronan, T.P. (1984). Application system development: A communication model for business users and DP personnel. *Data Base 16*(1), 21.26.

Engwall, M. (1998). The project concept(s): on the unit of analysis in the study of project management. In Lundin, R.A. & Midler, C. (Eds.), *Projects as areas for renewal and learning processes* (pp. 25-35). Boston: Kluwer.

European Information Technology Observatory Group (EITO) (2006). *European Information Technology Observatory 2006.* Berlin.

Ernst, B. & Kieser, A. (2003). In Search of Explanations for the Consulting Explosion. In. K. Sahlin-Andersson & L. Engwall (Eds.), *The Expansion of Management Knowledge: Carriers, Flows, and sources* (pp. 47-73). Stanford: Stanford University Press.

Faust, M. (2000). Warum boomt die Managementberatung? Und warum nicht zu allen Zeiten und überall. *SOFI_Mitteilungen, 28*(2), 59-85.

Fincham, R. & Clark, T. (2002) (Eds.), *Critical Consulting.* New Perspectives on the Management Advice Industry. Oxford: Blackwell.

Friedberg, E. (1995). *Ordnung und Macht.* Dynamik organisierten Handelns, New York/Franfurt a.M.: Campus Verlag.

Geister, S., Konradt, U. & Hertel, G. (2006). Effects of process feedback on motivation, satisfaction, and performance in virtual teams. *Small Group Research, 37*(5), 459-489.

Gevers, J.M.P. (2004). *It's about time we align. Meeting deadlines in Project Teams.* Eindhoven: Technische Universiteit Eindhoven.

Giddens, A. (1984). *The Constitution of Society.* Outline of the Theory of Structuration. Berkeley / Los Angeles: University of California Press.

Gillard, S. (2005). Managing IT-projects: communication pitfalls and bridges, in. *Journal of Information Science, 31*(1), 37-43.

Guzzo, Richard A. & Dickson, Marcus W. (1996). Teams in organizations: Recent research on performance and effectiveness. *Annual Review Psychology, 47*, 307-338.

Hochschild, A. R. (2003/1983). *The Managed Heart.* Commercialization of Humans Feelings, Berkeley/Los Angeles / London: University of California Press.

Hynsell, Deborah (2000). Global Teamwork for a global resource, in Professional Communication Conference, 2000. In *Proceedings of 2000 Joint IEEE International and 18th Annual Conference on Computer Documentation (IPCC/SIGDOC 2000).* Retrieved July 17, 2006 from, http://ieeexplore.ieee.org/servlet/opac?punumber=7114

Iding, H. (2000). *Hinter de Kulissen der Organisationsberatung.* Qualitative Fallstudien von Beratungsprozessen im Krankenhaus. Opladen: Leske und Budrich.

Joisten, M. (2005). Aneignung und Nutzung von Instant Messaging in Organisationen: Eine strukturationstheoretische Analyse, In C. Stary (Ed.), *Mensch und Computer 2005: Kunst und Wissenschaft—Grenzüberschreitung der interaktiven ART* (pp. 45-40). München: Oldenbourg Verlag.

Kennedy Information (2004). *The Systems Integration Marketplace: Key data, Forecasts & Trends Worldwide.* Executive Summary, Peterborough, NH USA: Kennedy Information.

Killer, R. & Kruse, S. (2005). Offshoring und betriebliche Interessenvertretung. Ein Bericht aus der Praxis (T-Systems). In. A. Boes & M. Schwemmle (Ed.s), *Bangalore statt Böblingen? Offshoring und Internationalisierung im IT-Sektor* (pp. 97-105), Hamburg: VSA-Verlag.

Koch, C. (2004). The Tyranny of Projects: Teamworking, Knowlegde Production and Management in Consulting Engineering. *Economic and Industrial Democracy, 25*(2), 277-300.

Kratzer, N. (2003). *Arbeitskraft in Entgrenzung. Grenzenlose Anforderungen, erweiterte Spielräume, begrenzte Ressourcen.* Berlin: Edition Sigma.

Krcmar, H., Böhmann, T. & Walter, S. (2005). Wissensmanagement im Kontext der IT Infrastructure Library (ITIL). In. N. Gronau, P. Pawlowski, T. Schildhauer, P. Schütt (Eds.). *KnowTech 2005. 7. Konferenz zum Einsatz von Knowledge Management in Wirtschaft und Verwaltung* (pp. 491-499), München.

Latniak, E. & Gerlmaier, A. (2006). *Zwischen Innovation und alltäglichem Kleinkrieg. Zur Belastungssituation von IT-Beschäftigten- Paper of IAT-Report* (2006, 4). Gelsenkirchen: Institut Arbeit und Technik.

Loose, Achim (2001). Netzwerkberatung und Beratungsnetzwerke—Strategischer Wandel durch externe Reflexion reflexiver Strukturation. In G. Ortmann & J. Sydow (Eds.), *Strategie und Strukturation. Strategisches Management von Unternehmen, Netzwerken und Konzernen* (pp. 235-270), Wiesbaden: Gabler.

Marwaha, S. & Willmott, P. (2006). Managing IT for scale, speed, and innovation. *McKinsey Quarterly, 12*(1), 14-21.

Markus, M. L. (2004). Technochange management: unsing IT to drive organizational change. *Journal of Information Technology, 19*(2004),3-19.

McKinlay, A. (2002). The limits of knowledge management. New Technology. *Work and Employment, 17*(2),76-88.

Mickler, O. & Kalkowski, P. (2002). Zwischen Emergenz und Formalisierung—Zur Projektifizierung von Organisation und Arbeit in der Informationswirtschaft. *SOFI-Mitteilungen 30*(4), 119-134.

Mingers, S. (1997). *Systematische Organisationsberatung.* Eine Konfrontation von Theorie und Praxis, Frankfurt am Main / New York: Campus Verlag.

Minssen, H. (2005). Challenges of Teamwork in Production: Demands of Communication. *Organization Studies 27*(1), 103-124.

Muhr, T. (2004). *Beratung und Macht. Mikropolitische Fallstudie einer Organisationsberatung, Dissertation Thesis, Bielefeld.* Germany, Retrieved May 10, 2006 from, http://deposit.ddb.de/cgi-bin/dokserv?idn=975390678

Newell, S., Bresnen, M., Edelmann, L., Scarbrough, H. & Swan, J. (2006). Sharing knowlegde across projects. *Management Learning, 37*(2),167-185.

Niedereichholz, C. (2000). *Internes Consuting. Grundlagen, Praxisbeispiele, Spezialthemen.* München / Wien: Oldenbourg.

Orlikowski, W. (1992, November). Learning from NOTES: Organizational Issues in Groupware Implementation. In *CSCW Proceedings, 362-369.*

Ortmann, G., Windeler, A., Becker, A., Schulz, H. J. (1990). *Computer und Macht in Organisationen.* Mikropolitische Analysen, Opladen: Westdeutscher Verlag.

Ortmann, G., Sydow, J. & Windeler, A. (1997). Organisation als reflexive Struktur. In. G. Ortmann, J. Sydow, K. Türk (Eds.). *Theorien der Organisation. Die Rückkehr der Gesellschaft* (pp. 315-354). Wiesbaden: Westdeutscher Verlag.

Rastetter, D. (2001). Emotionsarbeit—Betriebliche Steuerung und individuelles Erleben. In Schreyögg, G. & Sydow, J. (Eds.), *Emotion und Management, Managementforschung No. 11* (pp. 111-134). Wiesbaden/Germany: Gabler.

Rosenstiel, L. v. (2004). Kommunikation in Arbeitsgruppen. In. Heinz Schuler (Eds.) *Lehrbuch Organisationspsychologie* (pp. 387-438). Bern, Göttingen, Toronto, Seattle: Hans Huber.

Rothberg, D. (2006). *IT-consulting services hit a growth spurt.* In e-week enterprise news & reviews. Retrieved June 3, 2006 from, http://www.eweek.com/article2/0,1759,1950788,00.asp

Sapsed, J. & Salter, A. (2004). Postcards from the edge: Local communities, global programs and boundary objects. *Organization Studies, 25*(9),1515-1534.

Schreyögg, G. (2000). *Organisation.* Wiesbaden: Gabler Verlag.

Schulz von Thun, F. (2006). *Miteinander reden.* Störungen und Klärungen. Reinbeck bei Hamburg: Rowohlt Taschenbuch.

Soederlund, J. (2004). Building theories of project management: past research, questions fort he future. *International journal of project management, 22*(3),183-192.

Sosik, J. & Jung, D.I. (2003). Impression management strategies and performance in information technology consulting. The role of self-other rating agreement on charismatic leadership. *Management Communication Quarterly, 17*(2),233-268.

Sturdy, A. (1997). The Consultancy Process—An Insecure Business? *Journal of Management Studies, 34*(3),389-413.

Sydow, J., Lindkvist, L. & DeFilippi, R. (2004). Project-based organizations, embeddedness and repositories of knowlegde: Editorial. *Organization Studies, 25*(9), 1475-1489.

Symon, G. & Clegg, C. (2005). Construction identity and participation during technological change. *Human Relations, 58*(9),1141-1166.

Wedde, P. (2005). Rechtliche Handlungsmöglichkeith von betrieblichen Interessenvertretern. In A. Boes, & M. Schwemmle (Eds.), *Bangalore statt Böblingen?* Offshoring und Internationalisierung im IT-Sektor (pp. 119-1329). Hamburg: VSA-Verlag.

Wieandt, M. (2006). *Teamwork when implementing off-shoring: Exploring the German ICT sector.* Paper presented at the IWOT X Workshop in Groningen, The Netherlands, September 6-8 2006.

Wieandt, M. (2007). Information technology consulting in global information technology. In M. Raisinghani (Eds.), Global Information Management in the Digital Economy (chapter XVII). Hershey, USA: Information Science Reference. Forthcoming.

Wieandt, M. (2008). *Berater in IT-Offshoring-Projekten: Mitler und Partner.* Paper presented at the MKWI Conference in Munich, Germany, February 26-28, 2008.

Yin, R. (2003). *Case study research.* Design and methods. Charlotte, NC: B&T.

ADDITIONAL READINGS

Abrahamson, E. (1996a). Management Fashion. In *Academy of Management Review, 21,*254-285.

Abrahamson, E. (1996b), Technical and Aesthetic Fashion, In Czarniawska, B. and G. Sevón (Eds.), *Translating Organizational Change* (pp. 117-138). Berlin and New York: De Gruyter.

Abrahamson, E. (1991). Managerial fads and fashions: The diffusion and rejection of innovations. *Academy of Management Review, 18*(3),586-612.

Abrahamson, E. & Fairchild, G. (1999). Management fashion: Lifecycles, triggers and collective Learning Processes. Administrative Science Quarterly, 44 (6),708-40.

Alvarez, J. L. (Ed.), (1998). *The Diffusion and Consumption of Business Knowledge.* London: Macmillan.

Alvarez, J.L. (1998). The Sociological Tradition and the Spread and Institutionalization of Knowledge for Action, In, Alvarez, J.L. (Ed.), *The Diffusion and Consumption of Business Knowledge* (13-57). London: Macmillan.

Alvesson, M. (1993). Organization as rhetoric: Knowledge-intensive firms and the struggle with ambiguity. *Journal of Management Studies, 30,*997-1015

Alvesson, M. & Johansson, A. W. (2002): Professionalism and Politics in Management Consultancy Work, in: Clark, T. & Fincham, R. (eds.): *Critical Consulting. New Perspectives on the Management Advice Industry* (pp. 228-246) Oxford: Blackwell.

Amorim, C. & Kipping, M. (1999). Selling consultancy services: The Portuguese case in historical and comparative perspective. *Business and Economic History, 28*(1),45-56.

Arias, M.E. & Guillén, M. (1998). The Transfer of Organizational Techniques Across Borders: Combining Neo-Institutional and Comparative Perspectives. In Alvarez, J.L. (Ed.), *The Diffusion and Consumption of Business Knowledge* (pp. 110-137). London: Macmillan.

Armbrüster, T. (2000, July). *Towards a Political Economy of Management Consulting: The Case for a Macro Approach*, Paper presented at the 16th EGOS Colloquium, Helsinki.

Armbrüster, Th. & Kipping, M. (2003). Strategy consulting at the crossroads: Technical change and shifting market conditions for top-level advice. *International Studies of Management and Organization, 32,*19-42.

Beard, J.W. (1996). *Impression Management and Information Technology.* London: Quorum Books.

Berglund, J. and Werr, A. (2000). The Invincible Character of Management Consulting Rhetorics. *Organization, 7*(4),633-655.

Berthoin Antal, A., Lenhardt, U. & Rosenbrock, R.. Barriers to organizational learning. In Dierkes, M. et al. (Eds.), *Organizational Learning and Knowledge* (pp.865-885), Oxford: Oxford University Press.

Berthoin Antal, A. & Krebsbach-Gnath, C. (2001). Consultants as Agents of Organizational Learning: The Importance of Marginality. In Dierkes, M. et al. (Eds.), *Organizational Learning and Knowledge* (pp. 462-486), Oxford: Oxford University Press.

Bloomfield, B. P. & McLean, C. (1996). Madness and Organization: Informed Management and Empowerment, In Orlikowski, W. J., G. Walsham & DeGross, J. I. (Eds.), *Information Technology and Changes in Organizational Work* (pp. 371-393). London: Chapman & Hall.

Bloomfield, B. P. & R. Coombs (1992). Information technology, control and power: The centralization and decentralization debate revisited. *Journal of Management Studies, 29*,459-484.

Bryman, A. (1996). Leadership in Organizations. In Clegg, S., Hardy, C. & Nord, W. R. (Eds.), *Handbook of Organization Studies* (pp. 276-292), London et al.: Sage.

Burt, R. S. (2004). Structural holes and good ideas. *American Journal of Sociology, 110*(2),349-399.

Davidson, E. (2006). A technological frames perspective on information technology and organizational change. *The Journal of Applied Behavioral Sciences, 42*(1),23-39.

Dillon, J.T. (2003). The use of questions in organizational consulting. *The Journal of Applied Behavioral Sciences, 39*(4),438-452.

Dougherty, D. (1996). Organizing for Innovation. In Clegg, S., Hardy, C. & Nord, W. R. (Eds.), *Handbook of Organization Studies* (pp. 424-439), London et al.: Sage.

Faust, M. (2002). Consultancies as Actors in Knowledge Arenas: Evidence from Germany, In Kipping, M. & Engwall, L. (Eds.), *Management Consulting: Emergence and Dynamics of a Knowledge Industry* (pp. 146-163). Oxford: Oxford University Press.

Fincham, R. (1999*a*). The consultant-client relationship: Critical perspectives on the management of organizational change. *Journal of Management Studies, 36*(3),331-351.

Fincham, R. (1999*b*). *Business process reengineering: Ideas, interests and impact.* Paper presented at the International Conference on Professions and Management. University of Stirling.

Fincham, R. & Evans, M. (1999). The consultants' offensive: Reengineering—from fad to technique. *New Technology and Employment, 14*,32-44.

Fineman, S. (1996). Emotion and Organizing. In Clegg, S., Hardy, C. & Nord, W. R. (Eds.), *Handbook of Organization Studies* (pp. 526-542), London et al.: Sage.

Hardy, C. & Clegg, S.R. (1996). Some Dare Call it Power. In Clegg, S., Hardy, C. & Nord, W. R. (Eds.), *Handbook of Organization Studies* (pp. 622-641), London et al.: Sage.

Kieser, A. (2002). Managers as Marionettes? Using Fashion Theories to Explain The Success of Consultancies. In Kipping, M. & Engwall, L. (Eds.), *Management Consulting: Emergence and Dynamics of a Knowledge Industry* (pp. 167-183), Oxford: Oxford University Press.

Miller, S. Hickson, D.J. & Wilson, D. (1996). Decision-making in Organizations. In Clegg, S., Hardy, C. & Nord, W. R. (Eds.), *Handbook of Organization Studies* (pp. 293-312), London et al.: Sage.

Parker, B. (1996). Evolution and Revolution: from International Business to Globalization. In Clegg, S., Hardy, C. & Nord, W. R. (Eds.), *Handbook of Organization Studies* (pp. 484-505). London et al.: Sage.

Powell, W. (2001). The Capitalist Firm in the 21st century: Emerging Patterns. In DiMaggio, P. (Ed.), *The Twenty-first Century Firm (pp. 34-68),* Princeton: Princeton University Press.

Putnam, L. L., Phillips, N. & Chapman, P. (1996). Metaphors of Communication and Organization. In Clegg, S., Hardy, C. & Nord, W. R. (Eds.), Handbook of Organization Studies (pp. 375-407), London et al.: Sage.

Orlikowsky, W. J. (1992). The duality of technology: Rethinking the concept of technology in organizations. *Organization Science, 3*(3),398-427.

Roberts, K. H. & Grabowski, M. (1996). Organizations, Technology and Structuring. In Clegg,

S., Hardy, C. & Nord, W. R. (Eds.), *Handbook of Organization Studies* (pp. 276-292). London et al.: Sage.

Salaman, G. (2002). Understanding Advice: Towards a Sociology of Management Consultancy. In Clark, T. & Fincham, R. (Eds.), *Critical Consulting. New Perspectives on the Management Advice Industry* (pp. 247-259). Oxford: Blackwell.

Samra-Fredericks, D. (2005). Strategic practice, discourse and the everyday interactional constitution of power effects. *Organization, 12*(6),803-841.

Scheer, A. W. & Köppen, A. (2001) (Eds.), *Consulting. Wissens für die Strategie-, Prozess- und IT Beratung, Berlin, Heidelberg.* New York: Springer.

Schnelle, T. (2005). Durchsetzen von Strategien durch diskursive Beratung Anschlussfähigkeit in der Umsetzung von Strategien. In D. Seidl, W. Kirsch & M. Linder (Eds.), *Grenzen der Strategieberatung. Eine Gegenüberstellung der Perspektiven von Wissenschaft, Beratung und Klienten* (pp. 451-462). Bern/Stuttgart/Wien: Haupt Verlag.

Schwering, R.E. (2002). The IT audit assignment: Viewing technology in the organizational and strategic context. *Journal of Management Education, 26*(4),344-355.

Seidensticker, J. (2005). Über gewohnte Grenzen hinaus Strategieberatung zwischen Analyse und Umsetzung. In D. Seidl, W. Kirsch & M. Linder (Eds.), Grenzen der Strategieberatung. Eine Gegenüberstellung der Perspektiven von Wissenschaft, Beratung und Klienten (pp. 419-429), Bern/Stuttgart/Wien: Haupt Verlag.

Shadur, M.A., Kienzle, R., & Rodwell, J.J. (1999). The relationship between organizational climate and employee perceptions of involvement. The importance of support. *Group & Organization Management, 24*(4),479-503.

Shulman, A. (1996). Putting Group Information technology in its place: Comunication and Good Work Group Performance. In Clegg, S., Hardy, C. & Nord, W. R. (Eds.), *Handbook of Organization Studies* (pp. 357-374), London et al.: Sage.

Werr, A., Stjernberg, T. & Docherty, P. (1997). The functions and methods of change in management consulting. *Journal of Organizational Change Management, 10*(4), 288-307.

ENDNOTES

[1] According to Giddens (1984, p. 2), "Human social activity [...] is recursive. That is to say, they are not brought into being by social actors, but are continually recreated by them via the very means whereby they express themselves *as* actors. In and through their activities, agents reproduce the conditions that make these activities possible."(Emphasis as in original).

[2] According to Giddens (1984, p. 15) "we can say that action logically involves power in the sense of transformative capacity. In this sense, the most all-embracing meaning of 'power,' power is logically prior to subjectivity, to the constitution of the reflexive monitoring of conduct."

[3] It may also be the case that experience with IT consultants is not shared among several organizational units as Newell, (2006) reports.

[4] This differentiation is thought to be a continuum with the IT project approach on the one end and technochange at the other (Markus, 2004).

Chapter XIX
Digital Preservation by Design

Stacy Kowalczyk
Indiana University, USA

ABSTRACT

Current knowledge is produced, disseminated, and stored in digital format. This data will not be preserved by benign neglect; digital information will be preserved only through active management. This chapter will provide a theoretical foundation for digital preservation, an overview of current best practice for digital preservation, and a research agenda as well as a proscriptive framework by which to design digital preservation into a system.

INTRODUCTION

An ever-increasing percentage of data, information, and expertise is being documented and distributed in an exclusively electronic medium. Our cultural history is now digital. Not only are family histories now being created with digital cameras, almost all current events are captured digitally. Newspapers, magazines, and books are produced digitally. Virtually all published photographs are created digitally—35mm film is nearly extinct. All broadcast media is digital. Radio is recorded digitally—audiotape is nearly extinct. Television is produced and delivered digitally. Movies will be distributed digitally within the next few years. Not just cultural history, but predictions are that scholarly output will be exclusively digital by 2010.

Businesses, as producers of knowledge, create many documents that contribute both to our cultural history and to the scientific record. Contracts, white papers, marketing and promotional materials, audio and video documentaries of important occasions, and people in the company are important not only to the company but to the world. All types of research—from pharmaceutical and medical, to electronics and computer science, to new power fuel and energy technologies—are business activities, and all digital. From buildings to clothing, almost all design is digital. All commerce is digital. Current knowledge is produced, disseminated, and stored in digital format.

What is the problem? Isn't information in digital form more secure than paper? It is not a matter of degree, it is a matter of understanding the differences between a fixed media and digital. While paper can be put in a box on a shelf, digital objects are increasingly expensive to store because the media needs to be replaced on a three- to five-year schedule. Unlike paper which will remain useable if put in a relatively safe place, digital objects require constant and perpetual maintenance. Digital objects depend on and are bound to a technical environment and infrastructure. As the environment changes, so might the objects. And as the digital objects become more complex, the problems just increase. Data will not be preserved by benign neglect. Digital materials will only be preserved by active management.

Because so much information exists only in digital format, concern about our ability to keep this information available and usable for the future is increasing. In August, 2006, a prime example of a digital disaster made headlines. Tapes with very high-quality pictures of the first moon walk in 1969 have been reported as missing. To add insult to injury, the only remaining tape drive that can read these tapes is scheduled to be retired within the year. The missing tapes have a much higher quality picture than what was seen on, and recorded for, television (Macey, 2006). The loss is incalculable.

Businesses, governmental agencies, libraries, archives, and museums all need solutions to these problems. Over the past 10 years, digital preservation has emerged as an important area of research in both computer science and information science, at a national and international scale. Much of the research in digital preservation is coming from digital library programs more than from the traditional academic research community. Digital preservation is defined as:

...the managed activities necessary: (1) For the long-term maintenance of a byte stream (including metadata) sufficient to reproduce a suitable facsimile of the original document and (2) For the continued accessibility of the document contents through time and changing technology. (RLG & OCLC, 2002)

This chapter will provide a theoretical foundation for digital preservation, an overview of current best practice for digital preservation, and a research agenda.

DIGITAL PRESERVATION STRATEGIES

In a research area that is only 10 years old, it seems almost silly to talk of the "early days"; but in the early days, the focus of the conversation and theorizing revolved around preservation strategies. Three strategies emerged: technology preservation, technology emulation, and data migration. These are best defined though example. We will use the trivial example of a CD-ROM application that provides a virtual tour of the Vatican.

The technology preservation strategy proposes to save the technology platform for an application to preserve not only the data, but the "look and feel" as well. In our example, we would need to save the CD-ROM, a computer with a CD-ROM reader with the appropriate read speed as well as the correct operating system for the CD-ROM application software. In order to take the virtual tour, one would need to use that specific computer. Known as the museum-style approach (UKOLN, 2006), one can see the attraction to this model—it seems simple to just keep the hardware functioning. However, its simplicity is also its downfall. Depending on the number of applications to be kept functioning and the number of different platforms, the complexity will escalate until the cost becomes prohibitive. But the most significant failure point is that eventually, due to the increasing age, the hardware and storage media will fail irrevocably. Preserving the hardware as a scientific artifact for the future is a worthy goal. A number of museums are collecting computers. The Science Museum and the Computer Conservation Society in the UK are primary examples (UKOLN, 2006). But as a preservation strategy, because of its obvious weaknesses, it was never considered to be a serious option.

Like technology preservation, technology emulation is a strategy that has as its goal the preservation of the complete functionality of the original system. This strategy is based on the premise that system behaviors can be defined independently from its implementation. With the description of behavior, an engine could be developed that would re-create those behaviors. Alternatively, the source could be captured and saved and used as input into an emulation engine. As computers become faster and cheaper, the processing costs to deliver the information through an emulator would be negligible (Rothenberg, 1999a, 1999b; UKOLN, 2006). In our example, the CD-ROM would be copied in its entirety onto an emulation server. The server would need to know which operating system to emulate and how to invoke the software, as well as the wide variety of peripheral hardware interfaces. The server would also need to know the underlying formats of the data, images, text, and video in order to render them to a client application. While the technology preservation strategy was quietly dismissed as a viable option early in the discussion, emulation caused a firestorm of controversy (Bearman, 1999; Fleischhauer, 2003). Most critics cited the overwhelmingly daunting task of maintaining the requisite knowledge of a wide variety of hardware technologies, operating systems, databases, data formats, and other operating environments, as well as the functionality of each of the applications to be preserved. What was not widely discussed at the time, but which has become more obvious over time, is the confusion of presenting the data to consumers of the information preserved. How will future generations deal with command-level 1960s' mainframe applications or 1980s' game interfaces?

The data migration strategy proposes to move data into new formats as the old formats and/or systems become obsolete (Waters & Garret, 1996). The goal of this strategy is to preserve the data—the actual information—with as much of its functionality as possible. In our example, the data would be extracted from the CD-ROM. The text would be formatted into a useable format (today that would be an XML-based text file) with links (today that would be a URL-based link) to the images (today would be TIFF as a master file with a JPG deliverable file). A new system would need to be created that would be able to render a variety of XML-based text files. People using this new application would see the same data, but in a different environment with a different set of actions. Perhaps some specific functionality of the old system—perhaps an animated travel companion—would be lost. The emulation proponents decry the loss of functionality that the

proponents dismiss as trivial. What is universally considered to be a drawback to the migration strategy is the loss of data as a result of the migration itself. Moving from technical format to another often results in loss. If the image files were in the now obsolete PhotoCD format, migrating them to TIFF would result in irrevocable data loss. Even with these limitations, data migration is the predominate strategy to date.

OAIS REFERENCE MODEL

The open archival information systems (OAIS) reference model has become a foundation for discussing digital preservation. Like the OSI reference model, it is not a systems design but a set of high-level requirements built as a conceptual framework. It lays out what should be done in a digital preservation archive. It does not provide implementation instructions. OAIS uses the concept of an Information Package, a transaction, and/or data store that accompanies a digital object. An information package is a set of metadata that accompanies a digital object. OAIS uses the traditional meaning of metadata—data about (or describing) data. When data is brought into the system, the package is a SIP, a submission information package. It is modified as required to become an AIP, an archival information package. When the object is distributed for use, the information package is transformed again into the DIP, the dissemination information package (CCSDS, 2002). The OAIS was developed by the Consultative Committee for space data systems. The OAIS conceptual model has made two major contributions to the discussion of digital preservation. The first is the concept that preservation is a planned process that needs to be designed into a digital library from inception. The second is a common language for discussion digital preservation from submission to dissemination, from ingest to administration.

In the seminal paper on digital preservation, Waters and Garrett (1996) state:

For digital object, no less than for objects of other kinds, knowing how operationally to preserve them depends, at least in part, on being able to discriminate the essential features of what needs to be preserved...

Figure 1. OAIS functional entities (CCSDS, 2002; used with permission)

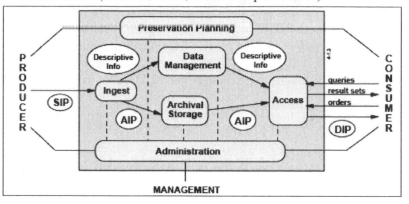

Whatever preservation method is applied, however, the central goal must be to preserve information integrity: that is, to define and preserve those features of an information object that distinguish it as a whole and singular work… including: content, fixity, reference, provenance and context.

THE FOUR GOALS OF PRESERVATION

Is this not a solved problem? Many think that if multiple copies exist in multiple locations, if the storage media is monitored for data degradation or technological obsolescence, if data center best practice that has been developed over the past 40 years is followed, then the data is "preserved." Unfortunately, "keeping the bits safe" is only the first, and the easiest, step in digital preservation. The longevity of digital information depends on more than good backups.

Waters and Garrett (1996) outlined four major goals of digital preservation: keeping the bits safe, keeping the files useable, keeping the integrity of the object, and keeping the context of the object. Fulfilling these goals will produce a trusted digital object which can prove the authenticity of its underlying bit-stream (Gladney, 2004). If we can design systems with preservation in mind, we can build trustworthy repositories for trusted digital objects.

Keeping the Bits Safe

Insuring the integrity of the bit-stream is the most basic function of digital preservation. Over the past 40 years, a body of best practice has been developed to preserve data at the bit-stream level. Fortunately, most businesses have implemented data center best practices. Best practice dictates a minimum of three copies of any file or record: one on active media, one on a near-line backup media, and one on a remote backup media. Unfortunately, creating the copies is not sufficient. One must manage these files. The media needs to be rotated and refreshed based on manufacturer's most conservative lifetime estimates. Media reliability degrades with the number of writes. Backup tapes or other removable media need to be rotated off the backup schedule after a certain number of uses. Offsite media need to be refreshed on a regular schedule. After some number of years (again, based on the manufacturer's recommendation), the offsite media need to be rewritten. But this schedule also needs to be managed. Will the organization have the necessary technology to rewrite the tapes? Thus, technology needs to be monitored to reduce the risk of obsolescence. When storage media is replaced, any removable media that uses that infrastructure must be replaced. This often greatly increases the cost and the complexity of a technology replacement project.

Storage

Storage—specifically choosing the technology—is always a concern as organizations begin to design a digital repository. The first question that I, as the assistant director for software development in the Harvard University Library Digital Initiative, was asked when I spoke about digital repositories was "What storage hardware are you using?" As I did then, I would like to discuss storage in the abstract—what issues need to be analyzed during the hardware selection process. The National Archives of England, Wales and the United Kingdom has developed an excellent set of selection criteria and a media scorecard in their second Digital Preservation Guidance Note. The six criteria are as follows:

- Longevity is not as important as one might expect since most storage media becomes obsolete before it degrades. The National Archives of England, Wales and the United Kingdom recommends a "proven lifespan" of 10 years (Brown, 2003b p. 5).
- Capacity is actually more important than longevity. Limiting the number of devices to manage is the key. Estimating the amount of storage required is the first and most difficult step.

- Viability describes the hardware-level data protection features of the storage media. Can the media be write protected? What types of read/write error detection are available? Is the media able to self-recover at failure?
- Obsolescence is, of course, a major concern. How does one decide between leading-edge and mature? We want to invest our limited resources in a technology that is both stable and has a high "cool" factor. Choosing technologies built on open standards with a high level of interoperability has a significantly higher probability of being usable longer.
- Cost has two major considerations, initial cost and total cost of ownership. The cost per gigabyte, the Mean Time Before Failure, as well as the personnel cost of administration should be factored into the total cost equation.
- Susceptibility is the term that describes the media's ability to withstand physical damage. Any media used should "be tolerant of a wide range of environmental conditions without data loss" (Brown, 2003b p. 5).

Creating an expandable and extendable storage architecture based on new but proven technologies, while seemingly more expensive, is more efficient

Figure 2. Functions of archival storage (CCSDS, 2002; used with permission)

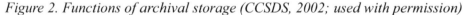

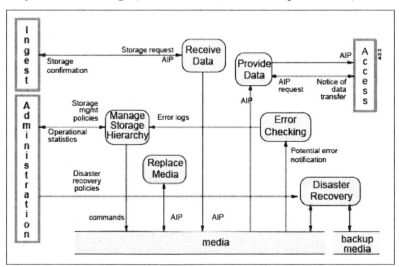

to manage and highly likely to have a lower total cost of ownership.

The OAIS archival storage model visually demonstrates that developing an architecture for preservation requires more than hardware. It requires process and management.

Archiving

Besides the body of best practice developed for data centers, more must be done to create the Trusted Digital Object that Gladney (2004) proposed. As work becomes more collaborative and more distributed, organizations find it increasingly difficult to manage their complex data. As a business develops new products, consultants in the U.S. develop business plans on a Microsoft platform, employees in Europe create the designs using CAD software, and the manufacturing plant in China uses proprietary systems to build the prototypes. While people are actively working on a project, information is e-mailed and documents are stored on a shared file system. When this company wants to harvest the knowledge and create a digital archive of the work products of the development, rather than a working dataset or file system, an archival digital object needs to be created. It then becomes the responsibility of the application to insure the integrity of the object—both its fixity and its validity at inception and over time.

Fixity is the term used to convey the notion that digital data is not immutable, that it can be changed easily, either maliciously or inadvertently. Regardless of intention, data cannot be considered to be preserved as a Trusted Digital Object if the repository cannot guarantee fixity—that the data has not been changed since it was archived. Technically, this is an insignificant task, but it does require a process to enforce. Each archived object needs to have a checksum or a digital signature. Because it is both simple and effective, many digital libraries use a simple MD5 checksum rather than the more cumbersome digital certificate. This checksum is then stored in a database with administrative data about the object. But a checksum is only useful if it is validated by a process that calculates the checksum for each digital file and compares it

to the saved checksum. If they do not match, an error needs to be sent to the appropriate staff for immediate action. Errors can be attributed to a number of factors: failing disk, ingest errors, file transfer errors, as well as malicious mischief. To insure fixity, a digital repository should implement a checksum or digital signature on archived files and validate them on a regular schedule.

IT Contingency Planning

Disaster recovery planning, business resumption planning, and IT contingency planning are considered to be synonymous terms. But regardless of the term, it is a process that allows the administrators of a system to know the tolerance for down time and provide a guide for restoring service under a wide variety of circumstances.

The National Institute of Standards and Technology (NIST, 2002) has developed a standardized model for developing a contingency plan:

1. Develop the contingency planning policy statement.
2. Conduct the business impact analysis (BIA).
3. Identify preventive controls.
4. Develop recovery strategies.
5. Develop an IT contingency plan.
6. Plan testing, training, and exercises.
7. Plan maintenance.

As is obvious from the NIST process described above, contingency planning is complicated. While the discussion could include hardware and network redundancy, automatic failover, and site mirroring, for the purposes of this chapter, disaster recovery planning will be limited to the issues of data preservation only.

To insure that a digital repository can "keep the bits safe," the data must not only be safe on the primary disk and backup media. The administrators of the system must be able to find the correct version, have access to the restored software, and have experience of restoring data. This requires an annual disaster recovery drill, which involves actually finding and retrieving a data file, restoring the file, and testing to insure data integrity. This should be incorporated into a larger disaster recovery and business resumption annual drill. A digital repository should institute an annual contingency plan drill within six months of its initial production date.

Keeping the Files Usable

Of the four digital preservation goals established in 1996 by Waters and Garret, keeping the files usable has turned out to be the most challenging because it depends on the complexity and transparency of file properties. Not only do digital objects depend on technology, they are bound to an environment and infrastructure. Changes to the environment or infrastructure might the objects. Abrams (2004) contends that "the concept of representation format permeates all technical aspects of digital repository architecture and is, therefore, the foundation of many, if not all, digital preservation activities." In other words, the technical format of a file determines its probability of being preserved. A format is defined as "the internal structure and encoding of a digital object, which allows it to be processed, or to be rendered in a human-accessible form" (Brown, 2006a, p. 3).

Formats need to be discussed within the context of the "levels of use." In digital preservation, we expect digital objects to be stored in different formats for different uses. In order to keep a file useable for the longest period of time, a digital object should be created in the format with the most information, in the most open format with the least risk of failure. The highest quality object with the highest level of fidelity is called an archival master file. Derivative files are made from the master file as necessary for more efficient delivery to applications. For images, current best practice would dictate that the master file be an uncompressed TIFF file and that images to be sent to a Web browser be a JPEG file. For audio file, current best practice would dictate that the master file be an uncompressed AIFF or Broadcast WAV, and that the files to be sent to a Web browser be an MP3 or a RealAudio file (Library of Congress, 2006b; TASI, 2006; National Library of Australia–Formats, n.d.).

Format Risk Assessment

How do organizations analyze the risk for an archival file format? Early projects, not surprisingly, discovered that the more open the format, the easier the process. But they also discovered that even open formats can have a proprietary and thus secret set of tags that may not be supported in a future version, or have any documentation for migration or emulation work (Lawrence, Kehoe, Rieger, Walters, & Kenney, 2000). Since the earliest projects, a number of organizations have developed different types of risk analysis.

The Library of Congress has developed a theoretical framework for assessing formats using seven sustainability factors (Arms & Fleischhauer, 2005):

1. **Disclosure:** Degree to which complete specifications and tools for validating technical integrity exist and are accessible to those creating and sustaining digital content. A spectrum of disclosure levels can be observed for digital formats. What is most significant is not approval by a recognized standards body, but the existence of complete documentation.

2. **Adoption:** Degree to which the format is already used by the primary creators, disseminators, or users of information resources. This includes use as a master format, for delivery to end users, and as a means of interchange between systems.

3. **Transparency:** Degree to which the digital representation is open to direct analysis with basic tools, such as human readability using a text-only editor.

4. **Self-documentation:** Self-documenting digital objects contain basic descriptive, technical, and other administrative metadata.

5. **External dependencies:** Degree to which a particular format depends on a particular hardware, operating system, or software for rendering or use and the predicted complexity of dealing with those dependencies in future technical environments.

411

6. **Impact of patents:** Degree to which the ability of archival institutions to sustain content in a format will be inhibited by patents.

7. **Technical protection mechanisms:** Implementation of mechanisms such as encryption that prevent the preservation of content by a trusted repository.

The National Archives of England, Wales and the United Kingdom has an alternative list of seven criteria by which formats could be judged: open standards, ubiquity, stability, metadata support, feature set, interoperability, and viability (Brown, 2003a). But both sets of criteria are aiming at a similar result—helping managers determine how to store their data for the long term. Archival formats should be:

•   Well documented, well understood, and not wholly owned by a single commercial entity.

•   Widely adopted to increase the probability of commercial tools for migration and to ensure a long usage cycle to avoid repeated, short-term migrations.

•   Self-contained, and not rely on a specific technical environment.

But beyond just format analysis, organizations need to be aware of other risks in the preservation process. The National Archives of Australia has developed a process called DIRKS–Designing and Implementing Recordkeeping System. This is an eight-step process defining the best practice standards and guidelines published by the National Archives as part of its efforts to preserve electronic information (it uses the term "e-permanence"). The DIRKS methodology is a basic waterfall requirements process that is designed to "help each organisation to determine such requirements and put in place procedures to reassess these needs over time" (National Archives of Australia, 2003b). The goal of the DIRKS methodology is a set of records that are authentic, reliable, complete and unaltered, useable, with integrity (National Archives of Australia, 2003b).

The multi-national library utility, OCLC, has developed the INFORM methodology for assessing the durability of formats for digital preservation which is based on six classes of risk that include both technology and organizational process (Stanescu, 2004, p. 3):

1. **Digital object format:** Risks introduced by the specification itself, but also including compression algorithms, proprietary (closed) vs. open formats, DRM (copy protection), encryption, and digital signatures.

2. **Software:** Risks introduced by necessary software components such as operating systems, applications, library dependencies, archive implementations, migration programs, implementations of compression algorithms, encryption, and digital signatures.

3. **Hardware:** Risks introduced by necessary hardware components including type of media (CD, DVD, magnetic disk, tape, WORM), CPU, I/O cards, and peripherals.

4. **Associated organizations:** Risks related to the organizations supporting in some fashion the classes identified above, including the archive, beneficiary community, content owners, vendors, and open source community.

5. **Digital archive:** Risks introduced by the digital archive itself (i.e., architecture, processes, organizational structures).

6. **Migration and derivative-based preservation plans:** Risks introduced by the migration process itself, not covered in any other category.

Format Registries

In one of the early investigations into file format risk analysis, the authors indicate that the biggest challenge in their research was compiling complete data about each of the formats under consideration (Lawrence et al., 2000). As other preservation-by-migration projects began, the problem of adequate format and persistent information became more obvious. In response, several institutions have initiated projects to create repositories of format information. Over the past several years, these have become known as "format registries." One of the major issues of format registries is the representation of information for format data, compression methods, character encoding schemes, and operating systems. The need for format registries is obvious when one looks at the general categories of formats that the National Library of Australia has outlined on its very useful online resource, Preserving Access to Digital Information: audio and audiovisual material, computer-aided design (CAD), databases, digital television, digital games, e-mail, geographic information system (GIS), networked digital material, physical format digital material, spreadsheets, virtual reality, and word processing documents (National Library of Australia–Formats, n.d.).

The National Archives of England, Wales and the United Kingdom has developed a format registry called PRONOM which provides information about data file formats and their supporting software products. Initially released in 2002, the system was developed for use by the National Archives but has recently been made available via the Web for public consumption. PRONOM holds information about software products as well as the file formats which each product can read and write. Currently, PRONOM only represents format information. The most interesting feature of the PRONOM system is the PRONOM persistent unique identifier (PUID). The PUID is a specific instantiation of the more generalized construct, the persistent identifier (PID), which will be discussed later in this chapter. In the specific case of the PRONOM system, the PUID is a persistent, unique, and unambiguous identifier for formats within the PRONOM registry:

Such identifiers are fundamental to the exchange and management of digital objects, by allowing human or automated user agents to unambiguously identify, and share that identification of, the representation information required to support access to an object. This is a virtue both of the inherent uniqueness of the identifier, and of its binding to a definitive description of the representation information in a registry such as PRONOM. (National Archives of England, Wales and the United Kingdom, 2006b)

The PUID is being used in the latest version of the E-Government Metadata Standard—providing a consistent method for describing file formats used throughout the UK government. While PIUDs can be expressed as uniform resource identifiers (URIs) using the "info:pronom/" namespace, they currently cannot be resolved to a URL, although the National Archives plans to implement this in the future (National Archives of England, Wales and the United Kingdom, 2006b).

The Digital Library Foundation (DLF) has sponsored an initial investigation into the creation of a global digital format registry (GDRF) to maintain format representation information. One of the most important contributions of this project is its international participation which includes the Bibliothque nationale de France, Harvard University, the Joint Information Systems Committee of the Higher and Further Education Councils in the United Kingdom (JISC), JSTOR, the Library of Congress, the Massachusetts Institute of Technology, the National Archives and Records Administration, the National Archives of Canada, the National Institute of Standards and Technology, New York University, the Online Computer Library Center, the University of Pennsylvania, Stanford University, the British Library, the California Digital Library, the Internet Architecture Board, the Internet Engineering Task Force, the Research Libraries Group, and the Public Records Office in the United Kingdom (Digital Library Federation, n.d.). The project is working on a long-term business model for sustaining the operation of the registry (Abrams, 2004). A prototype system is being developed by the University of Pennsylvania called FRED–Format REgistry Demonstration (Ockerbloom, 2004). This prototype is built on TOM, the typed object model. TOM is both an abstracted data model that describes the behaviors and representations of information sources such as file formats and information retrieval services, and a set of software services that use the model (Ockerbloom, 2005).

The Digital Curation Center (DCC) is an organization that is developing another repository. DCC is supported by the Joint Information Systems Committee (JISC) of the United Kingdom. Using the OAIS conceptual model that was described in the opening section of the chapter and which will be further explicated in the following section, the DCC is implementing what OAIS describes as a representation information registry/repository for digital data (Digital Curation Center, 2006). The DCC has architected the system for general applications of digital curation—format obsolescence—but is primarily interested in experimental scientific data which has significantly different properties than regular file formats and thus has more complex functional requirements than the format registries described above. As a minimum, the registry/repository needs format specifications, the details of the bit structure. But it also needs rendering and processing software source code, as well as binary executables along with an extensive set of metadata that is often considered data provenance, which will be discussed later in the chapter.

Redaction

There are many circumstances in which an organization will want to store a complete archival digital object that contains sensitive data while needing to make the non-sensitive data available to the employees or the general public. The process of removing content is a common occurrence in records management and is referred to as redaction. Redaction is "the separation of disclosable from non-disclosable information by blocking out individual works, sentences or paragraphs or the removal of whole pages or section prior to the

release of the document" (National Archives of England, Wales and the United Kingdom, 2006a, p. 4). The National Archives of England, Wales and the United Kingdom (2006a) has developed a set of five principles for redacting electronic records:

- The original file must not be altered. Redaction should be performed on a copy of the record.
- Redaction should "irreversibly remove the required information for the redacted copy of the record" (p. 13), not merely obstruct display.
- Redaction techniques should be fully tested for security.
- Redaction should be done in a controlled and secure environment.
- All intermediary states of the process should be deleted.

While redaction may be necessary, it is not recommended as a general practice on archived digital objects.

Data Ingest

Data ingest, as the name implies, is the process of getting data into a system. Best practice for all information systems is to get the data "right," right from the beginning. Fixing errors in data is always expensive. But for digital repositories, it is absolutely essential to get the correct digital file, intellectual metadata, and technical metadata at time of ingestion (National Archives of Australia,

Figure 3. Functions of ingest (CCSDS, 2002; used with permission)

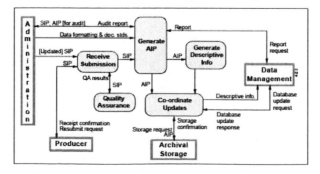

2003a). According to the National Archives of England, Wales and the United Kingdom, the cost of creating data for sustainability should be the goal because "attempts to bring electronic records into a managed and sustainable regime after the fact tend to be expensive, complex and, generally, less successful" (Brown, 2003a, p. 4).

In the OAIS model, ingest is the initial stage of preservation. When data is deposited in the repository, it must be accompanied by a submission information package (SIP). The SIP must have sufficient information about the object to be processed. The repository must confirm the quality of the data—both from the SIP and from the digital object itself. Upon successful ingest, the system must create an archival information package (AIP) to insure that sufficient data exists within the system to preserve the object. All data is stored and is actively managed over time.

The National Digital Information Infrastructure and Preservation Program (NDIIPP) of the Library of Congress is a 10-year, multi-million-dollar project to develop a distributed network of both public and private preservation partners. Ingest is a vital component of this initiative; the Archive Ingest and Handling Test (AIHT) is an NDIIPP project to test the ability of eight partner institutions to test the process of ingesting a common set of digital objects and later export and exchange with another partner. The major issues were not technical but developing a shared language and set of values (Smith, 2006).

Identification and Validation

We have already established the primacy of technical format in digital preservation. Ensuring that the digital repository knows with certainty that the file is what it purports to be and that the file conforms to all of the specifications of the format is vital. With the volume of objects that organizations need to process at ingest, an automated process to both identity and validate the format is required.

Identification is the first step. Most files self-identity via the file extension: .txt indicates a text file, .doc indicates a Microsoft Word file, .tif indicates a TIFF file, .jpg indicates a JPEG file; the list could continue for pages. But self-identification is unreliable and insufficient for a digital repository. Files are not always in the format that they claim to be. "Invalid objects can arise through the use of poor-quality software tools or as the result of accidental or deliberate corruption" (Brown, 2006a, p. 4). Not only does the repository need to know with certainty that the file is a TIFF file, it also needs to know that the file was created using the TIFF 6.1 specification.

Validation is the processes of determining the level of conformance to the encoding specification of a specific format. This process has two steps—the first step is to determine if the object is well-formed. Well-formed objects conform to the syntactic requirements for its format. In other words, it follows the grammar of the format. The second step is to determine its validity. Valid objects must conform to the semantic requirements of the format—does the object contain the meaningful content that is required. If a TIFF file has an eight-byte header followed by a series of Image File Directories (IFDs) made up of a two-byte entry count and a set of eight-byte tagged entries, it can be considered to be well formed. But to be considered valid, it must conform to additional rules that enforce more complex semantic rules—an RGB TIFF must have at least three sample vales per pixel (Harvard University Library, 2006).

While it might be possible to identify many file types via the UNIX file command using the "magic number" (Brown, 2006b), many feel that this is insufficient (Abrams & Seaman, 2003). Harvard University Library and JSTOR, a not-for-profit organization that creates and maintains a trusted archive of important scholarly journals, have collaborated through a Mellon-funded project to create a tool set to automate format-specific validation of digital objects. The software is named JHOVE—the JSTOR/Harvard Object Validation Environment (Harvard University Library, 2006). In addition to identification and validation, JHOVE also allows for characterization—the processes of determining the format-specific significant properties of an object. These actions are performed by modules which plug into a layered architecture that can be configured at the time of its invocation to include specific format modules and output handlers. JHOVE includes modules for arbitrary byte streams, ASCII and UTF-8 encoded text, GIF, JPEG2000, JPEG and TIFF images, AIFF and WAVE audio, PDF, HTML, and XML, as well as text and XML output handlers. JHOVE has been used by a number of digital libraries and archives. As of the writing of the chapter, JSTOR and Harvard were working with the Library of Congress to enhance the functionality and extend the architecture to improve the performance and the interoperability of the system (Harvard University Library, 2006).

The National Archives of England, Wales and the United Kingdom has developed an alternative method for identifying formats. The approach taken by the National Archives is to develop a format "signature." Using information about each specific format stored in the PRONOM format registry described above, the digital record object identification system analyzes the binary structure of a digital object and compares it with this pre-defined signature. The National Archives expects to extend this system to include format validation (Brown, 2006a).

A digital repository should optimize the probability of preservation by limiting the number formats accepted as archival quality or by reformatting the data upon ingest. A digital repository should validate digital objects when submitted for ingest. The validation should include format identification, validation, and characterization.

Data Provenance

Data provenance is a term that "broadly refer[s] to a description of the origins of a piece of data the process by which it arrived in a database" (Buneman, Khanna, & Tan, 2000, p. 2). Also know as lineage, provenance is a "special form of audit trail that traces each step in sourcing, moving and processing data" (Pearson, n.d.). In a repository, whether a generalized digital repository or a domain-specific repository, data provenance is difficult. Defining the data required to prove provenance is specific to each data type and/or domain. Developing these ontologies is a "crucial and thankless" task (Saltz, n.d.). Domain-specific provenance schemas are being developed—SNOMED and LOINC for medical research (Saltz, n.d.), and Karma for atmospheric research (Plale, Ramachandran, & Tanner, 2006; Simmhan, Plale, & Gannon, 2006) are but a few of the research efforts. But what is needed is a more generalized solution. Providing self-describing data and the software to process that data is not

Figure 4. JHOVE Schematic (Harvard University Library, 2006; used with the permission of the President and Fellows of Harvard College)

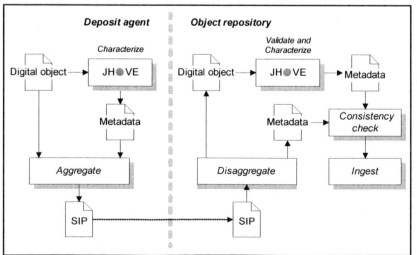

yet a reality. Chimera, a prototype generalized data provenance system, has attempted to abstract the data representation by using types, descriptors, and transforms. Types provide an abstraction layer for semantic content, the format of the physical representation, and the format's encoding; descriptors define an interpretable schema that defines the data—number of files, types of files, and so forth; and transforms are a generic, typed abstraction for computational procedures (Foster, Vockler, Wilde, & Zhao, 2002).

While much of the research on data provenance is in the scientific community, the issues surrounding data provenance permeate digital preservation and digital repositories. Unless repositories can fully describe how files have been transformed, either for research or for preservation, the objects will not be trustworthy. A digital repository should provide provenance information for all of its digital objects.

Persistent Identifiers

A persistent identifier (PID) is a unique, permanent, location-independent identifier for a network-accessible resource. A URL cannot be a persistent identifier because it conflates two important but separate functions—item location and item identification. By separating location from identification, PIDs help avoid the problem of broken links that is often referred to in the digital library community as the "404—not found" problem. Persistent identification is especially crucial for important resources that are referenced from scores of Web pages or are cited scholarly works. Basically, PIDs

are URLs that require a multi-phased resolution process. The first-level resolution is to find the right resolution server. Once the resolution server is located, the second-level resolution finds the resource. The second phase of the resolution is relatively simple. A database has both the persistent ID and a location of the object usually in the form of a URL. Using the PID as a key, the resolution service reads the database and redirects the http transaction using the location URL. As the problem of persistent identification of digital resources has become more prominent, a number of competing PIDs have been developed.

The Harvard University Library developed an early implementation of a persistent identifier system called the name resolution service (NRS). This service is based on the universal resource name (URN) syntax (WC3, 2001) with the expectation that Web browsers would ultimately support URNs as specified. But until that native browser support, the URN system needed to be delivered in URL syntax (Harvard University Library, 2003b). The Online Computer Library Center (OCLC) uses a PURL (persistent URL), a technology similar to the Harvard method but with a different syntax (Weibel, Jul, & Shafer, 1995). The Corporation for National Research Initiatives (CNRI) created another resolution system for its unique persistent identifier syntax named Handles. The Handle system is an open source, downloadable system with a set of open protocols and a namespace (Corporation for National Research Initiatives, 2006). The International DOI Foundation developed the digital object identifier (DOI) naming semantics that has been implemented using the Handle syntax and

Figure 5. Harvard University's Name Resolution Service (Harvard University Library, 2003b; used with the permission of the President and Fellows of Harvard College)

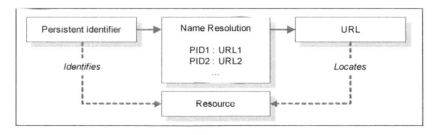

resolution system (International DOI Foundation, 2006). DOIs are used predominantly by publishers of electronic information to provide persistent and controlled access to journal articles. The California Digital Library has developed the archival resource key (ARK) which provides access to a digital information resource. The ARK is architected to deliver three parameterized services: the digital object metadata, the digital object content files, and a commitment statement made by the owning organization concerning the digital object (Kunze, 2003). A digital repository should implement a persistent identifier service to insure long-term unambiguous access to its digital objects.

Keeping the Integrity of the Object

More than fixity, the integrity of the object has referred to maintaining the intellectual wholeness of a digital object. Remember that a digital object is one or more files that constitute a logical entity. In a scientific application, a digital object could be several ASCII datasets with XML documentation and 10 visualizations stored as jpg images, as well as an XML workflow process file. In a medical application, it could be a series of x-rays, a treatment plan, a set of diagnostics, and a patient visit chart. For a digital book, it is a series of page images, OCR text files, a word/page coordinate file for highlighting a search hit on a displayed image, and a descriptive metadata record with author and title information. Examples of complex digital objects seem limitless.

Over the past several years, digital libraries have grappled with the issue of managing these complex objects. Initially, file-naming conventions were used to associate all of the files. That proved to be unsatisfactory and insufficient. After testing several different schemes, libraries developed a Metadata Encoding and Transmission Standard (METS) XML schema for maintaining the complex relationships between different files. A METS document consists of seven major sections (Library of Congress, 2006a):

1. **METS header:** The METS Header contains metadata describing the METS document itself, including such information as creator, editor, and so forth.

2. **Descriptive metadata:** Access metadata can be stored internally or have an external link, or both.

3. **Administrative metadata:** Provenance and other administrative data.

4. **File section:** Lists all files containing content which comprise the object.

5. **Structural map:** Provides a hierarchical structure for the digital object, and links the elements of that structure to content files and metadata that pertain to each element.

6. **Structural links:** Records the existence of hyperlinks between nodes in the hierarchy outlined in the structural map.

7. **Behavior:** Associates executable behaviors with content in the METS object.

Some digital libraries use METS internally; others use an RDBMS internally but export METS. But METS, or any other metadata schema, is not sufficient for insuring the integrity of an object. Many of the systems that manage digital objects, to be covered in detail in the following section, have a similar architecture—the data resides on a file system, and administrative and intellectual metadata reside in a database. While early attempts were made to keep the digital files in a database, this proved to be impractical. The huge file sizes caused the database to expand so rapidly that the database could not be backed up in a regular batch window. Other solutions, either database or hardware storage architectures, proved very costly. Thus the two-tiered architecture.

How can a repository insure object integrity with data residing in different systems? The Harvard University Library's digital repository system (DRS) has developed a set of procedures that insure the integrity of their digital objects. The DRS uses METS to keep intellectual control over the digital objects. When a complex object is ingested, the DRS creates a database record for each component file of the digital object and then uses the database's referential integrity enforcement to prevent one piece of the object from being deleted inadvertently. The DRS also developed a series of scripts that enforce integrity within the two-tiered architecture.

"The DRS has two main components the management database and the file system. Each object has a database record that maintains the administrative and technical metadata for the object. The database record knows the location of the primary digital file on the disk file system. Nightly, the DRS validates the integrity of both the database and the file system by verifying that every database record [in] the file system has a file and that every file has a database record." (Harvard University Library, 2003a)

A digital repository needs to maintain the relationships between all of the components of an object.

Keeping the Context of the Object

In 1996 when the list of digital preservation goals was proposed, keeping the context of the object seemed to be a huge issue. The major concern was that organizations would have terabytes of digital files that were not usable because no one knew what they were. Over the past 10 years, the fear of having 'orphaned' objects has decreased. But it is still important to maintain a strong association between the intellectual metadata and the logical object. Using a well-designed preservation system should solve this issue.

A preservation system, more commonly known as a "digital repository," is a system designed as an archive for digital objects. Much of the research in digital preservation, as well as in digital libraries, has been in this area. An early attempt to find a single architecture for a universal digital repository was the repository architecture Protocol (RAP)—a standard access protocol for digital repositories. RAP is a modular protocol that separates the byte stream from the data type, as well as the type definition from the type implementation. RAP is also extensible creating new types on demand (Blanchi & Petrone, 2001). While developed as an open source project, it is not yet clear that applications are using the RAP protocol.

Preservation System Models

Digital repository and institutional repository are two terms that are often used to describe a long-term preservation system. While very similar, there are fundamental differences that need explication. A digital repository has the connotation of a back-office function—a boring, batch-orientated system for collecting metadata and digital objects for general management and preservation for digital library organizations. A digital repository may have an access layer for general discovery, but it generally is thought of as a datastore. An institutional repository is both a publishing mechanism and a datastore. In opposition to a digital repository where the data generally comes from a set of trusted depositors, the institutional repository was conceived as a bottom-up, distributed data archive where data would come from the individual creators of the intellectual content—the actual authors would upload their data, create the metadata, and provide an intellectual organizational structure over their own content. While different in their focus, both require "most essentially an organizational commitment to the stewardship of...digital materials, including long-term preservation where appropriate, as well as organization and access or distribution" (Lynch, 2003, p. 2).

DSpace

A joint project of the Massachusetts Institute of Technology (MIT) and Hewlett-Packard, DSpace is an open source repository system which "captures, stores, indexes, preserves, and distributes digital research material" (MIT & HP, 2007). DSpace is a three-tiered system with an application layer, a business logic layer, and a storage layer. The layers have a strict hierarchy and can only communicate with their immediate neighbor; for example, the application layer can only talk to the business logic layer and may not talk with the storage layer directly. Each layer has its own API. Authentication and authorization is controlled at the application layer. Each application must insure that the people or external systems accessing the DSpace system

Figure 6. DSpace overview (MIT, 2004; used with permission from the Massachusetts Institute of Technology)

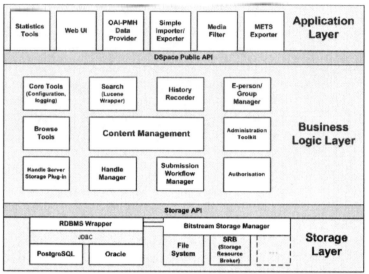

are who they say they are. DSpace is specifically designed to allow different communities within an organization to define their "space" with a set of depositors and an intellectual organization of the contents. Access to the content is through a minimally customizable Web portal (MIT, 2004).

Fedora

The flexible and extensible digital object repository architecture (Fedora)—is an open source digital repository system. Originally developed as a research project at Cornell University's Computer Science Department with funding by DARPA and NSF, it is now a joint project of the University of Virginia Library and Cornell funded by a grant from the Andrew W. Mellon Foundation (Lagoze, Payette, Shin, & Wilper, 2005).

A modular design, the Fedora architecture has an extendable object model which provides a fair amount of flexibility in representing complex objects and complex relationships between objects in two perspectives—an abstract model and a function (Lagoze et al., 2005). Since the earliest designs of Fedora, a central component of the system was a "disseminator"—the software that controlled the behaviors for metadata display and object rendering.

Disseminators allow the developers to abstract the format-specific constraints into layers that should allow for easier migration as the formats evolve.

The major features of Fedora are (Staples, Wayland & Payette, 2003):

- **XML submission and storage:** Digital objects are stored as XML-encoded files that conform to an extension of the metadata encoding and transmission standard (METS) schema.
- **Parameterized disseminators:** Behaviors defined for an object support user-supplied options that are handled at dissemination time.
- **Access control and authentication:** Although advanced access control and authentication are not scheduled until Phase II of the project, a simple form of access control has been added in Phase I of the project to provide access restrictions based on IP address. IP range restriction is supported in both the management and access APIs. In addition, the management API is protected by HTTP basic authentication.
- **Default disseminator:** The default disseminator is a built-in internal disseminator on every object that provides a system-defined behavior mechanism for disseminating the basic contents of an object.

Figure 7. Fedora object model (Lagoze et al., 2005)

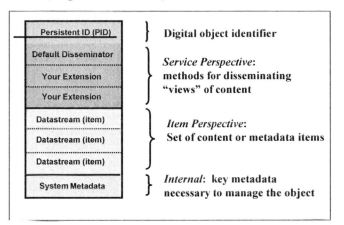

- **Searching:** Selected system metadata fields are indexed along with the primary Dublin Core record for each object. The Fedora repository system provides a search interface for both full-text and field-specific queries across these metadata fields.
- **OAI metadata harvesting:** The OAI protocol for metadata harvesting is a standard for sharing metadata across repositories. Every Fedora digital object has a primary Dublin Core record that conforms to the schema. This metadata is accessible using the OAI protocol for metadata harvesting, v2.0.
- **Batch utility:** The Fedora repository system includes a batch utility as part of the manage-

ment client that enables the mass creation and loading of data objects.

Additional functions to be added to Fedora are *component management, advanced access control* using an XML-oriented policy expression that can be used to enforce fine-grained object-level policies, *versioning,* and *preservation services* to monitor objects, provide alerts to vulnerabilities, and perform corrective actions.

Greenstone

Greenstone was developed by the University of New Zealand and first released in 2000. An open

Figure 8. Fedora architectural overview (Staples et al., 2003)

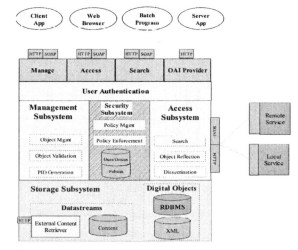

source system, it was built to be widely distributed as a means for access to digital collections. Its early tag line was, "What you see—you can get!" (Witten, Bainbridge, & Boddie, 2001, p. 12). It has a very low technology barrier and is often used in situations where the technical infrastructure is not mature. Its early implementation was not designed for preservation. The new implementation has a service architecture. The client service manager is the "Receptionist," while the server service manager is the "MessageRouter" (Don, Bainbridge, & Witten, 2002). This architecture is very modular and extendable, which should allow Greenstone to mature into a preservation system at some point.

Digital Information Archiving System (DIAS)

In 2000, the National Library of The Netherlands, the Koninklijke Bibliotheek (KB), began a project with IBM to create the technical infrastructure for a national digital repository for The Netherlands. Named the digital information srchiving dystem (DIAS), it is based on the OAIS preservation conceptual model (IBM/KB, n.d.). The system was developed using the universal virtual computer (UVC) developed by Raymond Lorie, an emulation engine that allows digital objects to be reconstituted in their original form. The UVC

Figure 10. DIAS Overview (IBM, n.d.)

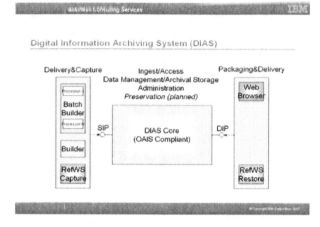

uses a logical data scheme with type description, a format decoder, and a logical data viewer (Lorie, 2000). Rolled out in 2003, the system, known at the KB as the e-Depot, is deigned to implement the library's "Safe Place Strategy" to ensure "the transfer of digital publications from their publishing environment to a dedicated archiving environment" (Steenbakkers, 2005). The KB has taken as its primary mission to preserve the published "Scientific Record"—journal articles directly from the publisher, CD-ROMs, and PDF files (Oltmans & van Wijngaarden, 2004).

DIGITAL REPOSITORY DISCUSSION

While each of the systems describe themselves as a digital repository, they each have very different goals, organizational structures, and preservation functions. DIAS and Fedora are similar in overall functional goals. Both of these systems expects to be the primary management environment for all of an organization's digital objects. They were both designed to be centrally administered, large backroom repositories with substantial batch processes for ingesting objects and their technical, structural, and intellectual metadata. DSpace has a very different overall functional goal. Its primary focus is gathering data from individuals who want to both save their files and provide public access to them. There is very little digital object management.

Figure 9. Greenstone architecture (Olson, 2003; used with permission from Waikato University)

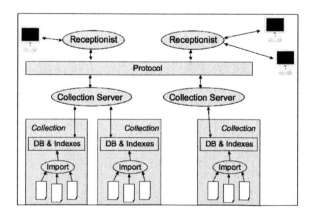

Rather than working in a batch mode, it expects individual online real-time data ingest from individuals who have some level of control over their own "space." Greenstone has yet another primary goal: to provide access to digital collections. Like DSpace, it has minimum administrative functions, but unlike DSpace, Greenstone is not designed for individuals to upload data on their own. It is more like a Web publishing application.

Although all of these repository systems were developed for universities, two, DIAS and DSpace, were developed in partnerships with commercial enterprises, while Fedora and were developed solely by the universities. DIAS is a joint project of IBM and Koninklijke Bibliotheek, the national library of The Netherlands, and DSpace is a project of MIT and Hewlett Packard. Even though both of these systems had commercial development partners, their business models seem to be very different. DSpace is an open source system, while DIAS is not. While there do not seem to be plans to immediately turn DIAS into a commercial product, it is certainly possible. DIAS, DSpace, and Greenstone all are turnkey systems. While they can be modified and customized, they are all designed for a simple implementation. Fedora, on the other hand, is not a fully formed system, but a set of tools and modules that need to be assembled by skilled programmers, which gives it great flexibility and power but limits its applicability for many organizations.

As with their goals and organizational structures, the preservation functions of these systems are quite different. Neither DSpace nor Greenstone has any real preservation functions other than a managed datastore. Fedora and DIAS were both designed as preservation systems. While not all of the functions have yet been implemented, Fedora was designed for migration. Using standard metadata schemas, Fedora captures both technical and structural metadata to aid in future format migration. DIAS is built to provide an emulation environment so that as formats become obsolete, they will continue to function with no need to migrate. Since both DIAS and Fedora are new systems with a small install base, neither of these preservation strategies as implemented has been applied in a real production environment. While there are strong opinions on both sides of the migration-emulation divide, neither has been proven or disproved. It is probable that both will be successful up to the next computing paradigm shift when all of our previously held assumptions are shattered.

A serious look at the architectures shows very similar structures. All are n-tiered client server designs. DIAS and DSpace have three explicit layers, while Fedora and Greenstone have four. All of them separate the access logic into a layer, as well as both processing logic and storage. Because of its extensive object modeling capability, Fedora has the most extendable architecture. With effort, Fedora should be able to model, store, and deliver almost any type of digital object.

Attributes of Digital Repositories

While much has been written on the subject of digital repositories and many fledging systems are taking wing, little has been done to create a comprehensive list of attributes that a digital reposi-

Table 1. Repository overview table

	DIAS	**DSpace**	**Fedora**	**Greenstone**
Organizational Ownership	IBM and Koninklijke Bibliotheek	MIT and Hewlett Packard	Cornell University and University of Virginia	University of New Zealand
Original Functional Goal	Digital Repository	Institutional Repository	Digital Repository	Digital Content Access System
Preservation Strategy	Emulation	None	Migration	None
Preservation Metadata?	Yes	No	Yes	No
Open Source?	No	Yes	Yes	Yes

tory should include.[1] The checklist presented here is a combination of the research presented as well as the practical experience of a systems manager. The ideal use of such a checklist is at systems design or during the request for proposal (RFP) process. Unfortunately, most of us do not live in ideal circumstances. We live in organizations with legacy systems, technical environments resistant to radical change, and tight resource budgets. These guidelines can be used to augment an existing infrastructure.

1. A digital repository should follow data center best practice including:
    a. Regular backups.
    b. Multiple copies of backups in multiple locations.
    c. Backup media rotation and migration.
    d. Developing a process by which files can be restored.
2. To insure fixity, a digital repository should implement a checksum or digital signature on archived files and validate them on a regular schedule.
3. A digital repository should institute an annual contingency plan drill within six months of its initial production date.
4. A digital repository should validate digital objects when submitted for ingest. The validation should include format identification, validation, and characterization.
5. A digital repository should use data formats that can be considered low risk based on the seven sustainability factors of disclosure, adoption, transparency, self-documentation, external dependencies, impact of patents, and technical protection mechanisms.
6. A digital repository should have processes to monitor the status of all of the file formats that the repository supports. A repository will need to determine when a change in a file format will require action for preservation.
7. A digital repository should store important technical characteristics that have been extracted from digital objects themselves.
8. A digital repository should provide provenance for all of its digital objects including a digitization date (or creation date if "born digital") and a process history

9. A digital repository should maintain the relationships between all of the components of an object with metadata and should enforce referential integrity for the entire digital object. The system should regularly verify that all components are present and accounted for.
10. A digital repository should implement a persistent identifier service to insure long-term unambiguous access to its digital objects.

CONCLUSION

Digital preservation is not just good data center management. Besides keeping the bits safe, there are three additional major goals of digital preservation: keeping the files useable, keeping the integrity of the object, and keeping the context of the object (Waters & Garrett, 1996). Preserving digital information is both a technical and an organizational problem. Over the past 10 years, a great deal of progress has been made. We have begun to identify the major issues and develop solutions. We have developed a number of repositories with different models, goals, and architectures. We have begun to develop community-based repositories for format information to aid preservation. We have begun to develop national strategies for preserving data. While much has been done, much more remains to be accomplished. What a wonderful opportunity for the research and the business communities to combine efforts to solve these challenges.

FUTURE RESEARCH DIRECTIONS

A report published jointly by the National Science Foundation and the Library of Congress (2003) developed a set of research challenges for digital preservation and archiving. The four main areas of research are technical architecture for repositories; the attributes of archival digital collections; tools and technologies for digital preservation; and organizational, policy, and economic issues. I have expanded on a number of these issues below.

While a number of these topics have been addressed within those broad categories, a number of substantial issues remain unexplored. Virtually all major digital preservation research initiatives have used the migration strategy. While migration will be the major strategic flow for the foreseeable future, emulation will become increasingly important, especially in the gaming and entertainment environments. Emulation could also provide a more generalized solution to the thousands of multimedia publications created during the 1980s and 1990s, as well as the 3D user interfaces of the systems of the future.

A major initiative needs to be undertaken to develop metrics for digital preservation. While some attempts have been made to theoretically define some metrics for risk, none have been tested in a scientifically rigorous method. We currently have no methodology of judging the quality of a preservation process. Can we measure effectiveness of a particular preservation process? How can we measure the quality of a digital object?

While format registries are an interesting start, we need much more research into understanding how to manage the multiple schema for describing both formats and metadata, much less the ontologies that describe the intellectual organization of disciplines. With the rapid proliferation of formats, schemas, and ontologies, how will we ever find anything? We need to develop more standard preservation quality formats for some of the rapidly developing technologies—audio and moving pictures, games, and interactive media.

While real, substantive work has been done in developing models of digital repositories, we have only scratched the surface. All of the repository models rightly assume other systems have created the objects. Perhaps we need to develop a theoretical and functional model for a preservation layer for generalized applications. Can we build a trusted digital object within an application prior to being sent to a repository?

Another major issue is awareness in organizations. How do we value digital assets to prioritize preservation within an organization? Can preservation become a part of information lifecycles? Beyond businesses and other information producers, can digital preservation be rolled out into consumer products? Can consumer software help preserve the millions of digital photographs and personal documents that could be lost?

And of course, the major issue for digital preservation, the elephant in the room that we do not really talk about, is funding models. This is a huge issue, not just for the not-for-profit organizations that have spearheaded digital preservation research, but for businesses as well. "While the costs associated with ensuring long-term access to digital information are difficult to predict quantitatively, they are generally agreed to be significant" (National Library of Australia–Costs, n.d.). Working with the ambiguous future makes this a difficult problem to define, much less solve. Nevertheless, we need to attempt to quantify total cost of ownership for a digital object.

NOTE

A draft evaluation criteria for digital repositories has been developed for a trusted external service agency called a "Certified Digital Repository" (RLG, 2005).

REFERENCES

Abrams, S.A. (2004). The role of format in digital preservation. *VINE, 34*(2), 49-55.

Abrams, S.A., & Seaman, D. (2003). Towards a global digital format registry. In *Proceedings of the World Library and Information Congress: 69th IFLA General Conference and Council*. Retrieved September 24, 2006, from http://www.ifla.org/IV/ifla69/papers/128e-Abrams_Seaman.pdf

Arms, C.R., & Fleischhauer, C. (2005). *Sustainability of digital formats: Planning for Library of Congress collections*. Retrieved September 24, 2006, from http://www.digitalpreservation.gov/formats/intro/intro.shtml

Bearman, D. (1999). Reality and chimeras in the preservation of electronic records. *D-Lib Magazine, 5*(4). Retrieved September 15, 2006, from http://www.dlib.org/dlib/april99/bearman/04bearman.html

Blanchi, C., & Petrone, J. (2001). *An architecture for digital object typing.* Corporation for National Research Initiatives. Retrieved September 15, 2006, from hdl.handle.net/4263537/4096

Brown, A. (2003a). *Digital preservation guidance note 1: Selecting file formats for long-term preservation.* Retrieved July 10, 2006, from http://www.nationalarchives.gov.uk/preservation/advice/digital.htm

Brown, A. (2003b). *Digital preservation guidance note 2: Selecting storage media for long-term preservation.* Retrieved July 10, 2006, from http://www.nationalarchives.gov.uk/preservation/advice/digital.htm

Brown, A. (2006a). *The national archives digital preservation technical paper: Automatic format identification using PRONOM and DROID.* Retrieved July 10, 2006, from http://www.nationalarchives.gov.uk/preservation/advice/digital.htm

Brown, G. (2006b). Virtualizing the CIC floppy disk project. In *Proceedings of the 2006 Fall Depository Library Conference.* Retrieved January 16, 2007, from http://www.access.gpo.gov/su_docs/fdlp/pubs/proceedings/06fall/brown.pdf

Buneman, P., Khanna, S., & Tan, W.C. (2000). *Data provenance: Some basic issues.* Retrieved April 28, 2006, from http://db.cis.upenn.edu/DL/fsttcs.abs

Consultative Committee for Space Data Systems. (2002). *Reference model for an open archival information system (OAIS), recommendation for space data system standards, CCSDS 650.0-B-1 (Blue Book).* Washington, DC: Author. Retrieved March 4, 2005, from http://public.ccsds.org/publications/archive/650x0b1.pdf

Corporation for National Research Initiatives. (2006). *Handle system.* Retrieved September 25, 2006, from http://www.handle.net/

Digital Curation Center. (2005). *About the DCC.* Retrieved October 4, 2006, from http://www.dcc.ac.uk/about/

Digital Curation Center. (2006). *Representation information in the DCC registry/repository version 0.4.* Retrieved October 4, 2006, from http://dev.dcc.rl.ac.uk/twiki/bin/view/Main/DCCRegRepV04

Digital Library Federation. (n.d.). *Digital preservation.* Retrieved on September 24, 2006, from http://www.diglib.org/preserve.htm.

Don, K., Bainbridge, D., & Witten, I.H. (2002). *The design of Greenstone 3: An agent based dynamic digital library.* Retrieved September 25, 2006, from http://www.greenstone.org/docs/greenstone3/gs3design.pdf

Fleischhauer, C. (2003). *Looking at preservation from the digital library perspective.*

Foster, I., Vockler, J., Wilde, M. & Zhao, Y. (2002, October). *The virtual data grid: A new model and architecture for data-intensive collaboration.* Proceedings of the Data Provenance/Derivation Workshop. Retrieved October 10, 2006, from http://people.cs.uchicago.edu/~yongzh/papers/CIDR.VDG.submitted.pdf

Gladney, H. (2004). Trustworthy 100-year digital objects: Evidence after every witness is dead. *ACM Transactions on Information Systems, 22*(3), 406-436.

Harvard University Library. (2003a). *DRS data verification process.* Internal Documentation.

Harvard University Library. (2003b). *Name resolution service: Introduction and use.* Retrieved April 28, 2006, from http://hul.harvard.edu/ois/systems/nrs/nrs-intro.html

Harvard University Library. (2006). *JSTOR/Harvard object validation environment.* Retrieved April 12, 2006, from http://hul.harvard.edu/jhove/

IBM. (n.d.). *Digital information archiving system.* Retrieved October 4, 2006, from http://www-5.ibm.com/nl/dias/index.html

IBM/KB. (n.d.). *IBM/KB long-term preservation study.* Retrieved October 4, 2006, from http://www-5.ibm.com/nl/dias/preservation2.html

International DOI Foundation. (2006). *Introductory overview: The DOI® system.* Retrieved September 24, 2006, from http://www.doi.org/overview/sys_overview_021601.html

Kunze, J. (2003). *Towards electronic persistence using ARK identifiers.* Retrieved October 4, 2006, from http://www.cdlib.org/inside/diglib/ark/

Lagoze, C., Payette, S., Shin, E., & Wilper, C. (2005). Fedora: An architecture for complex objects and their relationships. *Journal of Digital Libraries Special Issue on Complex Objects,* 124-138. Retrieved October 5, 2006, from http://www.arxiv.org/abs/cs.DL/0501012

Lawrence, G.W., Kehoe, W.R., Rieger, O.Y., Walters, W.H., & Kenney, A.R. (2000). *Risk management of digital information: A file format investigation.* Washington, DC: Council on Library and Information Resources. Retrieved September 24, 2006, from http://www.clir.org/PUBS/reports/pub93/pub93.pdf

Library of Congress. (2006). *Metadata encoding and transmission standard.* Retrieved April 28, 2006, from http://www.loc.gov/standards/mets/mets-home.html

Library of Congress. (2006). *Sustainability of digital formats: Planning for Library of Congress collections.* Retrieved April 21, 2006, from http://www.digitalpreservation.gov/formats/fdd/descriptions.shtml

Lorie, R.A. (2000). *Long-term archiving of digital information: IBM research report.* Retrieved September 29, 2006, from http://domino.watson.ibm.com/library/CyberDig.nsf/7d11afdf5c7cda94852566de006b4127/be-2a2b188544df2c8525690d00517082

Lynch, C.A. (2003). *Institutional repositories: Essential infrastructure for scholarship in the digital age.* ARL, 226. Retrieved September 24, 2006, from http://www.arl.org/newsltr/226/ir.html

Macey, R. (2006, August 5). One giant blunder for mankind: How NASA lost moon pictures. *The Sydney Morning Herald.* Retrieved August 8, 2006, from http://www.smh.com.au/news/national/one-giant-blunder-for-mankind-how-nasa-lost-moon-pictures/2006/08/04/1154198328978.html

MIT. (2004). *DSpace system documentation: Architecture.* Retrieved September 25, 2006, from http://www.dspace.org/technology/system-docs/architecture.html

MIT & HP. (2007). *Welcome to DSpace.* Retrieved April 13, 2007, from http://www.dspace.org/

National Archives of Australia. (2003a). *Appendix 10 recordkeeping cost-benefit analysis.* Retrieved September 25, 2006, from http://www.naa.gov.au/recordkeeping/dirks/dirksman/dirks_A10_cost_benefit.html

National Archives of Australia. (2003b). *The DIRKS methodology a users guide.* Retrieved September 25, 2006, from http://www.naa.gov.au/recordkeeping/dirks/dirksman/part1.html#bg3

National Archives of England, Wales and the United Kingdom. (2006a). *Redaction: Guidelines for the editing of exempt information from paper and electronic documents prior to release.* Retrieved July 10, 2006, from http://www.nationalarchives.gov.uk/preservation/advice/digital.htm

National Archives of England, Wales and the United Kingdom. (2006b). *The technical registry PRONOM.* Retrieved July 10, 2006, from http://www.nationalarchives.gov.uk/aboutapps/pronom/default.htm

National Institute of Standards and Technology. (2002). Contingency planning guide for information technology systems. In E.B. Lennon (Ed.), *Information technology laboratory.* Retrieved April 28, 2006, from http://csrc.nist.gov/publications/nistpubs/800-34/sp800-34.pdf

National Library of Australia–Costs. (n.d.). *Preserving access to digital information (PADI) initiative: Costs.* Retrieved July 15, 2006, from http://www.nla.gov.au/padi/topics/5.html

National Library of Australia–Formats. (n.d.). *Preserving access to digital information (PADI) initiative: Formats & media.* Retrieved September 25, 2006, from http://www.nla.gov.au/padi/topics/44.html

National Science Foundation & Library of Congress. (2003). *It's about time: Research challenges in digital archiving and long-term preservation.* Final Report: Workshop on Research Challenges in Digital Archiving and Long-Term Preservation.

Ockerbloom, J.M. (2004). *Meet Fred: Format Registry demonstration.* Retrieved October 4, 2006, from http://tom.library.upenn.edu/cgi-bin/fred?cmd=ShowDocu&&id=about

Ockerbloom, J.M. (2005). *The typed object model.* Retrieved October 4, 2006, from http://tom.library.upenn.edu/

Olson, T.A. (2003). *Building collections using Greenstone.* Retrieved April 10, 2007, from http://www.lib.uchicago.edu/dldc/talks/2003/dlf-greenstone/

Oltmans, E., & van Wijngaarden, H. (2004). *Digital preservation and permanent access: The UVC for images.* Retrieved October 8, 2006, from http://www.kb.nl/hrd/dd/dd_links_en_publicaties/publicaties/uvc-ist.pdf

Pearson, D. (2002, October). The grid: Requirements for establishing the provenance of derived data. In *Proceedings of the Data Provenance/Derivation Workshop.* Retrieved October 10, 2006, from http://people.cs.uchicago.edu/~yongzh/papers/Provenance_Requirements.doc

Plale, B., Ramachandran, R., & Tanner, S. (2006, January). Data management support for adaptive analysis and prediction of the atmosphere in LEAD. In *Proceedings of the 22nd Conference on Interactive Information Processing Systems for Meteorology, Oceanography, and Hydrology (IIPS).* Retrieved April 28, 2006, from http://www.cs.indiana.edu/~plale/papers/plale_IIPS06.pdf

RLG (Research Libraries Group). (2005). *An audit checklist for the certification of trusted digital repositories.* Mountain View, CA. Retrieved on October 6, 2006 from http://www.rlg.org/en/pdfs/rlgnara-repositorieschecklist.pdf

RLG & OCLC. (2002). *Trusted digital repositories. Attributes and responsibilities: An RLG-OCLC report.* Retrieved April 28, 2006, from http://www.rlg.org/longterm/repositories.pdf

Rothenberg, J. (1999). *Avoiding technological quicksand: Finding a viable technical foundation for digital preservation.* Retrieved July 15, 2006, from http://www.clir.org/PUBS/reports/rothenberg/contents.html

Rothenberg, J. (1999). *Ensuring the longevity of digital information.* Retrieved July 15, 2006, from http://www.clir.org/pubs/resources/articles.html

Saltz, J. (2002, October). Data provenance. In *Proceedings of the Data Provenance/Derivation Workshop.* Retrieved October 10, 2006, from http://people.cs.uchicago.edu/%7Eyongzh/papers/ProvenanceJS10-02.doc

Simmhan, Y., Plale, B., & Gannon, D. (2006). *A performance evaluation of the Karma Provenance Framework for Scientific Workflows.* Retrieved April 28, 2006, from http://www.cs.indiana.edu/~plale/papers/SimmhanIPAW06.pdf

Smith, A. (2006). *Distributed preservation in a national context: NDIIPP at mid-point.* D-Lib Magazine, 12(6). Retrieved October 11, 2006, from http://www.dlib.org/dlib/june06/smith/06smith.html

Stanescu, A. (2004). *Assessing the durability of formats in a digital preservation environment: The INFORM methodology.* D-Lib Magazine, 10(11). Retrieved July 15, 2006, from http://www.dlib.org/dlib/november04/stanescu/11stanescu.html

Staples, T., Wayland, R., & Payette, S. (2003). The Fedora project: An open-source digital object repository management system. *D-Lib Magazine, 9*(4). Retrieved October 5, 2006, from http://www.dlib.org/dlib/april03/staples/04staples.html

Steenbakkers, J.F. (2005). Digital archiving in the twenty-first century: Practice at the national library of The Netherlands. *Library Trends, 54*(1), 33-56.

Technical Advisory Service for Images (TASI). (2006). Choosing a file format. Retrieved October 11, 2006, from http://www.tasi.ac.uk/advice/creating/format.html#fo3

UKOLN. (2006). *Good practice guide for developers of cultural heritage Web services.* Retrieved July 15, 2006, from http://www.ukoln.ac.uk/interop-focus/gpg/

Waters, D., & Garrett, J. (Eds.). (1996). *Preserving digital information: Report of the task force on archiving of digital information.* Washington, DC/Mountain View, CA: Commission on Preservation and Access and the Research Libraries Group. Retrieved March 4, 2005, from http://www.rlg.org/ArchTF/

WC3. (2001, September). *URIs, URLs, and URNs: Clarifications and recommendations 1.0.* Report, W3C Note 21, W3C/IETF URI Planning Interest Group. Retrieved October 6, 2006, from http://www.w3.org/TR/uri-clarification/

Witten, I.H., Bainbridge, D., & Boddie, S.J. (2001). Greenstone: Open-source digital library software. *D-Lib Magazine, 7*(10). Retrieved October 5, 2006, from http://www.dlib.org/dlib/october01/witten/10witten.html

Weibel, S., Jul, E., & Shafer, K. (1995). *PURLs: Persistent uniform resource locators.* Retrieved October 8, 2006, from http://purl.oclc.org/

ADDITIONAL READINGS

Arms, W. (1999). Preservation of scientific serials: Three current examples. *Journal of Electronic Publishing, 5.* Available at http://www.press.umich.edu/jep/05-02/arms.html

Atkins, D.E. (2003). *Revolutionizing science and engineering through cyber-infrastructure: Report of the National Science Foundation Blue-Ribbon Advisory Panel on Cyberinfrastructure.* Directorate for Computer & Information Science & Engineering. Available at http://www.cise.nsf.gov/sci/reports/atkins.pdf

Barnett, B., Bishoff, L., Borgman, C., Caplan, P., Hamma, K., & Lynch, C. (2003). *Report of the Workshop on Opportunities for Research on the Creation, Management, Preservation and Use of Digital Content.* Available at http://www.imls.gov/pubs/pdf/digitalopp.pdf

Bearman, D. (1999). Reality and chimeras in the preservation of electronic records. *D-Lib Magazine, 5*(4). Available at http://www.dlib.org/dlib/april99/bearman/04bearman.html

Cantara, L. (2003). Introduction. In L. Cantara (Ed.), *Archiving electronic journals: Research funded by the Andrew W. Mellon Foundation.* Available at http://www.diglib.org/preserve/ejp.htm

Carlin, J.W. (2004). ERA: An archives of the future for the future. *Prologue, a Quarterly Publication of the National Archives and Records Administration, 36*(1). Available at http://www.archives.gov/publications/prologue/2004/spring/archivist.html

Cathro, W. (2004, November 9-11). Preserving the outputs of research. In *Proceedings of the Archiving Web Resources Conference,* Canberra, Australia. Available at http://www.nla.gov.au/nla/staffpaper/2004/cathro1.html

Crow, R. (2002). *SPARC institutional repository checklist & resource guide.* The Scholarly Publishing & Academic Resources Coalition, American Research Libraries. Available at www.arl.org/sparc

Davis, S. (2002). *Digital preservation strategy.* The National Archives of Australia Agency to Researcher Digital Preservation Project. Available at http://www.naa.gov.au/recordkeeping/rkpubs/fora/02nov/digital_preservation.pdf

Falk, H. (2003). Digital archive developments. *The Electronic Library, 21,* 375-379. Available at http://caliban.emeraldinsight.com

Flecker, D. (2001). Preserving scholarly e-journals.

D-Lib Magazine, 7(9). Available at http://www.dlib.org/dlib/september01/flecker/09flecker.html

Gadd, E., Oppenheim, C., & Probets, S. (2003). The Intellectual property rights issues facing self-archiving—key findings of the RoMEO project. *D-Lib Magazine, 9*(9). Available at http://www.dlib.org/dlib/september03/gadd/09gadd.html

Gilliland-Swetland, A., & Eppard, P. (2000). Preserving the authenticity of contingent digital objects. *D-Lib Magazine, 6*(7/8). Available at http://www.dlib.org/dlib/july00/eppard/07eppard.html

Granger, S. (2002). Digital preservation and deep infrastructure. *D-Lib Magazine 8*(2). Available at http://www.dlib.org/dlib/february02/granger/02granger.html

Harnad, S. (2001). The self-archiving initiative: Freeing the refereed research literature online. *Nature, 410*(April 26), 1024-1025. Available at http://www.ecs.soton.ac.uk/~harnad/Tp/nature4.htm

Hart, P.E., & Liu, Z. (2003). Trust in the preservation of digital information. *Communications of the ACM, 46*(6), 93-97. Available at http://doi.acm.org/10.1145/777313.777319

Harvard University Library. (2003) Report on the planning year grant for the design of an e-journal archive. In L. Cantara (Ed.), *Archiving electronic journals: Research funded by the Andrew W. Mellon Foundation.* Available at http://www.diglib.org/preserve/ejp.htm

Hedstrom, M., & Ross, S. (2003). *Invest to save: Report and recommendations of the NSF-DELOS working group on digital archiving and preservation.* Available at http://eprints.erpanet.org/archive/00000048/01/Digitalarchiving.pdf

Hunt, A., & Thomas, D. (2002). Software archaeology. *IEEE Software, 19*(2).

Inera, Inc. (2001). *E-journal archive DTD feasibility study.* Prepared for the Harvard University Library, Office of Information Systems, E-Journal Archiving Project. Available at http://www.diglib.org/preserve/hadtdfs.pdf

Kaplan, E. (2002). Response to "Preserving software: Why and how." *Iterations: An Interdisciplinary Journal of Software History, 1*(13), 1-3. Available at http://www.cbi.umn.edu/iterations/kaplan.html

Kling, R., Spector, L.B., & Fortuna, J. (2003). The real stakes of virtual publishing: The transformation of E-Biomed into PubMed central. *Journal of the American Society for Information Science and Technology, 55*(2), 127-148. Available at http://www3.interscience.wiley.com/

Library of Congress. (2003). *Preserving our digital heritage: Plan for the national digital information infrastructure and preservation program.* A collaborate initiative of the Library of Congress. Available at http://www.digitalpreservation.gov/about/planning.html

Lord, P., & Macdonald, A. (2003). *E-Science curation report: Data curation for e-science in the UK: An audit to establish requirements for future curation and provision.* The JISC Committee for the Support of Research. Available at http://www.jisc.ac.uk/uploaded_documents/e-ScienceReport-Final.pdf

Liu, Z. (2003). Trends in transforming scholarly communication and their implications. *Information Processing & Management, 39,* 889-898. Available at http://www.elsevier.com/

Maniatis, P., Rosenthal, D., Roussopoulos, M., Baker, M., Giuli, T.J., & Muliadi, Y. (2003). Preserving peer replicas by rate-limited sampled voting. In *Proceedings of the ACM Symposium on Operating Systems Principles Archive Proceedings of the 19th ACM Symposium on Operating Systems Principles Table of Contents.* Available at http://portal.acm.org/

Marcum, D.B. (2003). Research questions for the digital era library. *Library Trends, 51*(4), 636-651.

National Science Foundation Office of Cyberinfrastructure. (2005). *NSF's cyberinfrastructure vision of 21st century discovery.* Available at http://www.nsf.gov/od/oci/CI-v40.pdf

Pearson, D. (2001). Medical history for tomorrow—preserving the record of today. *Health Information and Libraries Journal, 18*. Available at www.blackwell-synergy.com/www.blackwell-synergy.com/

Pinfield, S., & James, H. (2003). The digital preservation of e-prints. *D-Lib Magazine, 9*(9). Available at http://www.dlib.org/dlib/september03/pinfield/09pinfield.html

Reich, V., & Rosenthal, D. (2004) Preserving today's scientific record for tomorrow. *BMJ: British Medical Journal, 328*(7431). Available at http://www.bmjjournals.com

Rosenthal, D., Lipkis, T., Robertson, T., & Morabito, S. (2005). Transparent format migration of preserved Web content. *D-Lib Magazine, 11*(1). Available at http://www.dlib.org/dlib/january05/rosenthal/01rosenthal.html

Smith, B. (2002). *Preserving tomorrow's memory: Preserving digital content for future generations.* International Preservation News, 29(May), 4-9. Available at http://www.ifla.org/VI/4/news/ipnn29.pdf

Spedding, V. (2003). *Data preservation: Great data but will it last?* Resource Information, 5(Spring).

Available at http://www.researchinformation.info/rispring03data.html

Waters, D. (2002). *Good archives make good scholars: Reflections on recent steps toward the archiving of digital information.* Council on Library and Information Resources. Available at http://www.clir.org/pubs/reports/pub107/waters.html

Waters, D. (2006) Preserving the knowledge Commons. In E. Ostrom & C. Hess (Eds.), *Knowledge as a commons: From theory to practice.* Understanding. Cambridge: MIT Press.

Wheatley, P. (2004). Institutional repositories in the context of digital preservation. *DPC Technology Watch Series Report, 4*(2). Available at http://www.dpconline.org/docs/DPCTWf4word.pdf

Woodyard, D. (2004). *Significant property: Digital preservation at the British Library. VINE, 34*(1), 17-20. Available at http://ninetta.emeraldinsight.com/Insight/viewContentItem.do?contentType=Article&contentId=862526

Zabolitzky, J.G. (2002). Preserving software: Why and how. *An Interdisciplinary Journal of Software History, 1*(13), 1-8. Available at http://www.cbi.umn.edu/iterations/zabolitzky.html

Chapter XX
Teaching Information Systems to International Students in Australia:
A Global Information Technology Perspective

Zhaohao Sun
Hebei Normal University, China

ABSTRACT

GIT and GIS have a significant impact on the undergraduate and postgraduate programs offered in universities in Australia. Further, how to teach IT and IS to international students has been becoming a significant issue for IT and IS programs offered in Australia, in particular in the context of a fiercely competitive market of international students and in the context of GIT and GIS. However, these topics have not drawn the attention of academic researchers so far. This chapter will fill this gap by examining the impact of global information technology on universities in Australia in such areas as curriculum development, textbooks and teaching, and looking at some issues in teaching information technology and information systems to international students from different countries with different IT and IS backgrounds based on the author's working and teaching experience in three different universities in Australia. This chapter also makes a daring prediction for the impact of GIT on international education in Australia and proposes a few viable strategies for resolving some issues facing international education for IT and IS in Australia. The proposed approach is very useful for research and development of GIT and GIS as well as for IT/IS programs in Australian universities.

INTRODUCTION

Global information technology (GIT) and global information systems (GIS) are not a new concept, because Manheim (1992) discusses the critical issues and strategic opportunities for globally competing firms using GIT and GIS. Palvia (1997) proposes a model of the global and strategic impact of information technology (IT). Palvia, Jain Palvia, and Whitworth (2002) also address some key issues of GIT and provide a model for analyzing global IT issues. Akmanligil and Palvia (2004) discuss strategies for GIS development, in which they consider GIS as it is used across one or more national borders. However, like global economy, GIT and GIS have a significant impact on the undergraduate and postgraduate programs offered in universities in Australia. In particular, the international students have dominated the student numbers that enrolled in IT and information systems (IS) in Australian universities. The majority of students enrolled in IT/IS postgraduate programs (by course work) are from Asia, mainly from China and India. For example, there were 16 students in a subject entitled Decision Support Systems taught by this author in Autumn 2006, and only one of these was Australian. The rest were from Asian countries. However, "global information technology in Australia" cannot be Googled in its "scholar" world, which implies that this topic has not drawn the attention of academic researchers so far. This chapter will fill the gap by examining GIT and its impacts on IT and IS education in Australian universities.

Further, how to teach IT and IS to international students has been becoming a significant issue for IT and IS programs offered in Australia, in particular in the context of a fiercely competitive market of international students and in the context of GIT and GIS. However, this issue has been technically ignored to some extent in universities in Australia. The administrators might believe that the key to teaching IT and IS in the international student-filled environment is to use flexible teaching methods in an online teaching and learning environment. This chapter will analyze some issues of teaching IT and IS international students based on my working and teaching experience in three different universities in Australia. My working and studying experience in China and Germany will certainly affect the discussion in the chapter.

The term IT is frequently used today not only within universities and colleges but also by individuals and governments. Strictly speaking, IT in Australia covers all disciplines of computing, at least from a viewpoint of immigration policies. Because there are some differences between IT

and IS within universities, I have used IT and IS or both in some contexts.

The rest of the chapter is organized as follows. The next section examines international education in Australia, followed by a look at IT and IS in Australian universities from a global viewpoint. I then discuss the impacts of GIT on IT and IS in Australia, as well as my experience teaching IT and IS in Australia as an example of GIT. The next section discusses the future trend for IT and IS in Australia. I end the chapter with some concluding remarks and by proposing future research directions.

INTERNATIONAL EDUCATION IN AUSTRALIA

This section will examine international education in Australia within a context of globalization. Therefore, GIT can be considered as a part of international education.

Harman (2002) considers Australia as a major higher education exporter. He also discusses internationalization of higher education within a context of globalization.

The higher education sector in Australia comprises 37 public and three private autonomous and self-accrediting universities, and four other autonomous and self-accrediting institutions. Internationalization of higher education in Australia has made significant progress since the 1980s. In 2004, 362,092 students commenced higher education in Australia, 107,142 of them being international students from overseas (DEST, 2005). This means that international students accounted for about 30% of the total new enrolled students in Australian universities in 2004.

Marginson (2004) points out that "between 1990 and 2002 the number of international students enrolled in Australian universities increased from 24,998 to 185,058." Lukic, Broadbent, and Maclachlan (2004) also noted that the enrollments of international students in Australian universities increased 123% from 1997 to 2002. Therefore, "international students are making up a substantial and growing proportion of Australian higher education students." At the same time, "by 2001 Australia spent only 0.8% of GDP on the public funding of higher education, which was half the level of public investment in 1975, although the national rate of participation in higher education had doubled since then" (Marginson, 2004). This also means that Australian higher education has been market-oriented. However, Australia provided scholarships to about 2% of the total international full-fee paying students, while the United States provided scholarships to 25% of its international students in 2002 (Marginson, 2004). This is why more than 50,000 postgraduate students of a total 60,000 international students from China are studying in universities in the U.S. Therefore, there is less financial support to international students including research students and PhD students in Australia. Nevertheless, Australian universities have been enjoying the success of the commercialization of education, because international education has become Australia's third largest services export. In 2002, universities earned $1.45 billion in student fees (13% of revenues), and Australia earned about $5 billion in total from international students spending on fees, food, transport, accommodations, living costs, and entertainment, on and offshore (Marginson, 2004).

International higher education "has provided Australian universities with large numbers of able and highly motivated students. This has been particularly important for research programs in fields such as engineering and IT" (Harman, 2002, p. 11).

Furthermore, Harman (2002) notes that in some departments and faculties, well over 50% of enrollments are from international students. Therefore, international students have been playing a critical role in Australian higher education and economy since then, although not all Australians share this common sense.

Marginson (2004) acknowledges that Australian international education is price dependent rather than quality dependent, because Australia commercializes its high education and tries to export its higher education as a product, in order to increase its revenue and improve its international reputation of higher education and at the same time promote international friendship and understanding

especially with its neighboring nations (Harman, 2002). Further, Asian students believe that Australia is one of the most important destinations for their international education, because their expectation for studying in Australian universities is to obtain a higher academic degree, improve their English, and possibly (many of them) to become a permanent resident in Australia or obtain a high-profit position after returning to their own country.

IT AND IS IN AUSTRALIA: A GLOBAL VIEWPOINT

This section reviews IT and IS in Australia, taking into account computing disciplines. This can be considered an impact of GIT on higher education in Australia from a general viewpoint.

Computing Classification and Its Impact in Australia

Significant developments have changed the landscape of the computing disciplines since the 1990s in the United States (CC, 2004). Computer engineering (CE) has become an independent discipline from electrical engineering (EE). Software engineering (SE) emerged as an area within computer science (CS) and now is a discipline unto itself. IS has become a discipline within business or an independent discipline. IT emerged in the context of business and CS, and also became a discipline in the later 1990s, as shown in Figure 1. This means that computing disciplines mainly consist of CS, CE, IS, EE, IT, and SE, although one normally uses IT to represent all these disciplines, as mentioned in the first section. Further, the CE, SE, IT, and IS shown in Figure 1 can be considered as the "overlapping" disciplines in the current classification. They have played a significant role in computing degree programs in higher education of Australia, because about one-third of computing degree programs in Australian universities are IT and IS programs. CE and SE degree programs are only offered in some universities such as at La Trobe University and the University of New South Wales.

The above classification (CC, 2004, 2005) of the Association for Computing Machinery (ACM), the Association for Information Systems (AIS), and the IEEE Computer Society (IEEE-CS) has been reflected in the configuration of faculty in some universities in Australia. For example, the Faculty of IT at the University of Technology Sydney (UTS) has three departments: Computer Systems, Software Engineering, and Information Systems (http://it.uts.edu.au/about/department/index.html), while the University of New South Wales has a School of Computer Science and Engineering (http://www.cse.unsw.edu.au/people/index.html). Information systems courses offered at this university are in the Faculty of Commerce and Economics. Some universities still use computing as the name of their faculty or school or department to cover any teaching and research activity of a technical nature involving computers (CC, 2005). Macquarie University has a Department of Computing. Some universities such as Griffith University use Computing and Information Technology as the faculty name, in order to keep the influence of traditional computing; at the same time, it does not like to lose the market of IT. Some Australian universities have not classified computing according to the disciplines as shown in Figure 1. For example, Internet computing and information security and intelligence have become relatively recent disciplines offered at universities in Australia such as www.ecu.edu.au. Information and knowledge management (IKM) has a

trend of separating itself from IS, although many Australian universities offer subjects or courses on IKM in the context of IS. Bond University has only offered Information Technology. The reason is that the degree programs of IT and IS offered at universities in Australia are very market oriented and always adjusted according to the change of market, which has been experienced in the past decade, because of significant ups and downs in IT and IS. It is difficult to predict that IT and IS can resume to the peak of 2000-2001 in Australia, although some IS and IT researchers believe that IT and IS have been recovering since 2005 in the United States.

IS and Its Programs in Australia

What is IS? This is a meta-question like, What is artificial intelligence (AI)? Generally speaking, IS is a discipline that integrates IT solutions and business processes to meet the information needs of businesses and other organizations, and enables organizations to achieve their objectives in an effective and efficient way (CC, 2005). While IT stresses T (technology), IS emphasizes I (information). In Australia, IT and IS are closer, compared with other computing disciplines (as shown in Figure 1).

IS as a discipline began more than 50 years ago to address the data processing needs of business in the areas of accounting, payroll, and inventory. The Association for Information Technology

Figure 1. Disciplines in computing based on CC 2005

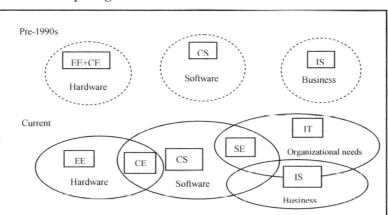

Professionals (AITP), founded in 1951, played an important role in the early development of IS, while the Association for Information Systems (AIS, https://www.aisnet.org/), founded in 1994, is playing an increasingly important role in global IS.

Before the 1990s, IS specialists had mainly ties with business or commerce schools and did not have much interaction with computer scientists and electrical engineers (CC, 2004). However, this has been changed in universities in Australia, because some IS programs have been offered in the Faculty of Information Technology, as does UTS. IS also has alternative names, such as Business Informatics offered at Murdoch University (http://handbook.murdoch.edu.au/courses /detail06.lasso?crscdhb=34225) or Business Information Technology (BIT) offered by the University of Adelaide, which claims that the Bachelor of BIT degree "offers students knowledge and skills in the application of modern IT within business. It integrates courses taught by the School of Commerce and the School of Computer Science. The degree program aims to develop knowledge, skills and understanding in the application of IT to developing business solutions" (http://www.adelaide.edu.au/programs/ug/prog/comm/#bitech). IS also has alternative names such as MIS (management information systems), which is offered by ECU (www.ecu.edu.au), and business information systems (BIS), which "recognizes the critical role of information and information systems in modern business practice," offered in the Faculty of Economics and Businesses at the University of Sydney (www.usyd.edu.au).

It should be noted that http://www.utas.edu.au/infosys/cgi/is_depts/ provides detailed information for IS programs offered at universities in Australia. From this Web site we can see that almost every university in Australia offers IT and IS programs for undergraduate and/or postgraduate students.

Global Information Systems in Australia

IT and IS have been affected by globalization. For example, the Association for Information Systems, located in the United States, has been influencing IS in Australia. Basically speaking, the AIS (2006) listed the following topics as the key areas of IS, at least for the Master's in Information Systems programs

- IT infrastructure.
- Introduction to programming.
- Algorithms and data structures.
- Data management.
- Analysis, modeling, and design.
- Enterprise models.
- IT governance.
- IT strategy and policy.
- Project and change management.
- IS sourcing.
- Ethical implications of IS/IT.
- Social and cultural aspects of IS.
- Global issues in IS.

All of these are reflected in the programs of IS education in Australia, because the textbooks are usually imported from the UK or United States directly, which will be discussed in more detail in the next section.

GLOBAL IT AND IS IN AUSTRALIA

This section will further examine GIT and its impacts on Australian universities from an IT and IS viewpoint.

Background

With the development of the Internet at the end of the last century, IT and IS are offered as undergraduate and postgraduate programs by almost all universities in Australia. The number of students enrolled in IT and IS programs reached its peak in 2002-2003 like other developed countries. Some universities offer IT and IS in the Faculty of Information Technology (e.g., www.uts.edu.au). Other universities offer them in different faculties (e.g., www.uow.edu.au). With the strong competition of educational markets of international students, it is said that the number of international students enrolled in IT and IS programs in universities in Australia has not been satisfactory in the past two years. In this case, some administrators have tried to improve the strategies of teaching methods, teaching/learning environments, programs offered, and reconstruction or reconfiguration of academic staff in order to attract international students. However, it seems that the strategies have not essentially changed the situation faced. As an academic staff member, I worked at a university in China for more than 13 years, at two German universities for more than three years, and at three Australian universities for more than seven years. What I can do is to try to understand the background of international students and improve my teaching art, in order to help the universities I worked for to attract international students. In a later section, I will go into each of them in greater detail.

Global IT and Its Impact on IT in Australia: An Immigration Viewpoint

Global information technology has drawn increasing interest and research since the end of the last century. GIT mainly consists of three components (Palvia et al., 2002): GIT-1: information systems and technology that are global in scope; GIT-2: information systems and technology in different cultures and different countries; and GIT-3: IT products and services that are built in one country and used in another. We will address each of them in what follows.

With the dramatic development of the Internet at the end of the last century, many developed countries carried out beneficial strategies to attract international students to study IT and IS in their own countries. For example, Australia uses immigration policies to attract international students to study IT or IS at Australian universities. More specifically, if one international student graduates from an IT or IS program at a university in Australia and applies for permanent residence in Australia, then he or she can get an immigration bonus, and his or her degree (bachelor or master) has also enjoyed relatively higher migration marks and his or her application can be processed within a relatively shorter time (three months) (2001-2003). This policy integrating computing and migration

attracted many Asian students to come Australia to study IT and IS programs. This belongs to GIT-2, because information systems and technology are taught to students from different cultures and different countries. It can be also considered as GIT-3, because the IT products and services available in Australia are used by students from other countries such as China. In this way, Australia helps the Chinese government with providing IT services to the young generation, although this is only applicable to some relatively rich Chinese families (which also belongs to GIT-3). Even so, it relieves the pressure resulting from the unmet social requirements from the higher degree education of China. At the same time, Australia received huge revenues from higher education export, as mentioned earlier.

Furthermore, like global economy, IT and IS have also experienced a process of globalization, because there are a growing number of globally mobile jobs in fields of business, computing including IT and IS, and scientific research (Marginson, 2004). Marginson (2004) demonstrates that:

"Australia has positioned itself as a high growth provider by good marketing and management, inventive off-shore engagement, a specialization in high-volume standard-cost training in business and IT, improving non-academic services, proximity to Asia, a friendly climate and a peaceful social atmosphere and a price advantage over the USA and UK deriving from a weak Australian dollar."

IT including CS, CE, EE, SE, and IS is one of the three most favorite fields for international students to study in universities in Australia (Lukic et al., 2004). The other two fields are management and health. The immigration policies of Australia promote this trend, because an international student with a higher degree from a university in Australia (master, bachelor) can easily obtain permanent residence in Australia, as mentioned earlier, which is still valid for the time being.

Global IT and Its Impacts on IT in Australia: A Comparative Viewpoint

Marginson (2004) notes that Australian education in IT is much the same as American or British education. This can be only considered as a high-level abstraction or summary. More specifically, the higher education system of Australia is inherited from that of Britain. For example, the bachelor for IT is a three-year program; it takes students in the United States and China four years in order to obtain a bachelor's degree in IT. This is because the superstructure of Australia is based on that of Britain. From a GIT viewpoint, this is a successful application of British IT and IS services and products to the higher education of Australia. Therefore, this belongs to GIT-3.

However, Americanization of higher education also has impressive influence on higher education in Australia. For example, a large number of textbooks for IT and IS undergraduate students are from the course technology publisher (http://www.course.com/). It is said that these textbooks can be considered a product of outsourcing IT and IS of the United States to Australia. Frankly speaking, the textbooks from this publisher are more teaching-friendly compared with other international publishers that I have encountered in the past years, because it provides the lecturer or instructor (http://www.course.com/irc/IR.cfm) with:

- An instructor manual with lesson plans and teaching tips.
- A sample syllabus including assignments, quizzes, and exams.
- PowerPoint presentation slides (although they usually must be revised, updated, and significantly extended).
- Figure files
- Solutions to exercises or problems.
- A test bank and test engine (based on the ExamView).

PowerPoint presentation slides are of practical significance, because they require lecturers to take a lot of effect and time. "Teachers are more and more expecting material and help from the authors and the publishers of a textbook" (Furbach, 2003). However, PowerPoint presentation slides provided by some publishers are not carefully and professionally designed or drafted taking into account class teaching and time arrangement. They usually must

be revised, updated, and significantly extended. For example, this author used a textbook for postgraduate students (BUSS 950). The publisher provides lecture slides for each chapter in the textbook. However, the number of the lecture slides for each chapter is only five or six, which is obviously not sufficient for a teaching period lasting 45 or 90 minutes. Therefore, this textbook will be not used in the future.

Further, it is obvious that the textbooks are not localized based on the characteristics of Australia, although the cover page of the textbook told the readers that it is an "International Student Edition not for sale in the U.S." (Satzinger, Jackson, & Burd, 2004). Further, other textbooks for IT and IS undergraduate and postgraduate students are published by a few international publishers located in the United States and UK such as Addison-Wesley (www.personed.uk), McGraw-Hill (www.mhhe.com), and Prentice Hall. In the past six years, I have used eight different textbooks for lecturing or teaching eight subjects for IT and IS undergraduate and postgraduate students at three universities in Australia. However, no textbooks are published by an Australian-owned publisher. Therefore, this belongs to GIT-1 and GIT-3. This is also the reason why the price of every textbook in Australian universities is very high, making it difficult for some students from developing countries to afford them. In this case, some students believe that it is very difficult for a lecturer to deliver "high-quality teaching" because he or she does not have his or her own published textbook, and therefore some lecturers can be easily considered as an "advanced photocopier"—photocopying knowledge, information, and data from textbooks for students without any further process or update, although these are extreme cases.

However, some universities in Australia still claim that they provide "high-quality teaching" to students and use it to attract international students. This has not drawn any attention in some academic staff of IT and IS in Australia. "Who cares" may be the answer from them, because they are enjoying the hegemony of culture and English. It seems the Australian government has also not provided sufficient money to support development of its own system of textbooks for IT and IS. One of the possible reasons for this is that Australia has a population of only about

20 million, and it is difficult and also not necessary to establish a perfect system of Australian-owned textbooks.

Based on the above discussion, we can come to a conclusion that one of the consequences of GIT is that the textbooks for IT and IS will be dominated by a few publishers from the UK and U.S.; at least this is true for the English-speaking world.

Global IT and Its Impacts on IT Curricula in Australia

The Association for Computing Machinery, Association for Information Systems, and IEEE Computer Society worked together and proposed Computing Curricula 2004 (CC, 2004) and 2005 (CC, 2005) in order to guide the undergraduate degree programs of computing offered by universities in the United States. These curricula have also influenced similar programs offered by the universities in Australia. The computing disciplines include computing engineering, computing science, information systems, information technology, and software engineering, as mentioned earlier.

CC 2005 listed 50 topics with values ranging between 0 and 5 and relative emphasis (min-max) for each kind of computing degree program for undergraduate students on each given topic. I examined the emphasis of IS programs on each of the 50 topics in order to help improve the existing curriculum in 2004. I used a three-level method for teaching and research of IS:

- **Level 1 topics with values not less than 4:** These are most important for teaching and research of IS.
- **Level 2 topics with the value of 3:** These are important for teaching and research of IS.
- **Level 3 topics with values less than or equal to 2:** These are less important, at least uncertain for teaching and research of IS. However, they can be involved in research.

Based on CC 2004 and CC 2005, I found that the first-level topics out of the mentioned 50 topics are as follows:

1. Programming fundamentals
2. Human-computer interaction
3. Information management (DB) practice
4. Management of IS organization
5. Organizational behavior
6. Legal/professional/ethics/society
7. Information systems development
8. Project management
9. Analysis of business requirements
10. E-business
11. Distributed systems
12. Systems integration
13. Mathematical foundations
14. Interpersonal communication

Each of the above 14 topics are emphasized in the IS program for undergraduate students in Australian universities, to some extent, except topic 13, because mathematical foundations are technically ignored in some IS programs in some universities in Australia. For example, I taught Information Systems Development at an Australian university using the same name as the subject for IT undergraduate students at another Australian university in the subject name of Systems Design and Architecture. From an Australian viewpoint, therefore, IT and IS are borderless. In other words, the curricula for IT and IS used in Australian universities have also been affected by the computing curricula designed by the special task force in the United States of ACM, AIS, and IEEE-CS, and therefore belongs to GIT-1 and GIT-3.

TEACHING IT AND IS TO INTERNATIONAL STUDENTS IN AUSTRALIA

As just stated, teaching IT and IS to international students in Australia belongs to GIT-1 and GIT-3. Therefore it is significant to describe the teaching experience of individuals and discuss some issues in the teaching activities in the context of GIT and GIS.

The universities in Australia promote a multicultural academic and learning environment in order to improve their international reputations or prestige, because international students have become more and more important to the Australian higher education system. However, there are still some members of the academic staff that do not care about the difference between international higher education students and their domestic counterparts. They have neither time nor interest to think about this difference, so they try to propose some corresponding strategies to improve their teaching in the environment of international education. In order to avoid this extreme case, I would like first to examine this difference, before going into the teaching of IT and IS to international students.

Lukic et al. (2004) have addressed these issues and emphasized that the range of cultures of international students is hugely diverse, and the range of educational expectations and requirements are equally diverse. They suggest that these should be taken into account when trying to attract international students to Australian universities and providing quality education services to the growing international market. However, they have not provided viable strategies for teaching international students.

In fact, English is not the first language of most international students, in particular from China, although English is not an issue for international students from India. As we know, Chinese and English belong to two different linguistic systems and lead to two different cultures—traditions and lifestyles, and working styles. Chinese culture shares some common values with the cultures of other countries such as Thailand and Korea. They are very sensitive to the hegemony, prejudice, and arrogance of language and culture that resulted from imperialism. In order to resolve these issues, a lecturer should be patient in the consultation of students, and carefully provide comments on the students' assignments, speaking English smoothly and slowly in lecture and tutorial time. A lecturer should supervise some research students from developing countries, in particular from non-English-speaking countries such as China, if possible, and can improve his or her patience and tolerance, and lessen the mentioned prejudice and arrogance of language and culture. The prejudice of language

and culture and the arrogance of behaviors can only damage the future of GIT and GIS and the future of the lecturer himself or herself.

In the first university in Australia, I taught Information Technology 2, Information Systems Development, and E-Commerce to undergraduate and postgraduate IT students. In the second Australian university, I lectured and tutored quantitative methods for information systems for undergraduate IS students. In the past two years, I satisfactorily taught the following subjects for either undergraduate students or postgraduate students:

- **BUSS218:** Systems design and architecture
- **BUSS211:** Requirements determination & systems analysis
- **BUSS 907:** Fundamentals of e-business
- **BUSS911:** Intelligent systems
- **BUS926:** Decision support systems
- **BUSS929:** Information systems research methods
- **BUSS 945:** Information systems research
- **BUSS950:** Systems development methodologies (as a coordinator and lecturer)

I also tried to realize my teaching philosophy, which consists of student-centered teaching activities, teaching informed by research, and integrating Who's Who theory and practice with respect to the subject at every lecture or tutorial. In what follows, we will look at each of these in some detail.

It should be noted that the teaching of many different subjects within a short time is not appropriate for a lecturer, although this is not seldom in Australian universities. This also implies that the academic staff in the field of IS and IT in Australia should be extended or improved or require more influence from GIS.

Teaching with International Vision

With the importance of ranking of world universities (annually) to the international prestige of a university, a university cannot always stay as a "local" or "regional" university, although this is still true for some universities in Australia or in China. The fierce competition of the educational market of international students requires a lecturer with international vision. That is, a lecturer should teach his or her students with international vision.

Teaching with international vision can encourage lecturers to train the students with international vision. Students will eventually participate in the competition of global economy. If one student has no international vision, it is difficult for him or her to effectively contribute to his or her business or organization in the context of global economy. Harman (2002) also shares the similar idea that "governments have come to see the need for their workforces to be internationally competitive as prerequisites to economic growth" (Herman, 2002, p. 4).

Teaching with international vision can encourage lecturers to patiently learn and understand different languages and different cultures from his or her native language and culture. Therefore, he or she can really know why patience, generosity, and friendliness—not from business, but from the heart—are most important in the teaching of international students from developing countries, in particular from those of past colonized or semi-colonized countries. In this way, the teaching of international students can be changed into "a form of foreign aid and cultural exchange rather than only a source of revenue" (Marginson, 2004).

Teaching with international vision can be considered an integrated part of global higher education. Teaching with international vision will lead a lecturer to undertake research and community engagement with international vision. Therefore, the international prestige of a university will eventually be improved.

Student-Centered Teaching Activities

Student-centered teaching activities are a necessary requirement from a nation, society, and student standpoint, because Australia is a multicultural and service-centered country. The service-centered community always requires customer-centered activities, like a sales assistant in a supermarket who always considers customer-centered activities. A student in a university in Australia is a special customer, and a lecturer is a special sales assistant. Therefore, student-centered teaching is a necessary condition for any successful teaching.

Student-centered teaching activities are also a requirement from a mass higher education standpoint. In elite higher education (e.g., that in the 1980s in China and Germany), teaching activities were lecturer-centered. Students generally had to follow the suggestions and decisions of lecturers to study and arrange all their study activities. However, it seems that elite higher education has been changed into mass higher education worldwide. In this case, students have more power in making compromise for the teaching/learning activities.

Student-centered teaching activities are also a requirement in a market economy. In market-oriented higher education, the student can select the subjects or programs which in turn force the lecturer or university to take into account the interest of students. In particular, in the case that international students become more and more important to higher education of Australia, student-centered teaching activities become more necessary. For example, one lecturer teaches a subject for IS undergraduates in a university in Australia, and the failure rate of his or her students passing the final examination of his or her subject is about 47%. The consequence is that the majority of students could not select this subject any more if the lecturer still coordinates and lectures it. Some international students called the lecturer "killer." In the long term, this will affect the number of international students at this university. Some universities or faculties are still suffering from such killers.

I have tried to do my best to realize this philosophy. For example, I used the online teaching tools (WebCT Vista) to let students access the lecture/tutorial materials/notes easily. I also used PowerPoint visuals to design lecture/tutorial notes. At the same time, I used e-mail twice for every subject that I lectured (one is in Week 4, another is in Week 8 or 9) through (SMP Central) to ask the students to e-mail what should be improved, what failed in the teaching activities, and what the expectation of the students is and how I could improve that from a student viewpoint. After receiving the e-mails from students, I would respond to each of them carefully and timely. Some students said "this is an excellent realization of student-centered teaching."

Integrating Who's Who, Theory, and Practice

Integrating Who's Who, theory, and practice with respect to the subject at every lecture or tutorial is of practical significance, because the textbooks for IS students (the second year or more) lack the personal histories of relevant people in the area. These are normally a simple stack of knowledge, theory, techniques, methods, and principles in a domain. For example, BUSS 218 used the textbook, *Systems Analysis & Design in a Changing World, Course Technology* (Satzinger et al., 2004). This is one of the excellent textbooks. However, it has no story about Who's Who for any science or knowledge discovery in the history of modern computing. This author had to add as many case studies and personal stories of relevant people in the area as possible to make the lectures more interesting for students while lecturing theory and helping the students with practice in the computer lab. For example, I introduced to the student many ACM Turing awards winners such as John McCarthy, H.A. Simon, Edgar F. Codd, Niklaus Wirth, and Andrew Chi-Chih Yao to name a few; I told them each of the winners is an important player in one area of computer science, IT, and IS, because each of them has made the contributions of lasting and major technical importance to the computer field. For example, when I lectured database design for undergraduate students, I told the story of Edgar F. Codd and his contributions to relational databases in the 1970s. When I lectured intelligent systems, I taught the story of John McCarthy and H.A. Simon and their contributions to artificial intelligence.

Just as one should never forget the past, a student of IT and IS should also know Who's Who in the field of computing. More importantly, the students can obtain lessons, experiences, and heuristics from the history of Who's Who in the field of computing and can go in a right direction based on the work of the successful pioneers in the

field. This is an important necessary condition for the future of students towards their research and development.

Teaching Informed by Research

Teaching informed by research usually appears in the job advertisement for an academic position of a university in Australia. It implies that the successful applicant should integrate his or her research into teaching. To my knowledge, teaching informed by research consists of at least two parts: (1) the lecturer should integrate his or her research activities into his or her teaching, and (2) the lecturer should create a research-oriented academic research and development (R&D) environment. Both parts are critical not only for students but also for academic staff.

The successful commitment to the first part can facilitate the constructing knowledge and understanding of students, and at the same time promote the further research of the lecturer. The successful commitment to the second part can facilitate the research curiosity of students and sometimes promote the R&D of both students and academic staff. The successful example in this case is that Bill Gates obtained necessary experience in the research-oriented academic R&D environment of Harvard University before he dropped out and founded Microsoft.

Further, teaching informed by research requires that the academic staff must proactively undertake research in related fields of IT and IS in general. In the past few years, this author has actively researched in the fields of experience management, knowledge management, case-based reasoning (CBR) and experience-based reasoning (EBR), intelligent systems, multi-agent systems, e-commerce, e-services, fraud and deception in e-commerce based on mathematical logic, fuzzy logic, artificial intelligence (AI), knowledge-based systems, and system development methodology—all of these belong to IT and IS. In the past, I have published in more than 60 international journals and high-quality international conference proceedings, many of which have been indexed in the ISI's Science Citation Index (SCI, 14 indices),

ISI Proceedings (6 indices), INSPEC (17 indices), and DBLP (12 indices). Since 2004, I published one monograph (Sun & Finnie, 2004), four international journal papers, two book chapters, and 15 international conference papers. All of these can be internationally visible.

Based on the above-mentioned research experience, this author has tried to involve his research expertise in every subject that I have taught. For example, he introduced a unified model for integrating algebraic systems, logical systems, and intelligent systems for BUSS911: Intelligent Systems. This model was later published as a paper in the *International Journal of Intelligent Systems* (Sun & Finnie, 2005). I taught a new perspective: human-like system development architecture to BUSS218 undergraduate students and BUSS950 postgraduate students. This architecture is to be published in the proceedings of an international conference. In fact, this architecture was motivated in the lecturing BUSS218. The students also motivated me to expose any innovative ideas, some of which have been converted into research projects or publications. Furthermore, I realized the "80/20 teaching principle" through this teaching approach—that is, 80% of contents are from the textbooks outsourced from the United States, while 20% are from this author's research expertise or other available teaching resources. This also avoids the allegation of "advanced photocopier of knowledge." The students—in particular, postgraduate students—favor such a philosophy. This has been proven by the increasing number of students enrolling in BUSS950 (from 24 to 38) and BUSS911 (from 6 to 16) in past years.

Teaching Related to Community Engagement

In the view of this author, development of modern science and technology depends on community engagement of a significant number of researchers and academic staff. Therefore, I have tried to commit to actively engaging in the community as much as possible. For example, I worked as a coordinator for the Information Systems Seminars

Series in 2005 in order to promote the research and development of IS and IT in the university at which I worked. At the time, I successfully completed the supervision of an Honors student in 2005, as well as supervised a PhD student with the Thai government scholarship. I supervised a master's student by research and co-supervised three master's students by research together with other colleagues. At the same time, I worked as a referee for 10 prestigious international journals including *IEEE Transactions on Knowledge and Data Engineering*. I also worked as a member of the program committee and as a reviewer for 12 international conferences, and won the Award for Best Paper Reviewer, "for providing reviews which demonstrated both insight and constructive feedback," at the 2nd International Conference on Information Management and Business (IMB, 2006). I chaired sessions at international conferences such as HIS2004 and KES2005, and delivered many outstanding presentations at international conferences. I was one of the co-chairs of the International Workshop on Experience Management and Engineering (EME 2006).

Outcome of Teaching IT and IS and Discussion

The teaching surveys demonstrated that this teaching at the university is excellent, because the average score of one teaching survey for lectures in BUSS911 (Autumn 2006) was 5.21 out of 6. The average score of another teaching survey for lectures in BUSS950 (Autumn 2005) was 4.91 out of 6. At the same time, the number of BUSS950 students increased from 24 in 2004 to 38 in 2005, and the number of BUSS911 students increased from 6 in 2004 and 2005 to 16 in 2006. All of this occurred even though the Australian IT and IS market is still experiencing a recession. However, there is still a long way to go for this author to improve my teaching art and performance, because English is not my first language. Teaching performance should be improved for life, because it is a life task for a university teacher. I will try enthusiastically to use more advanced techniques, tools, and strategies to attract students to study the subjects that I teach.

Further, with many years working and studying in China, Germany, and Australia, in my view, high-quality teaching cannot essentially improve the international or national reputation or prestige of a university. It cannot attract international students either. For example, in China, only a normal college emphasizes the priority of high-quality teaching. However, some universities in particular in Australia still use "high-quality teaching" to attract international students. Some heads of schools or departments also use "high-quality teaching" to realize the hegemony or arrogance or prejudice of English, which is an obvious consequence of colonialism and imperialism. This is a tragedy of that university. In the end, research in particular international visible research is the priority of a university. Otherwise, one cannot understand why Harvard University is famous not based on its "high-quality teaching," but based on its research activities. Furthermore, the well-known Academic Ranking of World Universities, published by Shanghai Jiaotong University (IHE, 2006) and which has drawn increasing attention in Australia, is based on the following criteria:(see Box 1).

At least we have not found "high-quality teaching" in the above table. In fact, an outstanding student wants to go to Harvard University, not based on that he likes the "high-quality teaching" at Harvard University but based on its international prestige. Therefore, appropriate use of "high-quality teaching" on a university campus is still a big issue for some universities in both Australia and other countries.

Some Secrets Revealed

According to Marginson (2004), "English-language nations enjoy a post-imperial advantage." In fact, some native-English-speaking students and academic staff are also enjoying English as a hegemony. I once met a Professor Xiks, who asked me, "Do you understand what I said to you?" while using an unfriendly gesture. Although I understood he had said, he did not show any patience and did not know that he was discriminating against a colleague. This is a typical language discrimination. This author also experienced a local postgraduate student whose native language was English. The student tried to do her best to command me as to what she liked to learn and to listen to. She even asked to stop the tutorial whenever she had no time to attend it. If I did not agree, she would use her hegemonic English to make an official complaint to my department head. Although these are the extreme cases, I have suffered in my teaching experience. However, I do realize that we are a long way from realizing the dream of global equality, of "everyone is equal." A multicultural academic environment is still an ideal or goal for Australia to struggle for, because we are still a long way from realizing that.

Flexible teaching and learning is also a popular concept in universities in Australia. It seems that a lecturer is required to use a flexible teaching approach in his or her teaching activities. Generally speaking, flexible teaching and learning approaches are (http://www.utas.edu.au/tl /supporting/flexible/index.html):

Box 1. Source: IHE (2006), http://ed.sjtu.edu.cn/rank/2006/ARWU2006Methodology.htm

Criteria	Indicator	Weight
Quality of Education	Alumni of an institution winning Nobel Prizes and Fields Medals	10%
Quality of Faculty	Staff of an institution winning Nobel Prizes and Fields Medals	20%
	Highly cited researchers in 21 broad subject categories	20%
Research Output	Articles published in Nature and Science	20%
	Articles in Science Citation Index-expanded, Social Science Citation Index	20%
Size of Institution	Academic performance with respect to the size of an institution	10%
Total		100%

- Learner-centered.
- About good teaching and learning practices for all students.
- Less time- and place-dependent than more traditional forms of teaching.
- Ones that increase the learner's responsibility for his or her own learning.

The first point is the same as the student-centered teaching activities mentioned earlier. The second point requires a lecturer to use effective teaching methods to teach students. The third point has been realized using e-teaching and learning environments (e.g., based on WebCT Vista), because a lecturer and the students can communicate using WebCT. The lecturer can upload his teaching materials to the WebCT Vista, and the students can access them using WebCT Vista. And the fourth point asks the students to learn in a more flexible way, in particular based on the e-teaching and learning environment. However, in practice, it is difficult to realize flexible teaching approaches. Sometimes, this approach easily leads to an arbitrary teaching and learning environment: A lecturer can complete his or her lecture earlier as expected. A student cannot attend a lecture without any kind of permission. WebCT can help a student to download the lecture notes or slides. However, no student has been told that he or she needs not attend the lecture because of WebCT. Even so, the attendance rate for a lecture is on average lower compared with that in the past. If one agrees with the idea that the face-to-face instruction is still dominating the teaching activities, this is a big issue. At least no practical method has been found in order to resolve this issue, in this author's opinion.

FUTURE TRENDS

Based on the previous examination, in particular the impact of GIT on higher education in Australia, we can see that the IT and IS programs in Australian universities will be further affected by those offered by the UK and U.S. through computing curricula and textbooks. At the same time,

Australian universities will further try to attract international students worldwide, in particular students from Asian countries, to enroll in their IT/IS degree programs.

With the further development of economy in China, Australia will play a more important role in training students from China and possibly establish some or many education training centers (one form of higher education cooperation) in China in order to train Chinese students in China. However, Australia cannot provide 100% Australian-owned IT/IS products or services to international students. The offered IT/IS products normally include computing curricula, textbooks, lecture notes, and examination materials provided by the UK and in particular by the U.S. Like other English-speaking nations, Australia will still "enjoy a post-imperial advantage" (Marginson, 2004) and use English as an important instruction media to promote the GIT and GIS in Australia and some countries in Asia, as shown in Figure 2.

However, Australia will face a more intense competition for attracting students from China, together with other English-speaking nations such as the U.S. and UK. The reason is that mass higher education (for undergraduate programs) in China has been carried out since the end of the last century, while the mass higher degree education (for master's programs and doctoral programs) in China are being changed into more flexible forms like in the U.S. in the past few years. Harman (2002) is also concerned about how quickly and successfully Asian nations expand and strengthen their own systems of higher education which will affect the international education of Australia. This trend will relieve the huge unmet demands of higher degree education from the society of China and at the same time will lessen the possible student potential source that can come to Australia to get similar higher degree education. This is a big issue, because postgraduate programs take a very high proportion of total international students.

Furthermore, in the near future, Australia will evolve into a national "advanced" training center like Singapore to train students from Asia, in particular from China; at least this is currently true in the field of IT and IS, because the majority of students enrolled in IT and IS are from China, Hong Kong (a special administrative region of China), and Taiwan (a province of China). For example, 38 students enrolled in this author's BUSS950 in 2005. Only one of them was Australian, and another was from Norway. The rest were from Asia, in particular from China. In 2006, 16 postgraduate students (by courses) enrolled in BUSS911. Only one student was Australian, and two students were from Thailand. The rest were from China, including Taiwan and Hong Kong. However, because of difference of superstructure and culture from Singapore and China, Australia should do more with attitudes and behaviors in this direction. Otherwise, young people from China will lose interest in IT and IS programs offered by universities in Australia, and instead they will turn their attention to the UK, United States, and Canada, like Japanese have. This is based on the fact that from a viewpoint of economy, the China of today is the Japan of yesterday. In the 1980s, the products of Japan were seen in every market in the world, like those made in China today. In 2002, 45,960 students from Japan enrolled in universities in United States as the fourth of the 10 principal sources of international students in the U.S. (see Table 1).

However, Japan was not listed in the 10 principal sources of international students in Australia in the same year. The last of the 10 principal sources of international students in 2002 for Australia is Taiwan with 3,977 students (Marginson, 2004). Japan has a population of 128 million, about six times the size of Taiwan (22 million). English is not the native language for either Taiwan or Japan. So, why are there not more than 4,000 students from Japan to enroll in universities in Australia? This case was marginally changed in 2004, because Japan became the tenth of the 10 principal sources of international students in Australia in that year, and the UK was excluded from the 10 principal sources as shown in Table 2. However, compared with the number of international students from Taiwan and the corresponding population, the number of students from Japan is still very low. This requires the policymakers of Australian higher education to do some serious contemplation. In my view, they now have no time to think about the consequences of this comparison, when one day the absolute majority of students from China leave Australia, and China is not listed in the 10 principal sources of international students in Australia. Will that day take a very long time to come? The reader can find the answer somewhere in this chapter. The majority of academic staff working in IT and IS areas in Australia have been thinking about this day for some time!

It should be noted that in comparing the number of international students in 2002 and 2004 (shown

Table 1. Ten principal sources of international students in the U.S. and Australia, 2002 (Marginson, 2004)

USA 2002-2003		Australia 2002	
India	74,603	Singapore	29,956
China	64,757	Hong Kong	26,956
Korea	51,519	Malaysia	23,725
Japan	45,960	China (Mainland)	19,596
Taiwan	28,107	Indonesia	11,981
Canada	26,513	India	8,390
Mexico	12,801	United States	8,325
Turkey	11,601	United Kingdom	5,752
Indonesia	10,432	Thailand	5,202
Thailand	9,982	Taiwan	3,977

in Tables 1 and 2), we find that Asian countries are the principal source of international students in Australia. Further, China and India are the most important driving forces for international education in Australia, because the number of international students from China and India increased 89% and 94% respectively, while the enrollments of international students in Australia increased 14% annually over the past three years (2002-2004) (DEST, 2005). These are also reasons why it is not yet the time to worry about that special day.

To avoid the early coming of that day, Australia immigration policy should not be changed significantly comparing with the current immigration policies. Otherwise, any new tougher immigration policies will encourage international students, in particular many students from China, not to select Australia as the destination for international education. Australian universities should provide more scholarships to international students in order to attract more talented students to study in Australia. Any academic staff should try to stop the direct or indirect hegemony of culture and English as much as possible on any occasion. They should also avoid any direct and indirect, intended or unintended prejudice, discrimination, and arrogance of culture and language, which does still exist to some extent and is ignored by researchers and policymakers. These are very sensitive for any student from a developing country, in particular from Asia.

FUTURE RESEARCH DIRECTIONS

This chapter examined global information technology and its impact on universities in Australia, and it also looked at some issues in teaching IT and IS to international students in the context of GIT and GIS based on the fact that different students from different countries have different IT and IS backgrounds. This chapter also made a daring prediction for the impact of GIT and GIS in Australia, and proposed a few viable strategies for resolving some issues facing international education for IT and IS in Australia. The proposed approach is very useful for GIT, GIS, and the university IT/IS training worldwide.

It is obvious that students from developed nations rarely enroll in universities of developing countries, except some special disciplines such as languages. However, the trend cannot be changed significantly in the near future. The students from the developing countries will receive increasing benefits from IT and IS, with the development of the Internet, GIT, and GIS. Australian universities will significantly contribute to the progress of GIT and GIS in Australasia and Asia through education export.

Finally, the future research directions and opportunities in related areas were briefly discussed. The results presented in previous discussions suggest a number of topics for future research. In

Table 2. Ten principal sources of international students in Australia, 2004* (DEST, 2005)

Country of Permanent Home Residence	Total Persons	% Increase Compared with 2002
China (excludes Hong Kong and Taiwan)	37,106	89.3
Malaysia	28,862	21.6
Singapore	28,290	-5.6
Hong Kong	27,461	1.8
India	16,320	94.5
Indonesia	11,316	-0.6
United States	9,522	14.3
Thailand	5,824	12.0
Taiwan	4,533	14.0
Japan	4,409	N/A

* *Includes only public funded universities*

what follows, I only describe three topics for future research, owing to space limitation.

One of the topics for future research is to examine major theoretical or conceptual frameworks in information systems education in Australian universities. The research into this topic will help better understanding of GIT and GIS in Australian universities' education. It can also help examine the interrelationship between theory and practice mentioned in an earlier section. Another topic for future research is the impact of development of higher education of China on IT and IS programs offered in Australian universities. We have mentioned this issue in this chapter. In fact, the development of mass higher degree (master's and PhD) education in China will have a significant influence on the IT and IS programs offered in Australian universities. One possible consequence is that the number of Chinese students that enroll the IT and IS postgraduate programs offered by Australian universities will be further decreasing, which will make the infrastructure of IT and IS in Australian universities shrink. Because of weak development of the manufacturing sector related to IT and IS in Australia, IT and IS programs will face a critical challenge in Australian universities in the near future. One possible chance is that Australian universities should accelerate the educational cooperation in the area of higher degree education cooperation with their counterparts in China, although the advances in this area are very slow at the moment.

The third topic for future research is to look at the contributions of Australian universities to GIT and GIS. This chapter focuses on the impact of GIT and GIS on IT and IS programs offered in Australian universities. In fact, Australian universities have also made huge contributions to GIT and GIS through international cooperation in research and teaching. Therefore, it is significant to examine how Australian universities themselves contribute to GIT and GIS worldwide.

ACKNOWLEDGMENT

The author thanks Professor Ann Hodgkinson of the University of Wollongong, Australia, Professor Gavin Finnie of Bond University, Australia, and Professor Jianqiang Li of Hebei Normal University, China, for their encouragement and support during the progress of this chapter.

REFERENCES

ACM. (2002). *IS 2002 model curriculum and guidelines for undergraduate degree programs in information systems.* Retrieved July 6, 2004, from http://www.acm.org

ACM Turing Awards. (n.d.). *Winners.* Retrieved October 20, 2006, from http://awards.acm.org/homepage.cfm?srt=all&awd=140

AIS. (2006). *Accreditation survey.* Retrieved October 19, 2006, from http//:atc.bentley.edu/resources/perseus5/surveys/accreditationsurvey.htm

AIS. (n.d.). *Information Systems Master's Program accreditation survey.* Retrieved October 19, 2006, from http://atc.bentley.edu/ resources/ perseus5/ surveys/accreditationsurvey.htm#%2025a

Allen, E. (2005). *Excellence in teaching: An international vision.* Retrieved October 20, 2006, from http://www.gradschool.duke.edu/student_life/finding_support/international_student_support/excellence_in_teaching.html

Akmanligil, M., & Palvia, P.C. (2004). Strategies for global information systems development. *Information & Management, 42*(1), 45-59.

Australian Universities. (n.d.). *Homepage.* Retrieved October 28, 2006, from http://www.australian-universities.com/

Avison, D.E., & Fitzgerald, G. (2003). *Information systems development: Methodologies, techniques and tools* (3rd ed.). London: McGraw-Hill International.

CC (Computing Curricula). (2004, June 1). *Joint Task Force of ACM, AIS and IEEE-CS over report.* Retrieved July 8, 2004, from http://www.acm.org

CC. (2005, April 11). *Joint Task Force of ACM, AIS and IEEE-CS education draft*. Retrieved October 20, 2006, from http://www.acm.org/education/Draft_5-23-051.pdf

Creaders. (n.d.). *Immigration*. Retrieved October 21, 2006, from http://news.creaders.net/immigration/newsViewer.php?id=685508

DEST (Department of Education, Science and Training). (2005). *Higher education sector in Australia*. Retrieved October 19, 2006, from http://www.dest.gov.au/sectors/higher_education/default.htm#Higher_Education_Report_2004-05

EDNA. (n.d.). *Homepage*. Retrieved October 16, 2006, from http://www.edna.edu.au/edna/browse/0,5390

Furbach, U. (2003). AI-A multiple book review. *Artificial Intelligence, 145,* 245-252.

IHE (Institute of Higher Education, Shanghai Jiao Tong University). (2006). *Academic ranking of world universities 2006*. Retrieved October 18, 2006, from http://ed.sjtu.edu.cn/ranking.htm

Harman, G. (2002, September 5-7). Australia as a major higher education exporter. *Proceedings of the Consortium of Higher Education Researchers 15th Annual Conference,* Vienna, Austria. Retrieved October 25, 2006, from http://www.iff.ac.at/hofo/CHER_2002/pdf/ch02harm.pdf

Lukic, T., Broadbent, A., & Maclachlan, M. (2004). *International higher education students: How do they differ from other higher education students?* Retrieved October 16, 2006, from http://www.dest.gov.au/ NR/rdonlyres/CB05180A-CC58-44EC-9DAF-A32CF84C06B1/1176/2.pdf

Marakas, G.M. (2002). *Decision support systems (2nd ed.)*. Englewood Cliffs, NJ: Prentice Hall.

Marginson, S. (2004). National and global competition in higher education. *The Australian Educational Researcher, 31*(2), 1-27. Retrieved October 16, 2006, from http://www.aare.edu.au/aer/online/40020b.pdf

Manheim, M.L. (1992). Global information technology: Issues and strategic opportunities. *International Information Systems, 1*(1), 38-67.

Nelson, B. (2002). *Higher education: Report for the 2003 to 2005 triennium*. Retrieved October 19, 2006, from http://www.dest.gov.au/sectors/higher_education/publications_resources/profiles/default.htm

Palvia, P.C. (1997). Developing a model of the global and strategic impact of information technology. *Information & Management, 32*(5), 229-244.

Palvia P.C., Jain Palvia, S.C., & Whitworth, J.E. (2002). Global information technology: A meta analysis of key issues. *Information & Management, 39*(5), 403-414.

Satzinger, J.W., Jackson, R.B., & Burd, S.D. (2004). *Systems analysis and design in a changing world* (3rd ed.). Thompson Learning.

Sun, Z. (2004, July 8). *IS: An individual perspective*. Seminar Presentation, School of Economics and Information Systems, University of Wollongong, Australia.

Sun, Z., & Finnie, G. (2004). *Intelligent techniques in e-commerce: A case-based reasoning perspective*. Heidelberg/Berlin: Springer-Verlag.

Sun, Z., & Finnie, G. (2005). A unified logical model for CBR-based e-commerce systems. *International Journal of Intelligent Systems, 20*(1), 29-26.

Sun, Z., Finnie, G., & Weber, K. (2004). Case base building with similarity relations. *Information Sciences: An International Journal, 165*(1-2), 21-43.

Sun, Z., Finnie, G., & Weber, K. (2005). Abductive case based reasoning. *International Journal of Intelligent Systems, 20*(9), 957-983.

UTAS. (n.d.). *IS departments*. Retrieved October 16, 2006, from http://www.utas.edu.au/infosys/cgi/is_depts/ (page no longer available).

ADDITIONAL READING

Adelsberger, H.H., Collis, B., & Pawlowski, J.M. (Eds.). (2005). *Handbook on information technologies for education and training.* Berlin: Springer-Verlag.

Avgerou, C. (2002). Information systems and global diversity. Oxford: Oxford University Press.

Desai, M.S., Desai, K.J., & Ojode, L. (2004). A global information technology model: Business applications in developing economies (case studies). *Information Management & Computer Security, 12*(5), 401–410.

Espinosa, J.A., DeLone, W., & Lee, G. (2006). Global boundaries, task processes and IS project success: A field study. *Information Technology & People, 19*(4), 345-370.

GlobIS: Global Information Systems Group. (n.d.). http://www.globis.ethz.ch/education/mpis

Hernandez, M.G., Equiza-Lopez, F., & Acevedo-Ruiz, M. (2006). *Information communication technologies and human development: Opportunities and challenges.* Hershey, PA: IGI Global.

Hunter, M.G., & Tan, F.B. (2005). *Advanced topics in global information management.* Hershey, PA: Idea Group.

Ives, B., & Jarvenpaa, S.L. (1991). Applications of global information technology: Key issues for management. *MIS Quarterly, 15*(1), 33-49.

Jones, C., Rathi, D., Twidale, M., & Li, W. (n.d.). *One system, worldwide: Challenges to global information systems.* Retrieved April 16, 2007, from http://www.isrl.uiuc.edu/~twidale/pubs/one_system_worldwide.pdf

Khosrow-Pour, M., & Loch, K. (1993). *Global information technology education: Issues and trends.* Hershey, PA: Idea Group.

Kurihara, Y., Takaya, S., & Yamori, N. (2006). *Global information technology and competitive financial alliances.* Hershey, PA: Idea Group.

Lacity, M.C., Willcocks, L.P., Lacity, M.C., & Willcocks, L. (2001). *Global information technology outsourcing: In search of business advantage.* New York: John Wiley & Sons.

Mena, E., & Illarramendi, A. (2001). *Ontology-based query processing for global information systems.* Berlin: Springer-Verlag.

Palvia, P., Palvia, S., & Roche, E.M. (Eds.). (2001). *Global information technology and electronic commerce.* Ivy League.

Palvia P.C., Palvia, S.C.J., & Whitworth, J.E. (2002). Global information technology: A meta analysis of key issues. *Information & Management, 39*(5), 403-414.

Palvia, P., Mao, E., Salam, A.F., & Soliman, K.S. (2003). Management information systems research: What's there in a methodology? *Communications of AIS, 11*(16), 1-33.

Peppard, J. (1999). Information management in the global enterprise: An organising framework. *European Journal of Information Systems, 8*(2), 77-94.

Raisinghani, M.S. (2001). Book review: Global information technology and electronic commerce: Issues for the new millennium. *Journal of Global Information Technology Management, 4*(4), 58-60.

Schneider, G. (2006). *Electronic commerce* (6th ed.). Australia: Thomson Course Technology.

Silberglitt, R., Anton, P.S. et al. (2005). *The global technology revolution 2020, in-depth analyses: Bio/nano/materials/information trends, drivers, barriers, and social implications.* Retrieved April 18, 2007, from http://www.rand.org/pubs/technical_reports/TR303/

Smith, M.M. (2002, August 18-24). Global information ethics: A mandate for professional education. *Proceedings of the 68th IFLA Council and General Conference.* Retrieved April 18, 2007, from http://www.ifla.org/IV/ifla68/papers/056-093e.pdf

Sun, Z., & Lau, S.K. (2006). Customer experience management in e-services. In J. Lu, D. Ruan, & G. Zhang (Eds.), *E-service intelligence: Methodologies, technologies and applications* (pp. 365-388). Berlin/Heidelberg: Springer Verlag.

Stair, R., & Reynolds, G. (2006). *Fundamentals of information systems* (3rd ed.). Thomson Course Technology.

Tan, F.B. (Ed.). (2002). *Global perspective of information technology management.* Hershey, PA: IRM Press.

Weforum. (n.d.). *Global information technology report.* Retrieved April 18, 2007, from http://www.weforum.org/en/initiatives/gcp/Global%20Information%20Technology%20Report/index.htm

Chapter XXI
Sampling Approaches on Collecting Internet Statistics in the Digital Economy

Song Xing
California State University, Los Angeles, USA

Bernd-Peter Paris
George Mason University, USA

Xiannong Meng
Bucknell University, USA

ABSTRACT

The Internet's complexity restricts analysis or simulation to assess its parameters. Instead, actual measurements provide a reality check. Many statistical measurements of the Internet estimate rare event probabilities. Collection of such statistics renders sampling methods as a primary substitute. Within the context of this inquiry, we have presented the conventional Monte Carlo approach to estimate the Internet event probability. As a variance reduction technique, Importance Sampling is introduced which is a modified Monte Carlo approach resulting in a significant reduction of effort to obtain an accurate estimate. This method works particularly well when estimating the probability of rare events. It has great appeal to use as an efficient sampling scheme for estimating the information server density on the Internet. In this chapter, we have proposed the Importance Sampling approaches to track the prevalence and growth of Web service, where an improved Importance Sampling scheme is introduced. We present a thorough analysis of the sampling approaches. Based on the periodic measurement of the number of active Web servers conducted over the past five years, an exponential growth of the Web is observed and modeled. Also discussed in this chapter is the increasing security concerns on Web servers.

INTRODUCTION

The Internet has grown tremendously from an early research prototype in 1969 connecting four computers to today's global communication system reaching all countries of the world. Businesses, educational institutions, government organizations, and individuals have become heavily dependent on its capability for rapid data communications and information exchange. One issue related to this continuous growth is the evident increase in numbers of hosts connected to the Internet, and also worth noting are the numerous public IP addresses being consumed by these computers.

Theoretically, the current IPv4 address space can identify 2^{32}, or 4.3 billion hosts. However, the two-level address structure (consisting of a network and a host) categorized into five classes imposes constraints that make the use of the address space inefficient. Subnetting and supernetting (or CIDR, Classless Inter-Domain Routing) approaches allow more efficient allocation of IP addresses than classful addressing, but these strategies make routing more complicated. Actually, since the release of IPv4, the Internet population grew to over 400 million hosts by the end of 2006 (ISC–Survey, n.d.), increasing far faster than anticipated. As the space of available addresses decreases, it becomes increasingly difficult to obtain new public IPv4 addresses. Furthermore, the pace of this growth is expected to continue for years to come.

In the short term, Dynamic Host Configuration (DHCP) and Network Address Translation (NAT) relieve the pressure for additional address space. By using private addresses that are reserved for local usage, NAT allows network administrators to hide large communities of users behind firewalls and NAT boxes. Since different multi-corporate networks can each reuse the same local private addresses, NAT reduces the need for new unique public IP addresses. Unfortunately, NAT is not a permanent solution. It addresses the needs of large communities of client systems, but it does not help the servers on the Internet as each requires a unique public address. Nor does it work for peer-to-peer communications for the same reason. What happens when we run out of public IPv4 address?

To improve IPv4's scalability, as well as its security, ease-of-configuration, and network management, the next-generation Internet Protocol (IPv6) has been proposed and is now a standard. As a long-term solution, IPv6 fixed the problem of the shortage of IPv4 addresses by increasing the IP address size from 32 bits to 128 bits. And IPv6 is expected to gradually replace IPv4 with the two addresses coexisting during a transition period. Therefore, it would be more realistic and helpful to predict when IPv4 address will eventually run out,

and when IPv6 will need to be widely implemented. Being able to map the growth of the Internet or take snapshots of its current size is certainly beneficial in planning the future evolution of IPv4 and the implementation of IPv6.

In addition, recent studies have stated that a historical analysis shows the phenomenal growth of Internet usage was slowed in recent times (Devezas, Linstone, & Santos, 2005; Modis, 2005). Specifically, Devezas et al. (2005) report the growth of Internet users is coming to the end of the fourth Kondratieff cycles downswing and will then embark on the fifth Kondratieff cycles upswing. Modis (2005) points out that the population trends and Internet-user trends have indicated that the percentage of the population using the Internet is decreasing everywhere despite large discrepancies in different regions in the world, and the boom years of Internet explosion are over. Similarly, Nielsen's (2006) report states that the early Web's explosive growth rate has slowed and the Web has experienced a "maturing" growth in the last five years. Whether the decreased Internet usage or the Web maturation, both arguments provide us some useful insights. On the one hand, it shows the Internet or the Web is no longer a marvel of innovation. On the other hand, it may implicate a nearly exhausted IPv4 address space. Hence having a reliable and accurate estimate of the present size of the Internet and of its growth rate would be very important and of interest both to network operators/engineers and to market analysts.

Be aware that the Internet is a decentralized and dynamic compilation of global networks. To evaluate the parameters or performance of such a complex system, analytical techniques may be applied. For example, Balchi and Mukhopadhyay (2004) have introduced several soft models—such as genetic algorithm, neural network, and fuzzy regression—to study and predict the Internet growth in several OECD[1] nations. However, the analytical techniques are usually very expensive, time consuming, and relatively inflexible. In addition, such techniques often require over-simplification of the system model, leading to uncertain and inaccurate estimates. Simulation is another powerful technology that plays a key role in exploring the scenarios that are difficult or impossible to analyze. However, it is difficult to generate simulation scenarios to map the growth of the Internet because of its heterogeneity, large scale, and rapid evolution. In contrast, actual measurements and experiments provide the means for a reality check of the current Internet to collect its growth statistics.

Nevertheless, what specific data should be estimated when measuring the Internet's growth is difficult to decide due to its nature as a loose collection of networks. It is worth noting that the explosive growth of the Internet in recent years has been dominated by the growth of the World Wide Web (WWW). Web communication is revolutionizing the way we acquire information, as today's Web browsers support a rich palette of media types. Although real-time traffic has increased and placed great burdens on the Internet, the Web has triggered explosive growth in the Internet. In this work, we have measured the number of hosts connected to the Internet which provide a given information service, such as the WWW. This measurement represents an important part of the current Internet.

Note that many statistical measurements of the Internet relate to estimating rare event probabilities. For example, we measure the density of information servers over the IP address space to estimate the number of information servers, or the rate of adoption of a new protocol. However, a scan of all IP address space is impractical for obtaining server density. This renders sampling methods in collecting such statistics.

A sampling approach is a technique that utilizes a form of random selection. The simplest form is the Monte Carlo Sampling method using uniform distribution, where all samples have an equal probability of being selected. Therefore, this method applies to problems whether there is an inherent probabilistic structure or not.

With the use of the Monte Carlo approach, we have sampled the IP address space uniformly and have probed each randomly selected address to determine if the host at that address provides the proper information service or not. Subsequently, an estimate for the number of information servers is the product of the density of information servers P (i.e., the proportion of probes that revealed an information server) and the size of the IP address space, 2^{32} for IPv4.

The Monte Carlo method has provided very accurate estimates if the number of samples is sufficiently large. Its main drawbacks are potentially slow convergence and large variance of the estimates observed for events occurring infrequently. As a result, it requires a considerable or even prohibitively computational effort for a reliable estimate.

Importance Sampling is a technique that permits sampling of low probability events with a significant reduction of computational effort (Glynn & Iglehart, 1989). The samples are from a non-uniform (biasing) distribution. The estimates become unbiased through weighting, taking into account the biasing distribution.

Importance Sampling successfully estimates the probability of rare sets. Current research has wide applications of Importance Sampling for problems with continuous random variables. For example, it estimates error probabilities and/or false alarm rates for high performance digital communications or detection systems (Orsak & Aazhang, 1989; Liu & Yao, 1988; Orsak, 1993), but it is rarely applied for a discrete event system as in our research collecting Internet statistics. For discrete event systems application, Importance Sampling attracts the most attention in simulations involving rare events in networking (queuing) systems, such as the estimator of the cell loss rate in ATM switches/multiplexers (Wang & Frost, 1993), buffer overflow probabilities (Glasserman & Kou, 1995), and blocking probabilities of WDM networks (Andrew, 2004).

Nevertheless, Importance Sampling has been used traditionally for simulations where all relevant statistics are known and controllable (Smith, Shafi, & Gao, 1997). However, we have faced problems in collecting Internet statistics due to the underlying distributions being usually unknown.

We have presented approaches based on Importance Sampling for measuring the size of the Internet (Xing & Paris, 2001, 2002). We have estimated the size of the IPv4 Internet by measuring the number of publicly accessible Web servers and FTP servers. In this chapter, we have extended our work to make more accurate measurements of the Internet and map its growth. We also have particularly included the measurement of the number of Web servers visible on the public Internet but not providing a public information service. A real problem herein is that the optimal unbiased Importance Sampling strategy is infeasible because of the unknown (or practically inestimable) underlying statistics of the set of all active Web servers.

In the following sections, we first present background on measuring the size and growth of the Internet. Specifically, the Monte Carlo Sampling and Importance Sampling approaches are introduced. Furthermore, we have extended our work to measure the number of all active Web servers, and track the prevalence and growth of the Web service. An improved Importance Sampling approach is presented to significantly reduce the sampling time, and it is integrated into a new estimation scheme to unbias the estimator. We show the numerical results for the presented Importance Sampling approach and compare it to Monte Carlo Sampling. In the conclusion, ideas for future work are described.

PRELIMINARIES

Recent work has shown increasing interest in Internet growth statistics. The commonly cited measures of the growth are the number of servers, domains, or hosts on the Internet. And the measurement approaches for obtaining these statistics are classified into two categories: hostname-based (Netcraft, 2007; ISC–Background, (n.d.); Telcordia NetSizer, n.d.) and IP address-based (Xing & Paris, 2001, 2002, 2004).

Related Work for Measuring the Growth of the Internet

Internet Systems Consortium (ISC), Telcordia Net-Sizer, and Netcraft conducted the Internet growth survey and Web growth survey via a hostname-based Internet growth measurement scheme. The works of ISC and Telcordia NetSizer are relevant for measuring the number of hosts. They discover named hosts—that is, computers with domain names—by querying the domain name system (DNS).

The latest VeriSign Domain Name Industry Brief, which highlights key industry data for worldwide domain name activity, has shown that the total domain name registrations reached 120

million across all of the Top-Level Domain Names at the end of 2006, representing a continued strong increase over past years (VeriSign, 2007).

With technical operations subcontracted to Network Wizards (NW, n.d.), which has reported the number of Internet hosts since 1981, ISC is able to collect data and publish its survey quarterly. The survey has shown the number of hosts continues to grow rapidly, and that growth has accelerated somewhat during recent years (ISC–Survey, n.d.). Specifically, its latest report counted hosts at 433,193,199 in January 2007.

This work has been done by a complete search of the DNS system. However, there is a problem with the accuracy of this approach because a host name with an assigned IP address does not guarantee the host actually exists or is active. Moreover, one-to-one mapping of IP addresses to domain names has been eliminated for modern Web applications where multiple Web domains are hosted by the same IP address (virtual hosting) or one Web site uses multiple IP addresses (load balancing). Although ISC only counts a host once if it maps to multiple IP addresses, its operations cannot detect multiple domains operating on the same IP address.

Netcraft has explored the Internet since 1995. Its latest Web survey found more than 110 million Web sites in March 2007 (Netcraft, 2007). This result shows that the Internet has almost doubled in size in the last two years, as the survey hit 60 million in March 2005. Based on Netcraft's Web survey, Nielsen concludes the Web has experienced **three growth stages** since its founding 15 years ago: **explosive** growth from year 1991 to 1997 with a yearly rate of **850%**, **rapid** growth from 1998 to 2001 with a yearly rate of **150%**, and maturing growth from 2002 to 2006 with a yearly rate of **25%** (Nielsen, 2006).

Netcraft's periodic survey on the number of Web sites is conducted by checking the Web server software usage, collecting and collating the hostnames providing the http service, and polling each one with an HTTP request for the server name. Apparently, this approach involves time-consuming data collection, and the accuracy of the survey might be affected depending on the amount of data collected. Moreover, not all of these Web sites are live: some are "parked" domains, while others are abandoned

Weblogs that have not been updated in ages. Also, Netcraft's approach cannot accurately figure out the number of "physical" Web servers due to the application of virtual hosting.

Thus, virtual hosting has become a common problem for the hostname-based approaches to detect the number of hosts or domains. Particularly, the regional Internet registries such as RIPE[2] strongly encourage the deployment of name-based virtual hosting rather than IP address-based virtual hosting to ease the demand for scarce IP addresses (Apache, APNIC, RIPE NCC). As a matter of fact, there is a significant increase in the number of organizations that do not have high-traffic Web sites and have turned to Web hosters to obtain a cost-efficient and reliable Web presence. Obviously, the number of hostnames or domains would not match to the number of active servers.

Alternatively, consider that each server or router connected to the Internet has a unique public IP address. A naive approach to accomplish our objective to measure the prevalence of a given information service on the Internet would be to probe the IP address space and count the number of information servers thus found. We have introduced our sampling methods using this IP address-based approach.

In addition, it is worth noting a revealed Web dynamic link feature. The Web continuously expands and grows through the addition of new nodes (pages) and hyperlinks that connect to nodes already present in the Web. Several empirical study results have shown that for the large-scale networks such as the WWW, the degree distribution $p(k)$, which represents the fraction of the number of nodes that have k links in the network, possesses a power-law tail (Barabási & Albert, 1999; Broder et al., 2000). With power-law degree distribution, several growing models for the Web have been discovered, including the scale-free models (Barabási & Albert, 1999; Pennock, Flake, Lawrence, Glover, & Giles, 2002) and those with community structure (Kimura, Saito, & Ueda, 2002; Flake, Lawrence, & Giles, 2000). These models describe the connectivity-based dynamics of the Web, but we aim to calculate the consumption of the existing IPv4 address space.

Before we end this discussion, one more issue to consider is the software utilities used for the "real-time" Internet measurement in a client-server manner. As such, we need to generate requests to access the remote information servers and count the responses for the number of active servers. One way for this to work may be simply using *ping* to detect whether or not a server is up. The *ping* program uses the ICMP (Internet Control Message Protocol) echo request and echo reply messages to test the reachability of remote hosts on a network. Similarly, the TCP-based (or UDP-based) *ping* program sends a TCP (or UDP) datagram to the TCP (or UDP) echo port of the target host and waits for a reply. The host is considered unreachable if it cannot be connected, if the reply datagram is not received, or if the reply differs from the original datagram.

However, some hosts have filtered the ICMP protocol at their routers, and *ping* would indicate such hosts are down even though they can be reached through other protocols. For example, *www.netscape.com* is generally alive but not ICMP "pingable." Similarly, many hosts have disabled their TCP and UDP echo services, causing TCP and UDP pings to fail.

Reaching 43,402 Web servers[3] through *ping* (shown on the left of Figure 1) illustrates the above point. The data points in the figure are the rate of acknowledgment of TCP SYN packages sent to the remote host's echo port within the specified timeout. We can see that there are 3% "unpingable" Web servers even if the timeout is as long as 44 seconds (i.e., up to four TCP retransmissions), whereas local hosts normally respond to pings within milliseconds. The bins shown on the right of Figure 1 illustrate that almost all TCP ACKs (99.85% over the echoed messages) for the TCP SYN *ping* package arrive within 8 seconds (i.e., at most two TCP retransmissions) during our test.

It seems that more efficient and effective means are required for our task, and so we are developing the strategies to probe the remote host's TCP well-known port 80 for measuring the prevalence of Web services on the Internet.

Monte Carlo Sampling

While the complexity of the Internet has made closed-form analysis of the estimated parameters of the Internet prohibitive, sampling methods are rendered as the primary substitute for collecting

Figure 1. Left: Reaching 43,402 publicly accessible Web servers through TCP SYN ping; Right: Distribution of RTT of TCP SYN-ACK over the pinged Web set in left; test date: November 11, 2002

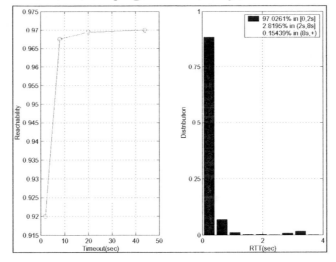

the Internet statistics. Monte Carlo Sampling is a numerical technique used for obtaining solutions to deterministic problems based on the principle of random sampling. In cases where a mathematical approach is intractable, a Monte Carlo approach is a key method due to its generality, flexibility, and ability to deal with arbitrarily complex systems.

Consider the problem of estimating the probability of a fixed event E, denoted by P(E) where P is the probability that E occurs on any particular trial. Suppose A is a discrete random variable with the probability measure g(a) on the measurable subsets of discrete domain Ω. Letting I(A) be an indicator function for the event E, $I(a_n)$ is 1 if E occurs on the n_{th} trial, and 0 otherwise. Then $P = P(E) = E[I(A)] = \sum_{a \in \Omega} I(a)g(a)$. In cases where I(a) is not available in closed form, P can be calculated by repeatedly generating N independent identically distributed (i.i.d.) random samples a_n with the probability mass function (pmf) g(a), and by counting the number that event E occurs. By the strong law of large numbers, it follows that with probability 1:

$$\hat{P} = \sum_{n=1}^{N} \frac{I(a_n)}{N} \rightarrow E[I(A)] = P(E) = P, \quad \text{as } N \rightarrow \infty. \tag{1}$$

Hence, P can be approximated as the sample average value of $I(a_n)$. This approach to approximat-

ing expectation is called Monte Carlo Sampling (Gentle, 1998), and its estimator is defined as:

$$\hat{P}_{mc} = \frac{1}{N_{mc}} \sum_{n=1}^{N_{mc}} I(a_n), \tag{2}$$

which is unbiased since:

$$E(\hat{P}_{mc}) = \frac{1}{N_{mc}} \sum_{n=1}^{N_{mc}} E[I(a_n)] \overset{a_n \text{ are } i.i.d.}{=} E[I(A)] = P. \tag{3}$$

The accuracy of this estimator may be illustrated by some cost associated with the estimate. The most commonly used cost is the mean squared error (MSE), or the estimator variance for an unbiased estimate, which is given by:

$$\text{var}(\hat{P}_{mc}) = E[(\hat{P}_{mc} - P)^2]$$

$$= E\left[\left(\frac{1}{N_{mc}} \sum_{n=1}^{N_{mc}} (I(a_n) - P)\right)^2\right]$$

$$= \frac{1}{N^2_{mc}} E\left[\sum_{i=1}^{N_{mc}} \sum_{j=1}^{N_{mc}} (I(a_i) - P)(I(a_j) - P)\right]$$

$$= \frac{1}{N^2_{mc}} \sum_{i=1}^{N_{mc}} \sum_{j=1}^{N_{mc}} (E[I^2(a_i)I(a_j)] - P^2)$$

$$= \frac{1}{N^2_{mc}} (E[I^2(A)] - P^2) \tag{4}$$

$$= \frac{1}{N^2_{mc}}(P - P^2). \tag{5}$$

The Monte Carlo approach is robust and easy to implement. It generates a high consistency—that is, the probability of the Monte Carlo estimator to be close to the estimated parameter increases as the number of trials increases. It can provide very accurate estimates if the number of samples is sufficiently large, but it also shows poor efficiency with a large variance of the estimator. More specifically, a small confidence interval for the estimated parameters requires a large sample size, which is computationally expensive.

To illustrate this, for a $\delta\%$ confidence interval of size η, the number of trials required is given approximately by (Papoulis, 1991):

$$N_{mc} = \left(\frac{2\sigma t_{1-\frac{\delta}{2}}}{\eta} \right)^2 \tag{6}$$

where, t_u is the u_{th} percentile of the Student-t distribution with $N_{mc} - 1$ degrees of freedom and σ is the sample standard deviation given by:

$$\sigma^2 = \frac{\sum_{n=1}^{N_{mc}}(I(a_n) - \overline{I(a)})^2}{N_{mc} - 1}$$

$$\approx \frac{\sum_{n=1}^{N_{mc}}(I(a_n) - P)^2}{N_{mc} - 1}$$

$$\approx \frac{1}{N_{mc}}\sum_{n=1}^{N_{mc}}(I(a_n) - P)^2$$

$$= P - P^2$$

$$\approx P, \quad \text{for a small } P. \tag{7}$$

For example, for a 95% confidence interval of [0.9P, 1.1P], the number of trials is approximately equal to $N_{mc} \approx \frac{420}{P}$. So as the active server address density P in the current IPv4 Internet is quite small (e.g., approximately 0.4% for the WWW service), the Monte Carlo approach requires more than 100,000 trials to sufficiently "hit" the rare events to estimate P.

In essence, the required number of Monte Carlo samples is directly proportional to $\frac{1}{P}$. Thus, it is especially true that Monte Carlo Sampling provides an inefficient estimate of the probability of rare events.

Therefore for estimating small P, it becomes necessary to consider the variance-reduction techniques to obtain reliable estimates using fewer samples than what would be required with the Monte Carlo approach.

Variance-Reduction Technique: Importance Sampling

There are two standard methods used for reducing the variance of raw or direct sampling estimators such as the use of a control variate (Lavenberg & Welch, 1981) and antithetic sampling (Hammersley & Morton, 1956). The former requires control variables that have known expectations and that are highly correlated with the estimators of interest. The latter seeks two unbiased estimators having strong negative correlation. The key problem for both techniques is that it is quite difficult to find these quantities. For our case to acquire the statistics of the Internet, it is not simplistic to determine control variables or a suitable bijection for antithetic sampling.

Importance Sampling, also called biased sampling, is another variance-reduction technique which can significantly reduce the number of Monte Carlo trials necessary for accurately estimating the probability of rare events.

In recognizing and rewriting the problem of estimating the value $P = E[I(A^*)] = \sum_{a^* \in \Omega} I(a^*)g(a^*)$, we introduce another pmf $p^*(a^*)$ such that $p^*(a^*) > 0$ whenever $g(a^*) > 0$ (this is called the absolute continuity condition). Then we can express P as:

$$P = \sum_{x^* \in \Omega} \frac{I(a^*)g(a^*)}{p^*(a^*)}p^*(a^*)$$

$$= E_*\left[\frac{I(A^*)g(A^*)}{p^*(A^*)} \right] = E_*[w(A^*)I(A^*)], \tag{8}$$

where the likelihood ratio $w(a^*) = \dfrac{g(a^*)}{p^*(a^*)}$ is called a weighting function. The notation $E_*[\cdot]$ indicates that the expectation is taken with respect to the probability measure $p^*(a^*)$.

It follows from equation (8) that P can be estimated by successively generating N independent identically distributed (i.i.d.) samples a^* of a random variable A^* drawn from the biased density $p^*(a^*)$, and then using the average of the values of $\dfrac{I(a^*)g(a^*)}{p^*(a^*)}$ as the estimator. Consideration can then be made as to how $p^*(a^*)$ may be chosen so that the random variable $w(a^*)I(a^*)$ has reduced variance to result in a more efficient estimator of P.

The aforementioned approach is called Importance Sampling (Glynn, & Iglehart, 1989) because the biased distributions minimize the Importance Sampling estimator variance. As a result, the observed frequency of the rare events is increased.

The Importance Sampling estimator is then defined as:

$$\hat{P}_{is} = \frac{1}{N_{is}} \sum_{n=1}^{N_{is}} w(a_n^*)I(a_n^*). \tag{9}$$

The definition of the weighting function $w(a^*)$ ensures an unbiased estimator. The resulting expectation:

$$E_*(\hat{P}_{is}) = E_* \left[\frac{1}{N_{is}} \sum_{n=1}^{N_{is}} w(a_n^*)I(a_n^*) \right]^{a_n^* \text{ are } i.i.d} =$$

$$E_*[w(A^*)I(A^*)] = P$$

Similar to $var(\hat{P}_{mc})$, the variance of the Importance Sampling estimator can be computed as:

$$var(\hat{P}_{is}) = \frac{1}{N_{is}}(\overline{W} - P^2), \tag{10}$$

where $\overline{W}$ is the second moment of $w(\cdot)I(\cdot)$, given by $\overline{W} = E_*[w^2(A^*)I(A^*)]$.

In essence, the intention of the Importance Sampling approach is to reduce dramatically the variance of the estimate, thereby decreasing sampling time for a given level of accuracy or improve drastically the estimator accuracy for a given limited number of samples. Hence, the performance of the biasing scheme can then be measured by a gain defined by the ratio of the cost of the Monte Carlo

Sampling estimator to the Importance Sampling estimator. Thus, the gain may be expressed as the ratio of the number of trials for a given variance, or equivalently as the ratio of the variances for a fixed number of iterations, given by:

$$\gamma = \frac{N_{mc}}{N_{is}} \bigg|_{var_{mc} = var_{is}} \tag{11}$$

or

$$\gamma = \frac{var_{mc}}{var_{is}} \bigg|_{N_{mc} = N_{is}} = \frac{P - P^2}{\overline{W} - P^2}. \tag{12}$$

It is clearly observed that the improvement achieved by using Importance Sampling over Monte Carlo Sampling is strongly influenced by the choice of the biasing pmf $p^*(\cdot)$. Comparison of equation (10) with equation (4) shows that $var(\hat{P}_{is}) \leq var(\hat{P}_{mc})$ if $I(\cdot)w(\cdot) \leq I(\cdot)$. This implies that a hit or a rare event would occur more frequently with Importance Sampling since the biasing pmf $p^*(\cdot)$ has to be greater than the original pmf $g(\cdot)$ when $I(a^*) = 1$—that is, when samples a^* produce hits.

Furthermore, using Jensen's inequality, the optimal biasing density $p_{opt}^*(a^*)$ given by:

$$p_{opt}^*(a^*) = \frac{g(a^*)I(a^*)}{P} \tag{13}$$

would have resulted in a perfect "estimate" of P for any sample size, even with only a single trial, thus maximizing the sampling efficiency. Unfortunately, this unconstrained solution is impractical because it assumes knowledge of the parameter P that we wish to estimate, and relies on an a priori knowledge of the function $I(a^*)$.

However, equation (13) provides some useful insights. For example, $p_{opt}^*(\cdot)$ contributes all of its mass to a promising area. In other words, a sampling distribution that is appropriately proportional to $g(a^*)I(a^*)$ would lead to a significant reduction in estimator variance. In fact, a nearly constant average weight over the promising regions would be obtained and in turn reduces the random fluctuations of the estimator. Therefore, an effective estimator should increase the relative frequency of promising samples which are more likely to yield hits. This observation has led us to introduce an improved Importance Sampling scheme.

AN IMPROVED IMPORTANCE SAMPLING SCHEME

Throughout the discussion in the previous section, we have recognized that if we only draw the probing samples from a promising sample set Ω_F, then it is expected that the improvement on the effectiveness of the estimator will be significant. Here, Ω_F is a subset of sampling space Ω and Ω contains the samples drawn from a biasing density p^* which satisfies the absolute continuity condition.

To be more specific, let weighting function $w(a^*) = \dfrac{g(a^*)}{p^F(a^*)}$ if $a^* \in \Omega_F$ and $w(a^*) = 0$ otherwise.

Here $p^F(a^*)$ is the biasing density over Ω_F. In general, $p^F(a^*)$ does not satisfy the absolute continuity condition—that is, it is not necessarily that $p^F(a^*) > 0$ whenever $g(a^*) > 0$.

Then, the expectation of this improved Importance Sampling estimator $\hat{P}_F$ for P is given by:

$$E(\hat{P}_F) = \frac{1}{N_{is}} \sum_{n=1}^{N_{is}} E_*[w(a_n^*)I(a_n^*)]$$

$$= \frac{1}{N_{is}} \sum_{\substack{n=1 \\ a_n^* \in \Omega_F}}^{N_{is}} E_*[w(a_n^*)I(a_n^*)]$$

$$= \sum_{\substack{a_n \\ a_n^* \in \Omega_F}} \frac{g(a_n^*)I(a_n^*)}{p^F(a_n^*)} p^F(a_n^*)$$

$$= P \sum_{\substack{a_n \\ a_n^* \in \Omega_F}} \frac{g(a_n^*)I(a_n^*)}{P}$$

$$= P \sum_{\substack{a_n \\ a_n^* \in \Omega_F}} p_{opt}^*(a_n^*), \text{ by (13)}$$

$$= PB,$$

$$\text{where } B = \sum_{a_n^* \in \Omega_F} p_{opt}^*(a_n^*) \le 1 \tag{14}$$

Thus, $\hat{P}_F$ is a biased estimator of P. This occurs due to the omission of the non-promising samples that contribute to small hit rates. Then the values of the random variable $I(a_n^*)$ ($a_n^* \in \Omega_F$) have been distributed according to a probability mass function that is not absolutely continuous with probability measure $g(a_n^*)$. Consequently, $\hat{P}_F$ (the weighted sample mean of $I(a_n^*)$, $a_n^* \in \Omega_F$) will not converge to P (the weighted sample mean of the values of $I(a_n^*)$, $a_n^* \in \Omega$).

We call B a bias factor. In general, an unbiased estimate of P may be obtained by correcting the bias factor B if it is found or estimated. The resulting variance of the biased estimator $\hat{P}_F$ is:

$$\text{var}(\hat{P}_F) = \frac{1}{N_{is}}(\bar{W}^F - P^2 B^2), \tag{15}$$

where the average weight $\bar{W}^F$ can be derived as follows:

$$\bar{W}^F = E_*[w^2(a_n^*)I(a_n^*)]$$

$$= \sum_{\substack{x_n \\ a_n^* \in \Omega_F}} \left(\frac{g(a_n^*)}{p^F(a_n^*)}\right)^2 I(a_n^*)p^F(a_n^*)$$

$$= P \sum_{\substack{a_n \\ a_n^* \in \Omega_F}} \frac{g(a_n^*)}{p^F(a_n^*)} \frac{g(a_n^*)I(a_n^*)}{P}$$

$$= P \sum_{\substack{a_n \\ a_n^* \in \Omega_F}} w(a_n^*)P_{opt}(a_n^*). \tag{16}$$

A high performance biased estimator $\hat{P}_F$ is obtained. To illustrate this, consider the estimator gain γ^F. Similar to equation (12), γ^F can be given by:

$$\gamma^F = \frac{P - P^2}{\bar{W}^F - P^2 B^2} \approx \frac{P}{\bar{W}^F} \text{ for a very small value of } P. \tag{17}$$

Clearly, the gain is mostly determined by $\bar{W}^F$.

For comparison, consider a conventional Importance Sampling scheme which gives:

$$\bar{W} = P \sum_{\substack{a_n \\ a_n^* \in \Omega}} \frac{g(a_n^*)}{p^*(a_n^*)} P_{opt}(a_n^*), \tag{18}$$

where p^* is the biasing density over set Ω. Rewrite the conventional estimator gain γ^C with equation (12) which gives:

$$\gamma^C = \frac{P - P^2}{\bar{W} - P^2} \approx \frac{P}{\bar{W}}. \tag{19}$$

We can construct the new biasing density $p^F(a_n^*)$ and make $p^F(a_n^*) > p^*(a_n^*)$ for $a_n^* \in \Omega_F$, and

$\Omega = \Omega_F + \Omega_{F^c}$, in general. Then:

$$\sum_{\substack{a_n^* \\ a_n^* \in \Omega_F}} \frac{g(a_n^*)}{p^F(a_n^*)} p_{opt}(a_n^*) < \sum_{\substack{a_n^* \\ a_n^* \in \Omega}} \frac{g(a_n^*)}{p^*(a_n^*)} p_{opt}(a_n^*).$$

Hence, $\overline{W}^F < \overline{W}$ and in turn $\gamma^F > \gamma^C$. The improvement of the biased estimator is achieved.

Since we only select promising samples to generate the biasing density p^F in order to achieve the best possible improvement, $\Omega_F \ll \Omega_{F^c}$ and then $\overline{W}^F \ll \overline{W}$. Thus, $\gamma^F \gg \gamma^C$ and the gain of the biased estimator over Monte Carlo Sampling γ^F will be much significant.

The improved Importance Sampling scheme is illustrated in Figure 2. As described above, the input samples a_n^* are generated from a promising sample set Ω_F. The biased estimator $\hat{P}_F$ is then scaled by the quantity $\frac{1}{B}$ to obtain an unbiased estimate of P.

MEASURING THE NUMBER OF ACTIVE WEB SERVERS

It is worth noting that the growth of the Internet has recently been dominated by the evolution of the World Wide Web. This section presents an Importance Sampling-based approach for tracking the prevalence and growth of the Web service. Specifically, we have developed approaches to measure the number of IP addresses with active Web servers.

Implementation of Importance Sampling Strategies

To measure the number of IP addresses with some servers, we may generate the IP addresses and send probes to the Internet to check whether or not there is a particular service server on that address or not. However, scanning the whole 2^{32} IP addresses A to probe the active Web servers is impractical. This renders sampling methods as a primary substitute. Assume the probability that a Web server found at an arbitrarily chosen IP address a_n is P_w, then the number of Web servers:

$$N_w = P_w \cdot \text{size of IPv4 address space} = P_w \cdot 2^{32}. \tag{20}$$

Hence, the objective is to estimate P_w using the IP address a_n as a sample unit of the random variable A.

With the Monte Carlo approach, we may sample the IP address space uniformly (letting the underlying density $g(a_n) = 2^{-32}$, $n = 1,..., 2^{32}$) and probe each randomly selected IP address a_n to determine if the host at that address provides the information service. Then the Monte Carlo estimator of P_w will be give by equation (2).

Since P_w in the current IPv4 Internet is quite small, Importance Sampling is introduced. Instead of uniformly selecting IP addresses, we draw N_{is} independent IP addresses a_n^* to be probed from a non-uniform biasing distribution p^*. More samples are taken from promising regions of IP address space which in turn produce more hits. We rewrite the Importance Sampling estimator of P_w as:

$$\hat{P}_{is} = \frac{1}{N_{is}} \sum_{n=1}^{N_{is}} w(a_n^*) I(a_n^*), \tag{21}$$

where $w(a_n^*) = \frac{2^{-32}}{p^*(a_n^*)}$.

The variance of the Importance Sampling estimator depends on the choice of biasing strategy $p^*(a_n^*)$. Typical Importance Sampling approaches use $p^*(a_n^*)$

Figure 2. The improved Importance Sampling scheme

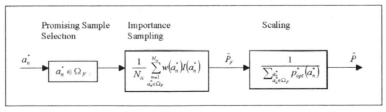

obtained by modifying the parameters of the underlying, or true, probability measure $p^*(a_n^*)$ of server addresses, where $p'(a_n')$ indicates the probability that $I(a_n^*) = 1$ for the n_{th} trial, given by:

$$p(a_n^*) = \frac{I(a_n^*)}{N_w} = \begin{cases} \dfrac{1}{N_w} & , \text{if } I(a_n^*) = 1 \\ 0 & , \text{if } I(a_n^*) = 0 \end{cases}. \qquad (22)$$

Furthermore, we can interpret the unconstrained optimal biasing density $p_{opt}^*(a_n^*)$ as the true probability measure $p(a_n^*)$, showing that:

$$p_{opt}^*(a_n^*) = \frac{2^{-32} I(a_n^*)}{P_w} = p(a_n^*). \qquad (23)$$

$\hat{P}_{is}$ is unbiased if we choose a biasing distribution $p^*(a_n^*)$ that is absolutely continuous with respect to the true probability measure $p(a_n^*)$. However, $p(a_n^*)$ is unknown without probing the entire IP address space. Instead, we try to obtain marginals of the true probability measure p, $p_j(b)$, by grouping the IP address using its conventional four-byte description (i.e., $a_n^* = b_1.b_2.b_3.b_4$), where:

$$p_j(b_j) = \sum_{\substack{a_n \\ j-th \text{ byte equals } b_j}} p(a_n^*), \qquad (24)$$

$j = 1, \ldots, 4$ and $b_j = 0, \ldots, 255$.

For probing the publicly accessible Web servers, $I(a_n^*) = 1$ if we receive a message with a response status code of 2XX, and $p_j(b_j)$ can be estimated from a large collection of known Web server addresses provided by the random URL service, such as http://www.randomWebsite.com. These addresses are used to form the following empirical distributions $p_j^{(e)}(b_j)$, which represents the fraction of the number of addresses with j_{th} byte equal to b_j.

$$p_j^{(e)}(b_j) =$$
$$\frac{\text{number of addresses with } j-\text{th byte equal to } b_j}{\text{total number of collected addresses}} \qquad (25)$$

And, we can approximate $p_j(b_j) \approx p_j^{(e)}(b_j)$.

The first byte empirical distributions of publicly accessible Web server addresses are depicted in the top of Figure 3. It captures the consequences of how

IP addresses are allocated. There are large numbers of Web servers in the relatively small "class C" address range. Significantly fewer servers are present in the "class B" and "class A" ranges, and no servers are found in the reserved address ranges (e.g., "class D" and "class E"). This matches the assignment of the first byte of IPv4 address space by IANA,[4] shown in the bottom graph of Figure 3 (IANA, n.d.; IANA–Multicast, n.d.).

Furthermore, $p_i^{(e)}$ and $p_j^{(e)}$, $i \neq j$, $i, j = 1, \ldots, 4$ appear to be fairly independent. This has been demonstrated in Xing and Paris (2001). Therefore, we may reasonably assume that the true probability measure for the pair of bytes p_i and p_j, $i \neq j$ are also independent. Hence, we focus on biasing distributions with independent bytes, that is, $p^*(a_n^*) = \Pi_{j=1}^4 p_j^*(b_j)$, where $p_j^*(b_j)$ is the byte biasing distributions. The overall weight becomes $w(a_n^*) = \Pi_{j=1}^4 w_j(b_j)$, where $w_j(b_j)$ is the byte weight.

Additionally, from equations (18) and (23), the average weight $\bar{W}$ for a conventional Importance Sampling scheme can be derived as:

$$\bar{W} = P_w \Pi_{j=1}^4 \sum_{b_j=0}^{255} w_j(b_j) p_j(b_j). \qquad (26)$$

Consider a single byte biasing. For example, only the j_{th} byte is biased of the IP address, and the other byte distributions are kept uniform. We will have $p_i^* \neq p_u$ (p_u is the uniform distributions over 256 IP byte addresses), and $p_i^* = p_u = \dfrac{1}{256}$ for $i \neq j$. Then, $w_j(b_j) = \dfrac{1}{256 \cdot p_j^*(b_j)}$ and $w_i(b_i) = 1$ for $i \neq j$. $\bar{W}$ becomes:

$$\bar{W}_j = \frac{P_w}{256} \sum_{b_j=0}^{255} \frac{p_j(b_j)}{p_j^*(b_j)}. \qquad (27)$$

Similarly, for the improved Importance Sampling scheme with independent bytes, the average weight $\bar{W}^F = P_w \Pi_{j=1}^4 \sum_{\substack{b_j=0, b_j \in F_j}}^{255} w_j(b_j) p_j(b_j)$. Here, F_j is a promising address set for the j_{th} byte IP address. And, the bias factor $B = \Pi_{j=1}^4 B_j$, where the byte bias factor:

$$B_j = \sum_{\substack{b_j=0 \\ b_j \in F_j}}^{255} p_j(b_j). \qquad (28)$$

Figure 3. Allocation of the first byte of IPv4 address space Top: Empirical distributions of publicly accessible Web servers; Bottom: IANA assignment on January 27, 2005 (http://www.iana.org/assignments/ipv4-address-space/)

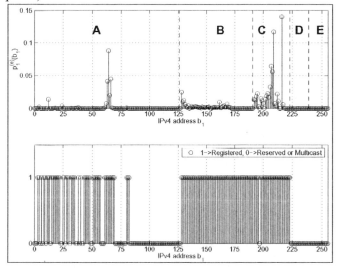

If we only bias the j_{th} byte of the IP address as mentioned above, $\bar{W}^F$ becomes the byte average weight $\bar{W}_j^F$, given by:

$$\bar{W}_j^F = \frac{P_w}{256} \sum_{\substack{b_j=0 \\ b_j \in F_j}}^{255} \frac{p_j(b_j)}{p_j^F(b_j)}. \tag{29}$$

And, $B_i = 1$ for $i \neq j$. Consequently, the bias factor $B = B_j$.

An optimal unbiased Importance Sampling strategy based on the marginal distribution p_j has been presented for measuring the number of publicly accessible Web servers with a gain of 7 (Xing & Paris, 2001). However, we have noted that the active Web servers should also include those which are not providing a public information service because of security concerns. Such Web servers either only respond to authorized users or are behind some kind of gateway or firewall. In addition to 2XX (successful requests), there have been other response codes we received for our probes that also indicate the presence of a Web server at that probed address. Table 1 lists the number of responses for HTTP HEAD requests that are sent to the TCP well-known port 80 of hosts. A total of 229,747 IP addresses have been probed in a Monte Carlo fashion, and the survey was conducted November 1-7, 2004.

From Table 1, we have found that besides the 2XX status codes, there are a considerable number of 4XX responses. Specifically, an HTTP status code 401 ("Unauthorized," authentication required), 403 ("Forbidden," usually because of file permissions), or 404 ("Not Found," commonly used when the server does not wish to reveal exactly why the request has been refused) was received in response to our HTTP HEAD request. These servers are configured reflecting security concerns. Some 4XX responses might also come from intermediate machines (e.g., proxy firewalls or gateways), rather than the Web servers themselves that operate behind these intermediaries. In order to count the total number of active Web servers, we must include these 4XX responses. In calculating the IP address consumption, the number of active Web servers would be closer to the actual size of the Internet.

Importance Sampling approaches are still utilized for effectively and efficiently estimating the number of active Web servers. A critical problem behind this extension is that the empirical data obtained from the Web crawler is incomplete for estimating the relative distribution of the number of Web servers with 4XX responses for a HTTP request, as the Web crawler acquires data by spidering or following all links found on the Web site, hence omitting the servers that do not provide a public information service. Therefore, we cannot estimate (or approximate) the marginals of the *true* probability measure for all active Web servers any longer via the empirical distributions $p_j^{(e)}$ and further devise an optimal unbiased Importance Sampling strategy based on these marginal distributions. However, we need to find an alternative biasing strategy to measure the number of active Web servers.

Choosing the Biasing Density

The improved Importance Sampling approach discussed in this chapter appears to be a powerful and a needed method to estimate the probability of rare events in discrete event systems, as in our case. The performance of the improved Importance Sampling approach will depend on the choice of a promising sample set, and the resulting biased estimator $\hat{P}_F$ is scaled by the quantity $\dfrac{1}{B}$ to obtain an unbiased estimate of P_w. To bootstrap the improved Importance Sampling approach to estimate the active Web server density P_w, we may find a *promising* byte address set F_j by thresholding empirically observed address distributions (Xing & Paris, 2002), that is:

$$F_j = \{b_j | p_j^{(e)}(b_j) \ge \theta_j,\ b_j = 0,\ \dots,\ 225\}, \quad (30)$$

where θ_j is the threshold set in the j_{th} byte ($j = 1,\dots,4$). The byte biasing density is,

$$p_j^F(b_j) = \begin{cases} \dfrac{p_l^{(e)}(b_j)}{\displaystyle\sum_{\substack{b_j=0 \\ p_j^{(e)} \ge \theta_j}}^{255} p_j^{(e)}(b_j)} & ,\ \text{if } b_j \in F_j \\ \\ 0 & ,\ \text{otherwise} \end{cases} \quad (31)$$

for $b_j = 0,\dots,255$.

As stated in the previous discussion, we cannot approximate the marginals p_j of the true probability measure of active Web servers via empirical distributions $p_j^{(e)}$ to obtain an estimate of the bias B this time. However, the empirical data provides us with a guide to determine the promising address set F_j since the publicly accessible Web servers (responding with a 2XX code) make up the majority of the active Web servers (refer to the number of 2XX vs. the number of 4XX in Table 1).

Furthermore, instead of proportionally weighting the promising samples as equation (31), we may draw the promising samples uniformly, hence obtaining the byte biasing density:

$$p_j^Q(b_j) = \begin{cases} \dfrac{1}{Q} & ,\ b_j \in F \\ \\ 0 & ,\ \text{for all other } b_j\text{'s} \end{cases} \quad ,\ b_j = 0,\dots,255, \quad (32)$$

where Q is the number of selected promising byte addresses.

Table 1. Number of responses vs. status code, November 1-7, 2004

Status Code	Number of Responses
200 (Successful Request)	684
400 (Malformed Request)	15
401 (Unauthorized)	123
403 (Forbidden)	105
404 (Not Found)	61
No Response	228,759

Then, for single byte biasing, from equation (29), $\bar{W}_j^Q = \frac{Q}{256} P_w B_j$ and the resulting variance of the biased estimator $\hat{P}_Q$ is:

$$var(\hat{P}_Q) = var(\hat{P}_F) = \frac{P_w B_j}{N_{is}} \left(\frac{Q}{256} - P_w B_j \right). \text{ (33)}$$

A significant gain is achieved compared to Monte Carlo Sampling (compare to equation (4)) since $Q < 256$, $B_j \leq 1$, and P_w is very small.

Equation (33) also indicates that size Q has to be as small as possible to minimize the variance. Conversely, increasing Q will reduce the bias. Hence, we can find a critical point of the number of promising samples Q_0, based on which an unbiased estimate is obtained without the need for calculating or estimating the bias (i.e., make $B_j = 1$). For single byte biasing, one solution of this value is $Q_0 = 256$. However, it turns to Monte Carlo Sampling which defeats the purpose of saving sampling time.

Another solution for Q_0 is based on the exploration of IP address allocation. Specifically, we focus on the first byte IP address allocation. This information can be obtained from IANA (IANA–V4, n.d.). Then, Q_0 is the number of allocated first byte IP addresses, which in turn result in a single byte biasing density p_1^A given by:

$$p_1^A (b_1) =$$

$$\begin{cases} \dfrac{1}{Q_0} & \text{, for allocated address } b_1 \\ 0 & \text{, for all other } b_1\text{'s} \end{cases}, \; b_1 = 0, \ldots, 255$$

$$(34)$$

However, the resulting gain γ^A of the IP address allocation-based sampling estimator $\hat{P}_A$ over Monte Carlo Sampling is not significant since:

$$\gamma^A \approx \frac{P_w}{\bar{W}_1^Q} = \frac{256}{Q_0}, \tag{35}$$

and the IPv4 addresses have been well assigned (large value of Q_0). As of January 27, 2005, for example, the IANA reserved 108 first byte IP addresses (Figure 3), thus $Q_0 = 148$.

Based on the above discussion, we have concluded an Importance Sampling estimator which combines the biased improved Importance Sampling estima-

tor $\hat{P}_F$ and the unbiased IP address allocation-based sampling estimator $\hat{P}_A$, to achieve an unbiased estimate of P_w and also a high gain. The corresponding single byte biasing density over the first byte of IP address is given by,

$$p_1^* (b_1) = \alpha \, p_1^F (b_1) + \beta \, p_1^A (b_1), \text{ for } b_1 = 0, \ldots, 255,$$

$$(36)$$

where α is a mixture factor, $\beta = 1 - \alpha$.

This combined approach will provide an unbiased estimator $\hat{P}_w$ for $0 \leq \alpha \leq 1$, and the performance of this approach is strongly influenced by the choice of α. The factor α is chosen to obtain the maximum gain γ of P_w over Monte Carlo Sampling, that is, $\alpha = \arg\max\{\gamma\}$.

To evaluate the gain γ as a function of α, let M denote the total number of trials, and B_1 (specifically the first byte) denote the bias factor for biased estimator $\hat{P}_F$. $\hat{P}_w$ must be composed of estimates obtained from trials related to $\hat{P}_A$ and $\hat{P}_F$, respectively. Then, we can form $\hat{P}_w$ by:

$$\hat{P}_w = \lambda \hat{P}_A(\beta M) + (1 - \lambda) \frac{\hat{P}_F(\alpha M)}{\hat{B}_1}, \quad 0 < \lambda \leq 1. \tag{37}$$

The optimal value of λ, λ_{opt}, which minimizes the variance of the estimator $\hat{P}_w$, is easily found by Lagrangian optimization of $\hat{P}_w$. Then the gain γ for λ_{opt} is given by:

$$\gamma = \frac{M}{P_w - P_w^2} \left(\frac{1}{var(\hat{P}_A(\beta M))} + \frac{1}{var\left(\dfrac{\hat{P}_F(\alpha M)}{\hat{B}_1} \right)} \right).$$

$$(38)$$

In equation (37), $var(\hat{P}_A(k)) = \frac{1}{k} \left(\frac{Q_0}{256} P_w - P_w^2 \right)$ and,

$$var\left(\frac{\hat{P}_F(k)}{\hat{B}_1} \right) = (var(\hat{P}_F(k)))$$

$$+ E^2(\hat{P}_F(k)))var\left(\frac{1}{\hat{B}_1}\right) + var(\hat{P}_F(k))E^2\left(\frac{1}{\hat{B}_1}\right),$$
(39)

where the moments of $\hat{P}_F$, $E(\hat{P}_F(k))$, and $var(\hat{P}_F(k))$ can be obtained by equations (14) and 33, respectively.

To obtain the moments of $\frac{1}{\hat{B}_1}$ in equation (39), consider a Monte Carlo Sampling to generate hits. We may express B_1 by a conditional pmf $P(F_1|H_1)$, where F_1 is the *promising* first byte IP address set, given by equation (30), and H_1 denotes the set of first byte IP address resulting in hits during the Monte Carlo trials, given by:

$$H_1 = \{b_1 \mid p_1(b_1) \geq 0, \quad b_1 = 0, \ldots, 255\}.$$
(40)

Then,

$$B_1 = \sum_{\substack{b_1=0 \\ b_1 \in F_1}}^{255} p_1(b_1) = P(F_1|H_1) = \frac{E(I(F_1))}{E(I(H_1))} = \frac{N_F}{N_H},$$
(41)

where N_F and N_H denote the number of hits corresponding to F_1 and H_1, respectively. And, the

moments of $\frac{1}{\hat{B}_1}$, $E\left(\frac{1}{\hat{B}_1}\right)$, and $var\left(\frac{1}{\hat{B}_1}\right)$ can be estimated via the conditional pmf $p(N_H|N_F)$.

Be aware that N_F is a binomial random variable having parameters (N_H, B_1). It is reasonable to approximate N_F by a Poisson arrival process for a large N_H and a small B_1(Ross, 1997). And the conditional pmf $p(N_H|N_F)$ is expressed by the discretized Erlang-like distributions, given by[5]:

$$p(N_H = n_h \mid N_F = n_f) = \frac{B_1^{n_f} n_h^{n_f-1}}{(n_f - 1)!} e^{-B_1 n_h}. \quad (42)$$

Figure 4 illustrates the predicted gain γ for the estimator $\hat{P}_w$. The curves at the bottom show γ vs. α for several given values of bias B_1 and number of promising samples Q. It provides a basis for selecting a proper mixture factor α. It also shows that the promising samples should be selected from a small set which includes only the addresses that are most likely to yield hits (small Q and large B_1).

Scaling the Biased Estimator

As we have seen from Figure 4, the gain γ of the combined approach for an unbiased estimate of P_w over Monte Carlo Sampling is modest. The improved Importance Sampling scheme will increase

Figure 4. Predicted gain γ for estimating P_w (M = 140,000, P_w = 0.003, and n_f = 75). Top: Gain γ as a function of α and B_1 for Q = 2; Bottom: Gain γ as a function of α for given values of B_1 and Q

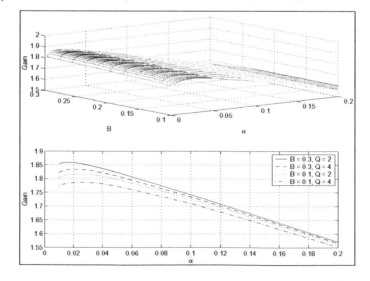

the gain significantly. Nevertheless, it results in a biased estimate of P_w. To obtain an unbiased estimate of P_w via the improved Importance Sampling approach, the bias B_1 (if only biasing the first byte) is required to be evaluated. Again, the marginals p_1 of the *true* probability measure of the active Web server addresses are not available to estimate B_1.

Alternatively, we may evaluate B_1 through Monte Carlo trials as mentioned by equation (41). But it is well known that a large number of hits N_F is required for a reliable estimate of B_1 via this Monte Carlo approach, leading to a long set of trials.

Recognize that the combined approach (see equation (36)) will alleviate this dilemma. Through the combined sampling trials, a fast convergence to B_1 will be achieved due to a large number of hits corresponding to the promising address set F_1, while the embedded IP address allocation-based sampling $\hat{P}_A$ will ensure an unbiased estimate of B_1. P_A will also save the sampling time as it draws samples from a reduced size of IP address space (see equation (35)).

Then, an unbiased estimate of B_1 is obtained and given by:

$$\hat{B}_1^{(IS)} = \frac{\sum_{b_1 \in F_1}^{M} I(a_n^*(b_1))w_1(b_1)}{\sum_{b_1 \in F_1}^{M} I(a_n^*(b_1))w_1(b_1) + \sum_{b_1 \in F_1^c}^{M} I(a_n^*(b_1))w_1(b_1)},$$

(43)

where the weight $w_1(b_1) = \dfrac{1}{256 p_1^*(b_1)}$, for $b_1 = 0,\ldots,255$.

Note that, although the aforementioned approach for evaluating B_1 will simultaneously provide an unbiased estimate of P_w after a long set of trials, it is still more efficient to perform two short runs: P_w is estimated by the improved Importance Sampling which follows the estimation of B_1. The total sampling time will be reduced for estimating both B_1 and P_w.

MEASUREMENT RESULTS

Figure 5 shows an experiment for estimating the active Web server density P_w, via the previously mentioned Importance Sampling approaches. Each point in the curves represents an estimate obtained by probing the remote host's TCP well-known port 80 for as many times as indicated on the x-axis. After each probe, the respective estimates are updated and plotted in each graph.

The curves in the top figure show the "running" estimates of bias B_1 via equation (40). In comparison, the Importance Sampling estimate settles clearly faster than the Monte Carlo Sampling estimate, reflecting a reduced variance.

An estimate of P_w via the improved Importance Sampling is shown in the middle figure. The biasing density in this second run is p_1^F (by equation (30)). An unbiased estimate of P_w is achieved by correcting B_1 at each point. An estimate of the gain of the improved Importance Sampling estimator over Monte Carlo Sampling is shown in the bottom figure.

Similarly, the curves in Figure 6 show that the standard deviation of the Importance Sampling estimator is significantly smaller than that of the Monte Carlo Sampling approach.

The experiments were conducted and completed in less than a day, in comparison to a week long of Monte Carlo Sampling! It was conducted on March 12, 2003, and estimated P_w to equal 0.351%. The standard deviation for the Importance Sampling estimate of P_w is $8.173 \cdot 10^{-5}$. For the Monte Carlo Sampling estimate, the standard deviation is $3.509 \cdot 10^{-4}$. An accurate estimate of the number of active Web servers $\hat{N}_w$ is given by:

$$\hat{N}_w = P_w \cdot \text{size of IPv4 address space}$$

$$= 3.51 \cdot 10^{-3} \cdot 2^{32} \approx 15.1 \; Millions \quad (44)$$

Based on the approaches presented above, we have made periodic measurements to map the growth of the Web. Figure 7 illustrates an immense growth of the number of IP addresses with active Web servers from January 2002 to March 2007. The growth rate for each year is listed in Table 2, showing the increase over the previous year.

From Figure 7 and Table 2, we have seen that the Web experienced the fastest growth in the year 2006 over the past five years. Our measurements have also presented that the Web continued to experience strong growth in the first quarter of 2007, showing a 9.5% increase over last year. Specifically, more than 27.7 million IP addresses related to Web servers were detected through our approaches by the end of March 2007. This effort indicates and suggests that the number of Web servers has doubled in the past five years.

However, in further analysis, this number is different from the measurement provided by, for example, Netcraft (2007) which counts *domains* or *hostnames*. The difference in these measurements can be explained (at least in part) by an increasing number of *virtual hosts*. At this time, our methods

do not provide means to detect multiple WWW domains operating on the same IP address, although our measurements bode well for concerns about exhaustion of the IP address space.

To be more specific, we have plotted the year-long growth of the Web for comparison. The growth curves for the period of December 2001 to February 2003 and the period of March 2003 to April 2004 are illustrated in Figure 8 (Xing & Paris, 2004), showing an exponential growth of the Web. The

Figure 5. Improved Importance Sampling vs. Monte Carlo estimation of active Web server density P_w on March 12, 2003. Top: First run for estimating B_1 on set $F_1 = [64\ 66\ 209\ 216]$, given $\alpha = 0.025$; Middle: Second run for estimating P_W given $B_1 = 0.256$; Bottom: Logarithmic gain of the estimator $\hat{P}_w$.

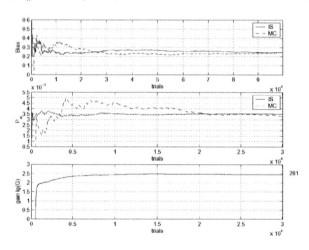

Figure 6. One-standard-deviation confidence interval for the estimates of P_w. Top: Improved Importance Sampling; Bottom: Monte Carlo Sampling; Test date: March 12, 2003

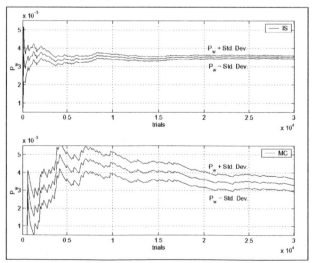

dashed lines in Figure 8 represent one-standard-deviation confidence interval for interpolated growth curve. The growth curves of the number of Web server IP addresses, shown in Figure 8, are well expressed by:

$$G1_w = 1.5086 \cdot 10^5 e^{0.2087m} + 1.2199 \cdot 10^7, \quad m \geq 0,$$
(45)

where m indicates the m-th month since January 2002, for the period of January 2002 to February 2003, and:

$$G2_w = 1.6131 \cdot 10^4 e^{0.3523m} + 1.4954 \cdot 10^7, \quad m \geq 0,$$
(46)

where m indicates the m-th month since January 2003, for the period of March 2003 to April 2004, respectively.

Table 2. Web sever address growth rate for 2002-2006

Year	Growth Rate (%)
2002	13.27
2003	15.24
2004	13.40
2005	14.13
2006	24.59

It gets interesting. The growth of the Web is not exponential in the year 2004, illustrated in Figure 7. However, the exponential growth of the Web continued after that period. The growth curve for the period of January 2005 to December 2006 is illustrated in Figure 9, which shows a continued exponential growth of the Web over the two years. Note again, the dashed lines in Figure 9 indicate one-standard-deviation confidence interval for interpolated growth curve. The growth curve of the number of Web server IP addresses, shown in Figure 9, is well expressed by:

$$G1_w = 0.2425 \cdot 10^7 e^{0.0678m} + 1.4972 \cdot 10^7, \quad m \geq 1,$$
(47)

where m indicates the m-th month since January 2005, for the period of January 2005 to December 2006.

In addition, the increasing security concerns on the Web server configuration have also been detected in our experiments. As we observe a period of the past three years, 2004 through 2006, we plotted the change of the numbers of Web servers with different status codes of 4XX for this period. These findings are illustrated in Figure 10. It showed an increasing number of Web servers configured to require user authentication for access, showing an increasing curve with 401 responses for the three

Figure 7. Number of IP addresses with active Web servers N_w from January 2002 to March 2007

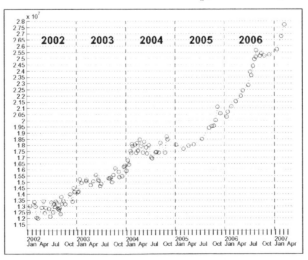

years. A slight decreasing number in 2004 and a significant increasing number in 2005 of "access refusal" are detected, shown by the down-up curve with 403 responses. Figure 10 further showed an increased number of servers "Not Found," showing an increasing curve with 404 responses for the past three years. It shows that more Web servers have turned to not making it available to the clients for the reason of access refusal and simply use "Not Found" instead.

CONCLUSION

This chapter has introduced the idea of collecting Internet statistics using sampling approaches. Certainly the Internet is decentralized and dynamic. To evaluate its parameters or performance, applying analytical techniques is usually very expensive, time consuming, and relatively inflexible. Additionally, many statistical measurements of the Internet

Figure 8. Number of IP addresses with active Web servers N_w. Left: From December 2001 to February 2003; Right: From March 2003 to April 2004

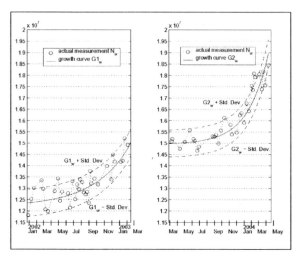

Figure 9. Number of IP addresses with active Web servers N_w from January 2005 to December 2006

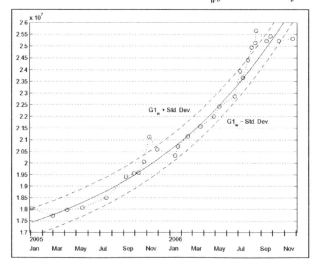

are related to estimating rare event probabilities. This renders sampling methods as a primary substitute to collecting such statistics.

We have presented the conventional Monte Carlo approach, which is the most straightforward sampling technique by directly counting the number of events in repeated trials. However, the problem is that the estimated probabilities are usually quite small, requiring numerous Monte Carlo runs to sufficiently hit the rare events to gain a reliable estimate. As a variance reduction technique, Importance Sampling is introduced. Importance Sampling is a modified Monte Carlo approach which can result in a significant reduction of the effort required to obtain an accurate estimate. The principle of Importance Sampling is to make the events of interest occur more frequently than in Monte Carlo Sampling. This is done by biasing the underlying probability measure from which samples are drawn, resulting in the events of interest having increased probability while others have a reduced probability. An unbiased estimate is then obtained by weighting the events appropriately. In addition, Importance Sampling works particularly well when estimating the probability of rare events compared to other variance-reduction techniques.

Therefore, it is extremely appealing to use Importance Sampling methods to estimate the Internet information server density. We introduced an improved Importance Sampling scheme. A thorough analysis of the proposed sampling approaches has been presented. We proposed Importance Sampling strategies to track the prevalence and growth of the Web service. A periodic measurement of the number of active Web servers was conducted over the past five years for mapping the growth of the Web. We observed and modeled exponential growth of the Web. We also discussed the increasing security concerns on the Web servers.

For further work, we plan to develop more sophisticated metrics for our measurement. In our current research, we group IP addresses utilizing the conventional addressing based on the four-byte partition of IPv4 addresses, and use empirical measurements to bootstrap the Importance Sampling procedure. Although using the adequate and simple four-byte description has produced efficiencies that are practically relevant for our probing endeavors, utilizing more specific Internet structures may provide improved sampling efficiency in our future research.

Figure 10. Number of IP addresses with active Web servers from January 2004 to December 2006. Upper left: 400 responses; Upper right: 401 responses; Lower left: 403 responses; Lower Right: 404 responses

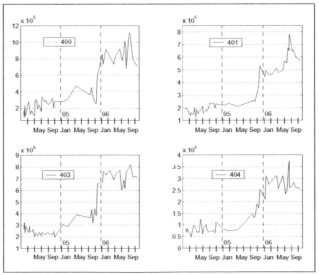

One method that recognizes clues from the topology of the Internet may be to group sets of IP prefixes associated with autonomous systems (ASs) by using, for example, BGP routing table dumps (e.g., collected by the Oregon route server (see University of Oregon, n.d.), RIPE, and RADB,[6] etc.). It would be reasonable to assume that persistence in any growth pattern of Internet service address density would be more accurately or succinctly related by AS boundaries than to a four-byte aggregation approach. Furthermore, by partitioning the measurement data of IP addresses into "domain subsets," it would expect much more information of the Internet topology being revealed, which could be exploited for more effective Importance Sampling.

Moreover, we will collect more dynamics of the Internet and estimate other relevant measures of the size and growth of the Internet in our future work. Lastly, we will assess the impact of IPv6 on our proposed approaches.

FUTURE RESEARCH DIRECTION

For further work, we plan to develop more sophisticated metrics for our measurements on the Internet growth. Rather than the Web, we will collect more dynamics of the Internet and estimate other relevant measures of its size and growth. We will also assess the impact of IPv6 on our proposed approaches. Details are described in the conclusion above.

REFERENCES

Andrew, L.L.H. (2004). Fast simulation of wavelength continuous WDM networks. *IEEE/ACM Transactions on Networking, 12*(4), 759-765.

Apache. (n.d.). *Name-based virtual host support*. Retrieved from http://httpd.apache.org/docs/1.3/vhosts/name-based.html

APNIC. (n.d.). *APNIC open address policy meeting*. Retrieved from http://www.apnic.net/meetings/amm2000/sigs/virtual-Web.html

Barabási, A.-L., & Albert, R. (1999). Emergence of scaling in random networks. *Science, 286,* 509-512.

Broder, A., Kumar, R., Maghoul, F., Raghavan, P., Rajagopalan, S., Stata, R., Tomkins, A., & Wiener, J. (2000). Graph structure in the Web. *Computer Networks, 33*, 309-320.

Devezas, T.C., Linstone, H.A., & Santos, H.J.S. (2005). The growth dynamics of the Internet and the long wave theory. *Technological Forecasting and Social Change, 72*(8), 913-935.

Flake, G.W., Lawrence, S., & Giles, C.L. (2000). Efficient identification of Web communities. In *Proceedings of the 6th ACM SIGKDD International Conference on Knowledge Discovery and Data Mining* (pp. 150-160).

Gentle, J.E. (1998). *Random number generation and Monte Carlo methods*. New York: Springer-Verlag.

Glasserman, P., & Kou, S.G. (1995). Analysis of an Importance Sampling estimator for tandem queues. *ACM Transactions on Modeling and Computer Simulation, 5*(1), 22-42.

Glynn, P.W., & Iglehart, D.L. (1989). Importance Sampling for stochastic simulations. *Management Science, 35*, 1367-1392.

Hammersley, J.M., & Morton, K.W. (1956). A new Monte Carlo technique: Antithetic variables. In *Proceedings of Cambridge Philosophical Society, 52*, 449-475.

IANA. (n.d.). *IP address services*. Retrieved from http://www.iana.org/ipaddress/ip-addresses.htm

IANA–Multicast. (n.d.). *Internet multicast addresses*. Retrieved from http://www.iana.org/assign-ments/multicast-addresses

IANA–V4. (n.d.). *Internet protocol V4 address space*. Retrieved from http://www.iana.org/assignments/ipv4-address-space

ISC–Background. (n.d.). *ISC Internet domain survey background*. Retrieved from http://www.isc.org/index.pl?/ops/ds/new-survey.php

ISC–Survey. (n.d.). *ISC Internet domain survey.* Retrieved from http://www.isc.org/index.pl

Kallol Baqchi, K., & Mukhopadhyay, S. (2004). Forecasting global Internet growth using fuzzy regression, genetic algorithm and neural network. In *Proceedings of the 2004 IEEE International Conference on Information Reuse and Integration, Las Vegas, NV.*

Kimura, M., Saito, K., & Ueda, N. (2002). Modeling of growing networks with communities. In *Proceedings of the 12th IEEE Workshop on Neural Networks for Signal Processing* (pp. 189-198).

Kleinrock, L. (1975). *Queueing systems, volume I: Theory.* New York: John Wiley & Sons.

Lavenberg, S.S., & Welch, P.D. (1981). A perspective on the use of control variables to increase the efficiency of Monte Carlo simulations. *Management Science, 27*(3), 322-335.

Liu, D., & Yao, K. (1988). Improved Importance Sampling technique for efficient simulation of digital communication systems. *IEEE Journal on Selected Areas in Communications, 6*(1), 67-75.

Modis, T. (2005). The end of the Internet rush. *Technological Forecasting and Social Change, 72*(8), 938-943.

Netcraft. (2007). *The Netcraft Web server survey.* Retrieved from http://www.netcraft.com/survey

Nielsen, J. (2006). *100 million Web sites.* Retrieved from http://www.useit.com/alertbox/Web-growth.html

NW. (n.d.). *Network wizards.* Retrieved from http://www.nw.com/

Orsak, G.C., & Aazhang, B. (1989). On the theory of Importance Sampling applied to the analysis of detection systems. *IEEE Transactions on Communications, 37*(4), 332-339.

Orsak, G.C. (1993). A note on estimating false alarm rates via Importance Sampling. *IEEE Transactions on Communications, 41*(9), 1275-1277.

Papoulis, A. (1991). *Probability, random variables, and stochastic processes (3rd ed.).* New York: McGraw-Hill.

Pennock, D.M., Flake, G.W., Lawrence, S., Glover, E.J., & Giles, C.L. (2002). Winners don't talk all: Characterizing the competition for links on the Web. In *Proceedings of the National Academy of Sciences of USA, 99,* 5207-5211.

RIPE NCC. (n.d.). *IPv4 address allocation and assignment policies for the RIPE NCC service region.* Retrieved from http://www.ripe.net/ripe/docs/ipv4-policies.html

Ross, S.M. (1997). *Introduction to probability models (6th ed.).* Academic Press.

Smith, P.J., Shafi, M., & Gao, H. (1997). Quick simulation: a review of Importance Sampling techniques in communications systems. *IEEE Journal on Selected Areas in Communications, 15*(4), 597-613.

Telcordia NetSizer. (n.d.). *Internet growth forecasting tool.* Retrieved from http://www.netsizer.com

University of Oregon. (n.d.). *University of Oregon Route Views Project.* Retrieved from http://www.routeviews.org

VeriSign. (2007). *VeriSign domain name industry brief.* Retrieved from http://www.verisign.com/Resources/Naming_Services_Resources/Domain_Name_Industry_Brief/page_002553.html

Wang, Q., & Frost, V.S. (1993). Efficient estimation of cell blocking probability for ATM systems. *IEEE Transactions on Networking, 1*(2), 385-390.

Xing, S., & Paris, B.-P. (2001). Importance Sampling for measuring the size of the Internet. In *Proceedings of the 35th Annual Conference on Information Sciences and Systems* (vol. 2, pp. 593-597), Baltimore, MD.

Xing, S., & Paris, B.-P. (2002). Measuring the size of the Internet via Importance Sampling—biasing through thresholding. In *Proceedings of the 36th*

Annual Conference on Information Sciences and Systems (pp. 796-801), Princeton, NJ.

Xing, S., & Paris, B.-P. (2004). On exponential growth of the Web. In *Proceedings of the 2004 International Conference on Internet Computing (pp. 510-516), Las Vegas, NV.*

ADDITIONAL READINGS

For more details about subjects discussed in this chapter, we recommend the following books and site, in addition to the reference list at the end of the chapter.

Books

Comer (2006) and Forouzan (2007) discuss the Internet, the Web, IP addressing, protocols, and Internet services. A good discussion of HTTP and the status codes can be found in the book of Gourley and Totty (2002). The book of Milton and Arnold (2003) is a broad survey of the issues on probability and statistics. Sampling techniques are discussed in the book of Govindarajulu (1999). Particularly, Kalos and Whitlock (1986) discuss the Monte Carlo methods, and Srinivasan (2002) and Bucklew (2004) discuss Importance Sampling.

Bucklew, J.A. (2004). *An introduction to rare event simulation.* New York: Springer-Verlag.

Comer, D.E. (2006). *Internetworking with TCP/IP volume I: Principles, protocols, and architecture (5th ed.).* Englewood Cliffs, NJ: Pearson Prentice Hall.

Forouzan, B.A. (2007). *Data communications and networking (4th ed.).* New York: McGraw-Hill Higher Education.

Gourley, D., & Totty, B. (2002). HTTP: *The definitive guide.* O'Reilly Media.

Govindarajulu, Z. (1999). *Elements of sampling theory and methods.* Englewood Cliffs, NJ: Prentice Hall.

Kalos, M.H., & Whitlock, P.A. (1986). *Monte Carlo methods (vol. 1).* New York: John Wiley & Sons.

Milton, J.S., & Arnold, J.C. (2003). *Introduction to probability and statistics: Principles and applications for engineering and the computing sciences (4th ed.).* New York: McGraw-Hill Higher Education.

Srinivasan, R. (2002). Importance Sampling*: Applications in communications and detection.* New York: Springer-Verlag.

Site

A good source of the Internet standards is the Web site of the Internet Engineering Task Force at http://www.ietf.org/.

ENDNOTES

[1] OECD stands for the Organization for Economic Cooperation and Development.

[2] RIPE stands for the Réseaux IP Européens; it is a collaborative forum open to all parties interested in wide area IP networks.

[3] Gathered from the Web crawler. Details will be discussed shortly.

[4] IANA stands for the Internet Assigned Numbers Authority; it manages the allocation of IP addresses to different organizations in various sized blocks.

[5] The result is presented in the Appendix.

[6] RADB stands for the Routing Arbiter Project; RIPE and RADB are two of the largest IRR (Internet Routing Registry) databases available.

APPENDIX: DERIVATION OF CONDITIONAL PROBABILITY MASS FUNCTION OF TRIALS N REQUIRED TO GET K SUCCESSES FROM A BINOMIAL PROCESS

Theorem 1: Suppose that the number of successes K is a binomial random variable having parameters (N, s), and further, the trial number N is large and "success" probability s is small. Then, the conditional probability mass function (pmf) of N given that $K = k$ is an Erlang-like distribution, given by:

$$p(N = n \mid K = k) = \frac{s^k n^{k-1}}{(k-1)!} e^{-sn}.$$

(48)

Proof: The proof starts with an introduction of the probability density function (pdf) $f_X(x)$ of the time interval X during which k arrivals from a Poisson process are collected. It can be described as the Erlang distributions family (Kleinrock, 1975), given by:

$$f_X(x) = \frac{\lambda(\lambda x)^{k-1}}{(k-1)!} e^{-\lambda x}, \quad x \geq 0,$$

(49)

where λ represents the average rate of Poisson arrivals.

Consider that the Poisson random variable K, taking on one of the values $0, 1, 2, \ldots, k, \ldots$ and having parameter λ, may be used to approximate a binomial random variable K with parameters (N, s) when the binomial parameter N is large and s is small (Ross, 1997). Thus, the proof proceeds to find a discretized form of equation (49). This may be done by subdividing the interval X into n small equal parts, each Δt units long, illustrated in Figure 11. Then $x = n\Delta t$, and the probability of one arrival in any interval Δt will be $s = \lambda \Delta t$.

Applying the above x and s to equation (49) yields:

$$f_X(x = n\Delta t) = \frac{s(sn)^{k-1}}{\Delta t(k-1)!} e^{-sn},$$

or, equivalently:

$$f_X(x = n\Delta t)\Delta t = \frac{s^k n^{k-1}}{(k-1)!} e^{-sn}.$$

(50)

Now, let $\Delta t \to 0$, then the left-hand side of equation (50) is approximated by a conditional pmf $p(N = n|K = k)$. Hence, equation (48) follows.

Figure 11. Time interval X in Poisson process

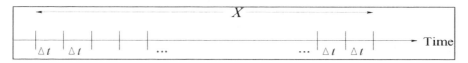

Chapter XXII
Natural Language Processing Agents and Document Clustering in Knowledge Management:
The Semantic Web Case

Steve Legrand
University of Jyväskylä, Finland

JRG Pulido
University of Colima, Mexico

ABSTRACT

While HTML provides the Web with a standard format for information presentation, XML has been made a standard for information structuring on the Web. The mission of the Semantic Web now is to provide meaning to the Web. Apart from building on the existing Web technologies, we need other tools from other areas of science to do that. This chapter shows how natural language processing methods and technologies, together with ontologies and a neural algorithm, can be used to help in the task of adding meaning to the Web, thus making the Web a better platform for knowledge management in general.

INTRODUCTION

At the end of 2005, the number of Internet users worldwide passed the 1 billion mark and is increasing steadily (de Argaez, 2006). The number of Web pages indexed, by the best search engines, is estimated to be 6 to 8 billion (Patterson, 2005), although both Yahoo and Google have, at times, claimed figures two or three times higher. No one seems to know the exact figure. The total number of Web pages, whether indexed or not, is estimated to be even higher, over 200 billion by Patterson (2005).

The Web in its current form provides a vast source of information accessible to computers but understandable only by humans. The research community has been looking at ways of making this information understandable to computers as well. In the Semantic Web (SW), different information structuring formats are used to make the information available for automatic machine processing. Ontologies and artificial learning techniques can help in this task of making the Web's full potential available. By now there are a great many ontology repositories with manually created ontologies, which can be used in various SW tasks, but due to the task-specificity, changing nature, and concomitant variety of ontologies that are required for these tasks, these repositories can only partially satisfy the demand.

Two basic avenues for solving the problem of knowledge acquisition bottleneck and construction and integration of various ontologies can be distinguished: ontology learning and ontology integration. These are not usually separate issues: the former plays the primary and the latter secondary role in this chapter. The need for semi-automatic ontology engineering and learning techniques in both approaches is dictated by time and money constraints. Ontologies can be learned from many different sources including free text, tagged documents, and databases, and by many different methods. To select a suitable ontology, it is useful to have some guidelines and comparative knowledge about the existing ontology learning applications. Instead of doing this comparative analysis here, we refer the reader to one of the state-of-art descriptions of ontology learning (Shamsfard & Barforoush, 2003) and merely present one of the many ontology learning applications, Text-To-Onto (Maedche & Staab, 2001), to exemplify the use of the comparison framework.

One thing that is often mentioned and just as often forgotten when we talk about the Semantic Web: people working on the SW-related research agree that manual document structuring (XML-related technologies) and semantic tagging (tech-nologies such as RDF and OWL, which are based on XML) are too complex and time consuming to ever become a popular pastime for your average Web user. One cannot force people to use something which they know very little of and which may be hard to learn. For this reason alone, we need to automate the Semantic Web and thus make the machines there understand each other and rid the human being from the boring details. This is, of course, easier said than done—we should never forget that human beings use natural language, and that most of the Web documents are only partially structured and written in natural language. Apart from creating standards based on XML, Web services, and so forth, we also need automated methods to understand and manipulate documents that are not tagged, that use natural language. The time is ripe to unify the research on natural language processing and on the Semantic Web, and reap the benefits that this can provide.

We believe that we will be seeing, in the near future, a gradual inclusion of NLP subsystems into the service of SW agents to form the backbone for new knowledge discovery systems. Many of the various SW technologies based on ontology-related annotations and utilizing various markup language standards have already established themselves as path setters for the future and can justify their place in the grand scheme of the Semantic Web. To discover new knowledge, however, a specialized agent network, capable of cooperation and able to process natural language, is needed to process raw text and refine it, through annotations, and make it digestible for other more generalized agents. This chapter, rather than trying to impose an artificial framework for such an agent network, instead reflects on the current developments in the area, pointing out some converging trends, highlighting the possibilities that new developments in the Semantic Web can offer, and drafting a possible information flow within the NLP agent framework gradually taking shape. The chapter emphasizes the fact that many of the natural language processing methods and technologies are readily adaptable for agent use, and what is needed, apart from new technological developments, is even deeper cooperation between the artificial intelligence community and the NLP community. For the benefit of those readers, who are not NLP practitioners, we have included what we think are the most relevant concepts in this field including linguistic analysis and clustering techniques.

For the Semantic Web to become a reality, a number of architectures have still to mature (Pulido et al., 2006):

- **Ontology learning:** It is important not to start an ontology from scratch.
- **Ontology editing:** Merging and integration tasks.
- **Ontelligent software:** Agents that carry out routine tasks for us.

We overview the current state of ontology learning and editing and the methods generally used in it, and consider the use of agents, natural language agents, and document processing agents in particular, in a novel architecture presented.

BACKGROUND

Ontologies and the Semantic Web

According to its pioneers, the Semantic Web "is an extension of the current Web in which information is given well-defined meaning, better enabling computers and people to work in cooperation" (Berners-Lee, Hendler, & Lassila, 2001). The SW stack has now become a well-known reference point (see Figure 1) when discussing the Semantic Web. Ontologies play a central role in the realization of the Semantic Web. User tasks are delegated to agents which need common vocabularies and standards to be able to successfully fulfill the role envisaged for them. Universal resource identifiers (URIs) are associated both with objects and relations, and provide the grounding for the whole SW stack. Resource description framework (RDF) (W3C, 1999), based on structured XML format (W3C, 2004a), and manipulating these objects and relations supports RDF-Schema (W3C, 2004c), which allows a disciplined representation of structured vocabularies (i.e., ontologies). Web ontology language, or OWL (W3C, 2004b), in its three available forms (Lite, DL, Full) increases the expressivity of RDF, allowing ontologies to be distributed and connected across the Semantic Web, and generally allowing better reasoning over and verification of ontologies. The rest of the stack is still under construction, and important progress is being made at the W3C organization each month.

Ontology Learning

A good starting point for classifying and comparing ontology learning systems that attempt to automate

Figure 1. The Semantic Web stack (based on W3C)

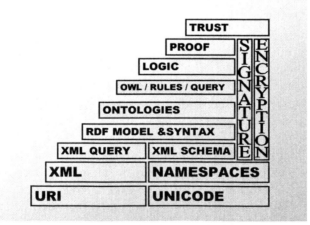

ontology building is Shamsfard and Barforoush (2003), the dimensions of whose ontology learning framework deal with what to learn, from where to learn it, and how it may be learned. These questions are expanded to derive six basic dimensions that the user can employ in selecting an ontology learning application that suits his or her purpose:

Q1. What kind of conceptual structure is obtained? What are the elements learned?

Q2. From where should ontology acquisition start, and from what should it be learned?

Q3. Is there any preprocessing to convert the input to a suitable structure to learn from?

Q4. What kinds of methods are used to extract knowledge?

Q5. What would the ontology and its resulting features be like?

Q6. How does one evaluate the learning methods or the resulted ontology?

As an example of how to position an ontology learning application to this framework, in order to assess the application's suitability for the Semantic Web, we consider Text-To-Onto workbench that is based on Maedche and Staab's (2001) ontology learning model. This workbench integrates a variety of disciplines, the foremost of which is machine learning. The model consists of five main steps: import, reuse, extraction, pruning, and refinement.[1]

The elements that Text-To-Onto learns (Q1) consist of concepts and relations between them. These relations might be taxonomic, obtained by the association rule algorithm measuring concept proximities, or non-taxonomic, obtained by the linguistic patterns algorithm that looks for common patterns in the text indicating relationships (Maedche, Pekar, & Staab, 2002). The discovered concepts and relationships are only potential, until the ontology engineer, on validating the results, decides whether to include or exclude the learned concepts and relations using the OntoEdit editing submodule for the task. This process takes place in the pruning and refinement step.

With Text-To-Onto the acquisition (Q2) can start from various sources, but it should be kept in mind that the workbench's linguistic processing is geared towards German texts. One can create a domain ontology simply by pruning, from an existing lexical resource such as WordNet (Fellbaum, 1998), the unwanted concepts and relations that fall outside the domain of concern. This is rarely sufficient, however. Other sources, apart from lexical databases, that can be used are natural language texts, WWW documents, and semistructured (XML, DTD) and structured data (DB Schema, ontologies). To deal with this great variety of ontology learning sources, Text-To-Onto integrates a variety of disciplines, the foremost of which is machine learning. This acquisition process takes place during import and reuse steps in the Maedche and Staab (2001) model.

Due to the great variety of sources, the preprocessing steps (Q3) in Text-To-Onto also can vary significantly depending on the resources used: HTML documents can be converted to free text; there are different preprocessing strategies for semi-structured sources such as dictionaries that might be converted into relational database structures or transformation rules for structured sources such as DB Schemas; ontologies can also vary a lot. For preprocessing natural language texts in German, shallow text-processing methods developed for SMES (Saarbrucken Message Extraction System) (Neumann, Backofen, Baur, Becker, & Braun, 1997) are employed: linguistically related pairs of words are identified and then mapped to concepts with the help of a domain lexicon.

The methods Text-To-Onto uses for extracting knowledge (Q4) are based on multiple strategies. The workbench contains a library of algorithms for the use of heuristics, association rules, formal concept analysis, and clustering techniques to learn different components of the ontology. Heuristic rules are often used to discover linguistic dependency relations. It should be kept in mind that many word sense disambiguation system components and their subsystems (morphology, syntax, etc.) used in linguistic analysis are often based, at least partially, in heuristics. Generally speaking, the Text-To-Onto learning methods can be described as semi-automatic (requiring human intervention, especially in pruning and refinement phases), interactive, and (balanced) cooperative (Morik, 1993).

The resulting ontology (Q5) can be viewed in the form of directed graphs or hierarchy independent of the underlying representation. As concept reference and denotation ("school" → building/institution/creed) can be expressed using separate entities, it allows the creation of very domain-specific ontologies. This separation of reference and denotation can also be easily expressed in RDF, making it suitable for the Semantic Web, where it prevents conflicts when merging ontologies.

The ontology generated can be empirically evaluated (Q6) by testing it against different domains, inputs, and methods. Shamsfard and Barforoush's (2003) framework, for example, which was used here, can be used for comparative testing with other ontology learning tools. It should be kept in mind, however, that the ontologies generated by the different systems would, most likely, not be comparable due to different domains, inputs, and backgrounds used. It is useful to keep in mind, in this respect, the various ontology learning approaches based on different domains (free text, dictionary, knowledge base, semi-structured data, and relational schemata) that the authors list in the survey part of their article. As pointed out, Text-To-Onto combines several of these approaches. Measuring recall and precision against predefined test sets might not do justice to the system accuracy or robustness. Ontology learning tools are undergoing constant development, and one needs to balance between the lack of desired features in more stable versions and the bugs in the later versions.

The Text-To-Onto ontology learning model is also still undergoing improvements and can be considered as a forerunner of more sophisticated applications still to emerge. Kavalec and Svátek (2005) further refine Text-To-Onto's capabilities in their study of automatic relation labeling which addresses non-taxonomic relation extraction, one of the subtasks in Maedhe's core ontology learning steps listed above. There may be various alternative relations and synonymous labels between two items that can be extracted from a text. For example the relations and synonymous labels between the con-

cepts Company and Product may include produce (manufacture, make); sell (trade, offer); and consume (buy, purchase). These concept-verb-concept triads and other frequent concept/word co-occurrence types can be extracted from text with known NLP techniques. The authors also elaborate on the second part of Q6 above: How does one evaluate the resulting ontology? The extracted relation labels are compared with a previously extracted collection of concepts arranged into taxonomy by experts (prior precision). The taxonomy is then augmented and modified by extracted concept relations that are judged correct and relevant by the experts, and matched again against the extracted relations (posterior precision).

In certain aspects, ASIUM (Faure & Nédellec, 1998) can also be considered as a predecessor to the described refinement to Text-To-Onto above. In ASIUM, taxonomic relations and subcategorization frames acquired are based on co-occurrences between verbs and concepts in text. The system can hierarchically cluster nouns based on verbs, or vice versa, but is based on a bag-of-words rather than named relations. In this respect, Kavalec and Svátek's (2005) extension to Text-To-Onto can be regarded as an improvement, and shows that ontology learning tool building as a whole is becoming more and more modular and extendible.

The best known of freely available ontology engineering tools that can be used for SW applications, however, is Protégé (Noy et al., 2001), developed at the University of Stanford for more than 20 years, with a plug-in architecture that allows incorporation of many new functionalities to its intended primary task, ontology design. The latest version includes the OWL plugin (Knublauch, Fergerson, Noy, & Musen, 2004) aimed specifically for the Semantic Web. Various knowledge sources, representation formats, user interfaces, and inference capabilities can be adapted to specific purposes including ontology learning. For example, OntoLT (Buitelaar, Olejnik, & Sintek, 2004) is the first Protégé OL plugin that can semi-automatically extract ontologies from text. The results of the ontology extraction from text obtained by the user with the help of predefined and modifiable rules are validated by the user before the concepts thus obtained are integrated into the ontology. OntoLT uses annotated text collections, the format of which integrates multiple levels of linguistic annotation which can be cross-indexed when defining rules for ontology building. Like Text-To-Onto, OntoLT was designed with German language in mind, but can be adapted to different other languages by adapting its linguistic parsing component to suit other languages. For those readers interested in further background in ontology learning, a review of related work can be found, for example, in Dey and Abulaish (2006).

Ontology Editing: Mapping, Merging, Aligning, and Refinement

Merging is usually defined as the creation of one ontology from two or more source ontologies. It should be distinguished from ontology aligning where two or more ontologies are joined to a so-called bridge ontology, that is, a view of the ontological correspondences between the two ontologies (see Figure 2). As we saw in the previous section, some of the ontology editing tools, such as Protégé, augment their base functions with various plugins including the OntoLT ontology learning tool. Predoiu et al. (2005) use another Protégé plugin, PROMPT (Noy & Musen, 2000), to exemplify ontology merging proper and contrast the tool with OntoMerge (Dou, McDermott, & Qi, 2002), which uses bridge axioms to map correspondences between ontologies. How-

ever, the fast pace in the ontology tool development is reflected in the fact that the most recent version of PROMPT now supports an explicit mapping mode also.

Mapping of ontologies can be one-to-one or global (see Figure 3). In one-to-one mapping all the ontologies are connected directly to all the others. In global mapping, there is a central shared ontology to which all the rest of the ontologies connect. There may also be mappings that are hybrids between the two, that is, ontologies are linked and may have locally centralized groups between the links.

After the mapping, merging, and aligning procedures, which themselves can be of various types and consist of several sub-processes, ontology refinement including pruning and other types of modifications as described in the previous section can be performed. The resulting ontology can then play the role of vocabulary for ontelligent applications.

There are many ontology editing tools with varying capabilities, including merging and aligning. These are under continuous development, and several comparative surveys of these tools can be found on the WWW, for example in Denny (2004).

Ontelligent Applications

We use the term "ontelligent" to describe ontology-aware applications and software that leverage ontologies in the SW environment. SW standards

Figure 2. Joining of ontologies

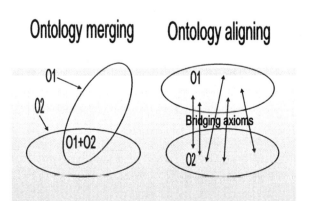

Figure 3. Mapping of ontologies

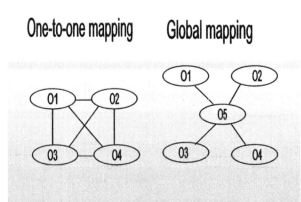

such as Web service standards are included within that description. As we saw above, ontologies can be created by many different methods and for many different purposes, but in today's SW context, these ontologies are mainly manipulated and used by Web services and agents.

Web Services

The prime example of ontelligent software is software and standards designed to implement and utilize Web services for machine-to-machine interaction over a network. Many different systems have been devised: common to all of them is that they are based on some underlying standard for interoperability and provide a particular service for the user. Generally, however, when we talk about "Web services" (W3C, 2004d), we refer to a system in which the service is given a structured description in the extended markup language (XML) (W3C, 2004a) format, where simple object access protocol (SOAP) (W3C, 2003) is used as a protocol to exchange these "enveloped" XML-based descriptions over a network, and where Web services description language (WSDL) (W3C, 2002) is used to describe public interfaces to the service. Another important piece is universal description,

discovery, and integration (UDDI) (OASIS, 2004), which allows businesses to register in a Web directory and advertise their wares. XML-based SOAP, WSDL, and UDDI thus form the core of the Web services (see Figure 4). To promote these standards among the public, the Web Services Interoperability (WS-I, 2006) consortium was established by the standards' industrial advocates.

One of the standard SOAP-based Web service examples is that of a travel agency. The service provider creates an interface with WSDL for its Web-based travel service. Another company, interested in providing a travel service to its employees, hires a developer to connect the company's processes to the application programming interface created and in a way integrates the service to the company's own systems. What happens beyond the interface provided by the travel service may involve other companies and other service providers with their own Web service interfaces: hotel booking service, car hire service, credit service, bank service, and others.

There are some publicly available lists of Web services, such as XMethods (2006), where anyone interested in trying one or subscribing to one can experiment. IBM, SAP, and Microsoft also had their own public Web service registries previously

Figure 4. A service requester first inspects any public UDDI registry to find a desired service. Having obtained a handle on the service provider's available methods, the service requester can then invoke a desired Web service through a SOAP message.

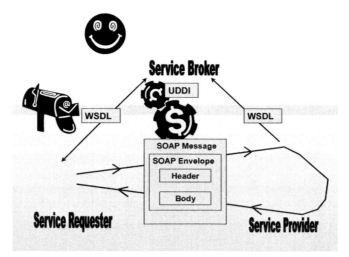

available from their Web sites, but have now integrated them with their products.

Agents

Agents in the Semantic Web are designed to use domain ontologies to undertake and complete tasks for their owners. A software agent can dynamically discover, combine, and execute a Web service depicted above (see Figure 4). Agents can also be made to assist in ontology learning itself. For example, an agent can incorporate a learning module with which it can update and extend its ontology database (Boicu, Tecuci, & Boicu, 2002; Boicu & Tecuci, 2004). A rule may state that a university teacher, if tenured, will not leave the university during the year. Nevertheless, there may be a tenured university teacher who will, in fact, leave, thus breaking the rule. The agent searches the ontology for pieces of knowledge that can be used to distinguish between the positive examples and negative exceptions. The rule is modified to eliminate the negative exception, and the ontology can be pruned and refined as the result. This process is facilitated by the application interface guiding the user in the selection of the distinguishing features. The ontology learning agents of this kind are semiautomatic and require expert intervention in the ontology learning process.

SW agents are usually thought of as autonomous and capable of some sort of goal-driven reasoning in order to accomplish tasks for their owners. Rather than being bound by any particular method or process in the way the Web services are, they may exercise choice in selecting whatever method or procedure or Web service to accomplish their goals. While their capabilities can range from very simple to extremely complex, they should conform to FIPA (2002b) specifications for building interoperable systems based on agents. FIPA governs, for example, the communication protocol (FIPA, 2002a) that agents use in FIPA agent communication language when coordinating their activities. In the Web services architecture specification (W3C, 2004d), agents are seen as software programs that drive Web services—they implement and access them on behalf of persons

or organizations—and personal agents often acts as a proxy in the process. This, however, should not be taken as limiting agent activities to Web services—the scope of agent activities can be much wider as we shall see.

Filling the Gaps

The Text-To-Onto ontology learning workbench presented above is one of the better examples of a promising approach to ontology learning. The work on it is continuing under various names, and both Open Source and commercial applications have been generated from the original described above.[2] Nevertheless, it is easy to point out the drawbacks inherent in a project where the question of ontology learning has been tackled head-on and in a wholesome manner. As discussed, Text-To-Onto uses a great variety of lexical sources, heuristics, and multiple strategies and methods. For sure, all these are needed, but intermingling them makes it hard to impose a disciplined modularized architecture on the product. This, in turn, makes it hard for outsiders to participate in the development of such a product, be it Open Source or not, unless that person is well acquainted with all or most of the disciplines involved. Potential contributors to the project might thus become excluded. This, it should be added, is not any peculiar drawback to Text-To-Onto; this state-of-affairs currently applies to any ambitious enough software project.

Many of the problems outlined could, however, be resolved with the use of agent technologies. One great advantage of the agent technologies is that once the person knows how to create a software agent, he can concentrate on a software method or process of his interest without worrying too much about how it will be used or which kind of application will incorporate it. For example, a person who is mainly interested in Russian morphology can create a morphological analyzer based on any of his favorite methods and then just leave it for others to use. He does not have to know anything about ontology learning or German, or English. There will presumably be other developers who will take care of these, and in turn, never worry about anything related to Russian language. Another person might be more worried about the language recognition aspect and develop a language recognition agent, for example. That agent might be able to recognize well a host of Indo-European languages but miserably fail in Fenno-Ugrian ones. Other developers would create competitive language recognition agents who would do a better job in this respect.

This would in a way distribute the development of software even better than the current Open Source practices, or at least contribute towards Open Source development. Agent communities developed by various persons in different countries could be organized to undertake complex tasks by combining task-specific agents' skills to achieve the desired results. The purpose of this section is to show a general SW architecture for this kind of development as applied to natural language processing.

To make the Semantic Web available to all the users and enable the incorporation of its masses of documents, it is imperative to automate methods that annotate Web data, and to do it in a manner that does not require user intervention. This has been pointed out by James Hendler (2001) and other pioneers of SW, who would like to see semantic annotation as an effortless by-product of computer use. You would need standards and

experts as you need them with the WWW, but the great majority of the users could be blissfully ignorant of the underlying technologies, about their personal agents communicating with other specialized agents to complete various user tasks, booking services, buying things, contacting bank accounts, downloading and uploading information as needed, and many other things.

Web users use natural language, and most of the documents on the Web are written in natural language. This is a fact that anyone working with SW technologies should acknowledge. Web services do have their place in the Semantic Web, the standards are necessary and inferencing a must—but these are aspects that an average user should be able to leave to trained professionals. Suppose I wanted to book a flight from Sydney to London. To get a good idea about Web services and to be able to avoid mistakes, one would need to complete a crash course on XML (a book of about 800 pages would give a fair idea) and other formats built on it, perhaps learn Java to understand JADE (Java Agents Distributed Environment) or some other programming language and agent network. One could learn more superficially through some Semantic Web for Dummies or Java for Dummies textbooks, but that would leave huge gaps in that person's knowledge and uncertainties related to

Figure 5. The relation of SW user's personal agent with Web service agents, NLP agents, and document processing agents. Only the principal agent entities are shown here.

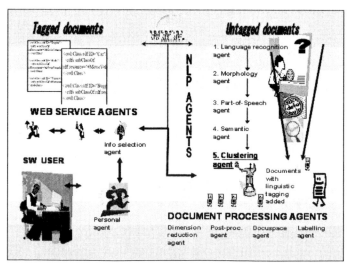

how to use the services. Basically, what I would like to do is to say something like "I want to book a flight from Sydney to London" and leave it to the Web agents to negotiate the best deal, recommend the hotel, make the reservation on finding a suitable deal, contact the bank, and take care of the payment. This is achievable and has been achieved with the present SW technologies, although rather than using a natural language, the user is directed to the goal through a host of selection menus, and perhaps needs to contact the banking and hotel reservations separately in the majority of cases.

The use of natural language technologies is much more apparent in cases where the information on the Web is not sufficiently well annotated to enable a personal agent to find what is needed. Search engines such as Google, Yahoo, or AltaVista are classifying search items better and better, and there are some specialized search engines that base their classifications on ontological structures. Human beings can get an idea about a document by looking at the text, its heading, context, and so forth. To eliminate the need of having to have a human being to validate each document retrieved, agents that are capable of dealing with natural language texts while retrieving them are needed. To build a monolithic software entity capable of taking care of everything that is needed to achieve the aim would be a formidable task for anyone. Instead a more gradualist approach of creating cooperating agents of various kinds might be more realistic, as it would facilitate the recruitment of various skills and interest of participating developers. Information, as in data mining, should be thought of as a primary material that needs various technologies to refine it—from the ore to the finalized product (see Figure 5). Semantic Web mining, using automated methods, is seen as one of the most promising research areas (Stumme, Hotho, & Berendt, 2006).

A raw untagged document could be subjected first to simple natural language technologies to separate the ore from the dirt, so to speak. Something along the line of text understanding agents (Java, Finin, & Nirenburg, 2006) could be adapted to the task. Various NLP techniques, using the background knowledge available on the Web, can refine the virgin information into something useable for cer-

tain applications. Suppose a preprocessing agent, looking at the context of a document, was able to decide whether the context is negative or positive as regards the keyword used in the search. The results of such simple negative/positive classification can be useful, for example, for an Air Force public relations officer worried about adverse publicity that flying practices might generate in the media, for politicians estimating the effects of their electoral campaigns, filmmakers wanting feedback, and so forth. In fact, the New York Times Web edition (Lipton, 2006) recently reported on a concerted effort that was being initiated by three large U.S universities to develop such sentiment analysis software for the U.S Homeland Security Department. A couple of days earlier, the same newspaper (Hafner, 2006) had reported a US$1 million price offered by Netflix for anyone substantially improving its movie rating system that could be based on a similar analysis. Other preprocessing agents could further process the results of this kind, refining the positively classified documents into objective and subjective with the help of context words. These further refined results could be used for example by an agent looking for learning objects (LOs) about a certain topic (keyword) that were positive and objective.

Refinement would continue, and at each refining step, before being passed to other requesting agents, the information in the documents would be annotated to a greater and greater degree by specialized agents, finally yielding well-annotated documents from which units of information could be extracted automatically for various tasks and organized into clusters or ontological structures for further use in a now refined form. Here we, in fact, talk about clustering. But before this kind of clustering or classification (= clustering + labeling) can take place, a more profound linguistic analysis might be needed.

NATURAL LANGUAGE PROCESSING AND SEMANTIC WEB AGENTS

Many of the natural language techniques that will be useful with the SW applications have not been specifically designed for the Semantic Web.

Nevertheless these key processing components dealing with linguistic analysis should always be kept in mind when dealing with natural language processing. Buitelaar and Declerck (2004) list these linguistic analysis steps as morphological analysis, part-of-speech (POS) tagging, chunking, dependency structure analysis, and semantic tagging. There are various language-specific software applications, specifically aimed for these various steps, that are available and can be easily adapted for the use of SW agents. We have selected these linguistic analysis steps to allocate the main tasks between our natural language agents, but it should be stressed here that this division is very general. Each agent task can be subdivided between various other agents (not shown in Figure 5), and the linguistic analysis process might be sequenced and subdivided differently. The idea here is not to give an exhaustive analysis of each of these possibilities, but to present a simplified, clear-cut example of a possible architecture for task allocation between SW agents.

Morphological Analysis

In linguistics, morphemes are regarded as the smallest meaningful units in language which can be subjected to morphological analysis. Roughly speaking, morphological analysis tries to separate the word stem from a full word form and can be divided into three main types:

1. Inflectional (variant forms of nouns, adjectives and verbs)
   - Person (first, second, third)
     TALKS → TALK +S
   - Number (singular, plural)
     HOUSE → HOUSE +S
   - Tense (present, future, past)
     TALKED → TALK + ED
   - Gender (male, female, neuter), for example, in German
2. Derivational (new word formation with or without an affix)
   - Verb → Noun (without affix)
     TALK → TALK

   - Noun → Verb (without affix)
     PROGRESS → PROGRESS
   - Verb → Noun (with affix)
     ADD → ADD + ITION
3. Compositional (new words formed by combining two or more words)
   - Adj + Adj → Adj
     BITTER + SWEET → BITTER-SWEET
   - Verb + Noun → Noun
     PICK + POCKET → PICKPOCKET

As can be seen, both the derivational morphology and the compositional morphology are related to part-of-speech information (verb, noun), which has bearing on chunking (see below). There are morphological parsers for most of the modern languages, based on various rules or statistical processing. Like ontology learning, morphology learning can also be automated: Goldsmith (2001), for example, uses the minimum description length (MDL) analysis to model unsupervised learning of the morphological segmentation of European languages. The related Linguistica software (Goldsmith, 2000) could be modified for the use of SW agents. Another interesting account related to automation in morphology learning is Schone and Jurafsky (2001), which utilizes syntactic information and other computational techniques.

One can imagine a language-specific morphological agent (morphological parser or morphology learner) digging into a document's content, annotating it and handing it over to the POS agent for further processing, or negotiating with POS agents over ambiguous items.

Part-of-Speech Tagging

Automated methods for the discovery of part-of-speech information have long been available and can be modified for SW use. These range from stochastic to rule-based and rely mostly on morphological information and various computational techniques.

POS tagging means classifying words according to their parts of speech such as verb, noun, adjective, and so forth, and usually relies on morphological analysis. To be able to determine whether each word variations of "talk" in the following sentences is a noun or a verb, a computer needs to do a POS analysis:

He talks with his boss.
His talk is about his boss.
He was talking with his boss.

There are three main types of POS analyses that can be used (Jurafsky & Martin, 2000):

1. **Rule-based:** This is usually based on a two-stage parser architecture. In the first stage no constraints or rules are applied, instead all the possible POS tags are applied. For example, in the sentence "His talk is about his boss," the word "talk" is tagged both as a verb (V) and a noun (N). In the second stage some rule or rules are used to determine the correct POS. In this case such a rule might be: if the keyword is preceded by a possessive pronoun (e.g., "His"–PP), then it is a noun and not a verb. This is a very simple example. Usually there are more rules that are applied, and they can form quite complex sequences.
2. **Stochastic:** Stochastic POS is based on statistical models, usually involving the frequency of word and the probability of occurrence within a certain distance from other POS tags. The simplest models consider only the frequency of the tag for the word in the training set, whereas more sophisticated models consider the frequency of other POS tags within a certain distance and in certain sequence from the word. Two well-known stochastic tagging algorithms are based on the Viterbi algorithm and hidden Markov model (HMM) (Bahl & Mercer, 1976).
3. **Transformational POS analysis:** Transformational POS analysis is an example of the transformation-based learning (TBL) (Brill, 1995) and combines aspects of both rule-based and stochastic analysis. There are three major stages. First every word is labeled by its most likely tag in a reference corpus.

Then a transformation rule that is based on the neighboring POS-tags is applied. Unlike in rule-based POS analysis where the rule set is manually created, these rules are induced automatically from data. Finally the word is retagged. Take the sentence "His talk is about his boss" for example. If the word "talk" is tagged as a verb (V) 65 % of the time and as a noun (N) 35% of the time in the corpus, then the word is initially tagged as a verb. Then a transformational rule such as "if the preceding word is PP, the word should be tagged as N" is applied. Several transformations can take place, and different rules are applied until some sort of stopping criteria is reached to get an optimal result.

Chunking

Chunking, known also as partial parsing or shallow parsing, is less ambitious than full parsing and cannot be used to provide a tree representation as in full parsing. Chunks of sentences forming phrases are tagged as a whole. For example the phrase "standard baseline measure" can be tagged as a noun phrase (NP) in shallow parsing, whereas it would be represented as a combination of adjective and two nouns (JJ+NN+NN) or perhaps erroneously by three nouns (NN+NN+NN) by a full POS parse. There are certain advantages to the shallow parsing approach. A chunk is usually a semantically integral piece of text and can be used as such for various information retrieval tasks. Psycholinguistic evidence also indicates that chunking may be a way humans process language (Gee & Grosjean, 1983). People look for key phrases (chunks) when reading; and when speaking, the intonation often corresponds to chunking units.

Dependency Structure Analysis

A dependency structure is made up of at least two linguistic units that immediately dominate each other in the syntax tree (Buiterlaar & Declerck, 2004). A chunk or a phrase such as "sample database query" can be understood in two different ways depending on the dominance structure: the phrase can either mean "a query on a sample database" or "a sample query on a database." The dependencies between heads, modifiers, and complements need to be unraveled to allow derivation of semantic and domain-specific information. The task of the dependency structure analysis is to describe correctly this dominancy relationship.

Semantic Tagging

Semantic relations between words are captured in ontological structures such as semantic networks, semantic lexicons, and thesauri. Semantic analysis may utilize all of the methods preceding it (see Figure 5) in an attempt to pinpoint the meaning of a word or concept. A semantic agent, before being able to take the full benefit of an ontological structure for meaning comparison task, would need to submit a free text to morphological, syntactic, and other relevant analyses through their corresponding agents. It should also be able to look at the content of a document, and for this reason it would perhaps use some clustering techniques through a clustering agent, for example. It should be kept in mind that ontology learning itself would rely on these language preprocessing agents, and this is one reason why the agents should be capable of independent action in the Semantic Web and not act as adjuncts to any particular ontology. It may be that another layer of specialized ontology representative agents is needed.

Clustering

Once we have the data analyzed and structured, we can use the structural and/or semantic features to cluster it for disambiguation, document classification, and other purposes. Clustering can, in principle, be used to create any types of groupings from the most simple to very complex. Various clustering methods have been applied in many fields of science, including linguistics. Clustering can be done on the basis of lexical and semantic information from existing sources such as standard upper merged ontology (SUMO) (Pease, Niles, & Li, 2002) or WordNet (Fellbaum, 1998), among others. Semantic similarity is based on the prox-

imity of concepts through their various relations. The WordNet relation most often used for this purpose is hypernymy (IS-A relation) (Lee, Kim, & Lee, 1993), but other WordNet relations such as synonymy (Nagao, 1992) and antonymy have been used also. In fact, clustering can be done on the basis of practically any kind of information, including semantic, morphological, part-of-speech, context, and other information. Clustering can refer to clustering of documents or to clustering of concepts within document(s). This is true in the case of the Semantic Web and SW agents also. In the simple clustering example above involving sentiment analysis and learning objects, context word occurrences were used. The example below shows a current state of our agent-based application in which clustering is done with SOM. Work is currently under way to improve the application with the kinds of NLP agents described above.

Example of Document-Level Clustering with SOM

The purpose of this section is to point out some of the difficulties in software development when trying to tailor existing software for the Semantic Web and show how a developer would benefit from the NLP agents described above if they were available. Another aim is to show that almost any kind of agent contributing to the overall task execution can be adopted to SW use: there may be alternatives, some better and some worse, but the choice can be left to the user.

Although our ontelligent software application is based on what is commonly known as document-level clustering, we should emphasize the fact that most of the techniques described can be applied to any piece of information, be it a just a small part of a document or an entire book chapter. How we go about it depends on the tasks we are planning to undertake. Also, our application is but a small piece in the envisaged cooperating NLP agent network corresponding roughly to the clustering agent in Figure 5.

Figure 6 depicts our system, which is based on the concepts of ontologies and self-organizing maps. A set of agents (spade) gather and process

Figure 6. Overview of the grubber/spade architecture

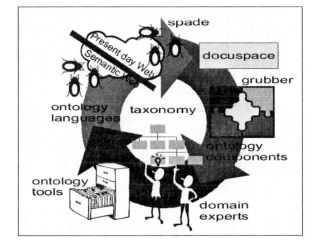

Web pages from a digital archive, and through self-organizing maps (grubber) a domain expert is able to visualize domain-specific ontology components. The software was written in Java, which offers robust, multi-platform, networking functionalities. Being an object-oriented programming language, it also facilitates code reuse.

Spade

This module consists of a number of agents that are used to gather and prepare the datasets extracted from the digital archive. These preprocessed datasets are then handed over to the grubber for further processing.

The Document Gatherer

The document gatherer retrieves hyperlinks from a predefined digital archive, for example, a Web site, and stores them for later use. This module starts with a root-hyperlink and by traversing html documents gathers only hyperlinks below the root. No repetitions are allowed. Only absolute and relative Web page hyperlinks within the domain are considered. Other hyperlinks, such as mailto and cgi, are disregarded. The URL list created is alphabetically ordered and stored for later use by the document analyzer.

The Document Analyzer

The obvious source of information for constructing an ontology is the words contained in the documents themselves. A Web page can be represented as a vector consisting of a suitable frequency count of terms. The document analyzer uses the list of URLs collected by the document gatherer and retrieves the actual HTML documents. Some hyperlinks are disregarded as they are broken links or contain no data, for instance HTML Frames are not considered.

Each HTML document is processed as follows:

1. HTML tags are removed (e.g., <html>,</html>).
2. Common words that carry little information (the, by, but) are pruned from the files using a stoplist.
3. Each remaining word is changed to lower case and its stem is obtained (Porter, 1980). For instance eas is the stem of easy, easier, easiest, easily.
4. If this stem does not exist in the lexicon, then it is added.
5. A vector space (docuspace) is then created.

The lexicon is an alphabetically ordered list of all the terms that comprise the digital archive. The number of terms in the lexicon may be quite large even for moderate document collections. The docuspace consists of m documents and n terms in the lexicon, which is created by the docuspace agent.

It is here that the concerns raised in previous sections need to be addressed. The document analyzer could be divided into several agent entities. Currently, only a small amount of linguistic preprocessing is done prior to creating a docuspace. Linguistic tagging would enrich the feature list attached to terms thus giving a better input for SOM.

The Docuspace Agent

Memory size is always an issue when dealing with huge amounts of data to be processed. As mentioned, documents can be described by their word histograms. The histograms are a useful statistical representation of the documents which is considerably compressed in comparison to the original data. Each document contains only a small percentage of the terms contained in the lexicon of the document collection which is highly dimensional. The docuspace is created by this agent with the individual vector spaces and the lexicon which were created by the document analyzer. The docuspace is characterized by a highly sparse document-term matrix with positive values and a significant amount of outliers.

The Dimensionality Reduction Agent

The dimensionality reduction agent shortens the docuspace size by using simple feature selection. Once the docuspace has been created, a dimensionality reduction is carried out on it. It is used for disregarding terms and documents that are not important within the document collection.

The Post-Processing Agent

The docuspace contains raw histograms of the documents from the digital archive. This agent produces some new docuspaces that are to be used by the grubber.

- **Transposed docuspace:** First, a transposed dataset from the original one is obtained. This is useful for a deeper analysis of the domain.
- **Normalized docuspaces:** Second, variables (columns) of both docuspaces (original and transposed) are normalized.
- **tf ×idf docuspaces:** Finally, a third pair of docuspaces is generated. This is the one that is fed into the grubber.

Grubber

This is the second of the two main applications that make up our system. This application processes docuspaces by using its histograms as input vectors and creates what we call the knowledge maps. Once the maps have been trained, the ontology components that have been clustered together can be visualized. Grubber is based on self-organizing maps (SOM) (Kohonen, 2001). The agents that comprise the grubber are described in turn.

The Labeling Agent

Labeling maps is an important feature of many systems that implement SOM. All systems we have surveyed use only one header file for labeling the maps. Our approach, on the other hand, takes into account both header files, the entity list (documents), and the attribute list (terms), for labeling maps. This allows us to provide users with more information about each cell and the knowledge that is contained in the maps as a whole. Either the info or ontology components are displayed depending on what docuspace, front or transposed view, we use to feed the grubber. For instance, the front view allows us to visualize has-relationships, as depicted in Figure 7.

The Coloring Agent

Another important feature of the grubber is coloring. The coloring of the maps is a visual help in identifying ontology components within the clusters. Java provides a special class for handling color spaces. This abstract class is used as a color space tag to identify the specific color space of a color object.

Many systems we have surveyed do not use coloring at all. Instead they only make use of text tables for displaying the knowledge of the maps (Merkl, 1999; Ritter & Kohonen, 1989).

The results of applying our system to the animal kingdom dataset are portrayed in Figure 8. A reduction of the dataset is not needed in the case of

Figure 7. The entity map relationships

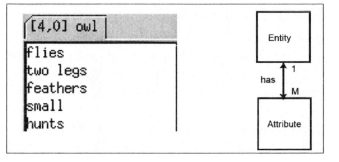

Figure 8. Animal domain mapped by SOM

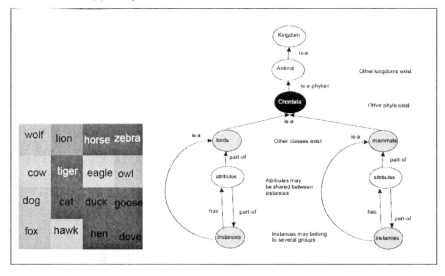

a domain as small as this. In order to validate our approach with larger datasets that reflect real-world properties, we applied the procedure to a search engine site and an academic site (see Figure 9) to test our ideas.

To automate the labeling of ontologies, and as a precursor for a semantic agent that uses WordNet as a lexical resource, a disambiguation application built on DGSOT (Luo, 2004) was created. DGSOT is a tree-structured self-organizing neural network that constructs a hierarchy from top to bottom by division, optimizing the number of clusters at each hierarchical level. DGSOT is impressive in its ability to organize data into their respective groups close to the desired granularity by modification of its parameters, but it needs some kind of disam-

biguation mechanism and a lexical or other source to create a labeled ontology. We used WordNet for the purpose and, using the animal dataset from the previous experiment, created, automatically, a hierarchical ontology (Figure 10) (Legrand & Pulido, 2004) which fully corresponds to the hierarchical structure of WordNet. The algorithm is simple but needs modification to extend its application to larger datasets. Nevertheless, our experiment shows that various agent type software can be gradually incorporated into an ontology tagging learning system: in our case, first the clusterer and then the semantic/labeling agent, which both presumably can be based on different methods and can benefit from other NLP agents higher up in the process flow.

Figure 9. Academic domain mapped by SOM

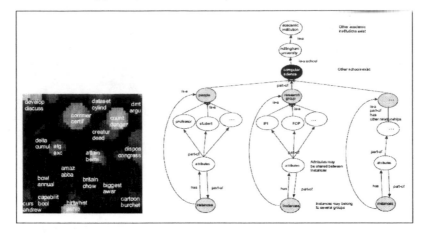

Figure 10. Hierarchical ontology structure

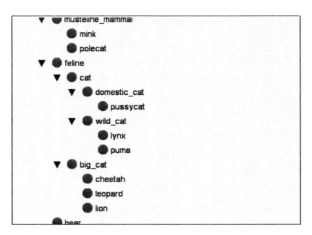

CONCLUSION

We have presented a draft model of cooperating natural language processing agents in the Semantic Web for knowledge management. We envisage cooperation between a number of scientists and hobbyists in different disciplines to make it happen. The idea is that each participant could concentrate on his or her area of strength when creating agents, and this evolutionary design model would gradually prune out the weakest components. We also expect that many of the already existing software applications will be gradually adapted to agent use.

Having such a vast array of agents of various kinds in the Semantic Web might seem overtly complicated and unnecessary. Why not, for example, create one monolithic language processing application that would take care of all that morphological, POS, semantic, and other processing mentioned above? We naturally need some sort of justification for the envisaged framework.

One such justification is historical. Looking at the present Internet, the WWW has grown over the years in an organic manner incorporating various communities and various interests in cooperative relationships. Just a couple of such communities—for example, Java and Perl—have had thousands and thousands of people cooperating, creating vast repositories of code and making them freely available to all users of these programming languages. Wikis, referred to below, have proved their mettle against commercial interests.

A monolithic system would probably work as well, but it would alienate most of the people now participating, people who want to do something about their hobby-horse, and people whose contributions can prove vital. Any monolithic imposed-above system would run counter to WWW and SW philosophy. We need standards and agreements, but most "Web savvy people" would probably agree that these should not come about through imposition but through negotiation and cooperation. Several standards would compete, of course, some dying out, some adapting to new constraints in the environments they operate, but that would be natural.

It is our belief that distributed, cooperative development of SW agents through various communities would be the most appropriate way to proceed, and in fact, perhaps the only reasonable way, taking into account the scale of the undertaking. Apart from harnessing the enthusiasm and skills of the participants, it would also create links between NLP, AI, and other scientific communities that are vital for the next stage of the Semantic Web outlined in this chapter. That would mean perhaps many dead ends (as can be witnessed by looking at the present WWW), redundancy, and downright failures, but evolution demands these, and just a few successes along the way can revolutionarize and energize the evolving SW landscape. Our spade and grubber application is just one of the countless other applications existing or still to come that either develop further and survive or die off through healthy competition in the evolutionary landscape of the Semantic Web.

FUTURE RESEARCH DIRECTIONS

When talking about future research directions on the Semantic Web, we need to keep in mind other evolving concepts in information management, such as Wikipedia (Krötzsch, Vrandecic, & Völkel, 2005). People championing wikis of all kinds hold to the view that in order to create a sufficient number of domain ontologies for the Semantic Web, one needs a huge number of volunteers for the task, and wikis have shown that this can be done by various kinds of collaborative knowledge structures created so far. Even the co-founder of Google, Sergey Brin, finds them impressive (Brin, 2005), although predictably still maintaining that Google may be the ultimate answer for the man's quest for knowledge. Many find both of these views wishful thinking and regard them just as an expected contention between commercial interest buying know-how and collaborative open sources massing man and brainpower for their cause. This reflects the fact that people all around the world recognize the coming of the Semantic Web and want to have a stake in it. There are many other collaborative efforts under way in the WWW that

could be used as a starting point for research on collaborative ontologies for NLP in SW.

Software tools are also an important means and an object for future research. We need better interfaces for the user, and better interfaces to connect various SW applications, NLP software, and ontologies. For most of the better-known applications, various APIs are available for further development. These include Protégé (Noy et al., 2000), WordNet (Fellbaum, 1998), and many others. There are many dedicated developers' sites, including OpenNLP (2007), for interesting NLP tools and tool development that could be used for SW.

Also hardware is developing constantly, and concepts such as the Semantic Grid will provide new types of platforms for agent and other software applications (Gil, 2006). Huge amounts of processing power needed to enable the Semantic Web can be harnessed in a distributed manner to serve both fixed and mobile terminals. These terminals can be parts of everyday consumer goods which allow machine-to-machine communication for monitoring, maintenance, and other purposes. Further ahead in time, attempts will be made to realize even more radical visions. Robots of human proportions or smaller with a distributed brain will become feasible as no King Kong of science fiction will be needed to lug around a large brain to provide enough computing power—the processing of huge amounts of data (visual, auditory, etc.) will take place in the Semantic Web/Grid through a mobile connection. Another commonplace scene in the future might be people from different countries conversing around a mobile device, each using his or her own mother tongue. A speech recognition software connected to language recognition software would feed a word sense disambiguation agent, and speech-to-text conversion and translation to another language would follow. Surgery by distance might become possible. These are truly radical visions, but already parts of these concepts have been realized with the existing technologies.

What is needed is close observation of synergies that are developing with the coming of the Semantic Web between various scientific disciplines. A lot that can be used in the Semantic Web already exists. NLP and other technologies can be leveraged as we have outlined, and it would be wise to consider converting existing NLP software to agent-based software in new SW designs.

REFERENCES

Bahl, L.R, & Mercer, R. (1976). Part-of-speech assignment by a statistical decision algorithm. In *Proceedings of the International Symposium on Information Theory, Ronneby, Sweden.*

Berners-Lee, T., Hendler, J., & Lassila, O. (2001). The Semantic Web. *Scientific American,* (May), 34-43.

Bisson, G., Nedellec, C., & Canamero, D. (2000). Designing clustering methods for ontology building. The Mo'K workbench. In *Proceedings of the ECAI 2000 Workshop on Ontology Learning (OL'2000).*

Boicu, C., Tecuci, G., & Boicu, M. (2002). Mixed-initiative exception-based learning for knowledge base refinement. In *Proceedings of the 18th National Conference of Artificial Intelligence, Edmonton, Alberta, Canada.*

Boicu, C., & Tecuci, G., (2004). Mixed-initiative ontology learning. In *Proceedings of the 2004 International Conference on Artificial Intelligence (IC-AI'2004)*, Las Vegas, NV.

Brin, S. (2005). *In Sims:141, search engines, technology and business [video].* Retrieved October 10, 2006, from http://video.google.com/videopla y?docid=7137075178977335350&q=google+berk eley&hl=en

Brill, E. (1995). Transformation-based error-driven learning and natural language processing: A case study in part-of-speech tagging. *Computational Linguistics, 21*(4), 543-566.

Buitelaar, P., & Declerck, T. (2004). Linguistic annotation for the Semantic Web. In S. Handschuh. (Ed.), *Annotation for the Semantic Web.* Amsterdam: IOS Press.

Buitelaar, P., Olejnik, D., & Sintek, M. (2004). A Protégé plug-in for ontology extraction from text based on linguistic analysis. In *Proceedings of the 1st European Semantic Web Symposium (ESWS),* Heraklion, Greece.

de Argaez, E. (2006). *One billion Internet users. Internet World Stats News, (014).* Retrieved October 10, 2006, from http://www.internetworldstats. com/pr/edi014.htm

de Chaelandar, G., & Grau, B. (2000). SVETLAN'—A system to classify words in context. In S. Staab, A. Maedche, C. Nedellec, & P. Wiemer-Hastings (Eds.), *Proceedings of the Workshop on Ontology Learning of the 14th European Conference on Artificial Intelligence (ECAI'00),* Berlin.

Denny, M. (2004). *Ontology tools survey, revisited.* Retrieved October 10, 2006, from http://www.xml. com/pub/a/2004/07/14/onto.html

Dey, L., & Abulaish, M. (2006). Ontology enhancement for including newly acquired knowledge about concept descriptions and answering imprecise queries. In D. Taniar, & J.W. Rahayu (Eds.), *Web semantics & ontology* (pp.189-225). Hershey, PA: Idea Group.

Dou, D., McDermott, D., & Qi, P. (2002). Ontology translation by ontology merging and automated reasoning. In *Proceedings of the EKAW 2002 Workshop on Ontologies for Multi-Agent Systems.*

Faure, D., & Nédellec, C. (1998). ASIUM: Learning subcategorization frames and restrictions of selection. In *Proceedings of ECML'98, Workshop on Text Mining.*

Fellbaum, C. (Ed.). (1998). *WordNet: An electronic lexical database.* Cambridge, MA: MIT Press.

FIPA. (2002a). *Agent Communication Language specifications.* Retrieved October 10, 2006, from http://www.fipa.org/repository/aclspecs.html

FIPA. (2002b). *FIPA specifications.* Retrieved October 10, 2006, from http://www.fipa.org/specifications/index.html

Gee, J.P., & Grosjean, F. (1983). Performance structures: A psycholinguistic and linguistic appraisal. *Cognitive Psychology, 15*, 411-458.

Gil, Y. (2006). On agents and grids: Creating the fabric for a new generation of distributed intelligent systems. *Web Semantics: Science, Services and Agents on the World Wide Web, 4*(2), 116-123.

Goldsmith, J. (2000). Linguistica: An automatic morphological analyzer. In *Proceedings of the Main Session of the Chicago Linguistic Society's 36th Meeting.*

Goldsmith, J. (2001). Unsupervised learning of the morphology of a natural language. *Computational Linguistics, 27*(2), 153-198.

Hafner, K. (2006). *And if you liked the movie, a Netflix contest may reward you handsomely. The New York Times, (October 2).* Retrieved October 10, 2006, from http://www.nytimes.com/2006/10/02/technology/02netflix.html?ex=1317441600&en=75c76fd0981113ee&ei=5090&partner=rssuserland&emc=rss

Hendler, J. (2001). Agents and the Semantic Web. *IEEE Intelligent Systems, 16*(2), 30-37.

Java, A., Finin, T., & Nirenburg, S. (2006). Text understanding agents and the Semantic Web. In *Proceedings of the 39th Annual Hawaii International Conference on System Sciences.*

Jurafsky, D., & Martin, J.H. (2000). *Speech and language processing.* Englewood Cliffs, NJ: Prentice Hall.

Kavalec, M., & Svátek, A. (2005). Study on automated relation labelling in ontology learning. In P. Buitelaar, P. Cimiano, & B. Magnini (Eds.), *Ontology learning from text: Methods, evaluation and applications* (pp. 44-58). Amsterdam: IOS Press.

Knublauch, H., Fergerson, R.W., Noy, N.F., & Musen, M.A. (2004). The Protégé OWL plugin: An open development environment for Semantic Web applications. In *Proceedings of the 3rd International Semantic Web Conference (ISWC 2004),* Hiroshima, Japan.

Kohonen, T. (2001). *Self-organizing maps (3rd ed.).* Berlin: Springer-Verlag.

Krötzsch, M., Vrandecic, D., & Völkel, M. (2005). Wikipedia and the Semantic Web—the missing links. In *Proceedings of Wikimania 2005 The 1st International Wikimedia Conference.*

Lee, J.H., Kim, M.H., & Lee, Y.J. (1993). Information retrieval based on conceptual distance in IS-A hierarchies. *Journal of Documentation, 49*(2), 188-207.

Legrand, S., & Pulido, J.R.G. (2004). A hybrid approach to word sense disambiguation: Neural clustering with class labeling. In P. Buitelaar, J. Franke, M. Grobelnik, G. Paaß, & V. Svátek (Eds.), *Proceedings of the Workshop on Knowledge Discovery and Ontologies of the 15th European Conference on Machine Learning (ECML)* (pp. 127-132), Pisa, Italy.

Lipton, E. (2006). *Software being developed to monitor opinions of U.S. The New York Times,* (October 4). Retrieved October 10, 2006, from http://www.nytimes.com/2006/10/04/us/04monitor.html?ex=1160798400&en=1f2f6f8007b8e411&ei=5070

Luo, F. (2004). *Mining gene microarray expression profiles.* PhD Thesis, University of Texas, USA.

Maedche, A., Pekar, V., & Staab, S. (2002). Ontology learning part one: Learning taxonomic relations from the Web. *Proceedings of the Web Intelligence Conference* (pp. 301-322). Berlin: Springer-Verlag.

Maedche, A., & Staab, S. (2001). Ontology learning for the Semantic Web. *IEEE Intelligent Systems, 16*(2).

Merkl, D. (1999). Document classification with self-organizing map. In E. Oja & S. Kaski. (Eds.), *Kohonen maps* (pp. 183-192). Amsterdam: Elsevier Science.

Morik, K. (1993). Balanced cooperative modeling. *Machine Learning, 11*(1), 217-235.

Nagao, M. (1992). Some rationales and methodologies for example-based approach. *Proceedings of the International Workshop on Fundamental Research for the Future Generation of Natural*

Language Processing (pp. 82-94), Manchester, UK.

Neumann, G., Backofen, R., Baur, J., Becker, M., & Braun, C. (1997). An information extraction core system for real world German text processing. In *Proceedings of the 5ᵗʰ Conference on Applied Natural Language Processing (ANLP-97)* (pp. 208-215), Washington, DC.

Noy, N.F., & Musen, M.A. (2000). Prompt: Algorithm and tool for automated ontology merging and alignment. In *Proceedings of the 17ᵗʰ National Conference on Artificial Intelligence* (AAAI2000), Austin, TX.

Noy, N.F., Sintek, M., Decker, S., Crubezy, M., Fergerson, R.W., & Musen, M.A. (2001). Creating Semantic Web contents with Protege-2000. *IEEE Intelligent Systems, 16*(2), 60-71.

OpenNLP. (2007). Retrieved March 10, 2007, from http://opennlp.sourceforge.net/projects.html

OASIS. (2004). *UDDI version 3.0.2*. Retrieved October 10, 2006, from http://www.oasis-open. org/committees/uddi-spec/doc/spec/v3/uddi-v3.0.2-20041019.htm

Patterson, A.L. (2005). *Multiple index based information retrieval system*. United States Patent Application, Patent Application Full Text and Image Database, U.S. Patent & Trademark Office. Retrieved October 10, 2006, from http://www.uspto.gov/patft/index.html

Pease, A., Niles, I., & Li, J. (2002). *The suggested upper merged ontology: A large ontology for the Semantic Web and its applications*. Working Notes of the AAAI-2002 Workshop on Ontologies and the Semantic Web, Edmonton, Canada.

Predoiu, L., Feier, C., Scharffe, F., de Bruijn, J., Martín-Recuerda, F., Manov, D., & Ehrig, M. (2005). *State-of-the-art survey on Ontology Merging and Aligning V2*. SEKT Deliverable D4.2.2, Digital Enterprise Research Institute, University of Innsbruck, Austria.

Porter, M. (1980). An algorithm for suffix stripping. *Program, 14*(3), 130-137.

Pulido, J.R.G., Ruiz, M.A.G., Herrera, R., Cabello, E., Legrand, S., & Elliman, D. (2006). *Ontology languages for the Semantic Web: A never completely updated review*. In Knowledge based systems. Science Direct.(pp. 489-497).

Ritter, H., & Kohonen, T. (1989). Self-organizing semantic maps. *Biological Cybernetics, 61*, 241-254.

Shamsfard, M., & Barforoush, A.A. (2003). The state of the art in ontology learning: A framework for comparison. *The Knowledge Engineering Review, 18*(4), 293-316.

Schone, P., & Jurafsky, D. (2001). Knowledge-free induction of inflectional morphologies. In *Proceedings of the 2ⁿᵈ Meeting of the North American Chapter of the Association for Computational Linguistics: Proceedings of the Conference* (pp. 183-191), Pittsburgh, PA.

Stumme, G., Hotho, A., & Berendt, B. (2006). Semantic Web mining, state of the art and future directions. *Journal of Web Semantics, 4*(2).

Sugiura, N., Shigeta, Y., Fukuta, N., Izumi, N., & Yamaguchi, T. (2004). Towards on-the-fly ontology construction—focusing on ontology quality improvement. *Proceedings of ESWS-04, Heraklion.*

WS-I. (2006). *Web Services Interoperability Organization*. Retrieved October 10, 2006, from http://www.ws-i.org/

W3C. (1999). *Resource description framework (RDF)*. Retrieved October 10, 2006, from http://www.w3.org/RDF

W3C. (2002). *Web Services Description Working Group*. Retrieved October 10, 2006, from http://www.w3.org/2002/ws/desc/

W3C. (2003). *SOAP version 1.2, part 1: Messaging framework*. Retrieved October 10, 2006, from http://www.w3.org/TR/soap12-part1/

W3C. (2004a). *Extensible markup language (XML) 1.1. W3C recommendation*. Retrieved October 10, 2006, from http://www.w3.org/TR/2004/REC-xml11-20040204/

W3C. (2004b). *OWL Web ontology language reference*. Retrieved October 10, 2006, from http://www.w3.org/2004/OWL/

W3C. (2004c). *RDF vocabulary description language 1.0: RDF Schema*. W3C recommendation. Retrieved October 10, 2006, from http://www.w3.org/TR/rdf-schema/

W3C. (2004d). *Web service architecture*. W3C Working Group note 11. Retrieved October 10, 2006, from http://www.w3.org/TR/2004/NOTE-ws-arch-20040211/

XMethods. (2006). *Recent listings*. Retrieved October 10, 2006, from http://www.xmethods.net/

ADDITIONAL READINGS

Alesso, P.H., & Smith, G.F. (2006). Thinking on the Web: Berners-Lee, Gödel and Turing. New York: John Wiley & Sons.

Aref, M.M. (2003). A multi-agent system for natural language understanding. In *Proceedings of the 2003 International Conference on Integration of Knowledge Intensive Multi-Agent System (KI-MAS'03)* (pp. 36-40), Boston.

Bontcheva, K., Cunningham, H., Kiryakov, A., & Tablan, V. (2006). Semantic annotation and human language technology. In J. Davies, R. Studer, & P. Warren (Eds.), *Semantic Web technologies trends and research in ontology-based systems* (pp. 29-50). Chichester, UK: John Wiley & Sons.

Bontcheva, K., Kiryakov, A., Cunningham, H., Popov, P., & Dimitrov, M. (2003). *Semantic Web enabled, open source language technology*. Proceedings of the Language Technology and the Semantic Web, Workshop on NLP and XML (NLPXML-2003), in conjunction with EACL 2003, Budapest.

Cimiano, P., Handschuh, S., & Staab, S. (2004). Towards the self-annotating Web. In *Proceedings of the International WWW Conference* (pp. 462-471), New York.

Di Marzo Serugendo, G., Foukia, N., Hassas, S., Karageorgos, A., Kouadri Mostéfaoui, S., Rana, O.F., Ulieru, M., Valckenaers, P., & Van Aart, C. (2004). *Self-organising applications: Paradigms and applications*. Proceedings of the Engineering Self-Organising Applications Workshop (ESOA'03). Berlin: Springer-Verlag (LNCS 2977).

Farrar, S., Lewis, W.D., & Langendoen, D.T. (2002). *An ontology for linguistic annotation. Semantic Web Meets Language Resources: Papers from the AAAI Workshop* (Technical Report WS-02-16, pp. 11-19). Menlo Park, CA: AAAI Press.

Fensel, D., Hendler, J., Wahlster, W., & Lieberman, H. (Eds.). (2002). *Spinning the Semantic Web: Bringing the World Wide Web to its full potential*. Cambridge, MA: MIT Press.

Hahn, U., & Kornél, G.M. (2002). An integrated, dual learner for grammars and ontologies. *Data & Knowledge Engineering, 42*(3), 273–291.

Hendler, J. (1999). Is there an intelligent agent in your future? *Nature Web Matters*, (3). Retrieved October 10, 2006, from http://www.nature.com/nature/webmatters/agents/agents.html

Horridge, M., Knublauch, H., Rector, A., Stevens, R., & Roe, C. (2004). *A practical guide to building OWL ontologies using the Protégé-OWL plugin and CO-ODE tools*. Retrieved March 10, 2007, from http://www.co-ode.org/resources/tutorials/ProtegeOWLTutorial.pdf

Huhns, M.N., & Stephens, L.M. (1999). Multiagent systems and societies of agents. In G. Weiss (Ed.), *Multiagent systems: A modern approach to distributed artificial intelligence* (pp. 79-120).

Ide, N., & Veronis, J. (1998). Word sense disambiguation: The state of the art. *Computational Linguistics, 24*(1), 1-40.

Kalfoglou, Y., Alani, H., Schorlemmer, M., & Walton, C. (2004). On the emergent Semantic Web and overlooked issues. In *Proceedings of the 3rd International Semantic Web Conference (ISWC'04), Hiroshima, Japan*.

Kilgarriff, A. (1997). "I don't believe in word senses." *Computers and the Humanities, 31*(2), 91-113.

Koehler, J., Philippi, S., Specht, M., & Ruegg, A. (2006). Ontology based text indexing and querying for the semantic Web. *Knowledge-Based Systems, 19,* 744-754.

Maedche, A. (2002). *Ontology learning for the Semantic Web.* Boston: Kluwer Academic.

Nwana, H.S. (1996). Software agents: An overview. *Knowledge Engineering Review, 11*(3), 1-40.

Nirenburg, S., & Raskin, V. (2004). *Ontological semantics.* Cambridge, MA: MIT Press.

Reeve, L., & Han, H. (2006). A comparison of semantic annotation systems for text-based Web documents. In D. Taniar & J.W. Rahayu (Eds.), *Web semantics ontology* (pp. 165-187). Hershey, PA: Idea Group.

Sen, S., & Weiss, G. (1999). Learning in multiagent systems. Multiagent systems and societies of agents. In G. Weiss (Ed.), *Multiagent systems: A modern approach to distributed artificial intelligence* (pp. 259-298).

Shamsfard, M., & Barforoush, A.A. (2003). The state of the art in ontology learning: A framework for comparison. *Knowledge Engineering Review, 18*(4), 293-316.

Su, X., & Gulla, J.A. (2004). Semantic enrichment for ontology mapping. In F. Meziane & E. Métais (Eds.), *Proceedings of Natural Language Process-*

ing and Information Systems, the 9th International Conference on Applications of Natural Languages to Information Systems (pp. 217-228), Salford, UK. Berlin: Springer-Verlag (LNCS 3136).

Walton, C. (2007). *Agency and the Semantic Web.* New York: John Wiley & Sons.

Wooldridge, M. (2000). Semantic issues in the verification of agent communication languages. *Autonomous Agents and Multi-Agent Systems, 3*(1), 9-31.

Wooldridge, M. (2002). *An introduction to multiagent systems.* New York: John Wiley & Sons.

ENDNOTES

[1] The importance of detailing the steps lies in that, unlike Text-To-Onto which performs the full cycle of tasks related to ontology learning, there are OL tools such as Doddle II (Sugiura, Shigeta, Fukuta, Izumi, & Yamaguchi, 2004) and SVETLAN (de Chaelandar & Grau, 2000) that only perform some of these steps.

[2] OntoEdit, the graphical user interface for Text-To-Onto with some add-ons, became OntoStudio and is now distributed by Ontoprise (http://www.ontoprise.de/content/index_eng.html); Text-To-Onto became Text2Onto and is now an Open Source SourceForge project (http://sourceforge.net/projects/text-toonto/).

Chapter XXIII
Integrating Mobile Technologies in Enterprise Architecture with a Focus on Global Supply Chain Management Systems

Bhuvan Unhelkar
University of Western Sydney, Australia

Ming-Chien Wu
University of Western Sydney, Australia

Abbass Ghanbary
University of Western Sydney, Australia

ABSTRACT

This chapter investigates opportunities to integrate mobile technologies within an organization's enterprise architecture (EA), with an emphasis on supply chain management (SCM) systems. These SCM systems exist within the overall EA of the business. SCM systems are further influenced by the increasing modern-day need for information and communications technologies (ICTs) within a business, to bring together all of its disparate applications. The resultant enterprise application integration (EAI) also stands to benefit immensely from the incorporation of mobile technologies within it. Traditionally, supply chain management systems have involved management of the flows of material, information, and finances in a complex web of networks that include suppliers, manufacturers, distributors, retailers, and customers. Thus, these traditional supply chain management systems have a great need for integration under the umbrella of EAI. Mobile technologies can provide time and location independence to these EAIs in terms of information in the supply chain systems, creating the possibility of multiple business processes that traverse diverse geographical regions. This chapter, based on the research conducted by the authors at the University of Western Sydney, discusses the opportunities that arise in supply chain management systems due to the time and location independence offered by mobility, and the resultant advantages and limitations of such integration to the business.

INTRODUCTION

A business enterprise uses a suite of different software applications to fulfill its various activities. These systems include supply chain management (SCM) systems, customer relationship management (CRM) systems, enterprise resource planning (ERP) systems, business intelligence (BI) systems, and other supporting financial and business systems. These enterprise systems do not operate in isolation. In fact, each of these systems depends on other systems, as well as large amounts of data in the background, to fulfill their own requirements. Specifically, supply chain management systems involve management of the flows of materials, information, and finance in a complex web of networks that include suppliers, manufacturers, distributors, retailers, and customers. The complexity of an SCM system requires it, as per Poirier (1999), to offer the right combination of data, products, and services to customers at the right time, right place, and right price. With rapidly increasing Internet access and business-to-business (B2B) connectivity, users of SCM are able to get their information needs easily—leading to what can be called electronic supply chain management (E-SCM) systems. E-SCM (Internet-based) systems are integrated together with all other enterprise applications, resulting in a comprehensive enterprise architecture (EA). Such an EA delivers the company a competitive advantage by opening up opportunities to streamline processes, reduce costs, increase customer satisfaction, and enable thorough strategic planning (Unhelkar & Lan, 2006). In today's modern business environment, it is important to further extend the advantages by incorporating wireless technologies and handheld devices in the organization's overall enterprise architecture. As Barnes (2002) mentions, the impact of wireless telecommunication on the Internet has taken a new turn. We use the mobile technology application for communications, working, banking, and shopping. The "time and location" independence provided by mobile technologies leads us into the era of mobile supply chain management (M-SCM) systems. It is important to understand these M-SCM systems within the context of the overall enterprise architecture. This chapter starts with a brief review of enterprise architecture and the issues related to enterprise application integration (EAI). This is followed by an understanding of the traditional SCM systems, together with the study of mobile technologies and applications. The chapter then describes the details of E-SCM and M-SCM. Finally, an outline of a model for integration of mobile technologies with SCM processes is then presented, together with its advantages and limitations.

ENTERPRISE ARCHITECTURE

An enterprise architecture represents the enterprise's key business, information, application, and technology strategies, and their impact on business functions and processes. EA consists of four key components: enterprise business architecture (EBA), enterprise information architecture (EIA), enterprise solution architecture (ESA), and enterprise technology architecture (ETA). The overall EA comprises software systems that may have been created using different programming languages and databases, and may be operating on different technology platforms. Figure 1 presents how EA is composed of different enterprise systems. However, Figure 1 also shows that users of the system want to see a unified view of the EA. This need for a unified view requires the enterprise to bring these various applications together, in an integrated fashion, resulting in enterprise application integration.

An enterprise business architecture that defines the enterprise business model and process cycles and timing also shows what functions should be integrated into the system. The enterprise information architecture focuses on which data and the corresponding data model should be integrated into the system. The enterprise solution architecture, also referred to as an application portfolio, is the collection of information systems supporting the EBA, which helps the user to easily understand and use the interface and components. Enterprise technology architecture is a consistent set of ICT standards which use infrastructures to support the EBA, EIA, and ESA. The infrastructures span across various different technical domain architectures, and include databases, applications, devices, middleware,

Figure 1. Enterprise application integration composed of different enterprise systems

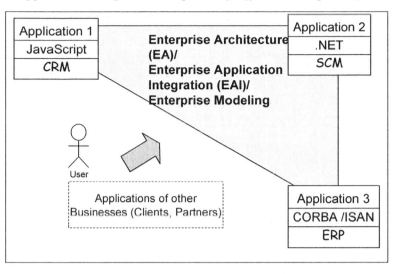

networks, platforms, security, enterprise service buses, hosting, WLAN, LAN, Internet connection, operation system, servers, systems management, and so on (Pulkkinen, 2006).

Enterprise application integration maintains data integration and process integration across multiple systems, and provides real-time information access among systems. EAI not only links applications together, but also provides more effective and efficient business processes to the enterprise. There are numerous technologies that can be used for enterprise application integration, such as bus/hub, application connectivity, data format and transformation, integration modules, support for transactions, enterprise portal, Web service, and also service-oriented architecture (Finkelstein, 2006). Most importantly, however, the technologies of Web services build on extensible markup language (XML), Web services description language (WSDL), and universal description, discovery and integration (UDDI), which provide an excellent basis for integrating the applications of the enterprise—particularly when they are on separate platforms.

Linthicum (2000) declared that EAI enables the original chaotic enterprise processes to reach a semblance of order after the integration is achieved, resulting in increased efficiency on process flows, data integration, and data transportation. Furthermore, EAI also makes a more effective extension of enterprise processes. Irani, Themistocleous, and

Love (2002) divided application integration into three categories: intra-organization, hybrid, and inter-organization. Intra-organizational application integrates packaged systems, custom applications, and EPR systems, and there are no transactions between external users or partners. Hybrid application integrates business-to–consumer (B2C) applications with IT infrastructure. Inter-organizational application integrates all processes between extended enterprises, such as the supply chain, and also can be a transaction between virtual enterprises, for example, e-procurement.

Further to the above discussion, in order to bring about a successful EAI, it is also important to create a model of such integration—called an enterprise model (EM). An EM would describe the objectives pursued by an enterprise and, as per Brathaug and Evjen (1996), focus on four aspects: process, product, organization, and systems. Doumeingts, Ducq, and Kleinhans (2000) defined enterprise modeling as the representation of enterprise activities at a global and a detailed level, using functions and processes in understanding its running. A good EM would take into account not only the technical aspects but also business, social, and human aspects of the enterprise. Such a comprehensive EM will also make it easier for the incorporation of mobility.

Kamogawa and Okada (2004) pointed out that integration of enterprise systems focuses on integrating collaboration agreements, collaboration profiles, business scenario integration, business process integration, and messaging technology. The three major applications—CRM, SCM, and ERP—are all shown in Figure 2. Figure 2 also shows how these applications are integrated through the enterprise model. Our aim is to further apply mobility to the enterprise model. However, in this chapter the discussion on the application of mobility to EM will be restricted to its application to SCM systems.

EA/EM/EAI all integrate enterprise applications. Such integration cannot only enable the enterprise to present a unified view of the system to its suppliers and clients, but also reduces errors and improves quality by reducing or even eliminating duplication of data entry. Enterprise application integration brings about not only internal integration, but through extension also offers much more efficiency to its external suppliers, customers, and other trading partners over the Internet. Thus, providing mobility to EAI, and especially the SCM system, will connect existing and new systems to enable collaborative operation within the entire organization in real time—providing new and improved services without location and time limitations.

EXISTING MODEL OF SUPPLY CHAIN MANAGEMENT

In order to successfully apply mobility to SCM, we consider SCM within the overall context of EM.

Traditional supply chain management involves the flows of material, information, and finance in a network, including suppliers, manufacturers, distributors, retailers, and customers. This is shown in Figure 3, where the various parties are connected to each other through the ability to supply goods, provide information about the goods, and deal with the financial aspects of those supplies.

The traditional supply chain is a push model. As outlined by Lee (2000), material flow includes both physical products flowing from the suppliers to customers through the chain and reverse flows via product returns, servicing, recycling, and disposal. Information flows involve order transmission and delivery status. Financial flows include credit terms, payment schedules, consignment, and title ownership arrangements. These flows cut across multiple functions and areas within a company and across companies (and sometimes industries); this leads to big challenges in terms of both technologies and business. Organization and integration of these flows within and across companies are important for effective supply chain management.

Supply chains can exist in both manufacturing and service organizations. In manufacturing organizations, they are mostly concerned with the flow of products and information between supply chain member organizations—procurement of materials, transformation of materials into finished products, and distribution of those products to end customers. However, in service organizations, supply chains

Figure 2. Enterprise model (based on Kamogawa & Okada, 2004)

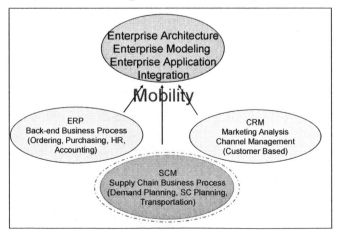

Figure 3. The supply chain flows (based on Lee, 2000)

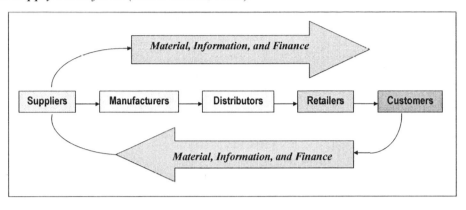

can focus on "values added" to the services being offered. Overall, the current information-driven, integrated supply chains enable organizations to reduce inventory and costs, to add product value, to extend resources, to increase speed time to market, and to retain customers (Burt, Dobler, & Starling, 2003).

There are complex relationships in supply chains, such as multiple suppliers serving multiple customers, or a supplier who may be a customer or even a competitor in different parts of the chain. This complexity is the reason why we refer to supply chains as "supply networks" or "supply webs." Because of the network complexity, correct quality and time transfer of information can be extremely difficult. In particular, the multiple layers in a supply chain have the potential to misrepresent order information. This misrepresentation can lead to numerous confusion and errors, such as excessive inventory, inactive capacity, high manufacturing and transportation costs, and increasingly dissatisfied customers. Achieving supply chain efficiency requires exact and timely information. And the longer and more complex the supply chain is, the greater the requirement is, according to Dong (2001), for the supply chain to have precision in terms of the quality and timing of information.

SCM systems primarily include the requirement for integration architecture; the varied objectives of all the participants in a supply chain; mutual collaborative functioning of interfacing systems; and the varied levels of functionalities required for customers, retailers, suppliers, and manufacturers.

A comprehensive supply chain management system can be an integration of a customer relationship management system, supplier relationship management system, order/purchasing system, delivery products management (logistics management) system, as well as time management systems.

The goal of supply chain management is to reduce inventories by optimizing material and information flow without sacrificing service level. SCMs have a responsibility to maintain sufficient inventory levels to satisfy the demands. Furthermore, increasingly, industries with short inventory and product cycles, such as high-tech and customer electronics, are highly reliant on SCM to provide them with the ability to interact with their numerous suppliers and retailers. SCM also allows high-quality customer service by delivering the right products to the right place at the right time.

MOBILE (EMERGING) TECHNOLOGIES

Mobile technologies can be considered as one set of the significant emerging technologies (as per Unhelkar, 2005) that have the potential to influence supply chains. Wireless technologies encompass any aspect of communication that is achieved without land-based or wired mechanisms. Thus, mobility, in a strict sense, is a subset of wireless technologies. This is because there can be some wireless communications that need not be mobile (for example, transmissions from a wireless radio tower or between two stationary servers). We consider a range of wireless technologies in this section that are likely to influence the various business processes of an organization. Later, we will discuss the specific mobile technologies (such as RFID) from the point of view of their usage in M-SCM.

Wireless Technologies

Wireless technology refers to technology without wires and phone lines that uses a multiplicity of devices for communications (IBM, n.d.). The term "wireless technology" can also be used to describe modern wireless connections such as those in cellular networks and wireless broadband Internet. In modern usage, wireless is a method of communication that uses low-powered radio waves to transmit data between the mobile terminals (Elliott & Phillips, 2003). The terminals, such as mobile phones, iPods, personal digital assistants (PDAs), global positioning systems (GPSs), watches, email-only devices, handheld computers, and "wearable" technology, are carried by individuals and are far more "personal" than mere desktop PCs. The latest and important wireless technologies that require a brief discussion in this section are:

- "3G" mobile network
- Mobile satellite network
- Infrared
- Bluetooth
- Wireless
- Local area network
- WiMAX
- Radio frequency identification

Third-Generation Mobile Network

The development of 3G-related technologies has overcome the limitation of the previous generation of mobile technologies by allowing higher transmission rates and more complex e-commerce interactions (Barnes, 2002). Kuo and Yu (2005) and Huber (2002) list three 3G standards, including wideband code division multiple access (WCDMA), code division multiple access 2000 (CDMA2000), and time division–synchronized code division multiple access (TD-SCDMA), approved by the International Telecommunication Union (ITU).

W-CDMA is the most popular 3G mobile network which is capable of transferring multimedia between terminals; it is the technology behind the 3G universal mobile telecommunications system (UMTS) standard, combined with the 2G global system for mobile communications (GSM) standard, which is mainly dominated by European and Japanese firms.

Due to the promotion of the GSM organization and the 60% popularity usage of the 2G system in the global market, CDMA2000 gained the attention of many companies, especially U.S. and Korean firms that mainly support it. One of the advantages of the CDMA2000 system is the upgradeability of the narrowband CDMA system, so the user does not need to change his or her mobile device—just upgrade his or her user plan.

The TD-SCDMA includes three main key technologies: (1) TDMA/TDD principle, (2) smart transmitter and receiver, and (3) joint detection/terminal synchronization. It is mainly supported by China's Datang Telecom, which advocates its low-cost infrastructure.

Mobile Satellite Networks

Mobile satellite networks represent the convergence of the latest mobile technologies with space technologies. Satellites are operated at microwave radio frequencies in various bands, which are allocated by the ITU (2001). Olla (2005) declared that integrating space technology into mobile communications offers two main advantages. The first advantage is in providing access to voice and data service anywhere in the world—of which the current popular application is Internet phone (Voice over IP–VoIP). The second advantage is the exact positioning of useful location-sensitive information used for direction-finding-based and map-reading-based services, the current popular application of which is a car GPS. These applications are becoming commonplace, with Fitch (2004) pointing out that the technique for interfacing satellite links to global networks is well developed, including methods to overcome timing problems.

Infrared

Infrared (IR) technology provides directional electromagnetic radiation for "point-to-point" communication within short range. The radiation wavelength of IR communication is approximately between 750 nm and 1 millimeter. IR data transmission is a mobile application for short-range communication between a computer terminal and mobile device, such as a PDA or a mobile phone. Infrared communications are useful for indoor use in areas of high population density. IR does not transmit through physical barriers such as a wall, and so it does not interfere with other devices in the vicinity. Infrared transmission is, therefore, the most common way for remote controllers to control physical machines. Furthermore, infrared lasers are used to provide the light for optical fiber communications systems; they are the best choice for standard silica fibers, as using infrared lasers can be a cheaper way to install a communications link in an urban area (Okuhata, Uno, Kumatani, Shirakawa, & Chiba, 1997).

Bluetooth

Bluetooth is a short-range radio technology developed to connect devices without wires. It is an effective technology for a new generation of Internet-capable mobile terminals. It enables numerous innovative services and applications, which function regardless of the mobile operator. The most important solution enabled by Bluetooth technology is synchronization between a PC server and one or more other mobile terminals. Synchronization has been particularly successful in cooperative applications, providing access to SCM systems (Paavilainen, 2001). Buttery and Sago (2004) describe the Bluetooth application as being built into more and more mobile telephones, allowing some very interesting m-commerce opportunities to be created. As people currently carry mobile phones with Bluetooth technology, these technologies can be used for making payments and related service concepts through simple downloads on their mobile devices. Retailers might also be able to provide samples of products to download via a Bluetooth link

located close to the actual item, potentially resulting in better customer service and an enriched shopping experience. Bluetooth can operate up to 10 meters (eventually up to 100 meters in future versions). Since Bluetooth technology is a radio transmission, it does not need line-of-sight with another Bluetooth-enabled device to communicate (Scheniderman, 2002). Once Bluetooth technology is in place, one can envisage consumers walking around and giving out messages wirelessly via Bluetooth in order to buy items from vending machines, or buying low-value tickets, or even making small-value "cashless" purchases, such as newspapers.

Wireless Local Area Network (WLAN)

WLAN technology is closer to the fundamental principle of the Internet, wherein anybody can establish an individual network as long as it follows the general intranet guidelines. The wireless links would provide a network connection to all users in the surrounding area, ranging from a single room to an entire campus. The backbone of such a WLAN network may still use cables, with one or more wireless access points connecting the wireless users to the wired network. Currently, laptop computers and some PDA devices can be attached to a WLAN network using a compact flash (CF) or a Personal Computer Memory Card International Association (PCMCIA) card. In the future, PDAs and mobile phones might support multiple network technologies. WLAN is expected to continue to be an important form of connection in many business areas. The market is expected to grow as the benefits of WLAN are recognized (Paavilainen, 2001; Burness, Higgins, Sago, & Thorpe, 2004).

WiMAX

WiMAX is defined as Worldwide Interoperability for Microwave Access by the WiMAX Forum. The forum describes WiMAX as "a standards-based technology enabling the delivery of last mile wireless broadband access as an alternative to cable and DSL." The forum also states that it "will be incorporated in notebook computers and PDAs by 2007, allowing for urban areas and cities to become 'metro zones' for portable outdoor broadband wireless access" (WiMAX Forum, 2006). WiMAX delivers 72 Mbps over 30 miles point-to-point and four miles non-line-of-sight (NLOS) (Ohrtman, 2005). Its purpose is to ensure that broadband wireless radios manufactured for customer use interoperate from retailer to retailer. The main advantages of the WiMAX standard are to enable the implementation of advanced radio features in a standardized approach, and provide people in a city with online access via their mobile devices.

Radio Frequency Identification

RFID is an emerging technology that has been increasingly used in logistics and supply chain management in recent years. RFID technology can identify, sort, and control the product and information flow, all through a supply chain. Today, RFID is a standard technology that uses radio waves to automatically identify people or objects. There are several methods of identification, the most common of which use RFID tags and readers.

Ngai, Cheng, Au, and Lai (2005) proposed that RFID is made up of two components: the transponder, which is located on the object to be identified; and the reader, which, depending upon the design and the technology used, may be a read or write/read device.

Roberts (2006) states that an RFID system will typically comprise the following three components, as shown in Figure 4:

- An RFID device (tag), which is a unique identifier for an object or person.
- A tag reader with an antenna and transceiver.

- A host system or connection to an enterprise system.

As Figure 4 shows, firstly we incorporate data inside an RFID tag. When the tag goes through a tag reader, the information inside the tag will automatically transfer to the host system. The host system is stored in a data center. After the data center analyzes and organizes the RFID tag information in the host system, specific useful tag information will be sent to a different enterprise SCM system.

Using an RFID system in the supply chain has been demonstrated by Asif and Mandviwalla (2005). Firstly, the SCM system constructs the item "where and when" during processing. When the items leave the manufactory and arrive at the place where they are to be read by the readers, the same information will be transferred directly to the distributor. The items are quickly sent to the correct trucks. As these items arrive at the retail outlet, they are read by the receiving RFID readers, and the retail outlet's inventories are updated automatically. Since the shelves at this outlet also have their own readers, they can directly increase replacement orders. However, using RFID technology in the SCM system, the items' quality can be automatically updated by the RFID reader sending into the SCM system. This provides highly location-based tracking, reduces the cost and human-error risks, and also improves the effectiveness and efficiency.

EPCglobal, a development of the earlier Auto-ID Center, is one of the two primary RFID standards setting groups. It proposed an Internet-based supply chain model that is aimed at improving supply chain end-to-end efficiency. A key component of the EPCglobal model is the Electronic Product Code or EPC. The manufacturer adds an RFID tag to every

Figure 4. Important parts of an RFID system (based on Roberts, 2006)

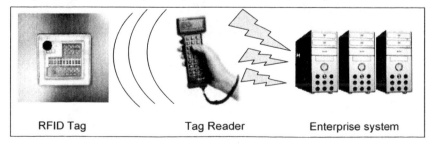

| RFID Tag | Tag Reader | Enterprise system |

item of its product line. Each tag contains a unique EPC, which is a 96-bit code that uniquely identifies objects (items, cases, pallets, locations) in the supply chain (EPCglobal, 2005).

APPLICATION OF MOBILE TECHNOLOGY IN SUPPLY CHAIN MANAGEMENT

Based on the literature surveyed so far, there appears to be a gap between what is considered traditional SCM, electronic SCM, and the potential offered by mobile SCM. The major gap in the current literature in the SCM domain appears to be a lack of discussion between the two types of commerce and, in particular, the value derived from the ability of mobility to provide time and location independence. As shown in Figure 5, SCM can be extended to the e-commerce environment and at the same time it can also be extended to M-SCM. However, there is also a potential, as again shown in Figure 5, for E-SCM to be extended to M-SCM. These are some of the important aspects of SCM systems studied in this chapter.

E-Supply Chain Management

E-commerce deals with a combination of hardware technologies, software applications, and changes to business processes and appropriate customer strategies. E-SCM can enable customers to use electronic connections to obtain the information and associated services from the organization's supply chain system. The objective of E-SCM is to understand customer demographics, purchasing patterns, inventories, orders, and order fulfillments, in order to enable customer satisfaction and creation of new business opportunities (Arunatileka & Unhelkar, 2003). E-commerce provides the basis for much more efficient supply chains that can benefit both customers and manufacturers. This is because e-commerce, through connectivity, brings together various parties involved in commercial transactions. In today's environment, customers are less forgiving of poor customer service and more demanding of customized products or services. As the competition continues to introduce new offerings modified to the special needs of different market sectors, companies have to respond by offering similar custom-made and highly personalized offerings. The ensuing production of various goods and services for multiple countries, customer sections, and distribution exits creates major challenges in forecast, inventory management, production planning, and after-sales service support. Internet-based E-SCM systems bring the companies a competitive advantage by opening up opportunities to streamline processes, reduce costs, increase customer satisfaction, and

Table 1. Mobile technology application comparison table

Mobile Technology	Functions and Applications
3G Mobile Network	• Application: mobile phone device • Higher transmission rate • Popular used and high marketing acceptance
Mobile Satellite	• Application: GPS device and Internet phone (Voice over IP–VoIP) • Space technology • Direction finding and map reading
Infrared	• Application: remote controller • Communication in short distance • Low cost
Bluetooth	• Application: Bluetooth device • Synchronization • Transfers data between a PC server and one or more other mobile device(s)
WiMAX	• Wireless online in urban areas by using mobile device or any computer
WLAN (Wireless Local Area Network)	• Wireless link PC or mobile device network connection in particular surrounding area
RFID (Radio Frequency Identification)	• Application: RFID tag and reader • Product tracking and controlling by automatically updating the RFID tag location through RFID reader

Figure 5. SCM to E-SCM and M-SCM

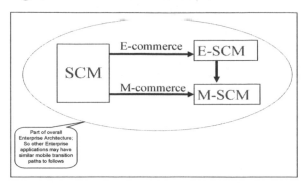

make possible thorough planning abilities (Unhelkar & Lan, 2006).

The supply-chain e-business model creates a virtual value chain, and information flows across the supply chain. All members of the supply chain have strong electronic systems, and the information sharing to the customer is very effective in the ordering process, product delivery, and other SCM issues (Arunatileka & Arunatileka, 2003).

The e-supply chain is a pull model; in a pull-based supply chain, production and distribution are demand driven so that they are coordinated with true customer demand rather than forecasted demand. This is enabled by fast information flow mechanisms to transfer customer demands to the various supply chain participants. This leads to a significant reduction in inventory costs and enhanced ability to control materials when comparing this to the equivalent push-based system (Levi, Kaminsky, & Levi, 2003).

M-Supply Chain Management

In the 21st century, we are in the era of wireless and handheld technologies, and the impact of the Internet and wireless telecommunication has taken a new turn (Barnes, 2002). Mobile technologies are at the core of the communication revolution. They have increased commercial efforts from the removal of physical connectivity for people, processes, and businesses, resulting in a significant impact on communication. Therefore, mobile devices can also be used to optimize the flow of information and materials. An increased number of mobile work-

ers and time sensitivity drive companies towards advanced mobile solutions.

Paavilainen (2001) highlights that the solutions of supply chain management systems are highly time sensitive. The requirement of the time sensitiveness is that SCM systems must have the ability to transact products as close to real time as possible—opening up opportunities for the application of mobile technologies. By incorporating mobility in the SCM system processes, monitoring and receiving of immediate messages from the market can be improved. M-supply chain management focuses on the shortened cycle time from making an order to the fulfillment of that order—which, in most cases, would be delivery of the product to the customer. With mobility, response and confirmation time are much quicker than with the use of the standard Internet connections. Automatic data-reading and updating can be accessed from any mobile devices without the restriction of time and place. Traffic control systems (GPRSs) can be used to deliver products in the supply chain, and also automatically detect the products and report cars' and trucks' locations.

Eng (2005) declares that three main concerns of M-SCM are:

1. a place for efficient distribution of products and services,
2. timing for meeting customer demand and managing logistics, and
3. service quality for responsiveness and customer satisfaction.

In Figure 6, the M-SCM architecture is divided into four parts—the RFID system, SCM system, e-commerce, and m-commerce—and as proposed by us is an extension to the original ideas of Ngai et al. (2005). They state that RFID technology can be integrated with wireless networks to send information to a supply chain management system through a portal to staff, customers, and partners. We define that M-SCM refers to integrating the RFID system, e-commerce, and m-commerce through the Internet portal and ICT communication into a supply chain management system in a mobile environment. Moreover, we declare the RFID system's contents and supply chain management system's contents, and how e-commerce and m-commerce will integrate the SCM through the portal.

The RFID system typically integrates RFID tags, readers, and the host system that will store the received tag information in the data center. After the database analysis process inside the data center, information will be transferred from the RFID tag of each product to each company's enterprise SCM system.

The comprehensive supply chain management system can be an integration of a customer relationship management system, supplier relationship management system, order/purchasing (financial) system, delivery products (logistics) management system, and time management system.

The e-commerce and m-commerce parts show how the communication can occur among customers, staff of enterprises, suppliers, and other supply chain management members to the SCM system. People can use e-mail via the Web to an Internet Web portal to access the SCM system to get information or conduct e-commerce. In addition, they also can use SMS via a mobile device to a mobile portal or SMS gateway to access the SCM system to get information or carry out m-commerce.

The aforementioned model can also be used to understand how existing supply chain processes transfer to incorporate mobility in them. These can be called "m-transformation of SCM" processes. When a company already has the supply chain management system in its enterprise architecture, we can help it add a mobile system and set up the Internet portal with ICT communication devices to upgrade the SCM to M-SCM. In M-SCM, the cooperation of real-time processes by using mobile technology applications provides a stable workflow of up-to-date information from both inside and outside the company. Mobile supply chain applications can also allow users to request information and conduct "ubiquity"—whatever they want, whenever they want it, wherever they want it, and how they want it.

INVESTIGATION INTO ADVANTAGE AND LIMITATION OF MOBILITY IN SCM

The traditional supply chain is a push model. However, the E-SCM and the M-SCM models that we are discussing in this chapter can be considered as pull models. Table 2 depicts the comparison of characteristics between the push and pull models of the supply chain, based on various factors.

Figure 6. Architecture of M-SCM systems (this model is proposed by these researchers as an extension to the original ideas of Ngai et al., 2005)

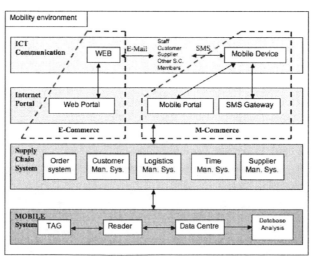

From Table 2, Levi et al. (2003) are quite clear in stating that traditional SCM focuses on reducing the cost and recording the location of products into the system. The information flow is based on a push model. As such, the traditional SCM process undergoes a long cycle, and the process time cannot be easily estimated. E-SCM focuses on customer service, and the process is totally based on responding to customers' orders and requirements. Every member of the supply chain can access the information flow from the E-SCM system at any time if they want to track it. Thus, E-SCM can be said to follow the "pull model" of information; it shortens the product cycle and lowers complexity compared with the traditional SCM (push model). The M-SCM can also be said to follow the "pull model," wherein information is extracted from the system when desired by the user.

Both E-SCM and M-SCM provide 24-hour information access, accurate and fast billing, less paperwork/fewer duplicated processes, on-site technical support, and trouble-shooting databases. However, in E-SCM, the users of the supply chain can only access the information of SCM when they connect to the Internet. It is limited by the location, in that members still need to sit inside the office to plug in their computers. M-SCM members can access the system at any time and anywhere by using mobile tools with a satellite connection. This brings huge benefits to people with a more convenient and comfortable environment to increase efficiency in their part of the value chain.

Following, we would like to list the advantages and limitations of mobility in SCM.

Advantages

The M-SCM system provides real-time data that can be accessed after logging into the system (Eng, 2005). Batten and Savage (2006) highlight that M-SCM will eliminate considerable duplication of data entry through simplified automated order placement, order status inquiries, delivery shipment, and invoicing. Mobility goes through data entry when it is created to reduce paperwork, document tracking, and human error. It also brings security control. The M-SCM system shortens the organization planning and production cycles, establishes one central data repository for the entire organization, and facilitates enhanced communications through all supply chain members communicating with each other by mobility (Paavilainen, 2001). Moreover, the M-SCM allows all users to request information, place orders for whatever they want, whenever they want it, wherever they want it, and how they want it.

The investigation of mobile technology application into the supply chain systems will bring benefits to all members of the supply chain, which includes suppliers, manufacturers, distributors, retailers, and customers.

Suppliers: The M-SCM system reduces paperwork, the number of administrative employees, and inventory costs, so the company reduces the cost of the products and brings in more customers as well as retaining its present customers. It also brings increased financial incomes to the suppliers (Unhelkar & Lan, 2006).

The RFID system stores the product contents when these have been acquired. When the product is about to expire, all details are contained in each RFID tag for each item. This can help suppliers to quickly obtain the information they need, simply by scanning the RFID tag once only. Also, this can help the suppliers to forecast the schedule arrangements to process the materials and prevent materials from expiring.

Table 2. Push and pull model of SCM (Levi et al., 2003, p. 127)

Portion	Push	Pull
Objective	Minimize cost	Maximize service level
Complexity	High	Low
Focus	Resource allocation	Responsiveness
Lead Time	Long	Short
Processes	Supply chain planning	Order fulfillment

Manufacturers: The M-SCM systems can provide the organization with shorter planning and production cycles, and establish one central data repository for the entire organization. Then manufacturers will know the amounts they need to produce, and save money on the products that nobody buys.

RFID has been used in manufacturing to identify items or groups of items, express production procedures, and ensure the correct product quality. It helps that the right materials arrive at the right place, and nothing will be lost (Duckworth, 2004).

Distributors: The M-SCM system ensures quicker time-to-market for the firm's products, provides the retailer with enough stock, and also reduces excessive stocks in the distribution center. A traffic control system can be used as a GPRS to deliver goods to customers/retailers, and also automatically detect control and report locations of cars and trucks.

RFID identifies the distributed items stored inside the containers or trucks, and helps the delivery process to be 100% correct to deliver the right items to the right place at the right time. It has been reported that the RFID program can estimate the need for physical cycle counting, saving companies hundreds of employee hours and days of down time (Mullen & Moore, 2006).

Retailers: No data need to be re-entered into the M-SCM system through the simplified automatic order placement, order status inquiries, delivery shipment, and invoicing. The RFID system processes automatic data-reading and reporting to the supply chain system of the products' location (Wyld, 2006).

The RFID system is also very useful in maintaining enough stock levels in retailers (Carayannis, 2004). It has the ability to automatically record sales, check inventories, and refill or order additional stock in order to reduce the amount of inventory. Some food or items with limited time span can be notified by the system to guarantee retailers having fresh products on the shelves all the time. In addition, it has been proven to reduce theft from the retailers' shelves during the product delivery process in the supply chain. Loss avoidance directly benefits the retailers by minimizing costs and improving selections (Mullen & Moore, 2006).

Customers: The M-SCM system improves customer service substantially by efficient distribution of products and service, timing for meeting customer demands and logistics managing, and service quality for responsiveness and customer satisfaction. It improves the firm's ability to attract new customers and also retain its original customers (Unhelkar & Lan, 2006).

Customers can access information about products via mobile gadgets, and also place/check their orders and pay their bills in the M-SCM system by mobility (Mei, 2004). The M-SCM also allows customers to enquire for information and purchase any products at any time, anywhere, by any method.

Limitations

Supply Chain Integration and strategic partnering: The limitation that has existed in traditional supply chain integration is "reliance and trust" among the partners (other supply chain members) in this mechanism. This is because when the supply chain system integrates all companies in the supply chain, the members need to consider how much information they should announce to other members. Moreover, the more information a company can share, the greater the efficiency and effectiveness of the system. Nevertheless, the company members of the supply chain depend on other members' reliance and trust to share the information. So, this is the critical limitation of the original supply chain integration.

Cost of M-SCM system and facilities implementation: When the companies in the supply chain want to install M-SCM systems in their companies, the cost of systems and facilities during the establishment period is an essential consideration. They need to prepare the project fee at the beginning, but this is not a small amount, and it is the reason why the companies in the supply chain always find it difficult to make decisions to implement the M-SCM system.

Different countries develop mobility at different levels—the Internet speed, WLAN population: As we mentioned earlier, the companies of a supply chain may not be only in one country. Different countries may develop mobile technology at different levels. Some countries are not able to provide wireless local area networks, and can only provide dial-up Internet speeds. In other words, there are many limitations for those companies that want to use the M-SCM systems in the whole supply chain.

Security and privacy issues: Sheng (2006) points out that the issue of security and privacy is indeed a great concern, especially when the members of a supply chain make payments by the m-payment system. The qualifications of any system to provide secure data transfer are regarded as an important standard for both existing and potential users of m-payment systems. The personal privacy of customer information is a major concern to the customer who is deciding whether to use the system or not.

Companies need to change their business process: When the members of a supply chain decide to install the M-SCM systems in their supply chain management system, the current business processes may not be available or suitable to use all the time. The system development team needs to go through the original business processes to modify the new business processes suitable for the M-SCM system users. Therefore, after the system implementation in the companies, the system team needs to prepare a training class for employees regarding the business processes change and the new system utilization in the future.

BENEFITS OF MOBILITY TO THE ENTERPRISE ARCHITECTURE

Enterprise architecture represents a technology-business philosophy that provides the basis for cooperation between various systems of the organization that could be inside or outside the organizational boundary. EA also facilitates the ability to share data and information with business partners by enabling their applications to "talk" with each other. Linthicum (2000) pointed out that many organizations would like to build their entire systems by using the emerging technologies of today, of which mobile technology is a crucial part. Using mobile devices in enterprise modeling can help real-time information access among systems, in production planning and control, inbound and outbound logistics, material flows, monitoring functions, and performance measurements (Rolstadas & Andersen, 2000).

According to Ghanbary (2006), by correct application of mobile technologies into the business processes, the business enterprises are likely to gain advantages such as increased profits, satisfied customers, and greater customer loyalty. These customer-related advantages will accrue only when the organization investigates its customer behavior in the context of the mobile environment.

It is very important to identify that not many organizations have existing mobile solutions. Umar (2005) states that next-generation enterprises (NGEs) rely on automation, mobility, real-time business activity monitoring, agility, and self-service over widely distributed operations to conduct business. Mobility is one of the most invigorating features, having an enormous impact on how communication is evolving into the future.

Enterprise application integration is a relevant approach to integrating core business processes and data processing in the organization. Lee, Siau, and Hong (2003) state that EAI automates the integration process with less effort. EAI is a business computing term for plans, methods, and tools aimed at modernizing, consolidating, and coordinating the overall computer functionality in an enterprise. With new achievements in information technologies, companies are vulnerable if they do not respond to technologies such as mobile technology in a fast and appropriate manner.

BENEFITS OF MOBILITY TO THE GLOBAL ENTERPRISE

In this globalization era, many enterprises in a supply chain are located in different countries. Enterprises in some countries can provide low labor costs, and some in different countries may have low material costs, or others in different countries may provide professional skills or ideas about product design. However, all enterprises want to sell their product globally. The resultant ability of businesses and customers to connect to each other ubiquitously—independent of time and location—is the core driver of this change (Unhelkar, 2005). It leads the supply chain management to global supply chain management. Mobile technologies are thus a key influence in any efforts towards the globalization of business (Unhelkar, 2004). The processes of such m-transformation can lead an existing business into the mobile business via the adoption of suitable processes and technologies that enable mobility and pervasiveness (Marmaridis & Unhelkar, 2005).

M-SCM can further enhance the global SCM by reducing timing and cost, increasing correct delivery and customer satisfaction, and allowing global enterprises to conduct their business at any time and anywhere. Long (2003) pointed out that international logistics management focuses on international ship delivery schedule management, time, place, and product quality management.

An M-SCM system covers from planning, purchase, and production, to delivery to the customer. Mobile technology raises global enterprises to a much higher level of efficiency and effectiveness. Global enterprises can conduct their business at any time and anywhere, and provide high-quality products at low cost, and also support customer service 24 hours a day, seven days a week, by using an M-SCM system.

COLLABORATIVE SUPPLY CHAIN MANAGEMENT IN AN ENTERPRISE ARCHITECTURE

Electronic collaboration has been studied and experimented on by many studies. In electronic collaboration, there has been ample focus on the effects of dynamic environment and the rapidly evolving technology on organizations. Undoubtedly, these changes cause organizations to restructure and introduce a new suite of business processes to enable them to collaborate with the business processes of other organizations.

There are some critical technological issues that could cause drawbacks in collaboration across multiple SCM organizations. These issues could be classified as collaborations between different platforms, managing technology and maintenance (hardware/software). Web services technology is the solution for the collaboration of applications on different platforms, also independent of their different environments.

The electronic collaboration of the business processes of different SCM organizations is causing many practical issues. These issues are as follows:

- The excess inventory and inefficiencies in the supply chain while different organizations are involved.
- Requesting information by understanding the specific organization's capability to handle the request.
- Collaboration can reduce waste in the supply chain, but can also increase market sensitivity and increase customer expectation.
- Customer satisfaction, which is directly related to the previous issue, as customers expect more.
- Competition among all members of the partnership.

As such, the SCM must also address the following problems:

- **Distribution network configuration:** Number and location of suppliers, production facilities, distribution centers, warehouses, and customers.
- **Distribution strategy:** Centralized vs. decentralized, direct shipment, cross-docking, pull or push strategies, third-party logistics.
- **Information:** Integrate systems and processes through the supply chain to share valuable information, including demand signals, forecasts, inventory, and transportation.
- **Inventory management:** Quantity and location of inventory including raw materials, work-in-process, and finished goods.

Collaboration should be taking place in order to make sure that all parties involved in the collaboration are satisfied. In the past, collaboration was inadequate, with retailers hesitant to share information with others; however, the technology is capable of providing more support for the collaboration. Based on Horvath (2001), collaboration requires individual participants to adopt simplified, standardized solutions based on common architectures and data models. The time to market is critical, and participants will have to forego the luxuries of customization and modification that characterized the proprietary infrastructures of the past.

CONCLUSION AND FUTURE RESEARCH DIRECTIONS

The chapter has introduced enterprise application integration as a part of a comprehensive enterprise model, followed by a discussion of supply chain management systems in the context of the EM. The traditional supply chain management system and investigation of the opportunities to integrate specific mobile technologies (such as 3G mobile network, mobile satellite network, Infrared, Bluetooth, WiMAX, and WLAN) with supply chain management systems have also been discussed. This chapter has further considered the advantages and limitations of such integration. The discussions in this chapter are important for understanding how and where mobile technologies fit into the overall concept of the enterprise architecture. The discussion on the collaborative nature of Web services and the ability of supply chain systems to capitalize on the connectivity of Web services is also important for globalization and appears in the global supply chain management system.

The aim of this discussion is to provide a solid theoretical basis for future research direction by the authors in the area of mobility and its incorporation in an organization's systems and architecture. Therefore, this chapter is a door opening to further research in the areas of mobile technologies in "enterprise architecture" and "SCM systems." The authors have provided more details of mobility SCM systems—actually enterprise architecture based

on contributing the integration of all the enterprise information systems. Our research is opening opportunities to future research in the area of investigating how mobile technologies influence integrating other systems of enterprise architecture such as enterprise resource planning, customer relationship management, customer order control and planning, material requirement planning, financial accounting, and so on. The team members of our group (MIRAG of AeIMS of UWS) are also investigating mobility influences on business process reengineering, Web services, and project planning. In addition, we still investigate our research into how and what should be included on contributing the comprehensive mobility enterprise architecture (M-EA) model.

REFERENCES

Arunatileka, S., & Arunatileka, D. (2003). E-transformation as a strategic tool for SMEs in developing nations. In *Proceedings of the International Conference on E-Government 2003,* New Delhi, India.

Arunatileka, D., & Unhelkar, B. (2003). Mobile technologies, providing new possibilities in customer relationship management. In *Proceedings of the 5th International Information Technology Conference,* Colombo, Sri Lanka.

Asif, Z., & Mandviwalla, M. (2005). Integrating the supply chain with RFID: An in-depth technical and business analysis. *Communications of the Association for Information Systems, 15,* 393-427.

Barnes, S.J. (2002). The mobile commerce value chain: Analysis and future development. *International Journal of Information Management, 22*(2), 91-108.

Batten, L.M., & Savage, R. (2006). Information sharing in supply chain systems. In Y.U. Lan (Ed.), *Global integrated supply chain systems* (ch. 5). London: Idea Group.

Brathaug, T.A., & Evjen, T.A. (1996). *Enterprise modeling.* Trondheim: SINTEF.

Burness, L., Higgins, D., Sago, A., & Thorpe, P. (2004). Wireless LANs—present and future. In

Mobile and wireless communications: Key technologies and future application (ch. 3). British Telecommunications.

Burt, D.N., Dobler, D.W., & Starling, S.L. (2003). *World class supply management: The key to supply chain management* (7th ed.). Boston: McGraw-Hill/Irwin.

Buttery, S., & Sago, A. (2004). Future application of Bluetooth. In *Mobile and wireless communications: Key technologies and future application* (ch. 4). British Telecommunications.

Carayannis, J.P. (2004, July). *RFID-enabled supply chain replenishment*. Cambridge: MIT.

Dong, M. (2001). *Process modeling, performance analysis and configuration simulation in integrated supply chain network design*. Faculty of the Virginia Polytechnic Institute and State University, USA.

Doumeingts, G., Ducq, Y., & Kleinhans, S. (2000, August 21-25). Enterprise modeling techniques in year 2000. *Proceedings of ITBM 2000, IFIP 16th World Computer Congress*, Beijing, China.

Duckworth, D.A. (2004). *Potential for utilization of RFID in the semiconductor manufacturing intermediate supply chain*. Cambridge: MIT.

Elliott, G., & Phillips, N. (2003). *Mobile commerce and wireless computing systems*. Boston: Addison-Wesley.

Eng, T.Y. (2005). *Mobile supply chain management: Challenges for implementation*. Elsevier.

EPCglobal. (2005). *Homepage*. Retrieved March 21, 2006, from http://www.epcglobalinc.org/

Finkelstein, C. (2006). *Enterprise architecture for integration: Rapid delivery methods and technologies*. Artech House.

Fitch, M. (2004). The use of satellite for multimedia communications. In *Mobile and wireless communications: Key technologies and future application* (ch.10). British Telecommunications.

Ghanbary, A. (2006). Evaluation of mobile technologies in the context of their applications, limitations and transformation. In B. Unhelkar (Ed.), *Mobile business: Technological, methodological and social perspectives*. Hershey, PA: Idea Group.

Horvath, L. (2001). *Collaboration: The key to value creation in supply chain management*. Retrieved October 12, 2006, from http://www.emeraldinsight.com/Insight/ViewContentServlet?Filename=Published/EmeraldFullTextArticle/Articles/1770060501.html

Huber, J.F. (2002). Towards the mobile Internet. *Communications of the ACM*, (October).

IBM. (n.d.) *IBM new to wireless technology*. Retrieved February 22, 2006, from http://www-128.ibm.com/developerworks/wireless/newto/#1

Irani, Z., Themistocleous, M., & Love, P.E.D. (2002). The impact of enterprise application integration on information system lifecycles. *Information and Management, 41*, 177-187.

ITU Radio Regulation. (2001). *Frequency allocation* (vol. 1, article 5). ITU.

Kamogawa, T., & Okada, H. (2004). Issues of e-business implementation from enterprise architecture viewpoint. *Proceedings of the 2004 International Symposium on Applications and the Internet Workshops* (SAINTW'04).

Kuo, Y.F., & Yu, C.W. (2005). *3G telecommunication operators' challenges and roles: A perspective of mobile commerce value chain*. Elsevier.

Lee, H.L. (2000, January). *Supply chain management review*. School of Engineering, Stanford University, USA.

Lee, J., Siau, K., & Hong, S. (2003). Enterprise integration with ERP and EAI. *Communications of the ACM, 46*(2).

Levi, D.S, Kaminsky, P., & Levi, E.S. (2003). *Designing and managing the supply chain: Concepts, strategies and case studies* (2nd ed.). New York: McGraw-Hill.

Linthicum, D.S. (2000). *Enterprise application integration*. Boston: Addison-Wesley.

Long, D. (2003). *International logistics global supply chain management*. Boston: Kluwer Academic.

Marmaridis, I., & Unhelkar, B. (2005). Challenges in mobile transformations: A requirements modeling perspective for small and medium enterprises (SMEs). *Proceedings of the M-Business International Conference,* Sydney, Australia.

Mei, Q.R. (2004). *RFID impact supply chain: Innovation in demand planning and customer fulfillment.* Cambridge: MIT.

Mullen, D., & Moore, B. (2006). Automatic identification and data collection. In *RFID: Applications, security, and privacy* (ch. 1). Boston: Addison-Wesley Pearson Education.

Ngai, E.W.T., Cheng, T.C.E., Au, S., & Lai, K.H. (2005). *Mobile commerce integrated with RFID technology in a container depot.* Elsevier.

Ohrtman, F. (2005). *WiMAX handbook: Building 802.16 wireless networks.* New York: McGraw-Hill.

Okuhata, H., Uno, H., Kumatani, K., Shirakawa, I., & Chiba, T. (1997). 4MBPS infrared wireless link dedicated to mobile computing. *IEEE,* 463-467.

Olla, P. (2005). *Incorporating commercial space technology into mobile services: Developing innovative business models.* Hershey, PA: Idea Group.

Paavilainen, J. (2001). *Mobile business strategies: Understanding the technologies and opportunities.* Wireless Press.

Poirier, C.C. (1999). *Advanced supply chain management: How to build a sustained competitive advantage* (1st ed.). Berrett-Koehler.

Pulkkinen, M. (2006). Systemic management of architectural decisions in enterprise architecture planning. Four dimensions and three abstraction levels. *Proceedings of the 39th Hawaii International Conference on System Sciences.*

Roberts, C.M. (2006). Radio frequency identification. *Computers Security, 25,* 18-26.

Rolstadas, A., & Andersen, B. (2000). *Enterprise modeling improving global industrial competitiveness.* Kluwer Academic.

Scheniderman, R. (2002). *The mobile technology question and answer book.* Amacom.

Sheng, M.L. (2006). Global integrated supply chain implementation: The challenges of e-procurement. In Y.U. Lan (Ed.), *Global integrated supply chain systems* (ch. 6). London: Idea Group.

Umar, A. (2005). IT infrastructure to enable next generation enterprises. *Information Systems Frontiers, 7*(3).

Unhelkar, B. (2004). Globalization with mobility. *Proceedings of ADCOM 2004, the 12th International Conference on Advanced Computing and Communications,* Ahmedabad, India.

Unhelkar, B. (2005). Transitioning to a mobile enterprise: A three-dimensional framework. *Cutter IT Journal, 18*(8).

Unhelkar, B., & Lan, Y.C. (2006). A methodology for developing an integrated supply chain management system. In Y.U. Lan (Ed.), *Global integrated supply chain systems* (ch. 1). London: Idea Group.

WiMAX Forum. (2006). *Frequently asked questions.* Retrieved from http://www.wimaxforum.org/technology/faq

Wyld, D.C. (2006). The next big RFID application: Correctly steering two billion bags a year through today's less-than-friendly skies. In *Handbook of research in mobile business: Technical, methodological and social perspectives* (ch. 54). Hershey, PA: Idea Group.

ADDITIONAL READING

Anckar, B., & D'Incau, D. (2002). Value added services in mobile commerce: An analytical framework and empirical findings from a national consumer survey. *Proceedings of the 35th Hawaii International Conference on System Sciences.*

Basole, R.C. (2004). *The value and impact of mobile information and communication technologies.* Atlanta: Georgia Institute of Technology.

Basole, R.C. (2005). Transforming enterprises through mobile applications: A multi-phase framework. *Proceedings of the 11th America's Conference on Information Systems,* Omaha, NE.

Bernard, H.B. (1999). *Constructing blueprints for enterprise IT architectures.* Wiley Computer.

Carbine, J.A. (2004). *IT architecture toolkit.* Englewood Cliffs, NJ: Prentice Hall.

Chopra, S., & Meindl, P. (2007). *Supply chain management: Strategy, planning & operation* (3rd ed.). Englewood Cliffs, NJ: Pernson Prentice-Hall.

Cook, M.A. (1996). *Building enterprise information architectures reengineering information systems.* Englewood Cliffs, NJ: Prentice Hall.

Cummins, F.A. (2002). *Enterprise integration: An architecture for enterprise application and systems integration.* Wiley Computing.

Dimitris, C.N. (2001). *Integrating ERP, CRM, SCM, and smart materials.* Boca Raton.

Eckfeldt, B. (2005). What does RFID do for the consumer? *Communications of the ACM, 48*(9).

Er, M., & Kay, R. (2005). Mobile technology adoption for mobile information systems: An activity theory perspective. *Proceedings of ICMB'05,* Sydney, Australia.

Garfinkel, S., & Rosenberge, B. (2006). *RFID: Applications, security, and privacy.* Boston: Addison-Wesley Pearson Education.

Gattorna, J.L., & Walters, D.W. (1996). *Managing the supply chain: A strategy perspective.* Palgrave.

Gershman, A. (2002). Ubiquitous commerce—always on, always aware, always pro-active. *Proceedings of the 2002 Symposium on Applications and the Internet.*

Guitton, A. (2004). *The value of RFID in transportation: from greater operational efficiency to collaboration transportation management.* Cambridge: MIT.

Hammer, M., & Champy, J. (2001). *Reengineering the corporation: A manifesto for business revolution.* London: Nicholas Brealey.

Hawryszkiewycz, I., & Steele, R. (2005). A framework for integrating mobility into collaborative business processes. *Proceedings of the International Conference on Mobile Business.*

Hoque, F. (2000). *E-enterprise: Business models, architecture, and components.* Cambridge: Cambridge University Press.

Jarvenpaa, S.L., Lang, K.R., Takeda, Y., & Tuunainen, K. (2003). Mobile commerce at crossroads. *Communications of the ACM, 46*(12), 41-44.

Kalakota, R., & Robinson, M. (2001). *E-business 2.0: Roadmap for success.* Boston: Addison-Wesley.

Knolmayer, G., Mertens, P., & Zeier, A. (2002). *Supply chain management based on SAP systems.* Springer.

Kou, W., & Yesha, Y. (Eds.). (2006). *Enabling technologies for wireless e-business.* Berlin/Heidelberg: Springer-Verlag.

Lan, Y., & Unhelkar, B. (2005). *Global enterprise transitions: Managing the process.* Hershey, PA: Idea Group.

Lyytinen, K., & Yoo, Y. (2002). Issues and challenges in ubiquitous computing. *Communications of the ACM, 45*(12), 62-65.

May, P. (2001). *Mobile commerce: Opportunities, applications, and technologies of wireless business.* Cambridge: Cambridge University Press.

Medvidovic, N., Mikic-Rakic, M., Mehta, N.R., & Malek, S. (2003). Software architectural support for handheld computing. *Computer, 36*(9), 66-73.

Murugesan, S., & Unhelkar, B. (2004). A road map for successful ICT innovation: Turning great ideas into successful implementations. *Cutter IT Journal, 17*(11), 5-12.

Myerson, J.M. (2005). *RFID in the supply chain: A guide to selection and implementation.* CRC Press.

Passerini, K., & Patten, K. (2005). Preparing IT organizations for the mobile revolution. *Cutter IT Journal, 18*(8), 19-27.

Ptak, C.A. (2000). *ERP: Tools, techniques, and applications for integrating the supply chain.* Boca Raton, FL: St. Lucie Press.

Raisinghani, M., & Taylor, D. (2006). Going global: A technology review. In Y.U. Lan (Ed.), *Global integrated supply chain systems.* London: Idea Group.

Rao, B., & Minakakis, L. (2003). Evolution of mobile location-based services. *Communications of the ACM, 46*(12), 61-65.

Sandoe, K., Cornitt, G., & Boykin, R. (2001). *Enterprise integration.* New York: John Wiley & Sons.

Senn, J.A. (2000). The emergence of m-commerce. *Computer, 33*(12), 148-150.

Sharif, A.M., Elliman, T., Love, P.E.D., & Badii, A. (2004). Integrating the IS with the enterprise: Key EAI research challenges. *Journal of Enterprise Information Management, 17*(2), 164-170.

Spewak, S.H., & Hill, S.C. (1992). *Enterprise architecture planning: Developing a bluepoint for data, applications, and technology.* New York: John Wiley & Sons.

Sun, J. (2003). Information requirement: Elicitation in mobile commerce. *Communications of the ACM, 46*(12), 45-47.

Unhelkar, B. (2004). Paradigm shift in the process of electronic globalization of businesses resulting from the impact of Web services based technologies. *Proceedings of IRMA 2004.*

Unhelkar, B. (Ed.). (2006). *Handbook of research in mobile business: Technical, methodological and social perspectives.* Hershey, PA: Idea Group Reference.

Urbaczewski, A., Valacich, J.S., Jessup, L.M., & Guest Editors. (2003). Mobile commerce: Opportunities and challenges. *Communications of the ACM, 46*(12), 30-32.

Varshney, U. (2000). Recent advances in wireless networking. *Computer, 33*(6), 100-103.

Varshney, U. (2003). The status and future of 802.11-based WLANs. *Computer, 36*(6), 102-105.

Varshney, U., & Vetter, R. (2002). Mobile commerce: Framework, applications and networking support. *Mobile Networks and Applications,* 185-198.

Vaughan-Nichols, S.J. (2003). Mobile IPv6 and the future of wireless Internet access. *Computer, 36*(2), 18-20.

Wang, Y., Van der Kar, E., Meijer, G., & Hunteler, M. (2005). Improving business processes with mobile workforce solutions. *Proceedings of the International Conference on Mobile Business,* Sydney, Australia.

Weilenmann, A. (2003). *Doing mobility.* Goteborg University, Sweden.

Wisner, J.D., Leong, G.K., & Tank, C. (2005). *Principles of supply chain management: A balanced approach.* Thomson South-Western.

Chapter XXIV
Influence of Mobile Technologies on Global Business Processes in Global Organizations

Dinesh Arunatileka
University of Western Sydney, Australia

Abbass Ghanbary
University of Western Sydney, Australia

Bhuvan Unhelkar
University of Western Sydney, Australia

ABSTRACT

Organizations are globalizing their business primarily due to the communications capabilities offered by Internet technologies. As a result, there are global business processes that span across multiple geographical locations and time zones. The influence of mobility on these global business processes does not appear to have been studied in sufficient detail. Furthermore, mobile technology goes far beyond its ubiquitous use as a mobile phone for voice communication or for the exchange of messages. This chapter discusses and recommends a model for transition and integration of mobility into global business processes. We also envisage the accommodation of mobile Web services in mobile transformations enabling business applications to collaborate regardless of their technological platforms.

INTRODUCTION

Technology has changed the way people and businesses communicate with each other. Information and communications technology (ICT) has made a big leap in communications in the previous decade. With the communications backbone of the Internet, ICT has influenced the very way of life for many people and organizations. As a result, the method and manner in which the organizations carry out their businesses have also changed. Ubiquity of business processes, as per Arunatileka (2006), is likely to play a major role in future business environments. This ubiquity is a result of organizations starting to collaborate electronically, paving way for collaborative global businesses, resulting in significant strategic advantages to these organizations. These advantages include business growth in the global market, and building strategic alliances and partnerships for business organizations (Arunatileka & Arunatileka, 2003). However, when it comes to extending and applying the concepts of collaboration through time- and location-independent mobile technologies, it appears that organizations are still relatively nascent. The paucity of literature in this regard provided us with the necessary impetus to study mobile technologies from the point of view of their application in global businesses.

This chapter accomplishes our aim of studying and applying mobility to global business processes. This chapter also reports on construction and application of corresponding models to enable mobile transformations (m-transformations). The lead author of this chapter has also validated and applied these models through "action research" at a real global organization. This well-thought-out application of mobility resulted in streamlining and speeding up of the existing processes, as well as exploration and creation of totally new business processes within that global organization.

Mobile Technology

The advancement of mobile technologies has created the opportunity for organizations to adapt this technology in their business processes. Per Schneiderman (2002), faster access to the corporate database and new applications that embody wireless and Internet connectivity are two great advantages that organizations can develop in terms of their business operations. The usage of mobile devices in the modern era is so important that their incorporation in business processes can be classified as one of the crucial factors in the survival and prosperity of a business. Birchler (2004) clearly points out that the exponential growth of

the Internet has challenged the prevailing understanding of network organizations and ownership. Therefore mobility, combined with the Internet, provides organizations with a powerful tool to be used strategically for connections in the electronic business world. Deshpande, Murugesan, Unhelkar, and Arunatileka (2004) describe the requirement of delivering the Web in a single composite device; their vision, under the auspices of the Device Independent Web Engineering (DIWE) Group, is to make the Web accessible to "anyone, anywhere, anytime, anyhow."

The use of portable computing through communications devices is forcing the reappraisal of the capabilities and future of wireless. In today's competitive markets, mobile technology is providing person-to-person communication, resulting in a new era of customer relationship management for organizations (Arunatileka & Unhelkar, 2003). Mobility, in the context of businesses, can be understood as the ability of processes to be executed anywhere and at anytime. Mobile technology encompasses the various devices and applications that have been put together to provide organizations and individuals with the ability to conduct businesses as per the DIWE vision mentioned earlier.

This study started with observing daily business activities of a global organization in order to ascertain how m-transformation could enhance their business processes. These processes were then modeled using the activity diagrams of the unified modeling language (www.omg.org). This modeling was followed by "re-engineering" of the business processes based on the theoretical m-transformation models formulated by the researchers. Thereafter, two selected business processes related to "timesheets" were transformed into mobile-enabled processes. The following sections describe the research problem and the approach taken in solving it in greater detail.

THE RESEARCH PROBLEM

The research problem was formulated to understand whether m-transformation of certain business processes of the company would result in improved efficiency and productivity. The initial effort was to identify such candidate business processes which could undergo m-transformation. Thereafter those processes were to be transformed using the theoretical model of m-transformation. Once the m-transformed processes are integrated into the mainstream of business processes, their functionality was to be further observed in order to achieve a smooth flow of business processes. Advantages and challenges in terms of this m-transformation were also to be studied, in order to improve and validate the model.

There were two processes that were identified as the potential processes for improvement. This identification was done in consultation with the managing director of the global organization (henceforth referred to as "the company"). The two processes initially observed for this research were: the timesheet operation and information gathering process.

The timesheet process was one of the most important processes since it involved the revenue generation for the branch office. The existing process for timesheet operation had a few lapses, which are described under the analysis. Mainly, there was no activity to initiate the timesheet process. The group leaders (GLs) who initiated the timesheets were too busy with their own work to be involved in this administrative process. The account manager (AM) who was the facilitator for this process only could call and remind the GLs regarding the timesheet. However the GLs had to find a time to sit down and send an e-mail to indicate the timings of each of the workers.

Information gathering was a process to gather information for future business. Again the busy GLs were given the task to find out whatever information they could from the project clients. There was no formal process for this either. Therefore there was no proper information kept regarding the current project status as well as other important information regarding future projects, deadlines, and so forth.

These two processes were carefully studied and modeled in order to analyze potential solutions for them to overcome the current lapses. Input from the AM and GLs was also used to verify the existing processes and workflow in order to get a correct picture.

Modeling of Existing Processes

Modeling of existing processes was carried out with use cases and activity diagrams of the unified modeling language (UML, n.d.). Use cases document, in a step-by-step manner, how actors (people and the system) interact with each other. These descriptions of use cases are used to further visually model them with the help of activity diagrams—graphically representing the documentations of the use cases.

Timesheet Operation

There were five use cases identified from the study of the existing timesheet operations. Once the use cases were described, the information therein was converted into activity diagrams. Thereafter mobile technology was introduced in order to convert the existing processes into a new suit of business processes.

Information Gathering

Whatever information is gathered at a branch office currently is collected in a very ad-hoc way. However there is a need for systematic gathering of information since the market is becoming more competitive and needs to have the constant attention of the marketing staff. Three main types of information required by the management were identified. Apart from the marketing people, the AM in this instance, the best people who could have access to such information were people working on a project such as the GLs. They could get information via the grapevine. However since they were extremely busy with their own expert contributions, a method to get such information was very important. However this area is not discussed in detail in this chapter.

THE COMPANY BACKGROUND

This action research was carried out in a truly global organization, headquartered in India and with operations around the world including in Australia. The company is a provider of professional services to technology organizations. The specific study was in the Sydney, Australia branch office.

The company in Australia is based mainly in Sydney and Melbourne. Its clients mostly include ICT technology providers. There are GLs in each of the projects, and they report to the AM in charge of that project. The AM is overall in charge of the project and reports to the regional director (RD). One AM could handle several projects; a project could be classified as the provision of the company expertise to a client organization in terms of technical expertise, project management, and other related services. One client could have several projects being run in parallel. Each project would have one group leader who is responsible to report to the account manager about the number of hours worked by each of the company employees attached to that project.

The objective of the branch office is to conduct business activities in Australia and New Zealand, and generate revenue for the parent company in India. The company has several areas of core business, namely: billing support systems, networks, mobility services, location-based services, and next-generation networks (NGNs).

Being an overseas company, the branch in Australia must outsource legal expertise in Australia. These outsourced services are in the area of accounting, including taxation, immigration laws, reporting procedures to the ASIC and other such government institutions, and other relevant local laws.

The company has a major challenge in collating the timesheets by its 50-plus consultants working in this region. It takes a while for the accounts manager to collect all the timesheets, collate them, consolidate them, and then send them across to the head office for invoicing to the clients in Australia and New Zealand.

The information gathering process is a proactive process where the GLs who work in various projects are expected to provide feedback for the company with regard to the projects. The information is rel-

evant to current projects as well as projects in the pipeline for the same client. GLs who work within the client companies are considered the best people to gather this type of information for the branch office. The following section briefly describes the theoretical background for action research.

METHODOLOGY: ACTION RESEARCH

This research carried out at the company followed the 'action research' approach in order to validate our theoretical presuppositions. Action research has been defined by Rapoport (1970) as follows:

"Action research aims to contribute both to the practical concerns of people in an immediate problematic situation and to the goals of social science by joint collaboration within a mutually acceptable ethical framework."

The action research at the company mainly concentrated on two business processes which were very significant and also had problems right now. These two processes of weekly timesheets and monthly information sheets were considered for this study. The managing director emphasized the need to streamline these processes to enable getting timesheets to the head office as quickly and efficiently as possible.

Action research was very appropriate for this research study because it:

- Established research method use in the social and medical sciences.
- Increased importance for information systems toward the end of 1990s.
- Varied in form and responded to particular problem domains.

In addition, its most typical form is a participatory method, and the fundamental contention of the action researcher is that complex social processes can be studied best by introducing changes into these processes and observing the effects of these changes.

There is widespread agreement by action research authorities, as indicated by Peters and

Robinson (1984), that it has four common characteristics:

- An action and change orientation.
- A problem focus.
- An "organic" process involving systematic and some times iterative stages.
- Collaboration among participants

The key assumptions underlying action research which were also applied in the company setting were that social settings cannot be reduced for study and action brings understanding.

Thus the existing processes were modeled using UML. Thereafter, the models of the existing processes were studied within the context of the m-transformation model in order to ascertain the areas within the process where mobility can be incorporated.

The existing procedure was first modeled drawing use cases in order to identify the interactions between various actors. The use cases were documented and then converted to activity diagrams. There were altogether five use case descriptions and five activity diagrams modeling the existing business process for timesheets. These activity diagrams were then verified by the RD and the AM at the branch office.

The action and change orientation in this instance were the two operations selected. The specific problems were the delays in timesheet operations and the unstructured nature of the current information gathering process. The use of UML for modeling provided the process involving systematic and sometimes iterative stages. The collaboration among participants was provided through various meetings held to verify the existing and proposed processes.

Thus action research offered a very scientific and subtle way of observing changes in an organization and introducing new changes without drastically changing the ongoing operations of the organization. The following section analyzes the current operation and uses the theoretical model for m-transformation to transform these processes.

ANALYSIS

Timesheet Operation

Once the existing timesheet operation was modeled through the activity diagrams, an industry survey was carried out through a literature survey. This survey revealed the existing technology available for projects of this nature. There were also discussions with the account manager, group leader, and director on which processes and areas to be improved. These discussions with the TML stakeholders also revealed various drawbacks with the existing timesheet operation, as follows:

- Timesheets were not submitted on time by the group leaders.
- There was no formal method of triggering this important activity.
- The client project manager was not involved in the current process.
- Discrepancies could take considerable time to be corrected.
- The proper monthly timelines—thus affecting the ERP software cycle (PeopleSoft) at the head office—are missed at times.
- Collection of account receivables goes on overtime due to the lapses in the process.

Information Gathering Process

The information gathering process was triggered by a form which could be sent to the AM by the GL at the end of each month. An short message service (SMS) reminder would be sent by the AM during the first week of the month for such information for the previous month. The information gathering process was fraught with lack of proper structure. This problem was further exacerbated by the fact that the GLs were overloaded with their own consulting work, resulting in lack of time to gather such information. This situation appeared to provide a rich opportunity for application of mobility for its alleviation. As a result, a form was proposed that would tell the GL the exact information that was required from the project. If the GL could observe such information even before the form was due in the month (e.g., hearing about a new project in the pipeline), the GL could immediately convey that to AM via SMS so that AM and the director had time to prepare themselves to talk to the client.

Mobile Transition Roadmap

While the aforementioned two processes were the focus of the study, it was also essential to provide a carefully thought-out approach to transforming these processes to mobile-enabled processes. The researchers created a model of the "mobile transformation roadmap," which provided the necessary and robust theoretical basis for transitioning the processes into mobile-enabled processes. Figure 1 illustrates the crux of this roadmap model. What is shown is a generic model to transform a business organization into a mobile-enabled organization by transitioning its business processes.

The business process transformation modeled in Figure 1 is further broken down into smaller and manageable steps when it is executed. In the business process transition area, factors internal to the organization are considered. The current operations of the organization are looked at in the

wake of customers and employees demanding new mobile technologies as well as easier and efficient work methods.

The technology transition, although a part of the overall business process transition, is focused on the application of emerging technologies, and corresponding new tools and applications that need to be incorporated into the mobile-enabled processes. The incorporation of such new technology in the business adds pressure for the organization to effectuate change in its technology usage. This leads to new thinking and new business processes to get the full effect of emerging technology.

The training of employees and the forming of the new-look organization creates a more customer-oriented work ethic. The transitioned organization is able to follow the well-known objective of being customer centric by making judicious use of mobile technology. As a result, the service standards, delivery periods, response times, and similar attributes change positively in the organization leading to a new business culture. Thus, three perspectives—namely, technology with regard to emerging technologies, methodology with regard to business processes, and sociology with regard to new business culture towards customer

Figure 1. The proposed mobile transition roadmap

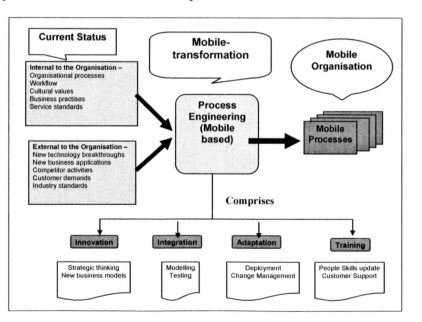

orientation—are identified in the transitioned organization.

The m-transformation roadmap points out the four action areas where process engineering should very carefully considered. These are innovation, integration, adaptation, and training. These key areas should be revisited—iteratively, incrementally, and parallel—until the new business processes are satisfactorily transformed. Furthermore, the m-transformation process can also be supported by corresponding computer aided software engineering (CASE) tools that can make the process easier as well as measured.

Innovation tools include brainstorming as well as critical evaluation of the current business processes. Furthermore, theoretical innovation models such as one by Rogers (2003) that include the five stages in the innovation-decision process—namely, knowledge, persuasion, decision, implementation, and confirmation—can also be of immense importance in m-transformation. In our case, they were applied in identification of the processes that had potential for m-transformation.

Integration required us to model the processes undergoing m-transformation to a stage where they could be studied, modified, and made ready for integration with the business itself. This required us to make use of the unified modeling language to model both existing as well as the new business processes that would result from m-transformation.

Adaptation involved the need to 'settle' the new processes in the business environment. While the integration stage required extensive modeling, the adaptation stage had a need to ensure that the freshly modeled processes were adaptable to the environment—including the business, its employees, and customers. This stage of the m-transformation processes was crucial in our exercise as it required us to make the employees aware of the proposed processes as well as putting together service standards and rules.

Training is the last and most crucial stage of the m-transformation process. This stage required us to provide training in the use of the mobile-enabled process to employees as well as customers

Figure 2. Proposed activity 1—account manager/group leader pre-timesheet activity

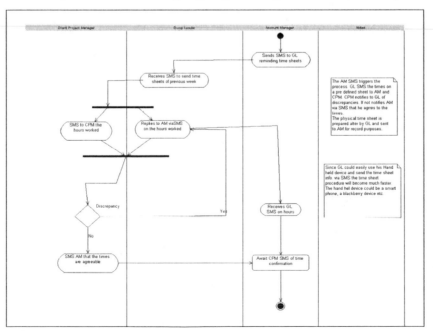

Figure 3. Proposed activity 2—timesheet preparation and verification

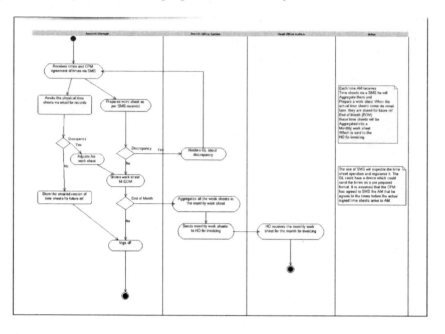

Figure 4. Proposed activity 3—head office invoice operation

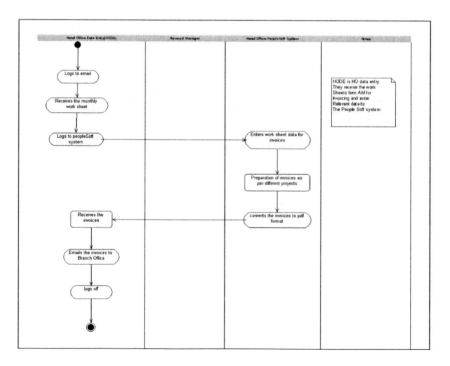

in order to understand and use the new processes in a smooth manner.

Having looked at the existing processes, new activity diagrams were drawn in order to highlight and rectify the drawbacks. There were four such new activity diagrams highlighting the introduction of mobile technology and the improvement of the business processes which are listed herein.

Proposed Process Activity Diagrams for Timesheet Process

Figure 2 depicts the initial timesheet process where the AM is triggering the process with an SMS message of billable time. The actual timesheet data is delivered by the GL to the AM via SMS. The AM sends back time data to the client project manager via SMS again for time confirmation. Therefore the whole process is based on SMS messages where all the unnecessary delays are reduced and the process is fast tracked since the SMS could be

sent anytime anywhere at the real time, with quick reactions, rather than delaying sending the data. Therefore any such delays in getting back to the office to send the e-mail and finding the time to do such action are minimized. See Figure 2 for the origination of a timesheet by the AM and the GL which shows the fundamental change effectuated by incorporation of mobility.

Further, since AM is triggering the timesheet operation by an SMS message in the proposed process, the GL has to reply to the SMS in order to send in the timesheet. Therefore the process is controlled at the branch office, as opposed to the current process where the control is with the GL, who is an employee of the company, but physically working in an outside client organization.

As depicted in Figure 3, the AM awaits the SMS reply from the GL. The difference in the proposed process as compared to the existing process is, the AM does not await the arrival of the actual timesheet, but instead prepares the Excel sheet

Figure 5. Proposed diagram 4—branch office and project client finalizing of invoices

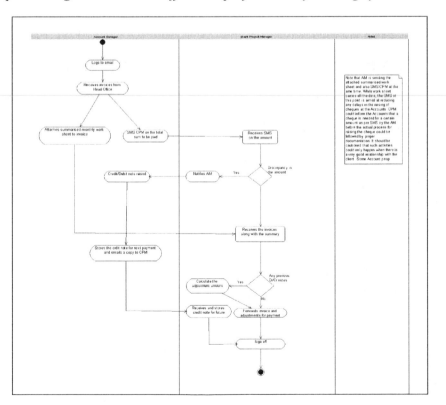

based on the agreed times transmitted through the SMS message. This process of recording the timings before the paper-based timesheets are received provides crucial advantage to the business at the end of the month. The AM could update any discrepancy every week until the end of the month with the actual timesheet data. However, at the end of the month he will forward the data in the Excel sheet and his last update would be based on an SMS message.

Figure 4 illustrates the process at the head office when it receives the Excel worksheet on work times. Since the AM forwards the Excel sheet with SMS-based data, for the last week of the month, there would be no delays in processing and sending invoice data to the head office.

Therefore every PeopleSoft cycle would be producing a set of invoices. Thus the invoicing operation is streamlined that each PeopleSoft cycle is printing a set of invoices to be sent to customers. Any discrepancies will be dealt with later through a process of credit and debit notes.

It should also be noted that Figure 4 would change very much if the mobile Web service, which is described as a future enhancement later in this chapter, is adopted by the company. The entire activity of manual entry of data into the PeopleSoft system would be taken care of by the mobile Web service.

Figure 5 illustrates the finalizing of the process with CPM that deals with sending the invoices to the accountant for payment. Note that a credit/debit note is provided within the process for any discrepancies for the previous accounting period since the actual invoice is partly based on the SMS data. This ability to provide a credit/debit note provides the necessary flexibility to amend errors that are likely to occur when the process is m-transformed with the use of SMS data.

EFFECT OF MOBILE TRANSFORMATION

Having considered how the selected business processes for the international organization under study would change as a result of m-transformation, we now do a brief comparison of the effect of such transformation on the organization itself. In our case, this comparison will be between the existing timesheet process and corresponding mobile-enabled timesheet process. This comparison showcases the difference between the two processes—without and with mobile technology—especially in the way in which it affects the roles played by people in the organization. There are five activities listed which are depicted in the

Table 1. The comparison of existing processes with proposed m-enabled processes

Activity	Current Process	Proposed Process
Group Leader (GL) Timesheet Operation	There are no official indications or reminders sent to GL for timesheets.	Account manager (AM) sends official reminder to GL via SMS, which prompts faster action.
Branch Office Timesheet Verification	AM awaits receipt of timesheet of GL to start filling out Excel worksheet to be sent to head office (HO).	AM is prompted by the times via SMS from GL and the confirmation from the client project manager (CPM).
Head Office Invoice Operation	HO awaits the Excel sheet with times for invoice preparations.	Still awaits Excel sheet, but it happens faster since the times are delivered via SMS to AM, vs. the current process where AM has to await for the e-mails.
Branch Office Dispatch of Invoices to Clients	The invoices are occasionally dispatched late due to delays in preparation and collection of timesheet data.	The invoices are dispatched more accurately based on SMS time data. There is provision for credit notes if there are any discrepancies for amounts invoiced, which are carried forward to the next period.
Invoice Operation at the Project Client	The invoices are checked by the CPM for any discrepancies at this point. If the invoice has been delayed due to delayed times sent to head office, this procedure would be around 2-3 months later than the actual month of invoicing.	There is no specific process needed at this point since the invoicing has been done and a credit/debit note could simply be raised to make the adjustment at this point. However, the invoicing would be completed within the next month due to the faster action via SMS messaging.

existing activity diagrams. These activities are then compared with the proposed timesheet operation activity diagrams.

Comparison of the Existing Process with the Proposed Process

In the action research work that was carried out at the company, application of mobile technology for the selected business processes of the organization resulting in new processes was proposed. The transformation of the business processes are guided by the m-transition roadmap, which is a generic model for transformation of business processes with the application of mobile technology. The roadmap looks both inward and external to the organization in deciding what is happening in the organization as well as in the industry sector in which the organization belongs. In this specific case, we looked at how the technology services providers work in a general way when deciding how to improve the business processes of the organization. By doing that, the organization is compared with other similar organizations in the same industry. Therefore it provides a guideline as to what new technology has to be introduced in order to keep pace with the competition.

A further improvement of the timesheet process could be looked at in terms of Web services and mobile Web services. A detailed description on how the business processes could be further improved by use of this emerging technology is discussed in the next section.

EMERGING TECHNOLOGIES

Based on our understanding, the company under study has an excellent opportunity to use emerging technologies to further enhance the processes modeled with mobility. Web services and mobile Web services are such technology which could be used to communicate with the PeopleSoft system directly. This would result in further improving the process by eliminating manual data entry and use the Web service to send the data directly to the PeopleSoft system. Therefore it is useful look at

Web services and mobile Web service technology for future expansion.

Web Services (WS)

Web services (WS) is a unit of business, software application, or a system that can be accessed over a network by extensible markup language/simple object application protocol (XML/SOAP) messaging. It is a delivery mechanism that can serve many different consumers on many different platforms at the same time. Stacey and Unhelkar (2004) describe WS technology as an enabler to connect incompatible standalone systems to integrate a complex distributed system in a way that was not possible with previous technologies, while Chatterjee and Webber (2004) believe that Web services represent a new architectural paradigm for applications. WS capabilities access other applications via industry standard network, interfaces, and protocols.

Web services are software programs that enable document applications to talk to each other. Taylor (2005) describes that although Web services are centered around the documents, they do not necessarily follow that such a document should be readable by people; this is reflected to be the core goal of WS.

Web services could be defined as open standard-based (XML, SOAP, etc.) Web applications that interact with other Web applications for the purpose of exchanging data. Initially used for the exchange of data on large private enterprise networks, Web services are evolving to include transactions over the public Internet (Lucent, n.d.).

A more specific form of WS using mobile technology is described next which is relevant to the organization under study.

Mobile Web Services (MWS)

A mobile application that is using the WS to transmit its data is classified as MWS. According to Pashtan (2005), mobile terminals and mobile services are an integral part of the extended Web that includes the wireless domains that facilitate automated interoperation between terminal and network services. WS can replace less flexible methods for information exchanging of specific transaction data. WS enables the building of software applications that execute on the Internet and use the same software paradigms that were successfully applied in the development of enterprise application.

According to the Australian Computer Society (ACS, 2005) report on MWS, with Web services, phones now have the potential to actually consume useful services. But before developing a mobile client, you might want to think twice before taking the simple object application protocol/hyper text transfer protocol (SOAP/HTTP) route. First of all, turning your phone into a SOAP client might have some performance costs related to slow data speeds and processing both HTTP commands and XML. Secondly, most phones do not come with Web services support built in. Finally, you can hide the Web services complexity and leverage existing technologies to make use of their widespread availability. This would require a gateway to sit in between the phone and the Web service to handle the passing and conversion of messages, but you no longer have to worry about client-side performance issues or even deploying a client (ACS, 2005).

Microsoft service providers define MWS as an initiative to create Web services standards that will enable new business opportunities in the personal computer and mobile space, and deliver integrated services across fixed (wired) and wireless networks. Mobile Web services use existing industry standard XML-based Web services architecture to expose mobile network services to the broadest audience of developers (http://www.microsoft.com/). The functionality of MWS is examined in the light of how MWS could enhance the current process enhancing its functionality to talk to the PeopleSoft system directly via Web eliminating the second data entry at the head office, which is happening during the current process.

Business Process Reengineering with the Global Company Perspective

Having discussed WS and MWS, an important question worth considering is how these technologies can be incorporated into the business processes of the company that is undergoing m-

transformation. Thus, the discussion on MWS is a part of re-engineering business processes with mobility. "Reengineering," as defined by Hammer and Champy (2001), is a fundamental rethinking and radical redesign of business processes to achieve dramatic improvements in the critical, contemporary measure of performance such as cost, quality, services, and speed. Reengineering a company's business processes ultimately changes practically all aspects of a company such as people, jobs, managers, and values that are linked together.

The global company under study has undergone m-transformation. However, the transformed business processes could be further enhanced by the use of mobile Web services. For instance, the process of sending the timesheet data to the head office for invoicing could be easily done through such mobile Web services. By using mobile Web services, the data could be directly sent using a mobile device. This would cut down on reentering the data into the PeopleSoft system if the MWS could be configured to talk directly to the PeopleSoft system. Such direct integration would make the process faster and also make it less error prone due to reducing of human intervention. Such integration could be used in all the offices of the organization globally, to communicate with the PeopleSoft system sending timesheet data. The security concerns arising could also be addressed through MWS itself by authenticating the invoice printing through a second MWS communication.

As has been mentioned earlier, the main focus of this research is to investigate the business processes to see how they could be made more productive. By reengineering the business processes, they could collaborate and integrate with the business processes of the other organizations, the head office, and branch offices in this context. As stated in ACS (2005), processes have linkage to each other; this research is concentrating on this linkage of the processes to another organization's processes that may not be known to each other. Thus the total global operation of the company could be integrated together using WS/MWS. These processes could help each other, thus the branch offices of the entire organization could automatically collaborate with each other without going through the head office.

CONCLUSION AND FUTURE RESEARCH DIRECTION

This research investigated the current systems at a global organization in order to look at possible solutions to enhance the business processes of the company under study. Selected business processes were studied in order to introduce mobile technology to those processes. This resulted in transformation of existing business processes to mobile-enabled business processes which would be integrated into the organization. The company is implementing this proposal systematically and carefully under the guidelines of the m-transformation roadmap, concurrently looking at adaptation and training issues. Once all the proposed business processes are fully operational, the actual impact of the m-transformation could be identified.

This research has a value to all the stakeholders who took part in it. We, the researchers, benefited by the overall research findings to understand how the organizational processes would change in order to accommodate mobile technology. The company benefited by implementing some outcomes from this research and streamlining its very important business processes. The company could further explore and get far-reaching benefits, if it would invest to implement WS/MWS technology into its business processes, which would benefit the global organization in communicating to the head office directly using MWS/WS, thus improving productivity of the global organization.

REFERENCES

ACS (Australian Computer Society). (2005, September 8). *Web services overview.* Retrieved November 10, 2005, from http://www.acs.openlab.net.au/content.php?article.131

Alonso, G. (2004). *Web services, concepts, architecture and applications.* Berlin: Springer-Verlag.

Arunatileka, D. (2006). In B. Unhelkar (Ed.), *Mobile business: Technological, methodological and social perspectives.* Hershey, PA: Idea Group.

Arunatileka, D., & Unhelkar, B. (2003). Mobile technologies, providing new possibilities in customer relationship management. In *Proceedings of the 5th International Information Technology Conference, Colombo, Sri Lanka.*

Arunatileka, S., & Arunatileka, D. (2003). E-transformation as a strategic tool for SMEs in developing nations. In *Proceedings of the 1st International Conference on E-Governance, New Delhi, India.*

Birchler, M. (2004). Future of mobile and wireless communications. In P. Smyth (Ed.), *Mobile and wireless communications: Key technologies and future applications.* UK: Institution of Electrics Engineers.

Cabrera, L.F., & Kurt, C. (2005). *Web services architecture and its specifications: Essential for understanding WS.* Redmond, WA: Microsoft Press.

Chatterjee, S., & Webber, J. (2004). *Developing enterprise Web services: An architect's guide.* Englewood Cliffs, NJ: Prentice Hall.

Deshpande, Y., Murugesan, S., Unhelkar, B., & Arunatileka, D. (2004). Methodological considerations and challenges: Moving Web applications from desk-top to diverse mobile devices. In *Proceedings of the Device Independent Web Engineering Conference,* Munich, Germany.

Ghanbary, A. (2006). Evaluation of mobile technologies in the context of their applications, limitations and transformation. In B. Unhelkar (Ed.), *Mobile business: Technological, methodological and social perspectives.* Hershey, PA: Idea Group.

Hammer, M., & Champy, J. (2001). *Reengineering the corporation, a manifesto for business evolution.* UK: Nicholas Brealey.

Lucent. (n.d.). *W-definitions.* Retrieved May 18, 2006, from http://www.lucent.com/search/glossary/w-definitions.html

Marmaridis, I., & Unhelkar, B. (2005). *Proceedings of the 1st MobiComm, Mobile Business Conference,*

Sydney, Australia. Retrieved from http://www. mbusiness2005.org/contact.html

Pashtan, A. (2005). *Mobile Web services.* Cambridge: Cambridge University Press.

Peters, M., & Robinson, V. (1984). The origins and status of action research. *Journal of Applied Behavioral Science, 20*(2), 113-124.

Rapoport, R.(1970). Three dilemmas in action research. *Human Relations, 23*(4), 499-513.

Rogers, E.M. (2003). *Diffusion of innovations* (5th ed.). New York: The Free Press.

Schneiderman, R. (2002). *The mobile technology, question and answers.* AMACOM.

Stacey, M., & Unhelkar, B. (2004). Web services in implementation. *Proceedings of the 15th ACIS Conference, Hobart, Australia.*

Taylor, I.J. (2005). *From P2P to Web services peers in a client/server world.* Berlin: Springer-Verlag.

UML. (n.d.). *UML 2.0.* Retrieved May 4, 2006, from http://www.uml.org/#UML2.0

Unhelkar, B. (2005). Transitioning to a mobile enterprise: A three-dimensional framework. *Cutter IT Journal, 18*(8), 5-11.

ADDITIONAL READING

ACMA. (2003, August). *Mobile commerce: Regulatory and policy outlook discussion paper.* Retrieved December 7, 2005, from http://www. acma.gov.au/ACMAINTER.4849984:STAN-DARD:1004384283:pc=PC_7126

Adam, O., Chikova, P., & Hofer, A. (2005). Managing inter-organizational business processes using an architecture for m-business scenarios. *Proceedings of ICMB 05, Sydney, Australia.*

Alag, H. (2006). Business process mobility. In B. Unhelkar (Ed.), *Mobile business: Technological methodological and social perspectives* (vol. 2, pp. 583-601). Hershey, PA: Idea Group.

Anckar, B., & D'Incau, D. (2002). Value added services in mobile commerce: An analytical framework and empirical findings from a national consumer survey. In *Proceedings of the 35th Hawaii International Conference on System Sciences.*

Archer, N. (2004). The business case for employee mobility support. In *Proceedings of the IADIS International Conference on E-Commerce, Lisbon, Portugal.*

Barjis, J. (2006). Overview and understanding of mobile business in the age of communication. In B. Unhelkar (Ed.), *Mobile business: Technological methodological and social perspectives* (vol. 2, pp. 719-726). Hershey, PA: Idea Group.

Barnes, S.J. (2002). The mobile commerce value chain: Analysis and future development. *International Journal of Information Management, 22*(2), 91-108.

Basole, R.C. (2004). *The value and impact of mobile information and communication technologies.* Atlanta: Georgia Institute of Technology.

Basole, R.C. (2005). Transforming enterprises through mobile applications: A multi-phase framework. In *Proceedings of the 11th America's Conference on Information Systems, Omaha, NE.*

Chan, J.C., & Hoang, D.B. (2005). Novel user-centric model for m-business transformation. In *Proceedings of the International Conference on Mobile Business.*

Cousins, K., & Varshney, U. (2001). A product location framework for mobile commerce environment. In *Proceedings of the Workshop on Mobile Commerce,* co-located with MobiComm2001, Rome.

Di Pietro, R., & Mancini, L.V. (2003). Security and privacy issues of handheld and wearable wireless devices. *Communications of the ACM, 46*(9).

El Kiki, T., & Lawrence, E. (2006). Government as a mobile enterprise: Real-time, ubiquitous government. In *Proceedings of the 3rd ITNG Conference, Las Vegas, NV.*

Er, M., & Kay, R. (2005). Mobile technology adoption for mobile information systems: An activity theory perspective. In *Proceedings of ICMB 05, Sydney, Australia.*

Falcone, F., & Garito, M. (2006). Mobile strategy roadmap. In B. Unhelkar (Ed.), *Handbook of research in mobile business: Technical, methodological, and social perspectives.* Hershey, PA: Idea Group.

Forouzan, B.A. (2004). *Data communications and networking* (3rd ed.). New York: McGraw-Hill.

Gershman, A. (2002). Ubiquitous commerce—always on, always aware, always pro-active. *Proceedings of the 2002 Symposium on Applications and the Internet* (SAINT 2002).

Guizani, M., & Raju, A. (2005). Wireless networks and communications security. In Y. Xiao, J. Li, & Y. Pan (Eds.), *Security and routing in wireless networks* (vol. 3, p. 320). New York: Nova Science.

Hawryszkiewycz, I., & Steele, R. (2005). A framework for integrating mobility into collaborative business processes. In *Proceedings of the International Conference on Mobile Business (ICMB 2005).*

Herzberg, A. (2003). Payments and banking with mobile personal devices. *Communications of the ACM, 46*(5), 53-58.

Hsu, H.Y.S., Burner, G.C., & Kulviwat, S. (2005). Personalization in mobile commerce. *Proceedings of IRMA 2005, San Diego.*

Huber, J.F. (2002). Toward the mobile Internet. *Computer, 35*(10), 100-102.

ITU. (2006a). *The regulatory environment for future mobile multimedia services.* Retrieved September 15, 2006, from http://www.itu.int/ITU-D/ict/partnership/index.html

Jarvenpaa, S.L., Lang, K.R., Takeda, Y., & Tuunainen, K. (2003). Mobile commerce at crossroads. *Communications of the ACM, 46*(12), 41-44.

Kalakota, R., & Robinson, M. (2002). *M-business: The race to mobility.* New York: McGraw-Hill Professional.

Lalis, S., Karypidis, A., & Savidis, A. (2005). Ad-hoc composition in wearable and mobile computing. *Communications of the ACM, 48*(3).

Lee, C. (2006). Mobile CRM: Reaching, acquiring, and retaining mobility customers. In B. Unhelkar (Ed.), *Mobile business: Technical, methodological and social perspectives.* Hershey, PA: Idea Group.

Lee, Y.E., & Benbasat, I. (2003). Interface design for mobile commerce. *Communications of the ACM, 46*(12), 48-52.

Lyytinen, K., & Yoo, Y. (2002). Issues and challenges in ubiquitous computing. *Communications of the ACM, 45*(12), 62-65.

Mallat, N., Rossi, M., & Tuunainen, V.K. (2004). Mobile banking services. *Communications of the ACM, 47*(5), 42-46.

Manecke, N., & Schoensleben, P. (2004). Cost and benefit of Internet-based support of business processes. *International Journal on Production Economics, 87*, 213-229.

McGregor, C., & Morris, B. (2006). A survey of recent research to support remote neonatal care via mobile devices. *Proceedings of the IMB Conference, Sydney, Australia.*

Patel, A. (2006). Mobile commerce in emerging economies. In B. Unhelkar (Ed.), *Mobile business: Technological, methodological and social perspectives.* Hershey, PA: Idea Group.

Raisinghani, M., & Taylor, D. (2006). Going global: A technology review. In Y.U. Lan (Ed.), *Global integrated supply chain systems.* London: Idea Group.

Rao, B., & Minakakis, L. (2003). Evolution of mobile location-based services. *Communications of the ACM, 46*(12), 61-65.

Sarker, S., & Wells, J.D. (2003). Understanding mobile handheld device use and adoption. *Communications of the ACM, 46*(12), 35-40.

Schwiderski-Grosche, S., & Knospe, H. (2002). Secure mobile commerce. *Electronics & Communication Engineering Journal, 14*, 228-238.

Sheng-Tzong, C., Jian-Pei, L., Jian-Lun, K., & Chia-Mei, C. (2002). A new framework for mobile Web services. *Proceedings of the Symposium on Applications and the Internet* (SAINT 2002), Nara, Japan.

Stafford, T.F., & Gillenson, M.L. (2003). Mobile commerce: What it is and what it could be. *Communications of the ACM, 46*(12), 33-34.

Stanoevska-Slabeva, K. (2003). Towards a reference model for m-commerce applications. *Proceedings of ECIS 2003, Naples, Italy.*

Sun, J. (2003). Information requirement: Elicitation in mobile commerce. *Communications of the ACM, 46*(12), 45-47.

Tarasewich, P. (2003). Designing mobile commerce applications. *Communications of the ACM, 46*(12), 57-60.

Tian, M., Voigt, T., Naumowicz, T., Ritter, H., & Schiller, J. (2004). *Performance considerations for mobile Web services. Computer Communications,*

27, 1097-1105. Retrieved December 3, 2006, from http://www.elsevier.com/locate/comcom

Tsai, H.A.B., & Gururajan, R. (2005). Mobile business: An exploratory study to define a framework for the transformation process. In *Proceedings of the 10th Asia Pacific Decision Sciences Institution (APDSI) Conference, Taipei, Taiwan.*

Urbaczewski, A., Valacich, J.S., Jessup, L.M., & Guest Editors. (2003). Mobile commerce: Opportunities and challenges. *Communications of the ACM, 46*(12), 30-32.

Varshney, U. (2002). Mobile payments. *Computer, 35*(12), 120-121.

Varshney, U. (2004). Vehicular mobile commerce. *Computer, 37*(12), 116-118.

Varshney, U., & Vetter, R. (2002). Mobile commerce: Framework, applications and networking support. *Mobile Networks and Applications,* 185-198.

Waegemann, P. (2006). Mobile solutions offer providers flexibility in managing care. *Managed Healthcare Executive, 16*(2), 58.

Wang, Y., Van der Kar, E., Meijer, G., & Hunteler, M. (2005). Improving business processes with mobile workforce solutions. In *Proceedings of the International Conference on Mobile Business, Sydney, Australia.*

Chapter XXV
Objects as the Primary Design Principle for International Information Systems

Hans Lehmann
Victoria University of Wellington, New Zealand

ABSTRACT

This exploratory research project set out to investigate the architecture and design principles of international information systems. Analysing six case vignettes in a modified grounded theory approach, a two-dimensional topology for international information systems—postulated from previous research as a seed concept—was confirmed as a useful architecture paradigm. In its terms, international information systems are configured from two elements: core systems (common for the whole enterprise) on the one hand, and local systems (specific only for each site) on the other. The interface between the two is a third component. The cases showed that achieving the correct balance between core and local can be a difficult political process and requires careful organisational engineering to be successful. One case vignette, in particular, highlights the logical and organisational difficulties in defining these systems elements. Object orientation as the fundamental design principle is investigated as an approach to provide a solution for this problem. Because it enables implementation differentiation and flexibility for future functional changes, it is conjectured that object technology is an optimal—technical—development strategy for international information systems. Directions for further research are outlined.

INTRODUCTION

The notion that globalisation is the only key to survival in a rapidly shrinking world has been a hackneyed cliché for many businesses since the early 1980s. Equally, the pivotal importance of information technology as a key business driver has not been seriously questioned in 30 years. Yet the obvious fusion of these two truisms, the application of information technology throughout global operations, is still widely ignored by academics (Gallupe & Tan, 1999) and largely misunderstood by practitioners. As a result, international information systems[1] projects over the last 20 years have often been downright disastrous.[2] Research into why these applications are difficult and how they could be mastered should be of high priority, but it is not: The ABI/INFORM database lists 32,919 papers with information systems as a keyword between 1985 and 2000. For the same time period, keywords to do with international information systems occur in 234[3] papers (i.e., in two thirds of 1 percent).

Furthermore, the sparse research efforts by the academic community have been sporadic and dispersed over many, disjointed and often irrelevant[4] topics (Palvia, 1998; Gallupe & Tan, 1999). This has left the field devoid of a firm theoretical base and framework from which to advise practitioners and to direct further applied research.

This exploratory paper first validates a generic architecture common to international systems. Selecting and building an appropriate IT architecture is considered an important building block for the successful development of any complex system (Earl, 1989). Because such an a priori architecture simplifies the design process, it has the potential to make the development of international information systems faster and less risky.

Validation of the architecture model then establishes a useful framework for further research into the nature of IIS. Combining the two-dimensional topology with the notion of object-oriented analysis, design and development of IIS provides a method for building IIS that is clearer, would avoid failure through destructive politics, and, thereby, removes a large portion of the risk associated with these systems. It, furthermore, provides eo ipso the flexibility required for the ever-changing information systems and technology environment within multinational enterprises.

The chapter is organised as follows:

- After a review of the (sparse) literature, previous research into the architecture of IIS is summarised.
- Next, the methodological backdrop to the approach used in the study—qualitative research, using grounded theory principles, especially the use of ideational concepts for sketching out a theory and its validation by re-casting these concepts—is introduced.
- The case vignettes are then described and their IIS structure expressed in terms of the postulated architecture model.

- Finally, the use, if the architecture model as a framework for analysing, designing and building IIS is brought out, and the benefits of an object-oriented approach are set out and demonstrated on examples drawn from the vignettes.

INTERNATIONAL INFORMATION SYSTEMS IN THE LITERATURE

The literature does not clearly identify a generally accepted term for information systems technology applied across borders. Often "global" is used (e.g., by Ives et al., 1991), but "transnational" is also in general use (e.g., by King et al., 1993, 1999) for such systems. The first inevitably invites associations of vast enterprises covering the planet, whereas "transnational" is open to possible confusion with the precise use of the term coined by Bartlett and Ghoshal (1989) for describing one specific style of a firm's operation in more than one country.

In this paper, therefore, the term "international"[5] is used. Furthermore, to distinguish international information systems (IIS) from other distributed systems, in this paper they are defined as:

The distributed information systems (within one firm) that support similar business activities in highly diverse environments, commonly found across country boundaries.[6]

Most reviews of international information systems in the literature[7] tend to agree that past research into IIS is sporadic and spread over a wide array of topics. Only in the last few years have researchers begun to direct their attention to the design and development of IIS.[8] Some of this recent research focuses on the structure and architecture of IIS (e.g., Gibson, 1994; Burn et al., 1996 ; Targowski, 1996 ; Grover et al., 1996; and Peppard, 1999) and the role of an information technology infrastructure in general (Weill, 1992, 1993; Weill et al., 1994a, 1994b, 1995, 1998; Broadbent et al., 1997). With the ever-increasing ubiquity of information technology and its ever-increasing pervasiveness, infrastructure has now acquired the role of the main technology architecture. This notion has been developed further by Weill et al. (2002) and Weill and Vitale (2002), is discussed in more detail by Ross (2003) and has been elaborately summarized by Tucker and Woolfe (2003).

This increasing interest in IIS, however, seems to be confined to academics in the information system discipline. IIS are still a very peripheral concern for international business researchers. Similarly, there is very little evidence in the practitioner literature—with Collins et al. (1999) perhaps one recent exception.

FRAMEWORKS AND ARCHITECTURE OF INTERNATIONAL INFORMATION SYSTEMS

Researchers of IIS architectures often use a framework for the classification of enterprises operating in more than one country that was developed by Bartlett and Ghoshal in 1989. Their model focuses on the level of global control vs. local autonomy:

- "Global" means high global control while "multinationals" have high local control;
- "Internationals" are an interim state, transiting toward a balance of local and global;
- "Transnational" organisations balance tight global control whilst vigorously fostering local autonomy. This strategy of think global and act local is considered optimal for many international operations;

Butler Cox (1991) also put a developmental perspective on the Bartlett and Ghoshal framework. In Butler Cox's terminology, companies seem to become active internationally first as exporter of their goods or services—usually applying a global[9]

business strategy. Increased activity in any one location encourages autonomy for local operations, taking on the role of national adapter, similar to the multinational classification. In the next phase, this degree of autonomy is counterbalanced by some global control as central coordinator, that is, an international firm. Finally, as global operations mature, firms move toward a status of global coordinator (equivalent to the transnational). Figure 1 below demonstrates the Bartlett and Ghoshal (1989) classification and shows the migration paths suggested by Butler Cox (1991).

A number of researchers have developed models of IIS with a direct, one-to-one relationship between Bartlett and Ghoshal's global business strategies and IT architectures as described in Table 2 below.

It seems that just as the *international* business strategy is an intermediary stage, so are the corresponding global information technology configurations. If these replicated/inter-organisational/intellectually synergy structures are regarded as embryonic *integrated* architectures, then three

Figure 1. Classification and migration through global business strategies

Table 1. Linkage between global business strategy and IT architecture

Bartlett & Ghoshal (1989)	Butler Cox (1991)	Karimi & Kosynski (1996)	Sankar et al. (1993)	Jarvenpaa et al. (1994[10])
Global	Centralised	Centralisation	Centralised	Headquarters-driven
Multinational	Autonomous	Decentralisation	Decentralised	Independent
International	Replicated	Inter-organisational	(Undefined)	Intellectual Synergy
Transnational	Integrated	Integrated	Integrated	Integrated

mutually exclusive generic architectures could be defined, namely:

- centralised
- decentralised (including autonomous and independent)
- integrated

Whilst the centralised and decentralised structures have been researched over a number of years and are by now well-understood, the nature of the integrated architecture has rarely been an object of empirical study. However, the very nature of the systems under investigation makes it possible to establish some common sense, a priori postulates as to the shape of their architecture.

International information systems support common functions across a number of local sites. The common-sense deduction from this is the obvious requirement that such systems would have parts that are common to all sites and other parts that are specific to individual localities. The basis of this concept, that is, the need for variation in international systems to accommodate differing local circumstances has been established by Keen et al. as early as 1982, when a paradigm of a common core'of information systems applications with local alterations was first articulated. There has been little further development of this model as far as the functionality of application systems is concerned and what researchers concluded

10 years ago, namely that "the literature offers little guidance for . . . local versus common applications" (Ives & Jarvenpaa et al., 1991), still holds today.

However, one exception is a set of conjectural papers published in the mid-1990s. Building on lived experience in the development and implementation of IIS, Lehmann (1996a, 1996b, 1997).

proposed a two-dimensional topology as an architecture model for international information systems:

- The topology would consist of a "common core" and "local variations" of the system, linked together by a "core/local interface," as shown in Figure 2 above;
- Each local implementation of the IIS consists of the core of applications and technology that are a common standard for all sites; and
- A varying configuration of local systems (as shown by the shaded "Local Variations").

These earlier postulates were subsequently validated in extensive case research with a number of large multinational enterprises (Lehmann, 1999, 2001a, 2001b,[11] 2002).

RESEARCH METHODOLOGY

The dearth of IIS research makes qualitative, theory building methods an appropriate choice. Such methods are well-established in organisational research and are becoming accepted in information systems research too (Galliers et al., 1987; Yin, 1989; Lee, 1989; Orlikowski et al., 1991). In particular, Eisenhardt (1989) describes the process of building theory, focusing especially on its inductive nature. In Sociology Press, Glaser and Strauss (1967) already had developed a specific inductive method, which they termed the "grounded theory" approach, where theory is left to "emerge" from the data—in which it is "grounded." Turner (1983) was one of the first to apply the grounded theory approach to management studies. Since 1984, grounded theory had been used in a number of business studies (Glaser, 1995). Orlikowski (1993, 1995) has pioneered grounded theory in information system (IS) research, followed

Figure 2. Conceptual architecture model for international information systems

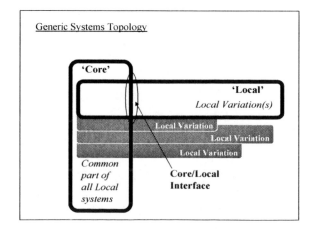

by Yoong (1996) and Atkinson (1997) with studies on group decision making.

Glaser and Strauss (1967) emphasise that not just large research projects, but also small informal cases and "anecdotal comparisons,", as long as they are the researcher's "lived experience," are a legitimate source for the conceptualisation of theoretical constructs (p. 67). In a later monograph Glaser and Strauss (1994) set out in more explicit terms how to use the grounded theory method with case histories. Fernandez and Lehmann (2005) build on this to show the mutual enhancement of rigour and relevance of this research practice for organisational cases. The approach selected for the study of case vignettes in this paper is based on these methodological foundations.

The following sections, thus, first contain brief descriptions of the case vignettes,[12] followed by an interpretation of the case facts using the postulated generic architecture (shown in Figure 2). Glaser and Strauss (1967) recommend this to see if a theoretical concept *works*, that is, if it can—just as well, or better—explain the case from the different perspective introduced by the postulated theoretical construct.

CASE VIGNETTE A: THE LEASING SUBSIDIARY OF AN INTERNATIONAL BANK (LEASING)

This UK firm with branches in the USA, the UK, and three European countries was acquired by an Asian international bank to give them a base in the leasing business. The central computer into which all offices were linked was in New York. The business in the various countries was firmly limited to installment credit transactions and differed mainly in magnitude. This premise of business being the same did, however, not translate into systems terms. While the lease set-up process was similar, the lease administration part, which makes up more than two thirds of the system, differed significantly from country to country.

- Local country modules would receive the basic data for input into the country-specific receivables and marketing modules, to cope with local languages as well as differing business

practices. Other than stringent data interface standards, the local offices had complete freedom to choose appropriate local software.

Support came from technical people at the centre and business-oriented applications managers at the local sites.

In terms of global business strategy, the leasing company balances strong global control with wide local autonomy to use the local environment to best advantage. This classifies[13] them as a transnational firm.

CASE VIGNETTE B: AN A USTRALASIAN MERCHANT BANK (BANK)

The business of this rapidly expanding New Zealand based merchant bank with substantial branches in Australia, Hong Kong, and London consisted mainly of money market dealing, investment banking, and stock broking. Information systems technology at the head office was fragmented, and the branches ran odd assortments of software and equipment, loosely linked by public networks. A newly appointed central Treasurer set out to install global systems and controls.

There were two levels of information and systems needs:

- A comprehensive management control system to monitor exposure and risk internationally as well as for each local firm.
- Operations, specifically in the money market and stock broking activities required more systems support.

The resultant IIS consisted thus of a narrow core that only contained detailed and stringent data interface and communication standards for input into the Treasurer's own global risk monitoring system. As an incentive to comply with the standards, an electronic mail and bulletin board service was offered on the core. The local systems were entirely composed of the best-suited local software, provided they could comply with the data and information interface requirements. The

Figure 3. The balanced topology of the Leasing Company

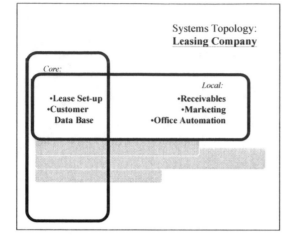

Figure 4. Dominance of local systems in the Merchant Bank's topology

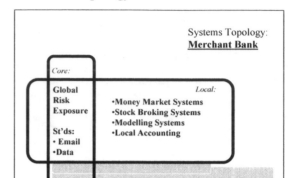

branches would rely entirely on local, and external, technical and applications support.

The merchant bank is low on global control and classified as a multinational.

CASE VIGNETTE C: A NEW ZEALAND COMMODITY EXPORTING BOARD (BOARD)

The Board had a virtual monopoly in the purchase of fruit from producers. It owned packing houses and cool stores in New Zealand, operated its own charter fleet and ran a number of European sales offices, while North American sales are controlled through an agency. Asia is an important target for development in the near future.

The Board's systems strategy focused on strong production systems with some marketing modules integrated into them. The international part is, however, the smallest part of the system and consists mainly of common messaging formats. The shipping system is designed to send shipment details and forecasts to the branches who return sales statistics back to the centre. Some of the overseas sales offices use sales order entry systems specific to their environment.

The architecture consists of:

Figure 5. Systems Topology of the Commodity Firm

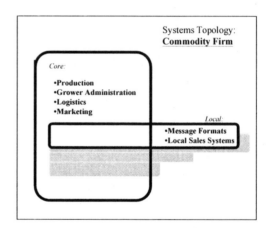

- A large core of extensive and sophisticated systems in the production, logistics, and marketing (forecasting and decision-support/modelling) areas.
- The messages and the independent sales and administration support systems at the branch offices are thus the only local parts in the topology of this international system.

The commodity firm is strong on global control, leaving relatively little autonomy to the local sales offices. This classifies them as a global operator.

CASE VIGNETTE D: A DANISH SHIPPING GROUP (SHIPPER)

SHIPPER has a very successful IIS with a core of clearly defined and centrally run IIS, which are compulsory for all local and regional offices. As an international shipping firm, SHIPPER relies on the effective management of a common operating resource, that is, the shipping fleet. Standardised access to a group of tightly integrated, common information systems, closely managed at the centre, is essential for this. Several (local) users need to be able to interpret, discuss, and manipulate information at the same time across the globe—a requirement termed *synchronicity*. The central stewardship of the information systems and databases meant that users could rely implicitly on the accuracy and integrity of the data/information they used.

This *synchronicity* requirement[14] defined unequivocally what data and functionality was required in the suite of core information systems. Furthermore, because the IT support thus provided was a critical—and very instrumental—necessity for their business operations, its functionality was largely undisputed. Similarly, any further, local, systems developments were put into the accountability of local management—all that was required was that they interfaced to the core systems without any problems. The investment would come out of the regional profit centre, implicitly assuring at once a clear focus on operational necessity and stringent economical justification for local systems.

Figure 6. SHIPPER's system topology

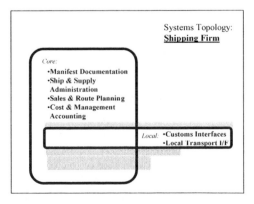

All this clearly classifies SHIPPER as a global enterprise.

CASE VIGNETTE E: AN AUSTRALASIAN FOOD PRODUCER'S CO-OP (CO-OP)

Similar to the previous vignette, the Australasian food producer's co-operative (the "Co-op") is a statutory monopoly for the export of its produce from the home country. The UK was its main market until that country joined the EC and severely restricted the Co-op's access. In response, however, the Co-op rapidly built a global network of sales offices. This helped it first to become a global exporter and later, as it included local manufacturing resources, it turned into a truly international operator of considerable size: It now ranks 15th among the world's food industry giants. Organised into regional enterprises with great autonomy, it found it difficult, however, to implement the global branding, which its competitors began to use to good effect during the last decade. Some 5 years ago, a new CEO began a strategic migration toward a transnational global business strategy, balancing the regions' power with a corresponding measure of central control over global product, marketing and branding policy.

The Co-op's IT people misunderstood this move as a return to a global strategy, that is, one aimed at minimising regional autonomy. For this reason, they set out to implement a globally standard IIS, with little local input and with hardly any information systems under local management—discarding the substantial regional information systems in existence. Figure 7 depicts this architecture.

Regional/local management had a different view of an appropriate IIS for the Co-op. Their vision was based on their existing systems, loosely linked by a common framework for production and marketing planning (Figure 8). They, furthermore, interpreted the IT proposal as a covert way to increase central control and resisted this attack on the independence of their local fiefdoms' vigorously. The IT people responded to this strong resistance from regional business management with political manoeuvres. This made the communica-

Figure 7. The globally standard IIS proposed by the IT people

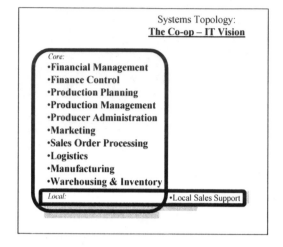

tion between the business and IT more and more antagonistic. Because of the diagonally juxtaposed visions of the IIS architecture most appropriate for the Co-op, they went through several iterations of a cycle of business rejection and political reaction from the IT people.

In the end, the CEO terminated the project and re-allocated the team's people and technology resources.

Figure 8. Dominance of local systems in the Merchant Bank's topology

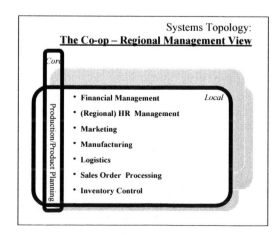

CASE VIGNETTE F: AN INTERNATIONAL FREIGHT FORWARDING GROUP[15] (FREIGHTER)

FREIGHTER, headquartered in Switzerland, has a history in information systems that goes back to the early 1960s. Forty years on they have reached a level of deep integration that does not just engender the fullest user acceptance, but has led to a strategic unity of IT and business. For FREIGHTER, their IIS are the very core competencies from which flow the ongoing development of new strategic products and services.

FREIGHTER has a clear understanding of what constitutes the *cCore,* that is, a common infrastructure of hardware platform, communications standards, and application systems that is a compulsory technology package for every one of the 260 offices (in 60 countries) in the group. It essentially comprises the consignment routing and tracking software together with the documentation generator, a very sophisticated and constantly adapted proprietary real-time information system.

The *local* part of their systems environment is of equal strategic importance: In addition to local logistics software it consists of electronic linkages to the local offices (and systems) of their major customers as well as to the transport providers and customs agencies in each international site.

The high level of user acceptance is accompanied (and caused by) the superior functional quality of their systems. To achieve both, they had put in place organisational structures and management processes that were designed to counteract any potential for *functional* as well as *political* conflict and rejection. Their project organisation assures the broadest possible base of central and local knowledge and has an escalating conciliation procedure if consensus over system functionality cannot be reached first time around—a procedure that explicitly introduces the win-win sort of politics to deflect and defuse the destructive win-loose political infighting so common in many multinational companies.

FREIGHTER is a truly *transnational* business.

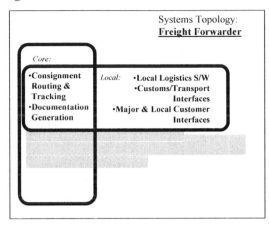

Figure 9. Systems Topology of the International Freight Forwarder

ARCHITECTURAL ANALYSIS OF THE CASE VIGNETTES

The usefulness of the architecture model can now be assessed from two viewpoints:

a. As a framework; first for describing the structure of a wide variety of international information systems supporting an equally wide variety of multinational businesses; and, second, whether it leads to an enhanced understanding of the nature of international information systems.

b. As a blueprint and/or template for the design of international information systems, especially with regard to its potential for economies[16] in the development and/or implementation of international information systems.

The following paragraphs assess and discuss both framework and blueprint perspectives in more detail.

A FRAMEWORK FOR DESCRIPTION AND UNDERSTANDING

The two dimensional topology is flexible and can implement all the architectures cited above:

- Centralised architectures have a small local part.
- Decentralised architectures have a small core part.
- Integrated architectures have a varying core to local ratio for the IIS used in each location.

The global business strategy, that is, the degree of balance between local autonomy and global control, of the case vignettes seems to be correlated to the topology of their international information systems. A topology of large local'technology, compared to thinner core'components seems to correlate to the higher degree of local autonomy and low level of global control as reflected in the Merchant Bank's organisational strategy. The balance in global vs. local control in the structure of the leasing company is reflected in a medium-to-large core and equally sized local systems. High global control and little autonomy for the branches in the commodity firm describe an architecture characterised by a large core of systems at the centre and only a thin smattering of local systems. The contradictory visions of what would be a suitable IIS structure held by the Co-op's IT people and local/regional management shows up as diametrically opposed. Figure 10 shows the position of the six case vignettes with respect to their topology and global business strategy.

DESIGN ECONOMIES FROM THE MODEL

CSC (1995), in a case study of the way in which a number of multinational firms deals with the issues of global information systems vs. local business requirements, summarise that building systems to satisfy a multiplicity of diverse business needs can take two different forms. The core system is formed around the lowest common denominator[17] of all the requirements (i.e., the sum of all local business system needs) in system building terms, however, this can be a disappointingly small proportion of the overall information system. The opposite stratagem, in CSC terms the grand design, attempts to specify a system that contains all the requirements of all local and global business

Figure 10. Link between global business strategy and the architecture (topology) of IIS

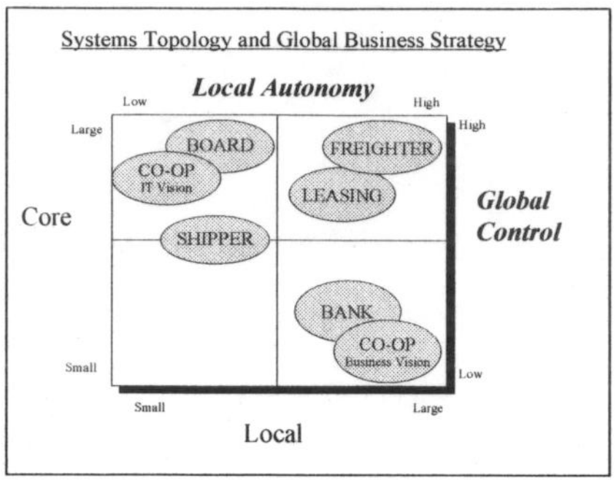

units and agglomerates them into one information system; in mathematical terms this may be called the lowest common multiple—and just as such a number can be alarmingly large, so can information systems built along this principle; some of the more spectacular information systems failures fall into this category: during the systems development time the business changed so much that there could never be a final version of the software.

In mathematics, however, there is a third possible stratagem for finding common elements among divergent number sets—multiples of common prime factors. In systems terms, these would be components in the form of building blocks that would be used to assemble systems. The components would carry the global standards, but their assembly could then follow individual local requirements. Information systems built in this way would satisfy both common and local needs and would avoid the conflicting trade-off stance altogether.

Such prime factors for the establishment of global commonality can be implemented in three ways:

1. As infrastructure to enable common basic applications (such as e-mail in the case vignette of the Merchant Bank); in this way, global standards are implemented in a form that would be immediately useful for the local business unit.

2. As a design template, that is, a set of design outlines and specifications for the global standard part of an application, from which the individual local systems can be built; the case vignette of the Leasing Subsidiary is a variation on this theme, with the template fairly firmly embedded in actual software templates.

3. As software components.

Both design templates and actual software components will consist of data and processes that clearly and unambiguously defines the resulting conglomeration as an object.

THE BENEFIT OF "OBJECT" QUALITIES FOR CORE SYSTEMS ELEMENTS

The paradigm of "object orientation" in the creation of information technology applications has been in force as a quasi-standard for systems development for some two decades now (Glass, 2002). It also seems to have progressed in the recent past from a predominantly programming tool to a wider spectrum of use as a systems—and business process—engineering method (Mentzas, 1997; Purao et al., 2001; Hassan, 2003; Watson et al., 2004; Liu & Stewart, 2004). On the other hand, object orientation in the systems building context has now reached the status of a firm theoretical base (Leontief et al., 2002; DeLoach & Hartrum, 2003) on the one hand, and is evolving further into aspect-oriented programming, a wider sphere of system process module generation (Diaz-Pace & Campo, 2002; Elrad et al., 2002).

There are three key qualities of object orientation with respect to the common/local issue in international information systems. They are discussed below:

1. Objects are defined as encapsulating both data and processes/functions in one unit. This combination makes them very useful for vehicles of global; standards, incorporating both data/information standards as well as prescribing standard ways of operating.

2. Objects communicate with other objects using messages. Polymorphism, defined as the capability of objects to deal differently with

Figure 11. The standard LEASE-SETUP 'message' acts on all objects, taking country variations into account

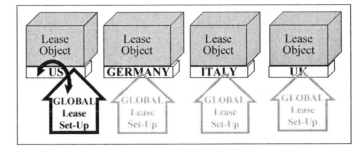

identical messages, is an essential quality for implementing local requirements onto standard processes. Examples are:

a. The application of direct/sales taxes where the local applicability rules, rates, and so forth, are kept with the local accounting object, reflecting the different local statutory and tax regimes.

b. If the 'Lease-Setup' part of global standard information system in the case vignette Leasing Subsidiary were an object-oriented system, one such a globally enforced message would have been the compulsory calculation and reporting of the profitability of each lease deal. Again, the processing modules in the message would act on local and individually different data (e.g., local cost-of-money rates, tax-rebate rules, etc.). Figure 8 depicts this.

3. Inheritance is the quality of objects to structure themselves hierarchically into super-classes and sub-classes to pass down characteristics (data and/or processes). This has two main uses in the global/local dichotomy:

a. Consider "Payments" transactions in the Leasing Subsidiary case vignette: whilst the gist of payment processing (application into a ledger, cash-book/bank reconciliations, etc.) is common, the operational detail of the payment process is not; each local object would inherit the common core processes from a standard Accounts Receivable module (the 'super-class'), but implement typical

local payment types (e.g., Direct Debits in the UK, Bank-Account-Transfers in Germany, negotiable promissory notes in Italy, etc.) in the local sub-class (denoted as the white squares); Figure 12 illustrates this.

b. The second use would be the introduction of new functionality across the organisation such as new or updated global standards or new operational software developed in one site but potentially useful elsewhere. In the Co-op case vignette the UK subsidiary developed a system of vendor-managed-inventory with a large supermarket chain that would pay for goods sold on the basis of their own point-of-sale records, without any orders

Figure 12. The PAYMENT transaction is applied differently in each country, although the accounting module/object is a global standard

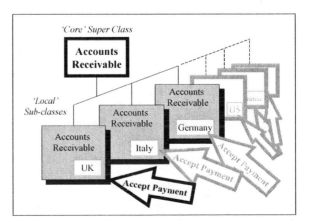

or invoices involved (the white VMI box in the UK sub-class). Implemented in object-oriented form, this functionality could have been incorporated as an attribute in the super class of the Sales & Inventory object. In this way, this functional module would have been instantly available to all other local sub-classes through inheritance from the super-class of the Sales & Inventory object. In the actual case, it was the Malaysia local office that used it to strong competitive advantage. This is illustrated in Figure 13.

The advantages of using an object-oriented approach to the design/definition of the common and local parts of an international information system are, however, not restricted to the building of the system. As Butler Cox (1991) postulates, the business style of multinational enterprises is fluid and changes with their development. Moreover, King and Sethi (1993) demonstrated that multinational enterprises are hardly ever homogenous—they work at the same time in different modes and at differing degrees of penetration into the local systems of different countries (e.g., applying a global

Figure 13. Once the Vendor-Managed-Inventory (VMI) system functionality (developed locally in the UK) becomes part of the Sales&Inventory super-class it is instantly available to any 'Local' sub-class – here demonstrated on Malaysia

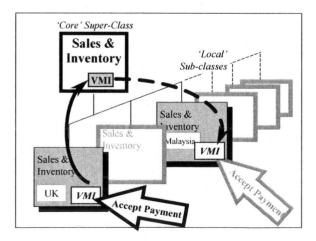

style in small subsidiaries and a transnational style in larger, more sophisticated local environments). The ease and flexibility with which an object-oriented information systems architecture can be maintained and changed would certainly seem to make such an object-oriented approach an essential design consideration.

CONCLUSION

Previous research into the nature of international information systems has led to the proposition of a generic architecture paradigm, consisting of a two-dimensional topology. The model configures any international information system as consisting of a core of information systems common for all and Local systems used in subsidiary sites. This generic structure model has been confirmed by applying it to the information systems of a set of four different multinational enterprises. It could be shown to be a practical and flexible tool to describe and understand the nature of international firms' information systems. It, therefore, may be concluded that the postulated architecture model may well be of use as a conceptual framework for future research into the structure of international information systems.

Because the architecture model prescribes a way of structuring international information systems it also could have significant implications for the modus of developing them. Using the notion of the two-dimensional topology, linked by a standard interface, as a framework for the building and implementation of international information systems would allow, in the first instance, a systematic accumulation of a body of knowledge about this process. Secondly, it enables a modular and parallel systems building approach, as Ccore and local systems and their interfaces could all be developed with significant independence. This could make the development of international information systems more predictable, shorter, and less risky. The two dimensional structure eo ipso also could provide for in-built flexibility for gradual future enhancement.

The goodness of the design for an international information system seems to hinge on how well the core systems (technology and applications) is designed, as this determines to a large extent how easy it will be to apply, maintain, and change the global standards of the enterprise. Local systems— and their interfaces—are contingent on, and complement the core's technology. Object orientation, as a base paradigm for the design of core elements, was found useful. In particular, the principles of encapsulation, polymorphism, and inheritance ensure that the core systems can be implemented in differing degrees of penetration. Furthermore, an object-oriented design is supposed to foster ease of maintenance, enhancements, and other changes as future business needs and the evolution of the international firm itself dictate. It is conjectured[18] that object orientation should be the preferred modus of analysis, design and development for international information systems.

FUTURE RESEARCH DIRECTION

To be of practical use, however, this architecture model now needs to be validated on a much larger, diversified and altogether more representative scale. More empirical research aimed at analysing the structure and architecture of international information systems, for which a grounded theory approach seems appropriate, is needed.

REFERENCES

Applegate, L. M., McFarlan, F. W., & McKenney, J. L. (1996). *Corporate information systems management, text and cases. (Ch. XII; 4th Ed.)* Chicago: Irwin.

Atkinson, G. J. (1996). *A study of perception of individual participants of a client group undertaking a series of meetings supported by a group support system.* Unpublished doctoral thesis, Curtin University of Technology, Perth, W.A., Australia.

Bartlett, C. A., & Ghoshal, S. (1989). *Managing across borders: The transnational solution.* Boston: Harvard Business School Press.

Broadbent, M., &Weill, P. (1997). Management by maxim: how business and IT managers can create IT infrastructures. *Sloan Management Review, 38*(3), 77-92.

Burn, J. M., & Cheung, H. K. (1996). Information systems resource structure and management in multinational organisations. In P.C. Palvia, S.C. Palvia, E.M. Roche (Eds.), *Global information technology and systems management-Key issues and trends* (pp. 293-324). Ivy League Publishing, Ltd.

Butler Cox plc. (1991). *Globalisation: The information technology challenge.* Amdahl Executive Institute Research Report. London.

Collins, R. W., & Kirsch, L. (1999). *Crossing boundaries: The deployment of global IT solutions.* Practice-Driven Research in IT Management Series™. Cincinnati, OH.

CSC Research and Advisory Services (1995). *Globalisation and localisation: Implications for IS.* CSC Foundation Final Report, London.

Deans, C. P., & Karwan, K. R. (Eds.) (1994). *Global information systems and technology: Focus on the organisation and its functional areas.* Harrisburg, PA: Idea Group Publishing..

DeLoach, S. A., & Hartrum, T. C. (2000). A theory-based representation for object-oriented domain models. *IEEE Transactions on Software Engineering, 26*(6), 500-517.

Diaz-Pace, J. A., & Campo, M. R. (2001). Analyzing the role of Aspects in software design. *Communications of the ACM, 44*(10), 66-73.

Earl, M. J. (1989). *Management strategies for information technology.* London: Prentice-Hall.

Eisenhardt, K. M. (1989). Building theories from case study research. *Academy of Management Review, 14*(4), 532-550.

Elrad, T., Filman, R. E., & Bader, A. (2001). Aspect-oriented programming. *Communications of the ACM, 44*(10), 28-32.

Fernandez, W. D., & Lehmann, H. P. (2005) Achieving rigour and relevance in information systems studies—Using grounded theory to investigate organsational cases. *Grounded Theory Review, 5*(1), 23-40.

Flowers, S. (1996). *Software failure: Management failure.* New York: John Wiley & Sons.

Galliers, R. D., & Land, F. F. (1987). Choosing appropriate information systems research methodologies. *Communications of the ACM, 30*(11), 900-902.

Gallupe, R. B., & Tan, F. B. (1999). A research manifesto for global information management. *Journal of Global Information Management, 7*(3), 5-18.

Gibson, R. (1994). Global information technology architectures. *Journal of Global Information Management. 2*(1), 28-38.

Glaser, B. G. (Ed.) (1995). *Grounded theory: A reader (Vols. I-II).* Mill Valley, CA: Sociology Press.

Glaser, B. G., & Strauss, A. L. (1994). Case histories and case studies. In B.G. Glaser (Ed.), *More grounded theory methodology: A reader* (pp. 233-245). Mill Valley: Sociology Press. (Reprinted from Anguish, by Glaser, B. G., & Strauss, A. L., 1970, Mill Valley: Sociology Press).

Glaser, B. G., & Strauss, A. L. (1967). *The discovery of grounded theory.* New York:Aldine Publishing Co., Hawthorne.

Glass, R. L. (1992). The universal elixir and other computing projects which failed. *Computing Trends.* Bloomington, IN.

Glass, R. L. (1998). *Software runaways.* Upper Saddler River, NJ: Prentice Hall PTR.

Glass, R. L. (2002). The naturalness of object orientation: Beating a dead horse? *IEEE Software, 19*(3), 103-104.

Grover, V., & Segars, A. H. (1996). The relationship between organizational characteristics and information system structure: An international survey. *International Journal of Information Management, 16*(1), 9-25.

Hamelink, C. J. (1984). *Transnational data flows in the information age.* Lund, Sweden: Studentlitteratur AB.

Hassan, M. D. (2003). Reengineering the process in the design of object-orientation using concepts of industrial engineering. *International Journal of Computer Applications in Technology, 16*(4), 167-180.

Ives, B., & Jarvenpaa, S. L. (1991). Applications of global information technology: Key issues for management. *MIS Quarterly, 15*(1), 33-50.

Ives, B., & Jarvenpaa, S. L. (1992). Air products and chemicals, inc. *International Information Systems, (April),* 77-99.

Ives, B., & Jarvenpaa, S. L. (1994). MSAS cargo international: Global freight management . In T. Jelass, & C. Ciborra (Eds.), *Strategic information systems: A European perspective.* New York: John Wiley and Sons.

Jarvenpaa, S. L., & Ives, B. (1994). Organisational fit and flexibility: IT design principles for a globally competing firm. *Research in Strategic Management and Information Technology, 1,* 39.

Karimi, J., & Konsynski, B. R. (1996). Globalisation and information management strategies. In C. Deans, & J. Jurison (Eds.), *Information technology in a global business environment* (pp. 169-189). London: Boyd & Fraser.

Keen, P. G. W., Bronsema, G. S., & Auboff, S. (1982). *Implementing common systems: One organisation's experience.* Systems, Objectives and Solutions, 2.

King, W. R., & Sethi, V. (1993). Developing transnational information systems: A case study. *OMEGA International Journal of Management Science, 21*(1), 53-59.

King, W. R., & Sethi, V. (1999). An empirical assessment of the organization of transnational information systems. *Journal of Management Information Systems, 15*(4), 7-28.

Lee, A. S. (1989). A scientific methodology for MIS case studies, *MIS Quarterly, 13*(1), 32-50.

Lehmann, H. P. (1996a). Towards a common architecture paradigm for the global application of information systems. In B.C. Glasson, D.R. Vogel, P.W. Bots, & J.F. Nunamaker (Eds.), *Information systems and technology in the international office of the future* (pp. 199-218). London: Chapman and Hall.

Lehmann, H. P. (1996b). Towards a specific architecture for international information systems: An exploratory study. *Journal of International Information Management 5*(1), 15-34.

Lehmann, H. P. (1997). A definition of research focus for international information systems. In *Proceedings of the Thirtieth Annual Hawaii International Conference on Systems Sciences*. Maui, HI.

Lehmann, H. P. (1999). Researching the development of an international information system Anatomy of a grounded theory investigation. In A.M. Castell, A.J. Gregory, G.A. Hindle, M.E. James, G. Ragsdell (Eds.), *Synergy matters: Working with systems in the 21st century*. London: Kluwer Academic/Plenum Publishers.

Lehmann, H. P. (2000). The fatal politics of multinational information systems: A case study. *Journal of Information Technology Cases & Applications, 2*(3). New York, NY.

Lehmann, H. P. (2001a). Using grounded theory with technology cases: Distilling critical theory from a multinational information systems development project. *Journal of Global Information Technology Management, 4*(1), 45-60. Memphis, TN.

Lehmann, H. P. (2001b). The Australasian food products co-op: A global information systems endeavour. In F. Tan (Ed.), *Cases on global IT applications and management: Successes and pitfalls*. Harrisburg, PA: Idea Group Publishing.

Lehmann, H.P. (2002) 'The Design of Information Systems for the International Firm: A Grounded Theory of Some Critical Issues'. In P. Palvia, S. Palvia and E. M. Roche (Eds.) *Global Information Technology and Electronic Commerce: Issues for the New Millennium*. Ivy League Publishing, Marietta.

Lehmann, H. P. (2004). The Australasian produce co-operative: A global information systems project. *Communications of the AIS (CAIS)*, (13), Article 17.

Lehmann, H. P. (2006). European international freight forwarders-Information as a strategic product. *Journal of Cases on Information Technology, 8*(1), 63-78.

Lehmann, H. P., & Gallupe, R. B. (2005). Information systems for multinational enterprises–Some factors at work in their design and implementation. *Journal of International Management, 11*(4), 28-49.

Leontiev, Y., Ozsu, M. T., & Szafron, D. (2002). On type systems for object-oriented database programming languages. *ACM Computing Surveys, 34*(4), 409-449.

Liu, D., & Stewart, T. J. (2004). Object-oriented decision support system modelling for multi-criteria decision making in natural resource management. *Computers & Operations Research, 31*(7), 985-999.

Mentzas, G. N. (1997). Re-engineering banking with object-oriented models: Towards customer information systems. *International Journal of Information Management, 17*(3), 179-197.

Orlikowski, W. J. (1993). CASE tools as organisational change: Investigating incremental and radical changes in systems development. MIS Quarterly, pp. 309-337.

Orlikowski, W. J., (1995). *Organisational change around groupware*. (Working Paper CCS 186). Massachusetts Institute of Technology.

Orlikowski, W. J., & Baroudi, J. J. (1991). Studying information technology in organisations. *Information Systems Research, 2*(1), 1-28.

Palvia, P. C. (1998). Global information technology research: Past, present and future. *Journal of Global Information Technology Management, 1*(2).

Peppard, J. (1999). Information management in the global enterprise: An organising framework. *European Journal of Information Systems, 8*(2), 77-94.

Purao, S., Jain H. K., & Nazareth, D. L. (2001). An approach to distribution of object-oriented applications in loosely coupled networks. *Journal of Management Information Systems, 18*(3), 195-234.

Ross, J. (2003). IT architecture as strategic capability: Learning in stages. *MIS Quarterly Executive, 2*(1), 31-43.

Sankar, C., Apte, U., & Palvia, P. (1993). Global information architectures: Alternatives and trade-offs. *International Journal of Information Management, 13*, 84-93.

Sethi, V., & Olson, J. E. (1993). An integrating framework for information technology issues in a transnational environment. In Global Issues in Information Technology, Harrisburg, PA: Idea Publishers. Simon, S. J., Grover, V. (1993). Strategic use of information technology in international business: A framework for information technology application. *Journal of Global Information Management, 1*(2), 29-42.

Targowski, A. S. (1996). *Global information infrastructure—He birth, vision and architecture.* London, UKJ: Idea Group Publishing.

Tractinsky, N., & Jarvenpaa, S. L. (1995). Information systems design decisions in a global versus domestic context. *MIS Quartely, 19*(4), 507-534.

Tucker, C., & Woolfe, R. (2003). The reality of IS lite. *Gartner Report.*

Turner, B. A. (1983). The use of grounded theory for the qualitative analysis of organisational behaviour. *Journal of Management Studies, 20*(3), 333-348.

Van den Berg, W., & Mantelaers, P. (1999). Information systems across organisational and national boundaries: Aan analysis of development problems. *Journal of Global Information Technology Management, 2*(2).

Watson, R.T., Zinkhan, G. M., & Pitt, L. F. (2004). Object-orientation: A tool for enterprise design. *California Management Review, 46*(4), 89-110.

Weill, P., & Vitale, M. (2002). What IT infrastructure capabilities are needed to implement e-business models? *MIS Quarterly, 1*(1), 17-35.

Weill, P. (1992). *The role and value of information technology infrastructure: Some empirical observations* (Working Paper No. 8). University of Melbourne, Melbourne, July.

Weill, P. (1993). The role and value of information technology infrastructure: Some empirical observations. In R. Banker, R. Kauffman, & M.A. Mahmood (Eds.), *Strategic information technology management: Perspectives on organizational growth and competitive advantage.* Middleton, PA: Idea Group Publishing.

Weill, P., & Broadbent, M. (1994a). Infrastructure goes industry specific. *MIS*, 35-39.

Weill, P., & Broadbent, M. (1998). *Leveraging the new infrastructure: How market leaders capitalize on information technology.* Harvard Business School Publishing, Boston, MA.

Weill, P., Broadbent, M., Butler, C., & Soh, C. (1995). Firm-wide information technology infrastructure investment and services. In *Proceedings of the 16th International Conference on Information Systems, Amsterdam.*

Weill, P., Broadbent, M., & St.Clair, D. (1994b). *I/T value and the role of I/T infrastructure investments.* In J. Luftman (Ed.), Strategic Alignment. Oxford University Press.

Weill, P., Subramani, N., & Broadbent, M. (2002). Building the IT infrastructure for strategic agility. *MIT Sloan Management Review, 44*(1), 25-31.

Yin, R. K. (1989). *Case study research: Design and methods.* Newbury Park, CA: Sage Publications.

Yoong, S. P. (1996). *A grounded theory of reflective facilitation: Making the transition from traditional to GSS facilitation.* Unpublished doctoral thesis, Victoria University of Wellington, New Zealand.

Yourdon, E. (1997). *Death march: The complete software developer's guide to surviving "Mission Impossible" projects.* Upper Saddler River, NJ: Prentice Hall PTR.

ADDITIONAL READING

The following, largely historical readings are recommended for further study to deepen understanding of the subject:

Applegate, L. M., McFarlan, F. W., & McKenney, J. L. (1996). *Corporate information systems management, text and cases* (Ch. XII; 4th Ed.) (pp. 684-691) Chicago: Irwin.

Bartlett, C. A., & Ghoshal, S. (1989). *Managing across borders: The transnational solutio* (Ch.2-5). Boston: Harvard Business School Press.

Burn, J. M., & Cheung, H. K. (1996). Information systems resource structure and management in multinational organisations. In P.C. Palvia, S.C. Palvia, & E.M. Roche (Ed.), *Global information technology and systems managemen—Key issues and trends* (pp. 293-324). Ivy League Publishing, Ltd.

Buss, M. D. J. (1982). Managing international information systems. *Harvard Business Review, 60*(5), 153-162.

Butler Cox plc. (1991). *Globalisation: The information technology challenge.* Amdahl Executive Institute Research Report (Chs. 3, 5 6). London.

Cavaye, A., Mantelaers, P., van de Berg, W., & Zuurmond, A. (1998). Towards guidelines for development and management of transnational information systems. *The Australian Journal of Information Systems, 5*(2), 34-58.

Chin, W. W., & Newsted, P. R. (1995). The importance of specification in causal modeling: The case of end-user computing satisfaction. *Information Systems Research 6*(1), 73-81.

Christmann, T. (1998). Developing a global information vision. *Information Systems Management, 15*(4), 46-54.

Collins, R. W., & Kirsch, L. (1999). *Crossing boundaries: The deployment of global IT dolutions.* Practice-driven research in IT management aeries™ (Chs. 4, 5). Cincinnati, OH.

Deans, C. P., & Karwan, K. R. (Eds.). (1994) *Global information systems and technology: Focus on the organisation and its functional areas* (Chs. 3, 5-8). Harrisburg, PA: Idea Group Publishing.

Deans, P. C., & Jurison, J. (1996). *Information technology in a global business environment–Readings and cases* (Chs. 5-7). New York: Boyd & Fraser.

Earl, M. J., & Feeny, D. F. (1996). Information systems in global business: Evidence from European multinationals. In N. Thomas, D. O'Neal, & J. Kelly, J. (Eds.), *Strategic Renaissance and Business Transformation* (pp. 183-210). Chichester: John Wiley & Sons.

Glass, R. L. (1998). *Software runaways* (Ch.3). Upper Saddler River, NJ: Prentice Hall PTR.

Ives, B., & Jarvenpaa, S. L. (1991). Applications of global information technology: Key issues for management, *MIS Quarterly,* 33-49.

Keen, P. G. W. (1992). Planning globally: Practical strategies for information technology strategies in the transnational firm. In S. Palvia, P. Palvia, & R. Zigli (Eds.), *The Global Issues of Information Technology Management* (pp. 575-607). Harrisburg, PA: Idea Group Publishing.

Keen, P. G. W., & Bronsema, G. S., & Auboff, S. (1982). *Implementing common systems: One organisation's experience. Systems, Objectives and Solutions,* (2), 125-142.

King, W. R., & Sethi, V. (1993). Developing transnational information systems: A case study. *OMEGA International Journal of Management Science, 21*(1), 53-59.

King, W. R., & Sethi, V. (1999). An empirical assessment of the organization of transnational information systems. *Journal of Management Information Systems 15*(4), 7-28.

Palvia, P. C. (1998). Global information technology research: Past, present and future. *Journal of Global Information Technology Management, 1*(2), 12-32.

Palvia, P. C. (1995). Global management support systems: A new frontier. *Journal of Global Information Management, 3*(1), 3-4.

Roche, E. M. (1992b). *Managing information technology in multinational corporations* (Chs.5, 8). New York: Macmillan.

Roche, E. M. (1996). The multinational enterprise in an age of the Internet and electronic commerce. In P.C. Palvia, S.C. Palvia, & E.M. Roche (Eds.),

Global Information Technology and Systems Management-Key Issues and Trends (pp. 424-440). Ivy League Publishing, Ltd.

ENDNOTES

[1] These also will be referred to as **IIS** throughout this paper. Similarly, **IS** will be used for information systems and **IT** for information technology.

[2] Most of the evidence for these failures is now contained as the (often historical) international cases in anthologies and monographs on large information systems failure (e.g., Glass, 1992 and 1998; Flowers, 1996); Yourdon, 1997; Collins et al., 1999).

[3] This compares well with Gallupe et al. (1999) who found 314 articles between 1990 and 1998, albeit in the wider field of *information management* and, therefore, in a wider spectrum of journals.

[4] Nearly 40% of the papers deal with domestic instances and issues of information technology, but in a country other than the author's—a category that Palvia (1998) expressedly excludes from the realm of global information technology research.

[5] This, too, has been used by Bartlett and Ghoshal (1989), but in a more general sense.

[6] For a fuller treatment of this definition refer to Lehmann (1996).

[7] The coverage of the literature is available in more detail in literature reviews and position papers elsewhere: Hamelink (1984) covers the early research; Sethi et al. (1993) give a very exhaustive overview; Lehmann (1997) brings it more up-to-date and Gallupe et al. (1999) establish a blueprint for future research.

[8] Such as King et al. (1993, 1999); Deans et al. (1994); Tractinsky (1995); Applegate et al. (1996); and, Van den berg et al. (1999).

[9] Italics denote the Bartlett and Ghoshal classification.

[10] Their classification also is supported by a series of case studies by Ives et al. (1991, 1992, 1994).

[11] One of the richer cases was subsequently remodelled as a teaching case, focusing (among others) on the importance of architecture and infrastructure in the design of IIS (Lehmann, 2004).

[12] In accordance with the wishes of the enterprises participating in this research, all cases are disguised. The first three vignettes are described in more detail in Lehmann (1996) and are presented here in abbreviated form. The fourth vignette is the summation of the architecture perspective of a large case, which is contained in more detail in Lehmann (2000).

[13] In the nomenclature of Bartlett and Ghoshal.

[14] The more detailed analysis of this concept is in Lehmann and Gallupe (2005). *Synchronicity* has been shown to be the critically instrumental element for deriving the core/local functionality balance in a rational, predictable and reasoning way.

[15] This case is described in more detail in Lehmann (2006).

[16] In terms of cost, effort, and time.

[17] Although, in strictly mathematical terms, this should be the *highest common factor*.

[18] So far, neither the literature nor the author's own experience and research have witnessed international information systems projects that use object orientation as the main design principle.

About the Contributors

Mahesh S. Raisinghani is an associate professor in the executive MBA program at the TWU School of Management. He is a certified e-commerce consultant (CEC) and a project management professional (PMP). Dr. Raisinghani was the recipient of TWU School of Management's 2005 Best Professor Award for the Most Innovative Teaching Methods; 2002 research award; 2001 King/Haggar Award for excellence in teaching, research and service; and a 1999 UD-GSM Presidential Award. His previous publications have appeared in *IEEE Transactions on Engineering Management, Information and Management, Journal of Global I.T. Management, Journal of E-Commerce Research, Information Strategy: An Executive's Journal, International Journal of E-Business Research, Journal of IT Cases and Applications, Information Resources and Management Journal, Journal of I.T. Theory and Applications, Enterprise Systems Journal, Journal of Computer Information Systems and Information Systems Management,* among others. Dr. Raisinghani is included in the millennium edition of *Who's Who in the World, Who's Who Among America's Teachers,* and *Who's Who in Information Technology.*

* * * * *

Dinesh Arunatileka is researching for his PhD at the University of Western Sydney in Australia, in the area of mobile technologies and its application to business processes. He also has been a teaching fellow at the same university for the past two-and-half years. He earned his BSc in computer science from the University of Colombo and his MBA from the University of Sri Jayewardenepura, Sri Lanka. Arunatileka has more than nine years of experience in business development in the computing and telecommunications industry. He has published and presented conference papers in the area of methodologies to introduce mobile technology into business practice.

Esther Ruiz Ben is assistant professor at the Institute of Sociology of the Technical University of Berlin. Since October 2005, she has been conducting a research project about the internationalization of the German ICT industry and the transformation of tasks and qualification profiles financed by the DFG (Deutsche Forschungsgemeinschaft). Esther also has worked and taught in the areas of professionalization in ICT environments, gender and technology, and technology and sustainability at the Institute of Informatics and Society of the University of Freiburg.

J. Michael Blocher is an associate professor of educational technology in Northern Arizona University's College of Education. Dr. Blocher also has been a member of the Western Governors University Education Program Council since 1998. Dr. Blocher earned his PhD in curriculum and instruction from Arizona State University with an emphasis in educational media and computers. He also holds an MA in curriculum and instruction from the University of Colorado, and an MA in industrial technology from the University of Northern Colorado. He was instrumental in the design, development, and implementation of Northern Arizona University's Educational Technology Master's Degree Program—a totally online degree program that was begun in 2000. His research interests include learner interaction within online learning environments and integrating technology into the re-K to12 instructional process. Dr. Blocher has co-authored a book, published in both scholarly and practitioners journals, and has presented numerous papers at international conferences.

Suvarna Cherukuri is an assistant professor of sociology at Siena College whose teaching and scholarly work focuses primarily on feminist criminology. She received her PhD in sociology from Kansas State University in 2003 and an MBA from the University at Albany in 2007. She is the author of the forthcoming book *Women in Prison: An Insight into Captivity and Crime* (Foundation Books). Her more recent research focuses on social implications of outsourcing in India.

Subhankar Dhar is a leading expert in information systems outsourcing, mobile and pervasive computing, and is a faculty member in the Department of Management Information Systems at the Lucas Graduate School of Business at San José State University. He also is a Lucas Fellow and serves as a member of the editorial board of the *International Journal of Business Data Communications and Networking*. He has received numerous awards and grants for his significant contribution in academic research. He also has given lectures and presentations to various international conferences and seminars. Prior to joining San Jose State University, Dhar was a member of the technical team at SAP Labs in Palo Alto. He received his PhD from the University of South Florida and has several years of experience in software development, enterprise resource planning, consulting for Fortune 500 and high-tech start-ups, including product planning, design, and information systems management. Dhar is a member of various professional organizations such as, IEEE, ACM, AIS.

Vera Eccarius-Kelly, assistant professor of political science at Siena College in Albany, NY, specializes in globalization studies and comparative Middle East and Latin American politics. Dr. Eccarius-Kelly was named interim director of globalization studies in 2005, after Siena College established its interdisciplinary program with the Schools of Business and Liberal Arts. She received a PhD from The Fletcher School of Law and Diplomacy at Tufts University in Boston in 2002. Among her recent publications are: "Counterterrorism Policies and the Revolutionary Movement of Tupac Amaru: The Unmasking of Peru's National Security State," in *Countering Terrorism in the 21st Century* (Praeger International, 2007); "Guatemalan Women's Cooperatives and State Neglect," in *Peace Review: A Journal of Social Science, 18*(2006), 37-43; "Political Movements and Leverage Points: Kurdish Activism in the European Diaspora," in *The Journal of Muslim Minority Affairs, 22*(2002), 91-118; and "Radical Consequences of Benign Neglect: The Rise of the PKK in Germany," in *The Fletcher Forum of World Affairs, 24*(2000), 161-174.

Abbass Ghanbary (Bachelor of Applied Science, Hons) is undertaking his PhD-level research at the University of Western Sydney (UWS) in Australia. His specific research focus includes the issues and challenges in incorporating Web services in businesses integration and creating a model for collaborative business process engineering. He will have earned his PhD by December 2007. Ghanbary has earned a scholarship from the University of Western Sydney to undertake his research. His investigation is mainly concentrated on the improvements of the Web services applications across multiple organisations. Ghanbary also teaches and tutors in UWS, and is a member of the emerging technologies sub-group with advanced enterprise information management systems (AeIMS), and Mobile Internet Research and Applications Group (MIRAG) at the University of Western Sydney. He also is a full member of the Australian Computer Society and is active in attending various forums, seminars, and discussion groups.

Stacy Kowalczyk currently is the associate director for projects and services for the Indiana University Digital Library Program. Prior to her current position at Indiana University, she managed the development of the technical infrastructure for Harvard's Library Digital Initiative. She has developed a large number of digital library applications from geospatial systems to digital repositories. Besides her work in the Digital Library Program, she also is a PhD student at Indiana University's School of Library and Information Science where her research interests are digital preservation and management of digital libraries.

Steve Legrand received a BSc from the Griffith University, Australia, in environmental science and worked after that in his own business. He completed an MSc in computer science at the University of Jyväskylä in Finland in 2000. His PhD dissertation ("Use of Real-world Background Knowledge for WSD in Semantic Web") is scheduled for the autumn of 2007. His main research interests are languages, XML-based technologies and representation languages, word sense disambiguation, and Semantic Web. His other interests include arranging business contacts between companies in Finland and Mexico (where he spent the last two years) with the help of the Web and novel Web technologies.

Hans Lehmann, Austrian by birth, is an information technology professional with some 35 years of business and academic experience with information systems. After a career in data processing line management in Austria in the early 1970s he became an information technology manager in the manufacturing and banking sectors in South Africa. After completing an MBA there, he joined Deloitte's and worked for 12 years in their international management consultancy firm in Zimbabwe, London, and New Zealand. Lehmann's work experience spans continental Europe, Africa, the United Kingdom, North America, and Australasia. He specialised in the management of the development and implementation of international information systems for a number of blue-chip multi-national companies in the financial and manufacturing sectors. In 1991, Lehmann changed careers and joined the University of Auckland, New Zealand, where his research focused on the strategic management of international information technology and systems, specifically for global supply chain management applications, in the context of transnational electronic business. He currently works as the associate professor of electronic business at Victoria University of Wellington in New Zealand.

Martina Maletzky, MA, was born in 1974 in Nürnberg, Germany. She completed her studies in sociology, cultural sciences and German literature at the Albert-Ludwigs-Universität in Freiburg, Germany, and currently works as a research associate at the Institute of Sociology at the Technische Universität of Berlin, Germany, where she is simultaneously working on her dissertation in the field of intercultural collaboration. She has worked at the Max Planck Institute for Foreign and International Criminal Law and Criminology in Freiburg, the Institute for Informatics and Society in Freiburg, and as a guest lecturer at the Universidad Autónoma de Mexico. Maletzky's research interests include the internationalization of the ICT sector; the specific working conditions within the ICT sector; globalization; intercultural collaboration and communication; virtual teamwork; organizational, industrial, and work sociology.

Scott McDonald (PhD, Northern Illinois University) is associate director and professor at the Institute for Policy and Economic Development, University of Texas at El Paso, where he is active in the graduate-level public administration and leadership programs. His work has resulted in reports and articles on a variety of public and not-for-profit issues related to innovation and economic and community development.

Xiannong Meng received his PhD in computer science from Worcester Polytechnic Institute in Worcester, MA, in 1990. He is currently a professor in the Department of Computer Science at Bucknell University in Lewisburg, PA. His research interests include distributed computing, data mining, intelligent Web search, operating systems, and computer networks. He is a member of ACM and IEEE.

Gerald Merwin holds a PhD in industrial/organizational and vocational psychology from North Carolina State University. He teaches public administration courses at Valdosta State University, Valdosta, GA. Dr. Merwin has served as a consultant to government, nonprofit, and for-profit organizations on issues related to information technology, economic development, and organizational change. His research is primarily in the area of e-government and information management.

Levy C. Odera holds a Master of Public Administration degree from Valdosta State University. He is pursuing a PhD in political science, with a specialty in international political economy, at the University of Florida. Odera's home is Nairobi, Kenya, and he intends to return there after completion of his graduate education. His plans include starting a nonprofit organization that will focus on promoting economic development in Kenya and continuing research on the IT infrastructure in Africa.

Bolanle A. Olaniran (PhD, University of Oklahoma, 1991) is a professor at Texas Tech University in the Department of Communication Studies. His research interest is in the area of computer-mediated communication and specifically exploring the role and effects of communication technologies in organizations along with cross-cultural implications of communication technology in global virtual teams. His works have appeared in several journals in the regional, national, and international arena. He also serves as a consultant to government agencies and private businesses and universities.

Shintaro Okazaki (PhD, Universidad Autónoma de Madrid) is an associate professor of marketing at the College of Economics and Business Administration, Universidad Autónoma de Madrid, Spain. His research focuses on the areas of international marketing, cross-cultural consumer behavior, electronic word-of-mouth, and mobile commerce. His work appears in *Journal of Advertising, Journal of Advertising Research, International Journal of Advertising, Journal of International Marketing, International Marketing Review, Internet Research, Information & Management, European Journal of Marketing, Computers in Human Behavior, Electronic Markets, Journal of International Consumer Marketing, Journal of Marketing Communications,* and *Psychology & Marketing*, among others.

Bernd-Peter Paris was born in Munster, Germany, in 1962. He received his Diplom-Ingenieur degree in electrical engineering from Ruhr-University Bochum, Germany (1986), and his PhD in electrical and computer engineering from Rice University, Houston, TX (1990). After being with the Public Switching Division at Siemens in Munich, Germany, for one year, he accepted a faculty appointment at George Mason University, Fairfax, VA, where he is currently an associate professor in the Electrical and Computer Engineering Department. Dr. Paris is engaged in research in the area of communication systems, with emphasis on mobile, wireless communication networks, and information theory. Dr. Paris is the recipient of a Fulbright Scholarship in 1986, of the NSF Research Initiation Award 1993-1996, and the Outstanding Teaching Award from George Mason University's School of IT&E. He is a member of the IEEE and of Eta Kappa Nu. He is the author or co-author of approximately 50 articles published in international journals and conferences.

Jorge Rafael Pulido has written a number of journal papers, conference papers, and books on the following topics: Semantic Web, ontologies, ontology learning, intelligent data mining, knowledge discovery, self-organizing maps, Internet computing, semantic information retrieval, and data visualization. He holds a PhD in computer science (2004) from The University of Nottingham, UK, an MSc in telematics (1999), and a BA in informatics (1995), both from The University of Colima, México.

Martin Schell was born in New York City and has spent the past 23 years in Japan, Thailand, and Indonesia. He has taught English in each of those countries, rewritten Japanese-to-English translations, designed distance learning materials in Thailand, and prepared economic and security assessments in Indonesia. Now based in his wife's hometown in central Java, he serves clients on several continents as a freelance editor, workshop trainer, and writing coach specializing in the fine points of strategic communication. He also is an adjunct faculty member at NYU's Stern School of Business, where he teaches an online course in business writing.

A.J. Gilbert Silvius (1963) is professor of business IT innovation at Utrecht University of Professional Education. His research covers the alignment between business and IT in organizations. Silvius studied business administration and applied economics at the Royal Military Academy in The Netherlands, the Erasmus University Rotterdam, and the Catholic University of Leuven in Belgium. He had more than 15 years experience in consulting work before joining the academic world.

Radoslav Škapa is an assistant professor at Masaryk University Brno, The Czech Republic. He has published papers in Czech journals and conference proceedings. His research interest lies in electronic commerce and new technology adoption.

Timothy M. Waema is an associate professor in the School of Computing and Informatics in the University of Nairobi. He lectures and does research in a variety of areas in Information Systems. He was instrumental in initiating many academic programmes when he was the director of the Institute of Computer Science, including MSc and PhD programmes in computer science and information systems. He also was key in building academic capacity by initiating funded training programmes at PhD level. As the immediate former director of ICT in the University, Professor Waema initiated and managed many large ICT projects, including creating local and wide area network infrastructure, development of corporate MIS applications, and enabling a sustainable Internet connectivity. At the university level, Professor Waema was very active in shaping the strategic direction of the university. He also has wide experience in consultancy in many areas of ICT and management, including strategic planning at both corporate and ICT levels, telecommunications, ICT systems development and implementation, project management, change management, results-based management, and national socio-economic development. His research interests are in information systems strategy, social issues in information systems development and implementation, ICT and national socio-economic development, software engineering, and management of change. Professor Waema is the lead researcher in Kenya for the Research ICT Africa (RIA!) network. He also is the research director of the Local Governance and ICTs Research Network for Africa (LOG-IN Africa), a new pan-African network of researchers and research institutions from nine countries focusing on local e-governance. He is involved in a number of ICT and development research projects, including e-readiness for higher educational institutions, ICT and local governance, ICT and poverty, and ICT and agriculture.

Zhaohao Sun holds a BSc (mathematics) and an MSc (applied mathematics) from Hebei University, China, an MSc (applied mathematics and computer science, Dipl.-Math.) from Brandenburg Technical University at Cottbus (BTU Cottbus), Germany, and a PhD (IT) from Bond University, Australia. He currently is a professor in the Department of Computer Science, College of Mathematics and Information Science, Hebei Normal University, China. He is a member of the IEEE (MIEEE) and the AIS (MAIS). Dr. Sun also undertook research and/or taught in the fields of soft-ware computing, applied mathematics, information technology, e-commerce, and intelligent systems at Hebei University, China; RWTH Aachen, BTU Cottbus, Germany; Bond University, Australian Catholic University, and University of Wollongong (UoW), Australia, sequentially. His monograph (with Professor Gavin Finnie): *Intelligent Techniques in E-Commerce: A Case-based Reasoning Perspective* was published by Springer-Verlag, Heidelberg/Berlin in 2004. He has more than 60 publications of national and/or international journals and conference proceedings. His current research interests include: e-commerce and e-business, intelligent techniques in e-commerce and e-services, experience-based reasoning, multiagent systems, Web intelligence and engineering, knowledge/experience management. He won the "Award for Best Paper Reviewer," awarded "for providing reviews which demonstrated both insight and constructive feedback," at IMB2006, 13-16 February, Sydney. His biography was listed in Marquis *Who's Who in Science and Engineering* (the 7th, 8th, and 9th editions).

Bhuvan Unhelkar (BE, MDBA, MSc, PhD; FACS) has more than 24 years of strategic, as well as hands-on, professional experience in ICT. He is the founder of MethodScience.com and has notable consulting and training expertise in software engineering (modelling, processes and quality), enterprise globalisation, Web services and mobile business. He earned his doctorate in the area of "object orientation" from the University of Technology, Sydney. In his academic role at the University of Western Sydney, he teaches, amongst other units, object oriented analysis and design and IT project management, and leads the Mobile Internet Research and Applications Group (MIRAG). He has authored/edited 10 books, and has extensively presented and published research papers and case studies. He is a sought-after orator, a fellow of the Australian Computer Society, life member of Computer Society of India, a rotarian and a previous TiE mentor.

Jacek Unold is an associate professor at the University of Economics in Wroclaw, Poland. He majored in civil engineering and managed many construction projects. In the 1990s, he was a chief executive officer of a big construction company in Poland. In 1997, having defended his PhD in economics, Dr. Unold joined the faculty. His research interests include information theory and management, information systems development, business process reengineering and technical analysis of financial markets. Dr. Unold has published 150 articles and three books, and participated in numerous program committees for international conferences. In 2001/2002, Dr. Unold was a Fulbright fellow in the USA and currently (2005-2008) is a recipient of the European Union scholarship (Marie Curie International Outgoing Fellowship) at Boise State University, USA. He is a life member of the Fulbright Association in Washington, DC.

Michaela Wieandt earned her master's degree in sociology, political science, and history at the Georg August University, Goettingen, Germany, and works as junior researcher at the Technical University of Berlin where she plans to earn her doctorate thesis in sociology on the issue of consulting and IT-offshoring. Currently, she works in a research project sponsored by the German Research Foundation (DFG) on the process of internationalisation of ICT Industry in Germany exploring impacts on categorization of job profiles and qualification. Her research interests include the developments of consulting, organizations, qualification/education in information technology sector.

Loong Wong teaches management studies in the School of Business and Government at the University of Canberra. He has taught and researched on e-commerce, international management and is particularly interested in the interplay of cultural, economic, and political forces. He has published in *Asian Business and Management, Prometheus, Peace Review, Critical Sociology*, amongst others, and previously had held senior positions in industry specializing in e-commerce practices.

Mindy Wu (Master of IT, major in information system management) is undertaking her PhD-level research at the University of Western Sydney (UWS) in Australia. Her specific research focus includes the issues and challenges in extending the enterprise architecture with mobility and creating a model for mobility enterprise architecture (M-EA). She is in the first year of her PhD studies. Wu is a member of the Emerging Technologies sub-group with Advanced Enterprise Information Management Systems (AeIMS) and Mobile Internet Research and Applications Group (MIRAG) research groups at the University of Western Sydney. She also is a student member of Australian Computer Society (ACS) and is active in attending various forums, seminars, and discussion groups. She has invited to join the young IT group to share ACS experience to school of computing and mathematics of University of Western Sydney students.

Song Xing received BS and MS degrees in electrical engineering from Southeast University, China (1985 and 1990, respectively), and a PhD in electrical and computer engineering from George Mason University (2003). From 1985 to 1995, he was a lecturer in the Radio Engineering Department at Southeast University, China, and also a researcher at the National Mobile Communications Research Laboratory, China (1990-1995). He was a visiting researcher in the Electrical and Computer Engineering Departments at the University of Michigan-Dearborn, MI (February 1995-April 1995), and at Boston University (May 1995-August 1996, respectively). In 2003, Dr. Xing joined California State University, Los Angeles, where he currently is an assistant professor in the Information Systems Department. His research interests include Internet traffic and performance measurement, communication networks and digital systems, importance sampling simulations of stochastic systems, and speech/image processing.

Robert C. Yoder is an associate professor of computer science at Siena College. He has a BS and MS in computer science and a PhD in information science, from the University at Albany, NY. His research interests include management information systems, globalization, and spatial data structures. His recent publications include "Using RFID in the Classroom to Teach Information Systems Principles," *Journal of Computing Sciences in Colleges, 21*(6), April 2006; "Migrating a Mainframe SNA Link to Ethernet using Communications Server Running on AIX," *z/Journal, 3*(6), December 2005; and "A Practical Algorithm for Computing Neighbors in Quadtrees, Octrees, and Hyperoctrees" (with Peter Bloniarz), *Proceedings, 2006 International Conference on Modeling, Simulation, and Visualization Methods*, Las Vegas, June 26-29, 2006, CSREA Press, edited by Hamid R. Arabnia.

Shafiz A. Mohd Yusof is an assistant professor at Faculty of Information Technology at University Utara Malaysia. He has a strong educational background in information technology where he received his bachelor's degree in IT from University Utara Malaysia. He continued to embark on his interest in

IT by receiving a master's degree in telecommunication and network management at School of Information Studies, Syracuse University. Yusof completed a PhD in information science and technology at Syracuse University. His dissertation investigated the social world of online gaming, the process of institutionalization, and how those factors impact the building of virtual communities. Equipped with several publications, and years of teaching experience, he continues to establish his research interests in areas such as virtual communities, e-learning, and user behavior. At current, Yusof is the director of the International Telecommunication Union–Universiti Utara Malaysia Asia Pacific Region Centre of Excellence (ITU-UUM ASP CoE) for Rural ICT Development. The key role of the CoE is the provision of high quality executive training and development programs pertaining to the issues of rural ICT development. Apart from that, the CoE provides one-stop knowledge repository to a wide range of materials relating to rural ICT development and also provides research and consultation activities.

Norhayati Zakaria is assistant professor at the Universiti Utara Malaysia in the Department of International Business, Faculty of International Studies. She received a PhD in information science & technology and MPhil in information transfer at Syracuse University, USA, an MSc in management of technology at Rensselaer Polytechnic Institute, USA and a bachelor's degree of business administration (human resource management) at Universiti Utara Malaysia. With the educational training, she has a unique combination of expertise in managing human and cultural factors as well as information communication technology. Her research program centers on issues of cross-cultural and intercultural communication and its impact on the effectiveness of managing expatriates, developing intercultural communication competencies through effective cross-cultural training for global virtual teams, and building culturally sensitive cyberinfrastructure collaboratories with the use of information communication technologies. She was a visiting professor in the School of Management in Syracuse University, USA (2000-2001) and a research associate for SISE (2001-2003) at the School of Information Studies, Syracuse University. She has been engaged (2005-current) in the Collaboratory on Technology Enhanced Learning Communities (Cotelco), a social research laboratory located in School of Information Studies, Syracuse University, USA. She currently is leading two research projects—(1) From Pawns to Partners Qualitative, and (2) United Nation Global Alliance on ICT and Development (GAID) under the research lab.

Index